343·099B

MEDIA LAW
CASES AND MATERIALS

LONGMAN LAW SERIES

GENERAL EDITORS

PROFESSOR I. H. DENNIS, *University College London*
PROFESSOR R. W. RIDEOUT, *University College London*
PROFESSOR J. A. USHER, *University of Edinburgh*

PUBLISHED TITLES

ERIC BARENDT & LESLEY HITCHENS

MEDIA LAW
Cases and Materials

An imprint of **Pearson Education**

Harlow, England · London · New York · Reading, Massachusetts · San Francisco
Toronto · Don Mills, Ontario · Sydney · Tokyo · Singapore · Hong Kong · Seoul
Taipei · Cape Town · Madrid · Mexico City · Amsterdam · Munich · Paris · Milan

Pearson Education Limited
Edinburgh Gate
Harlow
Essex CM20 2JE
England

and Associated Companies throughout the world

Visit us on the World Wide Web at:
http://www.pearsoneduc.com

First published 2000

ISBN 0 582 31719 3   PPR

British Library Cataloguing-in-Publication Data

A catalogue record for this book is available from the British Library

Set by 35 in 10/12pt Plantin
Printed and bound in Great Britain by Henry Ling Ltd.,
at the Dorset Press, Dorchester, Dorset

CONTENTS

v

PREFACE

Media law is now an established optional course at many universities and at the College of Law, a consequence to some extent of its growing importance in professional practice. Yet there are few books which adequately cover the range of topics comprising media law, and none, so far as we know, which attempts to present key materials with critical commentary. Our aim has been to provide a comprehensive course-book for students of media law, which can be used independently or in conjunction with other literature to which reference is made in the select bibliography.

The book contains extracts not only from legislation and leading decisions of the courts, but also from the reports and papers of Royal Commissions, departmental committees, regulatory authorities and other bodies whose work has done much to shape the development of media law. Inevitably we have had to be selective in our choice of material. Although we would have liked to include more extracts from periodical literature, we have decided to give priority to primary materials, particularly those which formulate significant principles in this area of law. The text is designed to introduce and provide commentary on these extracts, while the questions posed at various points in the book are intended to provoke discussion of difficult unresolved legal or policy issues.

We are aware that other authors might have provided space for topics omitted in this book. We chose those which are most central to the working of the principal mass media: the press and broadcasting media. Among the topics covered in the first part of the book are the principles of media regulation, in particular the special regulation of broadcasting, competition law applied to newspapers and the audio-visual media, and the control of advertising. Other chapters deal with the main restrictions on media freedom imposed by the law of libel and contempt and by statutory reporting restrictions. But we have omitted discussion of such topics as obscenity legislation, the regulation of hate speech, official secrets laws, freedom of information and data protection. They are generally well covered in civil liberties books and courses. Further, though they do have some impact on the media, they are less important than the topics we have included. We have also not covered copyright law, an important aspect of media and entertainment law practice, but one which is well served by the intellectual property literature.

Media law is subject to rapid change. This is partly attributable to the increasing role of European Community law which merits a separate chapter in the context of broadcasting regulation and a section of the chapter on competition law. The Human Rights Act 1998 will influence media law, perhaps by encouraging the formulation of a privacy right, a topic discussed in Chapter 11. There is also the impact of media convergence, explored in Chapter 8, which may call into question the boundaries between media law, information technology and telecommunications laws. Finally, there is always political and financial pressure to change the scope of media regulation, a phenomenon particularly noted in the chapters on broadcasting and programme regulation and on competition law.

Despite the difficulties posed by constant change, we have endeavoured to take account of all the material available to us by 31 July 1999, though in two instances – the Davies Report on Financing the BBC and the new edition of the British Codes of Advertising and Sales Promotion – material published after July has been incorporated. The House of Lords heard argument in the landmark *Reynolds* libel case in June 1999, but the judgments were only published in the autumn, so the case is noted in an Appendix.

We would like to thank Angela Hayes-Allen, Cyrene Siriwardhana, Sylvia Lough, Louisa Holt and Lesley Morris who helped by locating and photocopying material to be included in this volume. We are also grateful for the encouragement of the publishers, in particular Brian Willan who commissioned the book and Pat Bond, and to advice from Ian Dennis who enthusiastically supported the original proposal we made in the winter of 1996.

Eric Barendt
Lesley Hitchens
August 1999

ACKNOWLEDGEMENTS

We are grateful to the following for permission to reproduce the following material:

THE ADVERTISING STANDARDS AUTHORITY LTD AND THE COMMITTEE OF ADVERTISING PRACTICE for extracts from *British Codes of Advertising and Sales Promotion* (October 1999), clauses 1.4, 2.1–2.4, 2.8, 6.1, 7.1; 5.1–5.3, 12.1–12.2, 13.1–13.2, 13.4, 68.2, 68.6, 68.31–68.32, 68.39; *Annual Report 1996*, pp 1, 7; *Monthly Report (April 1999); Monthly Report (May 1999)*. A full set of the Codes and other background material is available free from www.asa.org.uk.

BLACKWELL PUBLISHERS for an extract from M Dockray, 'Courts on Television' (1988) 51 *Modern Law Review* 593, at 598–602.

THE BROADCASTING STANDARDS COMMISSION for extracts from Bulletin No 22 (June 1999) and Code on Fairness and Privacy (June 1998), paras 2–3, 7, 11–12, 22–23, 25–26

BOSTON UNIVERSITY SCHOOL OF LAW AND MILTON L SMITH for an extract from M L Smith, 'Space WARC 1985: The Quest for Equitable Access' (1985) 3 *Boston University International Law Journal* 229, at pp 237–241.

BUTTERWORTHS DIVISION OF REED ELSEVIER (UK) LTD for extracts from judgments of cases published in the All England Law Reports and for an extract from R Whish, *Competition Law*, 3rd ed (1993), pp 676–678.

CAMBRIDGE UNIVERSITY PRESS AND JUDITH LICHTENBERG for an extract from J Lichtenberg, 'Foundations and Limits of the Press', in J Lichtenberg (ed), *Democracy and the Mass Media* (1990), Chapter 3, pp 102–105.

CANADA LAW BOOK COMPANY, through the Canadian Copyright Licensing Agency (CANCOPY), for an extract from *Moyse v Alberta (Labour Relations Board)* (1989) 60 *Dominion Law Report* (4th) 1, at 4, 7–8 (judgment of Sopinka J, Supreme Court of Canada).

COLIN MUNRO for an extract from C Munro, 'The Banned Broadcasting Corporation' [1995] *New Law Journal* 518, at pp 519–520.

CTI LAW & TECHNOLOGY CENTRE, UNIVERSITY OF WARWICK for an extract from G Doyle, 'From "Pluralism" to "Ownership": Europe's Emergent Policy on Media Concentrations Navigates the Doldrums' (1997) 3 *The Journal of Information Law and Technology*, reproduced from website http://elj.warwick.ac.uk/jilt/commsreg/97–3doyl/.

DAVID J A GOLDBERG, J A W PROSSER AND STEFAN G VERHULST for extracts from D Goldberg, T Prosser and S Verhulst, *Regulating the Changing Media: A Comparative Study* (1998), pp 296–297, 298–299 and 314 and by permission of Oxford University Press.

ERIC BARENDT for an extract from E M Barendt, *Broadcasting Law: A Comparative Study* (1995), pp 5–9 by permission of Oxford University Press.

HER MAJESTY'S STATIONERY OFFICE for extracts from parliamentary copyright publications HCP 262 Home Affairs Committee 3rd Report; HoC Hansard, vol 308, 16 March 1998; HC 294 (1993). For extracts from Crown copyright publications Cmnd 6810 (1977); Cmnd 7772 (1979); Cm 2135 Calcutt Report; Cm 2918 (1995); Cmnd 9824 (1986); Cm 3152; The Future Funding of the BBC, July 1999; Cm 517 (1998); Cm 92 (1987); Cm 2946 (1995); Cmnd 2872 (1995); Listed Events Report and Recommendations, March 1998; Cm 4305 (1999); The Multi-Media Revolution, 4th Report; DTI Consultation Paper, January 1996; Cm 4022 (1998); DTI Regulating Communications: The Way Ahead (17 June 1999); Cmnd 5012 (1972); LCD Consultation Document, October 1996; Review of Access to and Reporting of Family Proceedings 1993; *The Pricing of Conditional Access Services for Digital Television*, OFTEL Consultative Document (October 1997); *The Regulation of Conditional Access for Digital Television Services: OFTEL Guidelines* (March 1997). Crown copyright is reproduced with the permission of the Controller of Her Majesty's Stationery Office.

HOWARD ANAWALT for an extract from H C Anawalt, 'Direct Television Broadcasting and the Quest for Communication Equality' in Michigan Yearbook of International Legal Studies, *Regulation of Transnational Communications* (1984), p 361, at pp 363–365.

INCORPORATED COUNCIL OF LAW REPORTING FOR ENGLAND AND WALES, London, for extracts from judgments of cases published in the Law Reports and the Weekly Law Reports.

INDEPENDENT TELEVISION COMMISSION for extracts from News Release 43/98, 28 April 1998; News Release 49/97, 24 June 1997; Television: The Digital Future (9 September 1998); News Release 118/98, 18 December 1998; The ITC Code of Advertising Standards and Practice (December 1998); Television Advertising Complaints Report (June 1997); Television Advertising Complaints Report (October 1997); Television Advertising Complaints Report (August 1998); Television Advertising Complaints Report (September 1998); Televisions Advertising Complaints Report (May 1999); Rules on the Amount and Scheduling of Advertising (December 1998); Review of ITC Code of Programme Sponsorship, Explanatory Memorandum (September 1996); ITC Code of Programme Sponsorship (September 1998); Review of ITC Code of Programme Sponsorship, Explanatory Memorandum (September 1996); ITC Programme Code (Autumn 1998); Code on Sports and Other Listed Events (January 1999); Consolidated Statement of ITC Rules on Cross-promotion of Digital Television Service; Competition Investigation into Channel Bundling etc, Consultation Document (April 1998); ITC Code of Conduct on Electronic Programme Guides (June 1997); Programme Complaints and Interventions Report (December 1997/January 1998); Programme Complaints and Interventions Report (February/March 1998); Programme Complaints and Intervention Report (August/September 1998); Programme Complaints and Interventions Report (April 1999); Programme Complaints and Interventions Report (May 1999).

INTERNATIONAL LAW STUDENTS ASSOCIATION AND A N DELZEIT AND R M WAHL for an extract from A N Delzeit and R M Wahl, 'Redefining Freedom of Speech under International Space Law: The Need for Bilateral Communications Alliances to Resolve the Debate Between the "Free Flow of Information" and "Prior Consent" Schools of Thought' (1995) *ILSA Journal of International and Comparative Law* 267, at 276–282.

INTERNATIONAL TELECOMMUNICATION UNION for extracts from the Final Acts of the Additional Plenipotentiary Conference, Geneva, 1992, Preamble, Article 1 and Nos 1001, 1003, 1012 of the Annex to the Constitution; International Telecommunication Convention, Nairobi, 1982, Provision 154, Article 33; International Telecommunication Convention, Malaga, Torremolinos, 1973, Article 33. The texts extracted from the ITU material have been reproduced with the prior authorisation of the Union as copyright holder; the sole responsibility for selecting extracts for reproduction lies with the beneficiary of this authorisation alone and in no way can be attributed to the ITU. The complete volume(s) of the ITU material, from which the texts reproduced are extracted, can be obtained from International Telecommunication Union, Sales and Marketing Service, Place des Nations, CH-1211 Geneva 20, Switzerland; e-mail: sales@itu.int; website: http://www.itu.int/publications.

THE MICHIGAN LAW REVIEW ASSOCIATION AND LEE C BOLLINGER for an extract from Lee C Bollinger, 'Freedom of the Press and Public Access: Toward a Theory of Partial Regulation' (1976) 75 *Michigan Law Review* 1, at 10–11, 13–16.

OFFICE FOR OFFICIAL PUBLICATIONS OF THE EUROPEAN COMMUNITIES, OP4—Sales and Copyright Management for extracts from judgments of cases published in the European Court Reports and for extracts from publications issued by the European Communities institutions.

OXFORD UNIVERSITY PRESS for extracts from B de Witte, 'The European Content Requirement in the EC Television Directive—Five Years After' in E M Barendt (ed), *The Yearbook of Media and Entertainment Law 1995*, pp 101–102, 104, 106–107, and 116–117; E M Barendt, 'Structural and Content Regulation of the Media: United Kingdom Law and Some American Comparisons' in E M Barendt (ed), *The Yearbook of Media and Entertainment Law 1997/8*, pp 89–90; R Wacks, 'Privacy in Cyberspace: Personal Information, Free Speech, and the Internet' in P Birks (ed), *Privacy and Loyalty* (1997), pp 93, 95–96, 97 and 102.

POLITY PRESS for an extract from R Collins and C Murroni, *New Media New Policies* (1996), pp 173–175.

PRESS COMPLAINTS COMMISSION for extracts from Press Complaints Commission Paper (July, 1996), p 12; Press Complaints Code of Practice, November 1997; PCC Report No 34 (1996), pp 5–8; PCC Report No 15 (1992), p 8; PCC Report No 27 (1994), p 11; PCC Report No 37 (1997), p 24; PCC Report No 40 (1997), pp 15–16; PCC Report No 40 (1997), p 16; PCC Report No 42 (1998), p 9; PCC Report No 43 (1998), pp 5–7, 10; PCC Report No 29 (1995), pp 6–7; PCC Report No 29 (1995), pp 30–31; PCC Report No 38 (1997), pp 9–12; PCC Report No 38 (1997), pp 9–12.

SOUTHERN METHODIST UNIVERSITY LAW REVIEW ASSOCIATION AND THE JOURNAL OF AIR LAW AND COMMERCE for an extract from J C Thompson, 'Space for Rent: The International Telecommunications Union, Space Law and Orbit/Spectrum Leasing' (1996) 62(2) *Journal of Air Law and Commerce* 279, at pp 290–292, 303–308.

SWEET & MAXWELL LTD for extracts from judgments of cases published in the Criminal Appeal Reports, European Human Rights Reports, European and Media Law Reports, Fleet Street Reports and for extracts from T Gibbons, 'Freedom of the Press: Ownership and Editorial Values' [1992] *Public Law* 279, at pp 290–291, 293–294; T Gibbons, *Regulating the Media*, 2nd ed (1998), pp 184–185, 223–225, 231–232, 301–302, 304.

TAYLOR & FRANCIS BOOKS LTD, INCORPORATING ROUTLEDGE, for an extract from J Curran and J Seaton, *Power Without Responsibility*, 5th ed (1997), pp 74–76.

While every care has been taken to establish and acknowledge copyright and contact the copyright owners, the publishers tender their apologies for any accidental infringement. They would be pleased to come to a suitable arrangement with the rightful owners in each case.

ABBREVIATIONS

BA	Broadcasting Act
BCC	Broadcasting Complaints Commission
BSC	Broadcasting Standards Commission
CCA	Contempt of Court Act
DA	Defamation Act
EC	European Community
ECHR	European Convention on Human Rights
ECJ	European Court of Justice
IBA	Independent Broadcasting Authority
ITC	Independent Television Commission
OFT	Office of Fair Trading
OFTEL	Office of Telecommunications
PCC	Press Complaints Commission
RA	Radio Authority

Barendt
E M Barendt, *Broadcasting Law: A Comparative Study* (Clarendon Press, 1995)

Gibbons
T Gibbons, *Regulating the Media*, 2nd ed (Sweet & Maxwell, 1998)

Robertson and Nicol
G Robertson and A Nicol, *Media Law*, 3rd ed (Penguin, 1992)

TABLE OF CASES

(*Note*: where a case is substantially extracted, the name is shown in heavy type. The page number is also in heavy type.)

UNITED KINGDOM

NON-UNITED KINGDOM CASES

AUSTRALIA

EUROPEAN FREE TRADE AREA COURT

GERMANY

NEW ZEALAND

UNITED STATES OF AMERICA

TABLE OF LEGISLATION

UNITED KINGDOM
STATUTES

STATUTORY INSTRUMENTS

1

THE PRINCIPLES OF MEDIA LAW

1. FREEDOM OF THE MEDIA

Although at first glance media law seems to consist of restrictions on the freedom of the press and broadcasters, that perspective can mislead. It is important to emphasise the central place of media freedom: the freedom to report and discuss matters of public interest. It is necessary for newspapers, broadcasters and other branches of the media to perform their vital role in the political and social life of a liberal society. So media freedom has been recognised in many constitutions (see Extracts 1.1.2 and 1.1.3) and by the European Court of Human Rights (see Section 2 of this chapter).

In the absence of a codified constitution or Bill of Rights, English law has hitherto taken a more limited view of the freedom. Two hundred years ago William Blackstone wrote that press freedom 'consists in laying no *previous* restraints upon publications and not in freedom from censure for criminal matters when published'.[1] The presumption against previous, or prior, restraints is discussed in the final section of this chapter. Dicey, the influential 19th century constitutional lawyer, agreed that the absence of any system of licensing was central to freedom of the press. He also emphasised other aspects of English press law.

Extract 1.1.1

A V Dicey, *An Introduction to the Study of the Law of the Constitution*, 10th ed (Macmillan, 1961), pp 246–247

Freedom of discussion is, then, in England little else than the right to write or say anything which a jury, consisting of twelve shopkeepers, think it expedient should be said or written. Such 'liberty' may vary at different times and seasons from unrestricted license to very severe restraint, and the experience of English history during the last two centuries shows that under the law of libel the amount of latitude conceded to the expression of opinion has, in

---

[1] 4 Bl Comm, 16th ed (London, 1825), p 151.

fact, differed greatly according to the condition of popular sentiment. Until very recent times the law, moreover, has not recognised any privilege on the part of the press. A statement which is defamatory or blasphemous, if made in a letter or upon a card, has exactly the same character if made in a book or a newspaper. The protection given by the Belgian constitution to the editor, printer, or seller of a newspaper involves a recognition of special rights on the part of persons connected with the press which is quite inconsistent with the general theory of English law. It is hardly an exaggeration to say, from this point of view, that liberty of the press is not recognised in England.

This account now seems complacent. First, it is surely wrong to rely on juries to safeguard freedom of the media; their members may be unsympathetic to the opinions of minorities or to the radical press and magazines.[2] Secondly, a number of restraints on the media may be imposed without their involvement. It is judges who determine whether to grant an injunction to restrain breaches of confidence (see Chapter 11) and whether to uphold applications to commit editors for contempt of court (Chapter 12). The broadcasting media may be subject to some degree of administrative censorship (see Section 5 of this chapter, and Chapters 3–4).

English law may be contrasted with that in other jurisdictions where media freedom is protected by the constitution.

Extract 1.1.2

The First Amendment to the US Constitution (1791)

Congress shall make no law . . . abridging the freedom of speech, or of the press . . .

Although the Supreme Court has never taken the absolutist approach that no regulation at all of the media is permissible, the First Amendment does mean that all types of regulation – the laws of libel and privacy, contempt of court and other reporting restrictions, broadcasting and cable regulation – can be reviewed by the courts to see that they do not infringe the freedoms guaranteed by it. The equivalent provision in the post-war German Basic Law (or Constitution) is much fuller.

Extract 1.1.3

Article 5 of the German Basic Law (1949)

(1) Everyone shall have the right freely to express and disseminate his opinion by speech, writing and pictures, and freely to inform himself from

---

[2] Moreover, juries have been responsible for the award of extravagant damages in libel cases: see Chapter 10, Section 6.

generally accessible sources. Freedom of the press and freedom of reporting by means of broadcasts and films are guaranteed. There shall be no censorship.

(2) These rights are limited by the provisions of the general laws, the provisions of law for the protection of youth, and by the right to inviolability of personal honour.

(3) [*Omitted*].

2. THE EUROPEAN CONVENTION AND THE HUMAN RIGHTS ACT 1998

(a) The Convention and the European Court of Human Rights

Press and media freedom are not explicitly guaranteed by the Convention, but they are covered by the right to freedom of expression protected in art 10.

Extract 1.2.1

European Convention on Human Rights and Fundamental Freedoms, art 10

(1) Everyone has the right to freedom of expression. This right shall include freedom to hold opinions and to receive and impart information and ideas without interference by public authority and regardless of frontiers. This Article shall not prevent States from requiring the licensing of broadcasting, television or cinema enterprises.

(2) The exercise of these freedoms, since it carries with it duties and responsibilities, may be subject to such formalities, conditions, restrictions or penalties as are prescribed by law and are necessary in a democratic society in the interests of national security, territorial integrity or public safety, for the prevention of disorder or crime, for the protection of health or morals, for the protection of the reputation or rights of others, for preventing the disclosure of information received in confidence, or for maintaining the authority and impartiality of the judiciary.

The importance of art 10 for the press, and the mass media generally, was made plain in the *Sunday Times* case. The House of Lords had granted an injunction to stop the publication of a newspaper article discussing the responsibility of the drugs company, Distillers, for the deformities caused by its thalidomide drug (see Chapter 12 and Extract 12.1.1). A majority of the European Court of Human Rights held that this restraint could not be justified as a 'necessary in a democratic society . . . for maintaining the authority of the judiciary'.

Extract 1.2.2

The Sunday Times v United Kingdom (1979) 2 EHRR 245, at 280–281 (European Court of Human Rights) (footnotes omitted)

As the Court remarked in its HANDYSIDE judgment,[3] freedom of expression constitutes one of the essential foundations of a democratic society; subject to paragraph 2 of Article 10, it is applicable not only to information or ideas that are favourably received or regarded as inoffensive or as a matter of indifference, but also to those that offend, shock or disturb the State or any sector of the population.

These principles are of particular importance as far as the press is concerned. They are equally applicable to the field of the administration of justice, which serves the interests of the community at large and requires the co-operation of an enlightened public. There is general recognition of the fact that the courts cannot operate in a vacuum. Whilst they are the forum for the settlement of disputes, this does not mean that there can be no prior discussion of disputes elsewhere, be it in specialised journals, in the general press or amongst the public at large. Furthermore, whilst the mass media must not overstep the bounds imposed in the interests of the proper administration of justice, it is incumbent on them to impart information and ideas concerning matters that come before the courts just as in other areas of public interest. Not only do the media have the task of imparting such information and ideas: the public also has a right to receive them.

To assess whether the interference complained of was based on 'sufficient' reasons which rendered it 'necessary in a democratic society', account must thus be taken of any public interest aspect of the case. The Court observes in this connection that, following a balancing of the conflicting interests involved, an absolute rule was formulated by certain of the Law Lords to the effect that it was not permissible to prejudge issues in pending cases: it was considered that the law would be too uncertain if the balance were to be struck anew in each case . . . Whilst emphasising that it is not its function to pronounce itself on an interpretation of English law adopted in the House of Lords, the Court points out that it has to take a different approach. The Court is faced not with a choice between two conflicting principles, but with a principle of freedom of expression that is subject to a number of exceptions which must be narrowly interpreted. In the second place, the Court's supervision under Article 10 covers not only the basic legislation but also the decision applying it. It is not sufficient that the interference involved belongs to that class of the exceptions listed in Article 10(2) which has been invoked; neither is it sufficient that the interference was imposed because its subject-matter fell within a particular category or was caught by a legal rule formulated in general or absolute terms: the Court has to be satisfied that the interference was necessary having regard to the facts and circumstances prevailing in the specific case before it.

---

[3] *Handyside v United Kingdom* (1979–80) 1 EHRR 737. The case involved an unsuccessful challenge to the application of UK obscenity legislation to a booklet addressed to adolescents, which advocated sexual freedom and liberal use of drugs.

Another important decision of the European Court of Human Rights was its ruling that Austrian defamation law violated the Convention when it required the defendant, the publisher of a satirical magazine, to prove the truth of an expression of opinion on the political manoeuvres of the Chancellor, Bruno Kreisky; the Court emphasised the importance of the press in fostering political debate.[4]

In one case the Court ruled that journalists enjoy freedom under the Convention to report offensive speech in respect of which the speaker himself could be prosecuted. The applicant, a Danish journalist, conducted a television interview with a youth group ('the Greenjackets'), in the course of which members of the group made racist remarks. The Court held that the journalist's conviction for aiding the spread of racist speech infringed art 10.

Extract 1.2.3

Jersild v Denmark (1995) 19 EHRR 1, at 215–218 (European Court of Human Rights) (footnotes omitted)

A significant feature of the present case is that the applicant did not make the objectionable statements himself but assisted in their dissemination in his capacity of television journalist for a news programme . . . In assessing whether his conviction and sentence were 'necessary', the Court will therefore have regard to the principles established in its case-law relating to the role of the press. . . .

In considering the 'duties and responsibilities' of a journalist, the potential impact of the medium concerned is an important factor and it is commonly acknowledged that the audio-visual media have often a much more immediate and powerful effect than the print media. . . . The audio-visual media have means of conveying through images meanings which the print media are not able to impart.

At the same time, the methods of objective and balanced reporting may vary considerably, depending among other things on the media in question. It is not for this Court, nor for the national courts for that matter, to substitute their own views for those of the press as to what technique of reporting should be adopted by journalists. In this context the Court recalls that Article 10 protects not only the substance of the ideas and information expressed, but also the form in which they are conveyed. . . .

News reporting based on interviews, whether edited or not, constitutes one of the most important means whereby the press is able to play its vital role of 'public watch-dog' . . . The punishment of a journalist for assisting in the dissemination of statements made by another person in an interview would seriously hamper the contribution of the press to discussion of matters of public interest and should not be envisaged unless there are particularly strong reasons for doing so. . . .

---

[4] *Lingens v Austria* (1986) 8 EHRR 407.

There can be no doubt that the remarks in respect of which the Greenjackets were convicted . . . were more than insulting to members of the targeted groups and did not enjoy the protection of Article 10. . . . However, even having regard to the manner in which the applicant prepared the Greenjackets item . . . it has not been shown that, considered as a whole, the feature was such as to justify also his conviction of . . . a criminal offence under the Penal Code.

The interpretation of art 10 poses problems in the context of the broadcasting media and the cinema. Under the third sentence of its first paragraph, states may establish licensing systems for these media. A relevant question is the relationship between this sentence and the terms of paragraph (2), which appears to allow restrictions on freedom of expression only when they are necessary for the protection of the rights and interests set out in that paragraph.

The Court addressed these issues in *Informationsverein Lentia*, where the issue was the compatibility of the Austrian public broadcasting monopoly with the Convention.

Extract 1.2.4

Informationsverein Lentia v Austria (1994) 17 EHRR 93, at 112–114
(European Court of Human Rights) (footnotes omitted)

As the Court has already held, the purpose of [the third sentence of paragraph 1] is to make it clear that States are permitted to regulate by a licensing system the way in which broadcasting is organised in their territories, particularly in its technical aspects. Technical aspects are undeniably important, but the grant or refusal of a licence may also be made conditional on other considerations, including such matters as the nature and objectives of a proposed station, its potential audience at national, regional or local level, the rights and needs of a specific audience and the obligations deriving from international legal instruments.

This may lead to interferences whose aims will be legitimate under the third sentence of paragraph 1, even though they do not correspond to any of the aims set out in paragraph 2. The compatibility of such interferences with the Convention must nevertheless be assessed in the light of the other requirements of paragraph 2.

The monopoly system operated in Austria is capable of contributing to the quality and balance of programmes, through the supervisory powers over the media thereby conferred on the authorities. In the circumstances of the present case, it is therefore consistent with the third sentence of paragraph 1. It remains, however, to be determined whether it also satisfies the relevant conditions of paragraph 2.

The Court has frequently stressed the fundamental role of freedom of expression in a democratic society, in particular where, through the press, it serves to impart information and ideas of general interest, which the public is moreover entitled to receive. Such an undertaking cannot be successfully accomplished unless it is grounded in the principle of pluralism, of which the State is the ultimate guarantor. This observation is especially valid in relation to audiovisual media, whose programmes are often broadcast very widely.

Of all the means of ensuring the these values are respected, a public monopoly is the one which imposes the greatest restrictions on the freedom of expression, namely the total impossibility of broadcasting otherwise than through a national station and, in some cases, to a very limited extent through a local cable station. The far-reaching character of such restrictions means that they can only be justified where they correspond to a pressing need.

As a result of the technical progress made over the last decades, justification for these restrictions can no longer today be found in considerations relating to the number of frequencies and channels available; the Government accepted this . . .

The Government finally adduced an economic argument, namely that the Austrian market was too small to sustain a sufficient number of stations to avoid regroupings and the constitution of 'private monopolies.'

In the applicant's opinion, this is a pretext for a policy which, by eliminating all competition, seeks above all to guarantee to the Austrian Broadcasting Corporation advertising revenue, at the expense of the principle of free enterprise.

The Court is not persuaded by the Government's argument. Their assertions are contradicted by the experience of several European States, of a comparable size to Austria, in which the coexistence of private and public stations, according to rules which vary from country to country and accompanied by measures preventing the development of private monopolies, shows the fears expressed to be groundless.

In short, like the Commission, the Court considers that the interferences in issue were disproportionate to the aim pursued and were, accordingly, not necessary in a democratic society. There has therefore been a violation of Article 10.

Questions for discussion

1. Does the *Jersild* case suggest that journalists and broadcasters have a right under the Convention to express, say, racist views, the expression of which by members of the public would be a criminal offence?

2. What are the implications of the 'principle of pluralism' referred to in *Informationsverein*? Does it require the state to intervene to promote a variety of media outlets or to ensure that broadcasters (and perhaps even newspapers) present a range of views?

(b) The Human Rights Act 1998

The European Convention on Human Rights has now been incorporated into UK law. The Human Rights Act 1998, which comes into force in October 2000, provides that it is unlawful for any 'public authority', including courts and persons, some of whose functions are 'of a public nature', to act incompatibly with the Convention rights set out in Sched 1 to the Act.[5] Legislation must be interpreted compatibly with them;[6] moreover, if that proves impossible, the High Court and appellate courts may declare legislation incompatible with the Convention.[7] But they have no power to invalidate an Act of Parliament for this reason.

Incorporation of the Convention is likely to have repercussions for media law. Courts will be required to interpret legislation restricting media freedom, such as the Contempt of Court Act 1981 (see Chapters 12–14) and the Youth Justice and Criminal Evidence Act 1999 (see Chapter 13), compatibly with the right to freedom of expression. Further, the decisions of such bodies as the Independent Television Commission and the Broadcasting Standards Commission (see Chapter 4) must also conform to the Convention. In determining the scope of Convention rights, UK courts must take account of decisions of the European Court of Human Rights.[8] During the passage of the measure through Parliament, the press expressed anxiety that it would lead inevitably to the development of a right to privacy which English law hitherto has not recognised.[9] Largely to meet this anxiety, it was amended to give special treatment to freedom of expression.

Extract 1.2.5

Human Rights Act 1998, s 12(4)

(4) The court must have particular regard to the importance of the Convention right to freedom of expression and, where the proceedings relate to material which the respondent claims, or which appears to the court, to be journalistic, literary or artistic material . . . , to—
    (a) the extent to which—
        (i) the material has, or is about to, become available to the public; or
        (ii) it is, or would be, in the public interest for the material to be published;
    (b) any relevant privacy code.

The significance of this provision for the development of privacy law will be explored in Chapter 11, while Section 5 of this chapter discusses the impact of other provisions of the HRA on prior restraints on the media.

---

[5] Human Rights Act 1998, s 6.
[6] Ibid, s 3.
[7] Ibid, s 4.
[8] Ibid, s 2.
[9] For further discussion, see Chapter 11 below.

3. THE SPECIAL REGULATION OF THE BROADCASTING MEDIA

The print media – newspapers, magazines, and books – are not subject to any licensing system. Their freedom is limited only by the criminal and civil law, aspects of which will be discussed in Chapters 10–13, and in the case of newspapers and magazines by a system of voluntary regulation operated by the Press Complaints Commission (see Chapter 2).

In contrast, broadcasters are additionally subject to a number of special restrictions. First, the company operating the channel must obtain a licence.[10] Secondly, programme restrictions go beyond the constraints imposed by the law, say, of obscenity and blasphemy. Finally, all broadcasters must show 'due impartiality', while some channels are required to show news bulletins and serious programmes.[11] There are no restrictions of these kinds on the press. A newspaper, for instance, is free to support a political party and may wholly ignore foreign affairs or other stories which in its view are of no interest to its readers.

Is there any justification for this radical divergence in the regulation of the principal branches of the mass media? A law review article by a prominent commentator in the USA has discussed the question against the background of two Supreme Court decisions. In *Tornillo*[12] it struck down a law providing for a 'right of reply' to newspaper columns as incompatible with freedom of the press, while in its previous ruling in *Red Lion* it had upheld the reply right granted by the Federal Communications Commission to personal attacks on radio and television.[13] The Court was persuaded that it was legitimate to regulate the latter because of the scarcity of frequencies for broadcasting.

Extract 1.3.1

Lee C Bollinger, 'Freedom of the Press and Public Access: Toward a Theory of Partial Regulation' (1976) 75 *Michigan Law Review* 1, at 10–11, 13–16 (footnotes omitted)

It is clear that the Court has not made explicit just what is so 'unique' about the broadcast media that justifies legislative action impermissible in the news-paper context. It is doubtful that the so-called scarcity rationale articulated in . . . *Red Lion* provides an explanation. Certainly the scarcity rationale ex-plains why Congress was justified in devising an allocation scheme to prevent the overcrowding of broadcasting frequencies. It may also serve to explain in part why the television industry is so concentrated. The scarcity rationale does

---

[10] See Chapter 3, Section 4.
[11] For full treatment of these topics, see Chapter 4 below.
[12] *Miami Herald Publishing Co v Tornillo*, 418 US 241 (1974).
[13] *Red Lion Broadcasting Co v FCC*, 395 US 367 (1969).

not, however, explain why what appears to be a similar phenomenon of natural monopolization within the newspaper industry does not constitute an equally appropriate occasion for access regulation. A difference in the cause of concentration – the exhaustion of a physical element necessary for communication in broadcasting as contrasted with the economic constraints on the number of possible competitors in the print media – would seem far less relevant from a first amendment standpoint than the fact of concentration itself. Thus, it might be argued that a person 'attacked' in the *Washington Post*, or one who holds a different viewpoint than that expressed in that newspaper, is able to publish a pamphlet or his own 'newspaper' in response. But does this have any more appeal than a similar argument with respect to the Columbia Broadcasting System?

It is true, of course, that a person with the requisite capital and inclination could, theoretically, always establish his own newspaper if the local print media refused to publish his point of view, whereas it is highly unlikely that he could establish his own broadcast station if the local stations refused to cover his viewpoint. But this seems a slim basis on which to predicate such dramatically different constitutional treatment. Even if we assume greater ease in entering the print media, however, the question remains why the purported openness of the newspaper market should not be considered an important factor in assessing the significance of concentration in the broadcast media. Why, this analysis asks, did the Court in *Red Lion* treat the broadcast media as separate and discrete? Why did the Court, in an exercise similar to defining the 'relevant market' in an antitrust case, narrow its focus to a particular segment of the mass media? Why did the Court not say that, so long as people can gain access somewhere within the mass media, there is no need for legislative action in any concentrated branch? The treatment of the broadcast media as discrete constitutes at least implicit acknowledgement that the newspaper and other major print media are also highly restricted. If anyone could set up a major newspaper, would we really care if entry into the broadcast media was physically precluded? Or is the explanation somehow hinged to the nature of the regulatory scheme itself?

. . .

In many important respects, television is today the most pervasive medium of communications in our society. Not only does virtually everyone have access to a television set, but more people watch it, even for purposes of obtaining news, and for longer periods, than read the publications of the print media. In addition, television is frequently considered to have a 'special impact' on its audience. Thus, many courts and commentators believe television is today the dominant means of influencing public opinion, not only because more people watch it than read newspapers, but also because it possesses some undefined and unquantifiable, but nevertheless unique, capacity to shape the opinions of the viewers in ways unrelated to the merits of the arguments presented. The television medium, it is also said, offers the opportunity to thrust information and ideas onto the audience. Unlike printed publications, which can be avoided by 'averting the eyes,' television provides the opportunity to force extraneous messages onto audiences gathered for other purposes. This medium, in short, may be the preeminent forum for the discussion of ideas and viewpoints in the society and it may offer opportunities to persuade that cannot be matched elsewhere within the system of expression. The greater concentration of power in television, therefore, may arguably represent more serious social and first amendment problems than the situation in the print media.

This line of argument, promising though it may seem, contains several serious problems. First, the analysis fails to explain why the current level of concentration in newspapers, even assuming that it is not as high as that in television, is not sufficiently troublesome by itself to justify governmental intervention . . .

Even more problematical, however, is the alleged special impact of television. Quite apart from any natural suspicions concerning the validity of the claim, given the frequency with which it seems to confront each new medium of communications, the impact thesis is a dangerously amorphous justification for regulation. It provides no clear limits to official authority and invites censorship as well as affirmative regulation. Further, in so far as the thesis rests upon the premise that regulation is more acceptable the greater the audience and the impact, it seems inconsistent with the underlying purpose of the first amendment, which presumably is to protect effective as well as ineffective speech. . . . Finally, there is simply no evidence at the present time to support the proposition that television shapes attitudes and ideas in ways so unprecedented as to require urgent remedial regulation. Thus, until more evidence exists to support the theory, or perhaps until a much wider consensus is formed in its support, it seems wise to avoid relying on the special impact theory.

It is at this point that conventional thinking about broadcast regulation largely stops. Once it is determined that the broadcast and print media are constitutionally indistinguishable, then it is concluded that the Court's theory of access regulation is without rational foundation and should be discarded at the earliest opportunity. Such a conclusion possesses a certain legalistic appeal, but it also may be an oversimplification. The very weakness of the scarcity rationale suggests that there is something more here than first meets the eye. The dual treatment of the press has been so long accepted even by persons known for their sensitivity to first amendment values, that the scarcity rationale may in fact be a convenient legal fiction covering more subtle and important considerations.

It is helpful, therefore, to adopt a less formalistic approach to the problem and to probe beyond normal legal analysis to account for this remarkable constitutional development. For even if broadcasting and the printing press are essentially the same, they nevertheless have different origins, have existed for different periods of time, and one has been controlled from its beginnings while the other has been left unrestricted. It is important, in short, that our analysis be sensitive to the historical process through which the present system has developed.

The crucial point, so far as Bollinger is concerned, is not whether broadcasting is really different from the print media, but the fact that they are generally considered to be different. But we will see from the next extract that he also attempted to justify the diverse treatment of the two mass media.

The arguments have also been considered in the UK, though here they lack the constitutional dimension they have in the USA and in Germany.

Extract 1.3.2

E M Barendt, *Broadcasting Law: A Comparative Study* (Clarendon Press, 1995), pp 5–9 (some footnotes omitted)

The [scarcity] argument is, however, less clear than appears at first sight. Does, for example, the scarcity of frequencies refer to the limited number *allocated* by the government as available for broadcasting or to the actual *numerical shortage* of broadcasting stations? If the former, it can be argued that the scarcity is an artificial creation of the government (rather than a natural phenomenon) since it reserves a number of frequencies for the use of the army, police, and other public services; government is then not in a good position to argue for restrictions on broadcasters' freedom. Further, economic liberals contend that if broadcasting licences were sold to the highest bidders (as happened in Britain in 1991), and they were then free to sell them, there would probably not be an excess of those wishing to broadcast over the supply of frequencies. That problem arises when a government chooses to award licences for nothing (or at below market price). On the alternative formulation of actual scarcity, it has been pointed out that in the United States there has been an increase in the number of broadcasting stations during the last twenty years, while there are fewer newspapers than there used to be.[i] Comparable developments have occurred in European countries in the same period, especially since the advent of cable and satellite.

The scarcity argument cannot easily be divorced from economic considerations. The German Constitutional Court, for instance, coupled them when it held positive regulation of the broadcasting media constitutionally necessary. The shortage of frequencies and the high costs of starting up broadcasting channels explained their dearth in comparison with the numbers (in 1961) of newspapers and magazines.[ii] However, it is now probably as difficult to finance a new newspaper as it is a private television channel, if not more so. Certainly that is true if a comparison is made between the costs of setting up a national newspaper and a local community radio station. Yet anybody rich enough to afford the former is free to publish what he wants, while there are (in most countries) limits on what the latter may broadcast. If, on the other hand, it is relatively easy to enter the press market, it may be hard to see why policy-makers should be so concerned about the prohibitive costs of instituting a broadcasting station: those unable to afford that would be able to communicate effectively in other ways.[iii]

Finally the scarcity argument is much less tenable now than it used to be. Cable and satellite have significantly increased the number of available or potentially available channels, so that there are more broadcasting outlets than there are daily newspapers (national and local), though it is harder to calculate the respective numbers of television or radio stations and specialist magazines. . . .

[Another] major argument for the differential treatment emphasizes the character of the broadcasting media. Television and radio, it is said, are more influential on public opinion than the press, or at least are widely thought to be. In the *Pacifica* case the United States Supreme Court majority said that they intrude into the home, are more pervasive, and are more difficult to control than the print media.[iv] In particular, it is hard to prevent children from being exposed to broadcasts, while it is relatively easy to stop them looking at magazines and papers (which in any case they may not be able to read or purchase). . . .

A somewhat different version of this argument has been formulated by the German Constitutional Court in the *Third Television* case:[v] regulation is necessary to guarantee pluralism and programme variety, whether or not there is now a shortage of frequencies and other broadcasting outlets. The free market will not provide for broadcasting the same variety found in the range of press and magazine titles. It follows that programme content should be regulated and that media monopolies should be cut down by the application of anti-trust laws. The implications of these propositions may differ from those which flow from the *Pacifica* rationale; but both the United States and German arguments lay stress on the power of television and its unique capacity to influence the public.

The arguments are difficult to assess. Broadcasting does not intrude into the home unless listeners and viewers want it to. From the point of view of constitutional principle, it is not easy to justify the imposition of greater limits on the medium on the ground that it is more influential than the written word. It cannot be right to subject more persuasive types of speech to greater restraints than those imposed on less effective varieties. On the other hand, the Court majority in the *Pacifica* case was probably right to regard broadcasting (particularly television) as a 'uniquely pervasive presence' in the lives of most people. Regrettable though it may be, much more time is spent watching television than reading; further, the presence of sound and picture in the home makes it an exceptionally potent medium. It may also be harder to stop children having access to 'adult material' on television than to pornographic magazines. . . .

These . . . justifications for broadcasting regulation are inconclusive. There may still be something to the scarcity rationale, and it is probably true that broadcasting is the most influential medium of communication. But it is doubtful whether the case is powerful enough to justify the radically different legal treatment of the press and broadcasting media. A separate question is whether it is appropriate to continue to treat radio in the same way as television. There is generally a large choice of local, if not national, radio programmes, and it is hard to believe that they exercise a dominating influence on the formation of public attitudes. A similar question arises for cable television.[vi] Although a permit must be obtained from a licensing authority, several franchises may be physically accommodated and a wideband cable system may be able to carry up to thirty or forty or even more channels. The scarcity rationale therefore seems inapplicable to cable, and, further, it is hard to believe that this mode of broadcasting exercises such a strong influence that stringent programme regulation is justifiable.

The last argument for the divergent treatment of the press and broadcasting media has been made by a leading American scholar, Lee Bollinger.[vii] He admits that there is no fundamental difference in the character of the two mass media. But they have been perceived as different, a phenomenon to be explained in terms of their history. Broadcasting is still a relatively new means of mass communication, and it is understandable that society has wanted to regulate it, just as it has treated the cinema with more caution than it has the theatre. Bollinger's case is, however, not based solely on tradition. He justifies the divergent treatment of the two media on the ground that society is entitled to remedy the deficiencies of an unregulated press with a regulated broadcasting system. That may be preferable to attempting to regulate both sectors. Regulation poses the danger of government control, a risk which is reduced if one branch of the media is left free.

This seems an unsatisfactory compromise. It does not appeal to the advocates of broadcasting deregulation. If regulation of the press is always wrong (and perhaps unconstitutional) and if there is no significant difference between its position and that of the broadcasting media, it follows that the latter should also be wholly unregulated. On those assumptions, Bollinger's case would appear to lack coherence.[viii] For it attempts to justify the unequal treatment of the liberties of broadcasters and newspaper proprietors and editors, when in all material respects their position is identical.

The argument is also unconvincing from the opposite perspective that regulation of the broadcasting media compensates for the weaknesses of an unregulated press. Suppose one shares Bollinger's view that there are powerful arguments for regulating the press, for example, by mandating in some circumstances rights of reply or access to it. His argument is that we have become used to an unregulated press and that there are good reasons for only regulating one part of the mass media. The question is then whether it makes sense to correct the (alleged) shortcomings of the press by regulating the broadcasting media to ensure that they are not repeated there. This is doubtful. In Britain, for instance, the press is overwhelmingly sympathetic to the Conservative Party, while broadcasters must not express their views and their programmes must be impartial. These latter restraints will only remedy a lack of balance in the newspaper industry on the assumption that otherwise broadcasters would also present predominantly Conservative programmes. However, the government imposed a tougher impartiality requirement in the Broadcasting Act 1990, because (some of) its supporters felt television and radio programmes were too left-wing!

[i] See Powe, [*American Broadcasting and the First Amendment*, Berkeley, California, 1987], 204–8.

[ii] See 12 BVerfGE 205, 262 (1961).

[iii] See Bollinger, 'Freedom of the Press and Public Access' [Extract 1.3.1 above], 11.

[iv] *FCC v Pacifica Foundation* 438 US 736 (1978) . . .

[v] 57 BVerfGE 295, 322–3 (1981).

[vi] The United States courts have been unsure whether to treat cable as similar to the press or to terrestrial broadcasting when ruling on the constitutionality of its broadcasting: see P. Parsons, *Cable Television and the First Amendment* (Lexington, Mass., 1987) . . .

[vii] See . . . 'Freedom of the Press and Public Access' [Extract 1.3.1 above] . . .

[viii] For the requirement of coherence and integrity in law, see R. M. Dworkin, *Law's Empire* (London, 1986), ch. 6.

Questions for discussion

1.   Do you agree with the view in the preceding extracts that the scarcity argument no longer justifies broadcasting regulation?

2.   Is it reasonable to impose greater constraints on television than on the print media, given the character of the former?

3.   Does Barendt do justice to Bollinger's argument for partial regulation of the media?

Considerations will be given to the implications of these arguments for the scope of broadcasting regulation in Chapter 3. Arguably, the case for this special regulation is further weakened by the growing convergence of broadcasting with telecommunications and with the Internet: see Chapter 8.

4. MEDIA FREEDOM AND FREEDOM OF SPEECH

Media freedom is intimately connected with freedom of speech. Dicey thought freedom of the press and the freedom of individual writers were substantially the same (see Extract 1.1.1 above). Although freedom of speech and freedom of the press are separately mentioned in the US and German constitutional provisions, it is unclear whether they have distinct meanings. On one view, press freedom is essentially the freedom of editors and journalists to express their views; similarly, broadcasting freedom is the freedom of radio and television commentators and producers to speak and make programmes. There is something to be said for this perspective. If the government bans a television programme or libel damages are awarded against a newspaper, both freedom of speech and freedom of the media are implicated.

But this perspective may fail to do justice to the complexity of media freedom. The difficulties can be exposed by posing some questions. Does an instruction by an editor to a journalist not to publish an article amount to an infringement of free speech, or is it an exercise of editorial freedom, an aspect of press freedom? Does a rule requiring broadcasters to show 'due impartiality' on matters of controversy, and not to express their own views, interfere with broadcasting freedom? Or should such a rule be defended as enhancing the access of viewers to a range of opinion and so protecting their freedom of speech?

The next two extracts broadly share the view that freedom of the press is a distinct concept. It certainly encompasses the freedom of individual writers to express their opinions, but it also gives editors and owners separate rights. The first is taken from the Report of the Royal Commission on the Press in 1977, the most recent of the three Commissions to investigate the position of newspapers after the Second World War. The second extract is from an article by Potter Stewart, a member of the Supreme Court, on the Free Press limb of the First Amendment (Extract 1.1.2).

15

Extract 1.4.1

Royal Commission on the Press, Cmnd 6810 (1977) Chapter 2: Functions and Freedom of the Press, paras 2.2–2.3

2.2 Freedom of the press carries different meanings for different people. Some emphasise the freedom of proprietors to market their publications, others the freedom of individuals, whether professional journalists or not, to address the public through the press; still others stress the freedom of editors to decide what shall be published. These are all elements in the right to freedom of expression. But proprietors, contributors and editors must accept the limits to free expression set by the need to reconcile claims which may often conflict. The public, too, asserts a right to accurate information and fair comment which, in turn, has to be balanced against the claims both of national security and of individuals to safeguards for their reputation and privacy except when these are overridden by the public interest. But the public interest does not reside in whatever the public may happen to find interesting, and the press must be careful not to perpetrate abuses and call them freedom. Freedom of the press cannot be absolute. There must be boundaries to it and realistic discussion concerns where those boundaries ought to be set.

2.3 We define freedom of the press as that degree of freedom from restraint which is essential to enable proprietors, editors and journalists to advance the public interest by publishing the facts and opinions without which a democratic electorate cannot make responsible judgements. However, some parts of the press are more subject to economic than to other forms of restraint. Anyone is free to start a daily national newspaper, but few can afford even to contemplate the prospect.

Extract 1.4.2

Potter Stewart, 'Or of the Press' (1975) 26 *Hastings Law Journal* 633–634

It seems to me that the Court's approach . . . has uniformly reflected its understanding that the Free Press guarantee is, in essence, a *structural* provision of the Constitution. Most of the other provisions in the Bill of Rights protect specific liberties or specific rights of individuals: freedom of speech, freedom of worship, the right to counsel, the privilege against compulsory self-incrimination, to name a few. In contrast, the Free Press Clause extends protection to an institution. The publishing business is, in short, the only organized private business that is given explicit constitutional protection.

This basic understanding is essential, I think, to avoid an elementary error of constitutional law. It is tempting to suggest that freedom of the press means only that newspaper publishers are guaranteed freedom of expression. They *are* guaranteed that freedom, to be sure, but so are we all, because of the Free Speech Clause. If the Free Press guarantee meant no more than freedom of expression, it would be a constitutional redundancy. . . .

It is also a mistake to suppose that the only purpose of the constitutional guarantee of a free press is to insure that a newspaper will serve as a neutral forum for debate, a 'market-place for ideas', a kind of Hyde Park corner for the community. A related theory sees the press as a neutral conduit of information between the public and their elected leaders. These theories, in my view, again give insufficient weight to the institutional autonomy of the press that it was the purpose of the Constitution to guarantee.

. . .

The primary purpose of the constitutional guarantee of a free press was . . . to create a fourth institution outside the Government as an additional check on the three official branches. Consider the opening words of the Massachusetts Constitution, drafted by John Adams:

'The liberty of the press is essential to the security of the state.'

The relevant metaphor, I think, is the metaphor of the Fourth Estate. What Thomas Carlyle wrote about the British Government a century ago has a curiously contemporary ring:

'Burke said there were three Estates in Parliament; but, in the Reporters' Gallery yonder, there sat a Fourth Estate more important far than they all. It is not a figure of speech or witty saying; it is a literal fact – very momentous to us in these times.'

In the following extract Judith Lichtenberg offers a different analysis. In her view, media freedom is valuable only insofar as it promotes the values underlying the fundamental human right to freedom of speech. It may follow that it is legitimate to regulate the media to foster pluralism and other values associated with that fundamental freedom.[14]

Extract 1.4.3

J Lichtenberg, 'Foundations and Limits of Freedom of the Press', in J Lichtenberg (ed), *Democracy and the Mass Media* (Cambridge University Press, 1990), Chapter 3, pp 102–105

I confess that I do not entertain that firm and complete attachment to the liberty of the press which is wont to be excited by things that are supremely good in their very nature.

Alexis de Tocqueville, *Democracy in America*[i]

Freedom of the press is guaranteed only to those who own one.

A. J. Liebling, *The Press*[ii]

Tocqueville and Liebling notwithstanding, freedom of the press in democratic societies is a nearly unchallengeable dogma – essential, it is thought, to

---

[14] Also see E M Barendt, 'Press and Broadcasting Freedom; Does Anyone have any Rights to Free Speech?' [1991] 44 *Current Legal Problems* 63, at 64–67.

individual autonomy and self-expression, and an indispensable element in democracy and the attainment of truth. Both its eloquent theoreticians and its contemporary popular advocates defend freedom of speech and freedom of the press in the same stroke, with the implication that they are inseparable, probably equivalent, and equally fundamental.

At the same time, we know that the press in its most characteristic modern incarnation – mass media in mass society – works not only to enhance the flow of ideas and information but also to inhibit it. Nothing guarantees that all valuable information, ideas, theories, explanations, proposals, and points of view will find expression in the public forum.[iii] Indeed, many factors lead us to expect that they will not. The most obvious is that 'mass media space-time' is a scarce commodity: Only so much news, analysis, and editorial opinion can be aired in the major channels of mass communication. *Which* views get covered, and in what way, depends mainly on the economic and political structure and context of press institutions, and on the characteristics of the media themselves.

These are some of the most important factors: (1) More often than not, contemporary news organizations belong to large corporations whose interests influence what gets covered (and, what is probably more central, what does not) and how.[iv] (2) News organizations are driven economically to capture the largest possible audience, and thus not to turn it off with whatever does turn it off – coverage that is too controversial, too demanding, too disturbing.[v] (3) The media are easily manipulated by government officials (and others), for whom the press, by simply reporting press releases and official statements, can be a virtually unfiltered mouthpiece. (4) Characteristics of the media themselves constrain or influence coverage; thus, for example, television lends itself to an action-oriented, unanalytical treatment of events that can distort their meaning or importance.

It is not surprising, therefore, that a great range of opinion and analysis outside the narrow mainstream rarely sees the light of the mass media. This lack of diversity manifests itself in two ways. One is simply lack of adequate exposure to information and ideas that are true or interesting or useful, that help us to understand the world better or make life more satisfactory in one way or another. The range of views considered respectable enough to appear regularly in the American mass media is extraordinarily narrow.[vi] As a result, we are more ignorant and more provincial than we could be, and we may be worse off in other ways as well.

The other consequence more directly concerns justice. The press, once thought of as an antidote to established power, is more likely to reinforce it, because access to the press – that is, the mass media – is distributed as unequally as are other forms of power. It is not, of course, that the less powerful never speak in the mass media or that their doings are never reported, or never sympathetically. But the deck is stacked against them, because the press is itself a formidable power in our society, allied intimately (although not simply) with other formidable powers. Displacing the attention of the media from the usual sources of news – the words and deeds of public officials and public figures – often demands nothing less than the politics of theater, for which those using such tactics may also be blamed.[vii] . . .

18

I believe that we have misunderstood what a modern democratic society's commitment to freedom of the press means and should be. Unlike freedom of speech, to certain aspects of which our commitment must be virtually unconditional, freedom of the press should be contingent on the degree to which it promotes certain values at the core of our interest in freedom of expression generally. Freedom of the press, in other words, is an instrumental good: It is good if it does certain things and not especially good (not good enough to justify special protections, anyway) otherwise. If, for example, the mass media tend to suppress diversity and impoverish public debate, the arguments meant to support freedom of the press turn against it, and we may rightly consider regulating the media to achieve the ultimate purposes of freedom of the press.

[i] vol. 1, chap. 11.

[ii] (New York, Ballantine Books, 1964), pp. 30–1.

[iii] This formulation is neat, but misleading. Viewed in purely quantitative terms, information is plentiful; indeed, the problem is that we are flooded with it and must take measures to stem the tide. When we are talking about enhancing or inhibiting the flow of ideas and information, then, we are thinking about quality and diversity, not mere quantity. Our concern is that we find less diversity in the mass media than we could and should, and than we found in the absence of *mass* media altogether.

[iv] See, e.g. Ben Bagdikian, *The Media Monopoly* (Boston: Beacon, 1983), esp. chap. 3; Tom Goldstein, *The News at any Cost* (New York: Simon & Schuster, 1985), chap. 5; Peter Dreier and Steve Weinberg, 'Interlocking Directorates,' *Columbia Journalism Review* (November–December 1979).

[v] For an extensively illustrated discussion of this and the third factor, see Jeffrey Abramson, 'Four Criticisms of Press Ethics,' this volume.

[vi] As compared, for example, with the European press . . .

[vii] Especially for a nonjournalist, specifying what of importance is not reported is fraught with paradox because it requires independent access to news sources. How do you know what is news except by following the usual sources? . . .

Questions for discussion

1. Which of these perspectives on media freedom do you agree with, and why?

2. On Lichtenberg's perspective, does it follow that it is legitimate to legislate for rights of reply to personal attacks in the press and broadcasting media? Or more radically for rights of access to publish or present articles or programmes which balance the coverage of the newspaper/television channel?

3. On her perspective, does the case for differential treatment of the press and broadcasting media collapse?

5. CENSORSHIP AND PRIOR RESTRAINTS

Blackstone and Dicey defined press freedom in terms of the absence of prior restraints: see Section 1 above. A newspaper or book publisher might be liable to a criminal prosecution or civil action for damages in respect of a work which has already been published, but pre-publication censorship is incompatible with the freedom.[15] It is objectionable since an official or committee is given authority, exercisable in private and on the basis of imprecise standards, to prevent a publication altogether. In these circumstances, the public has no opportunity to debate the wisdom of its proscription. In contrast, a criminal trial or civil action does involve a publication which has seen the light of day; further, in principle liability can only be imposed if there is a clear breach of relevant legal standards.[16]

(a) Judicial prior restraints

There is no provision in English law for the licensing or official censorship of newspapers and other printed media. But in some circumstances the courts may grant an injunction to prevent a publication, on the ground, for example, that it would amount to a breach of a confidence or contempt of court. In these cases there is a *judicial* prior restraint, which can be contrasted with the absence of provision for *administrative* censorship. The former is a less serious infringement of press freedom than the latter, since there is at least an opportunity to contest the grant of an injunction in open proceedings before an impartial tribunal.[17] As explained later in this book, the courts are reluctant to grant interim relief to restrain publication of material alleged to be defamatory: see Chapter 10, Section 6 below. On the other hand, they have generally been more willing to prevent publication of material obtained by the media in breach of a confidential relationship; see Chapter 11, Section 3. In *Fraser v Evans*, the Court of Appeal lifted an interlocutory injunction (now known as an interim injunction) which had been granted to restrain publication by *The Sunday Times* of an article containing on the face of it both defamatory allegations and extracts from a confidential report.[18] The passage indicates why courts are reluctant to prevent the release of a publication.

Extract 1.5.1

Fraser v Evans [1969] 1 QB 349, at 363 (CA)

LORD DENNING MR: There are some things which are of such public concern that the newspapers, the Press, and indeed, everyone is entitled to make known the truth and to make fair comment on it. This is an integral part of the right of free speech and expression. It must not be whittled away. 'The Sunday Times' assert that in this case there is a matter of public concern. They

---

[15] Also see Robertson and Nicol, pp 19–32, for the view that the rule against prior restraints is a fundamental principle of media law, albeit one which is far from absolute in practice.
[16] For fuller discussion, see E M Barendt, *Freedom of Speech* (Oxford University Press, 1987), pp 115–125.
[17] Ibid, 118–120.
[18] The applicant also claimed an interlocutory injunction to restrain a breach of copyright, but this too was rejected.

admit that they are going to injure Mr. Fraser's reputation, but they say that they can justify it; and that they are only making fair comment on a matter of public interest; and, therefore, they ought not to be restrained. We cannot prejudge this defence by granting an injunction against them. I think the injunction which has been granted should be removed. 'The Sunday Times' should be allowed to publish the article at their risk. If they are guilty of libel or breach of confidence, or breach of copyright, that can be determined by an action hereafter and damages awarded against them. But we should not grant an interim injunction in advance of an article when we do not know in the least what it will contain. I would allow the appeal accordingly and discharge the injunction.

The compatibility of prior restraints with the European Convention on Human Rights was considered by the European Court of Human Rights when two newspapers complained that injunctions granted against them on the basis of breach of confidence to prevent publication of allegations made in a book, *Spycatcher*, violated art 10 of the Convention.[19] The Court held that the maintenance of these injunctions after the time when the book became available in the USA could not be justified, as the allegations then ceased to be confidential.

Extract 1.5.2

The Observer and The Guardian v United Kingdom [1992] 14 EHRR 153, at 191 (European Court of Human Rights) (footnote omitted)

For the avoidance of doubt, . . . the Court would only add to the foregoing that Article 10 of the Convention does not in terms prohibit the imposition of prior restraints on publication, as such. This is evidenced not only by the words 'conditions,' 'restrictions,' 'preventing' and 'prevention' which appear in that provision, but also by the SUNDAY TIMES judgment of 26 April 1979[20] and its MARKT INTERN VERLAG GMbH AND KLAUS BEERMAN judgment of 20 November 1988.[i] On the other hand, the dangers inherent in prior restraints are such that they call for the most careful scrutiny on the part of the Court. This is especially so as far as the press is concerned, for news is a perishable commodity and to delay its publication, even for a short period, may well deprive it of all its value and interest.

[i] MARKT INTERN VERLAG AND BEERMAN *V* GERMANY (1990) 12 E.H.R.R. 161 [where the Court upheld the grant of an injunction by the German courts to restrain breach of unfair competition law.]

[19] The grant of interlocutory injunctions (now interim injunctions) had been approved by a majority of the House of Lords (*Attorney General v Guardian Newspapers* [1987] 1 WLR 1248), but the House subsequently refused permanent injunctions: *Attorney General v Guardian Newpapers (No 2)* [1990] 1 AC 109, discussed in Chapter 11, Section 3.

[20] (1979–80) 2 EHRR 245: see Extract 1.2.2 above.

However, five members of the Court said that prior restraints on publication, whether administrative or judicial, permanent or temporary, could never be justified outside wartime and national emergency.[21]

Questions for discussion

1. Do the arguments against administrative censorship apply as strongly to court injunctions?
2. In what circumstances, if any, might it be legitimate for a court to impose a prior restraint on publication of a newspaper, magazine or book?

(b) Human Rights Act 1998

As already discussed in Section 2 of this chapter, the Human Rights Act 1998 has incorporated the rights guaranteed by the European Convention on Human Rights into UK law, so courts will be required to consider their significance for media law. As a result of the press anxiety about the implications of incorporation, in particular of the Convention right to respect for private life (see Chapter 11 below), the measure was amended to ensure that courts paid particular regard to freedom of expression. A key provision has already been summarised (Extract 1.2.5); others will limit the availability of interim relief against the media.

Extract 1.5.3

Human Rights Act 1998, s 12(1)–(3)

12.—(1) This section applies if a court is considering whether to grant any relief which, if granted, might affect the exercise of the Convention right to freedom of expression.

(2) If the person against whom the application for relief is made ('the respondent') is neither present nor represented, no such relief is to be granted unless the court is satisfied—

    (a) that the applicant has taken all practicable steps to notify the respondent; or

    (b) that there are compelling reasons why the respondent should not be notified.

(3) No such relief is to be granted so as to restrain publication before trial unless the court is satisfied that the applicant is likely to establish that publication should not be allowed.

The particular impact of this provision on libel and breach of confidence actions will be considered later in the book. Overall its effect will be to make

---

[21] This was also the view of two members of the Supreme Court in the leading modern US case on prior restraint: *New York Times v US*, 403 US 713 (1971).

it harder to obtain an interim injunction against the media without an opportunity for them to contest its grant. More radically, courts are directed not to grant relief unless they consider it likely that a claimant's case is likely to succeed on full trial. Judicial prior restraints should become less frequent.

(c) Films, video, and broadcasting

Theatre censorship was finally abolished when the Theatres Act 1968 removed the power of the Lord Chamberlain to ban or demand cuts in stage plays. But films, radio and television, and most recently videos have all been subject to various censorship schemes. By statute local authorities must impose restrictions prohibiting the admission of children to 'unsuitable' films, while they have a general power to impose conditions on the use of licensed cinemas.[22] In practice, these responsibilities are delegated to the British Board of Film Classification (BBFC), which classifies films on the basis of their suitability for various age groups. Local authorities, however, must retain power to take the final decision; occasionally they permit a film refused a certificate by the BBFC or, more often, prevent its exhibition in their area, although it may be available in a neighbouring area where the council takes a different view.[23]

The principle of film censorship was approved by the Williams Committee.

Extract 1.5.4

Report of the Williams Committee on Obscenity and Film Censorship, Cmnd 7772 (1979), paras 12.1–12.2, 12.7–12.8, 12.11

12.1 ... The effect of the [censorship] system is broadly that what is regarded as objectionable, for reasons only partly connected with what the law prohibits, is never allowed to gain a showing in a public cinema, so that those who are responsible for enforcing the laws on obscenity and indecency on a 'subsequent punishment' basis scarcely have to concern themselves with investigating whether the law is being broken. The system therefore combines prior restraint with extra-legal control. ...

12.2 Despite the system's haphazard origins and despite the fact that this style of control is in this country peculiar to the cinema, it has many friends and few enemies. It has operated for a long time with a remarkable degree of public acceptance. Objections of principle to any idea of pre-censorship have to a large extent been suspended in favour of film censorship. It has

---

[22] See now the Cinemas Act 1985, s 1. For fuller treatment of film censorship, see Robertson and Nicol, pp 566–572, 583–590.

[23] An example of this phenomenon was the ban by Westminster Council of West End cinemas showing David Cronenberg's film *Crash*; it was however shown in cinemas licensed by Camden and other London boroughs.

undoubtedly been an effective system, both making it fairly certain what cinemas can legally show and under what conditions, and providing fairly watertight procedures to ensure that the rules are kept. . . .

12.7 . . . We think that the aim of treating all the media uniformly is misconceived; there is no reason why one solution should be expected to apply equally to a series of different problems. That the problems are different we have no doubt at all. No one can dispute that reading a magazine, watching a live show and watching a film are three very different experiences. We suggest that it is sensible and reasonable to apply three different standards of control, and not to hope, unrealistically, that the same control can be stretched to cover all three.

12.8 This conclusion, in rejecting the argument for parity of treatment, removes one type of objection to accepting the pre-censorship of films. We are taken further towards accepting it by the facts that the major part of our evidence supported the continuation of film censorship, that the present system has, in the main, worked effectively and well and that most other countries appear to regard film censorship as acceptable and desirable. What clinched the argument for some of us at least was the sight of some of the films with which the censorship presently interferes. We feel it necessary to say to many people who express liberal sentiments about the principle of adult freedom to choose that we were totally unprepared for the sadistic material that some film makers are prepared to produce. We are not here referring to the explicit portrayal of sexual activity or to anything which simply attracts charges of offensiveness. Films that exploit a taste for torture and sadistic violence do raise further, and disturbing, questions.

12.11 . . . We freely admit . . . that we are in part encouraged to favour pre-censorship by the fact that it is what already exists. What we have to consider is, realistically, not whether we would institute a system of censorship if it were a novelty but whether we should abandon a functioning system; or rather, to put it more exactly, whether we should continue to use the system for the protection of young audiences (as almost all our witnesses considered necessary), but at the same time refuse to use the system to control films for adult viewing. We were very much impressed, moreover, by a different kind of argument. The impact of a film can depend on very subtle factors, which will not at all be caught by simple statements of what is being shown on the screen, and because of this the law is too inflexible an instrument through which to impose a control. An *ad hoc* judgement, grounded on certain guidelines, is a more efficient and sensitive way of controlling this medium. All these considerations together led us to the conclusion that films, even those shown to adults only, should continue to be censored.

However, the Committee did propose transferring statutory film censorship powers from local authorities to the BBFC. Its recommendation has not been adopted.

The BBFC does enjoy statutory powers over videos. It is the authority designated under the Video Recordings Act 1984 to determine whether they are suitable for the issue of a classification certificate, 'having special regard to the likelihood of video works in respect of which such certificates have been issued being viewed in the home'.[24] A refusal to grant a certificate in effect bans distribution; it is an offence to supply a video for which none has been issued.[25] There is a right of appeal from BBFC decisions to a Video Appeals Committee.

The BBFC refused to grant a certificate for a short video, *Visions of Ecstasy*, on the ground that it might be liable to a prosecution for blasphemy as offensive to Christians. It depicted the erotic arousal of nun as she caressed the body of the crucified Christ. The majority of the European Court of Human Rights held the ban compatible with the Convention; Judge De Meyer dissented on the ground that it amounted to a prior restraint.

Extract 1.5.5

Wingrove v United Kingdom **(1997) 24 EHRR 1, at 36–37 (dissent of Judge De Meyer) (footnotes omitted)**

This was a pure case of prior restraint, a form of interference which is, in my view, unacceptable in the field of freedom of expression.

What I have written on that subject, with four other judges, in the OBSERVER AND GUARDIAN V THE UNITED KINGDOM case applies not only to the press, but also, *mutatis mutandis*, to other forms of expression, including video works.

It is quite legitimate that those wishing to supply video works be obliged to obtain from some administrative authority a classification certificate stating whether the works concerned may be supplied to the general public or only to persons who have attained a specified age, and whether, in the latter case, they are to be supplied only in certain places.

Of course, anything so decided by such authority needs reasonable justification and must not be arbitrary. It must, if contested, be subject to judicial review, and it must not have the effect of preventing the courts from deciding, as the case may be, whether the work concerned deserves, or does not deserve, any sanction under existing law.

Under the system established by the Video Recordings Act 1984 the British Board of Film Classification and the Video Appeals Committee may determine that certain video works are not suitable for being classified in any of its three categories, and they can thus ban them absolutely *ab initio*.

This was indeed what actually happened in respect of the piece at issue in the present case.

For reasons examined earlier in this chapter, broadcasting is subject to special regulation. For instance, a licence must be granted by the appropriate authority, the Independent Television Commission or the Radio Authority, for a television or radio station to broadcast. The current legislation, the

---

[24] Video Recordings Act 1984, s 4. For further discussion, see Robertson and Nicol, pp 575–583.
[25] Unless it is an 'exempted work', e.g. because it is designed to inform or educate, or it is concerned with sport, religion, or music: Video Recordings Act 1984, s 2.

Broadcasting Act 1990, does not require these authorities to preview or listen to programmes in advance of their transmission; neither body therefore has censorship powers.[26] On the other hand, the government does have such powers.[27]

Extract 1.5.6

Broadcasting Act 1990, ss 10(1), (3) and 11(3)

10.—(1) If it appears to him to be necessary or expedient to do so in connection with his functions as such, the Secretary of State or any other Minister of the Crown may at any time by notice require the Commission to direct the holders of any licences specified in the notice to publish in their licensed services, at such times as may be specified in the notice, such announcement as is so specified, with or without visual images of any picture, scene or object mentioned in the announcement; and it shall be the duty of the Commission to comply with the notice.

(2) [*Omitted*].

(3) The Secretary of State may at any time by notice require the Commission to direct the holders of any licences specified in the notice to refrain from including in the programmes included in their licensed services any matter or classes of matter specified in the notice; and it shall be the duty of the Commission to comply with the notice.

11.—(1), (2) [*Omitted*].

(3) Nothing in this Part [of the Act] shall be construed as requiring the Commission, in the discharge of their duties under this Part as respects licensed services and the programmes included in them, to view such programmes in advance of their being included in such services.

In fact, the government has rarely intervened. However, it used its censorship power in 1988 when it prohibited the BBC and the private channels from broadcasting the voices of members and supporters of terrorist organisations in Northern Ireland. A challenge in the English courts to the legality of the ban failed.

Extract 1.5.7

R v Home Secretary, ex parte Brind [1991] 1 AC 696, at 749 (HL)

LORD BRIDGE OF HARWICH: I find it impossible to say that the Secretary of State exceeded the limits of his discretion. In any civilised and law-abiding

---

[26] In contrast, the Independent Broadcasting Authority used to have power to preview programmes, though it is unclear whether this amounted to censorship: see Barendt, pp 37–38.

[27] For comparable radio provisions, see Broadcasting Act 1990, ss 94 and 95(3). The Secretary of State has a similar 'censorship' power over the BBC under the 1996 Agreement: see Chapter 3.

society the defeat of the terrorist is a public interest of the first importance. That some restriction on the freedom of the terrorist and his supporters to propagate his cause may well be justified in support of that public interest is a proposition which I apprehend the applicants hardly dispute. Their real case is that they, in the exercise of their editorial judgment, may and must be trusted to ensure that the broadcasting media are not used in such a way as will afford any encouragement or support to terrorism and that any interference with that editorial judgment is necessarily an unjustifiable restriction on the right to freedom of expression. Accepting, as I do, their complete good faith, I nevertheless cannot accept this proposition. The Secretary of State, for the reasons he made so clear in Parliament, decided that it was necessary to deny to the terrorist and his supporters the opportunity to speak directly to the public through the most influential of all the media of communication and that this justified some interference with editorial freedom. I do not see how this judgment can be categorised as unreasonable. What is perhaps surprising is that the restriction imposed is of such limited scope. There is no restriction at all on the matter which may be broadcast, only on the manner of its presentation. The viewer may see the terrorist's face and hear his words provided only that they are not spoken in his own voice. I well understand the broadcast journalist's complaint that to put him to the trouble of dubbing the voice of the speaker he has interviewed before the television camera is an irritant which the difference in effect between the speaker's voice and the actor's voice hardly justifies. I well understand the political complaint that the restriction may be counter-productive in the sense that the adverse criticism it provokes outweighs any benefit it achieves. But these complaints fall very far short of demonstrating that a reasonable Secretary of State could not reasonably conclude that the restriction was justified by the important public interest of combating terrorism.

The House of Lords also held that there was no obligation on the government to consider the compatibility of the ban with the Convention right to freedom of expression. Subsequently the Commission of Human Rights held a complaint by Brind inadmissible; in its view the ban was clearly justified in the interests of national security and to prevent disorder. But it was lifted in August 1994.

Questions for discussion

1. Could the UK film censorship system be challenged under the Human Rights Act 1998?

2. If the government were now to issue a broadcasting ban similar to that at issue in *Ex parte Brind*, could it be challenged successfully under the Human Rights Act 1998?

3. How important in that context should be the distinction drawn by Lord Bridge between restrictions on the matter of speech and on the manner of its presentation?

2

THE PRESS AND THE PRESS COMPLAINTS COMMISSION

1. THE RIGHTS OF OWNERS AND EDITORS

Whatever the meaning of press freedom and its relationship to freedom of speech (see Chapter 1, Section 4), it is far from clear who is entitled to exercise it. Is it a right of the newspaper editor or of its owner? On one view the important freedom is that of editors to choose the contents of the paper and its treatment of public issues.[1] But proprietors have often taken an active interest in these matters.[2] Further, like any proprietor, the owner of a newspaper is entitled to choose and dismiss his employees; owners may, therefore, hire and fire editors and journalists, subject only to the law of contract and the regulation of unfair dismissal. So even if press freedom is regarded as 'editorial freedom', in practice it may be more synonymous with the prerogatives of the press owners.

Indeed, at the beginning of the 20th century English newspaper owners were frequently termed 'press barons'. This was an accurate description of Lords Northcliffe, Rothermere, Beaverbrook and Kemsley, all of whom used their newspaper to try to influence the course of national politics. Recent years have seen a resurgence of interventionist owners of this kind.

Extract 2.1.1

J Curran and J Seaton, *Power without Responsibility*, 5th ed (Routledge, 1997), pp 74–76

Murdoch . . . imposed an editorial reorientation of his papers in Britain through a personalized style of management reminiscent of the earlier press barons. 'I did not come all this way', he declared at the *News of the World*, 'not to interfere.' Stafford Summerfield, its long-serving editor, found to his dismay that the new proprietor 'wanted to read proofs, write a leader if he felt like it,

---

[1] See *Miami Herald Publishing Co v Tornillo*, 418 US 241 (1974), where the Supreme Court unanimously ruled that a right of reply statute infringed editorial freedom.
[2] For a comprehensive history of the influence of proprietors on the evolution of the British press, see S Koss, *The Rise and Fall of the Political Press in Britain* (Fontana Press 1990).

change the paper about and give instructions to his staff'. A series of clashes with Murdoch, partly over the issue of whether the editor should be accountable to the paper's board or to Murdoch personally, hastened Summerfield's departure.

A subsequent editor of the *News of the World*, Barry Askew, also records Murdoch's extensive editorial interventions when he was in London. 'He would come into the office', Askew recalls, 'and literally rewrite leaders which were not supporting the hard Thatcherite line.' Askew, who was not a Thatcherite enthusiast, lasted only nine months.

Murdoch reconstructed the *Sun* by working closely with a talented but compliant editor, Sir Larry Lamb, whom he had handpicked for the job. But he adopted a more circumspect approach towards *The Times* and *Sunday Times*. During his bid for Times Newspapers in 1981, he was asked whether he would change their character. 'Oh no, no, I would not dream of changing them at all,' he had replied. But to assuage sceptical critics, Articles of Association and independent directors were imposed at Times Newspapers with the intention of preserving their editorial independence.

Although Murdoch never issued a direct editorial instruction to the editor of the *Sunday Times*, Frank Giles, he made his views forcibly known. 'Murdoch, the paper spread out before him,' Giles recollects, 'would jab his fingers at some article or contribution and snarl, "what do you want to print rubbish like that for?" or pointing to the by-line of a correspondent, assert that "that man's a Commie".' Further pressure was funnelled through Gerald Long, the new managing director appointed by Murdoch, prompting the editor to establish a dossier called the 'Long Insult File'. Undermined by a series of calculated humiliations (on one occasion, Murdoch entertained guests by firing an imaginary pistol at his editor's back), Frank Giles retired early. His replacement was a more reliably Conservative journalist, Andrew Neil, who moved the paper further to the right. 'Rupert expects his papers', according to Neil, 'to stand broadly for what he believes: a combination of right-wing republicanism from America mixed with undiluted Thatcherism from Britain. . . .'

. . .

Another active interventionist, Victor (later Lord) Matthews, became head of the Express Group between 1977 and 1985. 'By and large editors will have complete freedom,' he promised, 'as long as they agree with the policy I have laid down.' During his first flush of enthusiasm as proprietor, he forced his editors to endure lengthy discourses of homespun political philosophy, which then had to be recreated as editorials. Only the most outrageous *ex cathedra* judgements seem to have been resisted. 'I had to plead against the *Evening Standard*', remembers Simon Jenkins, its former editor, 'being expected to call for a nuclear first strike on Moscow, to rid the world of communism, just like that.' Lord Matthews' staff were also a little taken aback by his novel sense of news values. 'I would find myself in a dilemma', he publicly declared, 'about whether to report a British Watergate affair because of the national harm. I believe in batting for Britain.'

. . .

The third dominant personality to emerge in the national press was Robert Maxwell, a former right-wing Labour MP who acquired the Mirror Group in 1984. He brought to an end the relatively autonomous regime that had existed when the group was owned by Reed International during the 1970s and early 1980s. In the early days of his proprietorship, he was in the office almost every night phoning . . . as often as six times in the evening to staff who were working on political reports. 'I certainly have a major say', he declared, 'in the political line of the paper [*Daily Mirror*].' Running newspapers, he added on another occasion, 'gives me the power to raise issues effectively. In simple terms, it's a megaphone.'

However, his control over the megaphone slackened when he became involved in ever more desperate attempts to save his heavily indebted media empire, including stealing from his employees' pension fund. Facing imminent ruin in 1991, he slipped overboard from his private yacht in what appears to have been a suicide.

In 1977, a Royal Commission expressed concern about the interference with editorial freedom by proprietors, and the consequent dangers to diversity of opinion.

Extract 2.1.2

Royal Commission on the Press, Cmnd 6810 (1977), Chapter 16: Editorial Contracts, paras 16.1, 16.3–16.5 (footnote omitted)

16.1 In dealing with external pressures on publications it is the editor of the newspaper or magazine who carries the central responsibility. Complete editorial sovereignty is a myth. The results of the survey of editors carried out for us by Social and Community Planning Research would alone be enough to demonstrate that. The evidence from the Newspaper Publishers Association (NPA) stresses the limitations on editorial freedom which inevitably operate, but also points out that the editor is the only person able to deal authoritatively with the pressures which are brought to bear on newspapers:

'By convention an editor, once appointed and until removed, is the sole arbiter of what appears in the paper, both of advertising and editorial matter. This makes him the focus of the paper's identity, and therefore the man whose "freedom" from external pressures has to be defended. The doctrine of editorial responsibility, like that of ministerial responsibility, is both convenient and necessary. But, like ministerial responsibility, it cannot be assumed to operate with anything like theoretical purity.'

. . .

16.3 We believe it to be essential that an editor's rights should be guaranteed by his employers. We have recorded and take very seriously the possible dangers to diversity of opinion and expression which accompany the growth in concentration of ownership of newspapers. It can generate pressures which only editors can resist. Several managements of the large groups of newspapers have told us of a variety of means of formalising the rights of editors, including the adoption of an agreed description of duties and powers. If editors are to be independent, we believe that they should be assured of their basic rights. These are:

30

(*a*) the right to reject material provided by central management or editorial services;

(*b*) the right to determine the contents of the paper (within the bounds of reasonable economic consideration and the established policy of the publication);

(*c*) the right to allocate expenditure within a budget;

(*d*) the right to carry out investigative journalism;

(*e*) the right to reject advice on editorial policy;

(*f*) the right to criticise the paper's own group or other parts of the same corporate organisation;

(*g*) the right to change the alignment or views of the paper on specific issues within its agreed editorial policy; and

(*h*) the right to appoint or dismiss journalists and to decide the terms of their contracts of employment within the established policy of the organisation, and the right to assign journalists to stories.

16.4 We consulted a number of people in the press about a proposal that editors should be given a contract setting out these rights. It was generally agreed that the kinds of right mentioned were desirable, but some thought it was too constricting to try to frame them in terms that would permit their inclusion in a contract. Among people who took this view were those who claimed that many editors already enjoyed these rights in practice. Both from the management side and from editors, there was broad agreement that in reality editorial and managerial decisions were inseparable and must be made in a framework which gave the editor freedom within recognised constraints. Differences of opinion were more over means than over ends.

16.5 We know that it is difficult to define the elusive borderline between the responsibility of a proprietor and an editor. A precise job description for editors cannot be drawn up in such a way as to be appropriate for all the newspapers and periodicals in the country. However, we believe that the importance of publicly and explicitly guaranteeing editorial independence, in the context of concentration, chain ownership and monopoly, which we have described, is so great that publishers and editors should urgently consider ways of setting out and guaranteeing formally editorial independence from employers. Similarly, we stress the need to secure the independence of editors from their fellow journalists. . . .

In the next extract the author suggests how editorial freedom might be protected.

Extract 2.1.3

T Gibbons, 'Freedom of the Press: Ownership and Editorial Values'
[1992] *Public Law* 279, at 290–291, 293–294 (some footnotes omitted)

One way of enabling an editor to take an independent view, based upon standards of professional journalism and free from proprietorial pressure, is to incorporate some protection into his contract of employment. The third Royal

Commission on the Press identified a number of 'basic rights' for editors, including the right to reject material provided by central management, the right to determine the contents of the paper (within the bounds of reasonable economic considerations and the established policy of the publisher) and the right to criticise the paper's own group or other parts of the same corporate structure. It recommended that an agreed description of duties and powers should be drawn up for each editor and that editorial contrasts should incorporate a clause requiring 12 months notice of termination.

It is not likely to be easy, however, to enforce special recognition for the editor's status within the context of a commercial enterprise like the newspaper industry, although the Royal Commission was told that its catalogue of rights did represent existing practice. Proprietors will want to maintain control of the ventures that they have financed. . . .

An alternative approach is to secure some form of institutional protection for the editor. The model provided by broadcasting in this country, albeit imperfect, shows that such protection is workable, although this does not mean that it could simply be transplanted into the press. In broadcasting, the legal position in relation to ownership and control is formally similar to that in the press, but a set of conventional understandings have developed to provide greater autonomy for editors.

. . .

To what extent is it possible to introduce similar institutional constraints in the press? One way is to employ some form of external scrutiny of the relationship between an editor and his or her proprietor. One example is the arrangements for the ownership of *The Guardian*. The paper is owned by the Guardian and Manchester Evening News plc, which is owned, in turn, by the Scott Trust. Editors are employed on the basis that the paper 'shall be carried on as nearly as may be upon the same principles as they have heretofore been conducted.'[i] The Trust selects its own members, thereby perpetuating its own values, and it selects editors very carefully. But, once the editor is chosen, the trustees do not intervene in editorial policy, whether or not it will affect circulation figures. Indeed, the Trust is used to subsidise the newspaper in times of economic hardship.

. . . Another approach is to draft a company's articles of association in a manner that protects the editor's position. Harold Evans provides a fascinating account of the negotiations that took place between his editorial team at *The Sunday Times* and the new proprietor, Rupert Murdoch, to secure that protection. Yet Evans was well aware that the 'tradition' of editorial independence that had been enjoyed by himself and his predecessors was ephemeral and not easily reduced to rules.[ii] Furthermore, since a proprietor who wholly owns the company can easily change its articles of association, there may be no guarantee that editorial autonomy will persist.[iii]

In theory, the situation might be different where independent directors are appointed to safeguard editorial values. When the Thomson organisation (with extensive television interests and existing ownership of *The Sunday Times*) applied to buy *The Times* in 1966, it proposed that four independent directors should be appointed to the paper's board to ensure editorial independence. The Monopolies Commission was not impressed, however, and regarded the appointments as only symbolic. It considered that the national directors could not be expected to intervene in the highly technical process of producing a newspaper. 'Moreover, in the event of a dispute about the authority of an editor or the appointment or dismissal of an editor, there would be no assurance that national figures would take any different view of the best interests of the company from that of their fellow directors.'[iv] Nevertheless, the approach was used again when *The Times* and *The Sunday Times* were taken over by News International.

[i] See P. Schlesinger, *The Scott Trust* (1986), p. 7.
[ii] [H.] Evans [*Good Times, Bad Times*], Chap. 6.
[iii] In the event, Evans resigned after fundamental differences between himself and Murdoch: Koss, [*The Rise and Fall of the Political Press in Britain* (1990)], pp. 1110–1111.
[iv] Monopolies Commission, *The Times and Sunday Times* (1966–67, H.C. 273).

There is relatively little evidence to suggest that internal institutional restrictions – for example, the appointment of independent directors – provide an effective safeguard for editorial independence. In recent years editors have served only a short period in office; it is rare for someone to edit a national newspaper for decades, as used frequently to be the case. More attention has been paid to other matters: first, the prevention of ownership concentration, discussed in Chapter 6, and secondly, the voluntary regulation of newspapers in the interests of accuracy and personal privacy.

Questions for discussion
1. Do you think that press freedom should be regarded primarily as freedom of the editor?
2. What steps, if any, should be taken to protect editorial freedom?

2. VOLUNTARY REGULATION AND THE PRESS COMPLAINTS COMMISSION

(a) The Press Council and the Calcutt Report

Voluntary, or self, regulation of the press has a relatively long history.[3] As recommended by a Royal Commission,[4] the newspaper industry established a General Council of the Press in 1953.[5] Its principal functions were to promote press freedom and to consider complaints. Initially it was composed entirely of journalists and editors, with the owner of *The Times* as chairman.

[3] The term 'voluntary regulation' is preferred to 'self-regulation', since the latter suggests that the institution in question – in this instance, the press – regulates itself. The former implies only (and correctly) that the system of regulation is voluntary, rather than imposed under statute.
[4] First Royal Commission on Press, Cmd 7700 (1949).
[5] For a brief account of the history of the Press Council and the events leading to its replacement by the Press Complaints Commission, see Robertson and Nicol, pp 521–526. For a fuller account of the Council, see H Phillip Levy, *The Press Council* (Macmillan, 1967), and G Robertson, *People against the Press*, (Quartet Books, 1983), especially Chapter 1.

However, following criticism by another Royal Commission in 1962,[6] it changed its name to the simpler 'Press Council'; Lord Devlin, a retired Law Lord, was appointed as the first lay (non-press) chairman. (Others have included Sir Zelman Cowen, a former Governor-General of Australia, and Sir Louis Blom-Cooper, QC.) But its treatment of complaints was considered unsatisfactory. The Council often took months to reach a decision, while many complainants thought it was biased in favour of newspapers. The criticisms continued unabated despite the change in 1978 to parity of press and lay members. Adjudications were inconsistent and poorly reasoned. Newspapers sometimes failed to report adverse rulings or buried them in an inside page.

Matters came to a head in 1989 when the government invited Sir David Calcutt to chair a committee to consider whether to provide further protection for privacy against the press. Its report recommended the replacement of the Press Council by a Press Complaints Commission (PCC) to give 'one final chance to prove that voluntary self-regulation can be made to work'.[7] The PCC should differ from the Council in a number of respects; in particular, it should no longer be concerned to defend press freedom, but concentrate on the adjudication of complaints.

Extract 2.2.1

Calcutt Report of the Committee on Privacy and Related Matters, Cm 1102 (1990), paras 15.5, 15.7–15.8, 15.11–15.12, 15.15–15.16, 15.20–15.24

CODE OF PRACTICE

15.5 Prior to its internal review the Press Council had chosen not to publish a formal list of rules for good journalistic practice, but to identify standards of ethical practice through its adjudications and Declarations of Principle . . . Its review recognised that there have been changes in public attitudes and expectations. It therefore proposed that the Press Council should publish a code of practice and it put forward a draft code. It was envisaged that this would provide a general guide to good practice to which proprietors, editors and journalists should be prepared to subscribe and which members of the public would find valuable as an indication of what they are entitled to expect from the industry. . . .

15.7 The Press Complaints Commission must have a clear view of what is unacceptable press behaviour. It must also widely publicise its views to that potential complainants can gauge whether they have a good case. We therefore *recommend* that it should publish, monitor and implement a comprehensive code of practice for the guidance of both the press and the public. In

---

[6] Cmnd 1811 (1962).
[7] Calcutt Report on Privacy and Related Matters, Cm 1102 (1990), para 14.38.

relation to privacy, this should be more detailed and more specific than the code produced by the Press Council. . . .

ADDITIONAL POWERS

15.8 A significant proportion of the members of the public who submitted evidence wanted the Press Council to be able to discipline editors and journalists and fine or suspend publication of newspapers responsible for serious intrusions into privacy. Whatever the strength of feeling underlying these proposals, we consider them misguided. Although the self-regulating professions can discipline and expel members from the profession and journalists' trade unions can expel members, we would not wish to draw too close a parallel between journalism and other professions. It would be undesirable for the Press Complaints Commission to have such disciplinary powers. Any system of approved or registered publications and journalists is clearly incompatible with freedom of the press.

15.11 A hot line procedure . . . is probably the closest that anyone could come to prior restraint of publication under a system of non-statutory self-regulation. It is an imaginative proposal which has much to commend it. We consider that the procedure should also be available to a complainant being pursued by identifiable journalists or photographers against his wishes. To stand any chance of being effective, however, the proposed hot line procedure would need to be not only well publicised and adequately funded but also available to complainants on a 24-hour basis. We would emphasise that it would need the public commitment of the press. We *recommend* that the Press Complaints Commission should operate a hot line similar to that proposed by the Press Council review.

ENFORCEMENT

15.12 A number of witnesses complained to us that Press Council adjudications were not enforceable. The Chairman of the Press Council told us that, over 35 years, there have been only 10 occasions when a newspaper has declined to publish an adverse adjudication in whole or in part. On this evidence the Press Council review did not consider that it would be necessary or right to seek powers to enforce publication. It argued that the 'failure rate' in the past had not been unreasonable and did not indicate that self-regulation had broken down irretrievably. . . .

15.15 There can be no excuse for a newspaper or magazine refusing to publish a Press Council adjudication criticising its conduct. We accept, however, that the number of such instances has been small (see *paragraph 15.12*). They have tended to be highlighted by rival newspapers and other media. Furthermore, non-publication itself, while an indication of a newspaper's overall attitude, is not the fundamental issue.

15.16 Nevertheless, if the press wishes to retain non-statutory self-regulation, it must publicly commit itself to observing all the procedures and pronouncements of the Press Complaints Commission. Failure to give and to keep this commitment by any significant part of the press would, we consider, weaken the Press Complaints Commission and discredit self-regulation. . . .

MEMBERSHIP

. . .

15.20 We consider it essential that members of the Press Complaints Commission should not be nominated by industry bodies. For the Commission to be a credible adjudicating body its members must be independent and seen to be both independent and of high calibre. We therefore *recommend* that all appointments to the Commission should be made by an Appointments Commission. This should be given explicit freedom to appoint whoever it considers best qualified. The Appointments Commission itself should be independently appointed, possibly by the Lord Chancellor.

15.21 We note that parity of representation between press and lay members on the Press Council was finally achieved in 1978 following the recommendation to this effect by the third Royal Commission. We are aware that the argument for parity was based on the need to increase public confidence in the Press Council. However, a voluntary system of self-regulation must also attract the support and confidence of the profession or industry concerned. This is unlikely to be forthcoming unless a significant proportion of those responsible for adjudications have experience of the industry. We heard arguments for increasing the proportion of press members on the adjudicating body to, say, 75 per cent, on the grounds that editors and journalists are more likely to accept censure from their peers.

15.22 We consider that, once the press members are no longer representatives of the constituent bodies, the argument for precise parity of numbers becomes less powerful. The main need would be for the press members to be drawn from senior editorial levels of newspapers and publications and for the lay members to be people of high calibre. However, we would expect the majority of the members of the Commission to have experience at the highest level of the press.

PROCEDURES

15.23 The Press Complaints Commission should deal with complaints speedily. Its procedures should be clearly set out yet flexible enough to respond to different cases in different ways. The Press Council review recognised that the Press Council's adversarial approach tends to prolixity, but recommended its retention for the most contentious cases. For more straightforward cases it proposed a shortened process giving each side an opportunity to state its case. . . .

15.24 A general adversarial approach contributes significantly to delays in resolving complaints. In many cases the most satisfactory outcome for complainants would be to receive an apology without resort to the full adjudication process. We *recommend* that the Press Complaints Commission should have clear conciliation and adjudication procedures designed to ensure that complaints are handled with the minimum of delay. Whenever practical it should first seek conciliation. There should also be a fast track procedure for the correction of significant factual errors, on the lines of that provided now by the Press Council. The Commission should also have a specific responsibility and procedure for initiating inquiries whenever it thinks it necessary.

(b) The PCC: the merits of voluntary regulation

The Press Complaints Commission (PCC) replaced the Press Council at the beginning of 1991. But its institution has not ended the debate on the effectiveness of voluntary regulation. When it accepted the recommendation of the Calcutt Committee that the industry be given a final opportunity to make voluntary regulation work, the government intimated that it would review the new system after 18 months. It invited Sir David Calcutt himself to review the working of the PCC in 1991–92. He concluded that it was not an effective regulator. In particular, its members were not appointed by a fully independent Appointments Commission, while the Code of Practice had been drafted by a press committee, rather than by the PCC itself. Moreover, the contents of the Code differed in significant respects from that drafted by the Calcutt Committee (published as Appendix Q to the Report). Calcutt also found that PCC rulings were, like those of the Press Council, unpredictable and inadequately reasoned. Finally, on occasion tabloid newspapers had shown 'contemptuous treatment' of its adjudications.[8]

Sir David concluded that the PCC had failed to operate the system of voluntary regulation effectively, and that it would be right to replace it by a statutory press tribunal with power to draw up its own code of practice, to impose fines, to award compensation, and to require the printing of apologies and corrections. However, the National Heritage Committee of the House of Commons (now the Committee on Culture, Media, and Sport following the renaming of the Department in 1997) disagreed. It did not think it necessary to abandon voluntary regulation; the Committee recommended that the PCC should have broader responsibilities and powers, and that its work should be supported by a statutory Press Ombudsman.

Extract 2.2.2

Report of the National Heritage Committee, *Privacy and Media Intrusion* (HC 294, 1993), paras 74–78, 96–97 (footnotes omitted)

74. A further responsibility of the Press Commission again relates to its duty to complainants. **It is essential that, where factual errors or breaches of the Code have occurred, the Commission should be able to order the publication with due prominence of its adjudications and of a correction and appropriate apology.**

75. The two final responsibilities which the Committee believes ought to be given to the Press Commission have a financial impact. The first of these relates to the payment of compensation. It seems to the Committee unfair that where a complaint has been upheld there is nothing available to the complainant between an apology and expensive recourse to the Courts. **The Committee accordingly recommends that the industry should increase the powers**

---

[8] *Review of Press Self-Regulation* Cm 2135 (1993), paras 4.25–4.27, 4.41 and 5.23.

of the new Press Commission to allow it to require the payment of compensation. The press is of course *sui generis* and cannot be compared precisely with any other institution in the realm. Nevertheless, payment of compensation to an aggrieved person whose grievance has been confirmed after investigation would not be a unique or unprecedented step. The Solicitors Complaints Bureau, for example, can order an individual solicitor to pay compensation of up to £1,000. In the area of non-statutory Ombudsmen, the Banking Ombudsman, and the Insurance Ombudsman, can order the payment of compensation of up to £100,000.

76. The second of these responsibilities relates to the power to fine. Where a particularly blatant abuse of the Code has taken place, it seems inappropriate that the body charged with examining and adjudicating on the case should have no powers to fine the offending publication. . . .

77. The Committee can see circumstances in which the Press Commission itself might feel that a newspaper or journalist could be alleged to have reduced public confidence in newspaper publishing and might wish to impose a fine on such a publication. If the Press Commission is to exercise as much voluntary regulation as possible, it should be able to pre-empt the need for complainants to resort to the Ombudsman, and have the power to impose its own financial penalties on those newspapers which it judges have brought journalism into disrepute. The decision on whether to take such action should of course be a matter for the Press Commission. **The Committee therefore recommends that the industry should increase the powers of the new Press Commission to allow it to impose fines where it judges that a breach of the Code of Practice is such as to have brought journalism into disrepute.**

78. The Committee recognises that any imposition of a financial penalty must carry with it the possibility of seeking alleviation from that penalty. The Committee is therefore proposing that where any of the parties involved is not satisfied with the outcome they should have the right to seek a re-examination of the case by the Press Ombudsman, . . .

IV STATUTORY OMBUDSMAN

. . .

96. The Committee has decided that a regulatory level is needed beyond that of the Press Commission. Anyone dissatisfied with the outcome of an investigation, or whose complaint had been rejected without investigation, needs some further accessible and effective recourse. In the Committee's view this could best be provided by an Ombudsman. The weight of his or her work would be in direct proportion to the success or failure of voluntary regulation. The more successful that voluntary regulation turns out to be, the less the need for recourse to the Ombudsman. Nothing would please the Committee more than that self-regulation by the Press Commission should be so successful as to render the role of the Press Ombudsman a sinecure, at any rate so far as response to complaints is concerned.

97. Once the Committee had decided that the appointment of a Press Ombudsman would best meet the need to ensure that voluntary regulation

worked, it gave thought as to whether the position should be statutory or non-statutory. The Lord Chancellor did not make any recommendation in this area but he did concede that 'If it is a voluntary one, it would be effective only if the organs of the media were willing to give access to some of their documents and perhaps some of their information . . . [they] would be required to be willing to co-operate with the Ombudsman. As the Press Ombudsman would be called upon in general only when voluntary regulation had proved ineffective, this for the Committee proved a convincing argument in favour of a statutory Ombudsman. **The Committee therefore recommends that a statutory Press Ombudsman be appointed.**

The government did not react to the Heritage Committee's proposals for two years. On one view, it held back its response to see how the press and the PCC reacted to these proposals and to those in the Calcutt Review. A less charitable interpretation is that the government was anxious not to jeopardise its relations with the press before the General Election, eventually held in 1997. Alternatively, there may have been divisions within the government how to handle proposals of the Calcutt Review and the Heritage Committee Report to introduce a privacy law and statutory press control. At all events, it eventually concluded that voluntary regulation should continue.

Extract 2.2.3

Government Response to National Heritage Committee, *Privacy and Media Intrusion* Cm 2918 (1995), paras 2.5–2.6, 2.8–2.14

2.5   A free press is vital to a free country. Many would think the imposition of statutory controls on newspapers invidious because it might open the way for regulating content, thereby laying the Government open to charges of press censorship. Furthermore, the Government does not believe that it would be right in this field to delegate decisions about when a statutory remedy should be granted to a regulator such as a tribunal. For both these reasons, the Government does not find the case for statutory measures in this area compelling. It believes that, in principle, industry self-regulation is much to be preferred. That conclusion applies equally to Sir David Calcutt's statutory complaints tribunal and to the National Heritage Select Committee's statutory Press Ombudsman proposal.

2.6   In reaching this conclusion, the Government has been mindful also of a variety of improvements in procedures and practices which the PCC has introduced over the past two years. The Government welcomes these changes. It has, however, sought to address whether the changes go far enough and, in particular, pay sufficient heed to the criticisms of the PCC expressed by Sir David Calcutt and the National Heritage Select Committee. These questions are considered in more detail below.

. . .

2.8   In a statement responding to Sir David's review and the National Heritage Select Committee's report, issued on 4 May 1993, Pressbof [Press

Standards Board of Finance which funds the PCC] outlined a number of measures which were being or had been taken to strengthen self-regulation. These included:

- a majority of non-press members to be recruited to the Press Complaints Commission;

- additional independent members to be recruited to the Appointments Commission;

- the industry's Code of Practice to require ratification by the PCC; and

- changes to be made in the Code of Practice relating to 'bugging', long lens cameras, 'jigsaw' identification and the definition of public interest.

2.9 These changes, though welcomed by the Government at the time, fell far short of the recommendations of the National Heritage Select Committee and of Sir David Calcutt. The Government indicated that it would wish to keep a particularly close eye on how effectively and widely the new measures were implemented.

2.10 On 10 June 1993, the PCC announced the launch of a new helpline for members of the public concerned that the Code of Practice applied by the Commission was likely to be breached in a press investigation relating to them. On 15 July 1993. Pressbof announced changes to the Code, which had been ratified by the PCC on 30 June, covering long lens photography and 'jigsaw' identification in cases involving sexual offences against children. The revised Code slightly redefines the public interest, defines private property and emphasises the responsibility of editors to cooperate as swiftly as possible in PCC enquiries, and to ensure that journalists do not breach the provisions on harassment. On 12 November 1993, the PCC announced that the newspaper industry was now committed to the progressive incorporation of the Code of Practice into the individual contracts of all journalists and editors. Future grave breaches of the Code would become a matter on which employers could consider disciplinary action, including dismissal.

2.11 On 20 January 1994, the PCC announced the appointment of one of its lay members, Professor Robert Pinker, as Privacy Commissioner, with special powers to investigate urgent complaints about privacy and bring them to the Commission for decision under the Code of Practice. This followed a number of calls by Government Ministers for the industry to establish a voluntary press ombudsman. According to the announcement, the Commissioner has the power to investigate *prima facie* gross or calculated breaches of the Code, even if the complaint had been made by a third party or there has been no complaint at all. Professor Pinker will, at the request of the Press Complaints Commission, begin enquiries immediately a complaint is made, or, in high profile cases, as soon as the story breaks if there is no complaint. He consults all the parties and prepares a draft adjudication with a recommendation for the full Commission, which will publish the adjudication as soon as it is determined. Professor Pinker may also recommend that the Press Complaints Commission asks publishers to take disciplinary measures against an editor, and the Commission will monitor what action has been taken.

2.12 On 1 January 1995, Lord Wakeham was appointed Chairman of the Press Complaints Commission. He stressed the importance of a Commission independent of the newspaper industry. He has also argued that his organisation must build up the confidence of the public and be rigorous and consistent in dealing with issues. The Government considers that the recent appointment of four distinguished independent members to the PCC, the increase of numbers on the Appointments Commission from three to five, and the fact that both bodies have lay majorities, are encouraging signs.

. . .

2.13 Following informal contacts between the Chairman of the PCC and the then Secretary of State for National Heritage (Mr Stephen Dorrell), Lord Wakeham wrote to Mr Dorrell on 19 June to record the improvements which the industry had accepted, or which he hoped to implement. Following her appointment as Secretary of State for National Heritage on 5 July 1995, Mrs Virginia Bottomley responded welcoming these changes, but encouraging the industry to make further improvements . . .

2.14 The main points in the exchange are as follows:

(i) Appointments

Lord Wakeham stressed the independence of the self-regulatory system. The Appointments Commission which appoints the members of the Press Complaints Commission now has a clear lay majority, the PCC itself has a strengthened lay majority, and all adjudications are made by the full commission. Lord Wakeham will shortly bring forward proposals for discussion on the Code Committee, possibly including the introduction of a lay element into the Code Committee.

Government response. The Government welcomes the increased lay element in, and hence independence of, the self-regulatory machinery, and would wish to see the introduction of a lay element into the Code Committee.

(ii) Press Hotline

Lord Wakeham has initiated a comprehensive internal review of the PCC's procedures for dealing with more difficult matters, and, once this is complete, proposes to publish the basis on which the Commission intends to deal with matters in future.

Government response. The Government would wish to see the introduction of a hotline, whereby, in appropriate cases, the PCC or Privacy Commissioner might warn editors, thought to be likely to publish a story or photographs which might have been obtained in breach of the Code, of the consequences of doing so.

(iii) Other improvements to procedures

Lord Wakeham is prepared, in appropriate cases, to consider accepting third-party complaints, and to initiate enquiries. He will bring forward proposals for discussion on the adoption of Citizen's Charter-style performance targets, and, as already stated, he intends to set up an internal review of procedures.

Government response. The Government welcomes the indication that third party complaints will, in appropriate cases, be accepted and investigated. It would also welcome the adoption of performance targets, and commends to the PCC other principles of the Citizen's Charter. It also recommends the publication of fuller summaries of adjudications, and greater use of oral hearings.

(iv) Code written into contracts

Lord Wakeham reports that the Code is being progressively incorporated into the contracts of editors and some journalists, with the result that they may be subject to disciplinary action if they have been found in breach of it.

Government response. The Government welcomes the increased authority of the Commission. It awaits further evidence of disciplinary sanctions, for example, whether they include dismissal.

(v) Compensation fund

Lord Wakeham has set in motion an internal review of procedures, but he does not discuss the possibility of a compensation fund.

Government response. The Government wishes to see compensation paid to those whose privacy has been unjustifiably infringed by the press, from a fund set up by the industry.

Questions for discussion

1. Do you agree with the Government response that 'industry self-regulation' is preferable to statutory press regulation?
2. Should the PCC (i) have power to fine newspapers and (ii) operate a 'hotline' to advise (or tell) a newspaper not to publish an article or photograph?

(c) Composition and procedure of the PCC

The PCC has 16 members, nine of whom, including the chairman, are lay members, the other seven being editors of national or regional newspapers or of magazines. They are chosen by an independent Appointments Commission under the chairmanship of the present chairman of the PCC, Lord Wakeham, formerly a Conservative Cabinet Minister. The PCC is financed by the Press Standards Board of Finance, which collects registration fees from the newspaper and magazine publishing industries. Its annual costs total about £1.2 million.

One of the criticisms most frequently made of the Press Council was that it took months to reach a decision. The PCC in contrast prides itself on its speed. In 1998 about 72% of complaints had been resolved within 43 working days, and 85% within 64 days. The vast majority are resolved informally; complaints are referred to the editor of the newspaper or magazine, and are then subsequently dealt with to the complainant's satisfaction or withdrawn. Only a small minority (in 1998, 86 out of 1,595 investigated complaints and 2,601 received complaints)[9] are resolved by a formal adjudication.[10] Adjudications are made on the basis of written complaints and replies; the Commission retains the right to ask the complainant and editor to attend for an oral hearing, but this course is rarely, if ever, adopted. Details of its working procedures have been set out in an informal Commission paper.

Extract 2.2.4

Press Complaints Commission Paper (July, 1996), p 12

- The procedures of the Commission are as simple as possible. It meets every month; it rarely needs to hold formal hearings at which witnesses give evidence; nearly all complaints and adjudications are dealt with in writing; and the Commission accepts only those complaints which demonstrate a *prima facie* breach of the Code of Practice. Complaints must also be made within a reasonable time period. The PCC does not generally accept complaints made over a month after the publication of the original article unless a satisfactory explanation can be given for the delay.
- Complaints from third parties are accepted at the discretion of the Commission, and this is exercised when members of the Commission believe that they raise issues affecting the public interest which have not already been covered by interpretations of the Code.
- The Commission's primary aim in handling complaints is to ensure that complaints are dealt with swiftly and sympathetically by editors. Every letter which raises a *prima facie* breach of the Code is sent immediately to the editor of the publication concerned with the request to attempt a swift resolution of the difficulty if at all possible. The Commission takes much trouble to reconcile complainants and editors and thus to avoid the need for formal adjudications. Its task has been eased by the willing co-operation of all editors.
- Currently, some eighty five per cent of all complaints raising an issue under the Code are resolved without the need for an adjudication, to the satisfaction of the person making the complaint. This resolution may take the form of a published apology, correction or letter from the complainant.
- Only if it is impossible to achieve a resolution does the Commission proceed to a formal adjudication. Critical adjudications must be published by the newspaper or magazine in full and with due prominence.
- The outcome of each investigated complaint is published in a regular Complaints Report which is circulated to all newspapers and magazines as well

---

[9] Complaints are not investigated at all if they fall clearly outside the PCC's remit, e.g. because they concern matters of taste.

[10] These figures are taken from the PCC Annual Review 1998.

as to television and radio journalists, other regulatory bodies, political and trade organisations, law centres, consumer organisations, libraries and individuals with a particular interest in the work of the PCC. Over 2,000 reports are circulated free of charge and back copies are available on request.

3. THE CODE OF PRACTICE AND PCC ADJUDICATIONS

(a) The Code

Central to any evaluation of the Press Complaints Commission is the quality of the Code of Practice and of the decisions which apply it. The Calcutt Report had recommended that the Commission should adjudicate complaints on the basis of a published code. Ideally, its decisions should be coherent and well-reasoned, providing clear guidance to editors and journalists on the standards set out in the Code. On some occasions recently, the PCC has referred by name to previous decisions and has emphasised the importance of consistency.[11] However, according to its preamble, the Code is to be honoured in the spirit as well as the letter; it will not do for a newspaper to argue that it has complied with its strict terms, if it has failed to respect the moral standard underlying the text. The Code is more akin to an ethical code – a Ten Commandments for the press – than to an Act of Parliament.

The Code is drafted by a committee of senior editors.[12] This arrangement is justified with the argument that the press will be more inclined to respect a code drafted by editors than one imposed from outside or framed by laymen or women. But the Code Committee does take into account the PCC's views. Indeed, it was the chairman of the PCC, Lord Wakeham, who initiated the redrafting of the Code after the death of Diana, Princess of Wales in order to tighten the restrictions on press paparazzi. Moreover, since 1993 the PCC must ratify the Code and approve any amendments. Since its initial framing at the end of 1990, the Code has been revised on several occasions. The present Code is reproduced here.

Extract 2.3.1

Press Complaints Commission Code of Practice, November 1997

The Press Complaints Commission is charged with enforcing the following Code of Practice which was framed by the newspaper and periodical industry and ratified by the Press Complaints Commission, 26th November

---

[11] See the complaints concerning payments to criminals, Extract 2.3.9 below.

[12] Until his death in 1998, the Chairman was Sir David English, Editor in Chief of the *Mail* and the *Mail on Sunday*. The present Chairman is Leslie Hinton, Executive Chairman of News International.

1997. All members of the press have a duty to maintain the highest professional and ethical standards. This Code sets the benchmarks for those standards. It both protects the rights of the individual and upholds the public's right to know. The Code is the cornerstone of the system of self-regulation to which the industry has made a binding commitment. Editors and publishers must ensure that the Code is observed rigorously not only by their staff but also by anyone who contributes to their publications. It is essential to the workings of an agreed code that it be honoured not only to the letter but in the full spirit. The Code should not be interpreted so narrowly as to compromise its commitment to respect the rights of the individual, nor so broadly that it prevents publication in the public interest. It is the responsibility of editors to co-operate with the PCC as swiftly as possible in the resolution of complaints. Any publication which is criticised by the PCC under one of the following clauses must print the adjudication which follows in full and with due prominence.

1. Accuracy
(i) Newspapers and periodicals must take care not to publish inaccurate, misleading or distorted material including pictures.
(ii) Whenever it is recognised that a significant inaccuracy, misleading statement or distorted report has been published, it must be corrected promptly and with due prominence.
(iii) An apology must be published whenever appropriate.
(iv) Newspapers, whilst free to be partisan, must distinguish clearly between comment, conjecture and fact.
(v) A newspaper or periodical must report fairly and accurately the outcome of an action for defamation to which it has been a party.

2. Opportunity to reply
A fair opportunity to reply to inaccuracies must be given to individuals or organisations when reasonably called for.

*3. Privacy
(i) Everyone is entitled to respect for his or her private and family life, home, health and correspondence. A publication will be expected to justify intrusions into any individual's private life without consent.
(ii) The use of long-lens photography to take pictures of people in private places without their consent is unacceptable. Note – Private places are public or private property where there is a reasonable expectation of privacy.

*4. Harassment
(i) Journalists and photographers must neither obtain nor seek to obtain information or pictures through intimidation, harassment or persistent pursuit.
(ii) They must not photograph individuals in private places (as defined in the note to Clause 3) without their consent; must not persist in telephoning, questioning, pursuing or photographing individuals after having been asked to desist; must not remain on their property after having been asked to leave and must not follow them.

(iii) Editors must ensure that those working for them comply with these requirements and must not publish material from other sources which does not meet these requirements.

5. Intrusion into grief or shock

In cases involving grief or shock, enquiries must be carried out and approaches made with sympathy and discretion. Publication must be handled sensitively at such times, but this should not be interpreted as restricting the right to report judicial proceedings.

*6. Children

(i) Young people should be free to complete their time at school without unnecessary intrusion.

(ii) Journalists must not interview or photograph children under the age of 16 on subjects involving the welfare of the child or of any other child, in the absence of or without the consent of a parent or other adult who is responsible for the children.

(iii) Pupils must not be approached or photographed while at school without the permission of the school authorities.

(iv) There must be no payment to minors for material involving the welfare of children nor payment to parents or guardians for material about their children or wards unless it is demonstrably in the child's interest.

(v) Where material about the private life of a child is published, there must be justification for publication other than the fame, notoriety or position of his or her parents or guardian.

7. Children in sex cases

1. The press must not, even where the law does not prohibit it, identify children under the age of 16 who are involved in cases concerning sexual offences, whether as victims, or as witnesses.

2. In any press report of a case involving a sexual offence against a child—
   (i) The child must not be identified.
   (ii) The adult may be identified.
   (iii) The word 'incest' must not be used where a child victim might be identified.
   (iv) Care must be taken that nothing in the report implies the relationship between the accused and the child.

*8. Listening devices

Journalists must not obtain or publish material obtained by using clandestine listening devices or by intercepting private telephone conversations.

*9. Hospitals

(i) Journalists or photographers making enquiries at hospitals or similar institutions must identify themselves to a responsible executive and obtain permission before entering non-public areas.

(ii) The restrictions on intruding into privacy are particularly relevant to enquiries about individuals in hospitals or similar institutions.

*10. Innocent relatives and friends

The press must avoid identifying relatives or friends of persons convicted or accused of crime without their consent.

*11. Misrepresentation

(i) Journalists must not generally obtain or seek to obtain information or pictures through misrepresentation or subterfuge.

(ii) Documents or photographs should be removed only with the consent of the owner.

(iii) Subterfuge can be justified only in the public interest and only when material cannot be obtained by any other means.

12. Victims of sexual assault

The press must not identify victims of sexual assault or publish material likely to contribute to such identification unless there is adequate justification and, by law, they are free to do so.

13. Discrimination

(i) The press must avoid prejudicial or pejorative reference to a person's race, colour, religion, sex or sexual orientation, or to any physical or mental illness or disability.

(ii) It must avoid publishing details of a person's race, colour, religion, sexual orientation, physical or mental illness or disability unless these are directly relevant to the story.

14. Financial journalism

(i) Even where the law does not prohibit it, journalists must not use for their own profit financial information they receive in advance of its general publication, nor should they pass such information to others.

(ii) They must not write about shares or securities in whose performance they know that they or their close families have a significant financial interest without disclosing the interest to the editor or financial editor.

(iii) They must not buy or sell, either directly or through nominees or agents, shares or securities about which they have written recently or about which they intend to write in the near future.

15. Confidential sources

Journalists have a moral obligation to protect confidential sources of information.

*16. Payment for articles

(i) Payment or offers of payment for stories or information must not be made directly or through agents to witnesses or potential witnesses in current criminal proceedings except where the material concerned ought to be published in the public interest and there is an overriding need to make or promise to make a payment for this to be done. Journalists must take every possible step to ensure that no financial dealings have influence on the evidence that those witnesses may give. (An editor authorising such a payment must be prepared to demonstrate that there is a legitimate public interest at stake involving matters that the public has a right to know. The payment or, where accepted, the offer of payment to any witness who is actually cited to give evidence must be disclosed to the prosecution and the defence and the witness should be advised of this.)

(ii) Payment or offers of payment for stories, pictures or information, must not be made directly or through agents to convicted or confessed criminals or to their associates – who may include family, friends and colleagues – except where the material concerned ought to be published in the public interest and payment is necessary for this to be done.

THE PUBLIC INTEREST

There may be exceptions to the clauses marked * where they can be demonstrated to be in the public interest.

1. The public interest includes:
   (i) Detecting or exposing crime or a serious misdemeanour
   (ii) Protecting public health and safety
   (iii) Preventing the public from being misled by some statement or action of an individual or organisation.
2. In any case where the public interest is invoked, the Press Complaints Commission will require a full explanation by the editor demonstrating how the public interest was served.
3. In cases involving children editors must demonstrate an exceptional public interest to over-ride the normally paramount interests of the child.

Privacy complaints, the most controversial area of the PCC's work, are covered in Chapter 11; adjudications on a number of provisions, the interpretation of which has given rise to difficulty, are discussed here.

(b) Accuracy and the opportunity to reply

In both 1996 and 1997 approximately 54% of complaints concerned inaccuracy.[13] They are, therefore, brought under clause 1 of the Code of Practice, which imposes five related obligations.[14] Although at first glance these seem clear enough, some of them allow room for argument: when, for instance, is an inaccuracy sufficiently 'significant' to give rise to the duty of correction, and does a newspaper publish a correction 'with due prominence' if it is printed on an inside page when the inaccurate or misleading material appeared on the front page?

The difficulties of applying clause 1 were highlighted in the adjudication of one of the many complaints made by, or on behalf of, members of the Royal Family (most have involved privacy); it also raises interesting procedural issues.

---

[13] The 1998 Annual Report indicates that 62% of complaints were brought under clauses 1 and 2.
[14] Before the recent revision of the Code, a separate provision (clause 3) required the press to distinguish between comment, conjecture, and fact.

Extract 2.3.2

Complaint against *Business Age*, PCC Report No 34 (1996), pp 5–8 (Appendix omitted)

COMPLAINT

Charles Anson, Press Secretary to The Queen, complained that an analysis of The Queen's personal wealth and that of other members of the Royal Family included in a feature entitled 'The Rich 500' in the September 1995 issue of the magazine, Business Age, was inaccurate and misleading in breach of Clause 1 (Accuracy) and Clause 3 (Comment, conjecture and fact) of the Code of Practice.

Each year Business Age publishes a lengthy article about the personal assets of people who the compilers regard as the richest 500 individuals in the United Kingdom. The editorial to the September 1995 edition described 'The Rich 500' as, 'our definitive guide to wealth in Britain . . . And our research is exhaustive.' A column explaining how the list was compiled states that it 'details individual and not family wealth'. The magazine said that it made a judgement in each case as to the portion of family or trust wealth to allocate to individuals who are ranked according to the total estimate of their wealth made by the compilers.

In the issue concerned the magazine explained why The Queen, with an estimated wealth of £2.2bn, had risen in one year from 72nd to 1st place in the list. It said that in the previous year it had 'looked at what the Queen might walk away with in the event of a successful republican revolution. This consisted of her non-landed assets, valued at just £158m. This year, we have decided on a figure fourteen times higher. This is certainly not attributable to investment success. In fact it is mostly a matter of legal argument'. The magazine said that while assets readily identifiable as The Queen's private and personal wealth such as racehorses, stocks and bonds and bank deposits had been the basis of its valuation in the previous year, it had added in a large number of other assets which it had now attributed to the Monarch personally. These included some of the art treasures, jewellery and palaces belonging to the Crown. The magazine added, 'As we have discovered, royal retainers are willing to go to remarkable lengths to minimise estimates of the Monarch's personal wealth . . . Nevertheless our verdict stands.'

. . .

In correspondence, Business Age's solicitors raised a number of procedural matters with the Commission. They suggested that the matter should only proceed after a measure of disclosure from the Palace had been provided and an opportunity given to their clients to present their case, examine the complainant and tender expert evidence after its experts had been given the facility to inspect and value properties and other assets associated with The Royal Family. They also asked to be able to cross-examine the author of a letter (a copy of which had been provided by the Palace Press Office) who had personally written the previous year's article on the Queen's wealth.

ADJUDICATION

The Commission rejected all these requests. While the PCC is prepared to consider oral submissions, expert evidence and cross-examination where appropriate, the approach set out below does not, in its view, require any procedural change from the normal practice of considering complaints only on the basis of the written documentation submitted. In considering the complaint the Commission did not consider the letter mentioned above as being of any assistance to it as the author appeared to have no current knowledge of how the magazine arrived at its conclusions and the basis for the calculations adopted.

While complainants may be required to supply necessary information to satisfy the Commission that a complaint is well founded, the PCC did not accept the solicitors' contention that their clients and their representatives should be able to conduct a roving expedition into the facts and background. Such a course might not only cause inconvenience and expense to complainants but would allow newspapers and other media to print speculation under the guise of being factually correct as a means of flushing out information if a complaint was subsequently made. This cannot be right. It must be for the publication concerned to satisfy the Commission that either its statements are true and accurate, or that there is a reasonable factual basis for the material printed.

The Commission had considered carefully the approach which it should adopt in this case. The PCC is concerned not to inhibit investigatory journalism in the public interest, nor does it wish to criticise proper speculation by the press about matters which are unclear. Mr Anson did not contend that any investigation into the Queen's wealth was not a matter of public interest but he did argue that the magazine's conclusions had been reached without properly checking the facts with the relevant people concerned, were riddled with inaccuracies and presented supposition as authoritative fact.

The Commission accepted the magazine's contention that there were complicated matters of a legal and factual nature which may be the subject of legitimate discussion and argument in any assessment of the Queen's wealth. The Commission was pleased to note that the magazine had agreed to consult with the Buckingham Palace Press Office and others during the course of this year's investigation and trusted that this may enable the differences between the two sides to be narrowed. In considering the current complaint the Commission confined itself to a consideration of whether the magazine's claim that its research on the subject was exhaustive was justified and whether it may have indulged in speculation disguised as fact and without checking its conclusions with the relevant officials at Buckingham Palace.

The Commission considered that in increasing the total figure from £158m in 1994 to £2.2bn for 1995 the magazine should clearly have explained the basis on which the new figure was calculated. Only a limited breakdown was given in the magazine article without a clear description of how the final figure has been reached. However the magazine had supplied the Commission with a lengthy document together with a number of appendices which sought to set out the basis of the figures selected. The Commission agreed with a contention made by the Buckingham Palace Press Office that if there was insufficient information and understanding on which to base a valuation of the Queen's personal wealth this should have been reported, rather than presenting purely speculative numbers as established facts. . . .

In respect of a number of other items the magazine did admit that a number of errors had occurred and said it would correct these in its next valuation. In the view of the Commission this is unsatisfactory as periodicals have a clear obligation under the Code to correct promptly any errors which have occurred. In this case the magazine should have corrected any admitted errors in the next issue of the magazine. It did not do so.

. . .

The Commission concluded that to the extent set out above, the article presented speculation as established fact, the magazine failed adequately to check its facts and it made a number of errors which were not properly addressed.

On this basis, the complaint was upheld.

Questions for discussion

Do you agree with this decision? Should the PCC be prepared in these circumstances to consider oral evidence and allow cross-examination of witnesses?

Sometimes a charge of inaccuracy is accompanied by a complaint that the newspaper has refused the complainant an opportunity to reply, so violating clause 2 of the Code of Practice. These are, however, much less common than those brought under clause 1 alone, amounting to little more than 3% of the total number. The drafting of clause 2 should be noted: there is an obligation to provide a '*fair* opportunity to reply to inaccuracies . . . when *reasonably* called for'.[15] This amounts to a more modest obligation than that recommended by Sir David Calcutt in the Report of 1990, let alone that imposed by legally enforceable right of reply law common in continental European systems. Calcutt's draft Code provided for a 'proportionate and reasonable opportunity to reply to *criticisms or alleged inaccuracies*. . .'.[16]

The PCC's approach is shown in the following three extracts.

Extract 2.3.3

Complaint against the *Sunday Express*, PCC Report No 15 (1992), p 8

COMPLAINT

The Ramblers Association, of 1/5 Wandsworth Road, London SW8, complain that in the preparation of a report for the Sunday Express on April 19th 1992

---

[15] Emphasis added.
[16] Cm 1102, Appendix Q (emphasis added).

there was a failure to take care not to publish inaccurate, misleading or distorted material, contrary to Clause 1 of the Code of Practice and a breach of the duty to maintain the highest professional and ethical standards, in that subsequently a fair opportunity to reply was not given, in breach of Clause 2.

ADJUDICATION

The Sunday Express published an article 'Family lose home built across forgotten path. . . . Rambler's rights. . . . Couple and sons on the street.' The article stated that a family unknowingly built their house across an ancient public footpath and despite support from the local borough council, had failed to have the footpath removed because of opposition from the Ramblers' Association. Due to personal financial difficulties, the family tried to sell their house but said the decision that the footpath should be maintained deterred potential buyers. The house was subsequently repossessed and the article claimed that the house was now likely to be sold for less than half its original value.

. . .

The newspaper published a letter from the complainant a week after the article appeared which set out its objections to the article. The Association complained that the effect of its rebuttal was nullified by the newspaper including a footnote to the letter stating that Sunday Express stood by its original story.

. . .

The Commission find that the article wrongly gave the impression that the family had become homeless as a result of the objections of the Ramblers' Association, whereas the report of the Inspector made it clear that the Association was only one of a number of objectors. The substance and position of a quotation ascribed to a 'rambler', (in fact a Sunday Express reporter) further suggested that he was associated with the complainant. In the view of the Commission, there were errors and misleading statements in the article which deserved to be corrected. The publication of a letter by the newspaper containing the Ramblers' Association replies was largely negated by the footnote added by the newspaper.

The newspaper has made a number of technical points concerning the application of the Code of Practice to the facts of this case, all which the Commission rejects. The newspaper argues that the duty, set out in the introduction to the Code, to maintain the highest professional and ethical standards is not to be imported into each individual Clause of the Code. This is plainly wrong. It also argues that the Code does not prevent the newspaper placing its own comment after a corrective letter. The Commission holds that it will depend on the circumstances of each case as to whether such a comment will negate the effect of a fair reply provided under Clause 2 of the Code, as it does in this case.

The complaint is upheld.

Extract 2.3.4

Complaint against the *Sun*, PCC Report No 27 (1994), p 11

COMPLAINT

His Honour Judge Richard Cole, of Coventry Crown Court, complains that articles in The Sun, 'Judge jails dying dad for court row' of 26 May 1994 and 'Judges like this are a cancer on justice', a columnist's piece of 27 May, were inaccurate, unjustified and went beyond what would be recognised as fair comment. He further complains that the clarifying statement which The Sun offered to publish was an inadequate remedy. The complaints are raised under Clause 1 (Accuracy), 2 (Opportunity to reply) and 3 (Comment, conjecture and fact) of the Code of Practice.

The first article compared the sentencing by the complainant of two men to community service, for their attack on a young driver, with the three-month jail sentence on the driver's father for contempt of court following his shouting in court and attack outside on the two defendants. The judge said the father deserved a nine months' sentence but because of his illness he would reduce it. The column by Richard Littlejohn which appeared the next day expressed in robust terms a view that the jail sentence was unfair.

The complainant said it was inaccurate to say that the young man had been battered senseless when he had suffered only superficial physical injuries from the iron bar used. It was also inaccurate to say that the young man's father was suffering from stomach cancer and was dying. The judge said that evidence he had seen after the trial indicated that he was not dying and did not have stomach cancer. He also objected to the columnist's robust opinions that he was pompous, self-important and incompetent.

The newspaper responded at length to the complaint and stood by its story. Nevertheless, in order to try to resolve the complaint it offered to publish a statement* indicating the judge's rebuttal of the statements about the young man's battering and the assertions that his father was dying of stomach cancer.

ADJUDICATION

The Commission believes that this offer is an appropriate remedy under the Code and regrets that it was not accepted by the complainant.

The complaint is rejected.

---

* *On May 26 we reported that Judge Richard Cole let two vicious attackers walk free from court – then jailed their victim's dying dad for three months because he assaulted one of the freed attackers in the court precincts.*

The jail term against Melvin Sollors was later reduced to 14 days after The Sun backed his appeal.

Judge Cole has now complained to the Press Complaints Commission that although evidence was given to the court that Mr Sollors was suffering from intestinal cancer and had had heart attacks and a stroke, it was inaccurate to describe him as 'dying' even though the family told The Sun they believed this to be the case at the time.

The judge also complained that although evidence was given to the court that Mr Sollors' son, Christian, was struck on the head and arm with a metal bar, it was inaccurate to say he was 'battered senseless' as we reported.
We are pleased to put the record straight.

Extract 2.3.5

Complaint against the *Daily Telegraph*, PCC Report No 37 (1997), p 24

COMPLAINT

Sir Louis Blom-Cooper QC, Chairman of Victim Support, London, SW9 complained that an article in The Daily Telegraph of 26 September 1996, headlined 'Women must be forced to return to Room 101', contained significant inaccuracies, misleading statements and distortions in breach of Clause 1 (Accuracy) of the Code of Practice. In considering the complaint the Commission also had regard to Clause 2 (Opportunity to reply) of the Code of Practice.

A named writer had put forward her views on the work of Victim Support organisations, focusing on its witness service. The complainant alleged that a number of statements in the article misrepresented or distorted the position of the group. There were also significant inaccuracies including the writer's statements that the group had been started up by a grant from an anonymous American donor and that it was funded entirely by the Home Office. In correspondence with the editor the complainant had asked for space for an article in reply by Victim Support. While not ruling this out the editor offered publication of a letter responding to the points made, an offer which the complainant did not regard as satisfactory.

  . . .

ADJUDICATION

The Commission noted that the article was clearly presented as a comment piece. It considered that most of the complaints made concerned matters which were clearly presented as the named writer's personal opinions, which she was entitled to make, as they related to the interpretation and critique of Victim Support's work. The terms of the comparison between the system in the United States and the UK were clear. With regard to the factual complaints the Commission did not find any errors significant within the context of the article taken as a whole.

Any complaint about the article could have been dealt with through the newspaper's offer to publish a letter from the complainant. There was no obligation on the newspaper to give space to a reply article.

The complaint under Clause 1 was rejected.

Questions for discussion

1. Are these adjudications consistent? Do you think that the PCC provides complainants with an effective opportunity to reply to misleading or inaccurate articles?

2.   Might any of these complaints have been resolved differently if the Code had adopted the Calcutt draft?

3.   When is it reasonable for an editor to state that he does not agree with a letter sent in reply to 'inaccurate' allegations?

(c) Intrusion into grief or shock

Among the most sensitive aspects of journalists' work is the reporting of accidents, sudden deaths, and tragedies such as an air crash. Thankfully, this gives rise to relatively few complaints, no more than 2–3% of the total number. Clause 5 (formerly clause 10) covers these situations. The next extracts nicely show the situations where the PCC has to apply it.

Extract 2.3.6

Complaint against *Evening Chronicle*, PCC Report No 40 (1997), pp 15–16

COMPLAINT

Mr James McKeown of Jarrow, Tyne and Wear, complained of how a reporter questioned him and neighbours just twelve hours into a police search for his son, before it was known that he had drowned. The resultant report appeared the same day in the Evening Chronicle (Newcastle upon Tyne), 29 May 1997, headlined 'River swimmer is feared dead'. The complainant said the reporter asked for an interview about his son's death when the family hoped he was still alive. When told to leave, the reporter allegedly then shocked neighbours with questions about his son, also visiting the home of the two young friends who were with the complainant's son at the time of the accident. The complainant alleged breaches of Clauses 8 (Harassment) [now clause 4] and 10 (Intrusion into grief or shock) of the Code of Practice.

. . .

ADJUDICATION

The Commission first considered the complaint under Clause 8 of the Code. It noted that the newspaper's policy is to enquire once only at a home in such circumstances. This was a reasonable procedure – and it was clear from statements from the complainant and his neighbours that it had been followed to the letter, with the reporter leaving when asked to do so. On this point, the Commission therefore found no breach of the Code.

The Commission then considered the complaint under Clause 10, which seeks to ensure that in cases of grief or shock, enquiries are carried out with sympathy and discretion.

This part of the Code is designed to protect people who are particularly vulnerable at times of tragedy – by reminding reporters that they must be discrete. It is not there to stop legitimate newsgathering. The Commission recognises that even at times of shock, newspapers may wish to seek out information from those involved in a tragedy which may be in the public interest, and then to publish it. This often involves reporters approaching people who are grieving, or their neighbours, at a very early stage to seek comment. Although this form of newsgathering can cause great distress to those involved, it is right that it should happen – but only, as the Code makes clear, with sympathy and discretion.

While the Commission will always uphold the right of reporters to seek information in this way, it has always held that it is not the job of reporters to break the news of a death to the family or friends of those involved – particularly when it has not been confirmed. In a recent adjudication on a complaint under Clause 10, a newspaper was censured when it became clear that a reporter had informed a mother of the death of her daughter prior to the police contacting her with the tragic news.

In this case, the Commission had to consider not the practice of newsgathering in these circumstances, but the extent to which the reporter had compounded the grief of those involved by not acting with due discretion and breaking to them news which they had not already heard.

In deciding the matter, the Commission bore three facts in mind. First, it was quite clear that at the time the reporter called on the complainant the parents of the boy still hoped he was alive. They had not informed other relatives or neighbours that he was missing, nor had they given the police permission to reveal their son's name. However, as the newspaper confirmed, the reporter was acting on information that the boy had drowned – and the memory of the complainant was quite clear that he asked about the 'death' of his son.

Secondly, while the newspaper maintained that the reporter had not told neighbours about the death of the complainant's son, it was clear from their answers to the questions – printed in the newspaper – that the reporter had told them that the boy had drowned, not simply that he was missing. Indeed, the deputy editor had told the Commission that some neighbours wished to 'give tributes to the dead youth' – something they could not have done if the reporter had not broken the news. The quote from one neighbour in the newspaper article said that 'I can't believe it because he was such a lovely lad and he was only 20 as well.' The Commission therefore concluded that the reporter had himself informed neighbours about the death of the boy before it was confirmed, and before the parents had broken the news. Although it may have been inadvertent, the reporter had as a result informed the dead boy's uncle of the news – which was the first he had heard of the fact that his nephew was missing, let alone dead.

Thirdly, the newspaper published an article – which made quite clear that the boy had died – some eight hours before the family was informed by the police that a body had been found. The report said that 'frantic friends . . . jumped into the river to try to save him but he slipped from their grasp and went under.' Crucially, it quoted the mother of one of those friends talking about the boy's 'death'.

In all the circumstances, the Commission found that the newspaper could not have acted with the discretion due in these circumstances. News of the death – either directly or indirectly – had been broken to the parents, and to the boy's uncles, by the reporter and by the newspaper before they found out about it.

The complaint under Clause 10 was therefore upheld.

Extract 2.3.7

Complaint against *Bury Times*, PCC Report No 40 (1997), p 16

COMPLAINT

Mr Nigel Adams and his daughter Miss Sarah Adams of Holcombe Brook, Bury, complained that the visit made to their family by a representative of the Bury Times after the tragic death of James Adams, breached Clause 10 (Intrusion into grief or shock) of the Code of Practice.

The tragic road accident happened on the night of 15 October 1997, the complainants having been informed of the death at 3 a.m. the following morning, and returning home from the hospital at approximately 5.30 a.m. The reporter from the Bury Times arrived at 9.15 a.m. before the family had had time to take in the shock. Although he introduced himself and left immediately as requested, they considered he had behaved entirely without sympathy.

The group editor responded by saying that the accident had involved three fatalities. Further, while being a weekly newspaper meant fewer publication deadlines and therefore usually more leeway for timing visits, in the present case the reporter approached the family so soon after the accident trying to meet a deadline. However he had acted professionally, displaying necessary sensitivity by not returning. The group editor went on to explain that any approach to a grieving family ran the risk of being seen as intrusive.

ADJUDICATION

While the Commission noted the very sad circumstances and accepted that the family must have been suffering greatly when the reporter arrived, he was pursuing legitimate inquiries about a local tragedy. Further, the Commission had no evidence that he had conducted himself discourteously or without sufficient sympathy or discretion: he had left immediately when asked, apparently with little time to say more than his name and which newspaper he represented.

The complaint under Clause 10 was rejected.

Questions for discussion

1. Can you distinguish these two cases?
2. Is it relevant in the *Bury Times* case that the reporter was 'trying to meet a deadline'? Should it be?
3. Is it ethical for journalists to try to speak to close relatives after a fatal accident?

(d) Discrimination

There has been an increasing volume of complaints of racial and other prejudice. Many arose in the context of the 1996 European football championship with regard to the treatment by tabloids of the German team: 'Let's Blitz Fritz' and 'Here we go – bring on the Krauts' were two examples of their headlines. The PCC issued a statement, pointing out that clause 13 (then clause 15) is concerned with the pejorative treatment of *individuals* on the basis of their race, not abuse of national groups.[17]

This distinction between prejudicial treatment of individuals and abuse of national and other groups was drawn in a complaint about a tabloid leader concerning the allocation of Word Cup tickets. In this context, and in that of complaints concerning payments to criminals (discussed shortly), the PCC frequently exercises its discretion to consider complaints by third parties, that is, individuals not personally directly concerned by the press article.

Extract 2.3.8

Complaint against the *Daily Star*, PCC Report No 42 (1998), p 9

COMPLAINT

Dr R Waller, of The University of Liverpool, and six others complained that a short leader comment, 'Frogs need a good kicking', in the *Daily Star* of 2 March 1998 was discriminatory in breach of Clause 13 (Discrimination) of the Code of Practice. The comment said that the way in which the French had 'grabbed the lion's share of World Cup tickets is typical of their slimy continental ways . . . As we proved at Agincourt and Waterloo, a good kicking on their gallic derrieres is the only language the greedy frogs understand.' The complainant said the comment was racist, offensive and likely to incite violence.
. . .

ADJUDICATION

The Commission had considered a number of similar complaints about discrimination and incitement of football fans to violence during 1996. Then, three newspapers had covered the 'Euro 96 football tournament in a way which many people found tasteless and offensive. On that occasion, the Commission did not censure any newspaper for a breach of the Code. It believed that a considerable amount of nationalist fervour and jingoism was inevitable at a time of any significant international sporting event, and that newspapers were reflecting those emotions. However, the Commission had believed the reporting shrill and poorly judged, and a far cry from the tradition of tolerance and fair play that had previously characterised reporting of such events: editors themselves had recognised much of it as in bad taste and rightly apologised

---

[17] PCC Report No 35 (1996), pp 22–24.

for the offence they had caused. The Commission asked all editors to bear in mind the strong public reaction to this coverage in reporting in the future. The principles which underlay the Commission's decision then remain unchanged. Sporting events – and matters relating to them, such as ticketing arrangements – are bound to excite considerable emotion. Newspapers will inevitably reflect that – even if they do so in a way which some people will find offensive.

The Code is not intended to stop such robust comment. Indeed, the purpose of Clause 13 is to protect *individuals* from prejudice – not to restrain partisan comment about other nations. The Commission has noted before on a number of occasions that the Clause is rightly defined in this way to allow the press to make pointed and critical comment, if necessary, about events and people in a variety of circumstances. The leader comment on this occasion – reflecting partisan concern in a clearly tongue-in-cheek manner – had not therefore breached the Code, although its tone had been misjudged.

(e) Payment to criminals

Among the most controversial recent decisions of the PCC have been those interpreting the provision which prohibits payment to convicted criminals (except in certain circumstances). The next extract sets out the principles developed by the Commission in these cases, notably in a complaint concerning the serialisation of a book about Mary Bell, a convicted child killer.[18] (Their application to the second and third sets of complaints is omitted, as is the discussion of the impact on Mary Bell's daughter of the serialisation.)[19] In contrast to its resolution of these complaints, the PCC has upheld a complaint that the *Daily Telegraph* violated the provision when it made a payment to Jonathan Aitken's daughter for an article by her about the events preceding his conviction for perjury and its impact on her; the Commission concluded the article did not reveal material of public interest and payment was not necessary in that another newpaper had not paid her for the article.[20]

Extract 2.3.9

**Complaint against The Times, Mirror, Express, Daily Telegraph,
PCC Report No 43 (1998), pp 5–7, 10 (paras 1.0–1.3,
2.2–2.10, 3.0–3.2, 5.0–5.3, 6.0–6.1)**

1. THE COMPLAINTS

1.0 **The complaints.** The Commission considered three sets of complaints under Clause 16(ii) of the Code of Practice, which prohibits payments by

---

[18] Also see PCC rejection of a complaint regarding the payment by the *Daily Mail* to Louise Woodward after her conviction in the USA: see PCC Report No 44 (1998), p 12.

[19] Court injunctions had previously been obtained to stop publicity harmful to the welfare of Mary Bell's daughter: see Chapter 13, Section 7 below.

[20] Adjudication of 20 July 1999.

newspapers or magazines for stories to convicted or confessed criminals, except where publication of such stories is in the public interest.

1.1　The first set of complaints related to the serialisation by *The Times* of the book, *Cries Unheard*, by Gitta Sereny about the child killer Mary Bell. Serialisation took place from 29th April to 1st May 1998.

1.2　The second set of complaints related to articles in *The Mirror* and *The Express* setting out the story of Deborah Parry and Lucille MacLauchlan, both convicted of a killing in Saudi Arabia but released from prison there following a Royal Pardon. These articles were published in the week beginning 20th May 1998. . . .

1.3　The third set of complaints related to the serialisation by *The Daily Telegraph* of a book, *The Informer*, by convicted IRA terrorist Sean O'Callaghan. The serialisation began on 16th May 1998.

2. THE CODE AND THE LAW

. . .

2.2　**The legal framework.** The Code of Practice exists outside, and on top of, the legal requirements on editors. However, the Commission is aware that in dealing with the matter of payments to criminals, it is dealing not with an ordinary complaint – where there is a victim of a breach of the Code – but with a matter of general public policy. In considering the matter, the Commission has therefore thought it right to have regard to the existing legal structures in this area.

2.3　It has always been, and remains, a matter for Parliament to set down the framework within which people are not allowed to profit from their crimes. There is a good deal of statute in this area – most importantly, the Proceeds of Crime Act 1995, the Criminal Justice Act 1988 and the Drug Trafficking Act 1994, each of which prevents convicted criminals in certain circumstances from profiting from crime. There are geographical and chronological limits to that legislation. Statute does not stop criminals convicted in foreign jurisdictions from profiting from crime – except in very limited circumstances such as drug trafficking. And it does not apply after six years have elapsed following a crime.

2.4　All the cases considered by the Commission therefore fell outside the terms of the law – a point on which the Commission placed some weight. In the case of the nurses, the events and sentencing took place abroad. In the case of Mary Bell, the publication of *Cries Unheard* took place thirty years after the crime had been committed – well outside the time set in statute; in that of Sean O'Callaghan, the book was published eight years after he was convicted. The Commission was therefore mindful that, in interpreting the Code, it should hesitate before enforcing a censorious regime on newspapers beyond that which Parliament itself has put in place. It was also mindful that newspapers and magazines operate under a tough self regulatory regime to which book publishers and broadcasters are not subject: they are subject to the law alone.

2.5　**The purpose of the PCC Code.** The provisions of Clause 16 of the Code of Practice are not intended to stop all those who have ever been convicted of a crime from being paid for their story in every set of circumstances – for three reasons. First, as set out above, it is for Parliament to establish a legal regime which defines the extent to which criminals should be prevented from cashing in on their crimes through newspaper stories or otherwise. The PCC Code cannot work in isolation from that. Second, it would be unrealistic to demand that all convicted persons should be barred in perpetuity from writing for newspapers or book publishers about their crimes or indeed about other matters. The law itself recognises that offenders can be rehabilitated and convictions 'spent' – and it would be wrong of the PCC to take a different view. Indeed, this point was established in a Commission adjudication on the serialisation by *The Guardian* of a book by convicted drugs smuggler Howard Marks (*McFarquar v The Guardian*, PCC Report, October–December 1996). And third, the Commission recognises the importance of freedom of expression and of the public's right to know – both of which are currently being guaranteed by the Human Rights Bill before Parliament.

2.6 **The public interest.** While the Code is not designed to stop criminals being paid for their stories in all circumstances, it *is* designed to stop newspapers making payments for stories about crimes *which do not contain a public interest element*. Indeed, the philosophy of the Code is that a payment aggravates the case where there is no public interest, because the glorification of the crime is more of an affront if it is done for gain. The principle behind this is, of course, that it is wrong to glorify crime, not necessarily to write about it: there will be occasions on which the public has a right to know about events relating to a crime or criminals. The key to the Code is, therefore, public interest.

2.7 This is a point established by previous PCC adjudications. One adjudication concerned the publication by *Hello!* magazine of an interview with Darius Guppy, while he was still serving a prison sentence for fraud. The Commission could not accept that there was any public interest served by the article, which merely served to glorify the crimes that Guppy had committed. It therefore upheld the complaint on the grounds of inadequate public interest (*Huins v Hello!*, PCC Report, August–September 1993).

2.8 Another adjudication concerned the case of former Barings trader Nick Lesson, whose memoirs were serialised by *The Daily Mail* soon after he had started his prison sentence. Payment arose because of the television advertising of the book by the newspaper – thus increasing the royalties obtained from increased sales. The Commission concluded that, in this case, there was a public interest justification for the way in which the newspaper had dealt with the matter and rejected the complaints (*Gordon v The Daily Mail*, PCC Report, January–March 1996).

2.9 **Payments – and exclusivity.** In each of these cases, the Commission's judgements were determined on the issue of public interest alone. The Code also makes clear that if payment is to be made for a story that is in the public interest, payment must be 'necessary' for this to happen. The Commission acknowledges that payment is increasingly demanded by people (or their agents) whose stories the newspapers want; and that newspapers – which exist in a fiercely competitive environment – in their turn wish to require exclusivity because of the large sums demanded. Although such payments for exclusivity – and the size of them – may be distasteful and offensive, they do not in themselves involve a breach of the Code, because they must in such circumstances be judged as 'necessary'. Indeed, newspapers are not well known for making payments which are *un*necessary.

2.10 **The determining factors.** In looking at the complaints before it, the determining factors for the Commission are therefore freedom of expression and public interest. The issue of payment – regulated by Act of Parliament, and currently under review by the Government – is only relevant where no arguable public interest can be displayed by the newspaper: if there is no public interest, then payment is in breach of the Code; if there is a public interest, then there is no breach of the Code provided payment is necessary.

3. WAS THERE A PUBLIC INTEREST JUSTIFICATION?

3.0 **Mary Bell and *The Times*.** The Commission found the newspaper's public interest arguments in the case of the serialisation of *Cries Unheard* to be compelling. The newspaper summed up that public interest as something that 'runs like a spine through [Gitta Sereny's book] and was the reason why Sereny felt impelled to return to the case she covered at the time of the trial. Does the criminal justice system do real justice to such damaged children? If not, how can it be improved?'

3.1 Many specific issues of public interest were raised by the newspaper. They included: the circumstances in which a child who grew up in surroundings of depravity came to be a murderer; the connection between Bell's own crime and the abuse to which she herself was subjected; and the first authoritative account of how the penal system deals with child criminals. Indeed, the editor had summed up the public interest justification in a way the Commission found highly cogent: 'Only by trying to understand what could conceivably have driven an 11 year old girl to kill two small boys . . . can we come any closer to stopping these crimes.'

3.2 The Commission also noted that the newspaper was only serialising the work – and an argument of freedom of expression, and the public interest attaching to that, therefore also arose. The material had already been put into the public domain – as a result of the willing co-operation of Mary Bell herself – and what she had to say was original material of relevance to a wide range of issues relating to crime and punishment. As such the public – not just those who would buy her book – had a right to access the material. As the newspaper said, '*Cries Unheard* publishes information which should be put in the public domain for no more specific reason than that it is better for important facts to be available for dissection and discussion than for them to remain hidden.'

. . .

5. PAYMENTS

5.0 As set out above, the Code of Practice allows newspapers to make payments for material in the public interest – provided it is 'necessary' for it to be done. There were two ways for the Commission to look at this issue.

5.1 On one basis, the mere fact that a payment has been made means that it must, in all probability, have been 'necessary'. Individuals who want to give their story for free are able to do so – while newspapers are simply not in the habit of paying for material if they do not have to.

5.2 On another basis, the Commission could have hypothesised about what might have happened if no payment had been made. In the case of the two book serialisations, it would have meant that the material in the books would not have been made available to a wide public audience. In the case of the payments to Parry and MacLaughlan, the material might have emerged in time – perhaps in another country or in another medium – but it might not have emerged at all: the nurses could simply have declined to tell their story until they had written a book. They would have profited from that – perhaps to an even greater extent – and in the meantime the public would have been deprived of information that was in the public interest.

5.3 Looking at it either way, payment was – in the phraseology of the Code – 'necessary' to secure material by which the public interest was served *so far as it was possible for the Commission to determine.*

6. CONCLUSION

6.0 On the two matters before it – public interest and payment – the Commission did not find that any case had been made out for a breach of the Code. In each of the complaints there was a strong public interest justification. These were all matters on which the public had a right to know and about which wide debate was legitimate. Furthermore, payment was in all probability 'necessary' in the terms of the Code to secure the material – or at least it could not be proved that payment was unnecessary.

6.1 However, there was one further and general matter the Commission wished to address. Like many members of the public – and like many editors – the Commission believes that while payments may in some cases be necessary, they may at the same time be extremely offensive. However, that is a moral and subjective judgement which goes beyond the scope of the Commission and an objective Code at the heart of which is the public interest and the public's right to know. It is a matter of broader public policy for Government and Parliament.

Questions for discussion

1. Is the PCC right to hesitate to add to the legal restrictions on the press when it interprets the Code (see paragraph 2.4 of the above extract)?

2. Why is it relevant that a newspaper was serialising a book?

3. Do you agree with the PCC's treatment of the question whether 'payment is necessary'?

4. CONCLUSION: IS THE PCC EFFECTIVE?

Perhaps the most frequent criticism of voluntary regulation is that the PCC lacks effective sanctions. It cannot impose a fine. It has not accepted proposals for a 'hotline' procedure, under which it would advise an editor not to publish a story or photo if it was plain that publication would infringe the Code.[21] Admittedly, the Code preamble states that any publication criticised by the PCC 'is duty bound to print the adjudication . . . in full and with due prominence'. But the Calcutt Review found that on a few occasions tabloid papers had failed to comply with that obligation or had shown contempt for the Commission by reproducing material about which a complaint had been made.[22]

The preamble now requires editors and publishers to ensure that the Code is observed by both staff and outside contributors. Enlistment of the proprietor's support has been significant on at least one occasion: the PCC had found the *News of the World* in breach of the harassment provision (now clause 4) in a complaint brought by Earl Spencer.[23]

Extract 2.4.1

Complaint against *News of the World*, PCC Report No 29 (1995), pp 7–8

In January 1994 the Commission announced that it would in future bring instances of severe or calculated breaches of the Code of Practice (whose terms are incorporated into the conditions of employment of members of the staff of many newspapers) to the attention of publishers.

In accordance with this statement, the Commission has referred its adjudication in this case to the publisher of the News of the World.

Following the Commission's adjudication . . . Mr Rupert Murdoch, Chairman of News International plc, issued the following statement:

'. . . I have reminded Mr Morgan of his responsibility to the Code to which he as editor – and all our journalists – subscribe in their terms of employment. This company will not tolerate its papers bringing into disrepute the best practices of popular journalism which we seek to follow.'

---

[21] The PCC has not implemented the government's suggestion (Extract 2.2.3) for a hotline. But it does operate a telephone 'helpline' to advise individuals who fear a story about them may be published in breach of the Code.

[22] *Review of Press Self-Regulation*, Cm 2135 (1993), paras 4.25–4.28, 4.41.

[23] Also see Extract 11.5.4 below.

The editor immediately published a full apology.

The suggestion for the institution of a compensation fund from which awards could be made to complainants in appropriate cases (see Extracts 2.2.2 and 2.2.3) has not been taken up. There are difficulties to this proposal, even though awards might assuage some distress. First, it would be unfair to require the publishers of magazines and newspapers which rarely attract complaints to subsidise the excesses of the tabloids.[24] Secondly, if compensation were awarded, the newspaper would feel entitled to an appeal or review.[25] The power to award compensation would probably lead to more formal hearings, so sacrificing one merit of PCC procedures.

The PCC itself expresses satisfaction with the degree of compliance with its adjudications. In the last few years, apparently no newspaper has failed to publish a ruling fully. On the other hand, the threat of an adverse adjudication may not constitute a serious deterrent to a paper which is prepared to publish a good story irrespective of the Code. In that sense, it may be reasonable to question the effectiveness of the PCC in comparison, say, with legal rights of action for infringement of privacy and harassment. But even if such rights were instituted, there would be a place for the Commission. Informal systems of voluntary regulation set ethical standards; they are useful to resolve complaints, for example, concerning intrusion into grief or the publication of inaccurate (non-defamatory) material, which it would be inappropriate to bring before the courts. Moreover, the PCC provides a swift and costless remedy for people unwilling or unable to pay for a court action.

[24] The PCC Annual Reports do not distinguish complaints against tabloid papers from those brought against broadsheets. However, in the last three years 45–50% of all complaints are brought against national dailies and Sunday papers.
[25] The Court of Appeal has not decided whether the PCC is liable to judicial review: *R v Press Complaints Commission, ex parte Stewart-Brady* [1997] EMLR 185, at 189.

3

BROADCASTING STRUCTURE AND
REGULATION

1. INTRODUCTION

In addition to obligations imposed by the general law, broadcasting has been, and continues to be, subject to special regulatory obligations and restrictions (see Chapter 1, Section 3). Licences to broadcast are required while obligations are imposed upon broadcasters concerning the type and content of programmes broadcast. These are restrictions and obligations which would be regarded as intolerable if imposed upon the press, yet are generally accepted as necessary within the broadcasting context. Chapter 1 examined the traditional justifications for this differential treatment. This chapter looks at the regulatory framework for broadcasting activities in Britain, both public and private. There are however significant changes taking place which affect broadcasting. Digital technology is expanding the number of services, particularly in television, which are available to the public (see Section 6 of this chapter). Other developments are also occurring which affect both broadcasting and communications more generally. One such development is frequently described as 'convergence'. It is becoming increasingly feasible for content (such as, pictures, sound, or data) to be delivered by any medium (for example, television, computer, or telephone). This is presenting government and regulators with new difficulties in how broadcasting should be regulated: for example, should we continue to regulate broadcasting as a distinct sector or should there be common regulation of broadcasting and telecommunications? The regulatory implications of convergence will be considered in Chapter 8.

Whatever the validity of the traditional justifications, the pattern of British broadcasting regulation can be seen to reflect a belief that spectrum scarcity and the perception of broadcasting as a powerful and influential medium justify special regulation. In examining developments in broadcasting regulation, it can be seen that regulation of certain services has changed to reflect their increasing availability, and the likelihood that they will have a more limited influence on viewers. One question facing those responsible for developing broadcasting policy is the extent to which close regulation of broadcasting can still be justified. In moving from a broadcasting environment where only a limited range of broadcasting services is available to one where hundreds can be received, and with increased capacity for audience control over selection, are the traditional justifications for regulation valid or are there other grounds for regulation? It should be recalled that it was suggested in Chapter 1 that the regulation of broadcasting might be important for promoting media freedom. In this chapter, as already stated, the focus will be on the regulation of both public and private broadcasting. Chapter 4 will cover programme regulation (and enforcement of licences). The influence of European law on broadcasting will be examined in Chapter 5, and, in Chapter 6, rules on advertising. Finally, issues concerning the ownership and control of broadcasting will be examined in Chapter 7.

2. THE PUBLIC SERVICE BROADCASTING CONCEPT

The justifications for broadcasting regulation discussed in Chapter 1 not only meant that broadcasting was closely regulated, but also influenced the shape of the regulatory model. Although Britain differs from other European countries in having a long tradition of a broadcasting system offering both public and private commercial services, both these elements, until about 1990, were regulated in very much the same way. Both public and private broadcasting were required to observe the public service concept of broadcasting. This concept still forms the primary obligation of British Broadcasting Corporation (BBC) broadcasting. Even now that the private broadcasting sector is less bound by this concept, its influence can still be felt. Before examining in further detail the legal frameworks for the public and private broadcasting sectors, it is timely to examine this concept. Despite its influence, there is no one clear definition.

Extract 3.2.1

House of Commons, Home Affairs Committee 3rd Report,
***The Future of Broadcasting*, (HCP 262, 1987–88),**
paras 12 and 13 (footnotes omitted)

12. Although there may be differences of opinion about what precisely is public service broadcasting, the Home Office sees it as embracing the following features:
   '(a) broadcasting is a national asset which should be used for the national good, rather than for the benefit of particular interest groups;
   (b) responsibility for broadcasting should therefore lie with one or more broadcasting authorities, appointed as the "trustees for the national interest" in broadcasting;
   (c) viewers (or listeners) in all parts of the country who pay the same licence fee should be able to receive all public service channels; the concept of universality;

(d) the broadcasting authorities should be free of Government intervention in their day to day affairs and in the content of their programmes.'

13. In return for the allocation of scarce frequencies on the spectrum the broadcasters have been expected to accept public service obligations which have formed an integral part of the British tradition of public service broadcasting. In broad terms these obligations have required that:

(a) the service should inform and educate as well as entertain;

(b) high standards should be maintained in technical and other matters;

(c) programmes should cover a wide and balanced range of subject matter in order to meet all interests in the population;

(d) there should be a wide distribution for programmes of merit;

(e) a proper proportion of programmes should be of British (now European Community) origin and performance;

(f) a suitable proportion of material should be calculated to appeal specially to the tastes and outlook of the persons served by the station, including broadcasting in languages other than English (i.e. for ethnic minority or Gaelic or Welsh communities);

(g) local sound broadcasts in the same area should not consist of identical or similar material.

This public service broadcasting concept is also reflected in the legal sources of the BBC and the private broadcasting sector. A brief statement appears in the BBC Royal Charter (art 3(c)), which is elaborated in the BBC Agreement (clause 3) (these documents are discussed in Section 3 below). The Broadcasting Act 1990 (BA 1990) dispenses with the traditional summons to educate, inform, and entertain but something of the public service broadcasting ethos can still be discerned for the commercial sector. Note that here the obligation does not fall on to individual licensees but is directed at how the regulatory body, the Independent Television Commission (ITC), should carry out its duties.[1]

Extract 3.2.2

Broadcasting Act 1990, s 2(2)

2.—(2) It shall be the duty of the [Independent Television] Commission—

(a) to discharge their functions . . . as respects the licensing of the services . . . in the manner which they consider is best calculated—

---

[1] For radio, see BA 1990, s 85(2) and (3). In 1998, the Channel 3 licensees sought approval from the ITC to vary their licence obligations to enable them to replace the main news report (*News at Ten*) with two reports, at 6.30 pm and 11 pm. Before agreeing to the proposal, the ITC carried out a consultation and commissioned independent audience research: ITC, *ITC gives qualified approval to new weekday schedule on ITV* (News Release 105/98, 19 November 1998). The careful deliberation given to this request provides a good example of the close regulation which is still exerted by the ITC, despite the move away from public service broadcasting.

   (i) to ensure that a wide range of such services is available throughout the United Kingdom, and
   (ii) to ensure fair and effective competition in the provision of such
services and services connected with them; and
(b) to discharge their functions . . . as respects the licensing of television
   programme services and multiplex services . . . in the manner which
   they consider is best calculated to ensure the provision of television
   programme services which (taken as a whole) are of high quality and
   offer a wide range of programmes calculated to appeal to a variety of
   tastes and interests.

Gibbons has commented that the interpretation of public service has varied
over time, having been characterised by paternalism, elitism and, more recently, consumerism.[2] Certainly, there are difficulties in the notion of public
service broadcasting: how, for example, does one determine the 'national
good'; identify the interests of the population; determine what is a quality or
meretricious programme; decide what is the 'national identity'?[3] Whatever,
the vagaries of the notion, however, its principles have had a major influence
on broadcasting policy-making and regulation.

The Peacock Committee was established in the 1980s to consider BBC
funding, but it included in its examination the whole broadcasting sector. It
recommended a much more market-oriented approach to the regulation of
broadcasting and its Report was influential in bringing about the changes to
broadcasting regulation found in the BA 1990. The regulatory structure of
the BBC and of the private television sector is discussed in Sections 3 and 4
below. Meanwhile Extract 3.2.3, taken from the Peacock Committee Report,
illustrates an important point which permeates this chapter's examination of
the regulation of broadcasting: namely, that the maintenance of public service broadcasting is inexorably linked to the way in which broadcasting is
structured and financed. The Peacock Committee was of course reporting
prior to the 1990 changes, hence the reference to the ITV system describes
the private television sector.

Extract 3.2.3

Report of the Peacock Committee on Financing the BBC, Cmnd 9824 (1986), paras 580–581

580 The best operational definition of public service is simply any major
modification of purely commercial provision resulting from public policy. Defined in this way the scope of public service will vary with the state of broadcasting. If a full broadcasting market is eventually achieved, in which viewers

---

[2] Gibbons, p 58.
[3] See further T Burns, *The BBC: Public Institution and Private World* (Macmillan, 1977), p 40.

and listeners can express preferences directly, the main role of public service could turn out to be the collective provision . . . of programmes which viewers and listeners are willing to support in their capacity of taxpayers and voters, but not directly as consumers. These would include programmes of a more demanding kind with a high content of knowledge, culture, education and experiment (including entertainment).

581 But in the highly imperfect broadcasting market we have known, and which still exists, the role of public service is much wider. So long as the number of channels is severely limited by spectrum shortage, and there is no direct payment by viewers and listeners, an unregulated advertising-financed broadcasting system, so far from satisfying consumer demand can actually distort it. In particular it provides an inadequate supply of medium appeal and 'minority programmes', which most people want to see or hear some of the time . . . In these circumstances – quite apart from their role in stimulating a taste for demanding programmes – the Public Service institutions have been necessary to provide the viewer and listener with what he or she wants as a consumer. The BBC and the regulated ITV system have done far better, in mimicking the effects of a true consumer market, than any purely *laissez-faire* system, financed by advertising could have done under conditions of spec-trum shortage.

Question for discussion

Is the Peacock Report suggesting that the role of public service broadcasting is one of 'gap-filling'? Can other justifications be found?

3. PUBLIC BROADCASTING

(a) Introduction

When the BBC began broadcasting in 1922, under a licence granted by the government, it was as a private company, albeit operating as a monopoly, known as the British Broadcasting Company; its shares owned by British wireless manufacturing companies.[4] For the wireless manufacturers this was a necessary means of facilitating the sale of their radio equipment.[5] This structure continued until 1927 when it became a public corporation established under Royal Charter, and was renamed the British Broadcasting Corporation, following recommendations of the Crawford Committee that broadcasting should not be left to a commercial company.[6] It is important to remember that public broadcasting does not mean state broadcasting. If the public broadcaster is to be able to fulfil the public service mandate, then it will be important for it to be free not just of commercial pressures, but also of state influence and control. Hence the manner in which the public

---

[4] R H Coarse, *British Broadcasting: A Study in Monopoly* (Longman, 1950), p 15.
[5] Ibid, 15–16.
[6] Gibbons, p 57.

broadcaster is established and the terms under which it operates will be crucial. This is even more so in the UK which has lacked the type of constitutional protections found in countries such as Germany (see Extract 1.1.3).

(b) The structure of the BBC

The BBC is established by Royal Charter which, together with the Agreement made between the BBC and the Secretary of State (currently the Secretary of State for Culture, Media and Sport), sets out the constitution and terms of operation of the BBC.[7] The BBC's constitutional documents were last renewed in 1996: *Royal Charter for the continuance of the British Broadcasting Corporation*[8] (the Charter) and *Agreement Dated the 25th Day of January 1996 Between Her Majesty's Secretary of State for National Heritage and the British Broadcasting Corporation*[9] (the Agreement). The current Charter and Agreement are for a term of 10 years and replace the previous Charter and Agreement which had been granted in 1981. They differ considerably from their predecessors because much more detail is now provided about the BBC's role, structures of governance and obligations. The Charter, granted under Crown prerogative, sets out the objects and overall structure and functions of the BBC. The Agreement is more concerned with the day-to-day operations of the BBC.

Extract 3.3.1

Agreement Dated the 25th Day of January 1996 Between Her Majesty's Secretary of State for National Heritage and the British Broadcasting Corporation, Cm 3152 (1996), clauses 2.1, 2.3–2.5 and 6.1

2.1 The Corporation shall be independent in all matters concerning the content of its programmes and the times at which they are broadcast or transmitted and in the management of its affairs.

. . .

2.3 The Corporation may, subject to the prior agreement of the Secretary of State, vary the number or geographical coverage of its national television and sound programme services.

2.4 The Corporation may, subject to the prior agreement of the Secretary of State, provide multiplex facilities for digital television and sound broadcasting frequencies.

2.5 Unless prevented by circumstances beyond its control, the Corporation shall transmit efficiently programmes in the Home Services and the World

---

[7] For a discussion of the different types of structures canvassed for the BBC, See Burns, *The BBC: Public Institution and Private World*, pp 15–16.
[8] Cm 3248 (1996).
[9] Cm 3152 (1996).

Service from such stations as, after consultation with the Corporation, the Secretary of State and the Secretary of State for Foreign and Commonwealth Affairs may from time to time in relation to those Services respectively in writing prescribe.

. . .

6.1 The Secretary of State may from time to time by notice in writing give directions to the Corporation as to the maximum time, the minimum time, or both the maximum and the minimum time, which is to be given in any day, week or other period to broadcasts or transmissions in the Home Services and as to the hours of the day in which such transmissions are or are not to be given.

Both the Charter and the Agreement include powers of revocation in the event of breach (art 20(2) and clause 15 respectively). Article 8 of the Agreement, gives the government power to 'censor' BBC broadcasting in similar terms to BA 1990, s 10 (see Extract 1.5.6), but, as Extract 3.3.1 shows, there is also scope for government control through the ordinary affairs of broadcasting. Indirect influence can also be exerted on the BBC through appointments: art 8 of the Charter, provides that the governors, and the Chairman and Vice-Chairman shall be appointed by the government. Examining the structure of the BBC and its constitutional documents can show how vulnerable the BBC can be to government influence, both to direct pressure and to more subtle attempts to influence.[10]

(c) Funding of the public broadcaster

The way in which a public broadcaster is funded will also be important in ensuring its independence. Since its inception the BBC has been funded by licence fee. This is payable by those who possess a television set (Wireless Telegraphy Act 1949 (as amended), s 1(1)).[11] Although, the BBC does have greater flexibility now to undertake more commercial activities and to fund these by different means (see 1949 Act, s 3(e)), its major source of funding is still the licence fee.[12] Since 1990 the BBC has been responsible for its collection (BA 1990, s 180). It is generally assumed that a licence fee is a more secure means of providing funding, but it does not entirely guarantee that the broadcaster will be free from pressure. The following extract explains this, as well as other features of the licence fee. This extract is taken from a recent review of BBC funding which will be discussed below.

[10] For a discussion of how the structure of the BBC renders it vulnerable and an examination of alternative structures see E M Barendt, 'Legal Aspects of BBC Charter Renewal' (1994) 65(1) *The Political Quarterly* 20.

[11] Initially of course the licence fee applied to radio sets, but these have been exempt since 1971.

[12] For 1998–99, the licence fee provided 95% of all BBC income: BBC, *Annual Report and Accounts 98/99* (1999), p 40.

Extract 3.3.2

Department for Culture, Media and Sport, *The Future Funding of the BBC: Report of the Independent Review Panel* (July 1999), pp 140, 142–143

From the BBC's point of view, the licence fee is the best way to finance public service broadcasting. The security of this regular income allows the BBC to take a long-term perspective, nurturing creative and performing talent, carrying out research and development and investing in production skills and technology. However, the downside, as with all forms of guaranteed, tax-based revenue, is that it frees the BBC from the need to respond to changing consumer preferences. . . .

From a broadcasting point of view, therefore, the licence fee has much to recommend it. However, there is another side to the coin. The licence fee, correctly described, is a tax and a poor tax at that. It is levied on everyone who has a television set. It takes the same amount from every household, rich or poor. . . .

Partly in consequence, there are no grounds for complacency about the sustainability of the licence. Our poll indicates that opinion is divided on whether the licence fee provides good value for money – 45% agree, while 42% disagree. . . . Advertising, and not the licence fee, is the preferred way of funding the BBC amongst the public. . . .

Because the licence fee is unpopular with the public, it tends to be unpopular with politicians. Over a number of years now, it has been demonstrated that few governments are willing to put up the licence fee over a period of years by more than the retail price index. Moreover this means that the BBC is constantly forced to pay great regard to the views of politicians lest they punish it by cutting back the licence fee. This in turn can lead to perceptions that the Corporation is more susceptible than is desirable to political pressures, in turn jeopardising its reputation for impartiality.

The licence fee has been set, through linkage with the Retail Price Index, until 2002. Apart from its apparent unpopularity, the licence fee also appears less sustainable when, as now, there are a proliferation of services, compared with a period when the BBC was the only broadcaster or one of few. This may also make governments sensitive about licence fee funding. In October 1998, the government announced a review of BBC funding for the period up to renewal of the Charter in 2006. A review panel (the Review) was set up under the chairmanship of Gavyn Davies and it reported in July 1999 (the Davies Report). It is proposed that the government will conduct a consultation exercise and announce its plans in September 1999. The terms of the Review were quite narrow. First, the Review was instructed to assume that the licence fee is sustainable until the Charter's renewal. Secondly, it was not open to the Review to consider alternatives to the licence fee, only how it could be supplemented.[13] As part of its Review, the Davies Report considered other forms of funding.

---

[13] Department for Culture, Media and Sport, *Chris Smith announces terms for BBC Funding Review* (DCMS 256/98, 14 October 1998).

Extract 3.3.3

Department for Culture, Media and Sport, *The Future Funding of the BBC: Report of the Independent Review Panel* (July 1999), pp 63, 64 and 66–68

ADVERTISING ON BBC PUBLIC SERVICES

The introduction of advertising on BBC public services is superficially appealing. There is little doubt that it could generate very significant extra funds for the Corporation, making possible either a substantial cut in the licence fee, or comfortably funding the entire extra spending suggested in the BBC's [digital vision.] . . .

Nevertheless the Panel believes that the introduction of advertising on BBC public services is neither desirable nor practicable:

* introducing advertising on some or all of the BBC public services would be likely to alter the range and quality of BBC programmes, leading inexorably to a more populist and less distinctive schedule. The programmes would have to attract large or high-spending audiences, which advertisers pay to reach. This could force the BBC to cut back on challenging and innovative programming, programming of interest to older or poorer people who may spend less, or to reschedule minority programmes out of peak times;
* commercial pressures can also threaten the freedom and independence of programme makers and schedulers;
  . . .
* allowing the BBC to take advertising would reduce the revenues of Channel 4 and existing and prospective commercial television and radio services, and of the press . . .
* advertising becomes a less certain source of finance as the number of competing services grows;
* in a number of European countries, reliance by public service broadcasters on advertising has resulted in ratings wars, falling audiences and reduced revenues and there is some evidence of an adverse correlation between the extent to which the public service broadcaster is funded from advertising and the proportion of output dedicated to factual, children's and cultural programming, even when advertising is restricted to certain times . . . ;
* experience elsewhere in the EU suggests that taking advertising generates complaints from commercial broadcasters and raises regulatory queries about the legitimacy of public funding.

. . .

SPONSORSHIP

Sponsorship is another form of advertising limited to a statement in a programme that it is being financed by a particular organisation. Sponsorship would be less intrusive than advertising, but we would not recommend it for the following reasons:

- association with the BBC brand name could be attractive to sponsors, but there would be a risk that income from programme sponsorship might alter the balance of the BBC's programming, by putting pressure on the BBC to make more programmes which are attractive to sponsors;
- it would be unlikely to provide sufficient revenue to finance more than a small proportion of programmes and would cover only a fraction of the BBC's programme costs;
- it would inevitably draw advertising and sponsorship revenue away from Channel 4 and commercial broadcasters, or the arts and other sponsored events. The pot is not big to begin with: the sponsorship market in the UK is around £45 million. . . .

SUBSCRIPTION

Subscription could take several forms, ranging from a single fee for certain BBC services to paying to watch individual programmes. One advantage of subscription is that it could make a direct link between the providers and users of the services. Unlike the licence fee, subscription need not oblige television set owners to pay the same amount regardless of how many programmes or services they use. However, the downsides of subscription are:

- it would by definition be available only to those willing to pay and therefore negate the fundamental public purpose of free-to-air services and universal access for the nation as a whole;
- if programmes or services were encrypted to ensure payment of the subscription, this would discourage people from sampling a wide range of programmes and could reduce the availability of programmes for those less able to pay;
- there would be a financial incentive for the BBC to place its best offerings on pay channels, or single programme pay-per-view, which would further undermine the licence fee concept.

. . .

OTHER OPTIONS

We have also considered the possibilities of **direct funding** by Government either through taxation or grant and **mixed funding** systems. The former has, however, tended to create broadcasters that are inextricably linked to political moods and have the potential to lose management or editorial independence, while the latter undermines the principle of fixed and independent funding and would be vulnerable either to reductions in mandatory funding or eventual transformation into a full commercial broadcaster.

Our view is that each of these forms of supplementary funding, even if only providing funding at the margin, could change fundamentally the purpose and nature of the BBC's public services, both broadcast and online.

Question for discussion

Would these other methods of funding provide greater independence for the BBC compared with the licence fee?

The BBC had submitted to the Review proposals for an increase in the licence fee to provide it with an extra £650 million. Although, it considered that the BBC would make effective use of such additional funds, the Review adopted the principle that increases in the licence fee would only be justified if it was absolutely convinced that they were '. . . necessary to maintain a healthy broadcasting ecology in the UK'.[14] The Review was particularly conscious of the regressive nature of the licence fee, and felt that this constrained the amount by which it could increase. However, it did accept that, if the BBC was to fulfil its public service mission, it was essential for it to expand its involvement in digital broadcasting, and this could only be fulfilled if there was an increase in its funding.[15] The Review's proposal to provide the extra funding was to impose a supplement on the licence fee for digital receivers, starting at about £1.99 per month and falling to 99 pence by 2006. This supplement could provide additional funding until about 2010, when it was envisaged that the analogue system would have been switched off (see Section 6 below). The Review's reasons for favouring this option are set out in the following extract.

Extract 3.3.4

Department for Culture, Media and Sport, *The Future Funding of the BBC: Report of the Independent Review Panel* (July 1999), pp 74–76

The final option for extra funding, which is firmly in the tradition of how previous technological changes have been handled in the UK, is the introduction of a digital licence supplement for digital televisions, levied on the same basis as the current licence fee (i.e. on a per household basis, payable once a household had installed its first digital receiver or set top box). . . .

A digital licence supplement would have compelling advantages:

- it would continue the established practice that people should pay more when there is a major change in the technical capabilities of their main receiver – analogous with the introduction of television, and later the colour licence fee;
- it would reduce resentment among those who have not adopted digital technology that 10% of their licence fee was being spent on something from which they do not benefit;
- it would provide buoyancy for BBC revenues as digital take-up increases; and

---

[14] Department for Culture, Media and Sport, *The Future Funding of the BBC: Report of the Independent Review Panel* (July 1999), p 38.
[15] Ibid, p 58.

- once the initial decision was taken by Government, it would remove the BBC licence fee from the arena of political controversy for many years to come.

Against these some disadvantages have to be weighed:

- there are concerns among manufacturers, the platform operators, ONdigital and BSkyB, and others, that a higher licence fee for digital televisions might deter take-up of digital systems;
- it would add to the barriers to digital transfer faced by the poor;
- there may be enforcement difficulties, especially if many digital receivers were already in use before a digital licence supplement was introduced; and
- there would be uncertain effects on BBC revenue, dependent on the rate of digital penetration.

. . .

[The Report was aware that the most serious disadvantage was the possibility that it might deter take up of digital television. It went on to consider this issue and to review evidence provided on it:]

- The main obstacle to take up is the initial cost of the hardware and installation . . .
- take-up is determined more by the attractions of the technology than by its cost . . .
- a digital licence supplement at the levels suggested . . . is small compared with the cost of commercial subscription packages which range up to £29.99 a month.

. . .

- improved BBC digital services, and the marketing of these services on other BBC channels, would greatly add to the attraction of the digital package.

Questions for discussion

1. Is the digital licence supplement consistent with licence fee principles?
2. Is the digital licence supplement analogous with imposing a higher fee on colour television sets as the Review argued?

(d) Accountability

The range of tools through which the BBC may be made accountable range from the informal to the formal. The scope for the government to exert control over the BBC and its activities has already been mentioned. Consistent with a more consumerist approach, there are informal mechanisms such as programmes where viewers and listeners can comment on programmes, scheduling arrangements and so forth. Mechanisms may also arise internally or externally. The BBC is accountable to external bodies such as the Broadcasting Standards Commission (see Chapter 4, Section 4) and, increasingly, to the ITC in respect of its commercial activities. Finding ways to regulate and render accountable a public service broadcaster is complex and the mechanisms adopted can have an impact on the independence of the broadcaster.

(i) Reporting to audiences

The Annual Report includes an assessment of the BBC's performance, but it is the BBC itself which makes this assessment. This reflects the curious nature of the BBC. Notwithstanding, its potential vulnerability to government influence, it also exercises a self-regulatory role in respect of many of its activities. On this latter point, its position can be contrasted with the private broadcasting sector (Section 4 below). Clause 4.2 of the Agreement requires the BBC to report directly to the public by also publishing annually a Statement of Promises to Audiences.

(ii) Programme standards

Clause 5 of the Agreement imposes specific obligations on the BBC concerning programme standards. These obligations are similar to those imposed on the private broadcasting sector (Chapter 4). Detailed rules and guidance concerning these standards, and other aspects of programming, are set out in the *Producers' Guidelines* with which all programme makers are expected to comply.[16] The approach taken in these guidelines is similar to that adopted in the programme codes for private television and radio. There are several ways in which compliance with the programme standards is monitored. Within the BBC there is a Programme Complaints Unit which deals with complaints from the public from which appeals may be taken to a committee of the Governors of the BBC. The Governors also report on compliance with these standards in the Annual Report, as well as making an assessment of how well the complaints unit has performed. Viewers and listeners can also take complaints to the Broadcasting Standards Commission (Chapter 4, Section 4).

(iii) Government/Parliamentary scrutiny

Another form of accountability will come through parliamentary debate, although there is a fine line to be drawn between what is legitimate inquiry and what amounts to interference in day-to-day broadcasting decisions. Gibbons has made the following suggestion:

> One positive effect of the new BBC Charter and Agreement will be the provision of a set of criteria for judging the Corporation's actions without needing to defer to populist political pressure. Already it is more noticeable that when MPs or ministers express concern about the Corporation, they do so in terms of its formal obligations. The effect is to create a form of closure in respect of the BBC's existence and to move debate forward in terms of the application of its remit.[17]

---

[16] 3rd ed (1996).
[17] Gibbons, p 290.

A good example of this was an extensive debate over a BBC proposal, in conjunction with Camelot, the National Lottery operator, to broadcast a game programme which required potential members of the live audience to buy a scratchcard which could entitle them to attend the show. Some Members of Parliament considered that this breached the Charter, but the limits of such debates can be seen in the Secretary of State's response.

Extract 3.3.5

House of Commons Debates, *Hansard,* vol 308 (16 March 1998), cols 949–950

Mr Smith [Secretary of State for Culture, Media and Sport]: . . . [Any] contravention of the terms of the BBC's Charter and the terms laid down by the House is to be thoroughly deplored. However, the BBC asserts that the programme . . . does not contravene the terms of its charter. It is that precise question that I expect the governors of the BBC to address. Under its governing instruments, the royal charter and agreement, the BBC is, rightly, independent in all matters relating to the editorial content and scheduling of programmes. I cannot directly intervene in such matters; that is the job of the chairman and governors.

As part of its remit, the Review had to consider the commercial activities of the BBC (see Section 3(e) below). Although it did not consider that commercial activity conflicted with its role as a public service broadcaster, it did conclude that there was a lack of public confidence over the degree of separation of its public service and commercial operations.[18] As well as a number of medium-term recommendations dealing with this issue,[19] the Review proposed that, at its renewal, a new provision should be introduced into the Charter to give the National Audit Office the power to audit the BBC's accounts and its fair trading arrangements (which apply to its commercial activities). The following extract demonstrates the concerns of the Review and the BBC.

Extract 3.3.6

Department for Culture, Media and Sport, *The Future Funding of the BBC: Report of the Independent Review Panel* (July 1999), pp 146–147

Clearly, the BBC is subject to a number of outside controls. . . . Nevertheless, it is broadly a self-regulatory body. Its accountability is to the Corporation's Governors. . . .

---

[18] Note 14, above, p 105.

[19] For example, an inquiry by the Office of Fair Trading into the adequacy of the BBC's commercial policy guidelines, and reviews by the National Audit Office into BBC compliance with its fair trading policy and the transparency of its financial reporting: ibid, 107–108.

. . .

The most serious lacuna that results from this structure concerns financial control. The BBC is disposing of a substantial sum of what is essentially public money. One part of that money is subject to normal parliamentary controls. The Comptroller and Auditor General, Parliament's spending watchdog, can audit money paid to the BBC through the . . . annual grant to the BBC's World Service. But another and far larger part is not. The grant it gets from the Department for Culture, Media and Sport . . . [the licence fee] cannot be examined by the Comptroller, nor by the Committee of Public Accounts to whom he reports.

The BBC is sensitive about external regulation, in particular that it might undermine the Governors' role as the primary regulators . . . They fear that such audit would provide politicians with a handle with which to beat the Corporation, on its policy and even on its individual programmes. Rightly concerned for its independence, they oppose this. They also say that the knowledge that BBC executives might be second-guessed by politicians could result in timid and safety-first decisions by programme-makers.

. . . The Comptroller is appointed by Parliament, not by the Government. It is not his job to report on matters of policy and, in conducting its reviews, it should be made clear to the National Audit Office in its terms of reference that it must not cut across the proper independence of the BBC and, in particular, must not interfere in programming issues.

Questions for discussion

1. Does this proposal threaten the BBC's independence?
2. The BBC's Annual Report is reviewed by the Culture, Media and Sport Committee, and Parliament may engage in debate about the BBC. Would scrutiny by the National Audit Office differ from these forms of scrutiny?

(iv) Judicial review

There has been a growing readiness by private broadcasters to challenge decisions taken by the regulatory authorities through judicial review. Traditionally it was thought that the BBC was not subject to judicial review, in part because its constitutional documents did not set out legally enforceable standards, for example, in relation to impartiality. The position is now thought to be different, particularly since the Charter and the Agreement include detailed obligations. This opens the way for BBC practices and decisions on programming to be challenged. Certainly recent cases have proceeded on the basis that the BBC is subject to judicial review (see Chapter 4, Section 5).[20]

(e) The future of public broadcasting

One of the more recent developments for the BBC has been its strengthened ability to develop commercial activities. Its commercial activities are primarily

---

[20] See further Gibbons, pp 290–291 and *R Craufurd Smith, Broadcasting Law and Fundamental Rights* (Oxford University Press, 1997), pp 74–75.

operated through BBC Worldwide which sells programmes and related products, engages in publishing activities and the development of new programme channels. Another division, BBC Resources, providing broadcasting and technical facilities, has also been developing its commercial operations.[21] Any activities which the BBC engages in of a commercial nature which involve developing new broadcasting or programme services are licensed and regulated by the ITC or the RA. Section 136 of and Sched 8 to the Broadcasting Act 1996 (BA 1996) adapt the BA 1990 so that it applies to the BBC where necessary. The purpose of these commercial activities is to assist the BBC in securing additional funds for its public service activities. However, it is also important that it does not pursue these activities at the expense of its core role, or abuse its position by gaining unfair competitive advantages. The BBC has in place commercial policy guidelines and operates under a Fair Trading Commitment, set out in this extract.

Extract 3.3.7

BBC Worldwide, *Annual Report and Accounts 1998/99* (1999), p 22

This Fair Trading Commitment requires BBC Worldwide to:
– engage in commercial activities which are consistent with, and support, the BBC's role as a public service broadcaster;
– pay fair charges for any goods or services received from other parts of the BBC;
– charge prices which are a fair reflection of both costs incurred and market practice.

The Davies Report reviewed the BBC's commercial activities and noted concerns about the separation of its activities.[22] The BBC's success in its commercial activities could provide it with a further dilemma, as Gibbons suggests.

Extract 3.3.8

T Gibbons, *Regulating the Media*, 2nd ed (Sweet & Maxwell, 1998), pp 184–185 (footnotes omitted)

This idea of keeping the commercial activities distinct has the appearance of guaranteeing public finances, but the Corporation's very success in selling its (public service) products will eventually undermine the legitimacy of its public functions. It will be questioned whether public funding is needed at all to

---

[21] The Davies Report has recommended that these companies should be partly privatised: see note 14, above, Chapter 3.
[22] See note 14, above and Section 3(d)(iii) of this chapter.

sustain public service and commercial operators will come to regard it as a unfairly subsidised product which enjoys a competitive advantage in the marketplace. Although the licence fee will remain the principal source of income for the BBC in the short term, the general trend, then, is to push the BBC away from public service as an organisational aspiration to public service as a programming genre.

Question for discussion
How would the BBC differ if its public service mandate changed, as Gibbons suggests, from an organisational one to a focus on programming?

The Davies Report did not discount a future for the BBC in the digital world, but it was clear that one of the tasks of Charter renewal should be to define more precisely the role of public service broadcasting and the activities of the BBC. Broadcasting was not public service, simply because it was done by the BBC.[23]

4. PRIVATE TELEVISION BROADCASTING

(a) Introduction

Until the introduction of cable television in the early 1980s,[24] television broadcasting in the UK followed a largely unchanging pattern. The private television sector, the Independent Television Association (ITV), had secure funding to enable it to pursue a public service mandate because it did not have to compete with the BBC for advertising revenue. Even when Channel 4 commenced broadcasting, ITV's position remained secure because it controlled the sale of its advertising (see Section 4(g) below). The 'comfortable duopoly', as it was termed, continued until the BA 1990 introduced a new regulatory structure. Expansion of broadcasting services, through satellite and cable, has also changed the traditional pattern of regulation, and the media environment within which regulation must operate.

The structure of private broadcasting (which is also referred to as commercial broadcasting or independent broadcasting) was also rather curious. The Independent Broadcasting Authority (IBA) was both broadcaster and regulator for television and radio.[25] Although legally the broadcaster, in practical terms, the broadcasting was done by franchisees or 'programme contractors' as the legislation termed them. The pattern which was set at the outset for the regulation and operation of commercial television continued until the 1990 legislation. Although some changes were made, it remained a broadly

---

[23] Note 14, above, pp 139 and 140.
[24] Prior to the Cable and Broadcasting Act 1984, cable mainly existed only where reception of terrestrial television was poor.
[25] Prior to the introduction of local commercial radio in 1972, the body had been called the Independent Television Authority.

discretionary and largely unaccountable system.[26] In 1988, the government published a White Paper setting out proposals for reform of both television and radio broadcasting: *Broadcasting in the '90s: Competition, Choice and Quality*[27] (the White Paper). The proposals were made law through the BA 1990. The following extracts from the White Paper give an illustration of the government's approach and the tenor of the BA 1990.

Extract 3.4.1

Broadcasting in the '90s: Competition, Choice and Quality, Cm 517 (1988), paras 2.5–2.6, 4.1–4.2, 6.5 and 6.7

2.5 In a rapidly changing environment, the existing framework for broadcasting in the UK must change too. But change is desirable as well as inevitable. Through it the individual can exercise choice from a greater range and variety of services. The growth of choice means that a rigid regulatory structure neither can nor should be perpetuated. It would not be sensible for the Government to try to lay down a detailed blueprint for the future. The Government should not try to pick winners. It should enable, not dictate, choice. A new enabling framework must be flexible enough to allow for technological change. As new services emerge and subscription develops, viewer choice, rather than regulatory imposition, can and should increasingly be relied upon to secure the programmes which viewers want. Rules will still be needed to safeguard programme standards on such matters as good taste and decency and to ensure that the unique power of the broadcast media is not abused.

2.6 The principles underlying the Government's approach are these.

– Broadcasting services must remain independent of Government editorially and, to the greatest extent possible, in economic and regulatory terms.

– Because of broadcasting's power, immediacy and influence, there should be continued provisions, through both the law and regulatory oversight, governing programme standards, including the portrayal of violence and sex.

– There are significant differences between radio and television as broadcasting media which need to be reflected in their respective regulatory arrangements.

– There should be opportunities for new services to develop, as the market demands, and Government should not attempt to determine artificially the relative success of different technologies.

– There should be no unnecessary constraints on increasing the range, variety and quality of programmes from which viewers and listeners can choose.

– There should be increasing opportunities for direct payment for television programme services through subscription, whether on a pay per channel or pay per programme basis.

---

[26] See further T Prosser, *Law and the Regulators* (Clarendon Press, 1997), pp 242–244.
[27] Cm 517 (1988).

- There should be vigilance against uncompetitive practices and market distortions. Partly for this reason, and to limit barriers to the entry of new operators in the market, there should be a greater separation between the various functions which make up broadcasting and have in the past been carried out by one organisation. These include programme production, channel packaging and retailing, and transmission or delivery.
- The emergence of a production sector which is independent in that it neither controls nor has guaranteed access to a delivery system fits this objective and should be further encouraged.
- Broadcasting companies and organisations of all kinds should be briskly and efficiently run. They should give value for money to the viewer and listener and compete effectively with each other and abroad. The present duopoly can no longer be insulated from the disciplines necessary to bring this about.
- Through greater competition, downward pressure should be exerted on the costs to UK industry of television airtime.
- Wherever possible the Government's approach to broadcasting should be consistent with its overall deregulation policy. This is that the Government should help enterprises to set up, develop and meet the needs of consumers by removing unnecessary regulatory barriers. This implies both less regulation (removing restrictions which are outmoded or unnecessary) and better regulation (lighter, more flexible, more efficiently administered).

. . .

4.1 The Government agrees with the Peacock Committee . . . that we should move away from a highly regulated television duopoly towards a more competitive future, for the benefit of the viewer. This must be achieved without detriment to the variety, range and quality of programme services, and without debasing the content of programmes.

4.2 New programme services offer the prospect of wider choice of programmes for the viewer, additional outlets for TV advertising, business opportunities for the growing programme production sector, and a wider trial of subscription. The Government proposes that forthcoming legislation should create a liberalised enabling framework for the development of new services, subject to the necessary consumer protection requirements.

6.5 The Government thinks it right – as the Home Affairs Committee recommended . . . that all independent sector television services should be brought within the ambit of a single agency which can look across the board, rather than being limited, as the IBA and Cable Authority now necessarily are, to particular delivery technologies. The Government therefore proposes that there should be an Independent Television Commission (ITC). The ITC would apply lighter, more objective programme requirements. The way in which the Commission enforced them could be tested in the courts. The ITC would therefore adopt a less heavy handed and discretionary approach than the IBA necessarily does at present. . . .

6.7 The Government proposes that the ITC should be a licensing body rather than a broadcasting authority. This means that it will supervise, but not itself provide, programme services, applying broadly the same light touch regulation across the board.

In reviewing the regulatory structure created by this legislation, in the course of this chapter and the next, one should ask whether the government's aim of introducing a lighter (and less discretionary) regulatory system was achieved. Certainly this has been doubted by some commentators.[28]

(b) Independent Television Commission

The ITC differs from the IBA in a number of significant respects, although there are also similarities with the old system. Pursuant to the BA 1990, s 2(1), the ITC's principal role is the licensing and monitoring of commercial television (see also Extract 3.2.2). Probably the aspect of its functions which has attracted most attention has been the licensing process and, in particular, the licensing of Channel 3 and Channel 5. The licensing process for commercial television services is considered further below. There are two notable features of the current licensing regulatory system. First, the competitive tender process established for allocating some licences. Secondly, the licensing and regulation of services differs according to its availability.

The ITC is responsible for granting licences for a number of television services to be broadcast in the UK. Digital broadcasting services, which were introduced by the BA 1996, will be considered separately (see Section 6 of this chapter). Aside from digital services, the main services licensed by the ITC are:

- Channel 3 and Channel 5 – terrestrial commercial television services;
- Channel 4 – a specialised terrestrial commercial television service which is not owned privately or operated for profit-making;[29]
- satellite television services;
- licensable programme services – programme services licensed for distribution over local delivery services;
- local delivery services – generally cable, but, also, microwave systems, which deliver radio and television programmes;
- additional services – services such as teletext which use spare capacity on the terrestrial transmission signals;
- restricted services – these were introduced by the BA 1996, s 85, and copy a service available to radio broadcasters. A restricted service licence can be obtained to enable a broadcast for a particular location, establishment or event. A licence is of 56 days' duration for a specific event, and for a two-year period otherwise.

---

[28] See, for example, Barendt, p 13, and T Gibbons, 'Broadcasting in the '90s: Spoilt for Choice?' [1989] *Public Law* 213.

[29] There is a similar Welsh service known as S4C which has as one of its main functions to broadcast a substantial amount of programming in Welsh. However, this is not regulated by the ITC but by the Welsh Authority: BA 1990, Chap VI.

(c) Preliminary licensing requirements

All services to be licensed by the ITC[30] have to pass through certain 'pre-vetting' tests. These three tests are set out in ss 3(3) and 5(1) of the BA 1990. The disqualified person test (BA 1990, s 5(1)(a)) prohibits certain categories of persons, whether because of nationality, activity, or affiliation, from holding a licence: for example, religious bodies and advertising agencies. The list of disqualified persons is complex and detailed. Not all disqualified persons are disqualified from holding every type of licence. Section 5(1)(b) is a reference to the ownership restrictions on licences, which will be discussed in Chapter 7.

Extract 3.4.2

Broadcasting Act 1990, ss 3(3) and 5(1)

3.—(3) The Commission—
  (a) shall not grant a licence to any person unless they are satisfied that he is a fit and proper person to hold it; and
  (b) shall do all that they can to secure that, if they cease to be so satisfied in the case of any person holding a licence, that person does not remain the holder of the licence;

  . . .

5.—(1) The Commission shall do all that they can to secure—
  (a) that a person does not become or remain the holder of a licence if he is a person who is a disqualified person in relation to that licence by virtue of Part II of Schedule 2 to this Act; and
  (b) that any requirement imposed by or under Parts III to V of that Schedule are complied with by or in relation to persons holding licences in relation to which those requirements apply.

The fitness and propriety test provides a good example of the retention of broad discretionary powers by the ITC. There is little evidence of how the ITC applies this test. During the Channel 5 licensing process two of the applicants made identical cash bids. The ITC stated that if it had found evidence of collusion between the applicants it would have regarded them as not fit and proper.[31] (For an example of the Radio Authority using this test, see Section 5(c) below.)

---

[30] BA 1990, s 73(3) ensures that local delivery licences (which are granted by the ITC under Pt II of the 1990 Act) are also subject to these pre-vetting tests, which otherwise refer only to licences granted by the ITC under Pt I of the 1990 Act.
[31] ITC, *Annual Report and Accounts 1995*, pp 22–23.

(d) Licensing of Channel 3 and Channel 5

Channel 3 remains the predominant commercial television service available throughout the UK and the regulatory arrangements reflect this. It is subject to the most complex licensing and ongoing monitoring requirements. Programme contracts have been replaced by licences. Licences for Channel 3 are still awarded on a regional basis but with the intention of providing a nationwide service (see BA 1990, s 14), although there is one national service: GMTV Ltd, a breakfast service. Channel 5 which began transmission in 1997 is also intended to be a mainstream terrestrial commercial service and subject to similar licensing requirements, but one licence covers the entire transmission area. Although intended as a national service, it does not have the same geographical coverage as Channel 3 because its signal is weaker.[32]

Although the BA 1990 was intended to introduce a system of competitive tendering for Channel 3 and Channel 5 licences, the award of a licence is not made simply on this basis. As noted above, certain pre-vetting tests are involved. In addition, applicants for a licence will have to make promises of performance. For example, under s 15(3), an applicant will have to give details of its proposals for enhancing the enjoyment and understanding by hearing and sight-impaired people of the programmes included in the service; for location of its offices in the region served by the licence; and for the employment of persons in that same licence area. Section 16(2) (Extract 3.4.3) sets out other programming requirements which must also be satisfied.

One of the important aspects of an applicant's bid for a licence will be the cash bid because this represents the amount the applicant is prepared to pay for the licence. However, there are two further threshold tests which the applicant has to satisfy. These can be referred to as the quality threshold (BA 1990, s 16(1)(a)) and the financial sustainability threshold (BA 1990, s 16(1)(b)). The latter test is a recognition of the financial commitment needed to meet the programming obligations, and to sustain the regular payments required under the licence. In the Channel 3 licensing round 13 out of a total of 27 applicants failed the quality threshold, while three failed the financial test.[33] Section 86 of the BA 1996 gives the ITC new powers when awarding a licence under s 17 (Extract 3.4.4) to make the licence grant conditional on compliance with requirements, laid down by the ITC, concerning the financing of the service. It might be questioned whether this is consistent with the ITC's obligations under the financial sustainability test.

---

[32] The licensing procedures and requirements for Channel 5 are the same as Channel 3, with some modifications such as omission of the requirement to provide regional programming: BA 1990, s 29.
[33] Gibbons, p 164.

Extract 3.4.3

Broadcasting Act 1990, s 16(1)–(3)

16.—(1) Where a person has made an application for a Channel 3 licence in accordance with section 15, the Commission shall not proceed to consider whether to award him the licence on the basis of his cash bid in accordance with section 17 unless it appears to them—

    (a) that his proposed service would comply with the requirements specified in subsection (2) or (3) below (as the case may be), and

    (b) that he would be able to maintain that service throughout the period for which the licence would be in force,

    . . .

(2) Where the service to be provided under the licence is a regional Channel 3 service, the requirements referred to in subsection (1)(a) are—

    (a) that a sufficient amount of time is given in the programmes included in the service to news programmes and current affairs programmes which (in each case) are of high quality and deal with both national and international matters, and that such news programmes are broadcast at intervals throughout the period for which the service is provided and, in particular, at peak viewing times;

    (b) that a sufficient amount of time is given in the programmes included in the service to programmes (other than news and current affairs programmes) which are of high quality;

    (c) that a sufficient amount of time is given in the programmes so included—

        (i) to a suitable range of regional programmes, that is to say, programmes (including news programmes) which are of particular interest to persons living within the area for which the service is provided, and

        (ii) if the service is to include the provision of such programmes as are mentioned in section 14(3) [specialised local programming], to a suitable range of programmes for each of the different parts of that area or (as the case may be) for each of the different communities living within it, being in each case a range of programmes (including news programmes) which are of particular interest to persons living within the relevant part of that area or (as the case may be) the relevant community,

    and that any news programmes to included in accordance with subparagraph (i) or (ii) are of high quality;

    (d) that a suitable proportion of the regional programmes included in the service in accordance with paragraph (c) are made within the area for which it is to be provided;

    (e) that a sufficient amount of time is given in the programmes included in the service to religious programmes and programmes intended for children;

    (f) that (taken as a whole) the programmes so included are calculated to appeal to a wide variety of tastes and interests;

(g) that a proper proportion of the matter included in those programmes is of European origin; and

(h) that in each year not less than 25 per cent of the total amount of time allocated to the broadcasting of qualifying programmes in the service is allocated to the broadcasting of a range and diversity of independent productions.

(3) Where the service to be provided under the licence is a national Channel 3 service, the requirements referred to in subsection (1)(a) are such (if any) of the requirements specified in subsection (2) as the Commission may determine to be appropriate having regard to the nature of that service.

Question for discussion

To what extent does s 16(2) of the BA 1990 retain the elements of public service broadcasting? Compare with Extracts 3.2.1 and 3.4.8.

The cash bid is not a one-off payment for the licence but is a component of a tender payment which must be made by licensees annually (BA 1990, s 19). The tender payment has two parts. The first is a percentage of qualifying revenue (based on advertising and sponsorship income). The second part is the cash bid which is index-linked.[34] Licence fees are also paid to cover the ITC's costs (BA 1990, s 4(1)(b)).[35] These are levied according to the nature of the service and the degree of regulation which it requires.

If an applicant satisfies these threshold tests, its application is able to proceed to the next stage, the cash bid. When the White Paper published the proposals for awarding licences to the highest bidder, the process seemed simple. It was envisaged that this would be an objective, market-driven process.[36] Yet it is clear from the White Paper that the government never intended a completely objective process; the pre-vetting and threshold tests require the exercise of discretionary judgments. Even at the cash bid stage the ITC may be required to exercise its discretion. It is only when the ITC exercises its discretion under s 17(3) that it is required to give reasons (s 17(12)(c)). The cash bid was one of the most controversial aspects of the government's proposals. When the Bill was first published, it included the 'exceptional circumstances' provision, but gave no guidance as to how this should be interpreted. After intense lobbying it was expanded.[37]

---

[34] ITC, *Commercial Television: Revenues and Payments* (No 4, November 1997).

[35] Part of the licence fee is used to fund the Broadcasting Standards Commission: BA 1996, s 127.

[36] *Broadcasting in the '90s: Competition, Choice and Quality*, Cm 517 (1988) para 6.17.

[37] For a discussion of the difficulties presented by the cash bid system, see R Baldwin, 'Broadcasting after the Bill: Gold, Franchises and Murmurings of Discontent' (1990) 11 *Journal of Media Law and Practice* 2.

Extract 3.4.4

Broadcasting Act 1990, s 17(1), (3) and (4)

17.—(1) Subject to the following provisions of this section, the Commission shall, after considering all the cash bids submitted by the applicants for a Channel 3 licence, award the licence to the applicant who submitted the highest bid.

(2) [*Omitted*].

(3) The Commission may disregard the requirement imposed by subsection (1) and award the licence to an applicant who has not submitted the highest bid if it appears to them that there are exceptional circumstances which make it appropriate for them to award the licence to that applicant.

(4) Without prejudice to the generality of subsection (3), the Commission may regard the following circumstances as exceptional circumstances which make it appropriate to award the licence to an applicant who has not submitted the highest bid, namely where it appears to the Commission—

    (a) that the quality of the service proposed by such an applicant is exceptionally high; and

    (b) that the quality of that proposed service is substantially higher than the quality of the service proposed—

        (i) by the applicant who has submitted the highest bid, or

        (ii) in a case falling within subsection (2), by each of the applicants who have submitted equal highest bids;

and where it appears to the Commission, in the context of the licence, that any circumstances are to be regarded as exceptional circumstances for the purposes of subsection (3), those circumstances may be so regarded by them despite the fact that similar circumstances have been so regarded by them in the context of any other licence or licences.

In the next extract the 1991 Channel 3 licensing round is assessed. Prosser's reference to the 'quality threshold' includes reference to the financial threshold.

Extract 3.4.5

T Prosser, *Law and the Regulators* (Oxford University Press, 1997), p 258

The highest bid was by TVS, a franchise holder which had experienced serious business and financing problems, and was for £59,728,000. This was disqualified through use of the quality threshold, but the highest successful bid was for £43,170,000 for the London weekday licence. By contrast, two of the existing franchise holders gambled correctly that their bids would be unopposed, and so put in very low offers of £2,000 per year, one of these being for Central, one of the most important licences. As there was no reserve price set, both of these bids were accepted. These arbitrary valuations of licences led to a report by stockbrokers on the process to describe it as 'possibly the most ludicrous in corporate history'.[i]

Any expectation that the auctioning process as employed here would re-place administrative discretion with the formal rationality of the market proved to be ill-founded; the existence of the quality threshold proved of the utmost importance in the allocation of licences. Once more social aspects of regula-tion have proved to be more important than those which are essentially eco-nomic. Is this due to the peculiar circumstances of television, or of this allocation?

ⁱ 'Bids for TV Franchises Face Harsh Criteria', *Financial Times*, 12 Aug. 1991.

Questions for discussion

1.   How significant a role did the competitive bid play in the overall licens-ing process?
2.   How would you respond to Prosser's concluding question?
3.   Could a competitive bid system have been designed to ensure that bids reflected the value of the licence?

(e) Challenging ITC licensing decisions

In the Channel 3 licensing round, the ITC did not use the 'exceptional circumstances' provision and, therefore, was not required to give reasons. However, the retention of significant discretionary power provides oppor-tunities for discontent among unsuccessful applicants and the potential for judicial challenge. TSW Broadcasting Ltd (TSW), the incumbent programme contractor since 1981, had bid £16,117,000 for the south-west region licence. There had been three applications for the region's licence and the ITC awarded it to an applicant who had bid £7,815,000. One applicant had failed both threshold tests, while the ITC believed that TSW could not sustain the service under s 16(1)(b). TSW challenged this decision.

Extract 3.4.6

R v Independent Television Commission, ex parte TSW Broadcasting [1996] EMLR 291, at 300–301 and 303–305 (HL)

LORD TEMPLEMAN: TSW were understandably outraged when their applica-tion was rejected; they had been the licence holder of the south-west region since 1981 and had made profits. They believed in their projections. They had reason to suspect that they were the highest bidders. The ITC were not expressly bound to give reasons for their decisions and did not do so. I do not blame them for their initial caution but having regard to the unique position of TSW I consider that TSW were entitled to be told the reasons for their rejec-tion. The ITC agreed to provide an oral interview, a dangerous course to take, as my noble and learned friend Lord Keith of Kinkel observed in *R v Secretary of State for Trade & Industry, ex parte Lonrho* [1989] 1 WLR 525, 534, 535 . . . It would have been better if the ITC had given reasons in writing. Simon Brown J rejected TSW's application for leave to issue judicial review proceedings. On appeal, the Court of Appeal pointed out that in the circumstances of the present case it would have been appropriate for reasons in writing to be given. . . . The Court of Appeal by a majority, (Nolan and Steyn LJJ, Lord Donaldson of Lymington MR dissenting) rejected TSW's application for judicial review. TSW now appeal.

. . . In view of the evidence, I do not consider that there is any scope for the courts to interfere with the decision reached by the ITC with regard to TSW. The members of the ITC carefully considered the application of TSW and in particular the crucial forecasts of revenue, costs, profitability and the amount of the bid. Having given the matter their best consideration they found in the light of their general experience and in the light of their particular experience of 40 bids for Channel 3 licences that it did not appear to them that TSW would be able to maintain their proposed service throughout the period through which the licence would be in force. They were therefore bound to reject the application.

. . . In the present case, Parliament has conferred powers and discretions and has imposed duties on the ITC. Parliament has not provided any appeal machinery. Even if the ITC make mistakes of fact or mistakes of law, there is no appeal from their decision. The courts have invented the remedies of judicial review not to provide an appeal machinery but to ensure that the decision maker does not exceed or abuse his powers. For example, if the ITC decided to award a licence to TSW provided the ITC [sic.] reduced their bid from £16m. to £9m., that would be a decision which the courts would quash being a decision that it is not within the power of the ITC to make . . . If one of the members of the ITC were proved to be actuated by bias against TSW or to be financially interested in a rival applicant, then the decision of the ITC would be quashed because the ITC are bound by the rules of natural justice and cannot make a valid decision if the rules are broken. But the rules of natural justice do not render a decision invalid because the decision maker or his advisers makes a mistake of fact or a mistake of law. Only if the reasons given by the ITC for the decision to reject the application of TSW disclosed illegality, irrationality or procedural impropriety, then, in accordance with the speech of Lord Diplock in *Council of Civil Service Unions v the Minister of Civil Service* [1985] AC 374, and the judgment of Lord Greene MR in *Associated Provincial Picturehouses Ltd v Wednesbury Corporation* [1948] 1 KB 223, 228–229, could the decision be open to judicial review. This is not a case in which TSW can rely on any breach of the principle of proportionality or can require a close scrutiny of possible threats to human rights or fundamental freedoms.

Questions for discussion
1. What scope is there for courts to review decisions in the absence of published reasons?
2. Would the outcome have been different if reasons had been given in the *TSW* case?

Although TSW's challenge was unsuccessful, it is clear from this decision that the ITC cannot hide behind the legislation in deciding whether or not to give reasons. It did give reasons for its Channel 5 licensing decision although it was under no obligation to do so. Virgin Television Ltd, which had failed the quality threshold, was given leave to bring judicial review proceedings.[38] This challenge was also unsuccessful and the court indicated its reluctance to interfere in decisions taken by expert bodies, like the ITC.

(f) Duration and renewal of licences

Channel 3 licences commenced on 1 January 1993 and are for a term of 10 years. The procedure for their renewal is set out in BA 1990, s 20. Section 29 of the 1990 Act (not extracted) applies this procedure to Channel 5.

Extract 3.4.7

Broadcasting Act 1990, s 20(2), (4) and (6)–(7)

20.—(1) [Omitted]

(2) An application for the renewal of a Channel 3 licence under subsection (1) may be made by the licence holder not earlier than four years before the date on which it would otherwise cease to be in force and not later than the relevant date.

. . .

(4) Where an application for the renewal of a Channel 3 licence has been duly made to the Commission, they may only . . . refuse the application if—
- (a) they are not satisfied that the applicant would, if his licence were renewed, provide a service which complied—
  - (i) with the conditions included in the licence [. . . to deliver the promised service], and
  - (ii) with the requirements specified in section 16(2) or (3) (as the case may be); or
- (b) they propose to grant a fresh Channel 3 licence for the provision of a service which would differ from that provided by the applicant under his licence as respects either—
  - (i) the area for which it would be provided, or
  - (ii) the times of the day or days of the week between or on which it would be provided,
  or both.

. . .

(6) On the grant of any such application the Commission—
- (a) shall determine an amount which is to be payable to the Commission by the applicant in respect of the first complete calendar year falling within the period for which the licence is to be renewed; and
- (b) may specify a different percentage . . . as the percentage of qualifying revenue for each accounting period of his that will be payable by the applicant in pursuance of section 19(1)(c) during the period for which the licence is to be renewed.

---

[38] *R v Independent Television Commission, ex parte Virgin Television* [1996] EMLR 318 (CA).

(7) The amount determined by the Commission under subsection (6)(a) in connection with the renewal of a licence shall be such amount as would, in their opinion, be payable to them by virtue of [the cash bid] if they were granting a fresh licence to provide the Channel 3 service in question.

Question for discussion

In the light of the experience of the Channel 3 licensing round, can the ITC make any meaningful assessment under s 20(7)?

Under s 20(2) of the BA 1990, the renewal process can begin up to four years before the end of the licence period, and hence for Channel 3 began in 1998. Although the renewed licensees will still have an obligation to make tender payments, the legislation gives the ITC an opportunity to determine tender payments which more accurately reflect the value of the licences. Thus, the ITC proposed that Central, which originally bid £2,000, should pay £10.2 million and that its percentage of qualifying revenue should be increased from 11% to 14%, while Yorkshire's cash sum is to be reduced from £41.53 million to £7.670 million, and its percentage increased from 7% to 22%.[39] In effect, for this round of renewals, the ITC will be able to correct the competitive bid problems, although it is unlikely that this was what was intended when the legislation was drafted.

(g) Channel 4

Channel 4 commenced transmission in 1982. Its development followed a recommendation of the Annan Committee.[40] Although a commercially funded channel, it has a distinctive remit. Originally it operated as a subsidiary of the IBA, but under the BA 1990 it is established as a statutory corporation, licensed by the ITC. Despite the BA 1990's deregulatory theme, Channel 4 was allowed to continue its public service remit.

Extract 3.4.8

Broadcasting Act 1990, s 25(1), (2)(a) and (5)

25.—(1) The licence granted to the [Channel 4 Television] Corporation shall include such conditions as appear to the Commission to be appropriate for securing not only that Channel 4 complies with the requirements specified in subsection (2) but also—

---

[39] Central rejected these terms, which it was free to do. It can apply for renewal once more: ITC, *Annual Report and Accounts 1998* (1999), p 13.

[40] The Annan Committee conducted an inquiry into broadcasting in the 1970s. Part of its remit was to consider the establishment of a fourth channel: *Report of the Committee on the Future of Broadcasting*, Cmnd 6753 (1977) paras 15.3 and 15.18.

    (a) that Channel 4 programmes contain a suitable proportion of matter calculated to appear to tastes and interests not generally catered for by Channel 3, and

    (b) that innovation and experiment in the form and content of those programmes are encouraged,

and generally that Channel 4 is given a distinctive character of its own.

    (2) The requirements referred to in subsection (1) are—

    (a) that Channel 4 is provided as a public service for disseminating information, education and entertainment;

    . . .

    (5) The licence referred to in subsection (1) shall also include conditions requiring the Corporation not to be involved in the making of programmes to be broadcast on Channel 4 except to such extent as the Commission may allow.

One of the interesting features of Channel 4 has been its funding arrangements. When it began transmission it was subsidised by ITV, which had the right to sell advertising for transmission on Channel 4. This had two important consequences. It ensured that Channel 4 had a secure form of funding to enable it to fulfil its particular public service remit. Secondly, it ensured that ITV's commercial position was not threatened by having to compete for advertising revenue, and it could fulfil its own public service remit. The BA 1990 changed this approach in recognition of Channel 4's success in attracting audiences. It empowered it to sell its own advertising, thus making it a direct competitor with Channel 3. At the same time, a safety net was introduced to ensure that Channel 4's income did not fall below a certain minimum level. Because of the way these funding arrangements were set up, its success meant that it was having regularly to pay out large sums to its competitor. The BA 1996 has introduced greater flexibility into this system (see BA 1990, ss 26 and 27 and BA 1996, ss 82 and 83), so that from 1999 Channel 4 is no longer required to pay any surplus to Channel 3.[41] In return for this Channel 4 had to accept increased public service obligations.

Question for discussion

Notwithstanding Channel 4's reliance on advertising for its income, what characteristics of its structure ensure that it is able to meet public service obligations?

(h) Local delivery licences

Local delivery licences which enable a cable network to be provided are also licensed currently through a competitive bid system. As with Channel 3 and Channel 5 licences, local delivery licensees have been required to make

---

[41] For a more detailed explanation, see Gibbons, pp 187–188.

regular tender payments consistent with their monopoly status.[42] The licensing process, while similar to the Channel 3 and Channel 5 process, is much more straightforward. The quality threshold is replaced by a technical one which requires the applicant to provide a technical plan indicating: the area to be covered by the service; the timetable for achieving that coverage; and the technical means to achieve it (BA 1990, s 74(3)). It should be remembered that the preliminary licensing requirements must also be satisfied (see Section 4(c) above). The procedures for renewal of licences, which are granted for 15 years, follow a similar pattern to Channels 3 and 5.

Subscription to cable has been slow to develop and often there has been little competition for licences. In recognition of this, the ITC has frequently set the percentage of qualifying revenue (the first part of the tender payment (see Section 4(d) above for further explanation)), at 0%, at least for the first year. Depending upon demand for the licence for a particular region, there can be considerable variance in the amount bid. Thus the only applicant for one licence bid £11,[43] while, for another licence, the highest bid was £4.5 million.[44] To encourage expansion of cable, licensees have been allowed to provide telephone services, while British Telecom (BT) has been prohibited from supplying cable television. Licences were also allocated on an exclusive basis. In 1998, the government announced a change to this policy which has had a consequential impact on the ITC's licensing policy.[45] From 1998, BT (and other public telecommunication operators) have had the right to offer cable television services in areas not already subject to a local delivery licence. From 1 January 2001, they will be allowed to compete with existing cable operators throughout the UK. Over time these changes are likely to have a major impact on the cable landscape, as they will encourage further investment in the delivery networks and the exploitation of interactive and other communication services.

Extract 3.4.9

ITC, *ITC Announces New Local Delivery Licensing Policy* (News Release 43/98, 28 April 1998)

In response to the Government's announcement . . . , the ITC is revising its policy for future local delivery cable franchising.

---

[42] *Broadcasting in the '90s: Competition, Choice and Quality*, Cm 517 (1988) para 6.34.

[43] ITC, *Award of the Dumfries and Galloway Local Delivery Licence* (News Release 70/98, 27 July 1998).

[44] ITC, *BT Wins Milton Keynes Local Delivery Franchise* (News Release 43/97, 29 May 1997).

[45] Department of Trade and Industry and Department for Culture Media and Sport, *Broadband Britain: A Fresh Look at the Broadcast Entertainment Restrictions* (23 April 1998). The Broadcasting (Restrictions on the Holding of Licences) (Amendment) Order 1999 (SI 1999/122) removes the disqualification of public telecommunication operators from holding a local delivery licence.

Unfranchised Areas: In those parts of the country where there are no existing franchises, local delivery licences will be offered on a non-exclusive basis: so any number of applicants can come forward. As now, areas will be considered for advertisement only where a potential credible applicant has expressed interest. But the ITC will offer as many local delivery licences as there are applicants who can pass the statutory technical and financial tests specified in Section 75 of the Broadcasting Act 1990. For all those local delivery licences, the first part of the tender payment (percentage of qualifying revenue – PQR) will be set at zero.

Existing licences: Existing local delivery operators can opt to apply to the ITC to replace their present, exclusive licences with new licences. These will only be available on a non-exclusive basis, and newcomers will be able to apply for the same franchise area.

Questions for discussion

1.   Why is the ITC setting the percentage of qualifying revenue at zero?

2.   What role remains for a competitive cash bid?[46]

3.   What incentive will existing licensees have to replace their exclusive licences?

(i) Licensable programme services and satellite television services

Licensable programme services and satellite television services are the actual television programme services designed to be carried via cable and satellite. At the end of 1998, 91 licensable programme services and 201 satellite services had been licensed. The regulatory regime for these services is an acknowledgement that here spectrum scarcity is not a constraint. Content will be determined by the market rather than government policy, and so a quite different licensing procedure applies.

Under the BA 1990, it was intended that there would be two types of satellite licence: domestic satellite services and non-domestic satellite services. Domestic satellite services would transmit programmes using frequencies allocated to the UK, sufficient to provide five channels. These were to be allocated by a competitive bid process and to have public service broadcasting obligations. Such services are usually referred to as 'direct broadcasting by satellite' (DBS) because they use high-powered satellites dedicated to broadcasting. Non-domestic satellite services were services which used spare capacity on telecommunications satellites and were to be licensed essentially on demand with few licence obligations. The IBA had licensed British Satellite Broadcasting (BSB) to transmit on the allocated frequencies, and it commenced transmission in 1990. In the meantime, other satellite services were operating, most notably, Sky Television, using telecommunications satellites such as the Astra satellite. In November 1990 BSB and Sky merged,

---

[46] Applicants for the new non-exclusive licences have been making a nominal bid of £1: ITC, *Annual Report and Accounts 1998* (1999), p 24.

and announced that they would not broadcast using the allocated frequencies. Although the merger constituted a breach of BSB's programme contract, the IBA felt limited in what action it could take, believing that it was more important to secure continuity of service for those viewers who had purchased satellite dishes to receive BSB. It agreed to continue the programme contract for two years on condition that the merged service would continue to transmit on the allocated frequencies as well as via Astra.[47] Since this merger, no domestic satellite services have been licensed. One reason for this has been that the telecommunications satellites have improved in quality and capacity, and are now able to provide a comparable service to the more expensive DBS. As a result of a European Court of Justice judgment (see Chapter 5, Section 5(b) and Extract 5.5.2), the distinction between domestic and non-domestic satellite services was ruled invalid. In 1997, the government abolished the classification of domestic and non-domestic satellite services, replacing it with one category: satellite television services.[48]

<hr>

Extract 3.4.10

Broadcasting Act 1990, ss 43(1) and 45(1), (2) and (4)

43.—(1) In this Part 'satellite television service' means a service which—
  (a) consists in the transmission for general reception of television programmes by satellite; and
  (b) is provided by a person who for the purposes of Council Directive 89/552/EEC is under the jurisdiction of the United Kingdom [see Chapter 5].

45.—(1) An application for a licence to provide a satellite television service shall—
  (a) be made in such manner as the Commission may determine; and
  (b) be accompanied by such fee (if any) as they may determine.

(2) Where such an application is duly made to the Commission, they may only refuse to grant the licence applied for if it appears to them that the service which would be provided under the licence would not comply with the requirements of section 6(1) [the consumer protection standards].

(3) [*Omitted*].

(4) Any licence granted by the Commission to provide a satellite television service shall . . . continue in force for a period of ten years.

These licences are freely available subject only to the ITC being satisfied that the applicant will comply with certain programme requirements, known as the consumer protection standards (see Chapter 4 below). Licensable programme services follow a similar pattern to satellite television services (BA 1990, s 47).

<hr>

[47] IBA, *Final Report and Accounts, April–December 1990* (1991), pp 7–8.
[48] Satellite Television Service Regulations 1997 (SI 1997/1682). Further amendments were made in 1998: Television Broadcasting Regulations 1998 (SI 1998/3196).

The BA 1990 also refers to another type of satellite service, a 'foreign satellite service'. This service is not licensed by the ITC but it is one over which the government seeks to exercise control in certain circumstances. This will be discussed further in Chapter 5, Section 5(b).

5. REGULATION OF COMMERCIAL RADIO

(a) Introduction

Commercial radio is now licensed and regulated by the Radio Authority (RA) which was established by the BA 1990. It is an area of broadcasting which has expanded considerably, since the introduction of local commercial radio in 1972, although it has attracted less controversy and public concern than television. While, generally, the licensing and regulation of commercial radio follows a similar pattern to commercial television, the BA 1990 introduced significant differences. In 1987, the government published a Green Paper reviewing the future development of commercial radio broadcasting. Its conclusions have been largely incorporated into the BA 1990. Note the arguments used to justify a move away from public service obligations for commercial broadcasting.

Extract 3.5.1

Green Paper, *Radio: Choices and Opportunities*, Cm 92 (1987), paras 2.4 and 2.7

2.4 Underlying this wish for moves towards de-regulation is a genuine concern about the *financial basis* of the industry. Although successful in attracting audiences in competition with the BBC, ILR [Independent Local Radio] has not attracted advertising revenue to a corresponding degree....

2.7 The financial pressure on ILR has been reflected in programmes. The drama and education output has been limited. The need for economies in stations has had implications for the coverage of local news. None of this detracts from the real programme achievements of ILR in several fields, and different stations have different styles. But is it still sensible to expect each small independent local radio station to provide a microcosm of the public service broadcasting output of four BBC national networks?

(b) The Radio Authority

The BA 1990 established the RA as the regulatory body for all commercial radio services. Although there has been a move away from individual radio licensees having to provide public service broadcasting, as for the ITC, a remnant of the concept can be also discerned in the duties imposed upon the RA.

Extract 3.5.2

Broadcasting Act 1990, s 85(1)–(3)

85.—(1) Subject to subsection (2), the Authority may . . . grant such licences to provide independent radio services as they may determine.

(2) The Authority shall do all that they can to secure the provision within the United Kingdom of—

    (a) a diversity of national services each catering for tastes and interests different from those catered for by the others and of which—

        (i) one is a service the greater part of which consists in the broadcasting of spoken material, and

        (ii) another is a service which consists, wholly or mainly, in the broadcasting of music which, in the opinion of the Authority, is not pop music[49]; and

    (b) a range and diversity of local services.

(3) It shall be the duty of the Authority to discharge their functions as respects the licensing of . . . radio services in the manner which they consider is best calculated—

    (a) to facilitate the provision of licensed services (including digital sound programme services . . .) which (taken as a whole) are of high quality and offer a wide range of programmes calculated to appeal to a variety of tastes and interests; and

    (b) to ensure fair and effective competition in the provision of such services and services connected with them.

(c) Preliminary licensing requirements

As with commercial television, each applicant for a licence must pass certain 'pre-vetting' tests (see Section 4(c) above). The RA has had to act under the fitness and propriety provisions. In 1997, the majority shareholder in companies holding four local radio licences was convicted of rape and indecent assault. The RA determined that he was not a fit and proper person, and his shares were transferred to independent trusts.[50]

Question for discussion

What else should make it improper, or render a person unfit, to hold a licence?

(d) Licensing

Like television, radio uses a range of licensing mechanisms depending upon the type of service and its scarcity.

---

[49] 'Pop music' is defined in BA 1990, s 85(6).

[50] Radio Authority, *Radio Authority Agrees Transfer of Control of Licences Held by Owen Oyston* (News Release 28/98, 9 April 1998).

(i) National

There are currently three national services, offering programmes consistent with the requirement imposed upon the RA to provide services of different specified types: see BA 1990, s 85(2)(a) (Extract 3.5.2): *Classic FM* – a service providing light classical music; *Talk Radio* – a talk service; and *Virgin Radio* – a service providing rock and pop music. The availability of spectrum for national radio services is still relatively limited. However, digital broadcasting offers the prospect of more services at national level (see Section 6 below). The process for awarding a national radio licence shares similarities with the Channel 3 process. It requires a competitive bid, subject to an exceptional circumstances provision, and applicants have to pass threshold tests. However, there are also significant differences which are apparent if the provisions of the Broadcasting Act 1990 set out in Extract 3.5.3 are compared with those in Extracts 3.4.3 and 3.4.4.

Extract 3.5.3

Broadcasting Act 1990, ss 98(1)(b), (3)(a) and 100(3)

98.—(1) Where the Authority propose to grant a licence to provide a national service, they shall publish, in such manner as they consider appropriate, a notice—

. . .

(b) specifying—

(i) the period for which the licence is to be granted,

(ii) the minimum area of the United Kingdom for which the service is to be provided,

(iii) if the service is to be one falling within section 85(2)(a)(i) or (ii) [see Extract 3.5.2], that the service is to be such a service, and

(iv) if there is any existing licensed national service, that the service is to be one which caters for tastes and interests different from those already catered for by any such service (as described in the notice); . . .

(3) Any application made in pursuance of a notice under this section must be in writing and accompanied by—

(a) the applicant's proposals for providing a service that would both—

(i) comply with any requirement specified in the notice under subsection (1)(b)(iii) or (iv), and

(ii) consist of a diversity of programmes calculated to appeal to a variety of tastes and interests; . . .

100.—(3) The Authority may disregard the requirement imposed by subsection (1) [to award to highest bid] and award the licence to an applicant who has not submitted the highest bid if it appears to them that there are exceptional circumstances which make it appropriate for them to award the licence to that applicant; and where it appears to the Authority, in the context of the licence, that any circumstances are to be regarded as exceptional circumstances for the purposes of this subsection, those circumstances may be so regarded by them despite the fact that similar circumstances have been so regarded by them in the context of any other licence or licences.

(ii) Local

Here again there is a formal and detailed procedure for applicants,[51] but there are also marked differences in the licensing procedure compared with national radio.

Extract 3.5.4

Broadcasting Act 1990, s 105

105.—Where the Authority have published a notice under section 104(1) [proposing to grant a licence], they shall, in determining whether, or to whom, to grant the local licence in question, have regard to the following matters, namely—

(a) the ability of each of the applicants for the licence to maintain, throughout the period for which the licence would be in force, the service which he proposes to provide;

(b) the extent to which any such proposed service would cater for the tastes and interests of persons living in the area or locality for which the service would be provided, and, where it is proposed to cater for any particular tastes and interests of such persons, the extent to which the service would cater for those tastes and interests;

(c) the extent to which any such proposed service would broaden the range of programmes available by way of local services to persons living in the area or locality for which it would be provided, and, in particular, the extent to which the service would cater for tastes and interests different from those already catered for by local services provided for that area or locality; and

(d) the extent to which any application for the licence is supported by persons living in that area or locality.

Question for discussion

What factors might have contributed to the government's decision not to use a competitive bidding process for the award of local licences?

The broad discretion given to the RA for awarding local licences has been the subject of one unsuccessful challenge.[52] This was the first time that an

---

[51] The Radio Authority currently operates a policy whereby local licences are characterised as 'regional licences', which allow for specialised formats over a larger area to assist viability, and small-scale licences which are usually aimed at a distinct locality and cover an area smaller than the traditional local licence: Radio Authority, *Annual Report and Financial Statements for the Year ended 31 December 1997* (1998), p 5.

[52] *Re Trax FM Ltd*, 21 March 1996, LEXIS (CA).

applicant for a commercial radio licence had sought judicial review of a licensing decision.[53] Here again, the court showed its reluctance to intervene where broad discretionary powers have been given to a regulatory body. Since 1998, the RA has publishing reasons for its licensing decisions although under no obligation. However, because it provides only an appraisal of successful applicants, these reasons may be of limited value to unsuccessful applicants, and, as we have seen with television, providing reasons may not make the courts any readier to intervene.

(iii) Other services

There are several other kinds of services licensed by the RA which are comparable to those licensed by the ITC: licensable sound programme services, satellite services, restricted services and additional services. With the exception of additional services,[54] each of these services is essentially licensed on demand.[55]

(iv) Duration of licences

Compared with the ITC, the RA has greater freedom over the terms for which licences can be granted.[56]

Extract 3.5.5

Broadcasting Act 1990, s 86(1) and (3)

86.—(1) A licence shall be in writing and . . . shall continue in force for such period as may be specified in the licence.

(2) [*Omitted*].

(3) The following licences, namely—

(a) any licence to provide a national, local or satellite service,

(b) any licence to provide a licensable sound programme service, and

(c) any licence to provide additional services,

shall not continue in force for a period of more than eight years.

The national, local and additional licences have been granted for eight-year periods, while the other services referred to in s 86(3) are usually issued for five-year periods. Licence periods for restricted services can vary from 28 days to five years depending upon the type of service which has been licensed.

---

[53] Radio Authority, *Annual Report and Financial Statements for the Year ended 31 December 1995* (1996), p 7.

[54] Additional services are similar to television additional services and like the television services are licensed through a cash bid system. See BA 1990, ss 114–120.

[55] Licensing of satellite and restricted services is covered by BA 1990, s 104(6)(b).

[56] The BA 1996 introduced procedures for renewal of national and local licences: BA 1990, ss 103A and 104A as inserted by BA 1996, ss 92 and 94.

6. DIGITAL BROADCASTING

(a) Introduction

One of the main purposes of the BA 1996 was the creation of a regulatory framework to enable the introduction of digital terrestrial television and radio services. The introduction of digital television is likely to be the most significant broadcasting development for some time. To date, transmission of broadcasting services, whether terrestrial, satellite or cable, has used an analogue system, but it is anticipated that eventually digital transmission will replace analogue transmission. Not only does digital technology increase the number of channels available, but it can also provide interactive services, and facilitate the convergence of telephony, computer and broadcasting systems. Such developments have important implications for the regulation of broadcasting, an issue which will be addressed more fully in Chapter 8. The following text provides an overview of the digital broadcasting regulatory framework.

In August 1995, the government published a Policy Paper, *Digital Terrestrial Broadcasting: The Government's Proposals.*[57] Although digital technology affects terrestrial, cable and satellite broadcasting services, only digital terrestrial services required new legislation. This was because the BA 1990 made no provision for licensing new terrestrial services.

Extract 3.6.1

Department of National Heritage, *Digital Terrestrial Broadcasting: The Government's Proposals*, Cm 2946 (1995), paras 1.9–1.13

PRINCIPLES UNDERPINNING THE LEGISLATION

1.9   Terrestrial broadcasting is different from cable and satellite in two important ways.

1.10   First, it is an immensely powerful medium in that it provides a route into almost every home in the country. Although digital technology will allow considerably more channels, their number will still be very limited. The regulatory framework needs to reflect this, and ensure a variety of services while safeguarding standards of good taste and decency.

1.11   Second, the amount of spectrum available for terrestrial broadcasting is limited and valuable. The Government must ensure that there is an effective and efficient mechanism for allocating that spectrum. And in the long term the Government wishes to do all it can to release spectrum by switching off existing analogue transmission signals, should digital broadcasting be successful enough to allow it.

1.12   The Government attaches great importance to 'public service' broadcasting – in its broadest sense the services provided by the BBC (television

---

[57] Cm 2946 (1995).

and radio), ITV, Channel 4, S4C and, in the future, Channel 5 – which is a vital part of life in this country. It educates and entertains; it provides extensive and impartial news coverage and stimulates public debate; and it seeks to cater for the interests of the few as well as of the many. These channels are the envy of the world, and the Government wants them to have the opportunity to benefit from the new digital technology.

1.13 It is in the public interest that a fair and effective competitive market should develop at each stage in the chain from producer to consumer. No public interest would be served by erecting unnecessary regulatory barriers to entry into the market. But public service broadcasters have to comply with exacting standards which other broadcasters do not. Their costs are therefore much higher, and the regulatory regime has to allow for that.

Questions for discussion

1. What influence will the traditional justifications for regulation have on the regulation of digital broadcasting?

2. When reading Section 6(b) below, consider how the concerns expressed in paragraph 1.13 of the Policy Paper (Extract 3.6.1 above), have influenced the regulatory arrangements for digital television.

(b) Digital television

There is quite a contrast in the number of channels that each of the digital services can offer. Satellite television can provide about 200 channels, while digital terrestrial television only about 18–20, although there is scope for more. Cable, expected to commence late 1999, will also offer a large number of services. Digital cable services will be particularly useful for interactive services and will offer access to the Internet.[58] Until digital television sets become widely available, viewers will only be able to access digital television through a 'set-top' box or decoder (see Chapter 9, Section 2). The structure and regulation of digital terrestrial television has some curious features distinguishing it from the current licensing of television. There are three main components to digital terrestrial services. First, the programme services are carried on multiplexes. The second element is the programme services, which are carried by the multiplexes and are licensed separately. Finally, the multiplexes may carry additional services, such as Teletext, or interactive services, such as home shopping and banking.

(i) Multiplexes

The most complex aspect of the licensing regime is that applying to the provision of the multiplexes.[59] Part of this complexity arises because of the need to secure space on the multiplexes to enable existing analogue terrestrial

---

[58] Digital Television Group, *Switching to Digital*, 1 August 1998.
[59] Licences are for a term of 12 years: BA 1996, s 16(1).

broadcasters to transmit their free-to-air television services on digital. Of the six multiplexes, five are licensed by the ITC although the licensing regime varies as will be seen in this section. The policy behind reserving space for the terrestrial broadcasters was explained in the Policy Paper.

Extract 3.6.2

Department of National Heritage, *Digital Terrestrial Broadcasting: The Government's Proposals*, Cm 2946 (1995), paras 2.36–2.40

PRINCIPLES

2.36 The Government believes in the merits of public service broadcasting and wishes to safeguard it into the digital age. The Government therefore believes that it is essential to give public service broadcasters the opportunity of a place in the new technology. This will also enable them to offer an improved service, for example through widescreen television, and will be in the interests of digital terrestrial television as a whole, since the involvement of the existing broadcasters is likely to encourage consumers to move to digital.

2.37 The Government hopes that, in the long term, it will be possible to switch off the analogue signals in order to release part of the spectrum for other uses including, possibly, further digital broadcast services. That can only happen if the public service broadcasting, including regional variations, currently provided on analogue is equally widely available to viewers on digital television.

2.38 Public service broadcasters operate under stringent quality requirements, and their costs reflect that. The Government therefore wishes the ITC to make some digital slots available to such broadcasters on different terms from those which apply to broadcasters not operating under the same quality restrictions.

. . .

2.39 . . . In recognition of the rationale for the guaranteed places (that is, to maintain public service broadcasting and ultimately to allow analogue signals to be switched off), the great majority of programmes on the analogue channel should also be shown on the guaranteed digital channel. The Government therefore proposes that at least 80 per cent of the programme hours provided on the analogue channel should be shown on the guaranteed digital channel, the majority of these being 'simulcast', that is, shown at the same time. In areas of the UK where existing broadcasters provide a distinct national or regional service, and unless there are overriding technical obstacles, at least 80 per cent of these programme hours should also be shown on the digital channel.

2.40 The digital services of independent public service broadcasters on their guaranteed place will be bound by the specific conditions of their existing analogue licences. If such a broadcaster loses or gives up its analogue licence, its digital licence will be revoked. . . . The services offered by the BBC will be bound by its Charter and Agreement.

Section 28 of the BA 1996 and the Independent Analogue Broadcasters (Reservation of Digital Capacity) Order 1996 (SI 1996/2760) give statutory expression to this policy with regard to private broadcasters, the Secretary of State having directly allocated one multiplex to the BBC.[60] Curiously, although a multiplex is reserved for Channel 3 and Channel 4, and the Order stipulates that only a company controlled by them can apply, a formal licence application procedure must still be undertaken. The multiplex, known as the Channel 3/4 Multiplex, was awarded to Digital 3 and 4 Ltd. This multiplex which simulcasts Channel 3 and Channel 4 (as well as Teletext) also has space for the licensee to offer additional programme services. The other multiplex with reserved space, now known as Multiplex A, was granted to SDN Ltd (the only applicant). This licensee must carry Channel 5, S4C and some Gaelic programming.

The remaining multiplexes (Multiplexes B, C and D) have no obligations to carry any current analogue services. The licensing process, although competitive, differs markedly from the Channel 3 process (Extract 3.6.3). The move away from a competitive bid back to a discretionary allocation may be an acknowledgement that the former process was not a success, although it may also be a recognition of the uncertain commercial future for digital television, particularly terrestrial services.

Extract 3.6.3

Broadcasting Act 1996, s 8(1)–(2)

8.—(1) [... the Commission] shall in determining whether, or to whom, to award the multiplex licence in question, have regard to the extent to which, taking into account the matters specified in subsection (2) and any representations made to them [... from the public] with respect to those matters, the award of the licence to each applicant would be calculated to promote the development of digital television broadcasting in the United Kingdom otherwise than by satellite.

(2) The matters referred to in subsection (1) are—
- (a) the extent of the coverage area proposed to be achieved by the applicant as indicated in the technical plan submitted by him . . . ,
- (b) the timetables proposed by the applicant [... for coverage and commencement],
- (c) the ability of the applicant to establish the proposed service and to maintain it throughout the period for which the licence will be in force,
- (d) the capacity of the digital programme services proposed to be included in the service to appeal to a variety of tastes and interests,

---

[60] Under BA 1996, s 6 the Secretary of State assigns frequencies to the ITC for the provision of multiplex services.

(e) any proposals by the applicant for promoting or assisting the acquisition, by persons in the proposed coverage area of the service, of equipment capable of receiving all the multiplex services available in that area, and

(f) whether, in contracting or offering to contract with persons providing digital programme services or digital additional services, the applicant has acted in a manner calculated to ensure fair and effective competition in the provision of such services.

Two applications for the remaining multiplexes were received. The first applicant was British Digital Broadcasting plc (BDB) which was controlled by Carlton Communications plc, the Granada Group plc and BSkyB plc. The second applicant was Digital Television Network Ltd (DTN), a company owned by a cable operator. Both put in applications for all three licences, offering a range of specialist channels, pay-per-view services and, in the case of DTN, interactive and data services. The licences for the Multiplexes B, C and D were awarded to BDB, which now calls its service ONdigital. However, one issue was the presence of BSkyB.

Extract 3.6.4

ITC, *ITC Announces Its Decision To Award Multiplex Service Licences for Digital Terrestrial Television* (News Release 49/97, 24 June 1997)

AWARD OF MULTIPLEX LICENCES B, C AND D

. . .

The ITC has decided to award each of the licences for Multiplexes B, C and D to BDB, subject to the condition that, before the date of grant of the licences, the shareholding changes described below and already agreed by the shareholders should take place.

In reaching this decision, the ITC has had regard to the extent to which the award of each licence would be calculated to promote the development of digital television broadcasting in the United Kingdom otherwise than by satellite. The ITC has taken into account the matters specified in the Broadcasting Act including the representations made to the ITC in response to its public consultation in relation to the applications received.

The ITC has also taken into account its general duties under the Broadcasting Acts 1990 and 1996 concerning the exercise of its licensing functions, including its competition duties, and has had regard to relevant EC law.

In relation to the matters relevant to its decision specified in the Broadcasting Act 1996, the ITC's conclusions were briefly as follows:

Coverage and programme service timetables (section 8(2)(a) and (b))

. . . The ITC did not consider that the differences between the applicants' proposals were significant.

Ability to establish and maintain the service (section 8(2)(c))

The ITC considered that BDB's application offered a greater degree of assurance than that of DTN that the proposed services could be established and maintained throughout the period of the licences. The ITC considered that the revenue assumptions in BDB's business plan were more cautious than those of DTN, having regard to the nature of the programme services and additional services which each applicant proposed. Funding for BDB is to be provided from the internal resources of the shareholders, both of whom are substantial FTSE 100 companies. In the case of DTN, the business plan was dependant upon its parent company raising further debt.

. . .

The ITC's conclusion was that, on the basis of each applicant's business plan and funding proposals and the further information supplied by each applicant, there would be a higher degree of confidence in the ability of BDB to establish and maintain its services throughout the licence period.

Capacity of programme services to appeal to a variety of tastes and interests (section 8(2)(d))

Each applicant put forward acceptable proposals for appealing to a variety of tastes and interests but of a different character. BDB put forward proposals for programme services generally intended to appeal to broad audiences. On balance the ITC was more attracted by the innovative programme proposals (supported by additional services) designed to appeal principally to a wide range of different audiences which were put forward by DTN.

Promoting the acquisition of receiving equipment by viewers (section 8(2)(e))

Each applicant proposed substantial expenditure on the promotion of DTT, both in respect of the subsidy of domestic receiving equipment and in advertising and marketing costs. Although DTN proposed a higher level of expenditure on receiving equipment than BDB, this expenditure was dependant on a more optimistic estimate of subscriber numbers.

Contracting with service providers (section 8(2)(f))

The ITC did not consider that either application gave rise to concerns within the limited scope of this statutory provision.

Other matters taken into account by the ITC included the following:

Competition concerns

As a result of its consideration of the applications, including consideration of representations made in the course of public consultation, the ITC had concerns with respect to its competition duties about BDB's applications, but no such concerns about DTN's applications. The ITC had fundamental concerns stemming from the role of BSkyB as both a shareholder in BDB, thereby having an influence over BDB's choice of programmes, and a supplier of programmes to BDB, having regard to BSkyB's strength in the UK pay-television market, particularly in relation to premium film and sports channels. These concerns were supported by a number of responses to the ITC's public consultation. The ITC has no objection on competition grounds to the inclusion of programme services, such as those of BSkyB, whose ability to attract viewers and revenue is already well established.

The ITC consulted the Office of Fair Trading and the European Commission on these matters and took the preliminary views of those bodies into account. The ITC then put to BDB its concerns about competition. The ITC indicated to BDB that these concerns could be addressed by BSkyB ceasing to be a shareholder in BDB. The ITC made clear however that it would not be acceptable for BSkyB's programme services to be removed in connection with BSkyB's withdrawal as a shareholder since those services were part of the core proposals in BDB's application.

BDB informed the ITC that its shareholders had reached a legally binding agreement that BSkyB will withdraw as a shareholder in BDB and will continue to supply its programming as envisaged in BDB's application. Carlton and Granada have each agreed to acquire half of BSkyB's shareholding in BDB and to assume BSkyB's funding commitments. The ITC considered that it would be consistent with its competition duties and would not be in breach of European Community law to award these licences to BDB, subject to these changes in BDB's shareholding structure and the award of the licences is therefore conditional upon the changes taking place before the licences are granted. BDB's licences will contain a condition restricting Granada from acquiring control of BDB in the light of Granada's significant shareholding in BSkyB.

Receiver technology

Set-top box receivers are expected to be subsidised and to contain proprietary conditional access technology. However, for the new generation of TV sets which will have built in digital reception, the ITC supports open technical standards. The ITC will include in BDB's licence a requirement to do all they reasonably can to facilitate the introduction of such open standard TV sets, in cooperation with their chosen conditional access technology provider and with receiver manufacturers.

The possibility of split awards

Each applicant presented strong arguments in favour of the award of all three licences to a single party. However, in accordance with the Invitation to Apply, each applicant had submitted a separate application for each of Multiplex licences B, C and D, together with supplementary proposals in the event that the applicants were awarded more than one licence. The ITC considered these separate applications and supplementary proposals carefully, with a view to determining whether it would be desirable to award one or two licences to one applicant and the remaining licence or licences to the other applicant. The ITC considered that a split award would be likely to lead to a less focused and coherent promotional strategy to consumers and increase the risk of confusion in the development of receiving equipment, impacting adversely on the development and success of the whole digital platform. The ITC was clearly of the view that the development of digital terrestrial television in the United Kingdom would be better served by the award of all three licences to the same applicant.

CONCLUSION

The ITC has to consider the extent to which the award of each licence to each applicant would be calculated to promote the development of digital terrestrial television in the UK.

Digital terrestrial television is a new and high risk development, and one which is of key strategic importance to the future development of broadcasting in the United Kingdom. The ITC has therefore been mindful of the need for there to be a high degree of confidence that the successful applicant would have the resources necessary to ensure that despite the uncertainties and possible setbacks that attend a development of this kind, the new digital terrestrial platform can be successfully established.

The ITC has had to reach a view on whether the award of the licences for Multiplexes B, C and D to BDB or to DTN would be best calculated to promote the development of digital television broadcasting in the United Kingdom otherwise than by satellite. The ITC's conclusion is that the award of these licences to BDB would be best calculated to promote this objective.

Questions for discussion

1. What factors primarily influenced the ITC in its decision to award the licences to BDB?
2. The ITC considered that DTN was offering a more innovative set of programme proposals. Should more weight have been given to this assessment?
3. The ITC discusses its competition concerns about BDB. Should the ITC have been concerned also about BSkyB's provision of programme services?
4. Is the quality of the programmes being offered a relevant consideration in determining the award of a licence?

(ii) Digital programme services

The licensing of digital programme services, the 'content' of the multiplexes, is a straightforward process resembling that of satellite television services. Digital programme services will be those services broadcast only in digital form and terrestrially. There is no need for the cable and satellite services,[61] or existing analogue services (which are to be broadcast on digital also), to be licensed under these provisions. Under BA 1996, s 18 licences to provide a

---

[61] These will continue to be licensed under the BA 1990.

111

digital programme service are essentially available on demand, and for an indefinite period. A programme service provider will also have to find a place on a multiplex for that service to be broadcast. There is no technical reason why multiplex licensees could not provide programming themselves, however so far as Multiplexes B, C and D are concerned it is envisaged that a separation of programming and distribution will enable the development of a greater variety of programming.

Extract 3.6.5

Broadcasting Act 1996, s 19(1), (3)

19.—(1) Subject to the provisions of this Part [of the Act] and to section 42 of the 1990 Act as applied by section 23(8), a digital programme licence shall continue in force until it is surrendered by its holder.

(2) [*Omitted*].

(3) A digital programme licence shall also include such conditions as appear to the Commission to be appropriate for requiring the holder of the licence—

    (a) on entering into any agreement with the holder of a multiplex licence for the provision of a digital programme service to be broadcast by means of a multiplex service, to notify the Commission—

        (i) of the identity of the multiplex service,

        (ii) of the characteristics of the digital programme service to which the agreement relates,

        (iii) of the period during which it will be provided, and

        (iv) where under the agreement the holder of the digital programme licence will be entitled to the use of a specified amount of digital capacity, of that amount,

    (b) when any such agreement is varied so far as it relates to any of the matters mentioned in paragraph (a)(i), (ii), (iii) or (iv), to notify the Commission of the variation so far as relating to those matters, and

    (c) where he is providing a digital programme service to the holder of a multiplex licence in accordance with such an agreement as is mentioned in paragraph (a) but intends to cease doing so, to notify the Commission of that fact.

Question for discussion

Digital television separately licences distribution and content. Is there a precedent for this within the existing broadcasting structure?

(c) Digital terrestrial radio

As with digital television, digital radio offers improved quality of reception. It is also possible for digital radio to carry data on a screen. This could relate to programme information or advertising, or to entirely separate information.[62] However, there is less room for expansion owing to limited frequency space. The approach to the allocation of multiplexes and licensing of multiplexes and programme services is similar to digital television. There are to be seven multiplexes. Two will be national. One of these is allocated to the BBC. The other national multiplex will carry the three national commercial radio services, already being broadcast by analogue, as well as new digital programme services. In October 1998, the Radio Authority announced the award of the national commercial multiplex to Digital One Ltd, the only applicant for the licence. Unlike digital television, the analogue services (here called 'simulcast' services) do not have to be broadcast in their entirety (BA 1996, s 41(3)). This is in recognition of the more limited capacity available on the multiplex for the development of other services.

The remaining five multiplexes are to be used for local services and the RA is required to take into account local needs in determining licence awards (BA 1996, s 51(1)(d) and (e)). Although, there is provision for reservation of space on local multiplexes for BBC local radio, the arrangements are less clear-cut than we have seen so far in relation to television's guaranteed places. Under BA 1996, s 49(1) it is for the RA to decide how much space should be reserved for the BBC.

Digital sound programme services also follow a simple licensing process and are classified as either local or national (BA 1996, s 60). National and local multiplex licences are granted for a period of 12 years (with a renewal of 12 years) (BA 1996, s 58(1)), sound programme services for an indefinite period (BA 1996, s 61(1)).

(d) Relationship between analogue and digital broadcasting

It will be clear from the discussion of digital broadcasting that, for the present, terrestrial television and radio, will be available on both digital and analogue transmission. An important question for the future of digital broadcasting, and particularly television, is the date for a complete switch to digital broadcasting. This was addressed in the Policy Paper.

Extract 3.6.6

Department of National Heritage, *Digital Terrestrial Broadcasting: The Government's Proposals*, Cm 2946 (1995), para 2.37

The Government hopes that, in the long term, it will be possible to switch off the analogue signals in order to release part of the spectrum for other uses including, possibly, further digital broadcast services. That can only happen if

---

[62] Radio Authority, *Fact Sheet No 4: Digital Radio* (March 1998).

the public service broadcasting, including regional variations, currently provided on analogue is equally available to viewers on digital television.

The legislation has provided a procedure for determining this 'switch off'. Section 67 of the BA 1996 covers radio in the same terms.

Extract 3.6.7

Broadcasting Act 1996, s 33(1), (4)

33.—(1) For the purpose of considering for how long it would be appropriate for television broadcasting services to continue to be provided in analogue form, the Secretary of State—

    (a) shall keep under review the extent of—

        (i) the provision in the United Kingdom of multiplex services,

        (ii) the availability in the United Kingdom in digital form of the services specified in section 2(3), S4C Digital, the qualifying teletext service, and the television broadcasting services of the BBC, and

        (iii) the ownership or possession in the United Kingdom of equipment capable of receiving the services referred to in sub-paragraph (ii) when broadcast or transmitted in digital form,

    and the likely future extent of such provision, such availability and such ownership or possession, and

    (b) shall, on or before the fourth anniversary of the day on which the first multiplex licence is granted under section 8, and at such time or times thereafter as he thinks fit, require the Commission and the BBC to report to him on the matters referred to in paragraph (a).

    (2), (3) [*Omitted*].

    (4) For the purpose mentioned in subsection (1), the Secretary of State shall, on requiring reports under subsection (1)(b), consult—

    (a) such persons appearing to him to represent viewers as he thinks fit, and

    (b) such other persons as he thinks fit,

in connection with the matters referred to in subsection (1)(a) and also, if the Secretary of State thinks fit, as to the likely effects on viewers of any television broadcasting service ceasing to be broadcast in analogue form.

Viewers will require initially a 'set-top' box to access digital services, until integrated digital television sets become generally available, while radio listeners will have to purchase a digital radio set. There is an obvious tension here for the development of digital broadcasting. While the main services continue to be available in analogue form, viewers and listeners may have little incentive to purchase new digital equipment, unless they are attracted by better picture/sound quality or more services. This, in turn, may slow down demand for the new services, and delay the development of new equipment and the reduction of costs.

In February 1998, the government published a consultation document, *Television: The Digital Future* along with a study undertaken by National Economic Research Associates (NERA). The study was intended to act as a preliminary exercise to the s 33 review. NERA concluded that a shut down of analogue seemed feasible within 10 to 15 years and that an early announcement of a date for shut down could bring significant benefits.[63] However, in responding to the consultation document, the ITC was less optimistic about this time frame. It was also concerned about NERA's analysis of the benefits which could flow.

Extract 3.6.8

ITC, *Television: The Digital Future; The Independent Television Commission's View* (9 September 1998), para 15

The importance of any decision made about the timing of the switch-off of analogue terrestrial television broadcasting cannot be underestimated. That there would be some benefits from a relatively early switch-off we do not doubt, though these may be less than NERA suggest and will primarily flow to the Government,[64] equipment manufacturers and operators of new services. It is far harder to see much that would be of benefit to viewers who, in aggregate, have made an enormous investment in long-lived assets using current analogue technology.

Question for discussion
Apart from the financial burdens which might be placed upon the public, what other concerns might arise if analogue is switched off too early?

Although the formal review provided under the legislation will still have to take place, it is clear that the timing of the switch-off, and the timing of that decision, will not be without difficulty. Much will depend upon the success of the digital services which have recently been licensed by the ITC and the RA. If the Davies Report's recommendation of a digital licence supplement[65] is accepted, this, too, may have an impact on the timing of the switch-off.

---

[63] Radiocommunications Agency and Department for Culture, Media and Sport, *Television: The Digital Future, A Consultation Document* (http://www.open.gov.uk/radiocom/digittv/dtvcons.htm, February 1998), para 4.

[64] The analogue spectrum is a valuable resource which could be sold for other uses, such as mobile telephony.

[65] See Section 3(c) above.

4

PROGRAMME REGULATION

1. INTRODUCTION

There are two main aspects of the programme regulation regime. On the one hand, terrestrial broadcasters have to fulfil what might be termed 'positive programme requirements'. These relate to the promises of performance made by licence applicants. For example, as noted in Chapter 3, applicants for a Channel 3 licence have to make proposals about the programme matters referred to in BA 1990, s 16 (Chapter 3, section 4(d)). These promises of performance will form part of the licensee's obligations and will be monitored. The ITC publishes, with its Annual Report, detailed performance reviews of each Channel 3 licensee, Channel 4 and Channel 5. All broadcasters must also comply with the general programme requirements or 'consumer protection' standards, relating to matters such as taste and decency, and impartiality. Here too, the regulatory bodies, the ITC and the RA will be responsible for ensuring compliance.

One aspect of programme regulation which has caused concern has been the extent of regulatory overlap. As well as being responsible to the ITC or the RA, as the case may be, licensees (and the BBC) are also subject to the Broadcasting Standards Commission (BSC). The BSC adjudicates on complaints from the public on standards in broadcasting, such as the portrayal of violence, sexual conduct, and matters of taste and decency. It also deals with complaints concerning fairness of treatment and infringements of privacy.[1] The dilemma for broadcasters is that they may find a programme falls foul of one regulatory body, or, in the case of the BBC, the Programme Complaints Unit (see Chapter 3, Section 3(d)(ii)), but not the other.

This chapter is primarily concerned with the regulatory regime for private television programming, but it should be remembered that both radio and the BBC operate under similar rules. The discussion of the BSC and political and election broadcasting relates directly to public and private broadcasting. Only very brief coverage of the programme obligations can be given here, but the web sites (see Select Bibliography below) of the ITC, the RA and the

---

[1] The privacy aspect of the BSC's work will be considered in Chapter 11.

BSC provide good sources of information. Each web site includes the relevant code, and reports of adjudications are regularly published. The BBC web site provides more general information on programme compliance. Although applicable to more than just programme obligations, enforcement of licences will also be examined below.

2. REGULATION OF TELEVISION PROGRAMMING

(a) General programme obligations

The BA 1990 has developed a multi-streamed approach to licensing and ongoing obligations (see Chapter 3), but there is one area over which the government has chosen to retain a common level of regulation. The general programme obligations, or consumer protection standards, apply to all services regardless of their nature and with only minor variations.[2] These obligations are set out in BA 1990, s 6, and all services licensed by the ITC have to comply with these standards. Indeed, in the case of some licensed services, for example satellite television services and licensable programme services, the only ground for rejecting a licence application is the likelihood that the applicant will not comply with s 6.[3] Some of these programme obligations will be considered further in this chapter.

Extract 4.2.1

Broadcasting Act 1990, ss 6(1)–(6) and 7(1)–(3)

6.—(1) The Commission shall do all that they can to secure that every licensed service complies with the following requirements, namely—
- (a) that nothing is included in its programmes which offends against good taste or decency or is likely to encourage or incite to crime or to lead to disorder or to be offensive to public feeling;
- (b) that any news given (in whatever form) in its programmes is presented with due accuracy and impartiality;
- (c) that due impartiality is preserved on the part of the person providing the service as respects matters of political or industrial controversy or relating to current public policy;
- (d) that due responsibility is exercised with respect to the content of any of its programmes which are religious programmes, and that in particular any such programmes do not involve—
    - (i) any improper exploitation of any susceptibilities of those watching the programmes, or

---

[2] Additional services, but not Teletext, are the one exception to this: BA 1990, s 6(8).
[3] Subject also to an applicant having to satisfy the preliminary licensing requirements, see Chapter 3, Section 4(c).

(ii) any abusive treatment of the religious views and beliefs of those belonging to a particular religion or religious denomination; and

(e) that its programmes do not include any technical device which, by using images of very brief duration or by any other means, exploits the possibility of conveying a message to, or otherwise influencing the minds of, persons watching the programmes without their being aware, or fully aware, of what has occurred.

(2) In applying subsection (1)(c) a series of programmes may be considered as a whole.

(3) The Commission shall—

(a) draw up, and from time to time review, a code giving guidance as to the rules to be observed in connection with the application of subsection (1)(c) in relation to licensed services; and

(b) do all that they can to secure that the provisions of the code are observed in the provision of licensed services;

and the Commission may make different provision in the code for different cases or circumstances.

(4) Without prejudice to the generality of subsection (1), the Commission shall do all that they can to secure that there are excluded from the programmes included in a licensed service all expressions of the views and opinions of the person providing the service on matters (other than the provision of programme services) which are of political or industrial controversy or relate to current public policy.

(5) The rules specified in the code referred to in subsection (3) shall, in particular, take account of the following matters—

(a) that due impartiality should be preserved on the part of the person providing a licensed service as respects major matters falling within subsection (1)(c) as well as matters falling within that provision taken as a whole; and

(b) the need to determine what constitutes a series of programmes for the purposes of subsection (2).

(6) The rules so specified shall, in addition, indicate to such extent as the Commission consider appropriate—

(a) what due impartiality does and does not require, either generally or in relation to particular circumstances;

(b) the ways in which due impartiality may be achieved in connection with programmes of particular descriptions;

(c) the period within which a programme should be included in a licensed service if its inclusion is intended to secure that due impartiality is achieved for the purposes of subsection (1)(c) in connection with that programme and any programme previously included in that service taken together; and

(d) in relation to any inclusion in a licensed service of a series of programmes which is of a description specified in the rules—

(i) that the dates and times of the other programmes comprised in the series should be announced at the time when the first programme so comprised is included in that service, or

(ii) if that is not practicable, that advance notice should be given by other means of subsequent programmes so comprised which include

118

material intended to secure, or assist in securing, that due impartiality is achieved in connection with the series as a whole;

and those rules shall, in particular, indicate that due impartiality does not require absolute neutrality on every issue or detachment from fundamental democratic principles.

(7), (8) [*Omitted*].

7.—(1) The Commission shall draw up, and from time to time review, a code giving guidance—

(a) as to the rules to be observed with respect to the showing of violence, or the inclusion of sounds suggestive of violence, in programmes included in licensed services, particularly when large numbers of children and young persons may be expected to be watching the programmes;

(b) as to the rules to be observed with respect to the inclusion in such programmes of appeals for donations; and

(c) as to such other matters concerning standards and practice for such programmes as the Commission may consider suitable for inclusion in the code;

and the Commission shall do all that they can to secure that the provisions of the code are observed in the provision of licensed services.

(2) In considering what other matters ought to be included in the code in pursuance of subsection (1)(c), the Commission shall have special regard to programmes included in licensed services in circumstances such that large numbers of children and young persons may be expected to be watching the programmes.

(3) The Commission shall, in drawing up or revising the code under this section, take account of such of the international obligations of the United Kingdom as the Secretary of State may notify to them for the purposes of this subsection.

(4) [*Omitted*].

(b) Programme Code

Both of the codes required by the legislation are published by the ITC as the Programme Code, which was last revised in 1998.[4] The Programme Code is primarily concerned with giving guidance on the consumer protection standards, and includes sections on taste and decency, the portrayal of violence, matters of privacy and information gathering, the treatment of crime, terrorism and anti-social behaviour, the conduct of charitable appeals and the portrayal of religion. As well as monitoring compliance with these obligations, the ITC responds to viewer complaints. For the year ending 1998, the ITC received 3,257 complaints, the vast majority of which concerned terrestrial services. Of all the complaints received, the majority were about taste

---

[4] At the time of writing certain sections relating to political and election broadcasting are again under revision. Some examples of ITC adjudications on possible breaches of the Code, provided in this chapter, pre-date the current version of the Code, but in all cases the current provisions of the Code are applicable.

and decency matters (1,260).[5] However, it is worth noting also the number of complaints upheld: 'In 1998 the ITC upheld wholly or in part 361 complaints (11 per cent of the total received) about 69 individual programmes and intervened, without complaint, on a further 15.'[6]

Questions for discussion
(You may wish to consider these questions as you read through the rest of this section)
1. Is the system of programme regulation overly cumbersome when so few people appear to be disturbed about the programmes?
2. Given that the ITC has a general duty to ensure that programmes accord with certain standards, what is the role of viewer complaints?
3. To what extent do viewer complaints represent a confirmation of community agreement with these standards?

One aspect of the Programme Code which permeates most other areas is the family viewing policy. As required by BA 1990, s 7(1)(a) and (2), the ITC must take into account the likelihood that children and young people may be viewing programmes. Rules within specific sections of the Programme Code address this concern, but there is also a general policy covering the scheduling of programmes. The Programme Code prints specific rules in bold type and indented, so that all other text constitutes guidance,[7] although the ITC interprets the Code as a whole, and licensees are expected to be aware of the Code in its entirety.

Extract 4.2.2

ITC, *Programme Code* (Autumn 1998), 1.2(i)

1.2 Scheduling

1.2(i) Family Viewing Policy

. . .

> **Material unsuitable for children must not be broadcast at times when large numbers of children may be expected to be watching.**

However, the ITC accepts that, even though some children are always likely to be present in the audience, there should be a wide range of programmes appropriate for adults and including serious subject matter. The necessary compromise is embodied in the ITC's Family Viewing Policy which assumes a progressive decline throughout the evening in the proportion of children present in the audience. It requires a similar progression in the successive programmes

---

[5] ITC, *Annual Report and Accounts 1998* (1999), p 34.
[6] Ibid, p 35.
[7] Extracts from the Programme Code in this chapter follow the same pattern.

scheduled from early evening onwards; the earlier in the evening the more suitable, the later in the evening the less suitable.

Within the progression, 9.00 pm is normally fixed as the time up to which licensees will regard themselves as responsible for ensuring that nothing is shown that is unsuitable for children.

Not all daytime or early evening programming will be suitable for very young children. Licensees should provide sufficient information, in terms of regular scheduling patterns or on-air advice, to assist parents to make appropriate viewing choices.

After 9.00 pm and until 5.30 am progressively less suitable (i.e. more adult) material may be shown and it may be that a programme will be acceptable for example at 10.30 pm that would not be suitable at 9.00 pm.

Broadcasters must be particularly sensitive to the likelihood that programmes which start before 9.00 pm but which run beyond that time will continue to be viewed by a family audience.

Subscription television, through cable and satellite, has resulted in only limited and cautious departures from the general policy, despite its potential for programme specialisation and greater viewer control over what is delivered.

Extract 4.2.3

ITC, *Programme Code* (Autumn 1998), 1.2(ii)

1.2(ii) Premium subscription services

Where a programme service is only available to viewers on payment of a premium rate fee, its availability to children will be more restricted and the time at which parents may be expected to share responsibility for what is viewed may be shifted from 9.00 pm to as early as 8.00 pm. Material of a more adult kind than would be acceptable at the same time on a more broadly available channel may be shown after 10.00 pm and before 5.30 am on these services and on any service available solely to adult viewers who had specifically chosen it.

Pay-per-view television is cautiously given greater freedom, but only on a case-by-case, and, currently, an experimental, basis. These services do not have to follow the time-based watershed rules, provided that they have certain security mechanisms to control access in place.[8]

---

[8] Programme Code, Appendix 5. The ITC has recently extended this experiment by agreeing that '18' rated films, which could only be shown after 8 pm, can now be broadcast at any time on these services: ITC, *Changes to ITC Rules on Pay-per-View Film Scheduling* (News Release 49/99, 27 July 1999).

(c) Taste and decency

Taste and decency is an area where the family viewing policy will have particular relevance, but it is important to recognise that the legislation and the Programme Code are not concerned only with children. Clearly, regulation in this area can be sensitive as viewers will have differing views about what is acceptable for broadcast. It may be questioned whether adults need to have such protection provided for them. On the other hand, as we have seen, it is the area of taste and decency which attracts the most complaints, and it should be remembered that viewers may also be complaining to the BSC. The answer perhaps lies in the continuing influence of those beliefs which originally justified the close regulation of broadcasting, in particular, the perception that television has great power and comes uninvited into the household. The development of subscription television and pay-per-view services provides a greater opportunity for the viewer to exercise control over what is broadcast, but, as already noted, little allowance is made for the differing nature of these services, and, by and large, the Programme Code applies equally to such services. Viewers of cable and satellite television services tend to complain less about programmes compared with the terrestrial audience. This is so even allowing for the difference in audience size,[9] although the ITC noted that in 1998 the number of complaints concerning cable and satellite had increased more than three times compared with the previous year.[10]

Questions for discussion
1.   Given that the number of complaints for cable and satellite is less than for terrestrial television, does this provide the ITC with a mandate for adopting a more relaxed approach towards subscription television services?
2.   What factors might be contributing to the increase in complaints about cable and satellite programmes? How should this increase influence the ITC in deciding programme policy?

Extract 4.2.4 provides examples of two of the matters which are regarded by the ITC as relevant to 'taste and decency'. The legislation does not define 'taste and decency'; nor does the ITC provide any general guidance. This may be understandable given the difficulty of arriving at any absolute standard for these concepts. Extracts 4.2.5–4.2.7 illustrate the ITC's application of the Code. The programmes covered in the latter two extracts were also considered by the BSC, see Extracts 4.4.7 and 4.4.8 below.

---

[9] ITC, *Likely to Complain? Free-to-air Versus Subscription Channels* (1998), p 2.
[10] ITC, *Annual Report and Accounts 1998* (1999), p 34.

Extract 4.2.4

ITC, *Programme Code* (Autumn 1998), 1.4 and 1.5

1.4 Language

There is no absolute ban on the use of bad language. But many people are offended, some of them deeply, by the use of bad language, including expletives with a religious (and not only Christian) association.

If therefore the freedom of expression of writers, producers and performers is not to be jeopardised, gratuitous use of bad language must be avoided. It must be defensible in terms of context and authenticity, and should not be a frequent feature of the schedule.

Bad language (including profanity) should not be used in programmes specially designed for children.

The most offensive language should not be used before 9.00 pm. Its use after that must always be approved – where practicable in advance – by the licensee's most senior programme executive or the designated alternate.

1.5 Sex and nudity

Similar considerations apply. Much great drama and fiction has been concerned with love and passion which can shock or disturb. Popular entertainment and comedy have always relied to some extent on sexual innuendo and suggestive behaviour. But gratuitous offence should be avoided.

The portrayal of sexual behaviour, and of nudity, needs to be defensible in context and presented with tact and discretion. Of the greatest concern are scenes of non-consensual sexual portrayal, including rape, and particularly where there is graphic physical detail or the action is to any degree prolonged.

Representation of sexual intercourse should be reserved until after 9.00 pm. Exceptions to this rule may be allowed in the case of nature films, programmes with a serious educational purpose, or where the representation is non-graphic, and must be approved in advance by the licensee's most senior programme executive or the designated alternate.

Graphic portrayal of violent sexual behaviour is justifiable only very exceptionally. The same approval process must be followed.

Extract 4.2.5

ITC, *Programme Complaints and Interventions Report* (February/March 1998)

THE MARK THOMAS COMEDY PRODUCT: Channel 4
Wednesday 25 February: 11.00 pm

BACKGROUND   In this series, the comedian Mark Thomas looked at issues of public concern. In the second part of this particular programme, he discussed the subject of abortion.

ISSUE   Five viewers complained about the use of bad language when talking about such a serious issue.

ASSESSMENT   The ITC acknowledged that Mark Thomas's use of strong language in this context may not have seemed appropriate to some viewers. However, the programme went out well after the 9 pm watershed when it is generally accepted that stronger material which appeals to an adult audience may be shown. Although presented in a comedy format, the series sought to address issues of public concern. The ITC did not believe that most viewers would be surprised or offended by Mark Thomas's use of language.

CONCLUSION   Given Channel 4's special remit to provide original and innovative programming and the late transmission time, the ITC considered that this programme did not breach the Programme Code.

CATEGORY   Language

COMPLAINTS FROM   5 viewers (not upheld)

Extract 4.2.6

ITC, *Programme Complaints and Interventions Report* (April 1999), p 6

WHAT'S THE STORY?: Channel 5
Tuesday 23 March: 8.30 pm

BACKGROUND   This edition of the current affairs series considered three issues to do with 'sex for sale': the availability of pornography on the Internet, the legalisation of brothels in the Netherlands, and whether local authorities should license table-dancing clubs.

ISSUE   Six viewers felt the subject matter was unsuitable for transmission before the 9 pm watershed.

ASSESSMENT   The ITC noted that previous current affairs programmes had addressed topics of this kind, during early/mid evening, without evidence of widespread offence. The ITC therefore disagreed with those complainants who argued that the topic should be ruled out automatically before the watershed. As far as this particular programme was concerned, its treatment of its subject matter included no references or visual images of a graphic nature unsuitable for the time of transmission. Consistent with the programme's usual approach, a range of viewpoints was included, including those of commentators worried about developments in the sex industry.

CONCLUSION There was no breach of the ITC Programme Code.

CATEGORY Taste and decency

COMPLAINTS FROM 6 viewers (not upheld)

Extract 4.2.7

ITC, *Programme Complaints and Interventions Report*
(May 1999), pp 8–9

QUEER AS FOLK: Channel 4
Tuesdays 23 February–13 April: 10.30 pm

BACKGROUND This drama series, which was set in Manchester's 'gay village', centred on the lives of three young homosexual men.

ISSUE The ITC received over 160 complaints, most of which concerned the first episode, which showed a 15-year-old boy being introduced to homosexual activity by a promiscuous 29-year-old. Strong language also upset some viewers.

ASSESSMENT Channel 4 said that the under-age character, Nathan, was 'coming to terms with his sexuality', which included facing homophobia at his school and conservative parents at home. His age was essential to the storyline. The details of the sex scenes were brief, shot and edited responsibly, and no more graphic or explicit than many heterosexual scenes shown on terrestrial television. Their inclusion was approved at the highest level of the Channel's management and the first programme was preceded by a warning to viewers. The series fulfilled the Channel's remit to appeal to tastes and interests not catered for by ITV.

The ITC accepted that the series fell within Channel 4's statutory remit, and considered that most viewers would have had no difficulty with a series on this theme, scheduled at 10.30 pm, well after the 9 pm watershed. Indeed, the series was of high quality, well made, fast moving, and enlivened by a witty script and attractive score.

Nevertheless the ITC had concerns about the celebratory tone of the first episode, which left little room for any questions to be raised in viewers' minds about the rights and wrongs of the illegal, under-age relationship. A significant number of viewers clearly found this offensive. In addition, the decision to include three explicit sex scenes in the opening episode of the series had clearly shocked many viewers. Moreover, in the view of the ITC, Channel 4 had missed an opportunity in failing to provide any off-air support for the series, such as fact sheets or website material linking viewers to advice on young people and sexuality, and on safe sex. The ITC recommended that any repeat or further series should be enhanced by such responsible messages.

. . .

CONCLUSION The series was not in breach of the ITC Programme Code. However, the ITC expressed concern to Channel 4 about aspects of both the handling of the under-age relationship and the concentration of frank sex scenes in the opening episode.

CATEGORY Sexual portrayal

COMPLAINTS FROM 163 viewers (not upheld)

Questions for discussion
1. Is it possible to discern any pattern in the way that the ITC determines these complaints?
2. Should the quality of a programme be relevant in deciding a matter of taste and decency?

(d) Impartiality

The requirement imposed on licensees to present programmes with due impartiality and to avoid editorialising is one of the more direct infringements on a broadcaster's freedom of speech.[11] However, as Gibbons suggests, it can also be seen as relevant to the wider sense in which we talk of broadcasting freedom, because the rules prevent dominance by any particular interests,

[11] Barendt, p 100.

enabling the audience to obtain a variety of information and knowledge.[12] The legislation prescribes in some detail (Extract 4.2.1) the matters which the ITC must address in its Code. This was not the practice prior to the 1990 legislation. It is an irony of the BA 1990, that despite the government's intention to impose lighter regulation, the impartiality provisions produced more complex regulation. This was not what the government had intended, because the draft legislation had proposed the same legislative scheme which had operated under the Broadcasting Act 1981. However, pressure from the House of Lords during the passage of the Bill, resulted in this much more detailed regime.[13] The move for these changes illustrates the sensitivity of this aspect of programme-making, and the pressure which broadcasters, and, indeed, regulators, may be under in relation to current affairs reporting. This is so, even though very few complaints about impartiality are received from the public. Given the importance attached to impartiality, one can expect that this will be an area carefully monitored by the ITC, but generally it does not seem to cause any major regulatory issues.[14] The Programme Code's section on impartiality is, not surprisingly, one of the most detailed of the Code. The following extract is a sample only of the provisions.

Extract 4.2.8

ITC, *Programme Code* (Autumn 1998), sections 3.1, 3.2(i) and 3.3

3.1 Objectives

Licensees may make programmes about any issues they choose. This free-dom is limited only by the obligations of fairness and a respect for truth, two qualities which are essential to all factually-based programmes, whether on 'controversial' topics or not.

Impartiality does not mean that broadcasters have to be absolutely neutral on every controversial issue, but they should deal even-handedly with oppos-ing points of view in the arena of democratic debate. Opinion should be clearly distinguished from fact.

3.2 The legal position

3.2(i) Due impartiality

. . .

The term 'due' is significant; it should be interpreted as meaning adequate or appropriate to the nature of the subject and the type of programme. While

---

[12] Gibbons, p 94.

[13] For an account of the passage of the impartiality provisions see L Hitchens, 'Impartiality and the Broadcasting Act: Riding the Wrong Horse' (1991) 12(2) *Journal of Media Law and Practice* 48.

[14] Note 10, above, p 36.

the requirement of due impartiality applies to all areas of controversy covered by the Act, it does not mean that 'balance' is required in any simple mathematical sense or that equal time must be given to each opposing point of view, nor does it require absolute neutrality on every issue. Judgement will always be called for. The requirement will also vary with the type of programme; the considerations applying to drama, for example, are different from those applying to current affairs programmes. News and personal view programmes are also different in kind and bound by separate sets of rules. Similarly, the choice of participants in a research-led investigative report will be determined by the need to be fair to the subject matter, while participants in a political discussion programme will normally be chosen more with a view to reflecting the principal opposing viewpoints.

. . .

3.3 Impartiality over time

There are times when licensees will need to ensure that the principal opposing viewpoints are reflected in a single programme or programme item, either because it is not likely that the licensee will soon return to the subject, or because the issues involved are of current and active controversy. At other times, a narrower range of views may be appropriate within individual programmes. The ITC recognises that such issues call for editorial judgement based on the particular circumstances and that an impartial programme service does not necessarily have to ensure that in a single programme, or programme item, all sides have an opportunity to speak.

3.3(i) The 'series' provision

The Broadcasting Act's requirements about impartiality allow a series of programmes to be considered as a whole. For this purpose, the ITC defines a series as more than one programme broadcast in the same service, each one of which is clearly linked to the other(s) and which deal with the same or related issues.

It is not sufficient to claim that programmes on other channels or other media will ensure that opposing views will be heard.

Some series consist of programmes broadcast at regular intervals under the same title, but which may deal with widely disparate issues from one edition to the next. In this case, each programme should normally aim to be impartial in itself. Alternatively, producers may choose to deal with the same subject over two or more programmes or, for instance, offer separate in-depth interviews to the leaders of political parties and in this way achieve impartiality over time.

The intention to achieve impartiality in this way should be planned in advance and, wherever practicable, made clear to viewers.

Question for discussion

Why are broadcasters under an obligation to act with 'due impartiality' instead of with 'impartiality'?

The following extracts provide examples of adjudications on impartiality.

Extract 4.2.9

**ITC, *Programme Complaints and Interventions Report*
(August/September 1998), p 14**

**UTV LIVE INSIGHT: ITV (Ulster)
Thursday 2 July: 10.30 pm**

BACKGROUND Live Insight is UTV's weekly current affairs programme. This edition examined the Parades Commission's decision to refuse permission for the Orange Order to march from Drumcree Church along the predominantly nationalist Garvaghy Road. Part of the programme featured a studio discussion involving an Ulster Unionist MP, a spokesman for the Orange Order and a member of the SDLP. Breandan MacCionnaith of the Garvaghy Road Residents' Coalition joined the discussion by satellite link.

ISSUE Five viewers complained that the programme presenter failed to act impartially because he refused to allow Mr MacCionnaith to continue to take part after he had declined to withdraw an allegation implicating the Orange Order and its supporters in violence. By contrast, earlier remarks by the Ulster Unionist and Orange Order participants about violence by Garvaghy Road residents had gone unchallenged.

ASSESSMENT The ITC Programme Code reflects the Broadcasting Act requirement 'that due impartiality is preserved on the part of the person providing the service as respects matters of political or industrial controversy or relating to current public policy'. The format of this programme was clearly balanced, with a range of views being expressed by the four contributors to the discussion. In the ITC's view, the allegations made by the unionist speakers were not of the same order of seriousness as Mr MacCionnaith's. The ITC sympathised with the concerns expressed by viewers and agreed that the programme would have been better handled had the presenter's responses to the various points been more even. However, in the context of a live programme, the ITC did not consider that these shortcomings were serious enough to amount to a breach of the Code.

129

CONCLUSION   The programme was not in breach of the Programme Code.

CATEGORY   Impartiality

COMPLAINTS FROM   5 viewers (not upheld)

Extract 4.2.10

**ITC, *Programme Complaints and Interventions Report*
(December 1997/January 1998), p 8**

**NEWS; JIYANA GEL; NEWS: Med TV
3 June; 14 June; 9 October: Various times**

BACKGROUND   Med TV provides a service for Kurdish viewers in Europe, Turkey and the Middle East. **Jiyana Gel** is a series that throws light on life in remote regions. The programme on 14 June 1997 consisted entirely of coverage of a rally by the Workers' Party of Kurdistan (PKK) which is engaged in a guerrilla war with the Turkish authorities. The **News** programme on 9 October included comments on a list of terrorist organisations and the **News** on 3 June included comments from a reporter in the field.

ISSUE   ITC monitoring, and a complaint, drew attention to the fact that **Jiyana Gel's** coverage of the PKK rally included no context or balancing material to avoid the impression of partiality. Monitoring showed that in the **News** of 9 October remarks were made which appeared to represent editorial comment by the licensee on a list of terrorist organisations produced by the United States. Monitoring of the **News** of 3 June included personal comments from a Med TV reporter describing members of one Kurdish party as 'murderous and treacherous'.

ASSESSMENT   All three programmes were in breach of the ITC Programme Code requirement for due impartiality on the part of the broadcaster in respect of matters of political controversy. Med TV accepted that mistakes had been made in both **News** programmes, pointing out, in mitigation, that the reporter on 3 June had been under very great personal pressure following the loss of a colleague, and that the misjudgement on 9 October had been spotted and corrected in subsequent broadcasts. As far as **Jiyana Gel** was concerned, the

130

company argued that the programme had not been intended as propaganda but as a rare insight into the diverse life of a remote region. Even so, the ITC could see no justification for devoting a whole 40 minute programme to a rally by one party without any apparent attempt at balance.

CONCLUSION The ITC had expressed its concern to Med TV on numerous occasions about a lack of due impartiality and excessive coverage of the PKK. In November 1996, following a previous intervention on the grounds of failure to ensure due impartiality, a formal warning had been given to Med TV that any further such breaches would be likely to result in sanctions. The ITC viewed the three recent breaches as very serious and believed that financial penalties were appropriate in respect of each breach. The penalties incurred were: £50,000 in respect of **Jiyana Gel**; £25,000 in respect of the **News** on 9 October; and £15,000 in respect of the **News** on 3 June.

CATEGORY Impartiality

COMPLAINTS FROM 1 viewer (upheld)

There is a limited relaxation of the rules for some licensable programme services.

Extract 4.2.11

ITC, *Programme Code* (Autumn 1998), 3.9

3.9 The undue prominence rule for local licensable programme services

Under Section 47(4) of the Broadcasting Act 1990 the ITC may modify the provisions of Section 6 in respect of local licensable programme services by substituting in place of Section 6(1)(c) the following:

'(c) that undue prominence is not given in its programmes to the views and opinions of particular persons or bodies on matters of political or industrial controversy or relating to current public policy'.

The ITC will decide on a case by case basis whether the undue prominence requirement (rather than the impartiality requirement) should apply to particular licensees.

The following paragraphs constitute the Code on undue prominence...

No licensee is obliged to depart from maintaining due impartiality. Where it chooses to do so, however, and where the ITC permits it, it must still be even-handed, in accordance with the following guidelines:

On any channel which is permitted by its ITC licence to observe 'undue prominence' rather than 'due impartiality' an equality of opportunity must be offered which, were it to be taken up, would result in a balance of views across the channel as a whole. However, although equal access should be offered to individuals or groups wishing to express views different to those already broadcast, it is not necessary for the channel to solicit or commission such material. The channel should be open-minded about those political or religious groups to whom access might be allowed, and it should not merely invite, or grant facilities to, those whose views the channel shares or approves of.

Within this overall balance, there is scope for programmes to be allowed to convey a particular political view or reflect a particular philosophy. There is no need for individual programmes to be balanced in order to present an impartial approach, nor for a programme presenting one specific view to be balanced by another putting forward the opposing view. The general approach should be that, because the time available for programmes in a multi-channel environment is so considerable, there ought to be scope in a local context for many differing points of view to be expressed, even to the extent of allowing individual groups to present their own programmes espousing their views.

Questions for discussion

1. Why should there be a relaxation for local licensable programme services?

2. Given that some satellite services will be providing a more specialised service, often, addressing a specific audience, is there scope here for a different approach?

It might be questioned why an even more liberal regime does not apply to licensable programme services (local and otherwise), and possibly satellite services, if the traditional reasons for providing protection are less applicable? Paradoxically, it is likely to be services delivered by cable and satellite, because of their more specialist, interest group-based, nature, which may throw up more serious impartiality and balance problems, as Extract 4.2.10 illustrates.

Despite the concern about increased interference with broadcasters' freedom, the impartiality provisions, in their tightened form, do not appear to have caused great difficulty in practice. However, the problem of complex regimes in such an area is that broadcasters, fearing breach, may prefer not to make programmes or to make only 'safe' programmes. There may be a tendency to 'play safe', for example, by producing programmes which simply seek a balanced representation of the main political parties, rather than programmes which explore less mainstream points of view. The sensitivity of this area can best be seen in times of national crisis or when major national issues arise.[15] Broadcasters' attempts to be impartial may upset political

---

[15] During the Nato bombing of Serbia (in relation to the Kosovo conflict) in 1999, the government criticised the BBC frequently for its alleged partiality towards the Serbian point of view.

parties who will be quick to detect any incidents of bias, while the government of the day may even be concerned if broadcasters are too neutral. During the Falklands conflict, the then Prime Minister, Margaret Thatcher, was dissatisfied with the BBC because she regarded their coverage of the conflict as too even-handed.[16]

(e) Enforcement of licences

In ensuring compliance with the legislation, licence terms and ITC directions (and not just programme rules), the ITC has a range of sanctions which it can use.[17]

Extract 4.2.12

Broadcasting Act 1990, ss 40(1), (4)–(5), 41(1), (6), 42(1), (7) and 45A(1)

40.—(1) If the Commission are satisfied—
- (a) that the holder of a Channel 3 or Channel 5 licence has failed to comply with any condition of the licence, and
- (b) that that failure can be appropriately remedied by the inclusion in the licensed service of a correction or apology (or both) under this subsection,

they may ... direct the licence holder to include in the licensed service a correction or apology (or both) in such form, and at such time or times, as they may determine.

(2), (3) [*Omitted*].

(4) If the Commission are satisfied that the inclusion by the holder of a Channel 3 or Channel 5 licence of any programme in the licensed service involved a failure by him to comply with any condition of the licence, they may direct him not to include that programme in that service on any future occasion.

(5) This section shall apply in relation to Channel 4 as if any reference to a Channel 3 licence were a reference to the licence to provide Channel 4.

41.—(1) If the Commission are satisfied that the holder of a Channel 3 or Channel 5 licence has failed to comply with any condition of the licence or

---

[16] P Walters, 'The Crisis of "Responsible" Broadcasting: Mrs Thatcher and the BBC' [1989] *Parliamentary Affairs* 380, at 381–382. Michael Cockerell suggests that compared with the BBC, the Independent Television News (the provider of news programming for the private sector) adopted a much 'more supportive and unquestioning' approach, and that they were rewarded with an interview with Thatcher: M Cockerell, *Live from Number 10* (Faber and Faber, 1989), p 273.

[17] BA 1990, ss 40–42 are applied, with modifications, to other licensed services. For local delivery licences, see s 81; satellite television licences, s 45(5) and licensable programme licences, s 47(8). Enforcement of multiplex licences and digital programme licences are covered in BA 1996, ss 17 and 23 respectively.

with any direction given by the Commission under or by virtue of any provision of this Part, they may (subject to the following provisions of this section) serve on him—

    (a) a notice requiring him to pay, within a specified period, a specified financial penalty to the Commission; or

    (b) a notice reducing the period for which the licence is to be in force by a specified period not exceeding two years.

(2)–(5) [*Omitted*].

(6) This section shall apply in relation to Channel 4 as if—

    (a) any reference to a Channel 3 licence were a reference to the licence to provide Channel 4; and

    (b) subsection (1)(b) were omitted.

42.—(1) If the Commission are satisfied—

    (a) that the holder of a Channel 3 or Channel 5 licence is failing to comply with any condition of the licence or with any direction given by them under or by virtue of any provision of this Part, and

    (b) that that failure is such that, if not remedied, it would justify the revocation of the licence,

they shall . . . serve on the holder of the licence a notice under subsection (2) [which triggers the revocation process].

(2)–(6) [*Omitted*].

(7) If it appears to the Commission to be appropriate to do so for the purpose of preserving continuity in the provision of the service in question, they may provide in any such notice for it to take effect as from a date specified in it.

45A.—(1) If the Commission are satisfied—

    (a) that the holder of a licence to provide a satellite television service has included in the service one or more programmes containing material likely to encourage or incite to crime or to lead to disorder,

    (b) that he has thereby failed to comply with a condition included in the licence in pursuance of section 6(1)(a), and

    (c) that the failure is such as to justify the revocation of the licence,

they shall serve on the holder of the licence a notice under subsection (2) [which triggers the revocation process].

The range of sanctions ensures that the ITC can act in accordance with the degree of seriousness of the breach. One difficulty, however, in applying sanctions is that it may be the viewers who suffer. For example, a financial penalty may mean that funds which would have been available for programme-making will be sacrificed to the penalty. Revocation may deprive the viewer of a channel, although this is recognised in s 42(7) of the BA 1990.[18] The drastic consequences of losing a service, through revocation, may also inhibit the ITC's use of such a sanction. In the circumstances of the

---

[18] BA 1990, s 42(7) does not apply to local delivery licences, satellite television licences or licensable programme licences.

Sky merger with British Satellite Broadcasting (see Chapter 3, Section 4(i)), this was one of the concerns facing the regulatory body, even though there was a clear breach of the programme contract. As explained in Chapter 3 above, the BA 1990 introduced an important change in that, unlike the IBA, the ITC is not itself the broadcaster. Hence its relationship with licensees has become more formal in nature, although Gibbons has suggested that, while the ITC is active in monitoring licence breaches, it has not regularly imposed formal sanctions.[19]

Until recently the severest sanction it had imposed was the fine. In 1994 it fined Granada £500,000; the largest penalty then imposed and the only time a terrestrial licensee had been fined. More recent action by the ITC may indicate a greater willingness to impose heavy sanctions where it believes these to be warranted. In December 1998 it fined Central Television £2 million for a programme, *The Connection*. It had considered shortening the term of the licence.

Extract 4.2.13

**ITC, *ITC Imposes £2m Financial Penalty for 'The Connection'*
(News Release 118/98, 18 December 1998)**

The programme set out with ambitious claims to demonstrate the existence of a major new route for drug-running into the UK. But much of what was offered as evidence used to substantiate this was fake. In relation to this major section of the programme, little was as it seemed.

The size of the financial penalty imposed by the ITC reflects the scale of the programme's ambition and the consequent degree of deception of viewers.

Question for discussion
What factors might be relevant to determining the ambition of a programme?

In April 1999, the ITC revoked a licence, exercising its powers under BA 1990, s 45A (Extract 4.2.12).[20] The licence was for a satellite channel, Med TV, which broadcast across Europe and was aimed at a Kurdish audience. The licensee had received several formal warnings and had been fined on a number of occasions (see Extract 4.2.10 above).

Question for discussion
Might the nature of the service influence the ITC's willingness to revoke a licence? Should it?

---

[19] Gibbons, pp 258–259.
[20] ITC (News Release 28/99, 23 April 1999).

3. REGULATION OF RADIO PROGRAMMING

(a) Programme regulation

Although there are many similarities between the content regulation of television and radio, there are also differences which reflect the different regulatory approaches now taken towards the two arms of commercial broadcasting. Like television licensees, radio licensees must also comply with the consumer protection standards. Consistent, however, with the policy that the nature of a service will be relevant to the degree of regulation, there are differences in the way these standards are applied to radio.[21]

Extract 4.3.1

Broadcasting Act 1990, s 90(2)–(4)

90.—(2) The Authority shall, in the case of every licensed service which is a national, local, satellite or licensable sound programme service, do all that they can to secure that the service complies with the following additional requirements, namely—
  (a) the appropriate requirement specified in subsection (3);
  (b) that (without prejudice to the generality of subsection (1)(b) [obligation to present news with due accuracy and impartiality] or (3)(a)) there are excluded from its programmes all expressions of the views and opinions of the person providing the service on matters (other than sound broadcasting) which are of political or industrial controversy or relate to current public policy; and
  (c) that due responsibility is exercised with respect to the content of any of its programmes which are religious programmes, and that in particular any such programmes do not involve—
      (i) any improper exploitation of any susceptibilities of those listening to the programmes, or
      (ii) any abusive treatment of the religious views and beliefs of those belonging to a particular religion or religious denomination.
  (3) The appropriate requirement referred to in subsection (2)(a) is—
  (a) where the licensed service is a national service, that due impartiality is preserved on the part of the person providing the service as respects matters of political or industrial controversy or relating to current public policy;
  (b) where the licensed service is a local, satellite or licensable sound programme service, that undue prominence is not given in its programmes to the views and opinions of particular persons or bodies on such matters.
  (4) In applying subsection (3)(a) to a national service a series of programmes may be considered as a whole; and in applying subsection (3)(b) to a local,

---

[21] For digital sound programme services, see BA 1996, s 60(7).

satellite or licensable sound programme service the programmes included in that service shall be taken as a whole.

The RA must draw up codes giving guidance on programming (BA 1990, ss 90(5) and 91). There is a Programme Code (last revised in March 1998) and a News and Current Affairs Code (last revised in January 1994, but, at the time of writing, under revision). The approach towards programme regulation is similar to the ITC, although there is a greater reliance on listener complaints as the means of intervention.

(b) Enforcement of licences

As with television, there are a range of sanctions which the RA can use. The sanctions follow a similar pattern to television, although there are some differences. The most significant difference can be seen in BA 1990, s 109.

Extract 4.3.2

Broadcasting Act 1990, s 109(1)–(2)

109.—(1) If the Authority are satisfied that the holder of a licence . . . has failed to comply with any condition of the licence or with any direction given by the Authority . . . , they may serve on him a notice—
  (a) stating that the Authority are so satisfied as respects any specified condition or direction;
  (b) stating the effect of subsection (2); and
  (c) specifying for the purposes of that subsection a period not exceeding twelve months.
  (2) If, at any time during the period specified in a notice under subsection (1), the Authority are satisfied that the licence holder has again failed to comply with any such condition or direction as is mentioned in that subsection (whether or not the same as the one specified in the notice), the Authority may direct him—
  (a) to provide the Authority in advance with such scripts and particulars of the programmes to be included in the licensed service as are specified in the direction; and
  (b) in relation to such of those programmes as will consist of or include recorded matter, to produce to the Authority in advance for examination or reproduction such recordings of that matter as are so specified;
and a direction under this subsection shall have effect for such period, not exceeding six months, as is specified in the direction.

Questions for discussion

1. Is this power consistent with the regulatory policy for radio otherwise manifested in the broadcasting legislation?
2. Why should this power be thought necessary for radio, but not television?

4. BROADCASTING STANDARDS COMMISSION

(a) Jurisdiction

Prior to the BA 1996, two further bodies had authority over broadcasting programmes. The Broadcasting Standards Council (the Council) investigated complaints about standards of taste and decency, and the portrayal of violence or sexual conduct, while the Broadcasting Complaints Commission (the BCC) considered complaints of privacy and fairness. Despite the deregulatory intent of the BA 1990, the Council (established in 1988) was put on a statutory footing, while the BCC, established by legislation in 1981, was also allowed to continue. Pursuant to the BA 1996, these two bodies merged, to become the Broadcasting Standards Commission (the BSC). The merger came about largely to rationalise administrative costs and to overcome public confusion about the roles of these two bodies.[22] The BSC has responsibility for the same areas formerly covered by the BCC and the Council, but they are dealt with by separate panels and separate codes. The BSC's regulatory responsibilities for programme standards (the Code on Standards) and for fairness in broadcasting (the Code on Fairness and Privacy) are considered in the following text.[23] The BSC has jurisdiction over all broadcasters, public and private.

The BSC will not consider all complaints which are received. Time limits apply. Complaints about standards must be brought within two months of the date of a television broadcast, and three weeks of a radio broadcast (BA 1996, s 113(1)), although the BSC has a discretion to consider late complaints if there are circumstances making this appropriate. Fairness (and privacy) complaints do not operate under the same limitations, but there are other time restrictions. Under BA 1996, s 111(5), the BSC may refuse to consider a complaint if it was not made within a reasonable time after the last date of transmission. The BSC regards a reasonable time as three months for a television programme and six weeks for radio.[24] Further, it cannot consider a complaint about a programme, if it has been broadcast more than five years after the person's death, unless there are circumstances making it appropriate (BA 1996, s 111(4)). Further restrictions operate in relation to both standards and fairness complaints.

---

[22] T Gibbons, 'The Role of the Broadcasting Complaints Commission: Current Practice and Future Prospects' in E M Barendt (ed), *The Yearbook of Media and Entertainment Law 1995* (Oxford University Press, 1995), pp 129, 158.

[23] For BSC treatment of privacy, see Chapter 11, Section 5(b).

[24] BSC, *Annual Review 1997–98*, p 8.

Extract 4.4.1

Broadcasting Act 1996, s 114(2)

114.—(2) The BSC shall not entertain, or proceed with the consideration of, a fairness complaint[25] or a standards complaint if it appears to them—
- (a) that the matter complained of is the subject of proceedings in a court of law in the United Kingdom, or
- (b) that the matter complained of is a matter in respect of which the complainant or, in the case of a fairness complaint, the person affected has a remedy by way of proceedings in a court of law in the United Kingdom, and that in the particular circumstances it is not appropriate for the BSC to consider a complaint about it, or
- (c) that the complaint is frivolous, or
- (d) that for any other reason it is inappropriate for them to entertain, or proceed with the consideration of, the complaint.

Question for discussion

In exercising its discretion under s 114(2)(b), what matters would be relevant to its consideration?[26]

The BSC also has a wide jurisdiction under s 114(2)(d) to decide whether or not it will proceed with a complaint. In *R v Broadcasting Complaints Commission, ex parte Owen* (see Extract 4.4.2 below), David Owen, the leader of the then Social Democratic Party complained to the BCC that his party, and the Liberal Party, had received a disproportionately small amount of broadcast coverage during a certain period, compared with the Labour Party, having regard to the number of votes received at the previous General Election. The BCC ruled that it had no jurisdiction because it was required to consider complaints only where the actual content constituted unfair treatment, and not general editorial policy. Even assuming that it did have jurisdiction, the BCC decided that it was not an appropriate complaint for them to entertain. With some reluctance, the court held that the BCC did have jurisdiction in such a matter, but it held further that it had exercised its discretion properly in declining to consider the complaint. Among the reasons given by the BCC for not proceeding were that it was being required to formulate a criterion for determining whether a political party was a major political force; that it had

---

[25] 'Fairness complaint' here means also a privacy complaint.

[26] In a case concerning its predecessor, the BCC, the Court of Appeal has held that it would normally be expected to proceed with a complaint, and that a heavy burden rested on anyone who would seek to prevent the complaint proceeding (per Waller LJ). Once the BCC had satisfied itself that the complaint was not being brought for an improper purpose, and that there was no present intention to bring proceedings, it should normally proceed (per Oliver LJ): *R v Broadcasting Complaints Commission, ex parte BBC*, 16 May 1984, LEXIS (CA). In this section, the decisions extracted and discussed, although about the BCC are still applicable under the BA 1996.

no power to direct broadcasters to change their editorial policy, which was in effect what the complainant was seeking; and, that the principle of editorial freedom, which was embodied in the broadcaster's right to select programmes and programme material, should not be lightly infringed.

Extract 4.4.2

R v Broadcasting Complaints Commission, ex parte Owen [1985] QB 1153, at 1175

MAY LJ: The essence of the applicant's complaint is political and within it lies the thorny problem whether the voting system of this country should be changed ... In these circumstances I think that the stance taken by the commission ... is that the applicant's complaint was to the effect that the broadcasting authorities have, as a matter of editorial policy, taken a decision about how they will treat the ... [parties] in comparison with the Labour Party. The complaint would, in effect, require the commission to decide whether this editorial policy, if it exists, is fair and just. But by what criteria? They would have to express a view about a fundamental issue of British politics, not merely about alleged unjust or unfair treatment in a broadcast or television programme about which there are quite clearly strongly different views held by both the Conservative and Labour Parties.

The applicant's real concern is not to have the broadcasting authorities required to publish a comment by the commission on past programmes but to achieve a change of what he contends is editorial policy on the part of the broadcasting authorities in the future. That is not the type of relief that the commission is empowered to grant.

Another matter which may preclude the BSC from entertaining a complaint is the question of standing. This is a not a problem with complaints about standards because they apply generally to the community, and, therefore, anyone may make a complaint.[27] In fairness complaints, the question of standing has been more problematic.

Extract 4.4.3

Broadcasting Act 1996, ss 111(1), (7) and 130(1)

111.—(1) A fairness complaint may be made by an individual or by a body of persons, whether incorporated or not, but ... shall not be entertained by the BSC unless made by the person affected or by a person authorised by him to make the complaint for him.

---

[27] For privacy matters, the person whose privacy has been infringed has standing: BA 1996, s 130(1).

(2)–(6) [*Omitted*].

(7) The BSC may refuse to entertain—

    (a) a fairness complaint which is a complaint of unjust or unfair treatment if the person named as the person affected was not himself the subject of the treatment complained of and it appears to the BSC that he did not have a sufficiently direct interest in the subject-matter of that treatment to justify the making of a complaint with him as the person affected . . .

130.—(1) . . .

'the person affected'

    (a) in relation to any such unjust or unfair treatment . . . , means a participant in the programme in question who was the subject of that treatment or a person who, whether such a participant or not, had a direct interest in the subject-matter of that treatment . . .

In *R v Broadcasting Complaints Commission, ex parte BBC* (see Extract 4.4.4 below), Mrs Howard, an historian, had provided information to the BBC, and been interviewed and filmed, for a programme about Churchill's decision in 1943 to support Marshal Tito in Yugoslavia. The programme was made and broadcast, but it did not use any of the information which she had provided, nor include her interview. She complained to the BCC that she had been unfairly treated, because the omission of her research meant that other historians would infer that it had been unsatisfactory. The BCC upheld this complaint, but the BBC sought judicial review on the ground that it had no jurisdiction. Laws J agreed with the BBC and considered the appropriate way to determine whether a complainant was a 'person affected'. Since she was not a participant in the programme, the issue turned on whether she had a 'direct interest' (now BA 1996, s 130(1)).

Extract 4.4.4

R v Broadcasting Complaints Commission, ex parte BBC [1994] EMLR 497, at 505–506

LAWS J: In my judgment, however, the statutory words 'direct interest in the subject-matter of that treatment' require it to be shown that the complainant has a direct interest in the contents of the programme which arises not merely because he asserts that they treated him unfairly or unjustly; his interest must be in the subject-matter of the programme said to constitute unfair treatment whether or not that subject-matter is indeed unjust or unfair. . . . It is first necessary to identify what is the subject-matter of the unfair treatment. That exercise categorically does not consist in asking and answering the question whether the programme *was* unfair; it consists in identifying whatever is broadcast that is said to be unfair. It may be a particular part of a programme; it may be a whole programme; it may be . . . a series of programmes. When that exercise has been carried through, the next stage is to see whether the complainant has a direct interest in that subject-matter – as I say, irrespective of the question whether it can be shown to be unfair or not. If the complainant does have such a direct interest, the Commission has jurisdiction, and will then consider on the merits whether the treatment contained within that subject-matter is or is not unjust or unfair.

The result of this construction in the present case is that Mrs Howard had to demonstrate a direct interest in the contents of the programme as such. I do not understand her to have complained so much of specific excerpts from the programme, but rather that the effect of the programme as a whole was unfair to her. . . . In this case, therefore, the first question is whether she had a direct interest in the subject-matter of the programme as a whole. Obviously, she was interested in it; but in my judgment a 'direct interest' imports at least some connection or nexus between her and the contents of the programme itself. But there is none: the events of late 1943 cannot conceivably be said to have involved her directly . . . Her complaint is altogether in a different direction: it consists in the effect which the programme was said to have on the opinion which others might entertain of her later research. That is, in my judgment, altogether outside the conception of a direct interest in the subject-matter of what she says constituted unfair treatment.

It is clear from BA 1996, s 111(1) that fairness complaints are not confined to individuals, but what is the nature of the 'direct interest' required of a representative or campaigning group bringing a complaint about unfair treatment. In *R v Broadcasting Complaints Commission, ex parte BBC* (see Extract 4.4.5 below), the BBC had broadcast a *Panorama* programme about single parent families in Britain. The programme concentrated on young single mothers and their dependency upon welfare payments. The programme attracted much attention, particularly because at the time the government was expressing concern at the cost of welfare benefits for single parents. The National Council for One Parent Families (the Council), an organisation representing the interests of single parents, complained to the BCC that the programme had treated single parents unfairly. No person depicted in the programme complained, but the Council stated that it brought the complaint on behalf of all single parents in Britain, all of whom had been treated unfairly. The BCC upheld its complaint, and the BBC sought judicial review, again challenging the BCC's jurisdiction.

Extract 4.4.5

R v Broadcasting Complaints Commission, ex parte British Broadcasting Corporation [1995] EMLR 241, at 252, 257 and 261

BROOKE J: The main issue at the hearing before me was that the Commission had no jurisdiction to entertain the complaint at all and/or that it ought not to have assumed such jurisdiction. There are, however, . . . remaining features of the evidence to which I must refer.

. . . [All] three of the BBC's witnesses deposed to their concern if the Commission was held to have jurisdiction in this type of case. Ms Benson [editor of the programme] said that it may well be in the Council's interests to block off comment . . . , but if they are allowed to do so by making a complaint to the Commission, freedom of expression is subjected to an unnecessary and unjustified restriction. Programme-makers, she maintained, must be entitled to their own editorial line on an issue which may not be acceptable to pressure groups taking an interest in that issue. . . .

Mr Stevenson, the Secretary of the BBC, supported her. He said that the freedom to comment is extremely important to broadcast journalism and to the BBC. The BBC was concerned that the Commission's decision would hamper broadcasters from making future programmes about lone parents or other issues in which pressure groups take an interest. . . .

The present case is concerned with a . . . lower level of interference [with freedom of expression], since the only remedy available to this statutory Commission is to require the delinquent broadcaster publish a summary of its findings. It remains an interference nevertheless, and the evidence filed on behalf of the BBC, which I accept, shows it is an interference which any court concerned with questions of freedom of expression, would be bound to take seriously. If programme makers, who are concerned with handling controversial issues, are constrained to take into account, other than in wholly exceptional circumstances, not only issues of fairness and justice to individual people or organizations, but issues of fairness and justice to a large amorphous population of people, perhaps numbered in hundreds of thousands, then it is apparent that the public interest is likely to suffer if they feel themselves constrained on this account to play safe. . . .

My consideration of Article 10 of the Convention leads me to consider that it would need very clear language to identify a Parliamentary intention that a national body should be permitted to complain to the Commission about the treatment in a broadcast programme of very large numbers of unidentified people. A *fortiori* when none of them were shown to be subscribing members of that body or in some other way anxious to ensure that it promoted their interests if it, not they, believed that those interests had been harmed.

. . .

In my judgment, the Commission misdirected itself in law. The Council's interest in the subject matter of the allegedly unfair treatment was palpably an indirect interest.

Questions for discussion

1. What is the relationship between standing and freedom of expression?
2. What is the nature of the freedom of expression which is being considered in Extracts 4.4.4 and 4.4.5?

Compared with the ITC and RA, the BSC is limited in what action it can take if it upholds a complaint.

Extract 4.4.6

Broadcasting Act 1996, s 119(1)–(4)

119.—(1) Where the BSC have—

(a) considered and adjudicated upon a fairness complaint, or

(b) considered and made their findings on a standards complaint,

they may give directions of the kind specified in subsection (2).

(2) Those directions are—

(a) where the relevant programme was broadcast by a broadcasting body [BBC], directions requiring that body to publish the matters mentioned in subsection (3) in such manner, and within such period, as may be specified in the directions, and

(b) where the relevant programme was included in a licensed service, directions requiring the appropriate regulatory body [ITC and RA] to direct the licence holder to publish those matters in such manner, and within such period, as may be so specified.

(3) Those matters are—

(a) a summary of the complaint;

(b) the BSC's findings on the complaint or a summary of them;

(c) in the case of a standards complaint, any observations by the BSC on the complaint or a summary of any such observations.

(4) References in subsection (2) to the publication of any matter are references to the publication of that matter without its being accompanied by any observations made by a person other than the BSC and relating to the complaint.

Question for discussion

In *Owen* (Extract 4.4.2 above) it was argued that the BCC was being called upon to interfere with the broadcaster's editorial freedom. When the BSC rules on a standards or fairness complaint and requires the broadcaster to publish a notice, might this not be an interference with editorial freedom?

(b) Standards complaints

The BSC's Code on Standards addresses matters relating to standards concerning taste and decency, portrayal of sexual conduct and violence in similar form to the codes of the regulatory bodies and the BBC guidelines. Indeed, the regulatory bodies and the BBC are under a duty, in drafting their codes and guidelines, to ensure that they reflect the Standards Code (BA 1996, s 108(2)).[28] In the following two extracts, examples of the BSC's handling of matters concerning standards are provided. There is a notable absence of reasoning in these decisions. Both of the programmes dealt with here were also the subject of ITC investigations (see Extracts 4.2.6 and 4.2.7 above).

---

[28] The same duty applies in relation to fairness and privacy matters: BA 1996, s 107(2).

Extract 4.4.7

Broadcasting Standards Commission, *Bulletin No 22* (June 1999)
http://www.bsc.org.uk/bullitin/cn2406.htm

WHAT'S THE STORY? SEX FOR SALE
Channel 5, 23 March 1999, 2030–2100

The Complaint

Three viewers complained about images and scenes of a sexual nature, which they considered inappropriate for broadcasting before the Watershed.

The Broadcaster's Statement

Channel 5 explained there were three elements to the programme: the availability of pornography on the Internet; the legality of brothels in the Netherlands; and the licensing of table-dancing clubs. As to the Internet, the programme clearly distinguished between legal sites – with difficult access to them – and illegal pornography with ease of access. It also demonstrated how images can be involuntarily downloaded from cameras onto the computer screen, which the broadcaster considered to be in the public interest and should be dealt with in mainstream current affairs programming during peak viewing hours.

No explicit imagery or language was used in the item about legalised brothels in Amsterdam, which compared prostitution there – with its perceived advantages and disadvantages – with the same activity in the UK. The final item about 'table dancing' clubs dealt with opposition to such clubs and the limited powers of local authorities over licensing them.

The Commission's Finding

A Standards Panel watched the programme, and noted the broadcaster's statement about these issues forming relevant topics for a current affairs programme. It also noted, however, the extensive range of images and scenes portrayed of a detailed, sexual nature. It considered that the amount and nature of the material shown went beyond acceptable boundaries for a programme transmitted before the Watershed. The complaints were upheld.

Upheld

Extract 4.4.8

Broadcasting Standards Commission, *Bulletin No 22* (June 1999)
http://www.bsc.org.uk/bullitin/cn2142.htm

QUEER AS FOLK
Channel 4, February, March, and April 1999, 2230–2310 and 2315–2350

The Complaint

The Commission received 138 complaints about different aspects of this drama series. Some complained about bad language and the portrayal of drug use. But most complained about the portrayal of homosexuality, including stereotypical behaviour, and explicit sexual scenes, in particular with an underage character, which they believed encouraged and endorsed paedophilia. The majority of complaints were about the first episode; episode 2 attracted nine complaints; episode 3, five complaints; episode 4, two complaints and episodes 5, 6 and 7 three general complaints.

The Commission also received a number of letters praising the series.

. . .

The Commission's Finding

The Standards Committee watched the whole series to consider the complaints in the context of the developing storyline. It acknowledged the particular remit of Channel 4 to broadcast challenging and minority programmes and the ambition of the series to reflect something of the complexity and variety of gay life, as well as the adolescent exploration of sexual identity and its consequences for individuals and families.

It took the view that the series had neither encouraged nor condoned paedophilia. However, it was troubled by the explicit and graphic nature of the sexual encounter involving an underage character in episode one. That aspect of the complaints was upheld.

The Committee took the view that the portrayal of drug use had been realistic rather than glamorous, and that aspect of the complaints was not upheld. The Committee also considered that the language used generally in the series was unlikely to have exceeded the expectations of the majority of the audience.

However, in episode two, the Committee considered that the use of the phrase 'fucking bastard cunts' had exceeded acceptable boundaries, despite the dramatic context, given the severity with which such language is viewed by the majority of viewers. That aspect of the complaints was upheld.

In episode three, the Commission also took the view that the portrayal of troilism had exceeded acceptable boundaries.

Accordingly, the complaints were upheld in part.

Upheld in part

Question for discussion

Comparing these extracts with Extracts 4.2.6 and 4.2.7 above, can you discern any differences in the way that the ITC and the BSC have approached these complaints?[29]

---

[29] For a comparison of decisions made by the ITC, the RA, the BBC Programme Complaints Unit and the BSC (in fact, the Broadcasting Standards Council and the Broadcasting Complaints Commission) see J Michael, 'Complaints against the Media in 1996' in E M Barendt (ed), *The Yearbook of Media and Entertainment Law 1997/8* (Oxford University Press, 1997), p 335.

(c) Fairness complaints

Here again the BSC is concerned with programme matters that are also the subject of the other programme codes. Assessing whether a programme deals fairly with contributors or with the subject of the programme is important because it may also reflect upon whether the programme is balanced and impartial. This close connection between fairness and impartiality can be seen in the *Owen* complaint (Extract 4.4.2).

Extract 4.4.9

Broadcasting Standards Commission, *Code on Fairness and Privacy* (June 1998), paras 2–3, 7 and 11–12

General

2 Broadcasters have a responsibility to avoid unfairness to individuals or organisations featured in programmes in particular through the use of inaccurate information or distortion, for example, by the unfair selection or juxtaposition of material taken out of context, whether specially recorded for a programme, or taken from library or other sources. Broadcasters should avoid creating doubts on the audience's part as to what they are being shown if it could mislead the audience in a way which would be unfair to those featured in the programme.

Dealing Fairly with Contributors

3 From the outset, broadcasters should ensure that all programme-makers, whether in-house or independent, understand the need to be straightforward and fair in their dealings with potential participants in factual programmes, in particular by making clear, wherever practicable, the nature of the programme and its purpose and, whenever appropriate, the nature of their contractual rights. Many potential contributors will be unfamiliar with broadcasting and therefore may not share assumptions about programme-making which broadcasters regard as obvious.

Accuracy

7 Broadcasters should take special care when their programmes are capable of adversely affecting the reputation of individuals, companies or other organisations. Broadcasters should take all reasonable care to satisfy themselves that all material facts have been considered before transmission and so far as possible are fairly represented.

Opportunity to Contribute

11 Where a programme alleges wrongdoing or incompetence, or contains a damaging critique of an individual or organisation, those criticised should

normally be given an appropriate and timely opportunity to respond to or comment on the arguments and evidence contained within that programme.

Non-Participation

12 Anyone has the right to refuse to participate in a programme, but the refusal of an individual or organisation to take part should not normally prevent the programme from going ahead. However where an individual or organisation is mentioned or discussed in their absence, care should be taken to ensure that their views are not misrepresented.

The following complaint concerned a programme which was part of a BBC series, *Private Investigations*, which featured filmed reports by members of the public. The programme had been made by a former employee of the farming business, the subject of the programme, and he had been assisted by Viva!, a campaigning organisation. The complaint had also alleged infringement of privacy in the making and broadcasting of the film, which was upheld.

Extract 4.4.10

Broadcasting Standards Commission, *Bulletin No 22* (June 1999)
http://www.bsc.org.uk/bullitin/cnB22F3.htm

SUMMARY OF ADJUDICATION (issued 14.6.99)
Private Investigations, BBC2, 26 August 1998

The Broadcasting Standards Commission has upheld a complaint from John T. Fall Ltd about an item, broadcast on BBC2 on 26 August 1998, concerning standards of care in pig farming in the series Private Investigations. The item was presented by a former employee of the company and included filming at its pig unit and farmhouse.

In upholding the complaint, the Commission found that the BBC made an error of judgment in allowing a former employee, whose employment with the company had ended after a disagreement, to present the item. He was unlikely to have presented it impartially. He had said that he had more experience of pig farming than he actually had, and credited himself unduly for improvements at the unit. The role of the vegetarian organisation Viva!, in helping him make the item, had not been made clear.

The Commission found that there was insufficient evidence to support the impression given in the item that the pigs were overstocked, that the floor was unsafe and that appropriate procedures for the treatment of sick and dead pigs were not being followed. The programme was also misleading in that it failed to make clear that a recent government inspection had indicated that practices at the unit were for the most part satisfactory.

In all these respects the Commission found unfairness.

. . .

Accordingly, the complaint was upheld.

Extract 4.4.11

Broadcasting Standards Commission, *Bulletin No 22* (June 1999)
http://www.bsc.org.uk/bullitin/cnB22F2.htm

SUMMARY OF ADJUDICATION (issued 10.6.99)
Crime Report, Channel 5, 24 August 1998

The Broadcasting Standards Commission has upheld a complaint by Ms Kay Holder of unfair treatment in Crime Report, broadcast by Channel 5 on 24 August 1998, and in a trailer for the series.

The programme included an item about animal rights activists and the tactics employed by some of those within that movement. The item featured film of Ms Holder at a demonstration at Hill Grove Farm in Oxfordshire. The same piece of film was also used in a trailer to promote the programme and the series of which it was part.

The Commission considered that the trailer's narration, which emphasised that the Crime Report series would be reporting on major crime stories, combined with brief footage of Ms Holder, gave the clear and misleading impression that Ms Holder was involved in serious crime. It also considered that this suggestion was compounded by the trailer's statement that the series would 'expose the mechanics of the criminal mind', which had immediately preceded film of Ms Holder confronting police in riot gear. The Commission found that this was unfair.

The Commission took the view that the programme itself did not give a misleading impression of Ms Holder. However, viewers who saw both the trailer and the programme would have been left with the impression that Ms Holder was involved in serious crime. Therefore, the Commission found that the overall impression created by the combined trailer and programme was unfair.

Accordingly, the complaint was upheld.

Question for discussion
How do Extracts 4.4.10 and 4.4.11 illustrate the different types of harm which may result from unfair reporting?

(d) The role of the BSC

The largest number of complaints received by the BSC relate to standards. For 1998–99, 4,559 complaints on standards were received, compared with 333 for fairness. Of the 4,559 complaints, the BSC proceeded with 2,994 and upheld 31%, while 139 fairness complaints were taken forward and 63% upheld.[30] It can be seen that the complaints about standards are roughly comparable with those received by the ITC, while the BSC noted that for

---

[30] BSC, *Annual Review 1998/99*, pp 9–10. Of the 139 fairness complaints, nine related to privacy, and 37 to fairness and privacy.

1998–99, there had been a 42% increase in the number of complaints. Nevertheless, it must be questioned whether the BSC has any real function, at least in the areas we have been considered here, given the responsibilities of the ITC, the RA and the BBC.[31] It is difficult to envisage that commercial broadcasters would view a finding against them as having the same impact as one by the ITC or the RA. While, the opportunity for persons, dealt with unfairly, to complain and, if vindicated, have a statement broadcast, may be welcome to the public, this right offers nothing which could not already be achieved through the use of ITC and RA sanctions, and BBC practice. However, perhaps in one respect the broadcasters do heed the activities of the BSC. Despite, the very low number of fairness complaints, the broadcasters have been ready to challenge the BSC's jurisdiction. This may be because, here, the broadcasters are alive to the potential impact of fairness adjudications on broadcasting freedom, and seek to protect that freedom by monitoring closely the BSC's exercise of its remit.

Question for discussion
Might the BBC regard BSC adjudications more seriously?

5. POLITICAL AND ELECTION BROADCASTING

(a) Introduction

The obligation to ensure impartiality has already been considered. The rules on political and election broadcasting bear a relationship to this obligation because they aim to preserve a balance between the political parties and to avoid promotion of any one political party. The extent to which political and election broadcasting should take place is a difficult and sensitive matter. The pervasiveness of broadcasting makes it an attractive medium for politicians to put across their message, and there will be a temptation for political parties to try to ensure as much access as possible to radio and television outlets. However, equally, broadcasters may be sensitive to pressures being put on them by the politicians, and may wish to resist pressures for access in order to preserve their independence and the balance of their output.

It is important to be clear about the meaning of political broadcasts. Programmes such as news, current affairs, and those about political or current issues will be under the control of the broadcasters and will have to comply with the rules on impartiality and fairness. It is also important to distinguish political and election broadcasting from political advertising. Although some modern political and election broadcasting may have presentational styles more usually associated with advertising, paid political advertising is banned (see Chapter 6). A key consideration in the following discussion is what

[31] For an evaluation of the BSC, see Gibbons, pp 264–274.

provisions are made to allow political parties to broadcast messages during an election campaign and at other times. These are issues which affect public and private broadcasters. Once more it is an area which illustrates the differences between press and broadcasting regulation; the former not being under any constraints like those considered here.

Even accepting that it is important that political parties should have access to broadcasting outlets, there remain difficult questions to be resolved about who should have access and how much access should be allowed. Although there are specific statutory obligations, access is mainly resolved through negotiation between the political parties and broadcasters, leaving considerable discretion in the hands of the broadcasters and regulatory bodies. Some radio and television licensees have obligations, under their licences, to broadcast political messages (Extract 4.5.1).[32] The BBC Charter and Agreement do not include specific obligations, but the BBC regards itself, as part of its public service mandate, obliged to include such broadcasts.[33] Additional rules and guidance are given by the ITC and the RA in their programme codes, and the BBC sets out rules in the *Producers' Guidelines*. Both the BBC and the private broadcasters are subject to the same basic obligations although the legal sources of those obligations may differ.[34]

Extract 4.5.1

Broadcasting Act 1990, s 36(1), (3)

36.—(1) . . . any regional Channel 3 licence or licence to provide Channel 4 or 5 shall include—
  (a) conditions requiring the licence holder to include party political broadcasts in the licensed service; and
  (b) conditions requiring the licence holder to observe such rules with respect to party political broadcasts as the Commission may determine.
(2) [*Omitted*].
(3) Without prejudice to the generality of paragraph (b) of subsection (1), the Commission may determine for the purposes of that subsection—
  (a) the political parties on whose behalf party political broadcasts may be made; and
  (b) in relation to any political party on whose behalf such broadcasts may be made, the length and frequency of such broadcasts.

In the past the arrangements for allocating party political and election broadcast time were determined by the Party Political Broadcasting Committee,

---

[32] For radio, the obligation is imposed on national radio licensees pursuant to BA 1990, s 107.
[33] BBC, ITC, Radio Authority and S4C, *Consultation Paper on the Reform of Party Political Broadcasting* (January 1998), p 2.
[34] A E Boyle, 'Political Broadcasting, Fairness and Administrative Law' [1986] *Public Law* 562, at 568.

established in 1947.[35] The Committee was comprised of the main political parties, the BBC and the regulatory bodies. However, more recently, the Committee appears to have been something of a fiction; it had not met since 1983, and its business was carried out by the Secretary to the Government Chief Whip. During this period, the broadcasters themselves assumed increased responsibility for the allocation of broadcasting time, putting proposals to the 'Committee'. In June 1997, the broadcasters wrote to the Secretary of the Committee stating that in future they would receive representations directly from the political parties.[36] Conscious of the growing pressures for political broadcast time, arising out of developments such as devolution in Scotland and Wales, as well as the emergence of smaller, often single-issue, parties, the BBC, the ITC, the RA and the S4C Authority (responsible for the Welsh Channel) conducted a review of party political broadcasting which resulted in a Consultation Paper published in 1998, *Consultation Paper on the Reform of Party Political Broadcasting*. Some of the proposals from this review will be considered in the following sections, although at the time of writing some aspects are still under discussion. It needs to remembered that underlying all broadcasters' decisions about the allocation of political broadcast time will be the requirement that they observe the principles of impartiality and balance.

(b) Political broadcasts

The system which operated until now for party political broadcasts (PPBs) was that the broadcasters would make an annual offer of time to the political parties, the amount of air-time being based on a party's performance in a previous general election. As the Consultation Paper acknowledges, PPBs developed during a period when public access to politicians was much more limited.

Extract 4.5.2

BBC, ITC, RA and S4C Authority, *Consultation Paper on the Reform of Party Political Broadcasting* (January 1998), p 3

The annual series of PPBs was introduced for a different era before the televising of parliament and the expansion of broadcasting channels with an accompanying increase in news and current affairs programmes. The audience now has ample opportunity to see, hear and judge politicians on a wide range of subjects and in a wide range of situations, day by day and week by week; the PPBs now tend to draw more on the techniques of the advertising world than those of the public service broadcaster.

---

[35] Ibid, 575.
[36] Note 33, above, Appendix 1.

The Consultation Paper proposed that PPBs should cease, and that there should be an increase in the number of broadcasts at election times. This proposal was not acceptable to the political parties. One can appreciate the attraction of PPBs for political parties, given that they provide an opportunity for them to put their case to the public without the constraints and pitfalls of an interview.[37] However, audience interest for such broadcasts tends to be small. Moreover, politicians can no longer rely on a captive audience, because the rapid increase in the number of channels provides greater opportunities for audiences to 'switch-off'. The future of these broadcasts is not yet resolved. In June 1999, the ITC and the BBC, jointly, made further proposals which, at the time of writing, are under discussion with the political parties. Essentially the proposal is that PPBs continue, but their transmission should coincide with key events in the political calendar, such as the Budget, party conferences and the Queen's speech, when the public are likely to be more interested in party political messages.[38]

Questions for discussion
1.   Do PPBs have a role to play in the promotion of broadcasting freedom?
2.   Should audience interest be a relevant consideration?

(c) Election broadcasts

The allocation of election broadcasts has also been a matter left largely to the discretion of the broadcasting sector. The general practice has been that a party nominating at least 50 candidates at a General Election would be offered one five-minute broadcast by each broadcaster, and further broadcasts would be dependent upon previous electoral support. Arrangements were also in place for other elections. Understandably, election broadcast allocations have caused much more contention than the allocation of PPBs. There have been a number of challenges to the decisions made by the broadcasting bodies. In the 1997 General Election, a new party, the Referendum Party, challenged its allocation of one election broadcast per broadcaster.

Extract 4.5.3

R v British Broadcasting Company and Another, ex parte Referendum Party **[1997] EMLR 605, at 608 and 618–620**

AULD LJ: The Referendum Party argues that those allocations are irrational, and for that reason unlawful, because the broadcasters:

---

[37] Broadcasters do provide opportunities for ministerial broadcasts during events of national or international importance. Budget broadcasts are also carried. Opposition parties are offered an opportunity to reply to both types of broadcasts.

[38] ITC and BBC, *ITC and BBC Announce Revisions to Rules on Political Broadcasting* (28 June 1999).

1. wrongly included in the criteria for their decisions past electoral support, something that a new party could not show;

2. failed to take account of its electoral size and support, especially the large number of candidates it is fielding in the election.

. . .

The Referendum Party is a new political party . . . According to its manifesto, its purpose in contesting this parliamentary election is 'to obtain a full public debate on Britain's relationship with Europe followed by a fair referendum' and thereafter to dissolve. It has not previously contested any elections and, thus, has no record of previous electoral support. It has one sitting Member of Parliament, Sir George Gardiner, the Member for Reigate who transferred from the Conservative Party to it shortly before the election was announced. It claims to have written pledges of support from about 200,000 potential electors and recent opinion poll indications of present support of over 3 per cent, and growing, of the vote. It has a national office and is fielding candidates, supported by agents from constituency offices, in about 85 per cent of the United Kingdom constituencies, except for Northern Ireland. That is 547 out of 659. . . .

Mr David Pannick Q.C., for the BBC, and Mr Christopher Clarke Q.C. for the ITC made the following points in reply to this part of Mr Robertson's [counsel for the Party] argument on irrationality. First, . . . the broadcasters are subject to no criteria, statutory or otherwise, save that of impartiality in reaching their decisions, and there is no over-arching constitutional requirement by which they are to be judged. Second, Parliament has left them, as independent bodies, with a discretion to make the decisions, and the discretion is necessarily broad because the subject matter is difficult and potentially contentious. In such an area, they submitted, the courts should be slow to intervene. Third, as appears from the evidence which we have summarised, neither broadcaster treated the Referendum Party's unavoidable lack of previous electoral support as itself disqualifying it from allocation of more than one broadcast; that was one of a number of factors and they examined the others.

In our view, neither the broadcasters' inclusion of past electoral support as part of their general criteria for allocating party election broadcasts nor their treatment of the lack of it in this case was irrational. Impartiality in this context is not to be equated with parity or balance as between political parties of different strengths, popular support and appeal. See *Lynch v BBC* [1983] NI 193, QBD, *per* Hutton J at 202C–E; and *cf. Wilson v Independent Broadcasting Authority* [1979] SC 351, OH, *per* Lord Ross at 359 and 361–362. It means fairness of allocation having regard to those factors, yet making allowance for any significant current changes in the political arena and for the potential effect of the powerful medium of television itself in advancing or hindering such changes. Where it exists, past electoral support is obviously a relevant consideration, though only one, and an imprecise one at that, for assessing for this purpose the current strength of a political party relative to that of others. Clearly it would be absurd for broadcasters to allow it to be determinative or to regard it as a pre-condition for allocation of more than one party election broadcast. . . .

The second limb of Mr Robertson's argument is that, despite the protestations of the broadcasters to the contrary, they cannot have had any or any proper regard to the current strength of and support for the Referendum Party, in particular to the many candidates it is fielding. He submitted that the resultant disparity between allocations to it and to the other national parties is disproportionate. He suggested that its allocation is equivalent to that for a party contesting only about 8 per cent of the parliamentary constituencies instead of the 85 per cent that its 547 candidates constitute. . . .

As we have said, Mr Robertson placed most reliance on the number of candidates that the Referendum Party is fielding as the mark of its standing and support in comparison with the main national parties. Mr Pannick and Mr Clarke observed that, whilst the number of candidates was a factor, it was only one of a number and that it was for the broadcasters to determine its weight in conjunction with the other indications of support on which the Party relied. The broadcasters had taken all those matters into account, no doubt observing that, whilst the Party rivalled the three main candidates in the number of candidates, its claimed 3 per cent of committed support was well below the poll indications of any of theirs. In short, they argued that the broadcasters' assessment of the relevant factors and the individual and cumulative weight that they gave to them were essentially matters for their judgment . . .

In our view, Mr Pannick and Mr Clarke are correct in their submissions. The evidence before the Court shows that the Referendum Party, through its solicitors, made full representations to the broadcasters about its strength and support and that the broadcasters considered those representations. The broadcasters' criteria for allocation of further party election broadcasts where the threshold condition of 50 candidates is established are, in our view, reasonable – a combination of past electoral support, where there is any, and the present number of candidates.

Following the consultation, some changes have been agreed for allocating election broadcasts. Election broadcasts series have been introduced for Scottish Parliamentary and Welsh Assembly elections and for Northern Ireland. As before, parties will be offered broadcasts of five minutes, although, as requested by them, parties can now elect to have a three or four-minute slot. Election broadcasts must now be shown between 5.30 pm and 11.30 pm. Most significantly, the qualification threshold has been increased. A party must contest at least one sixth of the seats to qualify for at least one election broadcast. This means that for a General Election a party would now have to contest about 110 seats.[39] The Consultation Paper noted that in the 1997 General Election eight parties, not currently represented in Parliament, qualified for an election broadcast. None of these parties received more than 2.6% of the total vote and seven received less than 0.3%.[40] The factors discussed in Extract 4.5.3 will be still relevant to the broadcaster deciding whether to allocate further broadcasts to a party, not represented in Parliament.

[39] Note 33, above, p 5.
[40] Ibid, p 4.

In addition to the requirements to act impartially, the broadcasters are also subject to the constraints of the Representation of the People Act 1983. In particular, s 93 imposes restrictions on the broadcasting of items within constituencies. In its Annual Report for 1997, the ITC stated that it believed that s 93 should be repealed or reformed as it functioned as an 'obstacle to free and fair reporting'.[41]

Extract 4.5.4

Representation of the People Act 1983, s 93(1)

93.—(1) In relation to a parliamentary or local government election—
    (a) pending such an election it shall not be lawful for any item about the constituency or electoral area to be—
        [... broadcast ...]
        if any of the persons who are for the time being candidates at the election takes part in the item and the broadcast is not made with his consent; and
    (b) where an item about a constituency or electoral area is so broadcast pending such an election there, then if the broadcast either is made before the latest time for delivery of nomination papers, or is made after that time but without the consent of any candidate remaining validly nominated, any person taking part in the item for the purpose of promoting or so procuring his election shall be guilty of an illegal practice, unless the broadcast is so made without his consent.

Both the ITC's and RA's Codes have very detailed provisions covering these restraints, as does the BBC's *Producers' Guidelines*. One of the concerns expressed by broadcasters is that s 93 effectively ensures that candidates, even quite minor candidates, can veto programmes which could be of considerable value to the public. Equally, the provisions may operate as a restraint on programme making. In one general election, a broadcaster had to abandon plans to follow the progress of black candidates across the country because of concern that other candidates could veto their appearance.[42] During several by-elections plans to broadcast round-table debates with candidates had to be cancelled because of vetoes by some candidates.[43]

Questions for discussion
1. Is there a need for s 93 or would the impartiality rules be sufficient to ensure balanced coverage during elections?
2. What is the relationship between s 93 and freedom of expression?

---

[41] ITC, *Annual Report and Accounts 1997* (1998), p 36.
[42] *Press Gazette*, 30 August 1996, p 14.
[43] P Harding, 'Letter to the Editor', *Daily Telegraph*, 17 June 1996, p 21.

(d) Referendums

Referendums can be seen more clearly as simply requiring a balancing out of different sides of an issue.[44] However, difficulties can still arise. In the 1979 referendum on Scottish devolution, the IBA's approach to allocation of broadcasts was challenged. The IBA (and the BBC, although they were not a party to these proceedings) had allocated one political broadcast to each of the four main Scottish political parties using an approach similar to that used for election broadcasts. However, this was likely to result in three broadcasts advocating a 'yes' vote and only one 'no' vote broadcast. The petitioners successfully argued that the IBA had failed in its statutory duty to maintain a proper balance.

Extract 4.5.5

Wilson v Independent Broadcasting Authority 1979 SLT 279, at 283–284 (Court of Session, Outer House)

LORD ROSS: I accept that when arranging party political broadcasts in connection with a general election, all possible political viewpoints cannot be covered, and, for example, some participants in a general election and some minor parties may be excluded ... But, the situation is different with a referendum where the electorate is being invited to answer a question 'Yes' or 'No'. Where the subject-matter of programmes being broadcast is the referendum, I am of opinion that a proper balance must be maintained between programmes favouring 'Yes' and programmes favouring 'No'. It is plain from both the petition and the answers that the party political broadcasts with which the petitioners are concerned are not normal party political broadcasts but are to be devoted specifically to the issue to be put to the electorate in the referendum. This puts them in a special category and they cannot be treated as if they were ordinary political broadcasts.

Question for discussion

Does *Wilson* mean that during referendums, broadcasters can ignore parties' requests for broadcast time and concentrate entirely on the issue of the referendum?

Mindful of *Wilson* the broadcasters have refrained from introducing any set rules to allocate time during referendums.

(e) Impartiality

During election campaigns, broadcasters will still be required to observe the rules on impartiality. During the 1997 General Election campaign there was

---

[44] Barendt, p 178.

discussion about the possibility of a televised debate between the main party leaders. There were difficulties in reaching agreement about what would be fair between the parties, so the debate did not proceed.[45] However, before it was clear that the debate would not go ahead, the Scottish National Party, fearing that their party leader would not be included, commenced proceedings for an interdict (injunction) to prevent the debate on the ground that it would infringe the rules on impartiality. The application was dismissed by the Court of Session on the ground that the matter was hypothetical since no arrangements for the debate had been concluded. However, the court did consider the responsibilities of impartiality.

Extract 4.5.6

Scottish National Party v Scottish Television plc and Another, 15 April 1997, LEXIS (Court of Session, Outer House)

LORD EASSIE: It might also be said indeed that an interview with one political spokesman must by definition involve partiality and that where several viewpoints obtain, a programme which gives scope to only some of them, will, in isolation, also be partial. For that very practical reason also it is in my view plain that in judging whether a licensee is observing due impartiality, particularly in the context of political broadcasting in an election campaign, it is the generality or entirety of the broadcasting output in the relevant field to which one must look, rather than a single programme in isolation.

While the approach of the court appears to be a practical one, it may limit the scope for parties to challenge decisions taken by broadcasters. As Munro has commented:

> Once it is accepted that the obligation to preserve 'due impartiality' can only properly be judged across a range of programmes and over time, then there will in any event be difficulties in abstracting any particular programme or programmes, because there may always be others to put in the equation or additional or balancing programmes to be taken into account.[46]

However, in an earlier decision, the court has been prepared to prevent a programme proceeding which might have resulted in a lack of impartiality. In 1995, during a Scottish local election period, the BBC planned to broadcast an interview with the then Prime Minister, John Major on *Panorama*. The broadcast would have occurred three days before the election. The interdict, which prevented the broadcast in Scotland until the close of polls, was obtained only a few hours before the programme was due to be

---

[45] C Munro, 'The 1997 General Election and Media Law' (1997) 2(5) *Communications Law* 166, at 167.
[46] Ibid, at 168.

broadcast.[47] The following discussion by Munro provides a good overview of the issues.

Extract 4.5.7

C Munro, 'The Banned Broadcasting Corporation' [1995] *New Law Journal* 518, at 519–520 (some footnotes omitted)

The circumstances

. . . For the pursuers, it was argued that an extended interview with the party leader on the BBC's flagship current affairs programme would give the Conservatives an advantage, when corresponding opportunities had not been made available to Messrs Blair and Ashdown. For the defenders, counsel tried to deny that a searching interview need be viewed as advantageous, and tried to deny that the subject matter would be very relevant to local elections, whereas the pursuers had argued that it was naive to suggest that British political issues and local political issues were separable.

More generally, it was argued for the BBC that it was the *totality* of political coverage which fell to be considered, and that over time or over a series of programmes they would treat the political parties with due impartiality, as was always their aim.

However, the issue was crucially sharpened by the proximity of the local elections being held in Scotland on April 6, a few weeks ahead of elections in England. . . .

Significantly, the BBC also appeared to have failed to make arrangements to afford equal or reasonable prominence to other party leaders in the run-up to the election. . . .

Comment

Some caution is advisable, in case too much weight is given to the *Panorama* decision, which was, after all, only argued on an interim interdict basis, and hurriedly at that. That said, it needs to be remembered that applications for interim interdicts or injunctions are very important in practice, because matters often need not or do not proceed beyond that stage.

So far as the media are concerned, restraints on publication are erosions of their freedom, even when the ban is temporary rather than permanent. The United States Supreme Court has famously held that 'any system of prior restraint on expression comes to this court bearing a heavy presumption against its constitutional validity'.[i] In the absence of such fundamental guarantees as the First Amendment, we must hope that British courts will give proper weight to a presumption against prior restraints, but the decisions in the *Panorama* case were not encouraging in this respect.

---

[47] An appeal was dismissed only half an hour before the programme was due to be broadcast. The following day, leave to appeal to the House of Lords was refused: *Houston v British Broadcasting Corporation* 1995 SLT 1305.

Earlier decisions, in cases involving the Independent Broadcasting Authority, seemed to suggest something akin to a 'margin of discretion' for the broadcasters, with courts apparently reluctant to intervene except in the most flagrant circumstances. . . .

. . . [O]ne wonders if the Court of Session did not act rather precipitately in banning a single television programme of uncertain influence when, apart from other considerations, there was still a period of two clear days in which perceived imbalances or partiality might have been redressed. In the result, the courts have cast themselves in the role of censors, and their actions have formed an unattractive precedent. It is understandable that Mr Tony Hall (the BBC's Managing Director of News and Current Affairs) should regard the decision as an 'objector's charter', and that Mr Michael Grade (the chief executive of Channel 4) should fear that 'we are all going to be in the courts forever'.

[i] In *New York Times v US* 403 US 713 (1971), at p 729 (the 'Pentagon Papers' case).

Questions for discussion
1.   Do you agree with Munro that the court acted precipitately?
2.   Should it be a relevant consideration for the court, as Munro seems to suggest, that the influence of the programme might be uncertain?
3.   Comparing the *Scottish National Party* and the *Panorama* cases, do they suggest that it may be easier to establish a case the nearer one comes to the election date?

(f) Content of party political and election broadcasts

Although broadcasters are under obligations to ensure impartiality, the political parties are free to promote their own views during political broadcasts. However, broadcasts by political parties must comply with other programme standards as well as the general law.

Extract 4.5.8

ITC, *Programme Code* (Autumn 1998), 4.1(iii)

Editorial control of the content of PPBs and PEBs normally rests with the originating political party but licensees are responsible to the ITC for ensuring that nothing transmitted breaches Programme Code requirements on matters of offence to good taste and decency.

The 1997 General Election gave rise to some difficulties in this area. It is perhaps significant that these concerned single-issue parties. Political election broadcasts by the Pro-Life Alliance Party and the British National Party were subject to viewer complaints.[48] The complaints were not upheld. In agreeing to screen the Pro-Life broadcast, the broadcasters had obscured certain images. The Party, unsuccessfully, sought leave to bring judicial review proceedings. In its challenge, it argued that the right to freedom of expression had been infringed.

Extract 4.5.9

R v British Broadcasting Corporation, ex parte The Pro-life Alliance Party, 24 March 1997, LEXIS

DYSON J: Both the common law and the European Convention recognise that the right to freedom of expression is not totally untrammelled. It is subject to exceptions, and, quite rightly in my judgment, it was accepted by Mr Diamond [counsel for the Party] . . . that one of the limitations on that right arises where an untrammelled freedom of expression will interfere with another conflicting right, which is the right of members of the public not to be subjected to unduly offensive material. The striking of the balance between those two rights is a matter which sometimes calls for a difficult exercise of judgment. The decision-makers such as the BBC who operate in this sphere, have a margin of appreciation. Despite the arguments of Mr Diamond . . . , I am not persuaded that I ought to adopt an approach other than the conventional Wednesbury approach to these matters. I have in mind of course that freedom of expression is an important human right. Having read the affidavit of . . . [the BBC Chief Political Adviser] and having for myself seen the video of the offending part of the transmission, I am in no doubt that the decision of the BBC fell well within its margin of appreciation, notwithstanding that issues of freedom of expression are at stake in this case.

(g) The future of political broadcasting

Political broadcasting has the potential for unearthing many of the most central questions concerning the structure and regulation of broadcasting. The 1997 General Election resulted in more legal challenges than any other election that century.[49] With the changing political arena and the Human Rights Act 1998, it is not likely that this will be an isolated phenomenon. Munro's reservations about the desirability of judicial intervention should be taken seriously (Extract 4.5.7). Moreover, broadcasters may not welcome finding themselves regularly in court having their decisions challenged. However, given the sensitivities of political broadcasting, judicial review could bring a transparency to this area which might be welcome for both broadcasters and political parties.[50]

---

[48] ITC, *Programme Complaints and Interventions* (April/May 1997), pp 5 and 3, respectively. The former concerned 'taste and decency', the latter 'racial offence'.
[49] Munro, note 45, above, at 166.
[50] See also Gibbons, *Regulating the Media*, p 118.

5

EUROPEAN BROADCASTING LAW

1. INTRODUCTION

Traditionally, broadcasting regulation was a matter for the nation state and national governments. Who should be allowed to broadcast, and what could or should be broadcast were matters viewed as intrinsically linked with the language, culture and identity of the country in which the broadcast took place. In Europe, however, it was never quite as straightforward as this. Radio broadcasting signals were often received by countries with neighbouring borders, and as terrestrial television developed, the same phenomenon occurred. Broadcasting signals could not be neatly contained within national borders when so many countries existed in such close proximity, frequently sharing a common language. Germany, Austria and Switzerland, and the Netherlands and Belgium are obvious examples. However, these technical overspills were largely incidental to the broadcaster's main focus of coverage and did not create major difficulties. Indeed some countries, such as those just mentioned, benefited by establishing co-operation agreements enabling greater access to programme material.[1] Technological developments which enabled a more widespread transmission of broadcasting signals by cable, and, more particularly, satellite, created a greater incentive for broadcasters to reach a wider audience. This form of broadcasting raised a number of questions. Who should be responsible for regulating the broadcast and its content? Was the receiving country free to prevent transmission of a foreign broadcasting service, particularly if it was contrary to national rules on content or advertising? As satellite broadcasting developed, and viewers could receive such broadcasts directly, by means of their own receiving dishes, it was also apparent that governments might find it difficult to enforce regulation even where they considered it desirable or necessary.[2]

---

[1] F W Hondius, 'Regulating Transfrontier Television – The Strasbourg Option' (1988) 8 *Yearbook of European Law* 141, at 146.

[2] See, for example, the *Debauve* case (Extract 5.3.5 below) where the Belgian government did not enforce a law which it knew was being breached by cable operators, in part because it was aware that viewers were able to receive directly what was prohibited for retransmission by cable operators.

Within Europe, however, there was the potential for resolving these difficulties through co-ordinated regional action, given the existence of the European Community and the Council of Europe. In this chapter, the jurisdictional basis for action by the two organisations will be examined. The institutions of the European Community and the Council of Europe bring to the broadcasting sector a range of concerns about transfrontier broadcasting: economic; industrial; cultural; and human rights. In trying to develop a European regulatory framework for broadcasting, there were doubts about which was the appropriate organisation to have responsibility. The Council of Europe, with its particular concern for human rights protection, and its wider European membership,[3] would seem the logical choice; the European Community, with its narrower membership base, and its mandate for economic integration, might appear the less suitable. In fact, both organisations have produced legal instruments for the regulation for broadcasting. For the Council of Europe, there is the *European Convention on Transfrontier Television* (the Television Convention), and for the European Community, the *Television without Frontiers Directive* (the Television Directive). Despite their different origins, both instruments have substantial similarities. These instruments, but, particularly, the Television Directive, will be looked at later in this chapter.

2. THE COUNCIL OF EUROPE – JURISDICTION

The most important of the treaties entered into by the members of the Council of Europe is the European Convention for the Protection of Human Rights and Fundamental Freedoms (ECHR). Article 10 (see Extract 1.2.1) which guarantees freedom of expression is of particular relevance to broadcasting. However, the right to freedom of expression is not an unqualified right (see Chapter 1, Section 2(a)). In *Groppera Radio* the European Court of Human Rights had to consider the application of art 10 to transfrontier broadcasting. What scope would a state have for controlling transfrontier broadcasting? A Swiss radio company, via a subsidiary, had been broadcasting, intentionally into Switzerland, from Italy, radio programmes consisting mainly of light music and advertising. The programmes were received directly over the air and were also relayed by cable companies within Switzerland. The purpose in setting up the station had been to evade the Swiss state broadcasting monopoly. The Swiss government prohibited cable operators from broadcasting programmes which did not comply with the relevant international radio and telecommunication laws concerned with orderly use of

---

[3] All members of the European Community are also members of the Council of Europe. It has become common to use the terms 'European Community' and 'European Union' interchangeably. The matters under discussion in this chapter, however, concern the European Community.

the radio frequency spectrum. The applicants challenged the prohibition arguing before the European Court of Human Rights that the ban on cable constituted an infringement of their right to 'impart information and ideas ... regardless of frontiers' under art 10.

Extract 5.2.1

Groppera Radio AG and Others v Switzerland **(1990) 12 EHRR 321, at 337, 338–339, 340, 342–343 (footnotes omitted)**

As to the ... [Swiss Government's] submission [that the content of the programmes was not information or ideas], the Court does not consider it necessary to give on this occasion a precise definition of what is meant by 'information' and 'ideas.' 'Broadcasting' is mentioned in the Convention precisely in relation to freedom of expression. ... [T]he Court considers that both broadcasting of programmes over the air and cable retransmission of such programmes are covered by the right enshrined in the first two sentences of Article 10(1), without there being any need to draw distinctions according to the content of the programmes. ... [Having held that there was an interference by a public authority with the exercise of the Article 10 right, the Court had to consider whether that interference was justified. The answer to this turned on how the third sentence of Article 10(1) (entitling states to require licensing of broadcasting) was to be understood, and its relationship to Article 10(2).]
. . .
The insertion of the sentence in issue, at an advanced stage of the preparatory work on the Convention, was clearly due to technical or practical considerations such as the limited number of available frequencies and the major capital investment required for building transmitters. It also reflected a political concern on the part of several States, namely that broadcasting should be the preserve of the State. Since then, changed views and technical progress, particularly the appearance of cable transmission, have resulted in the abolition of State monopolies in many European countries and the establishment of private radio stations – often local ones – in addition to the public services. Furthermore, national licensing systems are required not only for the orderly regulation of broadcasting enterprises at the national level but also in large part to give effect to international rules ...

The object and purpose of the third sentence of Article 10(1) and the scope of its application must however be considered in the context of the Article as a whole and in particular in relation to the requirements of paragraph (2).
. . .
The Court observes that Article 19 of the 1966 International Covenant on Civil and Political Rights[4] does not include a provision corresponding to the third sentence of Article 10(1). The negotiating history of Article 19 shows that the inclusion of such a provision in that Article had been proposed with a view to the licensing not of the information imparted but rather of the technical

---

[4] See Extract 9.4.3 below.

means of broadcasting in order to prevent chaos in the use of frequencies. However, its inclusion was opposed on the ground that it might be utilised to hamper free expression, and it was decided that such a provision was not necessary because licensing in the sense intended was deemed to be covered by the reference to 'public order' in paragraph (3) of the Article.

This supports the conclusion that the purpose of the third sentence of Article 10(1) of the Convention is to make it clear that States are permitted to control by a licensing system the way in which broadcasting is organised in their territories, particularly in its technical aspects. It does not, however, provide that licensing measures shall not otherwise be subject to the requirements of paragraph 2, for that would lead to a result contrary to the object and purpose of Article 10 taken as a whole.

The sentence in question accordingly applies in the instant case inasmuch as it permits the orderly control of broadcasting in Switzerland. . . .

In sum, the interference was in accordance with the third sentence of paragraph 10(1); it remains to be determined whether it also satisfied the conditions in paragraph (2). . . .

Legitimate aim

The Government contended that the impugned interference pursued two aims recognised by the Convention.

The first of these was the 'prevention of disorder' in telecommunications. . . .

The Government submitted, secondly, that the interference complained of was for the 'protection of the . . . rights of others,' as it was designed to ensure pluralism, in particular of information, by allowing a fair allocation of frequencies internationally and nationally. This applied both to foreign radio stations, whose programmes had been lawfully retransmitted by cable. . . .

. . .

The Court finds that the interference in issue pursued both the aims relied on, which were fully compatible with Article 10(2) namely the protection of the international telecommunications order and the protection of the rights of others.

'Necessary in a democratic society'

The applicants submitted that the ban affecting them did not answer a pressing social need; in particular, it went beyond the requirements of the aims being pursued. It was tantamount to censorship or jamming.

The Government stated that it had no other recourse seeing that its representations to the Italian authorities continued to be fruitless. . . .

According to the Court's settled case law, the Contracting States enjoy a certain margin of appreciation in assessing whether and to what extent an interference is necessary, but this margin goes hand in hand with European supervision covering both the legislation and the decisions applying it; when carrying out that supervision, the Court must ascertain whether the measures taken at national level are justifiable in principle and proportionate.

In order to verify that the interference was not excessive in the instant case, the requirements of protecting the international telecommunications order as well as the rights of others must be weighed against the interest of the applicants and others in the retransmission of [the] . . . programmes by cable. The Court reiterates, firstly, that once the 1983 Ordinance had come into force, most Swiss cable companies ceased retransmitting the programmes in question. Moreover, the Swiss authorities never jammed the broadcasts . . . , although they made approaches to Italy and the International Telecommunications Union. Thirdly, the impugned ban was imposed on a company incorporated under Swiss law . . . whose subscribers all lived on Swiss territory and continued to receive the programmes of several other stations. Lastly and above all, the procedure chosen could well appear necessary in order to prevent evasion of the law; it was not a form of censorship directed against the content or tendencies of the programmes concerned, but a measure taken against a station which the authorities of the respondent State could reasonably hold to be in reality a Swiss station operating from the other side of the border in order to circumvent the statutory telecommunications system in force in Switzerland.

Questions for discussion

1. Would the Court have taken a different approach if the Swiss government had jammed the broadcasts?

2. What would the Court's reaction have been, if the Swiss government had banned, say the advertising content of the broadcasts?

In *Autronic AG v Switzerland*[5] the Court emphasised that ECHR, art 10 applied not only to content but also to the means of transmission or reception of the broadcast. In this case, the Swiss government was not justified in prohibiting reception by a dish aerial of satellite broadcasts received in uncoded form.[6] The decision was also a recognition that satellite broadcasting was becoming common.

The *Groppera* and *Autronic* decisions were significant because they reminded European governments that they would have to be able to justify any laws which restricted the flow of transfrontier broadcasting. Although in *Groppera* the Court had held that the Swiss government's actions had been justified under art 10, it was nevertheless clear that a government's scope for licensing and controlling broadcasting within its own borders could be limited. *Groppera* showed that a state could be justified in controlling broadcasting for technical reasons, and the Court, in *Informationsverein Lentia* (see Extract 1.2.4), provided further guidance on the type of matters which might be relevant to a state's licensing policy. However, it was clear that this pragmatic approach would not resolve all the difficulties which could arise as broadcasters sought to expand their activities and audiences. It was this

---

[5] (1990) 12 EHRR 485.
[6] The facts of this case concerned a broadcast via a telecommunications satellite, but, today, there is little practical difference between broadcasts using telecommunications satellites and those made by direct broadcasting satellites.

recognition which led to moves to reach agreement on a common framework for European broadcasting, which eventually resulted in the Television Convention. In the following extract, the relationship between the right to freedom of expression and the Television Convention is described.

Extract 5.2.2

**Hondius, 'Regulating Transfrontier Television – The Strasbourg Option'
(1988) 8 *Yearbook of European Law* 141, at 148 and 159–160
(footnotes omitted)**

In the Council of Europe, the existence of frontiers between States is accepted as a reality. Television, and in particular satellite broadcasting, can help to enhance the free flow of information and ideas across those frontiers and, as it stated in Article 10 . . . 'regardless of frontiers'.

. . .

The purpose of the Convention is to achieve a framework for the transfrontier circulation of television programmes. It does not seek to regulate the broadcasting activities, policies and structures of the Member States. It remains for every country to determine these in accordance with its own traditions. Nor does the Convention seek to impinge on the independence and autonomy of the broadcasters. Rather, it sets out a number of basic standards, notably on the rights of viewers, the duties of States, programming standards, advertising, and sponsorship. Under Article 4, parties to the Convention guarantee the non-restriction of the *re*-transmission of programme services conforming to these standards, it being understood that in any case there may be no interference with the transmission and direct reception of programme services, whether conforming or not. The latter principle follows from Article 10 of the European Human Rights Convention.

3. EUROPEAN COMMUNITY – JURISDICTION

The European Community, with its mandate for the establishment of the common market and the requirement that goods, services, and persons should have freedom of movement within the Community, made it perhaps inevitable that broadcasting would be brought within this framework. The European Community Treaty (the EC Treaty) contains no specific reference to broadcasting. Specific competence in the field of culture was only introduced by the Maastricht Treaty on European Union which came into force in 1993. Despite the specific mention of the audiovisual sector in art 151, this treaty provision has added little to the powers of the Community. The wording is rather vague and, at best, aspirational. Moreover, Article 151 seems to be more of a reminder to the Community of Member States' sovereignty, than an encouragement of Community action. It is notable that art 151(5) specifically excludes any harmonising measures, and requires incentive measures to have the unanimous consent of the Council.[7] Despite its limitations, art 151 may have a role in reminding the Community that cultural matters cannot be disregarded in the pursuit of the internal market. On 1 May 1999, the Treaty of Amsterdam, which amended the EC Treaty, came into force. As a result all articles of the EC Treaty have been renumbered. Extracts 5.3.1 and 5.3.3 refer to articles as renumbered, but the old numbering is given in brackets. References to EC Treaty provisions within other extracts in this chapter, such as judgments of the European Court of Justice will be to the old numbering.

Extract 5.3.1

EC Treaty, art 151 (1)–(4) (formerly 128)

1. The Community shall contribute to the flowering of the cultures of the Member States, while respecting their national and regional diversity and at the same time bringing the common cultural heritage to the fore.
2. Action by the Community shall be aimed at encouraging cooperation between Member States and, if necessary, supporting and supplementing their action in the following areas:
– improvement of the knowledge and dissemination of the culture and history of the European peoples;
– conservation and safeguarding of cultural heritage of European significance;
– non-commercial cultural exchanges;
– artistic and literary creation, including in the audiovisual sector.
3. The Community and the Member States shall foster cooperation with third countries and the competent international organisations in the sphere of culture, in particular the Council of Europe.
4. The Community shall take cultural aspects into account in its action under other provisions of this Treaty, in particular in order to respect and to promote the diversity of its cultures.

By the time of the Maastricht Treaty, it was already well-established that broadcasting came within the ambit of the EC Treaty. It was in 1974, in *Italy v Sacchi* (extracted below), that the European Court of Justice (ECJ) first had to consider the relationship between Community law and broadcasting. Sacchi was the owner of a cable undertaking which was transmitting television programmes, produced by the undertaking, or retransmitting programmes received by cable. Mr Sacchi had refused to pay the licence fee which was required from those operating apparatus enabling the reception of broadcasting transmissions. The Italian government had granted to Radio Audizione Italiana (RAI) a monopoly on television broadcasting and commercial television advertising and the licence fee was used to fund this operation. As a

---

[7] See, further, R Lane, 'New Community Competences under the Maastricht Treaty' (1993) 30 *Common Market Law Review* 939.

defence to proceedings brought for failure to pay the licence fee, Sacchi had argued that this monopoly restricted the reception into Italy of foreign programmes and advertisements, and, therefore, prevented the free movement of goods. The ECJ rejected this argument but, importantly, decided that broadcasting was covered by the EC Treaty.

Extract 5.3.2

Case 155/73 *Italy v Sacchi* [1974] ECR 409, at 427

In the absence of express provision to the contrary in the Treaty, a television signal must, by reason of its nature, be regarded as provision of services.

Although it is not ruled out that services normally provided for remuneration may come under the provisions relating to free movement of goods, such is however the case, ... only insofar as they are governed by such provisions.

It follows that the transmission of television signals, including those in the nature of advertisements, comes, as such, within the rules of the Treaty relating to services.

On the other hand, trade in material, sound recordings, films, apparatus and other products used for the diffusion of television signals are subject to the rules relating to freedom of movement for goods.

The EC Treaty provisions affecting broadcasting can be seen in the following extract.

Extract 5.3.3

EC Treaty, arts 46(1), 49 and 50

Article 46(1) (formerly 56(1))

1.   The provisions of this Chapter [right of establishment][8] and measures taken in pursuance thereof shall not prejudice the applicability of provisions laid down by law, regulation or administrative action providing for special treatment for foreign nationals on grounds of public policy, public security or public health.

Article 49 (formerly 59)

Within the framework of the provisions set out below, restrictions on freedom to provide services within the Community shall be prohibited in respect of nationals of Member States who are established in a State of the Community other than that of the person for whom the services are intended.

   . . .

---

[8] Article 55 applies this article to the Chapter of the Treaty on services.

Article 50 (formerly 60)

Services shall be considered to be 'services' within the meaning of this Treaty where they are normally provided for remuneration, insofar as they are not governed by the provisions relating to freedom of movement for goods, capital and persons.

. . .

The decision in *Sacchi* clearly brought broadcasting into European Community competence, by acknowledging that, to the extent that broadcasting had an economic or commercial function, it had a role to play in the completion of the internal market. However, it was less clear at that stage what scope there was for national control of broadcasting within the Community law framework. What was the relationship between Community law and national broadcasting law, particularly as much of the latter was framed to address particular national cultural and public interest concerns? What restrictions on broadcasting could be legitimately imposed? *SA Compagnie Générale pour la Diffusion de la Télévision, Coditel, and Others v SA Ciné Vog Films and Others* concerned the broadcasting of a film in Belgium by cable companies. They had picked up the television signal from Germany and relayed it by cable to their subscribers. The broadcast was an infringement of the exclusive rights held by a Belgian company to exhibit the film in Belgium at the cinema and on television, but the cable companies argued that exclusive rights were incompatible with the freedom to provide services. The ECJ rejected this argument.

Extract 5.3.4

Case 62/79 *SA Compagnie Générale pour la Diffusion de la Télévision, Coditel, and Others v SA Ciné Vog Films and Others* [1980] ECR 881, at 903

Whilst Article 59 of the Treaty prohibits restrictions upon freedom to provide services, it does not thereby encompass limits upon the exercise of certain economic activities which have their origin in the application of national legislation for the protection of intellectual property, save where such application constitutes a means of arbitrary discrimination or a disguised restriction on trade between Member States.

It was clear then from *Coditel* that the principle, free movement of services, did not prevent a Member State imposing restrictions on broadcasting. However, those restrictions could not discriminate between foreign and national broadcasters. The question of what scope there was for placing restrictions on this freedom again came before the ECJ, in *Debauve*, a case which also concerned Belgian law. At the time, Belgian law prohibited all advertising on television. This prohibition extended to foreign broadcasts relayed by cable for Belgian audiences, even though the inclusion of advertising was lawful in the country of original transmission. A number of the cable companies had ceased to remove the advertising transmitted with the foreign programmes. Many Belgian viewers were able to receive the programmes directly without the need for cable retransmission, although the Court did not consider that this rendered the law ineffective.

Extract 5.3.5

Case 52/79 *Procureur du Roi v Marc JVC Debauve and Others* [1980] ECR 833, at 856

From information given to the Court during these proceedings it appears that the television broadcasting of advertisements is subject to widely divergent systems of law in the various Member States, passing from almost total prohibition, as in Belgium, by way of rules comprising more or less strict restrictions, to systems affording broad commercial freedom. In the absence of any approximation of national laws and taking into account the considerations of general interest underlying the restrictive rules [in] this area, the application of the laws in question cannot be regarded as a restriction upon freedom to provide services so long as those laws treat all such services identically whatever their origin or the nationality or place of establishment of the persons providing them.

Question for discussion

In the *Coditel* and *Debauve* cases, what factors most influenced the Court in deciding that the restrictions were legitimate?

Although, the *Debauve* case showed that governments were free to restrict broadcasts according to the particular policies of that Member State, the ECJ had nevertheless made clear that such restrictions were only possible in the absence of harmonising legislation. In both *Coditel* and *Debauve*, the restrictions had been legitimate because they did not discriminate between national and foreign broadcasts. However, in *Bond van Adverteerders* the issue of discrimination was raised. Could discrimination between national and foreign broadcasters be legitimate if the purpose for that discrimination was to serve the Member State's public interest?

Dutch law prohibited cable companies broadcasting, by cable, advertising from outside the Netherlands which was intended for the Netherlands public, and programmes which were subtitled in Dutch. The rules were intended to prevent the de facto establishment of a commercial television service able to compete with the national service. The prohibition only applied to programmes transmitted by satellite and received by the cable companies for relay via cable. Although the cable companies also relayed programmes received

171

over the air, the Dutch government's view was that these were not covered by the prohibition because the cable companies were the passive receivers of programmes which could be received by viewers directly. Under Dutch law television advertising could only be arranged through a public monopoly (STER). The rules for the transmission of advertisements were strict, particularly with regard to the amount of time which was permitted for advertising. Many advertisers, feeling hampered by these rules, sought more flexible ways to reach the Dutch viewing public. The revenue from the sale of advertising arranged through STER was used primarily to subsidise Dutch broadcasting organisations. The advertisers sought to argue that the rules restricted the freedom to provide services within the Community. The ECJ held that the prohibitions were contrary to art 49 because they were discriminatory. The Court then had to consider whether the discrimination could be justified under art 46 (previously art 56 – see extract below).

Extract 5.3.6

Case 352/85 *Bond van Adverteerders and Others v The Netherlands State* [1988] ECR 2085, at 2135–2136

It must be pointed out that economic aims, such as that of securing for a national public foundation all the revenue from advertising intended especially for the public of the Member State in question, cannot constitute grounds of public policy within the meaning of Article 56 of the Treaty.

However, the Netherlands Government has stated that, in the final analysis, the prohibitions of advertising and subtitling have a non-economic objective, namely that of maintaining the non-commercial and, thereby, pluralistic nature of the Netherlands broadcasting system. . . .

It is sufficient to observe in that regard that the measures taken by virtue of that article must not be disproportionate to the intended objective. As an exception to a fundamental principle of the Treaty, Article 56 of the Treaty must be interpreted in such a way that its effects are limited to that which is necessary in order to protect the interests which it seeks to safeguard.

The Netherlands Government itself admits that there are less restrictive, non-discriminatory ways of achieving the intended objectives. For instance, broadcasters of commercial programmes established in other Member States could be given a choice between complying with objective restrictions on the transmission of advertising, such as a prohibition on advertising certain products or on certain days and limiting the duration or the frequency of advertisements – restrictions also imposed on national broadcasters – or, if they did not wish to comply, refraining from transmitting advertising intended especially for the public in the Netherlands.

. . .

It must therefore be held that [the] prohibitions of advertising and subtitling . . . cannot be justified on grounds of public policy under Article 56 of the Treaty.

4. THE DEVELOPMENT OF A COMMUNITY POLICY

As transfrontier broadcasting became more common, the harmonisation of broadcasting legislation also became more likely. The potential for cross-border trade and economic expansion could be halted or slowed if individual Member States imposed restrictive rules which made it economically unattractive for broadcasting undertakings to expand their operations. The development of a broadcasting Community policy can be traced back to 1982 with the Hahn Report.[9] This Report[10] on radio and television broadcasting was prepared by Hahn on behalf of the Committee on Youth, Culture, Education, Information and Sport. The Report, which was adopted unanimously by the European Parliament sought to assert the importance of information to the process of European unification. The response to the Hahn Report was two-fold. On the one hand there was a belief that European integration could best be assisted by means of a European television system. This was an idea which has so far failed.[11] The second, and more practical, response proposed that there should be a set of agreed safeguards and standards, whereby broadcasters having complied with these standards, would be free to broadcast Community-wide. In response, the European Commission (the Commission) presented a Green Paper, *Television Without Frontiers, Green Paper on the establishment of the Common Market for broadcasting, especially by satellite and cable*[12] (the Green Paper) which proposed four areas for harmonising legislation: advertising, protection of minors, copyright and right to reply. Some indication of why action was seen as being important can be gauged from the following extract taken from a summary prepared by the Commission on the Green Paper.

Extract 5.4.1

European Commission, *Television Without Frontiers, Green Paper on the establishment of the Common Market for broadcasting, especially by satellite and cable*, Summary, Communication from the Commission to the Council, COM (84) 300 final/2, paras 4–7

4 The Commission considers that action needs to be taken at the present time in the broadcasting field because of the importance of its effect, already considerable and steadily growing, on the process of European integration. This effect, actual and potential, is not only economic in character but also social, cultural and political.

---

[9] R Wallace and D Goldberg, 'The EEC Directive on Television Broadcasting' (1989) 9 *Yearbook of European Law* 175. See generally for history of the development of Community policy on broadcasting.
[10] European Parliament, *Report drawn up on behalf of the Committee on Youth, Culture, Education, Information and Sport on radio and television broadcasting in the European Community*, Working Documents, 1981–82, Doc 1–1013/81.
[11] See Wallace and Goldberg note 9, above, at 176.
[12] COM (84) 300 final.

5 Certainly broadcasting is a strategic sector of the Community's service economy, particularly as technical change increases the scope and availability of programmes and associated services including new information and communications services which will create many opportunities for innovation and employment. It constitutes one of the main factors accelerating the transition to an economy that will in large part be based on ready access to information and to rapid methods of communication. One of the principle [sic] components in the development of the infrastructure necessary for a modern information and communications network will be cable and satellite systems dedicated in substantial part to the broadcasting of a wide variety of programmes. The considerable investment in infrastructure and programme industries will be the more easily and rapidly found if, from the outset, those providing the new services can count on access to a single broadcasting area corresponding to the European Community as a whole.

6 But, equally clearly, broadcasting cannot be approached in exclusively technical and economic terms, even if its economic dimension is necessarily the starting point for policy making in an Economic Community. More fundamentally, broadcasting is a powerful medium for the communication of all kinds of information, ideas and opinion. It thereby influences the attitudes of almost all Community citizens, and provides the means by which they can influence the attitudes of others. . . .

7 . . . In this context, emphasis has been placed on the need to respect the European Convention on Human Rights and Fundamental Freedoms and, in particular, its provision the right to freedom of expression . . .

It can be seen from this extract, that the Commission's concerns were not purely economic. Nevertheless, it provides an insight into the Community's awareness of broadcasting's economic and industrial importance; an awareness which, in later Commission documents, has been much more explicit.[13] The need to build a Community-wide market for European audiovisual products, to improve competitiveness with the USA was also a strong motivating factor.[14]

Although some Member States, including the UK, had reservations about the need for legislation,[15] a proposal for a directive was produced in 1986.[16]

---

[13] See, for example, Commission of the European Communities, *Growth, Competitiveness, Employment, The Challenges and Ways Forward into the 21st Century*, White Paper, COM (93) 700 final and Commission of the European Communities, *Strategy Options to Strengthen the European Programme Industry in the Context of the Audiovisual Policy of the European Union*, Green Paper, COM (94) 96 final.

[14] In 1991, 77% of American exports of audiovisual programmes were exported to Europe (of which nearly 60% went to Member States), White Paper, note 13, above, p 120. Despite EC measures, the position does not seem to have improved greatly, and there has been a growing EC/US trade deficit in the audiovisual sector: European Commission, *The Digital Age, European Audiovisual Policy, High Level Group on Audiovisual Policy* (1998), p 15.

[15] Barendt, pp 232–233.

[16] Proposal for a Council Directive on the co-ordination of certain provisions laid down by law, regulation or administrative action in Member States concerning the pursuit of broadcasting activities, COM (86) 146/2 final.

While the Community was working on the draft directive, the Council of Europe was also engaged in preparations for a convention on broadcasting. There was, certainly, some rivalry between the two organisations during their respective drafting stages, and there was debate over which instrument should be settled first.[17] However, at a European Council meeting in December 1988,[18] it was agreed that the Television Convention should be settled first as it had a wider constituency. This would ensure that Council of Europe members would not be denied an opportunity to participate in the drafting of the Convention. The Television Convention was adopted on 5 May 1989[19] and the Television Directive on 3 October 1989.[20] Although the Community members are also signatories to the Television Convention, under art 27(1) of the Television Convention, they must comply with the Television Directive, except where the Television Convention covers a matter not dealt with by the Television Directive. The impact of the Television Convention is also limited because, like international law treaties, it lacks independent enforcement mechanisms, although some procedures are included in the Convention for settlement of disputes, but these rely largely on negotiation (see arts 25 and 26). The scope of the two instruments is broadly similar in that they both cover the areas of advertising, protection of minors, rights of reply and the promotion of European programming. Initially, it was envisaged that the Directive would cover radio and television, and that copyright would also be covered. However, both radio and copyright were dropped from the proposals.[21] For the remainder of this chapter, the focus will be on the Television Directive and its operation, although some points of comparison will be made with the Television Convention. Amendments to the Television Convention were adopted in October 1998,[22] and it should enter into force on 1 October 2000 unless accepted by all the parties prior to that date. References to the Convention in this chapter will be to the Convention as amended, unless otherwise stated.

---

[17] For accounts see Hondius, note 1, above and Schwartz, 'The EEC Directive on "Television without Frontiers"' (1988) 21 *Revue Belge de Droit International* 329.

[18] B de Witte, 'The European Content Requirement in the EC Television Directive – Five Years After' in E M Barendt (ed), *The Yearbook of Media and Entertainment Law 1995* (Oxford University Press, 1995), pp 101, 104.

[19] European Treaty Series, No 132.

[20] Council Directive 89/552/EEC of 3 October 1989 on the coordination of certain provisions laid down by law, regulation or administrative action in Member States concerning the pursuit of television broadcasting activities, [1989] OJ L298/23.

[21] Copyright had proved to be a matter too difficult on which to reach agreement: Barendt, p 232. Council Directive 93/83/EEC of 27 September 1993 on the coordination of certain rules concerning copyright and rights related to copyright applicable to satellite broadcasting and cable retransmission, [1993] OJ L248/15 was eventually enacted to deal with the copyright aspects of transfrontier broadcasting.

[22] Protocol Amending the European Convention on Transfrontier Television, European Treaty Series 171, 1 October 1998.

5. THE TELEVISION WITHOUT FRONTIERS DIRECTIVE

(a) Introduction

A directive amending the Television Directive became law on 30 July 1997.[23] In the following discussion references to the Television Directive will be references to the Television Directive as amended, unless otherwise indicated. The Television Directive was not substantially amended despite attempts by the European Parliament. However, Chapter II, which deals with jurisdictional matters was considerably amended to deal with difficulties which had arisen in the interpretation of its provisions (discussed in Section 5(b) below). A new provision to protect, for the general viewing public, major events, such as sport, was introduced (see Chapter 7 below). Increased protection for minors was also provided (Section 5(c) below), and amendments were made to the advertising rules (Chapter 6 below), and generally, to cover teleshopping programmes and channels. In addition, a Contact Committee was established (art 23a) to be made up of representatives of the Member States' competent authorities. The Contact Committee's role will include facilitating implementation of the Television Directive, and acting as a means for the exchange of information on regulatory activities.

(b) Jurisdiction and scope of the Television Directive

The focal point of the Television Directive can be found in Chapter II, and particularly art 2. Member States must ensure that all television broadcasts transmitted by broadcasters under their jurisdiction comply with the broadcasting law of that Member State, including, under art 3(2), the Television Directive. In addition, Member States must not restrict the reception of television broadcasts from other Member States in respect of any matter covered by the Television Directive (art 2a(1)). However, as an exception to this rule, a Member State may take action, including suspension of broadcasts, if a broadcast infringes art 22 or 22a, for example, because it contains pornographic material (see Section 5(c) below). But, the essential principle remains that broadcasts within the European Community should be allowed freedom of transmission and reception across borders. The Television Directive does not prevent a Member State requiring broadcasters within its jurisdiction to comply with stricter rules than those in the Television Directive (art 3(1)).

One area which caused difficulty in the Television Directive, as originally enacted, was the question of how Member States were to determine which broadcasters were under their jurisdiction. The following extract sets out the

---

[23] Directive 97/36/EC of the European Parliament and of the Council of 30 June 1997 amending Council Directive 89/552/EEC on the coordination of certain provisions laid down by law, regulation, or administrative action in Member States concerning the pursuit of television broadcasting activities, [1997] OJ L202/60.

relevant provisions as they were originally enacted. As can be seen they give little guidance in determining the question of jurisdiction.

Extract 5.5.1

Council Directive 89/552/EEC of 3 October 1989 on the coordination of certain provisions laid down by law, regulation or administrative action in Member States concerning the pursuit of television broadcasting activities (OJ 1989 L298/23), art 2(1)

Each Member State shall ensure that all television broadcasts transmitted
– by broadcasters under its jurisdiction, or
– by broadcasters who, while not being under the jurisdiction of any Member State, make use of a frequency or a satellite capacity granted by, or a satellite up-link situated in, that Member State,
comply with the law applicable to broadcasts intended for the public in that Member State.

The UK, under the Broadcasting Act 1990 (BA 1990), determined jurisdiction by the place of transmission. Hence, if transmission of a satellite broadcast took place from the UK, then the UK would take responsibility for licensing and controlling that broadcaster. The satellite television service, BSkyB, was licensed on this basis. However, the Commission and other Member States had taken the view that jurisdiction arose where the broadcaster was established. The European Commission brought infringement proceedings against the UK on the basis that it had failed to implement properly the Television Directive. One of the arguments which the UK government put forward was that its interpretation of art 2 was sensible because it meant that it was consistent with the parallel provisions of the Television Convention, which determined jurisdiction on the basis of place of transmission.

Extract 5.5.2

Case C-222/94 *Commission of the European Communities v United Kingdom of Great Britain and Northern Ireland* [1996] ECR I-4025, at 4070, 4072–4073, 4074, 4075–4076 and 4077–4078

The Directive contains no express definition of the phrase 'broadcasters under its jurisdiction'.

It is therefore necessary to consider first whether an interpretation in support of one or other of the parties' positions can be deduced from the text of Article 2(1).

. . .

The purpose of Article 2(1) . . . is to make sure that a Member State ensures that all television broadcasts made by broadcasters in relation to which it can assert the jurisdiction thereby conferred comply with the law applicable to broadcasts intended for the public in that Member State, including . . . the provisions of the Directive itself.

A Member State's power to enforce compliance with its laws is a function of its jurisdiction in relation to activities carried on in its territory and, subsidiarily, over persons or, as the case may be, physical objects such as spacecraft, linked to that State, even though located outside its territory.

The second indent of Article 2(1) refers to the situation in which a Member State may assert either its jurisdiction in relation to the use of a satellite or its territorial jurisdiction in relation to the use of an up-link, situated in that State, to a satellite which does not fall under its jurisdiction.

However, the second indent envisages the exercise of such jurisdiction only on condition that no other Member State has jurisdiction under the first indent of Article 2(1).

. . .

This interpretation is borne out by the wording of the first indent of Article 2(1) of the Directive in that it refers to broadcasters as being under the jurisdiction of a Member State without referring, in that context, to the place from which they transmit their broadcasts.

. . .

The United Kingdom argues that, although the Community is not itself a Party to the Convention, it would be absurd if the Community, by way of the Directive, sought to regulate intra-Community broadcasting in a manner radically different from that adopted by the Member States within the framework of the Convention.

That argument, considered in the light of a comparative analysis of the wording, scheme and aims of the Directive, on the one hand, and of those of the Convention, on the other, cannot, however, be accepted.

. . . [I]n order to determine which State is competent for ensuring compliance with the provisions relating to programme services, the Convention principally applies criteria based on transmission. It is only in the case of satellite transmissions, if responsibility cannot be established . . . [by the place of transmission] that Article 5(2) refers to the State in which the broadcaster has its seat. . . .

Under the first indent of Article 2(1) of the Directive, however, the Member State competent for ensuring compliance with the provisions relating to programme services is that under whose jurisdiction the broadcaster comes. According to the second indent of Article 2(1), it is only where the broadcaster does not come under the jurisdiction of any other Member State that the Directive uses criteria based on transmission.

It follows that Article 2(1) of the Directive and . . . the Convention use different criteria for determining the State that must ensure compliance with the provisions relating to television broadcasts. As the Commission has rightly observed, this substantive difference reflects a difference between the aims of the Directive and the aims of the Convention. Whereas, according to the second recital in the Directive's preamble, the Directive is designed to establish the internal market in television services, the Convention, according to Article 1 thereof, is designed to facilitate the transfrontier transmission and retransmission of television programme services.

Furthermore, there is no doubt that the Council was fully aware of the adoption of the Convention when it itself adopted the Directive, as is indeed clear from the fourth recital of the preamble. . . . It follows that, by adopting the Directive, the Community legislature chose to regulate television services in a way which differs from the path followed by the Convention.

. . .

[The United Kingdom had also argued that the Commission's interpretation of Article 2 was impractical because it could mean that broadcasters who had more than one place of establishment would be subject to the jurisdiction of more than one Member State.]

As to that point, the criterion contended for by the United Kingdom may produce problems in the delimitation of jurisdiction which, in its view, can be resolved only through the conclusion of international agreements between the Member States. Although the criterion of establishment may also give rise to difficulties, the Commission has stated, without being contradicted by the United Kingdom, that Member States may find a solution to the problem of double control, without the necessity of further legislation, by interpreting the criterion of establishment as referring to the place in which a broadcaster has the centre of its activities, in particular the place where decisions concerning programme policy are taken and the programmes to be broadcast are finally put together.

The United Kingdom also contends that the criterion of establishment involves a risk of abuse in that a broadcaster could move its seat to another Member State in order to avoid application of the legislation of a Member State.

As to that, the interpretation of the criterion of establishment advocated by the Commission . . . would considerably reduce the risk of abuse pointed out by the United Kingdom. The criterion advocated by the United Kingdom would, in any event, involve a comparable, if not greater, risk of abuse.

Questions for discussion

1. Does it follow, as the ECJ believes, that the different aims of the Convention and Directive result in different approaches to determining jurisdiction?
2. Do you agree that determining jurisdiction by establishment reduces the risk of abuse?

On the day that the ECJ delivered judgment in *EC Commission v United Kingdom*, it also gave judgment in another matter which concerned infringement proceedings brought by the Commission. Belgium had been operating a system of prior authorisation for programmes being relayed by cable from other Member States and, as part of this authorisation procedure, requiring broadcasters to meet certain conditions. The Commission argued this constituted an infringement of art 2(2) (now art 2a(1)) which requires that Member States '. . . ensure freedom of reception and shall not restrict retransmission on their territory of television broadcasts from other Member States . . .'. One of the arguments raised by the Belgian government was that it was necessary for Member States to ensure that broadcasts from other Member States complied with the Television Directive.

Extract 5.5.3

Case C-11/95 *Commission of the European Communities v Kingdom of Belgium* [1996] ECR I-4115, at 4164 and 4165

[T]he Belgian Government maintains that it is apparent from the recitals in the preamble to the directive, and from Article 2(1) thereof, that a television programme may circulate freely throughout the Community only if it complies with the applicable law of the originating State, including the provisions of the directive. It necessarily follows from that principle that the receiving Member State must be able to verify whether foreign television broadcasters applying for authorization to retransmit their programmes in the territory of the French Community of Belgium comply with the law of the originating State and are justified in calling for the application of Article 2(2) of the directive.

Having regard to the system whereby Directive 89/552 divides obligations between the Member States from which programmes emanate and the Member States receiving them, those arguments cannot be accepted.

. . .

It follows, first, that it is solely for the Member State from which television broadcasts emanate to monitor the application of the law of the originating Member State applying to such broadcasts and to ensure compliance with Directive 89/552, and, second, that the receiving Member State is not authorized to exercise its own control in that regard.

. . .

Only in the circumstances provided for in the second sentence of Article 2(2),²⁴ . . . may the receiving Member State exceptionally suspend retransmission of televised broadcasts, on the conditions laid down by that provision. Moreover, if a Member State considers that another Member State has failed to fulfil its obligations under the directive, it may, as the Commission has rightly observed, bring Treaty infringement proceedings . . . or request the Commission itself to take action against that Member State.

Difficult jurisdictional questions can arise when new technology, such as satellite transmission, enables a broadcaster to establish itself in one state while intending to broadcast to an audience in another state. In such circumstances, which Member State should have jurisdiction over that broadcaster? In the *VT4* Case, the broadcaster was established in the UK, operating through a company, incorporated in the UK, and licensed to broadcast under the BA 1990. Its television and radio programmes, however, were aimed at the Flemish Community, provided in Dutch, and transmitted by satellite. It also had an office in Flanders which was a point of contact for advertisers and local producers, and which also gathered local news. At the time the Belgian government permitted a monopoly over commercial television and television advertising in the Flemish Community. The Belgian authorities refused to allow cable network operators in the Flemish Community

---

²⁴ This refers to the power of the Member State (now art 2a(2)) to take action, including suspending transmission, for infringement of (now) arts 22 and 22a (see Section 5(c) below).

to retransmit VT4. They considered that VT4 had established itself in the UK in order to circumvent Flemish law, could not be regarded as being under the jurisdiction of another Member State, and, therefore, required a licence under Flemish law.[25]

Extract 5.5.4

Case C-56/96 *VT4 Ltd v Vlaamse Gemeenschap* [1997] ECR I-3143, at 3167–3168

Where a television broadcaster has more than one establishment, the competent Member State is the State in which the broadcaster has the centre of its activities. It is therefore for the national court to determine, applying that criteria, which Member State has jurisdiction over VT4's activities, taking into account in particular the place where decisions concerning programme policy are taken and the programmes to be broadcast are finally put together. . . .

It must also be emphasised that the mere fact that all the broadcasts and advertisements are aimed exclusively at the Flemish public does not . . . demonstrate that VT4 cannot be regarded as established in the United Kingdom. The Treaty does not prohibit an undertaking from exercising the freedom to provide services if it does not offer services in the Member State in which it is established.

It follows from the foregoing that Article 2(1) of the Directive is to be interpreted as meaning that a television broadcaster comes under the jurisdiction of the Member State in which it is established. If a television broadcaster is established in more than one Member State, the Member State having jurisdiction over it is the one in whose territory the broadcaster has the centre of its activities, in particular where decisions concerning programme policy are taken and the programmes to be broadcast are finally put together.

Paul Denuit[26] raised similar questions about the position of a broadcaster operating outside the Member State to which the broadcasts were directed. It concerned a refusal by the Belgian authorities to allow a Belgian cable operator to retransmit via cable a satellite programme service provided by a broadcaster situated in the UK. The programme service was a cartoon service called *TNT & Cartoon Network* which consisted mainly of American programme material. The Belgian authorities believed that the service did not comply with the Directive's rules on European content. The ECJ again confirmed that a Member State was not entitled to prevent retransmission of a broadcast which came under the jurisdiction of another Member State. The ECJ also ruled that the origin of the actual content was irrelevant in determining jurisdiction.

---

[25] The Belgian government has continued to insist that VT4 requires a licence under Belgian law. In July 1999, the Commission announced that it was initiating infringement procedures against the Belgian government on the ground that such a requirement would be in breach of the Television Directive (IP/99/455, 5 July 1999).

[26] Case C-14/96, [1997] 3 CMLR 943.

Although art 3(1) allows a Member State to impose, on broadcasters within its jurisdiction, stricter requirements than those set by the Directive, *VT4* and *Paul Denuit* illustrate the practical difficulty for a Member State trying to enforce a particular broadcasting policy. Given a broadcaster's ability to migrate to another jurisdiction, national governments may be under pressure to relax their particular rules, bringing them in line with the minimum standards set by the Directive, in order to ensure that employment and other business opportunities are not lost. Article 3(1) offers only a weak concession to Member State autonomy, and, its weakness, serves as a reminder that the underlying aims of the Television Directive are economic.

Article 2 of the Television Directive has been amended to clarify the issue of jurisdiction. It is worth noting that the amended Television Convention now adopts the same approach, as the Directive, to determining jurisdiction. In its second Application Report, the Commission emphasised the importance of the principle that Member States must exercise control of broadcasters established under their jurisdiction: 'The Commission assigns the greatest importance to the correct application of the principles of free movement and non-discrimination in this field. It would particularly stress the increased importance of a correct application of the so-called *"home country control"* principle (according to which broadcasters are subject only to the law of the country in which they have their principal place of business) in an audiovisual environment which – thanks to the proliferation of broadcasting capacities due to digital technology – favours the growth of transnational services.'[27]

Extract 5.5.5

Television Directive, Unofficial consolidated version prepared by the services of the Commission, http://europa.eu.int/comm/dg10/avpolicy/ twf/tvconse.html, art 2(1)–(4) and (6)

1. Each Member State shall ensure that all television broadcasts transmitted by broadcasters under its jurisdiction comply with the rules of the system of law applicable to broadcasts intended for the public in that Member State.

2. For the purposes of this Directive the broadcasters under the jurisdiction of a Member State are:

– those established in that Member State in accordance with paragraph 3;

– those to whom paragraph 4 applies.

3. For the purposes of this Directive, a broadcaster shall be deemed to be established in a Member State in the following cases:

---

[27] Commission of the European Communities, *Second Report from the Commission to the Council, the European Parliament and the Economic and Social Committee on the application of Directive 89/ 552/EEC 'Television without frontiers'*, COM (97) 523 final, p 5. Under the Television Directive, the Commission is required to report regularly on its implementation.

(a) the broadcaster has its head office in that Member State and the editorial decisions about programme schedules are taken in that Member State;

(b) if a broadcaster has its head office in one Member State but editorial decisions on programme schedules are taken in another Member State, it shall be deemed to be established in the Member State where a significant part of the workforce involved in the pursuit of the television broadcasting activity operates; if a significant part of the workforce involved in the pursuit of the television broadcasting activity operates in each of those Member States, the broadcaster shall be deemed to be established in the Member State where it has its head office; if a significant part of the workforce involved in the pursuit of the television broadcasting activity operates in neither of those Member States, the broadcaster shall be deemed to be established in the Member State where it first began broadcasting in accordance with the system of law of that Member State, provided that it maintains a stable and effective link with the economy of that Member State;

(c) if a broadcaster has its head office in a Member State but decisions on programme schedules are taken in a third country, or vice-versa, it shall be deemed to be established in the Member State concerned, provided that a significant part of the workforce involved in the pursuit of the television broadcasting activity operates in that Member State.

4. Broadcasters to whom the provisions of paragraph 3 are not applicable shall be deemed to be under the jurisdiction of a Member State in the following cases:

(a) they use a frequency granted by that Member State;

(b) although they do not use a frequency granted by a Member State they do use a satellite capacity appertaining to that Member State;

(c) although they use neither a frequency granted by a Member State nor a satellite capacity appertaining to a Member State they do use a satellite up-link situated in that Member State.

. . .

6. This Directive shall not apply to broadcasts intended exclusively for reception in third countries, and which are not received directly or indirectly by the public in one or more Member States.

Question for discussion

In what circumstances will art 2(4) apply?

(c) Protection of minors and unacceptable programming

As already explained, Member States are prohibited from preventing the reception and retransmission of broadcasts from other Member States, even if they believe that the broadcast does not comply with the Directive. However, arts 22 and 22a provide the circumstances in which an exception is made to this strict rule. Under art 2a(2), Member States have a limited right to derogate from the obligation to permit the free movement of broadcasts.

Extract 5.5.6

Television Directive, Unofficial consolidated version prepared by the services of the Commission, http://europa.eu.int/comm/dg10/ avpolicy/twf/tvconse.html, arts 2a, 22 and 22a

Article 2a

1. Member States shall ensure freedom of reception and shall not restrict retransmissions on their territory of television broadcasts from other Member States for reasons which fall within the fields coordinated by this Directive.

2. Member States may, provisionally, derogate from paragraph 1 if the following conditions are fulfilled:

(a) a television broadcast coming from another Member State manifestly, seriously and gravely infringes Article 22(1) or (2) and/or Article 22a;

(b) during the previous 12 months, the broadcaster has infringed the provision(s) referred to in (a) on at least two prior occasions;

(c) the Member State concerned has notified the broadcaster and the Commission in writing of the alleged infringements and of the measures it intends to take should any such infringement occur again;

(d) consultations with the transmitting Member State and the Commission have not produced an amicable settlement within 15 days of the notification provided for in (c), and the alleged infringement persists.

The Commission, shall, within two months following notification of the measures taken by the Member State, take a decision on whether the measures are compatible with Community law. If it decides that they are not, the Member State will be required to put an end to the measures in question as a matter of urgency.

3. Paragraph 2 shall be without prejudice to the application of any procedure, remedy or sanction to the infringements in question in the Member State which has jurisdiction over the broadcaster concerned.

Article 22

1. Member States shall take appropriate measures to ensure that television broadcasts by broadcasters under their jurisdiction do not include any programmes which might seriously impair the physical, mental or moral development of minors, in particular programmes that involve pornography or gratuitous violence.

2. The measures provided for in paragraph 1 shall also extend to other programmes which are likely to impair the physical, mental or moral development of minors, except where it is ensured, by selecting the time of the broadcast or by any technical measure, that minors in the area of transmission will not normally hear or see such broadcasts.

3. Furthermore, when such programmes are broadcast in unencoded form Member States shall ensure that they are preceded by an acoustic warning or are identified by the presence of a visual symbol throughout their duration.

Article 22a

> Member States shall ensure that broadcasts do not contain any incitement to hatred on grounds of race, sex, religion or nationality.

The procedure set down in art 2a is essentially as it was originally enacted (then art 2(2)), but there has been one interesting amendment. Article 2(2) had referred specifically to a right of temporary suspension of broadcasts, and this was the only action mentioned. The amended Television Directive is no longer as specific, referring only to 'measures taken by the Member State'. It may be that the Commission is keen to encourage Member States to consider less draconian measures when faced with infringements of art 22 or 22a, although the Directive clearly contemplates the possibility of suspension of broadcasts, because it refers to derogation from the obligation to ensure freedom of reception and retransmission. The limited right of Member States, under the Television Directive, to derogate from the freedom of reception obligation can be contrasted with the Convention. Article 24 of the Convention allows, according to a procedure set down in the article, a Party to suspend retransmissions of broadcasts not only in situations similar to the Television Directive, but also where breaches of some advertising rules have occurred. Interestingly, the amendments to the Television Convention have introduced a new art 24 *bis* which enables a party to the Convention to take action where a broadcaster, who is intentionally broadcasting to that party's territory, has established itself in another party's state, in order to evade the laws in the areas covered by the Convention. Parties must first proceed through a settlement procedure, but, if this fails, the Convention allows the party, receiving the broadcast, to take further action, provided that it complies with ECHR, art 10.

Question for discussion

To what extent do these rights to take action under the Directive and the Convention reflect the different aims of these two instruments?

To date, the UK has made the most active use of the art 2a procedure. The first occasion concerned Red Hot Television (formerly known as Red Hot Dutch), a satellite service, which was broadcast from a satellite up-link located in Denmark by a Dutch company, Continental Television BVio. An English company, Continental Television plc, was licensed by the Dutch company to act as the marketing branch in England. Prior to December 1992, it had been transmitting from an up-link in the Netherlands. The Red Hot Television case demonstrated that there were some difficulties in the interpretation of the Television Directive, which the amended Directive has now sought to address. Red Hot Television was a subscription service, broadcasting, in a form which required viewers to have a decoder, on Saturday and Sunday nights from midnight until 4 am. According to the Broadcasting

Standards Council (now the Broadcasting Standards Commission) Red Hot Television was broadcasting 'hard-core pornography on a regular basis'.[28]

The UK government proceeded to act against Red Hot Television under the BA 1990 provisions covering foreign satellite services.[29]

Extract 5.5.7

Broadcasting Act 1990, s 177(1)–(4) and (6)(a)

177.—(1) Subject to the following provisions of this section, the Secretary of State may make an order proscribing a foreign satellite service for the purposes of section 178.

(2) If the Independent Television Commission or the Radio Authority consider that the quality of any relevant foreign satellite service which is brought to their attention is unacceptable and that the service should be the subject of an order under this section, they shall notify to the Secretary of State details of the service and their reasons why they consider such an order should be made.

(3) The Independent Television Commission or (as the case may be) the Radio Authority shall not consider a foreign satellite service to be unacceptable for the purposes of subsection (2) unless they are satisfied that there is repeatedly contained in programmes included in the service matter which offends against good taste or decency or is likely to encourage or incite to crime or to lead to disorder or to be offensive to public feeling.

(4) Where the Secretary of State has been notified under subsection (2), he shall not make an order under this section unless he is satisfied that the making of the order—

  (a) is in the public interest; and

  (b) is compatible with any international obligations of the United Kingdom.

(5) [*Omitted*].

(6) In this section and section 178—

'foreign satellite service' means—

  (a) a service which is provided by a person who is not for the purposes of Council Directive 89/552/EEC under the jurisdiction of the United Kingdom and which consists wholly or mainly in the transmission by satellite of television programmes which are capable of being received in the United Kingdom, . . .

---

[28] Broadcasting Standards Council, *Report to the Secretary of State for National Heritage under section 153(5) of the Broadcasting Act 1990, Foreign Satellite Channels* (November 1992), p 3.

[29] The Red Hot case also raised the same problems about determining jurisdiction already examined in this chapter. The UK treated the service as a foreign satellite service because it regarded the place of up-link (at this time, Denmark) as conferring jurisdiction. However, Denmark (and the Netherlands) considered that the UK had jurisdiction over this service applying the establishment test. These doubts have now been resolved because BA 1990, s 177 has been amended in the light of the *EC Commission v United Kingdom* decision (see Extract 5.5.2 above).

The effect of an order under s 177(1) is to make it a criminal offence, under s 178, for anyone to assist with the supply of equipment or programme material, to advertise the service, or to advertise on the service. An order was made proscribing Red Hot Television. Continental Television plc sought judicial review of this order on the grounds that the Secretary of State had no power to make the order as it was in breach of the Television Directive. It will be noted that the Secretary of State cannot make a proscription order, unless satisfied that it is compatible with international obligations. It was in the course of these proceedings that the difficulties with the interpretation of what was then art 2(2) and art 22 were raised before the High Court. The first issue concerned the meaning of the term 'retransmission'. Did the term cover satellite services directly received by viewers? The second issue concerned the interpretation of art 22 as it was originally enacted:

> Member States shall take appropriate measures to ensure that television broadcasts by broadcasters under their jurisdiction do not include programmes which might seriously impair the physical, mental or moral development of minors, in particular those that involve pornography or gratuitous violence. This provision shall extend to other programmes which are likely to impair the physical, mental or moral development of minors, except where it is ensured, by selecting the time of the broadcast or by any technical measure, that minors in the area of transmission will not normally hear or see such broadcasts.

Could broadcasts which contained pornographic material be broadcast if measures were taken to ensure that minors would not be likely to see the broadcast? The English courts did not resolve these issues as the proceedings were ordered to be referred to the ECJ, under EC Treaty, art 234 (formerly art 177), for a preliminary ruling on the interpretation of the Directive provisions. The following extract, from the High Court judgment, is useful, however, in illustrating the arguments raised concerning the interpretation of the Television Directive. No preliminary ruling was ever given as the applicants went out of business and did not pursue the proceedings before the ECJ.

Extract 5.5.8

R v Secretary of State for the National Heritage, ex parte Continental Television BV and Others [1993] 2 CMLR 333,[30] at 340, 341, 344–345

LEGGATT LJ: . . . [T]he Commission having confirmed its view that a member-State has the ability to take action to discourage reception of a direct satellite broadcast if the conditions in Article 2(2) of the directive are satisfied, the letter [from the Commission] went on to explain that the view was the result of various considerations which are then set out in the letter. The first such consideration was that:

---

[30] The decision was upheld on appeal although there was no appeal from the matters dealt with in this extract: [1993] 3 CMLR 387.

Article 2(2) of the directive establishes the principle of freedom of reception and the term 'retransmission' is only used here to make it clear that the principle applies to broadcasts coming from another member-State. . . .

. . . As a rule, what matters is that the signals should come from one member-State and be broadcast in another; the manner in which the signals cross the internal frontier is irrelevant . . .

. . .

Mr Pannick [counsel for the applicants] argues that Article 2(2) does not apply in the circumstances of the present case because as a matter of construction, it requires Member-States to ensure freedom of reception whilst prohibiting restrictions of re-transmission. He contends that there is no re-transmission by Red Hot Television in the United Kingdom by any means whatsoever, that is to say whether by cable or otherwise. All that happens is that the programmes are received here. . . . Mr Pannick submits that although the Directive does not itself define the term 'retransmission', it is to be noted that Article 2(2) refers not only to re-transmission but also to reception, and must, therefore, have intended a distinction between the two. . . .

It is convenient at this stage, before proceeding further to evaluate the arguments on the first issue, to mention those relating to the second, that is as to the true construction of Article 22 of the directive. Mr Pannick argues that the closing words of the first part of Article 22, which refer to ensuring 'by selecting the time of broadcast . . . that minors in the area of transmission will not normally hear or see such broadcasts', in effect govern the opening sentence which, as will be recalled, provides that 'Member-States shall take appropriate measures to ensure that television broadcasts . . . do not include programmes which might seriously impair the . . . moral development of minors', in particular those that involve pornography.

He contends that the result of that method of construction is that the moral development of minors is not to be regarded as seriously impaired if, by reason of the time of transmission, they will not normally see it. I am bound to say that, as a matter of construction, had the Article been reproduced in an English statute, I should have thought it too plain for argument that the Article is divided, for present purposes, into two distinct parts. The first, which is free-standing, is concerned with the serious impairment of moral development of minors, in particular by those broadcasts which involve pornography. But, by contrast, the second part, as it says, extends to other programmes and, in relation to them but not to those in the first part, there is engrafted the exception clause relating to ensuring by selecting the time of broadcast that minors will not normally see them. . . .

Mr Pannick next contends that, assuming that Article 2(2) is applicable, Article 22 cannot apply because the time of reception is in any event such as would make it unlikely for the broadcast to be seen by minors. . . . Unfortunately, the timing of transmission and the need to purchase decoding equipment cannot, in reality, ensure that minors are unlikely to see the transmissions. The very fact that they occur in the small hours of morning makes it likely that the programmes will be recorded by prospective viewers, there is no prohibition on the sale of decoding equipment to minors, except insofar as there may be by virtue of the Secretary of State's order a general prohibition, nor can minors necessarily be prevented from viewing recordings made by others or, indeed, using equipment belonging to others. It seems to me indisputable that, if seen by minors, the material is such as might seriously impair their moral development.

Questions for discussion

1. Do you find the Commission's explanation of the term 'retransmission' satisfactory?

2. In the light of the opinion expressed by Leggatt LJ, will it be easy to take measures which will ensure compliance with art 22(2) (Extract 5.5.6)?

Although the ECJ was not given an opportunity to rule on these issues, art 22, as amended (Extract 5.5.6 above) does provide a response to the arguments raised in this case. To date, the Commission has upheld the proscription orders made by the UK as compatible with Community law,[31] but there is obviously a fine balance to be maintained. Where the UK proposes to act under BA 1990, s 177 in relation to a service, which is also under the jurisdiction of another Member State, it will be necessary for the Secretary of State to be satisfied, not only that the service comes within s 177, but, also, that it breaches art 22 (or, of course, art 22a). Ultimately, whether a service is in breach of Article 22 or 22a will be a matter for the Commission to decide. Under the amended Television Directive, the Commission might also wish to consider whether the measures taken by a Member State are proportionate to the harm occasioned by the breach of these articles.

Although other Member States have apparently not found it necessary to use the art 2a procedure, it is clear that since the Television Directive was first enacted concern has grown about the need to protect children from certain types of broadcasting. This has led to amendments to the Television Directive, although not on the scale sought by the European Parliament which wanted all programmes to be classified according to their likely detrimental effect on children, and all television receivers to be equipped with a device for filtering programmes.[32] The European Parliament did not achieve these amendments, but art 22(3) (see Extract 5.5.6 above) now requires some form of identification for certain types of programmes. Further, art 22b requires the Commission to report on measures which could facilitate parental control of programmes watched by children.[33]

---

[31] D Goldberg, T Prosser and S Verhulst, *EC Media Law and Policy* (Addison Wesley Longman, 1998), pp 66–67.

[32] P Keller, 'The New Television without Frontiers Directive' in E M Barendt (ed), *The Yearbook of Media and Entertainment Law 1997* (Oxford University Press, 1997), pp 177, 191.

[33] The report published in response to this requirement, *Final Report: Parental Control of Television Broadcasting*, can be seen at http://europa.eu.int/comm/dg10/avpolicy/key_doc/parental_control/index.html.

(d) Programme quotas

One of the most controversial group of provisions in the Television Directive contains measures designed to promote the production of programme material. Chapter III, entitled 'Promotion of distribution and production of television programmes', covers obligations aimed at increasing the quantity of European programmes being broadcast (art 4), and the amount of independently produced programme material (art 5). Article 7 is concerned with ensuring that cinematographic works are allowed an adequate period in which to be exhibited at the cinema before being broadcast on television. It is art 4 which has proved the most controversial of these three measures, while art 5, which sets a quota (at least 10%) for independent productions, does not appear to have caused any significant problems.[34] Article 7 of the amended Television Directive has been considerably watered down. In its original form, it imposed specific time periods which had to elapse between a film's first cinema exhibition and its television broadcast, unless otherwise agreed between the holders of the intellectual property rights to the film and the broadcasters. In its amended form, it seems to be a statement of the obvious.

<hr>

Extract 5.5.9

<hr>

Television Directive, Unofficial consolidated version prepared by the services of the Commission, http://europa.eu.int/comm/dg10/ avpolicy/twf/tvconse.html, arts 4(1), 6 and 7

Article 4

1. Member States shall ensure where practicable and by appropriate means, that broadcasters reserve for European works, within the meaning of Article 6, a majority proportion of their transmission time, excluding the time appointed to news, sports events, games, advertising, teletext services and teleshopping. This proportion, having regard to the broadcaster's informational, educational, cultural and entertainment responsibilities to its viewing public, should be achieved progressively, on the basis of suitable criteria.

Article 6

1. Within the meaning of this chapter, 'European works' means the following:
(a) works originating from Member States;
(b) works originating from European third States party to the European Convention on Transfrontier Television of the Council of Europe and fulfilling the conditions of paragraph 2;
(c) works originating from other European third countries and fulfilling the conditions of paragraph 3.

<hr>

[34] Commission of the European Communities, *Communication from the Commission to the Council and the European Parliament on the application of Articles 4 and 5 of Directive 89/552/EEC 'Television without Frontiers'*, COM (96) 302 final, p 74.

Application of the provisions of (b) and (c) shall be conditional on works originating from Member States not being the subject of discriminatory measures in the third countries concerned.

2.   The works referred to in paragraph 1(a) and (b) are works mainly made with authors and workers residing in one or more States referred to in paragraph 1(a) and (b) provided that they comply with one of the following three conditions:

(a) they are made by one or more producers established in one or more of those States; or

(b) production of the works is supervised and actually controlled by one or more producers established in one or more of those States; or

(c) the contribution of co-producers of those States to the total co-production costs is preponderant and the co-production is not controlled by one or more producers established outside those States.

3.   The works referred to in paragraph 1(c) are works made exclusively or in co-production with producers established in one or more Member States by producers established in one or more European third countries with which the Community has concluded agreements relating to the audiovisual sector, if those works are mainly made with authors and workers residing in one or more European States.

4.   Works that are not European works within the meaning of paragraph 1 but that are produced within the framework of bilateral co-production treaties concluded between Member States and third countries shall be deemed to be European works provided that the Community co-producers supply a majority share of the total cost of the production and that the production is not controlled by one or more producers established outside the territory of the Member States.

5.   Works which are not European works within the meaning of paragraphs 1 and 4, but made mainly with authors and works residing in one or more Member States, shall be considered to be European works to an extent corresponding to the proportion of the contribution of Community co-producers to the total production costs.

Article 7

Member States shall ensure that broadcasters under their jurisdiction do not broadcast cinematographic works outside periods agreed with the rights holders.

As already mentioned, the European quota has occasioned considerable controversy. Even the imprecise wording of art 4 seems to attest to the political compromise which produced this article. Indeed, it is doubtful whether art 4 would even be legally enforceable.

Questions for discussion

1.   What aspects of the drafting of art 4 would render its enforceability doubtful?

2.   What determines whether a programme is European or not? To what extent does art 6 indicate that the European quota is more concerned with industrial policy goals rather than cultural policy goals?

3.   What other aspects of the way in which art 4 is drafted are likely to limit its effectiveness?

There was certainly disagreement among Member States as to whether or not the quota was desirable or necessary. In the following extract, de Witte reviews the background to the quota.

Extract 5.5.10

B de Witte, 'The European Content Requirement in the EC Television Directive – Five Years After' in E M Barendt (ed), *The Yearbook of Media and Entertainment Law 1995* (Oxford University Press, 1995), pp 101–102, 104, 106–107

The intricate formulation and hesitant tone of Article 4 have led some authors to criticize the provision for being an example of symbolic legislation devoid of practical effects and incapable of achieving its stated objective of promoting the development of the European audio-visual industry. Yet most authors have criticized the European content requirement for opposite reasons, and regard it as an example of ill-conceived protectionism towards the outside world and undue interference with national cultural policies.

. . .

A European quota had not been envisaged by the Commission in its 1984 Green Paper, but was part of its 1986 proposal. It caused most of the political problems which arose during the very acrimonious and complicated negotiation process of the Television Directive.[i] The political bargaining which took place between single-market supporters, who wanted the adoption of the Directive in order to liberalize the market for broadcasting, and cultural and industrial policy-makers, who made the quota a condition for agreeing to the text of the Directive, led to the inclusion of European television programme content requirements in the Directive which was eventually adopted in 1989.[ii]

. . .

The European content requirement is a *corpus alienum* within this internal-market context. None of the Member States had ever thought of imposing quota requirements on *foreign* broadcasts, and the fact that Member States may have different views on whether, and to what extent, to impose programming requirements on their *own* broadcasters is not capable of hindering the cross-border *diffusion* of television programmes. Therefore, the inclusion of the European content requirement signals that the TV Directive is not *merely* one of the 300 pieces of the internal market mosaic, but also an instrument of *economic regulation* and of *cultural policy*. It was inspired by the will, most clearly expressed by the French Government but eventually also endorsed by the Commission and most other Member States, to take legislative action at the Community level in order to curb the massive dominance of American audio-visual productions on the European market. The final text of Article 4 of the Directive forms an uneasy compromise between, on the one hand, the ambitious aims held by the Commission, the European Parliament, and, above all, the French Government, who all wanted binding quotas, and, on the other hand, the strong misgivings of the private television groups and some other governments like those of the United Kingdom and Germany, which would have preferred to have no European content requirement at all.

---

[i] The negotiation process is described by P. Delwit and C. Gobin, 'Etude du cheminement de la directive télévision sans frontières: synthèse des prises de position des institutions communautaires' in G. Vandersanden (ed.), *L'espace audiovisuel européen* (Editions de l'Université de Bruxelles, 1991), 55.

[ii] R. Collins, 'The Screening of Jacques Tati: Broadcasting and Cultural Identity in the European Community' (1993) 11 *Cardozo Arts & Entertainment LJ* 361, 371.

As de Witte suggests art 4 was motivated by both industrial and cultural concerns. However, doubts can be cast on how effective art 4 is in contributing to either policy objective. For example, apart from excluding some programmes, it does not specify the type of programming which is to satisfy the quota obligation. Thus, broadcasters might be tempted to concentrate on the more inexpensively produced 'flow' type of programmes, for example, studio discussion programmes, which can satisfy the quota but have only a very short shelf life, and, therefore, do not contribute to the development of a library of programmes which can be rebroadcast or sold. For this, 'stock' programmes are required, for example, fiction series, but these are more expensive to produce, particularly compared with the American product. Article 4 does nothing to try to encourage this type of programming to be developed, yet it is stock programmes which are necessary for the development of programme catalogues, a need recognised by the Commission.[35] Similarly, as a tool of cultural policy, art 4 has its limits. The article is silent on transmission times. Broadcasters may be tempted to transmit European works at less popular viewing times, in order to leave free the prime viewing periods for those productions likely to gain a wider audience. Article 4 determines a work as 'European' essentially on the basis of location and/or nationality. Again, a question must be raised as to how this contributes to the development of television programmes about European culture or identity. Nationality and location alone will not ensure that programmes are produced which reflect European or national identity. This of course illustrates the inherent difficulty of trying to introduce measures which will promote a certain type of programming. To attempt to define in the regulation what is acceptable content for the purposes of promotion of cultural policy would almost certainly constitute an interference with broadcasting freedom. Quota requirements, such as art 4, are at best a crude instrument.

The quota has also been controversial for other reasons. Doubts have been raised about art 4's legal validity. There have been three main attacks on its validity. First, that it constituted an infringement of ECHR, art 10, discussed

---

[35] Commission of the European Communities, *Strategy Options to Strengthen the European Programme Industry in the Context of the Audiovisual Policy of the European Union*, Green Paper, COM (94) 96 final, p 8.

in Extract 5.5.11 below. Secondly, that there was no competence under Community law to introduce quotas, and thirdly, that it was incompatible with international trade obligations. Now that the Directive (and art 4) has been in force for some 10 years, these arguments have become less significant. Certainly, while there is no specific competence to justify the quotas, it can be argued that the Community, in addition to its express powers to deal with specific sectors, has functional powers which enable it to legislate in other areas in order to achieve Community objectives, such as the creation of the single market.[36] The US strongly objected to the introduction of the European quota, arguing that it acted as a barrier to free trade under the General Agreement on Tariffs and Trade (GATT). One of the points of disagreement between the US and the European Community was whether GATT covered trade in the audiovisual sector, the latter adopting the position that the audiovisual sector represented trade in services, not goods. When the General Agreement on Trade in Services (GATS) was agreed in 1994, the European Community and its Member States refrained from making any commitments under GATS in respect of audiovisual services, which effectively means that, for Member States, audiovisual services are excluded from their GATS obligations.[37] Negotiations for the further liberalisation of trade in services are due to begin in 2000, however, the US has indicated that it will not reopen the debate over the position of the European quotas.[38]

Extract 5.5.11

B de Witte, 'The European Content Requirement in the EC Television Directive – Five Years After' in E M Barendt (ed), *The Yearbook of Media and Entertainment Law 1995* (Oxford University Press, 1995), pp 101, 116–117 (some footnotes omitted)

International human rights treaties and the constitutional traditions of the Member States of the European Union form a source of inspiration for those unwritten general principles of Community law which, according to the case law of the ECJ, are binding for the Community institutions.[i] An act of Community law such as the Television Directive must therefore be compatible with freedom of expression, and the legality of Article 4 of the Directive must also be appraised in the light of the general principle of freedom of expression embodied in Article 10 of the ECHR,[ii] which guarantees the right to 'receive and impart information and ideas without interference by public authorities and regardless of frontiers'. The question, therefore, is whether Article 4 constitutes

---

[36] de Witte, note 18, above, pp 117–119.
[37] Ibid, pp 119–121.
[38] European Commission, *GATS 2000/WTO New Round*, http://europa.eu.int/comm/dg10/ avpo . . . nternat/gats2000/consultdoc_en.html. The negotiations are likely however to produce considerable debate over the definition of 'audiovisual' services, a sensitive issue in the light of the growing multimedia market.

194

an interference by the EC with somebody's rights of expression. One might argue that the quota requirement limits the European broadcasters' right to *impart* information and ideas, as well as the public's right to *receive* information and ideas. It is true that the quota requirement does not restrict the diffusion of any *specific* television programme and does not interfere with the transmission of any *particular* information or idea.[iii] Yet it is difficult to deny that Article 4 of the Directive is a general interference with the freedom of broadcasters to decide what to broadcast, and therefore a *prima facie* interference with the rights granted by Article 10 of the ECHR.

The second paragraph of Article 10 allows for restrictions of freedom of expression if they are prescribed by law and necessary for the protection of one of a listed number of public interests. Economic regulation and the protection of cultural identity, the fundamental objectives of the quota rule, are not listed among those public interests and this has led some legal writers to conclude that Article 4 is in breach of the Convention.[iv]

However, one should be aware of the fact that programme obligations are quite common in national broadcasting law. Although a direct challenge against them based on Article 10 of the Convention has not yet been brought before the Commission and Court of Human Rights, it is difficult to imagine that all such programme rules, intended to guarantee pluralism of opinions and ideas in the media, would be in breach of international human rights standards. The justification for such rules should probably be sought in the notion of 'rights of others', which is among the public interests mentioned in Article 10(2). Those rules limit the broadcasters' freedom to draw up their own schedule, but they do so in order to guarantee the access of viewers to a wide range and variety of ideas and cultural expressions. The same reasons could also justify the interference imposed by Article 4 of the Directive.[v]

[i] See e.g. A. Clapham, *Human Rights and the European Community. A Critical Overview* (Nomos, 1991); and, with specific reference to the area considered here, J.P. Jacqué, 'Liberté d'information' in A. Cassese, A. Clapham, J. Weiler (eds), *Human Rights and the European Community: The Substantive Law* (Nomos, 1991), 309; and B. De Witte and H. Post, 'Educational and Cultural Rights', *ibid.*, 123.

[ii] See particularly Case C-260/89, *Elliniki Radiophonia Tileorassi* [1991] ECR I-2925, in which the ECJ recognized freedom of expression, as embodied in Art. 10 of the ECHR, as a general principle of Community law.

[iii] V. Salvatore, 'Quotas on TV Programmes and EC Law', (1992) 29 *CML Rev.* 967, 986.

[iv] A. Von Bogdandy, 'Europäischer Protektionismus im Medienbereich' (1992) 9 *Europäische Zeitschrift für Wirtschaftsrecht* 15; C. Engel, *Privater Rundfunk vor der Europäischen Menschenrechtskonvention* (Nomos, 1993), 335.

[v] See J.P. Jacqué, note i above, 309, 342.

Questions for discussion

1. Do you find the defence of art 4 presented by de Witte convincing?

2. There are weaknesses in the drafting of art 4. If you were to redraft the article to redress these weaknesses, how might ECHR, art 10 limit that redrafting exercise?

Despite the concerns about the quota's validity, it has survived the Directive's amendment process, and it might be argued has become a firm component of industrial policy. The Commission had proposed that art 4 should continue only for a further period of 10 years.[39] However, this proposal was not adopted although art 25a requires an independent study of the impact of arts 4 and 5 to be carried out. The Commission is required to report every two years on the implementation of arts 4 and 5. Although in these reports the Commission has noted a general improvement in the quantity of European works being transmitted, it is also apparent that this improvement does not apply to all forms of television delivery. Subscription/pay channels, which are usually special-interest channels, frequently fail to meet the quota requirements.[40] Generally, the Commission, in its reports, has been fairly circumspect in its conclusions about the effectiveness of the quota and, as previously noted, the weaknesses of art 4 mean that an increase in the number of European works will not necessarily result in a successful contribution to the Community's industrial and cultural policy objectives.

(e) Right of reply

Article 23 provides a right of reply to natural or legal persons. Although the Application Report of the Commission[41] did not list any difficulties or problems with this provision, it has been amended to provide that there must be no unreasonable terms or conditions, hindering the exercise of the right of reply, and that it must be transmitted within a reasonable time, and at a time and in a manner appropriate to the offending broadcast.

Extract 5.5.12

**Television Directive, Unofficial consolidated
version prepared by the services of the Commission,
http://europa.eu.int/comm/dg10/avpolicy/twf/tvconse.html, art 23(1)**

1. Without prejudice to other provisions adopted by the Member States under civil, administrative or criminal law, any natural or legal person, regardless of nationality, whose legitimate interests, in particular reputation and good name, have been damaged by an assertion of incorrect facts in a television programme must have a right of reply or equivalent remedies. Member States

---

[39] Commission of the European Communities, *Report on Application of Directive 89/552/EEC and Proposal for a European Parliament and Council Directive amending Council Directive 89/552/EEC on the coordination of certain provisions laid down by law, regulation or administrative action in Member States concerning the pursuit of television broadcasting activities*, COM (95) 86 final, p 35.

[40] European Commission, *Third Communication from the Commission to the Council and the European Parliament on the application of Articles 4 and 5 of Directive 89/552/EEC 'Television without Frontiers' for the period 1995–96 including an overall assessment of application over the period 1991–96*, COM (98) 199 final, para 2.3.

[41] Note 39, above, p 23.

shall ensure that the actual exercise of the right of reply or equivalent remedies is not hindered by the imposition of unreasonable terms or conditions. The reply shall be transmitted within a reasonable time subsequent to the request being substantiated and at a time and in a manner appropriate to the broadcast to which the request refers.

Question for discussion
Refer to BA 1996, s 119, see Extract 4.4.6. Do the powers given to the Broadcasting Standards Commission under s 119 fulfil the UK's obligations under art 23?

6

ADVERTISING REGULATION

1. INTRODUCTION

Advertising has an important role within the media because it is a significant revenue source for both broadcasting and the press. Generally, the press is funded by a combination of advertising revenue and newspaper sales. Private broadcasting channels have been primarily funded by advertising, thereby enabling their programme services to be delivered free to the viewer.[1] Although, with the development of satellite and cable services (and more recently digital terrestrial television), subscription television has emerged as a source of funding, advertising revenue is presently still the major funding source for broadcasters, and even subscription services usually rely on a combination of advertising and subscription revenue. Commercial radio broadcasting has also depended on advertising for revenue, and the introduction of national commercial radio has probably increased advertisers' interest in radio. While the general law of course governs all advertisements, the specific regulation of advertising depends upon whether it appears in the broadcast or non-broadcast sector. To some extent regulation of advertising reflects a pattern similar to the regulation of press and broadcasting. As was seen in earlier chapters, press and broadcasting are regulated quite differently. Press advertising (as well as cinema, video, Internet, magazines, direct mail and so forth), is controlled mainly through a self-regulatory system by the Advertising Standards Authority (the ASA). Broadcast advertising is subject to legislative controls, administered through the relevant regulatory bodies, namely the Radio Authority (RA) and the Independent Television Commission (ITC).

Several issues arise concerning the relationship between advertising and the media, particularly in the case of broadcasting. Clearly advertisers will have an incentive to place as much advertising as they can, and the non-broadcast media are free to accept as much as they wish, subject only to commercial constraints such as how much advertising readers will tolerate.

---

[1] The Peacock Committee reported that revenue from advertising provided approximately 95% of the income of independent television companies and most of the income of the independent local radio stations: *Report of the Committee on Financing the BBC*, Cmnd 9824 (1986) para 80.

However, in the case of television, there are strict limits on the amount and frequency of advertising. Although radio is not subject to such specific rules, licensees might find themselves in breach of their licences if they were to broadcast an undue amount of advertising, so that the nature of their service changed.[2] The advertising rules imposed on broadcasters can be seen as a reflection of the familiar justifications for broadcasting regulation (Chapter 1, Section 3). Advertisers, despite their importance to broadcast funding, cannot have unlimited access, and they will be subject to restrictions on the amount of advertising, what can be advertised, and how it can be advertised.

A more significant issue is the relationship between advertising and what is broadcast. Advertisers have an interest in reaching as many viewers or listeners as possible during any given advertising slot, while broadcast companies will, in the interests of being able to charge higher advertising rates, have an incentive to present programming which will deliver the largest possible audience to the advertisers. These interests can have an effect on programme quality and diversity. To some extent, this risk is compensated for by the structure of broadcasting; for example, the BBC is a public broadcaster, not dependent upon advertising, and therefore able to provide diversified and minority programming (see Chapter 3). Commercial broadcasters cannot simply succumb to advertisers' pressure, as they also have to meet certain programme standards. Finally, the advertising rules, which will be examined in this chapter, also try to limit the temptation of broadcasters to cater for advertisers' needs. However, the impact of advertising on the quality and range of programming is a serious concern. With growing competition for audiences and advertising, broadcasters may feel under increased pressure to produce programming aimed at a mass audience. This could also lead to pressure on regulators to relax advertising rules. In the following extract, the Peacock Committee, which was established to examine BBC financing, but which also looked more widely at broadcast financing, discusses these concerns.

Extract 6.1.1

Report of the Committee on Financing the BBC, Cmnd 9824 (1986), para 421

Under an advertising-supported broadcasting system, broadcasters are effectively attracting an audience by their programmes that will also be an audience to advertisers. An advertising-supported system will lead to programme diversity only to the extent that different advertisers are willing to pay to associate their messages with different programmes. The important point from an efficiency perspective is that there is no reason why the value of programmes to

---

[2] Advertising agencies are also prohibited from holding radio and television licences: BA 1990, Sched 2, Pt II, para 6.

advertisers should correspond to the value attached to the programmes by viewers and listeners. In fact, the value to advertisers and the value to the audience of a particular programme may well differ markedly. The reason for this is that under an advertising-supported system, people can only express their preferences either by watching or not watching a particular programme, whereas the value to all viewers is measured by their aggregate willingness to pay which measures the intensity of their preferences ... In the broadcasting case, advertisers can bid for the service of supplying a message to a particular size and type of audience, but the audience has no way of bidding for programme services apart from watching or not watching a programme. The commercial viability of a programme in an advertising system means that the programme must generate a sufficiently large audience to induce advertisers to pay enough to cover the cost of showing the programme. This may lead to programmes being shown because they are popular numerically, even though programmes that are less popular numerically but more intensely demanded are not shown.

Question for discussion

Many of the new broadcasting services are special-interest services; does this alter the Committee's analysis?

This chapter will examine the regulation of both non-broadcast and broadcast advertising, and also consider the impact of European regulation.

2. REGULATION OF NON-BROADCAST ADVERTISING

(a) Background

The ASA's primary concern is to ensure industry observance of the British Codes of Advertising and Sales Promotion (the BCASP). While, there are specific industry voluntary codes, such as the Proprietary Association of Great Britain's *Code of Standards of Advertising Practice on the Public Advertising of Non-Prescription Medicines*, the BCASP constitutes a unified set of rules for the entire advertising industry, in the same way that both television and radio broadcasting have codes governing advertising. Although, the BCASP contains quite detailed rules, the essential obligation is to ensure that advertisements are 'legal, decent, honest and truthful'.

The ASA was established in 1962 by the advertising industry largely to stave off the threat of statutory regulation, arising from a report of the Moloney Committee on Consumer Protection,[3] which had criticised the voluntary system then operating. The BCASP, first drafted in 1961, is based upon the International Code of Advertising Practice of the International Chamber of Commerce.[4]

---

[3] C Munro, 'Self-regulation in the Media' [1997] *Public Law* 6, at 9.
[4] P Thomson, 'Informal Resolution of Disputes in Advertising – The Role of the Code of Advertising Practice Committee' (1982) 1 *Trading Law* 233.

It represented the first attempt at co-ordinated rules for the entire non-broadcast advertising industry. At the same time a Committee of Advertising Practice (CAP) was established, made up of advertising industry representatives. Review of the BCASP is one of its main responsibilities, while the ASA's central role is the investigation of alleged breaches of the BCASP.

Extract 6.2.1

The British Codes of Advertising and Sales Promotion (October 1999), clauses 68.2, 68.6 and 68.31–68.32

68.2 The strength of the [self-regulatory] system depends on the long-term commitment of all those involved in commercial communications. Practitioners in every sphere share an interest in seeing that advertisements and promotions are welcomed and trusted by their audience; unless they are accepted and believed they cannot succeed. If they are offensive or misleading they discredit everyone associated with them and the industry as a whole.

. . .

68.6 The ASA investigates complaints from any source against advertisements and promotions in non-broadcast media. Advertisers are told the outcome of the ASA Council's rulings and, where appropriate, are asked to withdraw or amend their advertisements or promotions.

. . .

68.31 Members of the public who complain may be asked by the ASA for a formal, written assurance that they have no commercial or other interest in registering a complaint. If they do have an interest, this will be disclosed to the advertiser and may be included in the ASA's published report.

68.32 Complaints are normally not pursued if the point at issue is the subject of simultaneous legal action. In certain cases it may be more appropriate for an investigation to be undertaken by other consumer protection bodies. If so, the ASA will provide information or will try to redirect the complainant to the most appropriate qualified source of assistance.

Question for discussion
Why should the commercial sector be allowed to complain?

(b) British Codes of Advertising and Sales Promotion

(i) Introduction
The current edition of the BCASP came into force on 1 October 1999 (the tenth). The BCASP contains a number of general principles as well as specific rules about specific products,[5] claims and audiences, for example, alcoholic drinks, children, motoring, environmental claims, slimming methods and

---

[5] 'Products' has a broad definition under the BCASP. It includes '. . . goods, services, ideas, causes, opportunities, prizes or gifts': BCASP, clause 1.3(a).

products, and financial services and products. There is a special code for cigarette and tobacco advertising which has been agreed between the ASA, the Department of Health, and the tobacco industry. The Cigarette Code has been incorporated into the BCASP, and operates as part of it. It differs, however, in one particular respect, because under clause 66.9, cigarette and tobacco advertisements have to be cleared by the CAP before publication. The following extract illustrates aspects of the BCASP's operation.

Extract 6.2.2

The British Codes of Advertising and Sales Promotion (October 1999), clause 1.4

1.4 The following criteria apply to the Codes:
  a the ASA Council's interpretation of the Codes is final
  b conformity with the Codes is assessed according to the advertisement's probable impact when taken as a whole and in context. This will depend on the medium in which the advertisement appeared, the audience and their likely response, the nature of the product and any additional material distributed to consumers
  c the Codes are indivisible; advertisers must conform with all appropriate rules
  . . .
  h the rules make due allowance for public sensitivities but will not be used by the ASA to diminish freedom of speech.

The BCASP contains two separate codes: the Advertising Code which covers advertising generally, and the Sales Promotion Code which covers promotional marketing techniques. The latter Code operates in conjunction with the Advertising Code and so the principles of the Advertising Code also apply where appropriate (clause 1.4, see Extract 6.2.2). In addition to the BCASP and the Cigarette Code, there are also sets of specific rules covering particular product categories or types of selling. The BCASP applies also to these specific areas. In the following extract some of the general principles and rules of the Advertising Code can be seen.

Extract 6.2.3

The British Codes of Advertising and Sales Promotion (October 1999), clauses 2.1–2.4, 2.8, 6.1 and 7.1

Principles

2.1 All advertisements should be legal, decent, honest and truthful.
2.2 All advertisements should be prepared with a sense of responsibility to consumers and to society.

2.3 All advertisements should respect the principles of fair competition generally accepted in business.

2.4 No advertisement should bring advertising into disrepute.

. . .

2.8 The Codes are applied in the spirit as well as in the letter.

Honesty

6.1 Advertisers should not exploit the credulity, lack of knowledge or inexperience of consumers.

Truthfulness

7.1 No advertisement should mislead by inaccuracy, ambiguity, exaggeration, omission or otherwise.

In 1998, there were 12,217 complaints covering 8,343 advertisements. Of these, the ASA ruled that 623 should be withdrawn or amended.[6] Consistently, it is issues of taste and decency which draw the highest number of complaints.

(ii) Decency

Extract 6.2.4

The British Codes of Advertising and Sales Promotion (October 1999), clauses 5.1–5.3

5.1 Advertisements should contain nothing that is likely to cause serious or widespread offence. Particular care should be taken to avoid causing offence on the grounds of race, religion, sex, sexual orientation or disability. Compliance with the Codes will be judged on the context, medium, audience, product and prevailing standards of decency.

5.2 Advertisements may be distasteful without necessarily conflicting with 5.1 above. Advertisers are urged to consider public sensitivities before using potentially offensive material.

5.3 The fact that a particular product is offensive to some people is not sufficient grounds for objecting to an advertisement for it.

In its 1996 Annual Report, the ASA referred to one particular advertisement (part of a Gossard Glossies campaign) as having attracted the highest number of complaints (321) for 1996.[7] The current decency rules are identical to the previous edition and therefore are relevant to the discussion in this section.

---

[6] Advertising Standards Authority, *Annual Report 1998*, p 17.
[7] Advertising Standards Authority, *Annual Report 1996*, p 25.

Extract 6.2.5

Advertising Standards Authority, *Annual Report 1996*, I

Complaint: Objections, including one from an MP and one from Leeds City Council, to posters headed 'Who said a woman can't get pleasure from something soft'. It featured a photograph of a woman wearing a translucent black bra and briefs and lying, arms outstretched, in long grass. The complainants objected that the advertisement was sexist and offensive.
Adjudication: Complaints not upheld.
The advertisers said that they had conducted group discussions among women in the 20–34 year old target market. The women had not found the advertisement offensive and had assumed that it would appear on posters. The Authority acknowledged that, although some people had been offended, the advertisement was, in the context of the advertised product, acceptable.

Questions for discussion
1. How successfully did the ASA apply the decency rules to this adjudication?
2. Is evidence of the target audience relevant to a poster campaign?

This advertisement, and the ASA's ruling, caused considerable controversy in the press, and one national newspaper encouraged readers to complain to the ASA. The ASA commented on its approach.

Extract 6.2.6

Advertising Standards Authority, *Annual Report 1996*, p 7

The taste and decency provisions of the Codes present advertisers with special difficulties because what is tasteless or indecent to some people may be perfectly acceptable to others. While journalists voice their own opinions in the columns of their newspapers, public opinion is not always so firmly rooted in absolute terms. The essential balance that the Council must achieve in judging such advertisements could not be impartial if the ASA was influenced solely by media pressure or lobbying.

It is not obvious what weight the ASA gives to the number of complaints received about a particular advertisement. For some rules the number of people complaining would be irrelevant; however, for decency, the number of complaints received may be some indication of the degree of offence caused. The ASA did not appear to be unduly influenced by the number of complaints which it had received about the Gossard advertisement, although, understandably, the weight to be attributed to them may have been lessened by the press encouragement to complain. However, the ASA did seem to be impressed by the number of complaints received in relation to an advertisement run by Club 18–30, a holiday company, which carried the slogan

'Girls, can we interest you in a package holiday?' above a graphic depiction of a man wearing boxer shorts: '490 complaints gave a clear indication that the public regarded these posters as obscene, irresponsible and offensive'.[8] Here, of course, a distinction can be made between the two advertisements because of the nature of the product being advertised (see clause 5.1). However, referring to the ASA's handling of complaints about decency, Munro suggests that there may be some inconsistency along gender lines.

Extract 6.2.7

C Munro, 'Self-regulation in the Media' [1997] *Public Law* 6, at 11

Pity the poor adjudicators who must pick their way through these considerations and counter-considerations [referring to the wording of the decency clause]. In 1995 billboard advertisements for Club 18–30 ('Beaver Espana', 'You get two weeks for being drunk and disorderly' and 'Girls, can we interest you in a package holiday?', the last displayed above a photograph of a man with a prominent bulge in his boxer shorts), notwithstanding their humour, were condemned by the A.S.A. as 'offensive' and 'irresponsible in advocating sexual and alcoholic excess.' There had been several hundred complaints received, but others regarded the verdicts as hypocritical. It is sometimes difficult to find a thread of consistency between the decisions. Complaints about Wonderbra advertisements ('Hello boys', 'We've been apart too long') were dismissed, while a proposed advertisement for underpants which featured a genitally well endowed male ('The Loin King') was disapproved on the ground that it treated the male body like a piece of meat.

The BCASP's rules on decency shows what a fine line may have to be drawn in balancing the freedom to communicate and public reaction. The next extract provides a good example of this balance. The complaint was made about a poster, part of an advertising campaign run by the Commission for Racial Equality. Forty-seven complaints were received.

Extract 6.2.8

Advertising Standards Authority, *Monthly Report* (May 1999)

Complaint: Objections, including one from the General Dental Council and several from dentists, to a poster that pictured the face of a black man next to the headline 'Scared?'. Directly beneath in smaller print, it stated 'You should be. He's a dentist'. The complainants objected that the poster:
1. was offensive in assuming that people should be either scared of black people or surprised to find them in a qualified position; and

---

[8] Advertising Standards Authority, *Annual Report 1995*, p 21.

2. denigrated the dental profession and discouraged children from visiting the dentist.

Adjudication: ... The advertisers said the advertisement was part of their 'Personal Responsibility Campaign' intended to encourage people to consider their attitudes and prejudices. ... They ... maintained that, despite ... advances, ethnic minorities and institutions alone could not fight what they considered was continuing racism; they had designed the advertisement to encourage readers to take responsibility for challenging racism. They thought that by using the humorous and ironic stereotype about dentists they would dispel readers' harmful and insulting stereotypes of ethnic minorities, black men in particular. The Authority accepted that fear of dentists was a long-established, humorous cliché and the portrayal of a dentist would not denigrate the dental profession. It concluded that, because of the prominence given to the face, which it considered sinister, and to the headline, the advertisement could be seen as advocating the negative stereotype that black men should be feared. The Authority considered that, although some readers would see the advertisement as a challenge to their prejudices and would not be offended by that stereotype, others would be seriously offended. The Authority noted, however, that the Committee of Advertising Practice had, as part of the poster industry's self-imposed mandatory pre-vetting procedure,[9] advised that it believed the ASA Council was unlikely to uphold complaints against the poster on grounds of offence. The Authority asked the advertisers to take particular care when devising future campaigns.

Questions for discussion

1. There is an inference in the adjudication that, had it not been for CAP's advice, the ASA would have upheld the complaint. Do you agree with the ASA's analysis?

2. Did the ASA correctly take into account the criteria stated in clause 5.1 for judging compliance?

3. Can an advertisement intend to offend as part of its message, and be in compliance with the BCASP?

(iii) Privacy

Extract 6.2.9

British Codes of Advertising Practice and Sales Promotion (October 1999), clauses 13.1–13.2 and 13.4

13.1 Advertisers should not unfairly portray or refer to people in an adverse or offensive way. Advertisers are urged to obtain written permission before:

---

[9] The pre-vetting procedure was introduced in June 1998, and applies to poster advertisers who have previously been found in breach of the taste and decency, inter alia, rules: note 6, above, p 28.

a referring to or portraying members of the public or their identifiable possessions; the use of crowd scenes or general public locations may be acceptable without permission

b referring to people with a public profile; references that accurately reflect the contents of books, articles or films may be acceptable without permission

c implying any personal approval of the advertised product; advertisers should recognise that those who do not wish to be associated with the product may have a legal claim.

13.2 Prior permission may not be needed when the advertisement contains nothing that is inconsistent with the position or views of the person featured.

13.4 Members of the Royal Family should not normally be shown or mentioned in advertisements without their prior permission. Incidental references unconnected with the advertised product, or references to material such as books, articles or films about members of the Royal Family, may be acceptable.

The previous edition of the BCASP urged advertisers to obtain prior written permission before portraying or referring to individuals in advertisements. However, under clause 13.2, it also appeared to accept that advertisers were unlikely to obtain prior permission of public figures portrayed in advertisements:

Advertisers who have not obtained prior permission from entertainers, politicians, sportsmen and others whose work gives them a high public profile should ensure that they are not portrayed in an offensive or adverse way. . . .

The new edition seems to place a stronger onus on advertisers to obtain such permission, but much may depend upon the interpretation of the new clause 13.2. The following adjudication, which was reached under the previous edition of the rules, concerned breaches of clauses 5.1 and 13.2. Would the new clause 13 have any effect on the outcome of the adjudication?

Extract 6.2.10

Advertising Standards Authority, *Monthly Report* (April 1999)

Complaint: Objections to an advertisement, in the Times, for a football match on Channel 5. It showed Gordon Brown asking Peter Mandelson 'Do you fancy Laudrup for tonight?' and Peter Mandelson replying 'Yes, I think he should get an outing.' The advertisement continued 'Will Laudrup play tonight? Copenhagen v Chelsea. Live only on Channel 5.' The complainants believed the advertisement perpetuated recent speculation about Peter Mandelson's sexuality. They objected that the advertisement was offensive generally and to Peter Mandelson.

Adjudication: Complaints not upheld. The advertisers . . . said the advertisement promoted the European Cup Winners Cup match between Copenhagen and Chelsea and they explained that there had been considerable speculation whether the Chelsea player, Brian Laudrup, would play that evening;

the term 'outing' was a football term meaning to play a game. They believed the advertisement was a humorous and entertaining play on words linking the match to speculation about Peter Mandelson's sexuality, that resulted from a comment on BBC's Newsnight a few days earlier.[10] The advertisers said they did not refer to Peter Mandelson's sexuality or comment adversely about it. They said they had received no complaints. The publishers said they had received no complaints and believed the advertisement did not breach the Codes' requirements on taste and decency. The Authority considered that the advertisement was unlikely to offend, either readers generally or Peter Mandelson and did not invade his privacy.

Questions for discussion
1. Was it relevant that the matter of Peter Mandelson's sexuality had not been commented upon by him in public? Should it have been relevant?
2. Will the length of an advertising campaign be relevant? Would it have played a part in this adjudication?
3. Does clause 13 provide any privacy protection for public figures?

(iv) Political advertising
One type of advertising which the ASA has been ambivalent about regulating has been party political advertising. In previous editions of the BCASP political advertising campaigns had to comply with the BCASP, although they were exempt from some parts of the Codes, including obligations to substantiate claims and to be truthful. In 1996, a political advertisement, run by the Conservative Party, attracted the second largest number of complaints (167) for that year. The advertisement showed a picture of Tony Blair, then Leader of the Opposition, revealing red, demonic-looking eyes and captioned 'New Labour new danger'.

Extract 6.2.11

Advertising Standards Authority, *Annual Report 1996,* I

Complaints upheld [in part]

Although it did not consider that readers in general would think the advertisement attributed satanic qualities to Tony Blair, the Authority reminded the advertisers that the Codes prohibited the portrayal, without permission, of politicians in an adverse or offensive way. Because it considered that the advertisement depicted Tony Blair as sinister and dishonest, the Authority asked for it not to be used again.

---

[10] The comment was not made by Peter Mandelson, nor had he commented on these speculations.

One might question whether a system, which is primarily concerned with commercial advertising, is really appropriate for dealing with political advertising.

In giving evidence, in 1998, to the Neill Committee on Standards in Public Life, CAP expressed the view that it was inappropriate for the BCASP to apply to party political advertising.[11] The new edition of the BCASP excludes completely party political advertising from the self-regulatory system.[12]

Extract 6.2.12

British Codes of Advertising Practice and Sales Promotion (October 1999), clause 12.1–12.2

12.1 Any advertisement, whenever published, whose principal function is to influence voters in local, regional, national or international elections or referendums is exempt from the Codes but advertisers are urged to make their identity clear.

12.2 There is a formal distinction between government policy and that of political parties. Advertisements by central or local government, or those concerning government policy as distinct from party policy, are subject to all the Codes' rules.

Questions for discussion

1. Are there standards, beyond the application of the general law, with which political advertising should have to comply?
2. Do we need a system for monitoring political advertising?
3. Does it make sense to have government advertising (of the type referred to in clause 12.2) regulated along with commercial advertising?

(c) Sanctions

As a self-regulatory body, the ASA is limited in the sanctions available to it. Essentially, it must rely upon the co-operation of the industry to enforce its rulings. Most commonly, it will require the offending advertisement to be amended or withdrawn. However, clause 68.39 supplements these sanctions, and it will be used where an advertiser has failed to respond to the ASA's inquiries or adjudication.

---

[11] Note 6, above, p 25. The Neill Committee chose to make no recommendation as to whether there should be a specific code for political advertising, but exhorted the political parties to agree a code with the advertising industry: *Fifth Report of the Committee on Standards in Public Life, The Funding of Political Parties in the UK*, Cm 4057-I (1998) para 13.24.

[12] Ibid.

Extract 6.2.13

British Codes of Advertising Practice and Sales Promotion (October 1999), clause 68.39

A number of sanctions exist to counteract advertisements and promotions that conflict with the Codes: the media, contractors and service providers may withhold their services or deny access to space; adverse publicity which acts as a deterrant may result from rulings published in the ASA's Monthly Report; pre-vetting or trading sanctions may be imposed or recognition revoked by the media's, advertiser's, promoter's or agency's professional association or service provider and financial incentives provided by trade, professional or media organisations may be withdrawn or temporarily withheld.

In relation to misleading advertisements or promotions, the ASA does have another avenue for action. Under the Control of Misleading Advertisements Regulations 1988 (SI 1988/915) the Director General of Fair Trading has a duty to act where the ASA's procedures have failed to resolve the matter. The Misleading Advertisements Regulations were introduced to give effect to an EC Directive on misleading advertising.[13] The Directive does not exclude self-regulatory control of advertising, provided that there are mechanisms for recourse to appropriate legal proceedings.[14]

Extract 6.2.14

Control of Misleading Advertisements Regulations 1988 (SI 1988/915), regs 2(2), 4, 5 and 6

2.—(2) For the purposes of these Regulations an advertisement is misleading if in any way, including its presentation, it deceives or is likely to deceive the persons to whom it is addressed or whom it reaches and if, by reason of its deceptive nature, it is likely to affect their economic behaviour or, for those

---

[13] Council Directive 84/450/EEC of 10 September 1984 relating to the approximation of the laws, regulations and administrative provisions of the Member States concerning misleading advertising, [1984] OJ L250/17. This Directive was amended in 1997 to cover also comparative advertising: Directive 97/55/EC of the European Parliament and of the Council of 6 October 1997 amending Directive 84/450/EEC concerning misleading advertising so as to include comparative advertising, [1997] OJ L290. A further directive, affecting the Misleading Directive, has been passed: Directive 98/27/EC of the European Parliament and of the Council of 19 May 1998 on injunctions for the protection of consumers' interests, [1998] OJ L166/51. This Directive when implemented will enable 'qualified entities' from other Member States to seek injunctions in the UK for breaches of, inter alia, the Misleading Directive. The government plans to consult in November 1999 on its implementation into national law.

[14] Unlike non-broadcast advertising, the Director General has no jurisdiction over misleading broadcast advertising (reg 4(2)). Instead, the ITC (and the RA) have a duty to investigate complaints about misleading advertisements (reg 8(1)).

reasons, injures or is likely to injure a competitor of the person whose interests the advertisement seeks to promote.

4.—(1) Subject to paragraphs (2) and (3) below, it shall be the duty of the Director [General of Fair Trading] to consider any complaint made to him that an advertisement is misleading, unless the complaint appears to the Director to be frivolous or vexatious.

(2) [*Omitted*].

(3) Before considering any complaint under paragraph (1) above the Director may require the person making the complaint to satisfy him that—

(a) there have been invoked in relation to the same or substantially the same complaint about the advertisement in question such established means of dealing with such complaints as the Director may consider appropriate, having regard to all the circumstances of the particular case;

(b) a reasonable opportunity has been allowed for those means to deal with the complaint in question; and

(c) those means have not dealt with the complaint adequately.

(4) In exercising the powers conferred on him by these Regulations the Director shall have regard to—

(a) all the interests involved and in particular the public interest; and

(b) the desirability of encouraging the control, by self-regulatory bodies, of advertisements.

5.—(1) If, having considered a complaint about an advertisement pursuant to regulation 4(1) above, he considers that the advertisement is misleading, the Director may, if he thinks it appropriate to do so, bring proceedings for an injunction (in which proceedings he may also apply for an interlocutory injunction) against any person appearing to him to be concerned or likely to be concerned with the publication of the advertisement.

6.—(1) The court on an application by the Director may grant an injunction on such terms as it may think fit but (except where it grants an interlocutory injunction) only if the court is satisfied that the advertisement to which the application relates is misleading. Before granting an injunction the court shall have regard to all the interests involved and in particular the public interest.

. . .

(5) The court shall not refuse to grant an injunction for lack of evidence that—

(a) the publication of the advertisement in question has given rise to loss or damage to any person; or

(b) the person responsible for the advertisement intended to be misleading or failed to exercise proper care to prevent its being misleading.

The following extract provides an example of an application for an injunction under the Misleading Advertisements Regulations. The advertisements, which had appeared in a national newspaper, were for a slimming aid. The ASA ruled that they were misleading, but they continued to be published unamended. It was alleged that they made six misleading claims either because they were wrong or unable to be substantiated.

Extract 6.2.15

Director General of Fair Trading v Tobyward Ltd and Another
[1989] 2 All ER 266, at 268 and 270–271

HOFFMANN J: . . . If a complaint is referred to the director and he considers the advertisement to be misleading, he may apply to the court for an injunction. The regulations provide no other legal remedy. They do not make the publication of misleading advertisements unlawful. The only sanction is that, once an injunction has been made, the publication of an advertisement in breach of its terms will be a contempt of court and punishable as such . . .

'Misleading', as I have said, is defined in the regulations as involving two elements: first, that the advertisement deceives or is likely to deceive the persons to whom it is addressed and, second, that it is likely to affect their economic behaviour. In my judgment in this context there is little difficulty about applying the concept of deception. An advertisement must be likely to deceive the persons to whom it is addressed if it makes false claims on behalf of the product. It is true that many people read advertisements with a certain degree of scepticism. For the purposes of applying the regulations, however, it must be assumed that there may be people who will believe what the advertisers tell them, and in those circumstances the making of a false claim is likely to deceive. Having regard to the evidence . . . , there is in my judgment a strong prima facie case that these advertisements were likely to deceive in each of the six respects of which complaint is made. The other element, namely that the advertisement is likely to affect the economic behaviour of the persons to whom it is addressed, means in this context no more than that it must make it likely that they will buy the product. As that was no doubt the intention of the advertisement, it is reasonable to draw the inference that it would have such a result. I am therefore satisfied that the court has jurisdiction under reg 6 to make an injunction in this case.

The making of the injunction is, however, a matter of discretion, and I must consider whether in this case it would be appropriate to do so. There are two reasons why I think I should. First, the regulations contemplate that there will only be intervention by the director when the voluntary system has failed. It is in my judgment desirable and in accordance with the public interest to which I must have regard that the courts should support the principle of self-regulation. I think that advertisers would be more inclined to accept the rulings of their self-regulatory bodies if it were generally known that in cases in which their procedures had been exhausted and the advertiser was still publishing an advertisement which appeared to the court to be prima facie misleading an injunction would ordinarily be granted. The respondents did offer undertakings to the director which could not have been enforced by any legal process other than the making of an application such as this for an injunction. But they were in terms which the director thought to be inadequate. . . .

Second, in my view the interests of consumers require the protection of an injunction pending trial of the action. It does not seem to me that the respondents could complain of any legitimate interference with their business if they were restrained from making claims of the kind to which the director is here taking objection.

Questions for discussion

1. Do you agree with his Lordship's view that the Director General's power reinforces the self-regulatory system?

2. Should the power to apply for an injunction be extended to breaches of other BCASP rules?

(d) Review of Advertising Standards Authority decisions

ASA adjudications are subject to judicial review.

Extract 6.2.16

R v Advertising Standards Authority Ltd, ex parte The Insurance Service plc (1990) 2 Admin LR 77, at 81–82 and 86

GLIDEWELL LJ: The principal authority in support of the submission that the [Advertising Standards] Authority's decisions are susceptible to judicial review is the decision of the Court of Appeal in *R. v Panel on Take Overs and Mergers, ex parte Datafin PLC & Anr* [1987] Q.B. 815. . . .

In his judgment, Sir John Donaldson, M.R. said of it [the Take-over Panel] at p.826:

'"Self-regulation" is an emotive term. It is also ambiguous. An individual who voluntarily regulates his life in accordance with stated principles, because he believes that this is morally right and also, perhaps, in his own long term interests, or a group of individuals who do so, are practising self-regulation. But it can mean something quite different. It can connote a system whereby a group of people, acting in concert, use their collective power to force themselves and others to comply with a code of conduct of their own devising. This is not necessarily morally wrong or contrary to the public interest, unlawful or even undesirable. But it is very different.

The Panel is a self-regulating body in the latter sense. Lacking any authority *de jure*, it exercises immense power *de facto* by devising, promulgating, amending and interpreting the City Code on Take-overs and Mergers, by waiving or modifying the application of the code in particular circumstances by investigating and reporting upon alleged breaches of the code and by the application or threat of sanctions. These sanctions are no less effective because they are applied indirectly and lack a legally enforceable base.'

. . .

The characteristics of the Advertising Standards Authority are in many ways similar to those of the take-over panel. The Authority has no powers granted to it by statute or at common law, nor does it have any contractual relationship with the advertisers whom it controls. Nevertheless, it is clearly exercising a public law function which, if the Authority did not exist, would no doubt be exercised by the Director General of Fair Trading. . . . I, therefore, have no hesitation in concluding that the decisions of the authority are susceptible to control by the court by way of judicial review.

213

The ASA has been in place now for over 30 years, and has clearly become established as part of the regulatory framework for ensuring that advertisements conform to certain recognised standards. It is common to compare the effectiveness of self-regulatory systems with statutory regulation. Frequently, it is claimed that a self-regulatory system has the advantage of expertise; that it is able to act flexibly, with speed, and with less cost to the public; and that it attracts industry confidence. However, there is no reason why these advantages cannot also be built into a statutory system, and the ITC and the RA provide reasonably good examples of statutory bodies which incorporate many of these features. Unlike self-regulation, statutory regulation will have the advantage of enforceable sanctions. Overall, there is no clear-cut case to be made for self-regulation.[15] Although it might be thought curious that there should be statutory regulation for broadcast advertising and a self-regulatory system for non-broadcast advertising, this seems less so when one reflects that it is consistent with the divergent regulatory patterns for broadcasting and the press. At the time of the ASA's establishment, the Moloney Committee was doubtful about the effectiveness of a self-regulatory, industry-regulated body, but there are now fewer doubts about its effectiveness. For the present, in any event, it seems unlikely that a different system will be put in place.

3. REGULATION OF BROADCAST ADVERTISING – TELEVISION

(a) Introduction

The Broadcasting Act 1990 (BA 1990) has little to say about the control of advertising, apart from prohibiting certain types of advertising, and requiring the ITC to draw up codes governing advertising. It is in these codes that the detailed rules are found. These codes also implement the rules on advertising and sponsorship found in the European Community's Television Directive, and to the extent that the Directive does not cover the matter, the Council of Europe's Television Convention (for background to these European instruments, see Chapter 5). Although these codes cannot be considered in detail here, the matters covered will illustrate the close scrutiny to which broadcast advertising is subject. Here again, the continuing influence of the theme that the unique power of broadcasting justifies regulation is apparent, although, one might question whether this underestimates the discrimination of the viewing audience.

---

[15] For a thorough review of self-regulation and an evaluation of the ASA and the Press Complaints Commission (discussed in Chapter 2), see Munro, note 3, above.

Extract 6.3.1

Broadcasting Act 1990, ss 8(1)–(2) and 9(1), (5)–(8)

8.—(1) The Commission shall do all that they can to secure that the rules specified in subsection (2) are complied with in relation to licensed services.

(2) Those rules are as follows—

    (a) a licensed service must not include—

        (i) any advertisement which is inserted by or one behalf of any body whose objects are wholly or mainly of a political nature,

        (ii) any advertisement which is directed towards any political end, or

        (iii) any advertisement which has any relation to any industrial dispute (other than an advertisement of a public service nature inserted by, or on behalf of, a government department);

    (b) in the acceptance of advertisements for inclusion in a licensed service there must be no unreasonable discrimination either against or in favour of any particular advertiser;[16] and

    (c) a licensed service must not, without the previous approval of the Commission, include a programme which is sponsored by any person whose business consists, wholly or mainly, in the manufacture or supply of a product, or in the provision of a service, which the licence holder is prohibited from advertising by virtue of any provision of section 9.

9.—(1) It shall be the duty of the Commission—

    (a) after the appropriate consultation, to draw up, and from time to time review, a code—

        (i) governing standards and practice in advertising and in the sponsoring of programmes, and

        (ii) prescribing the advertisements and methods of advertising or sponsorship to be prohibited, or to be prohibited in particular circumstances; and

    (b) to do all that they can to secure that the provisions of the code are observed in the provision of licensed services;

and the Commission may make different provision in the code for different kinds of licensed services.

(2)–(4) [*Omitted*].

(5) The Commission may, in the discharge of a general responsibility with respect to advertisements and methods of advertising and sponsorship, impose requirements as to advertisements or methods of advertising or sponsorship which go beyond the requirements imposed by the code.

(6) The methods of control exercisable by the Commission for the purpose of securing that the provisions of the code are complied with, and for the purpose of securing compliance with requirements imposed under subsection

---

[16] The ITC has upheld a complaint by BSkyB under this provision in relation to ITV's rejection of an advertisement for Sky Digital. ITV had argued that it had rejected it because it breached ITC rules, although it had accepted an advertisement from ONdigital (the terrestrial digital television service) which breached the same rules. Several ITV companies had an interest in ONdigital: ITC, *Television Advertising Complaints* (March 1999), pp 12–13.

(5) which go beyond the requirements of the code, shall include a power to give directions to the holder of a licence—

    (a) with respect to the classes and descriptions of advertisements and methods of advertising or sponsorship to be excluded, or to be excluded in particular circumstances, or

    (b) with respect to the exclusion of a particular advertisement, or its exclusion in particular circumstances.

(7) The Commission may give directions to persons holding any class of licences with respect to the times when advertisements are to be allowed.

(8) Directions under this section may be, to any degree, either general or specific and qualified or unqualified; and directions under subsection (7) may, in particular, relate to—

    (a) the maximum amount of time to be given to advertisements in any hour or other period,

    (b) the minimum interval which must elapse between any two periods given over to advertisements and the number of such periods to be allowed in any programme or in any hour or day,

    (c) the exclusion of advertisements from a specified part of a licensed service,

and may make different provision for different parts of the day, different days of the week, different types of programmes or for other differing circumstances.

Since it is the broadcasters, the licensees under the BA 1990, over whom the ITC has regulatory authority, it is they who are responsible to the ITC for compliance with the advertising rules. Compliance with the codes is a condition of a broadcaster's licence, and the ITC has power to impose sanctions for breaches (see Chapter 4, Section 2(e)). There are two codes: *The ITC Code of Advertising Standards and Practice* (the Advertising Code), last revised in December 1998; and *The ITC Code of Programme Sponsorship* (the Sponsorship Code), last revised in September 1998. There is also a set of rules governing quantitative controls over advertising, *The ITC Rules on the Amount and Scheduling of Advertising* (the Scheduling Rules), last revised in December 1998.[17] Like the ASA, the ITC sets down a number of general principles, supplemented by specific rules covering content; certain types of audiences, such as children; specific goods and services; and certain types of selling practices. With regard to programme compliance, the ITC is not prepared to rule on whether advertisements comply with the codes prior to their broadcast (see Chapter 4). There is, however, an independent body, supported by most television broadcasters, the Broadcast Advertising Clearance Centre (BACC), which will vet advertisements (in script or film version) to ensure compliance with the ITC codes.

In 1998, there were 7,855 complaints about 2,560 advertisements. Over half of these complaints (4,279) concerned offensive advertising. However, the ITC upheld only 122 complaints; only nine of these related to offensive content.[18]

---

[17] These rules were formerly known as the *Rules on Advertising Breaks*.

[18] ITC, *Annual Report and Accounts 1998*, p 39.

The ITC noted, in its Annual Report for 1998, that the number of complaints, compared with the previous year, had risen by 25%, although the number of complaints upheld did not increase in proportion.[19] The ITC attributed the increase to increased viewer awareness of the right to complain, and the willingness of advertisers '. . . to risk offending or upsetting viewers not in their target audience in an effort to create maximum impact amongst those who are. This is supported by the fact that complaints about offensive advertising rose by 56% . . .'.[20] The number of complaints received is generally less than the number received by the ASA. However, this needs to be put into perspective: there are approximately 30 million press advertisements and 100,000 posters per year;[21] while for television there were, in 1998, over 20,000 different advertisements.[22] These figures show that the number of complaints, and breaches, is very small compared with the overall amount of advertising in both sectors.

(b) Advertising standards and practice

(i) General

The Advertising Code contains a statement of general principles, which is similar to those contained in the BCASP.

Extract 6.3.2

ITC, *The ITC Code of Advertising Standards and Practice* (December 1998), rules 1–4

1. Television advertising should be legal, decent, honest and truthful.
2. Advertisements must comply in every respect with the law, common or statute, and licensees must make it a condition of acceptance that advertisements do so comply.
3. The detailed rules . . . are intended to be applied in the spirit as well as the letter.
4. The standards in this Code apply to any item of publicity inserted in breaks in or between programmes, whether in return for payment or not, including publicity by licensees themselves, and the term 'advertisement' is to be so construed for the purposes of this Code.

As well as rules about the content and presentation of advertisements, the Advertising Code includes rules about the advertising (including prohibition)

---

[19] Ibid.
[20] Ibid.
[21] Advertising Standards Authority, *Annual Report 1998*, p 4.
[22] Note 18, above.

of certain specific goods and services. These rules implement the Television Directive, but also have a wider coverage. For example, the Television Directive prohibits the advertising of tobacco and cigarette products (art 13), and certain medicinal products (art 14), while the Advertising Code prohibits, in addition, a number of other goods and services, such as private investigation agencies, breath-testing (for alcohol levels) devices, and the occult (rule 18). The Television Directive has rules on how alcohol products may be advertised (art 15). Here again, the Advertising Code has a wider remit, including restrictions on how products and services, such as motor cars (rule 21), financial services (rule 42), introduction and dating agencies (rule 39), can be advertised. The Advertising Code, like the other ITC Codes, supplements the rules with guidance on their interpretation. On occasion, the ITC will also issue statements about particular aspects of television advertising if it is concerned by advertising practices in that product category. For example, in 1997, the ITC issued a lengthy statement as a result of a series of complaints concerning car advertisements. The statement is valuable in illustrating the rationale for close regulation of advertising, particularly certain types. It also hints at the pressure which advertisers are likely to exert in order to avoid the advertising restrictions.

Extract 6.3.3

ITC, *Television Advertising Complaints Report* (June 1997), pp 1–2 and 3

A question sometimes asked is: why should car advertising be subject to so many rules when there is crazy driving shown in lots of television programmes and feature films? The answer is that television is a particularly powerful advertising medium and the most effective commercials usually focus on one simple selling proposition which is then reinforced by repeated showing. If the glamour of speed is what an advertisement is promoting, that is likely to have much more impact than a film, for example, where driving will usually be only one amongst many elements. And at least in drama we sometimes see the *consequences* of irresponsible driving. We never do in car advertising!

. . .

Car commercials tend to be relatively expensive to produce and advertisers are therefore particularly likely to contest regulatory decisions and claim the benefit of interpretive doubt once an investment has been made. Given the highly competitive nature of the sector these pressures, if unchecked by intervention, could easily lead to a wholesale drift in standards away from the relatively demanding ones in the current guidelines (which, as already explained, have their origin in a wider public policy context). Whereas the ITC will be prepared to review with the motor industry and road safety interests from time to time the detail of the guidelines it has a clear duty, which it intends to fulfil, to ensure that at all times they are applied in the manner intended.

(ii) Separation of programmes and advertisements

A fundamental rule of the Advertising Code, which is also laid down by the Television Directive (art 10(1)), is rule 5, which requires recognisable distinctions to be made between programmes and advertising.

Extract 6.3.4

ITC, *The ITC Code of Advertising Standards and Practice* (December 1998), rules 5(a)–(b) and 6

Rule 5

(a) Advertisements and programme promotions must be clearly distinguishable as such and recognisably separate from the programmes.
(b) Situations, performances and styles reminiscent of programmes must not be used in such a way as to risk confusing viewers as to whether they are watching a programme or an advertisement. In marginal cases the acceptability of such an advertisement may depend on positive indication that it is an advertisement. Where an advertisement imitates or parodies a particular programme it must not appear in the breaks in or adjacent to that programme.

Rule 6

(a) In order to ensure that the purpose of the rules prohibiting certain kinds of sponsorship is not circumvented, no advertisement may feature a person who appears in any current programme which the advertiser would be precluded from sponsoring by virtue of the *ITC Code of Programme Sponsorship.*
(b) No advertisement may feature, visually or orally, persons who regularly present news or current affairs programmes on any UK television service.
(c) With limited exceptions, advertisements which include a person who also appears, other than in a minor or incidental capacity, in a programme may not be scheduled in breaks in or adjacent to that programme. For the avoidance of doubt, a programme promotion is deemed to be a programme for the purposes of this part of the rule.

Extract 6.3.5

ITC, *Television Advertising Complaints Report* (October 1997), p 9[23]

Complaint from: 1 viewer
Nature of Complaint: A member of an ITC Viewer Consultative Committee reported seeing a British Telecom commercial featuring Nick Berry next to the

---

[23] Extracts of ITC adjudications which predate the revised codes remain relevant, under the revised rules.

programme 'Heartbeat', in which he stars. He thought that this conflicted with the ITC's rules that commercials and programmes featuring the same artists should be separated.

Assessment: TSMS, the sales house which sells airtime on behalf of a number of broadcasters, reported to the ITC that it had warned Meridian Broadcasting of the potential problem. Meridian acknowledged that human error had resulted in the warning not being acted upon.

Decision: Complaint upheld.

Question for discussion

Why is it important that viewers should be able to distinguish between advertisements and programmes?

(iii) Offensive advertising

Like the non-broadcast sector, complaints about offensive advertising dominate broadcasting.

Extract 6.3.6

ITC, *The ITC Code of Advertising Standards and Practice* (December 1998), rule 13

No advertisement may offend against good taste or decency or be offensive to public feeling and no advertisement should prejudice respect for human dignity.

NOTES:

. . .

(ii) An advertisement does not necessarily become unacceptable simply because a given number of complaints is received. The Commission will take into account all relevant considerations in making determinations under this rule.

The following two extracts offer examples of the different types of advertisements which can come before the ITC. The first advertisement (Extract 6.3.7) attracted the highest number of complaints (519) ever received about a television advertisement.[24] The second (Extract 6.3.8) was made for the NSPCC, a children's charity. It received 150 complaints.

Extract 6.3.7

ITC, *Television Advertising Complaints Report* (August 1998), p 19

Nature of Complaint: An advertisement for Levi Jeans showed a pet hamster, called Kevin, running on his treadmill. The wheel fell over and broke and the hamster was shown staring at the broken wheel. A voice-over said: 'Kevin

---

[24] Ibid.

grew bored. . . . and died.' It then showed a 'dead' hamster being pushed over with a pencil. Broadcast of the advertisement was heavily concentrated over a single weekend.

309 adult viewers complained that they had been upset by the advertisement or thought it was in bad taste. 163 further complaints were from parents stating that their children had been upset, or from children themselves saying how they had been upset because their own pet hamster had recently died. 47 viewers protested about possible cruelty to animals either in filming, or by children being encouraged to prod pets with pencils.

Assessment: The advertising agency argued that their intention was not to cause upset or shock to viewers, but to make a humorous observation on 'living your life in an original way'. The advertisement was not targeted at children but at a late teen audience and, in keeping with a BACC scheduling restriction, had not been shown in or adjacent to children's programmes.

The ITC was satisfied that there had been no cruelty to any animal used in the filming of the commercial and did not believe that it was likely to encourage people to mistreat their pets. While recognising that the humour was not to everybody's taste the ITC did not think the imagery used was likely to cause significant offence to the majority of adult viewers. However, the somewhat flippant depiction of the apparent death of a household pet, filmed in a realistic way, had triggered an immediate and unprecedented level of upset to children. While the potential for upsetting children had been recognised when the BACC had imposed their initial scheduling restriction, the ITC had no doubt that the overwhelming evidence from complainants was that this dimension had been underestimated and the advertisement had been scheduled in such a way that large numbers of children likely to be upset were exposed to it. Although the agency indicated that there were no plans for the advertisement to return the ITC required that, should it do so, it should not be broadcast before 9 pm.

Decision: Complaints not upheld except in relation to scheduling.

Extract 6.3.8

ITC, *Television Advertising Complaints Report* (May 1999), p 7

Nature of Complaint: NSPCC advertising aimed at encouraging viewers to report suspected abuse of children showed various symbols of childhood (teddy wallpaper, Rupert the Bear mug . . .) while the voices of unseen adults are heard abusing a child in different ways (screaming hysterically at one; threatening violence against another; humiliating one; and preparing to molest another sexually).

46 viewers reported that they had been abused when younger and that they found the reminder too distressing.

Other complainants raised a number of further objections, the most common being:

– that the advertising was too hard-hitting, particularly for children to see;
– that the campaign implied that only parents abuse children;
– that it could encourage abusers by stimulating them or reassuring them that their reactions are normal.

Assessment: The ITC had sympathy for those who found the reminders of their own suffering distressing but is generally prepared to allow stronger material to be shown in the context of charity or public service advertising. The ITC's experience is that most viewers are willing to tolerate uncomfortable viewing if they accept that the advertising is for an important issue, and also the advertisers in these cases are likely to have an understanding of the sensitivities of the groups involved.

. . .

Although the campaign was powerful and emotive, the ITC judged that it was likely to be found generally acceptable, given its objectives. The BACC had restricted the campaign to after 9 pm and the ITC judged that this was sufficient to keep the advertising away from younger children who, whether victims of abuse or not, might find it particularly disturbing.

The ITC did not agree that the advertising suggested that only parents abuse children or that it was likely to encourage abuse.

The ITC concluded that the advertising should be allowed to continue.

Decision: Complaints not upheld.

Questions for discussion

1. What influence did the number of complaints have on the ITC in Extract 6.3.7?

2. Is there a difference in the ITC's handling of commercial and public advertising complaints?

3. Do you discern any differences in the ASA's approach (Extract 6.2.8) compared with the ITC's approach in Extract 6.3.8?

(c) Quantity controls on television advertising

The Scheduling Rules, which are directed to the amount of advertising, its frequency and placement, also incorporate the Television Directive. The ITC imposes stricter rules where it considers it appropriate, and its rationale for this is explained in the following extract.

Extract 6.3.9

ITC, *Rules on the Amount and Scheduling of Advertising* (December 1998), Foreword, paras (d)–(e)

(d) The ITC has decided that for the time being there is no case for imposing substantially greater restrictions than those required by the EU Directive on services other than Channels 3–5.[25] Rules in this area are principally concerned with limiting interference to programmes from too much or too frequent advertising, and with ensuring that the time set aside for advertising does not curtail excessively the time available for programmes proper.

---

[25] The ITC has also acknowledged that advertising rules for digital, and interactive television, services will have to be modified: Foreword, para (h).

These matters relate to the quality and value to viewers of the services concerned. The ITC does not have a remit to influence programme quality on services other than Channels 3–5; its role is confined to enforcing consumer protection standards in areas defined by the Act and implementing the United Kingdom's obligations under international instruments.

(e) In the case of Channels 3–5 the ITC's remit does extend to the quality and value these services provide to viewers and the ITC believes that in some cases more demanding standards than those required by the European Directive remain justified.

Question for discussion

What is the relationship between scheduling rules and programme quality?

The Scheduling Rules are very precise and detailed (see Extract 6.3.10 below). There are also rules which, although less precise, prescribe when certain types of advertising are or are not permitted. For example, liqueur chocolates cannot be advertised during or adjacent to children's programmes (rule 4.2.1(d)(ii)). Certain programmes are prohibited from including any advertising: for example, news programmes of less than 30 minutes duration (rule 3.2). Central to the Scheduling Rules are the rules on how much advertising is allowed, which are found in Section 1. However, there has been considerable liberalisation of these rules in relation to one type of programming. The Television Directive gives greater recognition to home shopping channels and segments, defined in the Directive as 'teleshopping', and increases the total amount of time allowed for teleshopping segments ('windows') from one hour per day to three hours (art 18a). Teleshopping channels are, of course, not subject to these rules. Section 8 of the Scheduling Rules applies the Directive, although Channels 3–5 are only allowed to run long-form advertisements between midnight and 6 am, and must still comply with the Section 1 rules on the daily amount of airtime permitted for advertising (rule 8.1.4).

Extract 6.3.10

ITC, *Rules on the Amount and Scheduling of Advertising* (December 1998), Section 1, rules 1.1 and 1.2 and Section 5, rules 5.1–5.2

SECTION 1: AMOUNT OF ADVERTISING

Amount Per Day 1.1
(Channels 3–5 only)

1.1.1(A)
(a) The total amount of advertising in any one day must not exceed an average of seven minutes per hour of broadcasting.[26]

---

[26] In certain exceptional situations, there may be scope for transferring advertising entitlement from one day to another; for example, if all advertising had been foregone for programme reasons, such as the death of a member of the Royal Family.

. . .

(b) For the purposes of this rule a day's broadcasting is deemed to commence at 06.00 and run for the following 24 hours.

(c) In the periods 6 am [read 6 pm]–11 pm and 7 am–9 am the total amount of advertising must not, without the Commission's prior permission, exceed an average of seven and a half minutes an hour on any one day.

(Other Services)

1.1.2(B)

(a) The total amount of spot advertising in any one day must not exceed an average of nine minutes per hour (15 per cent) of broadcasting.

(b) This may be increased by a further three minutes per hour (5 per cent) devoted to teleshopping spots, but this additional 5 per cent must not be used for other forms of spot advertising.

. . .

Maximum Amount In Any One Hour 1.2

In any one clock hour there must be no more than 12 minutes of advertising spots and/or teleshopping spots. . . .

SECTION 5: INTERNAL BREAKS IN PROGRAMMES

Placing of Breaks 5.1

Breaks within programmes may be taken only at a point where some interruption in continuity would, in any case, occur (even if there were no advertising) and such natural breaks[27] must not damage the integrity or value of the programme in which they occur.

Programmes with 'Autonomous Parts' 5.2

In programmes made up of autonomous parts (e.g. magazine format programmes) breaks may only be taken in between the separate parts.

When adjudicating complaints about scheduling, there is less scope for subjective assessments compared with content complaints. While breaches of the Scheduling Rules might occur unintentionally, given their complexity, the ITC appears to adopt a firm attitude to all scheduling breaches, emphasising the broadcaster's responsibility to have in place proper monitoring and compliance procedures. In February 1999, the ITC fined Telewest, a cable service, £10,000 for repeated scheduling errors and a lack of monitoring procedures.[28] In the following extract, Zee TV, a satellite service, broadcasting mainly in the Hindi language, is issued with a formal warning.

---

[27] Guidance on natural breaks is given in the Scheduling Rules, Section 6.

[28] ITC, *Television Advertising Complaints Report* (February 1999), pp 6–7.

Extract 6.3.11

ITC, *Television Advertising Complaints Reports* (September 1998), p 11

Assessment: During the course of routine monitoring staff identified numerous breaches of the rules governing the number of advertising breaks permitted in programmes of various lengths and the positioning of breaks within programmes. Specific examples included centre breaks inserted incorrectly in a number of news programmes of less than 30 minutes duration . . . [Scheduling Rules, rule 3.2(viii)] and other programmes where breaks were significantly less than the required 20 minutes apart . . . [rule 5.4].

Zee TV said that in at least some cases the rules relating to programmes made up of autonomous parts should apply . . . [Rule 5.2]. Zee TV further said that the programmes originated from India and they believed that the breaks were natural breaks and were in the interest of viewers. The ITC was unable to identify any case where Rule 5.2 was relevant and did not accept that the overseas origin of programme material absolved a licensee from the responsibility to apply the distribution rules, which derived mainly from the European Directive on Broadcasting.

During the course of this investigation ITC staff became concerned with the interpretation of the underlying regulatory principles and the failure of the broadcaster to supply adequate and timely responses to regulatory enquiries. The broadcaster recognised that there were inadequacies in their existing procedures and assured ITC staff that steps were being taken to rectify the situation. The matter was referred to the Commission who considered the current issues in the light of a series of breaches of rules going back to 1995. As a result, on 18 September the Commission issued Zee TV with a formal warning that further breaches of ITC Codes and rules may result in the imposition of statutory sanctions.

(d) Sponsorship of programmes

Programme sponsorship was prohibited in the UK until the BA 1990, out of a concern that sponsors might try to influence programme content.[29] The first Code of Programme Sponsorship was introduced in January 1991, and the third revision of the Code entered into force in spring 1997, as a result of a review carried out by the ITC (see Extract 6.3.12 below). The Sponsorship Code was reissued in September 1998, incorporating minor changes arising from amendments to the Television Directive. As with the Advertising Code and the Scheduling Rules, the provisions of the Sponsorship Code are detailed and precise. Although, sponsorship is now accepted as a means of funding commercial television, and sponsorship revenue is growing,[30] it is clear that there is still a concern to prevent any undue influence on programme content.

---

[29] Barendt, p 205.
[30] ITC, *Annual Report and Accounts 1998*, p 38.

Extract 6.3.12

ITC, *Review of ITC Code of Programme Sponsorship, Explanatory Memorandum* (September 1996), paras 4–5

4. The ITC accepts that any restrictions which deny broadcasters potential commercial revenue must be clearly justified by the interests of viewers; and their scope and effects must be proportionate to the problems they are designed to address. However, we remain convinced that there is a continuing need for careful regulation in this area.

5. The ITC's principal objective in regulating sponsorship is to ensure that the development of this source of revenue and programme finance does not alter the character of programme services in such a way that they become adversely influenced by commercial considerations. This applies both to the content of individual programmes and the range of programmes and programme types on offer. It also relates to editorial or creative agendas and integrity, to the quantitative balance between commercial communication and programme material and the way in which the two are integrated, including the degree of transparency to viewers.

The Sponsorship Code has two main aims: to ensure that programmes are not influenced by sponsorship; and to ensure that sponsorship is not used to circumvent the advertising rules. The following extract illustrates how these concerns are embodied in the rules. Some programmes cannot be sponsored, for example, news and current affairs (rule 6), while certain sponsors may not be able to sponsor certain types of programmes (rules 4.2 and 7). In addition, some persons may be prohibited from sponsoring, for example, political bodies, and tobacco manufacturers and suppliers (rule 4.1). To the extent that it is relevant, the Advertising Code also applies to sponsorships and to sponsorship credits (Sponsorship Code, rule 2.3).

Extract 6.3.13

ITC, *ITC Code of Programme Sponsorship* (September 1998), rules 1.1, 2.1–2.2, 3, 8.4 and 9.1

1.1 A programme is deemed to be sponsored if any part of its costs of production or transmission is met by an advertiser with a view to promoting its own or another's name, trademark, image, activities, products or other direct or indirect commercial interest. . . .

2.1 One of the main principles governing the regulation of programme sponsorship is maintaining the distinction between advertising and sponsor credits, in order to ensure that credits are not used as a means of extending allowable advertising minutage.

2.2 Advertising which refers to sponsorship

Advertising which refers to sponsorship of a specific programme may not be transmitted in advertising breaks within or immediately adjacent to that programme. . . .

3. Scheduling

Without the previous approval of the Commission, no sponsored programme may be broadcast at a time or in circumstances where the sponsor would be restricted from advertising under the . . . [Scheduling Rules].

8.4 Sponsorship message

The front credit, or where there is none, the end credit, must identify the sponsor and explain the sponsor's actual connection with the programme, for example: 'sponsored by', 'in association with' or 'produced by'. It must not suggest that the ITC licensee's broadcasting responsibilities have been ceded to the sponsor or compromised in any way.

9.1 Sponsor influence

A core principle of this Code is the preservation of programme integrity by not allowing programme agendas to be distorted for commercial purposes. No sponsor is permitted any influence on either the content or the scheduling of a programme in such a way as to affect the editorial independence and responsibility of the broadcaster.

As shown above, there are restrictions on the credits which can be used by sponsors (rule 8.4). While a credit can indicate the sponsor's business (rule 8.5), a sponsor is prohibited from including, in the credit, any visual reference to its specific or branded product or service (rule 8.7). It may not always be easy to draw the line between an acceptable credit and one in which the credit clearly shows a representation of the sponsor's product. This is a difficulty to which the ITC is alive.

Extract 6.3.14

ITC, *Review of ITC Code of Programme Sponsorship, Explanatory Memorandum* (September 1996), para 8.7

A difficulty of interpretation which we have experienced . . . is in determining where to draw the line on product representations. For example, should an animated representation of a cartoon character drinking a cup of tea be regarded as a product representation if the sponsor is a tea-bag manufacturer? If a type of confectionery is sold in packets of a distinctive shape should the appearance

227

in stylised cartoon form of packets of this shape count as product representation even if they are of a different colour from that of the actual packaging?

Question for discussion

Would it be permissible for a coffee manufacturer to show in the credit a person drinking coffee?

Although the ITC has relaxed some of the rules by, for example, allowing more opportunities for distinctive branding,[31] the Code retains its adherence to the main aims for regulation of sponsorship. The detailed rules may seem pedantic, but it is fair to say that sponsorship credits, located as they are so closely at the beginning and/or end of programmes and advertising breaks, allow the viewer less opportunity to distinguish and control the commercial message, compared with advertisements. Advertisements coming in blocks, can be more readily distinguished, and even ignored by the viewer. However, the revision of the Sponsorship Code introduced one significant development, 'masthead programming'. This is programming, funded by a publisher of, for example, a magazine, which bears the name of the publication and carries content similar to the publication. Although rule 10.6 allows a broadcaster to use masthead programming, a specific programme cannot be a version of a specific edition of the publication, and there must be no references to the publication within the programme. Initially, the ITC was not prepared to allow masthead programming on Channels 3–5,[32] but rule 10.6 applies to all licensed services and Channels 4 and 5 have included such programmes in their services.

Questions for discussion

1.   Given the general principles found in the Sponsorship Code, such as rules 2.1 and 9.1, is the Sponsorship Code unnecessarily detailed?
2.   What risks might masthead programming present?

(e) Surreptitious advertising

With pressure on broadcasters to raise revenue through advertising, and the incentive for advertisers to maximise advertising opportunities, there is obviously a risk that advertisers might try to circumvent advertising rules. Subtle circumvention can occur by means of undue product prominence, product placement and 'perimeter' advertising, and there are rules in place to prevent such surreptitious advertising (as it is described by the Television Directive). This is an area which overlaps both advertising and sponsorship.

There are a number of rules which affect this area. Product placement, which occurs when branded products are deliberately included or referred to

---

[31] Independent Television Commission, *Review of ITC Code of Programme Sponsorship, Explanatory Memorandum* (September 1996), p 5.
[32] Ibid, pp 8–9.

in programmes, is prohibited (Sponsorship Code, Section 12, see Extract 6.3.15 below). Related to the practice of product placement, is the practice of giving undue prominence to products or services. This is prohibited by the Programme Code (rule 10.6, see Extract 6.3.16 below). Less blatant than product placement, it may nevertheless be a much more insidious form of advertising, and liable, at least according to the ITC, to lead to product placement, unless closely controlled. The ITC also considers that references to a sponsor in a sponsored programme will be difficult to justify editorially (Sponsorship Code, rule 10.2). The Programme Code also contains rules on product promotions occurring during programmes (Section 10.3). Another form of surreptitious advertising can occur with the coverage of an event, such as a sporting competition, at which there may be advertising (sometimes called 'perimeter' advertising). The competitors may be wearing branded uniforms or there may be advertising signs or hoardings. A particularly common way of advertising is around the perimeter of a cricket field or motor-racing track. Again, detailed rules cover this (Sponsorship Code, Section 13, see Extract 6.3.15 below). It is perhaps no accident that motor-racing has received substantial funding from tobacco companies through sponsorship, bearing in mind that broadcast advertising of tobacco products is prohibited. Under rule 13.4 of the Sponsorship Code, coverage of tobacco-sponsored events, or events where there is advertising for a tobacco company, must comply with a voluntary agreement which is in place between the government and the Tobacco Manufacturer's Association.[33]

Extract 6.3.15

ITC, *Code of Programme Sponsorship* (September 1998), rules 12.1–12.2 and 13.1–13.2

12. PRODUCT PLACEMENT

12.1 Definition

Product placement is defined as the inclusion of, or reference to, a product or service within a programme in return for payment or other valuable

---

[33] Pursuant to a European Community Directive, all advertising and sponsorship by tobacco products manufacturers are to be banned from 30 July 2001. Member States can defer implementation for one year in the case of the press, and for two years in respect of sponsorship. There is also scope for Member States to allow existing sponsorship arrangements to continue until 1 October 2006, in the case of events organised at world level. For this additional extension to apply, the amounts devoted to such sponsorship must decrease over that period, and there must be in place voluntary measures to restrict the visibility of advertising at such events. Directive 98/43/EC of the European Community and of the Council of 6 July 1998 on the approximation of the laws, regulations and administrative provisions of Member States relating to advertising and sponsorship of tobacco products, [1998] OJ 213/9. The validity of the directive is being challenged. The ECJ is expected to give judgement in November 2000: *R v Secretary of State for Health and Others, Ex parte Imperial Tobacco Ltd and Others* (1999) *The Times*, 17 December, CA.

consideration to the programme maker or the ITC licensee (or any representative or associate of either). This is prohibited.

12.2 Restrictions on donated goods and services

Where their use is clearly justified editorially products or services may be acquired at no or less than full cost. Provision of the article must not be conditional on any specific agreement as to the manner of its appearance in the programme.

. . .

13. COVERAGE OF EVENTS

13.1 Sponsored events

Programme coverage of events and locations (e.g. the Foster's Oval) which have been sponsored, or at which advertising or branding is present, may itself be sponsored. An event or location sponsor may also be the programme sponsor.

13.2 Advertising at events

Visual or aural references to any advertising, signage or branding at an event must be limited to what can clearly be justified by the editorial needs of the programme itself.

   Such advertising or branding is acceptable providing the event has a bona fide non-television status. Three conditions of that status must be satisfied:
 (i) the development and running of the event must be done by a body whose existence is independent of television, advertising and promotional interests;
 (ii) television coverage must not be the principal purpose of the event;
 (iii) the event must be open to members of the public irrespective of whether or not it is televised.

Extract 6.3.16

ITC, *The ITC Programme Code* (Autumn 1998), rule 10.6

10.6 Undue prominence

No undue prominence may be given in any programme to a commercial product or service. In particular, any reference to such a product or service must be limited to what can clearly be justified by the editorial requirements of the programme itself. An important practical yardstick is that no impression be created of external commercial influence on the editorial process. In no circumstances may the manner of appearance of a product be the subject of negotiation or agreement with the supplier. Branded products should not, as a general rule, be referred to in audio by brand name, or shown in close-up or from an angle which displays the branding to best advantage, or for any significant length of time.

As the following extract demonstrates, the ITC takes seriously even the appearance of advertiser interference with programming. In 1994, Granada, a Channel 3 licensee, was fined £500,000 for repeated breaches of the Programme and Sponsorship Codes by a programme, *This Morning*. Although the extract is referring to previous editions of the Codes, the references to the rules are unaffected.

Extract 6.3.17

J Michael, 'Complaints against the Media' in E M Barendt (ed),
Yearbook of Media and Entertainment Law 1995
(Oxford University Press, 1995), p 311, 328

In 1993 the ITC had investigated a horoscope telephone line promoted on the programme [*This Morning*] and found that 'neither the service arrangements nor the messages on the line appeared to be linked to the programme or under the editorial control of Granada Television'. . . . Another premium rate hotline featured on the programme was found to promote a commercial product that could not be defined as programme support material under section 10.3 of the [Programme] Code. Another *This Morning* programme on 6 May 1993 was found to have breached section 10.6 of the [Programme] Code by giving undue prominence to a new range of Heinz baby foods. Although the ITC were assured that no paid-for product placement had been involved, the Commission reminded Granada to avoid creating any impression of advertiser influence upon the editorial process. *This Morning* on 21 February and 17 March 1994 was found to have breached the Code by sponsorship of a viewers' competition and in the undue prominence given to a new perfume.

In its April–June 1993 report the Commission commented on these and other interventions for breaches of the 'under prominence' rule. The Commission commented that 'it is unlikely that such offers [of products and services], even in the absence of any specific financial inducement, will come entirely without strings attached – without, that is, some understanding of the *degree* of prominence with which the product is likely to be displayed in a programme'. The Commission continued that

'A production environment in which "undue prominence" is tolerated is also one in which "product placement" is more likely to flourish. The risks of detection will seem smaller, and the temptation to make a clandestine deal correspondingly greater.'

(f) Freedom of movement of services and television advertising

Some of the early difficulties over transfrontier broadcasting arose because of divergent national policies on advertising (see, for example, Extracts 5.3.5

and 5.3.6). The Television Directive sets down minimum standards for advertising in order to promote the free movement of broadcasting services within the European Community. However, difficulties have continued to arise in relation to national advertising laws. In its first report on the Television Directive, the Commission reported no serious difficulties with the advertising provisions, or their implementation into national law.[34] However, in its second report, it noted that it was investigating complaints of non-compliance with the advertising and sponsorship rules in several Member States.[35]

The first occasion on which the ECJ was called upon to decide a question on the Television Directive concerned the relationship between national advertising laws and the Directive's advertising provisions. *Societé D'Importation Edouard Leclerc-Siplec v TF1 Publicité SA and Another*[36] concerned a French law which prohibited television advertisements concerning the distribution of goods. The law was intended to protect regional daily press in France by ensuring that it had access to advertising revenue. The ECJ confirmed the entitlement of Member States to impose, under art 3(1), stricter rules on advertising in respect of broadcasters within their jurisdiction.[37]

The facts in the *Leclerc* case involved a fairly straightforward application of the Directive, since it only affected broadcasters under French jurisdiction. The question which arose in the next case was whether a Member State could act in relation to broadcasts from another Member State, which did not comply with national laws on misleading advertising and advertising directed at children.[38] The matter concerned, first, advertisements placed by Swedish companies on two television channels: TV3, a satellite service licensed in, and broadcast from, the UK, to Sweden; and TV4, a broadcaster operating within Sweden. The advertisements were for a children's magazine, each issue of which contained a model dinosaur part which could be collected. Under Swedish broadcasting law advertising directed at children

---

[34] European Commission, *Report on Application of Directive 89/552/EEC and Proposal for a European Parliament and Council Directive amending Council Directive 89/552/EEC on the coordination of certain provisions laid down by law, regulation or administrative action in Member States concerning the pursuit of Television Broadcasting Activities*, COM (95) 86 final (31 May 1995), p 21.

[35] European Commission, *Second Report from the Commission to the Council, the European Parliament and the Economic and Social Committee on the Application of Directive 89/552/EEC*, COM (97) 523 final (24 October 1997), pp 8–9.

[36] Case C-412/93, [1995] 3 CMLR 422.

[37] The ECJ had to decide the relationship between art 3(1) and art 19, which enabled a Member State to impose stricter rules on certain advertising matters. Article 19 has now been repealed.

[38] This was an issue which had previously come before the EFTA Court: Cases E-8 and E-9/94 *Forbrukerombudet v Mattel Scandinavia S/A (1) and Lego Norge S/A (2)* [1994–1995] EFTA Court Report 113. For a discussion of this case see M Pullen, 'TV Advertising within the EU and the EEA' [1995] 16 (8) *European Competition Law Review* 478. The EFTA Court hears matters concerning countries which are not members of the European Community, in this case Norway, but which are members of the European Economic Area (EEA). The Television Directive applies in the EEA.

under 12 years of age was prohibited. The advertisements were also alleged to be in breach of the Marketing Practices Act, Swedish legislation dealing with unfair and misleading advertising. The other matter also concerned alleged misleading advertisements broadcast by TV3 and by Homeshopping Channel, a broadcaster also operating under Swedish law. In this case, the advertisements were direct sales for skin-care products by means of 'infomercials'.

Extract 6.3.18

Joined Cases C-34–36/95 *Konsumentombudsmannen (KO) v De Agostini (Svenska) Forlag AB and TV-Shop I Sverige AB* [1997] ECR I-3843, at 3888–3889 and 3894–3895 (footnotes omitted)

[laws on misleading advertising]

. . .

Although the Directive provides that the Member States are to ensure freedom of reception and are not to impede retransmission on their territory of television broadcasts coming from other Member States on grounds relating to television advertising and sponsorship, it does not have the effect of excluding completely and automatically the application of rules other than those specifically concerning the broadcasting and distribution of programmes.

Thus the Directive does not in principle preclude application of national rules with the general aim of consumer protection provided that they do not involve secondary control of television broadcasts in addition to the control which the broadcasting Member State must carry out.

Consequently, where a Member State's legislation such as that in question . . . which, for the purpose of protecting consumers, provides for a system of prohibitions and restraining orders to be imposed on advertisers, enforceable by financial penalties, application of such legislation to television broadcasts from other Member States cannot be considered to constitute an obstacle prohibited by the Directive.

According to . . . [the advertisers] and the Commission, the principle that broadcasts are to be controlled by the State having jurisdiction over the broadcaster would be seriously undermined in both its purpose and effect if the Directive were held to be inapplicable to advertisers. They argue that a restriction relating to advertising has an impact on television broadcasts, even if the restriction concerns only advertising.

In response to that objection, it is sufficient to observe that Council Directive 84/450 relating to . . . misleading advertising, which provides in particular in Article 4(1) that Member States are to ensure that adequate and effective means exist for the control of misleading advertising in the interests of consumers as well as competitors and the general public, could be robbed of its substance in the field of television advertising if the receiving Member State were deprived of all possibility of adopting measures against an advertiser and that this would be in contradiction with the express intention of the Community legislature. . . .

It follows from the foregoing that the Directive does not preclude a Member State from taking, pursuant to general legislation on protection of consumers against misleading advertising, measures against an advertiser in relation to television advertising broadcast from another Member State, provided that those measures do not prevent the retransmission, as such, in its territory of television broadcasts coming from that other Member State.

. . .

[prohibition on advertising aimed at children]

Application of such a domestic provision to advertising broadcast by a television broadcaster established in the same State cannot be contrary to the Directive since Article 3(1) of that provision does not contain any restriction as regards the interests which the Member States may take into consideration when laying down more strict rules for television broadcasters established in their territory. However, the situation is not the same where television broadcasters established in another Member State are concerned.

. . . [t]he Directive contains a set of provisions specifically devoted to the protection of minors in relation to television programmes in general and television advertising in particular.

The broadcasting State must ensure that those provisions are complied with.

This certainly does not have the effect of prohibiting application of legislation of the receiving State designed to protect consumers or minors in general, provided that its application does not prevent retransmission, as such, in its territory of broadcasts from another Member State.

However, the receiving Member State may no longer, under any circumstances, apply provisions specifically designed to control the content of television advertising with regard to minors.

If provisions of the receiving State regulating the content of television broadcasts for reasons relating to the protection of minors against advertising were applied to broadcasts from other Member States, this would add a secondary control to the control which the broadcasting Member State must exercise under the Directive.

It follows that the Directive is to be interpreted as precluding the application to television broadcasts from other Member States of a provision of a domestic broadcasting law which provides that advertisements broadcast in commercial breaks on television must not be designed to attract the attention of children under 12 years of age.

Questions for discussion

1. Will this decision satisfy those Member States who want stricter laws on advertising?

2. What action can a Member State take in respect of misleading advertising broadcast from another Member State?

3. Does the judgment provide an incentive for Member States to draft national laws in such a way as to achieve the desired end, while avoiding apparent conflict with the Television Directive?

4. REGULATION OF BROADCAST ADVERTISING – RADIO

The regulation of advertising on radio follows a generally similar pattern to television. Advertising is under the regulatory authority of the RA which has, under BA 1990, s 93, a duty to draw up and subsequently review a code governing standards and practices in advertising and sponsorship. The RA has one code, the Advertising and Sponsorship Code (the Radio Advertising Code), last revised in March 1997. It follows a similar pattern to the television codes, covering (although with much less detail) general principles, standards for presentation and content of advertisements, restricted and prohibited goods and services, and rules about sponsorship. However, there are no rules about the amount, length and frequency of advertisements. There are also no rules covering the length of sponsorship credits although rule 7 (Radio Advertising Code, Section C) requires that they be brief. Like television, radio advertising has in place a copy clearance system funded by radio broadcasters, the Radio Advertising Clearance Centre (RACC). The RACC clears advertising scripts at the request of broadcasters, although the Radio Advertising Code requires advertisements within specified categories, such as alcoholic drinks, food and nutrition claims, and those directed at children, to have advance RACC clearance.

Although the Radio Advertising Code generally displays a more relaxed approach to advertising than television, it is in the area of sponsorship where the differences in approach become particularly marked (see Section 3(d) above).

Extract 6.4.1

Radio Authority, *Advertising and Sponsorship Code* (March 1997), Section C, rules 2–6 (practice notes omitted)

Rule 2 Sponsorable Programmes

All programmes may be sponsored, with the exception of news bulletins.

Rule 3 Direct Links

A direct link between the sponsor's commercial activities and the programme's subject matter is acceptable in all sponsored programmes.

Rule 4 Editorial Control

Ultimate editorial control of sponsored programmes must remain with the licensee.

Rule 5 Programme Contribution from Sponsors

Sponsors may contribute to the editorial content of all sponsored programmes, except:

news features;
news magazines;
current affairs;
business/financial news or comment;
programmes/documentary items addressing matters of political or industrial
controversy or relating to current public policy.

Rule 6 Product Endorsement

Endorsement of a sponsor's product or service within editorial is not permitted.

The RA investigates complaints about possible breaches of the Radio Advertising Code. Compared with television and non-broadcast advertising, however,
the number of complaints received is very low. For the year end 1998, 336
complaints were received, and 72 were upheld.[39] However, there has been a
gradual increase since 1991 in the number of radio advertising complaints.
Apart from a general willingness to exercise rights of complaint, which is also
reflected in the increasing number of television and non-broadcast complaints,
the increase for radio can also be attributed to the growth of commercial radio
stations, and, particularly, the introduction of national commercial radio.

Like television, political advertising is prohibited on radio (BA 1990, s 92,
see Extract 6.4.2 below). This prohibition was considered by the Court of
Appeal when Amnesty International sought judicial review of decisions refusing to allow certain advertisements, designed to raise awareness about its
campaign publicising human rights violations, particularly violations which
had occurred in Rwanda and Burundi. Under the Radio Advertising Code,
the advertisements were subject to pre-clearance. The RA had concluded
that they were by a body having objects of a mainly political nature, and,
that, therefore, any radio advertisements by Amnesty were prohibited. The
application for judicial review was dismissed by the Divisional Court, and
Amnesty appealed. Amnesty International (British Section) (AIBS) campaigns
against human rights violations. It works closely with Amnesty International
(British Section) Charitable Trust (AIBSCT), which it had set up. The
objects of these bodies included, in addition to campaigning against human
rights violations, education and research in the human rights field.

Extract 6.4.2

R v Radio Authority, ex parte Bull and Another [1997] 3 WLR 1094, at 1096, 1100, 1101–1102, 1103–1104 and 1106 (CA)

LORD WOOLF MR: Section 92 contains a number of rules. Section 92(1)
provides that: 'The authority shall do all that they can to secure that the rules

---

[39] Radio Authority, *Annual Report and Financial Statements for the year ended 31 December 1998*, p 19.

specified in subsection (2) are complied with in relation to licensed services.' Section 92(2)(a) comprises one of the rules. This rule prohibits the inclusion in a licensed service of:

'(i) any advertisement which is inserted by or on behalf of any body whose objects are wholly or mainly of a political nature, (ii) any advertisement which is directed towards any political end . . .'

. . .

The final decision of the authority of 7 October 1994 contains the following paragraphs:

'Following closer scrutiny of the objects of A.I.B.S., the authority maintains that it regards A.I.B.S.'s objects as being "mainly of a political nature" and has concluded, therefore, that radio advertising by A.I.B.S. should remain unacceptable . . . The authority noted the humanitarian objects of A.I.B.S. and those activities which A.I.B.S. regards as charitable. However, the authority concluded that such objects and activities cannot be reasonably separated from those objects and activities of A.I.B.S. which the authority regards as "political". In the light of further clarification of A.I.B.S.C.T.'s objects, however, the authority decided that the trust's objects may be described as *not* being mainly political. Advertising by the trust of its charitable work in the field of human rights is therefore acceptable under the authority's Advertising Code. If you decide to pursue this option, your radio advertisement may, for example, inform listeners of human rights violations, highlight the charitable trust's activities and appeal for donations while also clearly identifying the advertiser as "the Amnesty International British Section Charitable Trust".' . . .

In the first paragraph of the letter which I have cited, it will be observed that the approach of the authority appears to be to look at the objects of A.I.B.S. as a whole.

. . .

Section 92(2)(a)(i), as we have already seen contains a restriction on advertising by a 'body' whose 'objects' are 'wholly or mainly' of a 'political' nature . . . There is no statutory definition of 'objects,' 'wholly or mainly' or 'political.' The proper meaning of each of these words is important in determining the outcome of this appeal.

. . .

Where there is more than one object and some are political and others are not then it may be essential to go beyond the mere formal statement of the objects in order to decide whether the objects are mainly political. It needs to be remembered that if the body is not considered at least of a mainly political nature it is not subject to the prohibition.

'Wholly or mainly' is a phrase the meaning of which is not free from ambiguity. Clearly it requires a proportion which is more than half. But how much more? 51 per cent. or 99 per cent. and anything between are candidates . . .

Here it has to be construed as a part of a provision which restricts the ability of A.I.B.S. to promote itself on the media by advertising. This constitutes a restriction on freedom of communication. Freedom of communication is protected alike at common law and by the European Convention for the Protection of Human Rights and Fundamental Freedoms (1953) (Cmd. 8969):

237

Derbyshire County Council v Times Newspapers Ltd [1993] A.C. 534. The restriction is a general one in the sense that it applies a blanket ban on any advertising by the body concerned, and applies no matter how desirable a particular advertisement which the body may wish to broadcast is. In this sense it is a restriction which is significantly more intrusive than that contained in the second rule contained in section 92(2) which requires a judgment to be reached as to whether a particular advert offends the rule.

The issue is not whether the restriction contained in the first rule is justifiable but how the restriction should be construed having regard to its blanket or dis-criminative effect in relation to a political body. In view of this . . . restriction the ambiguous words 'wholly or mainly' should be construed restrictively. By that I mean they should be construed in a way . . . which limits the application of the restriction to bodies whose objects are substantially or primarily political. This corresponds with the *Shorter Oxford English Dictionary's* meaning of 'mainly' as being 'for the most part, chiefly or principally.' Certainly a body to fall within the provision must be at least midway between the two percentages I have iden-tified, i.e. more than 75 per cent. This approach to the interpretation of a pro-vision which impedes freedom of communication corresponds with the general approach of the courts of this country, the European Court of Human Rights and many Commonwealth courts in this area; see e.g. *Ming Pao Newspapers Ltd v Attorney-General of Hong Kong* [1996] A.C. 907, 917, *Attorney-General v Guardian Newspapers Ltd (No. 2)* [1990] 1 A.C. 109, 283–284, *Observer and The Guardian v United Kingdom* (1991) 14 E.H.R.R. 153 and *Australian Capital Television Pty Ltd v The Commonwealth of Australia* (1992) 177 C.L.R. 106.

[His Lordship accepted that a campaign to change existing law or govern-ment policy came within the meaning of 'political'.]

The authority having accepted that A.I.B.S. was a body with dual objects, was then faced with the difficult task of having to weigh the respective import-ance of the non-political and political objects. The authority . . . , 'was not persuaded that the question of whether the objects of A.I.B.S. were mainly political should depend on the allocation of its budget as between political and [non-]political activities.' If . . . [it was] meant by this that it should not wholly depend on the budget, this would be correct. But to ignore the respective expenditure would fail to take into account a relevant consideration. After all the director of Amnesty had attributed in excess of 70 per cent of the budget for 1994 on charitable objects of which 30 per cent was spent directly on behalf of the A.I.B.S.C.T. If the expenditure was not used as a guide on what basis did the authority come to its decision? We are not told and with or without this information it does appear that a very material proportion of the objects in fact being pursued by A.I.B.S. are non-political.

Because of the factors to which I have drawn attention, I suspect that, . . . the authority did not go about reaching its decision in the way that it should. Despite this . . . I have come to the conclusion it would not be right to allow this appeal and quash the decision of the authority and require it to reconsider its decision. My reasons for coming to this conclusion are as follows.
(a) The authority is a regulatory body consisting of lay members which is intended to take a broad brush approach to its task. In the words of section 92(1) it was required to 'do all that they can to secure that the rules, specified in subsection (2) are complied with . . .' This rather

     unusual statutory provision does not create an absolute obligation but instead places an obligation to do its best.

(b) The onus is on A.I.B.S. to show that the authority transgressed. If the authority did go wrong, which is not clear, it was not because of want of trying to reach the right result. . . .

(c) From an examination of the different elements of section 92(a)(i) it is apparent that it is difficult to identify with precision the parameters of the paragraph. The language of the provision therefore allows the authority a reasonable degree of tolerance in its application.

(d) Because of its lay nature and the terms of section 92(1) the court should be prepared in this situation to allow the authority a margin of appreciation and only interfere with its decisions when there is a manifest breach of the principles applied on application for judicial review.

(e) A.I.B.S. is entitled to make a fresh application.

Although Amnesty was unsuccessful in its appeal, the RA did seem to leave it with some room for manoeuvre.

Questions for discussion

1.   Can the RA's decision prohibiting the advertisement be justified?

2.   Was Lord Woolf right to take into account the fact that the RA was composed of lay members?

3.   In deciding to dismiss the appeal, did Lord Woolf give sufficient weight to the freedom of expression guarantee?

4.   Can a prohibition on (non-party) political advertising still be justified?

5. THE RELATIONSHIP BETWEEN ADVERTISING AND FREEDOM OF EXPRESSION

In Extract 6.4.2 the Court of Appeal considered the restrictions on advertising in the context of a right to freedom of expression. What impact will the European Convention on Human Rights, now incorporated into English law, have on advertising regulation? In *Casado Coca* a lawyer challenged a ban on advertising his services, as a violation of art 10 of the Convention. It was argued by the Spanish government that advertising which served only the advertiser's private interests, and not the public interest, was not protected by art 10.

Extract 6.5.1

***Casado Coca v Spain* (1994) 18 EHRR 1, at 20, 23–24, and 25
(European Court of Human Rights) (some footnotes omitted)**

The Court would first point out that Article 10 guarantees freedom of expression to 'everyone'. No distinction is made in it according to whether the type of aim pursued is profit-making or not[i]. . . .

In its *Barthold v Germany* judgment of 25 March 1985[ii] the Court left open the question whether commercial advertising as such came within the scope of the guarantees under Article 10, but its later case law provides guidance on this matter. Article 10 does not apply solely to certain types of information or ideas or forms of expression,[iii] in particular those of a political nature; it also encompasses artistic expression, information of a commercial nature as the Commission rightly pointed out – and even light music and commercial transmitted by cable.[iv]

In the instant case the impugned notices merely gave the applicant's name, profession, address and telephone manner. They were clearly published with the aim of advertising, but they provided persons requiring legal assistance with information that was of definite use and likely to facilitate their access to justice.

. . .

The applicant contended that the . . . [prohibition] was not 'necessary in a democratic society', because it constituted a disproportionate interference with his right to impart commercial information, a right which members of the Bar, like other citizens, were guaranteed under Article 10. He added that such a restriction was permissible only if it reflected a freely and democratically accepted willingness to exercise self-restraint; that was not so in the instant case.

. . .

Under the Court's case law, the States parties to the Convention have a certain margin of appreciation in assessing the necessity of an interference, but this margin is subject to European supervision as regards both the relevant rules and the decisions applying them.[v] Such a margin of appreciation is particularly essential in the complex and fluctuating area of unfair competition.[vi] The same applies to advertising. In the instant case, the Court's task is therefore confined to ascertaining whether the measures taken at national level are justifiable in principle and proportionate.[vii]

For the citizen, advertising is a means of discovering the characteristics of goods and services offered to him. Nevertheless, it may sometimes be restricted, especially to prevent unfair competition and untruthful or misleading advertising. In some contexts, the publication of even objective, truthful advertisements might be restricted in order to ensure respect for the rights of others or owing to the special circumstances of particular business activities and professions. Any such restrictions must, however, be closely scrutinised by the Court, which must weigh the requirements of those particular features against the advertising in question. . . .

In the present case, . . . [the] Court notes that . . . [the] rules allowed advertising in certain cases – namely when a practice was being set up or when there was a change in its membership, address or telephone number – and under certain conditions. The ban was therefore not an absolute one.

. . .

The wide range of regulations and the different rates of change in the Council of Europe's Member States indicate the complexity of the issue. Because of their direct, continuous contact with their members, the Bar authorities and the country's courts are in a better position than an international court to determine how, at a given time, the right balance can be struck between the various interests involved, namely the requirements of the proper administration of justice, the dignity of the profession, the right of everyone to receive information about legal assistance and affording members of the Bar the possibility of advertising their practices.

In view of the above, the Court holds that at the material time – 1982/83 – the relevant authorities' reaction could not be considered unreasonable and disproportionate to the aim pursued.

[i] See *mutatis mutandis, Autronic AG v Switzerland (A/178)*; (1990) 12 EHRR 485, para. 47. [See chap 5, s 2.]

[ii] (1985) 7 EHRR 383, para. 42.

[iii] See *Markt Intern. Verlag Gmbh and Klaus Beermann v Germany*, Series A, No 165; (1990) 12 EHRR 161, para. 26.

[iv] See *Groppera Radio AG v Switzerland (A/193)*; (1990) 12 EHRR 321, paras 54–55. [See Extract 5.2.1.]

[v] See, *inter alia, Markt Intern. Verlag*, note iii above, para. 33.

[vi] *Ibid.*

[vii] *Ibid.*, and see, *inter alia, Barthold*, note ii above, para. 55.

Question for discussion

In 1998, the European Community imposed a ban on all forms of tobacco advertising and sponsorship (see Section 3(e), note 33, above). Can this be justified under ECHR, art 10?

7

COMPETITION LAW

1. INTRODUCTION

Although the preceding chapters have already described a detailed broadcasting regulatory structure, there is still another area which attracts considerable regulatory attention, and that is the extent to which individuals and companies should be allowed to own and/or control the media. There are essentially two concerns here. On the one hand, regulators wish to ensure that media companies, like other companies operating in the commercial sector, do not engage in any unfair competitive behaviour. Anti-competitive practices are usually left to the control of general competition law, although as will be seen in this chapter, but also in Chapter 8, responsibility for competition regulation is becoming more diffuse. The second concern is that ownership concentration may limit the diversity of sources of information and views. This is a risk which can apply to all media, and it has led to specific regulation to promote pluralism (see Chapter 1, Sections 1–3). However, as established in earlier chapters, different approaches have been used for broadcasting and the press. The growth of private broadcasters and the development of new forms of broadcasting delivery have meant that concerns about concentration of ownership have increased both within the UK and the European Community. This chapter will examine both specific and general regulation of media ownership, comparing the non-broadcast and broadcast sectors. It will also consider the expanding role for European law. With developing technology and the convergence of broadcasting and telecommunications, regulation of these matters is becoming more complex. This is something which will be taken up more directly in Chapter 8. Two questions are central to the matters covered in this chapter. First, can the divergent regulatory treatment of press and broadcasting ownership continue to be justified? Secondly, does the complex structural regulation of broadcasting ownership and control really serve to ensure pluralism?

2. REGULATION OF NEWSPAPER MERGERS

The relationship between newspaper proprietors and editorial policy has been considered above (see Chapter 2, Section 1). In this chapter the measures adopted to prevent concentration of press ownership are of particular interest. The point has already been made that the regulation of the press has followed a different pattern compared with broadcasting. In the case of radio and television, pre-emptive controls may be imposed which limit, for example, the number of broadcasting licences which can be held (see later in this chapter). However, in the case of newspapers there are no pre-emptive rules; instead, a case-by-case approach is adopted. The focus is on whether an existing newspaper proprietor can acquire further titles. Newspaper mergers are subject to a specific regime set down in the Fair Trading Act 1973, which reflects an awareness that there might be public concern if press ownership was to become too concentrated. As can be seen in the legislative provisions, its key element is the requirement that mergers of a certain size require consent.

Extract 7.2.1

Fair Trading Act 1973, ss 58(1)–(4) and (6), 59(3)[1] (as amended)

58.—(1) Subject to the following provisions of this section, a transfer of a newspaper or of newspaper assets to a newspaper proprietor whose newspapers have an average circulation per day of publication amounting, together with that of the newspaper concerned in the transfer, to 500,000 or more copies shall be unlawful and void, unless the transfer is made with written consent given (conditionally or unconditionally) by the Secretary of State.

(2) Except as provided by subsections (3) and (4) of this section . . . , the consent of the Secretary of State under the preceding subsection shall not be given in respect of a transfer until after the Secretary of State has received a report on the matter from the Commission.

(3) Where the Secretary of State is satisfied that the newspaper concerned in the transfer is not economic as a going concern and as a separate newspaper, then—

(a) if he is also satisfied that, if the newspaper is to continue as a separate newspaper, the case is one of urgency, he may give his consent to the transfer without requiring a report from the Commission under this section;

(b) if he is satisfied that the newspaper is not intended to continue as a separate newspaper, he shall give his consent to the transfer, and shall give it unconditionally, without requiring such a report.

---

[1] As a result of the Competition Act 1998, the Monopolies and Mergers Commission (MMC) was replaced by the Competition Commission on 1 April 1999. References in the text will generally be to the Competition Commission (CC), although of course it is the MMC which has been dealing with the newspaper mergers considered in this section.

(4) If the Secretary of State is satisfied that the newspaper concerned in the transfer has an average circulation per day of publication of not more than 50,000 copies, he may give his consent to the transfer without requiring a report from the Commission under this section.

(5) [*Omitted*].

(6) In this section 'satisfied' means satisfied by such evidence as the Secretary of State may require.

59.—(1), (2) [*Omitted*].

(3) On a reference made to them under this section (in this Act referred to as a newspaper merger reference) the Commission shall report to the Secretary of State whether the transfer in question may be expected to operate against the public interest, taking into account all matters which appear in the circumstances to be relevant and, in particular, the need for accurate presentation of news and free expression of opinion.

Although the Secretary of State is generally required to obtain a report from the Competition Commission (CC) before giving consent, he or she is not bound by it.[2] However, one would normally expect that the Secretary of State would be guided by its conclusions. Some commentators have expressed concern about the operation of the newspaper merger provisions, particularly since there has been growing concentration in the newspaper market.[3] One concern is the role that the Secretary of State plays; it may not be desirable to have a politician making decisions in such a sensitive area.[4] He or she could be influenced by the impact the decision could have on the reporting of the government's activities by the newspapers in question. A more specific concern has been the number of mergers which have not required a reference, as a result of the exercise of discretion under s 58(3) of the Fair Trading Act 1973. This point is considered in the following extract.

Extract 7.2.2

R Whish, *Competition Law*, 3rd ed (Butterworths, 1993), pp 676–678 (some footnotes omitted)

On two occasions the MMC has considered mergers involving major national newspapers. Its first report was upon the proposed transfer of *The Times* to the Thomson Organization, which already owned the *Sunday Times*[i]. There were several arguments raised against the takeover: that the two papers would cease to be distinct, that they would be subject to editorial control by Thomson, that there would be an undesirable concentration of press ownership in the Thomson Organization and that the special status of *The Times* would go. However the MMC concluded that the transfer would not operate

---

[2] R Whish, *Competition Law*, 3rd ed (Butterworths, 1993), p 674.

[3] See Robertson and Nicol, pp 502–506 and Gibbons, pp 207–211.

[4] In August 1999, the Secretary of State reconfirmed his intention to retain his role in newspaper mergers: *Mergers: A Consultation Document on Proposals for Reform* (6 August 1999).

against the public interest. It accepted that *The Times* was in poor financial condition (faced with competition from other quality papers its revenue had declined considerably), and that it would benefit from being part of a larger concern with proven managerial ability in the field. Lord Thomson had given the MMC various assurances on matters such as editorial independence and it was therefore of the opinion that the takeover should not be prevented. When similar assurances were given to the ... [Secretary of State] the transfer was given unconditional consent. In 1980 the Thomson Organization sold both newspapers to News International. The Secretary of State, in the exercise of his discretion, chose not to refer this newspaper merger to the MMC, although certain conditions were imposed upon the purchaser.

In 1981 the proposed transfer of *The Observer* from Atlantic Richfield to George Outram (itself a part of the Lonrho organization) was considered by the MMC which concluded that it would not be against the public interest, provided that the transfer was made subject to certain conditions[ii]; these conditions should ensure that the editorial independence of *The Observer* would be safeguarded against a potential conflict of interest arising from Lonrho's extensive commercial interests. The transfer was permitted by the Secretary of State subject to conditions similar to those imposed when the Thomson Organization transferred *The Times* and *Sunday Times* to News International in 1980. A subsequent transfer of the *Observer* to Guardian Newspapers Ltd was cleared without a reference as the *Observer* was considered not to be economic as a going concern.

Although the basic structure of the Act is that newspaper mergers should be referred to the MMC, many transfers have been permitted without reference to the MMC under the terms of s 58. ...

Some of the instances where the Secretary of State refrained from making a reference to the MMC have led to fierce political argument. In 1980 the transfer of *The Times* and *Sunday Times* to News International, the publisher of *The Sun* and *The News of the World* (which for the purpose of the FTA qualify as newspapers) was permitted without a reference to the MMC, on the ground that the papers were not economic as going concerns and that the case was one of urgency. The decision not to refer was the cause of criticism, in particular as it was far from clear that *The Times* and *Sunday Times* were not economic as going concerns. The Secretary of State allowed the merger, subject to conditions. In particular News International Ltd was required to amend the Articles of Association of Times Newspapers Ltd in such a way that the editorial independence of the newspapers' editors would be assured and their exclusive right to give instructions to journalists would be respected. Removal of the editors was not to be effected without the approval of a majority of the six 'independent national directors' who would be appointed by the Secretary of State. Also it was required that *The Times* and the *Sunday Times* should continue to be published as separate newspapers. The success of these conditions came into question when the editor of *The Times*, Harold Evans, resigned in acrimonious circumstances.

Against this background there followed further controversy when News International acquired another national daily, *Today*, to add to its folio of *The Sun*, *The News of the World*, *The Times* and the *Sunday Times*. A better example of the concentration of press ownership it would be hard to imagine;

with this acquisition News International added a 'middle-market' paper to its 'popular' and 'quality' titles. Yet again no reference to the MMC was made as the Secretary of State was satisfied that *Today* was not economic as a going concern[iii]. The transfer of three national newspapers to the same newspaper proprietor without any scrutiny does raise the question of the effectiveness of the special provisions contained in the FTA. There would be much to be said for removing the element of political discretion in this area by making all newspaper mergers referable to the MMC, subject to a de minimis exception.

. . .

In the 1988 review of mergers policy some attention was paid to criticisms of the newspaper provisions[iv]. After that report the Secretary of State announced that the procedure for investigation would be speeded up; for example, the reference of *Parrett and Neves Ltd/EMAP plc*[v] required the MMC to report within two months, whereas in the past the normal period was three, and two months has become the standard period. An advantage of speeding the process up is that it will make it less easy to argue that a case is one of financial urgency, as matters will hardly be delayed at all by a reference[vi].

[i] HCP (1966–67) 273.
[ii] HCP (1980–81) 378; one member of the MMC was absolutely opposed to the transfer.
[iii] 1987 Annual Report of the DGFT [Director General Fair of Trading] p 81.
[iv] *Mergers Policy* (1988) paras 5.15–5.19.
[v] Cm 454 (1988).
[vi] *Mergers Policy* para 5.16.

The concentration of the newspaper market, and, in particular, the dominance exercised by Rupert Murdoch's News International has caused increasing concern. However, when the government conducted a review of media ownership and control in 1994 (see Section 4 below) only limited attention was given to press mergers and the only recommendation was for liberalisation of the de minimis exception (Fair Trading Act 1973, s 58(4)).[5] In 1998, the government introduced wide-ranging legislative reform of UK competition law. The Competition Act 1998 is modelled closely on Community competition law, EC Treaty, art 81 (anti-competitive agreements) and art 82 (abuse of dominant position).[6] However, the system for newspaper mergers has been retained. During the passage of the legislation, attempts were made, unsuccessfully, to introduce specific provisions regulating predatory pricing[7] in the newspaper market. This arose because of concerns that News International was trying, through pricing practices, to drive out of the market other national titles, such as *The Independent. The Times* had been

[5] Department of National Heritage, *Media Ownership: The Government's Proposals*, Cm 2872 (1995), paras 4.16 and 6.42.
[6] On 1 May 1999, the Amsterdam Treaty came into force. One of the consequences of this is that the numbering of the EC Treaty has changed. Thus the familiar arts 85 and 86 are now, respectively, arts 81 and 82. The Competition Act prohibitions, modelled on arts 81 and 82, will come into force on 1 March 2000.
[7] Predatory pricing involves price cutting to such a degree that other competitors are forced out of the market or deterred from entering. Those engaged in predatory pricing may be selling at below cost or subsidising their costs from other parts of their business.

investigated on three occasions (1993, 1994 and 1996) for predatory pricing, which on each occasion was not proven.[8] In July 1998, as a result of complaints from *The Independent, The Daily Telegraph* and *The Guardian* the Office of Fair Trading (OFT) launched an investigation into these alleged anti-competitive practices. The OFT concluded that News International had deliberately made a loss, selling *The Times*, and that this had affected competition. News International has agreed to submit to the OFT detailed business statements within 10 days of any future price cut.[9]

3. REGULATION OF OWNERSHIP AND CONTROL – TELEVISION AND RADIO

(a) Introduction

Unlike the press, specific rules are imposed on the organisation of broadcasting companies, what may be termed 'structural regulation', as a means of promoting pluralism or 'external pluralism'. In Chapter 4 the programme obligations of broadcasters designed to provide access to a range of programmes were examined. These various obligations concentrate on achieving internal pluralism, while, here attention is drawn to the rules promoting external pluralism, in other words, ensuring that a number of companies, rather than one or two, will be engaged in broadcasting. It is believed that the goal of broadcasting pluralism cannot be left to general competition law.

Extract 7.3.1

Department of National Heritage, *Media Ownership: The Government's Proposals*, Cm 2872 (1995), para 1.4

General competition legislation is mainly concerned with securing economic objectives, although it can also encompass other non-economic objectives. However, wider objectives are important so far as the media are concerned. A free and diverse media are an indispensable part of the democratic process. They provide the multiplicity of voices and opinions that informs the public, influences opinion, and engenders political debate. They promote the culture of dissent which any healthy democracy must have. In so doing, they contribute to the cultural fabric of the nation and help define our sense of identity and purpose. If one voice becomes too powerful, this process is placed in jeopardy and democracy is damaged. Special media ownership rules, which exist in all major media markets, are needed therefore to provide the safeguards necessary to maintain diversity and plurality.

---

[8] Office of Fair Trading, Press Release No 30/98 (2 July 1998).
[9] Office of Fair Trading, *Newspaper Pricing: News International Gives Assurance*, Press Release No 17/99 (21 May 1999).

Until 1990, when there was a major revision of broadcasting law, the legislation conferred wide discretionary powers on the regulatory body with a mandate to secure adequate competition.[10] Apart from specific provisions, concerning, for example, cross-ownership of media, little direction was given to the regulatory authority. The lack of legislative detail enabled the Independent Broadcasting Authority (IBA) to exercise a very wide discretion in monitoring the ownership and transfer of broadcasting franchises.[11] As Gibbons suggests there were both positive and negative aspects to this: '. . . the approach provided flexibility, but it also brought some uncertainty about the standards being applied and the need to rely on the discretion of an agency that did not always find it easy to resist commercial pressures . . .'.[12]

(b) Broadcasting Act 1990

During the 1980s, the traditional broadcasting environment was undergoing change, with the emergence of cable and satellite broadcasting offering the prospect of increased channel capacity. The BA 1990, which was designed to take these changes into account, introduced a new system for regulation of media ownership. Instead of the broad mandate and wide discretion conferred on the IBA, it imposed detailed quantitative rules governing the accumulation of mono-media and cross-media interests. The legislation, supplemented by secondary legislation, prevented anyone accumulating licences beyond certain limits. Thus, not more than two regional Channel 3 licences could be owned by the one person, with the further limitation that the two London licences could not be held by the same person. Only one national radio licence could be held, and, while, there were limits on ownership of local radio licences these were much more generous compared with television. Further limitations applied to cross-interests; thus, for example, a Channel 3 licensee could not hold an interest of more than 20% in certain other licensed services.

Extract 7.3.2

T Gibbons, 'Aspiring to Pluralism: The Constraints of Public Broadcasting Values on the De-regulation of British Media Ownership'
(1998) 16 *Cardozo Arts and Entertainment Law Journal* 475, at 485
(footnotes omitted)

. . . [t]he ownership provisions of the 1990 Act were very complex in an attempt to be all-inclusive and to trace corporate ownership to the controlling interest as far as possible. Predictability was obtained, but at the expense of

---

[10] Gibbons, pp 211–212. See, for example, Broadcasting Act 1981, s 20(2)(b).
[11] Cable and satellite were regulated by the Cable Authority under the Cable and Broadcasting Act 1984. The legislative approach was similar.
[12] Gibbons, note 10, above, p 212.

excessive rigidity and the need to anticipate all difficulties in advance in order to avoid loopholes.

The ITC was concerned that the legislation did not take sufficient account of the different attributes of the licensees.

Extract 7.3.3

Independent Television Commission, *Memorandum on Media Ownership*, 25 February 1994, paras 15 and 17.

15 The ownership rules in Schedule 2 to the Act in their present form prevent the holding of specific combinations of licences. The basis of the limitations is holding the particular type of licence, without regard for its attributes (for example size of audience or revenue or percentage share in either audience or revenue). The Commission questions whether . . . this is in fact a sensible approach.

17 However, the problem with this approach is illustrated by the situation of Yorkshire-Tyne Tees (YTTTV) . . . In the case of YTTTV, the maximum of two licences was already held, so that it was impossible in that case for a further take-over or merger to occur involving another Channel 3 licensee. Yet, taking both its regions together, YTTTV's share of audience amounts to little more than half that of either Carlton or Central, which have now merged . . . As this example shows, the . . . [rules have] served to emphasise disparities in the regional Channel 3 system.

A further difficulty with the 1990 scheme was the definition of 'control', which, because of its lack of flexibility, enabled companies to avoid the spirit of the law by literal compliance.[13] The definition of 'control' was one of the matters addressed by the BA 1996, with new powers to the regulatory authorities to examine functional control.

(c) Cross-media ownership and control

In recent times one of the most contentious aspects of media regulation has been cross-media interests, that is, the holding of interests across different media sectors. An example of a cross-media interest would be a newspaper proprietor also having an interest in a company holding a television licence. Until 1990, regulation of cross-media interests was not generally at the forefront of concern, but they became controversial because the BA 1990 provisions had

---

[13] *R v Radio Authority, ex parte Guardian Media Group plc; R v Radio Authority, ex parte Trans World Communications plc* [1995] 2 All ER 139 provided an example of this. Here the parties to a merger had devised a 'deadlocking' arrangement which gave each party an equal share, thereby precluding either of them being in 'control'. The RA concluded, correctly in the court's view, that it was powerless to do other than confirm the arrangement.

the effect of favouring Rupert Murdoch's media interests. News International was able to maintain its satellite interests (then Sky Television) while already controlling extensive press interests.

Extract 7.3.4

T Gibbons, 'Aspiring to Pluralism: The Constraints of Public Broadcasting Values on the De-regulation of British Media Ownership' (1998) 16 *Cardozo Arts and Entertainment Law Journal* 475, at 489

One aspect of the policy underlying the 1990 Broadcasting Act was an acceptance that companies have been eager to develop interests in different sectors of the media and that large consolidations of corporate power, especially at the international level, have become regarded as a precondition to competitive success. The new rules responsed [sic] to this trend by protecting the position of the quasi-public service channels, but liberalizing cross-holdings more generally. Proprietors of national newspapers could not have more than a 20% interest in a Channel 3 or 5, or national radio service, and a 5% interest in any second holding.[14] . . . With respect to all these services, there were broadly reciprocal restrictions on licensees' interests in newspapers. A notable omission, however, was the relationship between newspapers and satellite service. . . . [The] objection was raised that existing newspaper interests were being given preferential treatment and being allowed to develop undue concentrations of media power; not only News International but also Mirror Group Newspapers had major interests in Astra [satellite] services. The Government argued,[15] however, that imposing restrictions would curtail investment or that, in any event there is such diversity in Astra services that the newspaper proprietors would be unable to secure a dominant position for their own channels.[i] This disingenuously ignored the impact of the services on the United Kingdom market, together with the danger that a common corporate policy is likely to create pressure for more homogenized editorial positions or as has occurred cross-media promotion.

[i] See Hansard, Standing Committee F., Broadcasting Bill, Jan. 25–30 1990, cols 358–90.

Question for discussion
Are you persuaded by the government's arguments for not regulating cross-interests between newspapers and satellite services?

The failure to regulate newspaper and satellite cross-interests resulted in considerable debate when the legislation was introduced, and continued to be a source of discontent until the 1996 reforms.

---

[14] Local media was also subject to cross-media rules.
[15] The government also argued that if it had imposed restrictions on satellite services, the owners could have moved their operations elsewhere in Europe, with an inevitable loss of jobs. They could have continued to broadcast into the UK, but without being subject to its jurisdiction: Barendt, p 132.

4. BROADCASTING ACT 1996

Concerns about the rigidity of the 1990 regime and the position of News International were factors which led the government to set up its review of media ownership and control in 1994. Many within the media industry also lobbied for a relaxation of the rules, believing that media consolidation and growth was necessary to compete internationally, and to take advantage of new media opportunities. Digital broadcasting would also require changes to the ownership regime. In May 1995 the government published its Policy Paper, *Media Ownership: The Government's Proposals*.

Extract 7.4.1

**Media Ownership: The Government's Proposals, Cm 2872 (1995)
paras 6.1 and 6.5**

6.1 The Government believes that the existing structure of media owner-ship regulation, relying as it does on prohibitions which reinforce the traditional segmentation of the media market, is insufficiently flexible to allow media companies to exploit to the full the opportunities offered by the new technolo-gies, particularly in view of the expansion of media services which will follow the introduction of digital broadcasting. The Government recognises that these technologies are making the traditional segmentation of the market increas-ingly anachronistic and that media businesses need to be able to regard the provision of media services as a single activity. This Government therefore believes that media ownership regulation needs to evolve to reflect these changes in the shape of the industry. . . .

6.5 The Government believes that the long term regulatory regime must:
– continue to safeguard the public interest in a free and diverse media;
– allow the media industry to evolve in a way that exploits the opportunities created by technological change; . . .

Questions for discussion

What different goals is the government pursuing? Are these conflicting?

To meet these goals, the government proposed the idea of 'market share' as a means of determining the degree of interest which should be allowed. As Gibbons suggests, the approach attempts to measure media influence by, for example, measuring size of audience, and is less crude than one which simply adds up the number of licences held.[16] The government initially proposed that the traditional segmentation of media should be replaced with a system whereby a media company would be allowed a certain share of the total media market, irrespective of the media sector or sectors in which it held

---

[16] T Gibbons, 'Aspiring to Pluralism: The Constraints of Public Broadcasting Values on the De-regulation of British Media Ownership' (1998) 16 *Cardozo Arts and Entertainment Law Journal* 475, at 490.

its interests. The size of media markets would be determined by audience or revenue share, but each media sector would have a weighting in order for its influence to be compared with other sectors. This 'exchange rate' mechanism recognised that some sectors would carry greater influence than others.[17] The government eventually abandoned this scheme as too complex, but did introduce a market share approach based on audience share for broadcasting and sale figures for newspapers. The new legislative system seeks to meet some of the ITC's concerns (see Extract 7.3.3 above), while also redressing the imbalances of the 1990 regime. It introduces a new definition of 'control' and provides a degree of discretionary power. Extracts 7.4.2 to 7.4.5 set out the main elements of the legislative scheme.[18] Schedule 2 to the BA 1990 sets out the ownership rules. Part III of the Schedule covers accumulations of mono-media interests, both radio and television, and Pt IV deals with cross-media interests including newspapers. Parts III and IV of the BA 1990 were repealed and replaced by the BA 1996, while Pt I (definitions, including 'control') of Sched 2 was amended.[19] The references below to the BA 1990 are to that Act as amended by the BA 1996.

The key provisions for regulating television are set out in Extract 7.4.2. It will be seen that the scheme uses a combination of market share and limits on accumulations. Audience time is calculated by reference to all television services that can be received in the British Isles (BA 1990, Sched 2, Pt III, para 3). The ITC has some discretion over whether it includes or ignores some aspects of the statistics. In addition, to the key provisions there are also some other restrictions on television ownership. A national Channel 3 service cannot be held with a Channel 5 licence and a regional Channel 3 licence cannot be held with another regional Channel 3 licence covering the same area (BA 1990, Sched 2, Pt III, para 4). There are also restrictions affecting digital television. No more than three television multiplex licences can be held (BA 1990, Sched 2, Pt III, para 5). There are also limits on the provision of television digital programme services overlapping with certain analogue services and limits on the number of digital programme service licences which can be held (BA 1990, Sched 2, Pt III, paras 6 and 7).

Extract 7.4.2

Broadcasting Act 1990, Sched 2, Pt III, paras 1(1)–(2) and 2(1)–(2)

1.—(1) In this Part of this Schedule 'relevant Services' means any such services as are mentioned in sub-paragraphs (2) and (3) and, for the purposes

---

[17] Department of National Heritage, *Media Ownership: The Government's Proposals*, Cm 2872 (1995), Chapter 6.

[18] The legislation is lengthy and detailed and it is only possible here to give an overview of the scheme. Reference should be made to the legislation for a comprehensive understanding of the provisions.

[19] Part II deals with persons who are disqualified from holding a licence, see Chapter 3, Section 4(c).

of this Part, relevant services shall . . . be divided into the sixteen categories specified in those sub-paragraphs.

(2) In the case of services licensed by the Commission, the categories are—

    (a) regional and national Channel 3 services and Channel 5;

    (b) restricted services . . . ;

    [(c) repealed]

    (d) satellite television services;

    (e) licensable programme services;

    (f) additional services . . . ;

    (g) television multiplex services;

    (h) digital programme services; and

    (i) digital additional services . . .

2.—(1) No one person may, at any time when his audience time in respect of the period of twelve months ending with the last day of the preceding calendar month exceeds 15 per cent. of total audience time in respect of that period—

    (a) hold two or more licences to provide relevant services falling within one or more of the categories specified in paragraph 1(2)(a),(d),(e) or (h),

    (b) be a participant with a qualifying interest [20%][20] in two or more bodies corporate each of which holds a licence, or two or more licences, to provide services falling within one or more of those categories,

    (c) hold any licence to provide a relevant service falling within any of those categories and be a participant with a qualifying interest in any body corporate which holds such a licence or two or more such licences, or

    (d) provide a foreign satellite service and either hold any licence to provide a relevant service falling within any of those categories or be a participant with a qualifying interest in a body corporate which holds such a licence or two or more such licences, or

    (e) hold a licence to provide relevant services falling within the category specified in paragraph 1(2)(h) and provide two or more such services.

(2) For the purposes of sub-paragraph (1) a person's audience time at any time ('the relevant time') in respect of any period is the aggregate of—

    (a) the audience time attributable in respect of that period to each relevant service falling within any of the categories specified in paragraph 1(2)(a), (d) or (e) provided under a licence held by him at the relevant time,

    (aa) the audience time attributable in respect of that period to any relevant service falling within paragraph 1(2)(h) which is provided by him by means of a television multiplex service . . . ,

    (b) one half of the audience time attributable in respect of that period to any relevant service falling within any of the categories specified in paragraph 1(2)(a), (d) or (e) provided under a licence held by a body corporate which he does not control, but in which he is at the relevant time a participant with a qualifying interest,

---

[20] An interest refers to a beneficial entitlement to shares or possession of voting power.

(bb) one half of the audience time attributable in respect of that period
to any relevant service falling within paragraph 1(2)(h) which is
provided—
(i) by means of a television multiplex service [. . .], and
(ii) by a body corporate which he does not control, but in which he
is at any relevant time a participant with a qualifying interest, and
(c) the audience time attributable in respect of that period to any foreign
satellite service provide by him at the relevant time.

The following extract describes the rules for radio ownership (BA 1990,
Sched 2, Pt III, paras 8–15), which show a quite different approach compared with television.

Extract 7.4.3

E M Barendt, 'Structural and Content Regulation of the Media: United Kingdom Law and Some American Comparisons' in E M Barendt (ed), *The Yearbook of Media and Entertainment Law 1997/8* (Oxford University Press, 1997), pp 75, 89–90 (footnotes omitted)

The position with regard to radio is more complicated, and is worth detailed
exposition because of the explicit statutory references here to pluralism and
diversity. There is no longer a numerical limit on the total holdings of local
radio licences by any group throughout the country, although the points system (introduced by the 1990 legislation) has been retained; no group may hold
licences which cumulatively account for more than 15 per cent of the points
attributable to all radio services in the areas for which the licences have been
awarded. (Points are allocated according to size of the *potential* audience
over 15 years old in the coverage area, in contrast to the calculation of actual
audience for television licences.) This is supplemented by another rule to limit
radio concentrations in each local area; up to three licences may be held by
the same group, provided there is at least one licence on each of the AM and
FM wavebands. But the ownership of a second licence on the same wave-
band, and a third licence, is subject to a 'public interest' test to be applied by
the Radio Authority (RA) before its grant.

The Authority must have regard to 'any reduction in plurality of ownership'
which would result from a cumulation of licences and the likely effect of the
decision to award a licence on the range of programmes and the diversity of
opinions expressed on the radio services received in the area. In the exercise
of its discretion the RA must in effect look at all three aspects of the concept
of 'pluralism' identified in the previous section, viz. multiplicity of speakers,
diversity of opinion, and range of programmes. It is worth noting in this context
that local radio services are not subject to the strict impartiality rule applicable
both to regional television and to national radio, but to a lower duty not to give
'undue prominence' to the expression of the views of particular persons and
institutions. Nor is each local radio service required to observe internal pluralism; rather the RA is bound to ensure 'a range and diversity' of local services.

In other words, local radio regulation is concerned with the diversity of different programme services, and the new concentration rule is designed to support that policy. But it cannot be characterized as a purely structural rule, for the Radio Authority is also obliged to take account of the character of the licence's service, including the extent to which the views expressed on it will balance the range of opinion available on other channels.

As has been mentioned before, the most problematic area of media ownership has been cross-media interests. Two key aspects of the 1996 amendments are the provisions limiting the extent of newspaper interests in radio and television using a market share test, and the use of a public interest test.

Extract 7.4.4

Broadcasting Act 1990, Sched 2, Pt IV, paras 3(1), 4 and 5(1)–(4)[21]

3.—(1) For the purposes of this Part of this Schedule a person runs a national or local newspaper if—
    (a) he is the proprietor of the newspaper, or
    (b) he controls a body which is the proprietor of the newspaper.
(2) [Omitted].

4.—(1) No person who runs a national newspaper which for the time being has, or national newspapers which for the time being together have, a national market share of 20 per cent. or more may hold a licence to provide—
    (a) a regional or national Channel 3 service or Channel 5, or
    (b) a national or local radio service.

(2) A licence to provide a regional Channel 3 service may not be held by a person who runs a local newspaper which for the time being has, or local newspapers which for the time being together have, a local market share of 20 per cent. or more in the coverage area of the service.

(3) A licence to provide digital programme services may not be held by a person who runs a local newspaper which for the time being has, or local newspapers which for the time being together have, a local market share of 20 per cent. or more in the coverage area of any digital programme service provided under the licence.

(4) For the purposes of this paragraph a person shall be treated as holding a licence if the licence is held by a person connected with him.

5.—(1) No proprietor of a national newspaper which for the time being has, or of national newspapers which for the time being together have, a national market share of 20 per cent. or more shall be a participant with more than a 20 per cent. interest in a body corporate which is the holder of a licence to provide any of the services specified in sub-paragraph (4).

(2) No person who is the holder of a licence to provide any of the services specified in sub-paragraph (4) shall be a participant with more than a 20 per cent. interest in a body corporate which runs a national newspaper which has,

---

[21] There are further provisions covering cross-interests in local radio and local newspapers: BA 1990, Sched 2, Pt IV, paras 6 and 7.

or two or more national newspapers which together have, a national market share of 20 per cent. or more.

(3) No body corporate in which a person who runs a national newspaper which has, or national newspapers which together have, a national market share of 20 per cent. or more is a participant with more than a 20 per cent. interest, shall be a participant with more than a 20 per cent. interest in a body corporate which holds a licence to provide any of the services specified in sub-paragraph (4).

(4) The services referred to in sub-paragraphs (1), (2) and (3) are—

    (a) a regional or national Channel 3 service or Channel 5, and

    (b) national or local radio services.

The public interest test arises in two circumstances, specified in Sched 2, Pt IV, paras 9(1) and 9(2). Paragraph 13 of Sched 2 sets out the elements of the public interest test.

Extract 7.4.5

Broadcasting Act 1990, Sched 2, Pt IV, paras 9(1)–(4) and 13(1)

9.—(1) A licence to provide any of the services specified in sub-paragraph (4) may not be granted to a body corporate which is, or is connected with, the proprietor of a national or local newspaper if the relevant authority [the ITC or RA] determine that in all the circumstances the holding of the licence by that body corporate could be expected to operate against the public interest.

(2) Subject to sub-paragraph (3), a body corporate which holds a licence to provide any of the services specified in sub-paragraph (4) shall not become, or become connected with, the proprietor of a national or local newspaper and continue to hold the licence if the relevant authority determine within the permitted period [three months] that in all the circumstances the continued holding of the licence by that body corporate operates, or could be expected to operate, against the public interest.

(3) Sub-paragraph (2) does not apply in any case where the body corporate holding the licence—

    (a) is already the proprietor of some other national or local newspaper, or is already connected with such a proprietor, and

    (b) does not become connected with any other person who holds a licence to provide any of the services specified in sub-paragraph (4).

(4) The services referred to in sub-paragraphs (1) to (3) are—

    (a) a national Channel 3 service or Channel 5,

    (b) a national radio service, and

    (c) national digital sound programme services.

. . .

13.—(1) The matters to which the relevant authority shall have regard in determining, . . . whether the holding of a licence by a body corporate which is, or is connected with, the proprietor of a newspaper operates, or could be expected to operate, against the public interest include—

(a) the desirability of promoting—
(i) plurality of ownership in the broadcasting and newspaper industries, and
(ii) diversity in the sources of information available to the public and in the opinions expressed on television or radio or in newspapers,
(b) any economic benefits (such as, for example, technical development or an increase in employment or in the value of goods or services exported) that might be expected to result from the holding of the licence by that body but could not be expected to result from the holding of the licence by a body corporate which was not, and was not connected with, the proprietor of a newspaper, and
(c) the effect of the holding of the licence by that body on the proper operation of the market within the broadcasting and newspaper industries or any section of them.

Questions for discussion

1. What objectives have to be balanced in determining the cross-media 'public interest' test?
2. Compare the cross-media 'public interest' test with the radio accumulations 'public interest' test (Extract 7.4.3 above). How do these tests differ, and why?

Both the RA and the ITC[22] have had to apply the public interest tests. As yet no determination has been made that a transaction would be against the public interest, although the RA has sometimes imposed conditions, such as maintenance of separate news operations. In each of these cases the arrangements have concerned local media.[23]

The 1996 regime is still relatively new and it is too early to reach firm conclusions about its effectiveness. Gibbons assesses the new regime and questions whether there is even still a place for such sector-specific regulation.

Extract 7.4.6

T Gibbons, *Regulating the Media*, 2nd ed (Sweet & Maxwell, 1998), pp 223–225 (some footnotes omitted)

A number of questions may be raised about the new scheme, although it is too early to assess its full impact. One is the choice of 15 per cent as the threshold figure for television and radio services. It appears to have materialised as the intuitively correct indication of diversity in radio, but without a

[22] See for example ITC, *United News and Media Merger with MAI: ITC Determination* (News Release 11/97, 30 January 1997) and ITC, *ITC Concludes Provision of Digital Programme Service in Scotland Will Not Be against Public Interest* (News Release 12/99, 4 March 1999).
[23] See for example RA, *Proposed Acquisition of Kent and Sussex Radio Ltd by DMG Radio Ltd* (Public Interest Determination, 5 November 1998), RA, *Proposed Acquisition of Kent Coast Radio Ltd by Kent Messenger Ltd* (Public Interest Determination, 4 March 1999).

rational base. Given that public broadcasters account for around 55 per cent of audience share, the threshold effectively means that a commercial licensee cannot acquire more than one third of the remaining audience. Putting it differently, it is considered that media pluralism can be secured by ensuring that the internal pluralism offered by the public broadcasters is complimented by at least three 'players' in the commercial sector. The reasons for a 20 per cent threshold for newspaper cross-holdings are equally obscure, although it has had the effect of excluding the two largest current press interests, News International and the Mirror Group, from owning quasi-public service licences.

. . .

Another issue is the decision to include public service broadcasting in the total audience used as the basis for calculating the share reached by each programme service. This has the effect of depressing the audience share (and apparent market power) of other, commercial operators. Whether that is justified depends on whether there is an identifiable market for television and radio programming as a whole. If some commercial sectors are thought to constitute a separate market, for example, pay-t.v., the inclusion of public service broadcasters in the base may conceal the possible dominance of relatively small companies in such a market.[i] Since the public service broadcasters already cater for internal pluralism, there is a case for focusing entirely on the commercial sector when determining thresholds of concentration.

. . . More generally, there are doubts as to whether continued regulation of the structure of the industry can really deliver pluralism of information and opinion. Diversity of ownership may not provide such pluralism if the tendency in the market is for most companies to compete to provide essentially the same kind of product.[ii] Yet again, as the media markets converge, the detailed regulation of the terrestrial broadcasting sector may become less significant compared to the relatively unregulated cable and satellite sectors. As it happens, current regulation of television and radio does not depend on a structural approach to achieve its aims. Greater reliance is placed on designating the attributes of each service through licence conditions. It would appear to be possible, then, to dispense with ownership regulation in those sectors altogether, provided the regulators could be trusted to maintain programming standards. Indeed, to assist the ITC in that task, it have [sic.] been given additional powers to ensure that the quality of service in Channel 3 does not deteriorate when changes of ownership occur.[iii] However, although there is relative freedom to transfer ownership, the logic of that path has not been pursued. There is a feeling – basically caution – that an imposed pluralism is not a substitute for a diversity of creative sources and that commercial pressure by a limited number of powerful companies might be too much for the regulators to resist.

[i] According to the figures for January 1998, BBC 1 had 30.8 per cent of the audience share, BBC 2 had 11.5 per cent, Channel 3 combined had 29.1 per cent and Channel 4 had 10.1 per cent. By contrast the Sky channels together accounted for 5.53 percent. Of the cable and satellite channels, only Sky One (1.3 per cent) and Sky Sports (1.1 per cent) had a share of greater than 1 per cent. See ITC, News Release: 'Television audience share figures' (1998) 13/98.

[ii] See E. Barendt, 'Structural and Content Regulation of the New Media' (1997–98) 3 Yearbook of Media and Entertainment Law 75–95.

[iii] Under s. 21A of the 1990 Act, inserted by s. 78 of the 1996 Act.

5. EUROPEAN COMPETITION LAW

A number of developments have ensured that media ownership can no longer be easily left to national regulation. Technological developments, in particular satellite, have meant that broadcasting cannot be confined within national boundaries (see Chapter 5). At the same time, the Television Directive and the promotion of the European single market have encouraged broadcasting companies to look beyond national borders for investment opportunities. Regulation of media concentration has been added to the European Community's agenda. Like the UK, there are two approaches here: one is to rely on general competition law; while the second is to devise specific legislation.

(a) Community competition law

In the absence of specific media ownership regulation, the Community has relied on general competition law. Articles 81 and 82 of the EC Treaty (formerly arts 85 and 86), which deal with anti-competitive practices and abuse of dominant position respectively, and the Merger Control Regulation (Regulation (EEC) 4064/89, hereafter MCR) are the main tools available to the Commission for the regulation of media concentration. The MCR empowers the Commission to block mergers if competition within the single market is likely to be affected, although the Commission only has jurisdiction if the merger is of a certain size, and has a Community dimension. It also acknowledges the special nature of media.

Extract 7.5.1

Council Regulation (EEC) 4064/89 of 21 December 1989 on the control of concentrations between undertakings (as amended), [1989] OJ L395 (amended by [1990] OJ L257/13), art 21

Article 21

1.   Subject to review by the Court of Justice, the Commission shall have sole jurisdiction to take the decisions provided for in this Regulation.
2.   No Member State shall apply its national legislation on competition to any consideration that has a Community dimension.
. . .
3.   Notwithstanding paragraphs 1 and 2, Member States may take appropriate measures to protect legitimate interests other than those taken into consideration by this Regulation and compatible with the general principles and other provisions of Community law.
Public security, plurality of media and prudential rules shall be regarded as legitimate interests . . .

The MCR has probably become the most significant weapon for Community regulation of media concentration. The Commission has direct responsibility for competition matters and has made a number of decisions (many negative) and informal recommendations concerning the media industry.[24] Extract 7.5.2 provides an example of an early Commission decision concerning a joint venture of three powerful German media companies. The joint venture, Media Services GmbH (MSG), was established by Bertelsmann AG (Bertelsmann), Deutsche Bundespost Telekom (Telekom) and a company belonging to the Kirch media group (Kirch). Bertelsmann is Germany's main media company, having interests in television, recording and publishing while Kirch is the largest German controller of films and other programme material. Telekom controlled public telecommunications and almost all cable television networks in Germany. The purpose of the joint venture was to offer, through MSG, technical and administrative services for pay television. These would include conditional access and subscriber management services (see Chapter 8, Section 2 for a fuller description) which enable a supplier of pay television services to access viewers and to ensure they receive the services for which they have subscribed. At the time of establishing the joint venture, the only pay television service in Germany was controlled jointly by Kirch, Bertelsmann and another company, Canal Plus; however, it was envisaged that MSG's services would be offered to other pay television companies entering the market. The Commission decided that three separate markets would be affected by MSG: the market for administrative and technical services; the market for pay television (which included pay-per-channel, pay-per-view, and near video-on-demand); and the market for cable television networks. It concluded, in relation to each of these markets, that MSG would create or strengthen a dominant position hindering effective competition. The following extract sets out the Commission's conclusions on the administrative and technical market and the pay television market.

Extract 7.5.2

Commission Decision 94/922/EC of 9 November 1994 relating to a proceeding pursuant to Council Regulation (EEC) 4064/89 (IV/M.469 – MSG Media Service), [1994] OJ L364/1, paras 56, 60, 81–85, 87, 89–90 and 101

[Technical and Administrative Services]

(a) *Elimination of potential competition*

(56) ... [E]xperience in other countries shows that pay-TV suppliers or cable network operators are the most likely suppliers of technical and administrative

---

[24] For a comprehensive review of Commission competition decisions concerning media activities and Commission competition policy, see A Harcourt, 'Regulation of European Media Markets: Approaches of the European Court of Justice and the Commission's Merger Task Force' (1998) 9(6) *Utilities Law Review* 276.

260

services for pay-TV. In Germany, the only pay-TV supplier at present is Premiere, which is jointly controlled by its three shareholders, Bertelsmann, Kirch and Canal Plus. Premiere at present provides the necessary technical and administrative services for its pay-TV operation itself. On the other side there is Telekom, which holds a monopoly under public law on the broadband cable network, and which is virtually the sole cable network operator in Germany. Over 90% of cable networks in Germany are operated by Telekom. With the setting up of MSG there is therefore a concentration of those enterprises which would each otherwise have had to install an infrastructure for digital pay-TV and provide the corresponding services. The most likely potential competition is thus excluded already in the development phase of the market.

(b) *Partitioning of the market*

(60)   It appears scarcely conceivable that competing suppliers in Germany could enter the market for technical and administrative services for pay-TV once MSG had established itself on that market. The installation of an alternative infrastructure would require a large amount of investment that would be undertaken by other suppliers or groups of suppliers only if there was a chance of market penetration. However, such a chance would scarcely exist if MSG had already occupied the market. An alternative supply of services would have to impose itself against the combined competitive advantages and specific strengths of Telekom on the one hand and Bertelsmann/Kirch on the other. This appears hardly possible.

. . .

[Pay-TV]

(81)   . . . Bertelsmann/Kirch already at present has an extraordinarily strong position on the pay-TV market.

. . .

(82)   If . . . MSG achieves on a lasting basis a monopoly position as an operator of a digital infrastructure for pay-TV, all pay-TV suppliers that may enter the pay-TV market following digitalization will be forced to take the services underlying pay-TV from an enterprise controlled by the pay-TV suppliers that are already in a leading position. Future pay-TV competitors of Bertelsmann/Kirch would have the choice of either accepting MSG' conditions or staying out of the market. This assessment is supported by the results of the hearing and by a large number of responses from enterprises surveyed.

(83)   The parties argue in response to this that each pay-TV programme supplier has the alternative of providing this service themselves, as is currently generally usual. This is incorrect. A look at the present situation shows that any new programme supplier entering the market is obliged to make use of the services of that pay-TV supplier which is already established on the market with technical infrastructure. This follows from the fact that the economic risk is normally too great for a programme supplier to install its own new infrastructure for a new programme. Experience has shown that, for example,

261

a new programme supplier in the United Kingdom is dependent on BskyB's infrastructure and a new supplier in France on that of Canal Plus. With the setting up of MSG under its current shareholder structure, a comparable situation would also arise for digital pay-TV in Germany.

(84)   Via MSG, therefore, Bertelsmann/Kirch could significantly influence competition from future pay-TV suppliers and to a large extent shape it as they wished. Through their controlling influence in MSG, they can ensure that MSG's terms and conditions and in particular the price structure are arranged in a way that is advantageous to their own programmes and disadvantageous to those of their competitors. Bertelsmann/Kirch could also derive benefit from artificially high prices, since unlike their competitors they have a share in MSG's earnings.

(85)   There would furthermore be the possibility, citing technical constraints that could be verified only with difficulty, of supplying MSG's services in such a way that the market access of programmes that ran counter to the interests of Bertelsmann/Kirch was at least delayed. The same also applies to Telekom's input of programmes into the cable network. It cannot be ruled out that, if it is concentrated with Bertelsmann/Kirch in MSG, Telekom will also take its partners' interests into account. The difficulties previously encountered in feeding programmes broadcast via Astra into Telekom's cable network suggest that, citing technical constraints, it can influence access to the cable network without in any provable way infringing the neutrality requirement.

. . .

(87)   Bertelsmann/Kirch also have the possibility of influencing via MSG the location of their competitors' programmes. The large number of possible programmes in digital television makes it necessary to establish a system of user guidance to help the viewer locate individual programmes in the 'programme jungle'. Since the necessary on-screen modulator is contained in the decoder box, such user guidance will probably be operated by whoever installs the decoder base. The control of user guidance enables the operator to place programmes of competing pay-TV suppliers on positions in the programme menu which make them less attractive. In this context, it is important, for example, how many operating steps are required to get access to a certain programme.

. . .

(89)   Lastly, Bertelsmann/Kirch could acquire substantial informational advantages through MSG. This applies in respect of planned new programmes, but in particular also in relation to the customer structure and viewer behaviour of the subscribers handled by its subscriber management system. Bertelsmann/Kirch do not even have to acquire access to individual customer data. It is sufficient for them to obtain access to non-personal data giving, for example, information on the age structure of the viewers of the relevant programmes. In the case of interactive pay-TV services such as pay-per-view, moreover, it can be ascertained from non-individualized data which specific group prefers what specific programme contents and to what extent. Such information confers substantial competitive advantages since it makes it much easier to develop target-group-oriented programmes or programme packages.

(90)   The parties counter this by arguing that it could not be in the interest of MSG's shareholders to act to the prejudice of other pay-TV suppliers as this

would endanger the economic success of MSG. This argument appears questionable, since MSG is, as was stated above, expected to achieve a monopoly position. Other pay-TV suppliers will be dependent on the services supplied by MSG even if the conditions are unfavourable and there are possibilities of prejudice. . . .

(101) This hindering of effective competition does in fact make even the achievement of technical and economic progress questionable. It is extremely doubtful whether, under the conditions given, the establishment of a digital infrastructure for pay-TV by MSG will actually contribute in a positive manner to the development of technical and economic progress. It is to be feared that, in view of the effects of the concentration described above, potential suppliers of digital pay-TV will not decide to enter the market to the same extent as would be the case with a service supplier whose shareholder structure would ensure strict neutrality. The successful spread of digital television would, in such a situation, be hindered rather than promoted. This assumption is underpinned by a series of opinions from the enterprises surveyed, which have stated that, in the event of the concentration being carried out, they would have to review and possibly abandon existing plans or thoughts on future pay-TV supply in the digital television area.

Questions for discussion

1. Does the MSG decision indicate that the Commission takes into account other effects of the joint venture, as well as its impact on competition?
2. How might the MSG joint venture, if allowed to proceed, have affected media pluralism?

While the Commission has been willing to adopt a tough approach to mergers and joint ventures in emerging media markets, even where this might slow development of new media services,[25] there are still concerns, even expressed by the Commission, that reliance on competition law alone is not sufficient to ensure pluralism.

Extract 7.5.3

A Harcourt, 'Regulation of European Media Markets: Approaches of the European Court of Justice and the Commission's Merger Task Force' (1998) 9(6) *Utilities Law Review* 276, at 288

Despite the increased use of competition policy in regulating Europe's media industry, there have been concerns that it fails adequately to control media concentration due to problems of market definition, and that even large cross-media mergers are not caught by DGIV[26] turnover thresholds. DGIV's reliance

---

[25] V Rose and D Aitman, 'EC and United Kingdom Competition Law Developments' in E M Barendt (ed), *The Yearbook of Media and Entertainment Law 1995* (Oxford University Press, 1995), pp 423, 430.
[26] The Directorate-General within the Commission responsible for competition policy.

on instruments designed to guarantee the economic functioning of the single market cannot encompass issues of pluralism. Even with the new 1997 changes to the Merger Regulation,[27] without specific rules for the media industry, DGIV is experiencing difficulties in justifying media decisions and an increasing number are confronting appeal.

At a recent conference, Commissioner Van Miert remarked, 'As a direct result of the Single Market there are many, many more cases, particularly in multi-media . . .'[i] It was expressed that faced with a growing number of media decisions, the European Competition taskforce (DGIV) is understaffed. With media companies expanding into adjacent markets, the definition of media markets is becoming increasingly difficult, making judgments controversial. When asked if he was in favour of a draft harmonising media concentration, Van Miert stated:

'My personal opinion is that I am convinced of a need for European legislation on media concentration. From a democratic point of view, it is necessary. . . . We cannot use competition rules to govern democratic issues.'

[i] Future of Merger Control in Europe Conference, European University Institute, Florence, 26 September 1997 by Committee C (Antitrust and Trade Law) of the International Bar Association.

Questions for discussion
1. Why is the definition of the 'market' important?
2. What impact did the identification of the markets have in MSG?

(b) Sector-specific regulation

The recognition of the limits of competition law, and the expansion of the European-wide media industry have produced calls for Community regulation of media ownership. Initially coming from the European Parliament, they resulted in a Green Paper entitled, *Pluralism and Media Concentration in the Internal Market: An Assessment of the Need for Community Action*[28] (the Green Paper). It canvassed three options: no action; measures to improve transparency of information about ownership; and, thirdly, harmonising media ownership legislation. Although proposals have been discussed within the Commission, no legislation has resulted. There are considerable difficulties facing Community legislation. As with the Television Directive, it is debatable whether the Community has legislative competence. One approach is to argue that the lack of specific legislation hinders completion of the internal market. However, legislation framed with that end may fail to protect pluralism. There has also been considerable opposition among some Member States, including Germany and the UK, and industry groups to the idea of legislation.[29]

---

[27] The turnover threshold was lowered from 5 to $2\frac{1}{2}$ million ecu, effective from 1 March 1998.
[28] COM (92) 480 final (23 December 1992).
[29] A Harcourt, 'Regulating for Media Concentration: The Emerging Policy of the European Union' [1996] 7 *Utilities Law Review* 202, at 208.

Within the Commission there has also been differing views about the desir-ability of such regulation.[30] Finally, there are practical problems in trying to design regulation which will be appropriate for countries with very different media industries, in terms of size and stage of expansion.

Extract 7.5.4

G Doyle, 'From "Pluralism" to "Ownership": Europe's Emergent Policy on Media Concentrations Navigates the Doldrums' (1997) (3) *The Journal of Information Law and Technology*, http://elj.warwick.ac.uk/jilt/commsreg/97_3doyl/

In spite of the obstacles and objections to the advancement of a pan-European media ownership policy, DG XV [responsible for the internal market] managed to take a small step forward in July 1996 with the first draft of a possible EC Directive on Media Pluralism.

The Commission's proposals involved a 30 per cent upper limit on monomedia ownership for radio and television broadcasters in their own transmission areas. In addition, the draft Directive suggested an upper limit for total media ownership – i.e. ownership of television, radio and/or newspapers – of 10 per cent of the market in which a supplier is operating. All market shares would be based on audience measures . . . The proposed derogations would allow mem-ber states to exclude public service broadcasters from these upper limits, if they so wish.

. . .

In principle, the imposition of a 30 per cent upper limit on monomedia radio, television or newspaper ownership plus a 10 per cent upper limit on total media ownership, does not seem unreasonable. If pluralism is to exist, then a minimum of four suppliers each in the radio, television and newspaper sectors or ten different suppliers in the market as a whole may seem like an appropri-ate requirement. In practice, however, because of different rules and differing levels of resources available for media provision in each country, some of the member states of Europe would already fall foul of these proposals, even in terms of diversity of ownership at the *national* level. For example, Finland has only two national broadcasters, each with a market share in excess of 30 per cent.[i]

. . .

A revised set of proposals put forward by DG XV in Spring 1997 has introduced two small but significant modifications.[ii] First, the title of the pro-posed Directive has been changed from 'Concentrations and Pluralism' to 'Media Ownership' in the Internal Market. This signals a move to deflect the focus away from pluralism (where the Commission's competence would be in question) towards the aim of removing obstacles to the Internal Market.

Secondly, a 'flexibility clause' has been introduced. This adds, to the pro-posed derogations, the flexibility for individual member states to exclude any

---

[30] Ibid, at 206–208.

broadcaster they wish from the (unchanged) upper limits, provided that the broadcaster in question is not simultaneously infringing these upper thresholds in more than one member state and, also, provided that other 'appropriate measures' are used to secure pluralism. 'Appropriate measures' might include establishing, within any organisation which breaches the limits, 'windows for independent programme suppliers' or a 'representative programming committee'.[iii]

In effect then, as the switch of title suggests, the Directive is no longer about guaranteeing an equal right to pluralism (as represented by diversity of media ownership) for all EU citizens, irrespective of which European markets they live in. Although, in theory, the proposed Directive introduces a uniform set of media ownership restrictions throughout the EU, it is clear that, in practice, the 'flexibility clause' would allow member states to maintain whatever upper restrictions on ownership are affordable – either economically or politically – in their own territories. What, then, is the point of introducing a harmonising initiative?

[i] J. Barnard, V. Broomhead, L. Godwin and A. Smith, *Top Fifty European Media Owners* (Zenith Media, 1996).
[ii] I. Gabara (1997), 'The EU should leave media rules to Member States', *The Wall Street Journal,* 25 March 1997.
[iii] European Commission, *Explanatory Memorandum* (Media Ownership in the Internal Market), DG XV (February, 1997).

Whether there will be specific European regulation of media ownership is uncertain, but increasingly it will be difficult, at the national level, for regulators to ensure adequate control, and the question must remain whether it is sufficient to look only to Community competition law. The issue is further complicated by the increasing trend towards convergence of technology within the media industry. The MSG joint venture had a telecommunications operator as a member. The Community proposals for media ownership legislation are confined to the traditional media sectors; but should it be addressing the relationship between media and telecommunications companies?

(c) Public broadcasting

Community competition law is also applicable to public broadcasters. Article 86 of the EC Treaty requires Member States to ensure that public undertakings, enjoying special or exclusive rights, comply with competition (and free movement) rules. Public broadcasters have traditionally occupied a protected position to enable them to fulfil their public service mandate. The application of Community rules could challenge that position.[31] Article 86(2) offers some concession, but this is limited.

[31] R Craufurd Smith, 'Getting the Measure of Public Services: Community Competition Rules and Public Service Broadcasting' in E M Barendt (ed), *The Yearbook of Media and Entertainment Law 1997/8* (Oxford University Press, 1997), pp 147, 151.

Extract 7.5.5

EC Treaty, art 86(1)–(2) (formerly 90(1)–(2))

1. In the case of public undertakings and undertakings to which Member States grant special or exclusive rights, Member States shall neither enact nor maintain in force any measure contrary to the rules contained in this Treaty, in particular to ... [competition rules].

2. Undertakings entrusted with the operation of services of general economic interest or having the character of a revenue-producing monopoly shall be subject to the rules contained in this Treaty, in particular to the rules on competition, in so far as the application of such rules does not obstruct the performance, in law or in fact, of the particular tasks assigned to them. The development of trade must not be affected to such an extent as would be contrary to the interests of the Community.

It will be recalled from Chapter 5, that the *Sacchi* decision (see Extract 5.3.2 above), which concerned a state broadcasting monopoly, established that broadcasting was subject to Community law. In the following case, the ECJ had to consider the position of a Greek state broadcaster, Elliniki Radiophonia Tileorassi AE (ERT), with a public service mandate, which had an exclusive right to broadcast its own programmes, and to relay foreign broadcasting services. The proceedings had arisen because a local mayor and a company had unlawfully, under Greek law, set up a television station. The proceedings were referred to the ECJ for a ruling on the interpretation of the Treaty.

Extract 7.5.6

Case C-260/89, *Elliniki Radiophonia Tileorassi AE v Dimotiki Etairia Pliroforissis and Sotirios Kouvelas* [1991] ECR I-2925, at 2957 and 2961–2963

In ... *Sacchi* ... the Court held that nothing in the Treaty prevents Member States, for considerations of a non-economic nature relating to the public interest, from removing radio and television broadcasts from the field of competition by conferring on one or more establishments an exclusive right to carry them out.

Nevertheless, it follows from Article 90[86](1) and (2) ... that the manner in which the monopoly is organized or exercised may infringe the rules of the Treaty, in particular those relating to the free movement of goods, the freedom to provide services and the rules on competition.

The reply to the national court must therefore be that Community law does not prevent the granting of a television monopoly for considerations of a non-economic nature relating to the public interest. However, the manner in which such a monopoly is organized and exercised must not infringe the provisions of the Treaty on the free movement of goods and services or the rules on competition.

... [It] should be borne in mind that an undertaking which has a statutory monopoly may be regarded as having a dominant position within the meaning of Article 86[82] ... and that the territory of a Member State over which the monopoly extends may constitute a substantial part of the common market ...

Although Article 86[82] ... does not prohibit monopolies as such, it nevertheless prohibits their abuse. ...

In that regard it should be observed that, according to Article 90[86](2) of the Treaty, undertakings entrusted with the operation of services of general economic interest are subject to the rules on competition so long as it is not shown that the application of those rules is incompatible with the performance of their particular task (see ... *Sacchi* ...).

In that respect it should be observed that Article 90[86](1) ... prohibits the granting of an exclusive right to retransmit television broadcasts to an undertaking which has an exclusive right to transmit broadcasts, where those rights are liable to create a situation in which that undertaking is led to infringe Article 86[82] of the Treaty by virtue of a discriminatory broadcasting policy which favours its own programmes.

The reply to the national court must therefore be that Article 90[86](1) of the Treaty prohibits the granting of an exclusive right to transmit and an exclusive right to retransmit television broadcasts to a single undertaking, where those rights are liable to create a situation in which that undertaking is led to infringe Article 86[82] by virtue of a discriminatory broadcasting policy which favours its own programmes, unless the application of Article 86[82] obstructs the performance of the particular tasks entrusted to it.

The matter was referred back to the national court, for it to determine whether, on the facts, there was a breach of the Treaty.

More recently, Community law has had a more significant practical effect, as the arrangements of the European public broadcasters, to enable them to fulfil their public service mandate, have been subjected to judicial scrutiny. In this instance, it was the European Broadcasting Union (EBU), an organisation of public broadcasters, which was affected. The broadcasting of sporting events is regarded by public broadcasters as an essential part of their public service mandate.[32] However, increasingly, they find themselves outbid by commercial broadcasters for rights to sporting events (see further Section 6(a) below). One of the EBU's functions is to help the joint acquisition of rights to important international sporting events (the Eurovision Scheme). The Eurovision Scheme had been under investigation by the Commission, but in 1993 it granted the Scheme an exemption from art 81(1) (formerly art 85(1)), pursuant to art 81(3) (formerly art 85(3)), on the basis that the Scheme '... facilitated the production and distribution of goods, offered a fair share of resulting benefits to consumers, and neither imposed indispensable

---

[32] Ibid, p 152. Craufurd Smith also suggests that some public broadcasters, dependent upon advertising for their funding, regard broadcasting of sporting rights as essential to their survival because it attracts large audiences and hence increased advertising revenue.

restrictions on members nor eliminated competition altogether . . .'.[33] Four commercial television broadcasters challenged the Commission's decision and the European Court of First Instance (CFI) annulled the decision. An appeal is pending. One of the issues before the CFI was whether the Commission had been entitled to consider the public mission of EBU's members. The references in the judgment to articles 85 and 90 should now be read as references to articles 81 and 86 respectively.

Extract 7.5.7

Joined Cases T-528/93, T-542/93, T-543/93 and T-546/93 *Métropole Télévision SA and Others v EC Commission* [1996] 5 CMLR 386, at 413–414 (footnotes omitted)

According to the [Commission's] Decision, the particular public mission is characterised in particular by the 'obligation to provide varied programming including cultural, educational, scientific and minority programmes without any commercial appeal and to cover the entire national population irrespective of costs'. The Decision therefore essentially takes over the elements of the particular mission of operating services of general economic interest provided for in Article 90(2) of the Treaty, as it has been interpreted by the Community Court . . . In order to hold that the condition relating to Article 85(3)(a) . . . was fulfilled, the Commission therefore took account of factors falling within the field of application of Article 90(2) . . .

However, inasmuch as, according to the Decision itself, Article 90(2) is not applicable, factors coming essentially within the ambit of that article cannot in this case constitute a criterion for the application of Article 85(3) in the absence of other justification.

Admittedly, in the context of an overall assessment, the Commission is entitled to base itself on considerations connected with the pursuit of the public interest in order to grant exemption under Article 85(3) . . . However, in the present case it should have shown that such considerations required exclusivity of rights to transmit sports events, which the Decision authorises for the benefit of members of the EBU, and that that exclusivity was indispensable in order to allow them a fair return on their investments.

However, [the Commission] . . . merely stated that below a certain 'threshold' the acquisition of television rights to sports events at very high prices 'is no longer economically justifiable' and that the 'concept of fair returns cannot be expressed as a precise figure' but corresponds instead to an 'overall financial equilibrium on the part of the broadcasters'.

. . .

In any event, the Commission would not be justified in taking into account, for the purposes of exemption . . . the burdens and obligations arising for the members of the EBU as a result of a public mission, unless it also examined, carefully and impartially, . . . the other relevant aspects of the case, such as

---

[33] Ibid, p 154. The decision is reported at [1995] 4 CMLR 56.

the possible existence of a system of financial compensation for those burdens and obligations . . .

. . .

It follows that, by using in this case as a criterion for granting exemption . . . simply fulfilment of a particular public mission defined essentially by reference to the mission of operating services of general economic interest referred to in Article 90(2) . . . , the Commission based its reasoning on a misinterpretation of Article 85(3) of the Treaty. That error of law is likely to have distorted the assessment which it made of the indispensable nature of the restrictions of competition for which it granted exemption.

Questions for discussion

1. What will the Commission have to establish if it is to take public interest considerations into account when considering an art 81(3) exemption?
2. What is meant by 'a system of financial compensation'?

Another potential Community law threat arises in relation to state funding of broadcasters. This is because art 87(1) (formerly art 92(1)) in some circumstances prohibits state aid.

Extract 7.5.8

EC Treaty, art 87(1) and (3)(d)

1. Save as otherwise provided in this Treaty, any aid granted by a Member State or through State resources in any form whatsoever which distorts or threatens to distort competition by favouring certain undertakings or the production of certain goods shall, insofar as it affects trade between Member States, be incompatible with the common market.

. . .

3. The following may be considered to be compatible with the common market:

. . .

(d) aid to promote culture and heritage conservation where such aid does not affect trading conditions and competition in the Community to an extent that is contrary to the common interest;

This raises concerns about whether funding, either through direct grants or licence fees, is compatible with the common market. Paragraph (3)(d) of art 87 was added by the Maastricht Treaty on European Union, and it could be used to support the funding of state broadcasters. However, one must take into account that there are other broadcasters, such as Channel 4, who must also meet public service obligations, but who have to rely on commercial sources of revenue. This may weaken the support which art 87(3)(d) can offer public broadcasters.[34] The relationship between public broadcasters,

---

[34] Ibid, at 167.

their sources of funding and Community law is a complex one, particularly at a time when public broadcasters, like the BBC, may be developing commercial activities to support their mission. The Commission has been investigating public broadcast financing in Spain, France and Italy, and, in July 1999, announced that it would open proceedings against France in relation to capital increases and ad hoc cash subsidies granted to the two public broadcasters. However, at this stage, the proceedings do not include aid given through the licence fee.[35]

Despite the Commission's investigations, there does appear to be a greater willingness to acknowledge the role of public broadcasters.

Extract 7.5.9

European Community, *Treaty of Amsterdam Amending the Treaty on European Union, The Treaties Establishing the European Communities and Certain Related Acts* (2 October 1997), Protocol on the system of public broadcasting in the Member States

THE HIGH CONTRACTING PARTIES,
CONSIDERING that the system of public broadcasting in the Member States is directly related to the democratic, social and cultural needs of each society and to the need to preserve media pluralism,
HAVE AGREED UPON the following interpretative provisions, which shall be annexed to the Treaty establishing the European Community,
  The provisions of the Treaty establishing the European Community shall be without prejudice to the competence of Member States to provide for the funding of public service broadcasting insofar as such funding is granted to broadcasting organisations for the fulfilment of the public service remit as conferred, defined and organised by each Member State, and insofar as such funding does not affect trading conditions and competition in the Community to an extent which would be contrary to the common interest, while the realisation of the remit of that public service shall be taken into account.

Questions for discussion
1. Would the Protocol have had any impact on the *Métropole* decision?
2. How might it protect public broadcasters from the impact of Community law?

6. ANTI-COMPETITIVE AGREEMENTS AND PRACTICES

Broadcasters may be tempted to make arrangements, for the acquisition of exclusive rights, or to engage in practices, like the promotion of related

---

[35] European Commission, IP/99/531, 20 July 1999. The proceedings are brought under art 88(2) of the EC Treaty (formerly art 93(2)) which applies when the Commission considers that improper aid has been given.

media interests, in order to gain advantages in the market and to secure audiences. However, these could be anti-competitive, and they may also constitute restrictions on the freedom to broadcast or receive broadcasts.

(a) Exclusive agreements

With the growth of cable and satellite television over the last decade exclusive arrangements have attracted a lot of attention, partly because of the increased number of competing channels, but also because they can be crucial in attracting audiences. Obtaining exclusive rights to broadcast popular sporting events has been a useful way of winning over viewers to subscription television. Another attractive area for exclusive agreements is films, and BSkyB has contracted with a number of film studios to secure rights to distribute films on satellite television.[36] Equally, events of national significance such as a coronation or a state funeral could become subject to exclusive rights.[37] However, it has been sporting events which have occasioned most concern both within the UK and the European Community.[38] The amended Television Directive now includes a provision covering major events. Under art 3a Member States can take measures to ensure that broadcasters cannot broadcast, on an exclusive basis, major events, if that would deprive a substantial proportion of the public the opportunity to see the events on free-to-air television, by either live or deferred coverage.[39]

In the UK exclusive agreements for major events were not prohibited, but regulation was in place to protect the terrestrial broadcasters, for example by giving them rights of first refusal.[40] The BA 1990 introduced a major relaxation. Terrestrial broadcasters were no longer given preferential rights, although pay-per-view broadcasts were prohibited for certain events, known as 'listed' events because a list of the protected sport and national events was drawn up by the Secretary of State (BA 1990, s 182). The BA 1990 coincided with the expansion of satellite and cable services, and these broadcasters were able to obtain valuable rights for major sporting events. In 1996 the

---

[36] Office of Fair Trading, *The Director General's Review of BSkyB's Position in the Wholesale Pay TV Market* (December 1996), para 4.63.

[37] Barendt, p 137.

[38] It has been suggested that exclusive agreements over sporting events have the greatest impact compared with film rights, because they are perishable goods. Films will experience greater competition because the same film can be shown at different times, whereas the greatest value of a sporting event will be in its live form: M Williams, 'Sky Wars: The OFT Review of Pay-TV' [1997] 18(4) ECLR 214, at 218.

[39] The revised Television Convention also includes more detailed provisions for the protection of such events. The government proposes to introduce regulations in 2000 implementing the Television Directive, art 3a. The regulations will amend the legislative provisions discussed in this section.

[40] See, for example, Broadcasting Act 1981, s 30(1) and Cable and Broadcasting Act 1984, s 14.

Office of Fair Trading (OFT) conducted an investigation into BSkyB's position in the pay-television market, as a result of the acquisition of sporting and film rights. The OFT concluded that, although BSkyB had not acted anti-competitively, it did occupy a powerful position because of these rights,[41] and that this impaired the competitive process. Undertakings were accepted from BSkyB concerning its arrangements with other broadcasters, particularly cable.[42]

One of BSkyB's most valuable contracts is with the Footall Association Premier League. A new contract for the period 1997 to 2001 grants it the right to broadcast live Premier League soccer matches, and the BBC, the right to show highlights. Some 380 Premier matches are played each year, although BSkyB only broadcasts 60 of these. However, the Premier League has agreed that none of these other matches will be shown live on any other UK channel.[43] The agreement was referred to the Restrictive Practices Court (RPC) by the OFT because it considered that the agreement represented an anti-competitive cartel and was against the public interest.[44] In July 1999, the RPC held that the arrangements for collective negotiation and exclusivity were not unlawful and operated in the public interest. In the court's view, they ensured an equitable division of revenue among the clubs, and were the most practical way of ensuring that viewers had access to a representative selection of the matches played during the season.[45]

Question for discussion
How does the restriction on other matches being broadcast, operate in the interests of the soccer clubs and the public?

Public concern and a defeat in the House of Lords, caused the government to include in the BA 1996 new protection for sporting events.[46] It applies not just to sporting events, but, as before, it is these which have received most attention. The new provisions are much more extensive than those in the 1990 legislation, and aim to give terrestrial broadcasters an opportunity to broadcast live events.

---

[41] BSkyB had pay TV rights to over 90% of major first run films: note 36, above, para 2.22.

[42] *Fair Trading*, Autumn 1996, p 1. For a critique of the OFT's review see Williams, note 38, above.

[43] Williams, note 38, above, at 218.

[44] *Fair Trading*, Issue 18, 1998, p 4.

[45] *In the Matter of the Restrictive Trade Practices Act 1976 and in the Matter of an Agreement between the Football Association Premier League Limited et al and in the Matter of an Agreement relating to the Supply of Services facilitating the Broadcasting on Television of Premier League Football Matches and the Supply of Services consisting in the Broadcasting on Television of such Matches*, 28 July 1999, http://www.courtservice.gov.uk/pljmtint.htm, paras 312–315, 321–322, 339–340 and 346–347.

[46] House of Lords, vol 570 (5 March 1996), col 162 (Lord Inglewood).

Extract 7.6.1

Broadcasting Act 1996, s 98(1)–(2) and ss 99–101(1)

98.—(1) For the purposes of this Part [of the Act] television programme services shall be divided into two categories as follows—

    (a) such of the services specified in subsection (2) as are provided without any charge being made for the reception of programmes included in the service, and

    (b) all television programme services not for the time being falling within paragraph (a).

(2) The services referred to in subsection (1)(a) are—

    (a) regional and national Channel 3 services,

    (b) Channel 4, and

    (c) the television broadcasting services provided by the BBC.

(3),(4) [*Omitted*].

99.—(1) Any contract entered into after the commencement of this section under which a television programme provider acquires rights to televise the whole or any part of a listed event live for reception in the United Kingdom, or in any area of the United Kingdom, shall be void so far as it purports, in relation to the whole or any part of the event or in relation to reception in the United Kingdom or any area of the United Kingdom, to grant those rights exclusively to any one television programme provider.

(2) In this Part 'television programme provider' means the BBC, the Welsh Authority or any person who is the holder of any licence under Part I of the 1990 Act [that is, all television services, other than local delivery] or a digital programme licence under Part I of this Act.

(3) For the purposes of this section rights to televise the whole or any part of an event live for reception in any area granted to a television programme provider are granted exclusively if the person granting them—

    (a) has not granted any such right to any other television programme provider, and

    (b) is precluded by the terms of the contract from doing so.

100.—(1) Any contract entered into after the commencement of this section shall be void so far as it purports to grant to a television programme provider rights to televise the whole or any part of a listed event live for reception in the United Kingdom, or any area of the United Kingdom, unless the contract complies with subsection (2).

(2) A contract complies with this subsection if the terms of the contract allow the television programme provider to include the live coverage of the listed event—

    (a) only in a television programme service falling within paragraph
        (a) of subsection (1) of section 98, or

    (b) only in a television programme service falling within paragraph
        (b) of that subsection.

101.—(1) A person providing a service falling within either of the categories set out in subsection (1) of section 98 ('the first service') for reception in the United Kingdom or in any area of the United Kingdom shall not, without the previous consent of the Commission, include in that service live coverage of the whole or any part of a listed event unless—

(a) another person, who is providing a service falling within the other category set out in that subsection ('the second service'), has acquired the right to include in the second service live coverage of the whole of the event or of that part of the event, and

(b) the area for which the second service is provided consists of or includes the whole, or substantially the whole, of the area for which the first service is provided.

Questions for discussion

1. Why is Channel 5 not included in the first category of television programme services under BA 1996, s 98(1)(a)?

2. Does the 1996 regime guarantee coverage of live events on free-to-air terrestrial television?

Section 102 of the BA 1996 empowers the ITC to impose financial penalties on broadcasters acting in breach of s 101, although it does not have power to impose fines on the BBC and Welsh Authority. Instead, under s 103 it must report them to the Secretary of State. Section 104 requires the ITC to draw up a code of guidance on what constitutes a 'live' broadcast and the matters it will take into account when exercising its discretion (Extract 7.6.3 below).

In June 1998, the Secretary of State announced a new list of sporting events (see Extract 7.6.3) following the report of an Advisory Group, established by him, under the chairmanship of Lord Gordon. The Report highlights some of the tensions surrounding sporting broadcasts.

Extract 7.6.2

The Advisory Group on Listed Events, Report and Recommendations (March 1998), pp 2–3

The matters on which we have been asked to provide advice arouse strong emotions. The organisers of some sporting events resent any interference with what they regard as their right to secure the highest price for broadcasting coverage in a completely open market. Broadcasters divide somewhat predictably between certain established terrestrial broadcasters, who have traditionally covered such events and wish to continue to do so, and new services available on subscription or pay-per-view, who have regarded the securing of exclusive rights to live coverage of the most popular sporting events as an important means of increasing the number of subscribers to their services.

Most important of all, the great majority of the population who do not at the moment subscribe to satellite or cable services sometimes feel that they are being almost blackmailed into doing so if certain key sporting events become exclusively available on these channels . . .

... Terrestrial television services, with an obligation to provide a wide range of programming, cannot or should not be able to cover lengthy sporting events in full, without unacceptable disruption to normal services and consequential disappointment for viewers who are not aficionados of the sport in question. The logical place for complete live coverage of events of long duration must surely be on channels specifically catering for sport ... The fact that one has to pay for access to such a service should not be any more offensive to the devotee of the sport than the fact that an admission charge would be made for entry to the event itself.

There are, however, some events which clearly ... have a 'national reson-ance' and represent a shared fixed point on the national calendar. Wide-spread enjoyment of such events on generally-available terrestrial television is a force for cohesion in society. We recommend that such events continue to be listed.

Questions for discussion

1. Is it sufficient for the Committee to rely on the fact that sporting events require an admission charge to justify its approach?

2. In view of the likely growth in pay television, with the introduction of digital broadcasting, can a case still be made for regulating viewers' access to these events?

3. Are there other events which should be listed?

There are now two lists of events. List A is covered by the 'listed events' legislative provisions, but events in List B can be provided by exclusive live coverage, provided the ITC is satisfied that there is adequate provision for secondary coverage, such as delayed coverage or edited highlights. The fol-lowing extract, illustrates the matters relevant to the ITC's exercise of discre-tion under BA 1996, s 101.

Extract 7.6.3

**ITC, *Code on Sports and other Listed Events*
(January 1999), para 12 and Appendix 2**

12. In deciding whether to give its consent it may be sufficient for the ITC to establish that the availability of the rights was generally known and no broad-caster in the other category had expressed an interest in their acquisition to the rights holder, or had not bid for the rights. However, the ITC will wish to be satisfied that broadcasters have had a genuine opportunity to acquire the rights on fair and reasonable terms and, in reaching a view, will take account of some or all of the following criteria:

– any invitation to express interest, whether in the form of public advertise-ment or closed tender, in the acquisition of the rights must have been communicated openly and simultaneously to broadcasters in both categories;

- at the beginning of any negotiation the documentation and/or marketing literature must set out in all material respects the process for negotiating and acquiring the rights and all material terms and conditions, including what rights were available;
- if the rights to the listed event were included in a package of rights, the package must not have been more attractive to broadcasters in one of the two categories. Preferably, the rights should be capable of being purchased independently of other rights, e.g., to highlights, delayed transmissions, other events;
- the conditions or costs attached to the acquisition of the rights (for example, production costs) must have been clearly stated and must not be preferential to one category of broadcaster;
- the price sought for the rights must have been fair, reasonable and non-discriminatory as between the two categories of broadcaster. What is a fair price will depend upon the rights being offered and the value of those rights to broadcasters. A wide range of prices is likely to be regarded as fair but when required to make its own judgement on the matter the ITC will have regard to, inter alia:
    - previous fees for the event or similar events;
    - time of day for live coverage of the event;
    - the revenue or audience potential associated with the live transmission of the event (e.g., the opportunity to sell advertising and sponsorship; the prospects for subscription income);
    - the period for which rights are offered; and
    - competition in the market place.
  . . .

APPENDIX 2: LISTED SPORTING EVENTS

GROUP A

The Olympic Games
The FIFA World Cup Finals Tournament
The FA Cup Final
The Scottish FA Cup Final (in Scotland)
The Grand National
The Derby
The Wimbledon Tennis Finals
The European Football Championship Finals Tournament
The Rugby League Challenge Cup Final
The Rugby World Cup Final

GROUP B

Cricket Test Matches played in England
Non-Finals play in the Wimbledon Tournament
All Other Matches in the Rugby World Cup Finals Tournament

Five Nations Rugby Tournament Matches Involving Home Countries
The Commonwealth Games
The World Athletics Championship
The Cricket World Cup – the Final, Semi-finals and Matches Involving Home
    Nations' Teams
The Ryder Cup
The Open Golf Championship

While the 1996 provisions appear more comprehensive, and make a more concerted attempt to protect listed events for free-to-air television, much will depend upon how the ITC exercises its discretion. It may also be that some broadcasters already have such a competitive advantage that they will be able to compete more effectively for rights.

(b) Networking

Channel 3 operates on a regional basis with only one independent terrestrial broadcaster for each region, although now it is more likely that a company will control the licence for more than one region. A curious feature of commercial broadcasting has been the existence of networking arrangements whereby regional broadcasters sell programmes to the national network, that is for all the regional Channel 3 licensees. On the one hand, this seems a sensible option because, with limited competition in the region, it produces competition for programmes through the network, and broadens programme sources. On the other hand, it could squeeze out smaller companies attempting to sell programmes. If the networking arrangement can be dominated by a few companies, then there is a risk that sources of programming become limited. The networking arrangements have been somewhat problematic, partly because they were dominated by a few of the larger licensees.[47] Section 39 of and Sched 4 to the BA 1996 introduced a tougher, more competitive scheme for control of networking arrangements. The arrangements, which are drawn up by the licensees, must be approved by the ITC and the Director General of Fair Trading (DGFT). The former must be satisfied that the arrangements enable Channel 3 to compete with other television services (BA 1996, s 39(1)). The DGFT must be satisfied that they do not restrict, prevent or distort competition, or if they do, that there are counterbalancing benefits (BA 1996, Sched 4, para 2). The first networking arrangements made under the BA 1990 were rejected by the DGFT as anti-competitive, and, after a referral to the Monopolies and Mergers Commission, revised arrangements were made.[48] Despite the improvements, concerns are still felt about networking.

---

[47] For a history of these arrangements see Gibbons, pp 133–138.
[48] Monopolies and Mergers Commission, *Channel 3 Networking Arrangements* (April 1993).

Extract 7.6.4

T Gibbons, *Regulating the Media*, 2nd ed
(Sweet & Maxwell, 1998), pp 231–232

Generally, the new networking arrangements are a distinct improvement on the old agreement which operated prior to the 1990 Act. They provide much wider opportunities for a diversity of programming to reach a national audience, and on a much more competitive basis. However, if the arrangements are tested against the principle of freedom in communication, the benefits are not so obvious. The need to satisfy the Network Centre's schedulers means that the programmes which succeed are those which maximise audience figures during peak viewing times, and that will not necessarily provide a plurality of material. There is a deep tension in the networking arrangements, however. The licensees and the ITC tend to justify them with arguments about regionalism and the traditions of the independent television sector. But the tendency of the current arrangements is to undermine that tradition and, interestingly, the Director-General of Fair Trading did not appear to be convinced about its continued relevance.[i] The major advantage of the agreement, of course, is commercial; it enables companies which are relatively small, by international standards, to share costs, and it strengthens their position against the larger organisations which are tending to dominate the market.

[i] See Director-General of Fair Trading, *Channel 3 Networking Arrangements* (1992) December 3, paras 11.49–11.55.

(c) Cross-media promotion

There is a danger that a media group may use one of its companies to promote the interests and activities of another media company within the group. Equally, there could be a temptation to influence the reporting of news about the media group. The issue achieved prominence in the late 1980s, particularly with the competition for subscribers between British Satellite Broadcasting and Sky Television, before their merger. British Satellite Broadcasting complained to the DGFT about Sky's promotion through newspapers owned by News International plc. The DGFT's investigation was pre-empted by the government's announcement of an inquiry into cross-media promotion to be carried out by John Sadler. Although Sadler expressed concerns about cross-promotion practices, his Report recommended only the establishment of a self-regulatory code.[49] No further action was taken on this.

In the past few years cross-media promotion has received less attention, but the practice has not ceased. Newspapers will, in the guise of news reporting, give prominence to the launch, for example, of some new broadcasting

[49] J Sadler, *Enquiry into Standards of Cross Media Promotion: Report to the Secretary of State for Trade and Industry*, Cm. 1436 (1991).

service with which the newspaper is linked.[50] Reporting of matters connected with BSkyB, and with the Murdoch family, in newspapers owned by News International, regularly differs in terms of prominence and substance from that in other non-connected newspapers. More recently, the development of digital television (see Chapter 3, Section 6) has sparked concern about cross-media promotion between analogue and digital services. The licensing arrangements for digital terrestrial services mean that current terrestrial analogue broadcasters have interests in digital broadcasting (see Chapter 3). The ITC has published a code on the cross-promotion of all digital services, terrestrial, cable and satellite, which describes the circumstances in which cross-promotion, outside advertising time, is permitted.

Extract 7.6.5

Independent Television Commission, *Consolidated Statement of ITC Rules on Cross-promotion of Digital Television Service* (October 1998), paras 3 and 5

3. *Analogue terrestrial licensees* (Channels 3–5) may promote their own 'qualifying' service (i.e. the simulcast digital version of their analogue service) and any other service they provide on the 'gifted' digital capacity on the same multiplex as their 'qualifying' service. They may not, however, promote outside advertising minutage any other digital services.

5. Analogue terrestrial licensees may also broadcast outside advertising minutage material promoting digital terrestrial television generically i.e. without referring to specific channels or programmes.

The ITC has had to act to enforce this code. In November 1998, it ordered Channel 3 to withdraw all promotions of digital terrestrial television on the grounds that it was denigratory to the satellite platform, and in breach of paragraph 5 because references were made to ONdigital (a digital service owned by two Channel 3 licensees).[51] It is clear that with the intense competition for audiences to digital television, broadcasters (and related newspapers) will face temptation in the methods they adopt to attract those audiences. Digital television may test whether there is sufficient regulation for cross-media promotion.

(d) Bundling

Pay television introduces another practice, bundling, which may restrict viewers' choice and access to programmes, by forcing them to take channels which

---

[50] For examples of cross-media promotion and a discussion of the matter generally see D Glencross, 'Television Ownership and Editorial Control' in E M Barendt (ed), *The Yearbook of Media and Entertainment Law 1996* (Oxford University Press, 1996), p 3.

[51] ITC, *ITC Requires ITV Promotions for Digital To Be Pulled* (News Release 106/98, 20 November 1998).

they may not want. Essentially, bundling is the practice by which programme providers, package a group of channels and require subscriptions to the whole package. Bundling can occur at both the retail (the supply to viewers) and the wholesale level (the supply to satellite and cable operators).[52] Bundling frequently occurs with premium channels, which are usually the most attractive channels to viewers, and those for which they will be willing to pay a 'premium'. These will usually be broadcasting live coverage of popular sporting events or first television showing of major films. A pay television operator will view these channels as the most important element in securing a subscriber base.[53] Offering a package of cable telephone and television channels is another form of bundling, and the ITC and OFTEL (the telecommunications regulator) have recently published a consultation document exploring whether this may give rise to anti-competitive practices.[54]

Not surprisingly, many of the concerns about bundling practices have been connected with BSkyB, largely because of its dominance in the premium channels market. The OFT's inquiry into BSkyB's position in the pay-television market (see Section 6(a) above) involved its supply terms to cable operators, including premium channel bundling.[55] In November 1996, the ITC also began an investigation into premium channel bundling in response to a complaint about the Disney Channel. A cable operator had complained that it could only acquire the Disney Channel from BSkyB, and offer it as part of a bundle of three premium channels, although the other two channels could be acquired separately.[56] The ITC decided that it should investigate the matter of premium channel bundling more widely pursuant to its powers under the BA 1990.[57]

Extract 7.6.6

Broadcasting Act 1990, s 2(2)(a)(ii)

(2) It shall be the duty of the Commission—
   (a) to discharge their functions . . . in the manner which they consider is best calculated—

   . . .

   (ii) to ensure fair and effective competition in the provision of such [television] services and services connected with them . . .

---

[52] OFTEL, *Bundling in the Pay Television Market, Submission by the Director General of Telecommunications to the Independent Television Commission* (December 1997), paras 2.1 and 3.18.
[53] Ibid, para 3.17.
[54] ITC and OFTEL, *The Bundling of Television and Telephony: Competition Issues* (April 1998).
[55] Note 36, above.
[56] ITC, *Competition Investigation into Premium Channel Bundling in the Pay-TV Market*, Consultation Document (November 1996), para 7.
[57] Agreement was later reached to allow the Disney Channel to be acquired separately.

Initially it proposed confining itself to the retail market, but in July 1997 it announced a broadening of its investigation to include bundling practices more generally and the wholesale market.[58] In April 1998 it published a Consultation Document setting out the results of its investigation. This describes other bundling practices.

Extract 7.6.7

ITC, *Competition Investigation into Channel Bundling in the Retail Pay-TV Market*, Consultation Document (April 1998), paras 15–17 and 19

Basic Bundling and Minimum Carriage Requirements (MCRs)

15. Our investigation revealed that a significant influence on the size of basic channel packages was the minimum carriage requirements (MCRs) which commonly form part of the supply agreements between retailers (cable and satellite companies) and wholesalers (channel providers). An MCR essentially binds the retailer into showing the wholesaler's basic channel to a minimum proportion of subscribers. In that respect MCRs are unique, as other forms of bundling permit the retailer to decide the form, extent and level of bundling employed. Tiering obligations, e.g. a requirement to place a channel in a basic tier, have the same effect as MCRs.

16. Following the OFT's review of BSkyB's position in the wholesale pay-TV market, BSkyB lowered its MCRs for the supply of its basic channels from 100 per cent to 80 per cent. This has become the industry norm. In essence, the norm means that neither BSkyB (in its retail business) nor cable companies have much flexibility to offer viewers anything other than big basic channel packages since 80 per cent of subscribers must take each channel. Only 20 per cent of subscribers could be offered an alternative and this is probably uneconomic (at least on the basis of existing contractual arrangements).

17. The justifications advanced by proponents of MCRs relate to the assistance they provide to smaller niche channels entering the market, and the income security they provide to programme suppliers with high fixed costs. Our analysis suggests, however, that the economic characteristics of channels do not justify special arrangements, like MCRs. The costs of entering the market or producing channels are not particularly high and the argument that a high proportion of costs is fixed is also difficult to sustain. In any event, there are alternative payment mechanisms which would achieve the same financial objective without the anti-competitive impact of MCRs.

Buy-through

19. The removal of MCRs and tiering obligations should facilitate the creation of smaller basic packages. This will go a considerable way to mitigating

---

[58] ITC, *ITC Extends Review of Bundling in the Pay TV Market* (News Release 66/97, 30 July 1997).

any adverse effects on viewers of buy-through obligations, i.e., the obligation to buy basic channels before premium ones. Given the expressed demand for some basic channels (illustrated by viewing data), together with premium channels, and the prevalence of buy-through in other pay-TV markets, the ITC believes that it is difficult to conclude unambiguously that buy-through is anti-competitive in effect. Consequently, the ITC does not propose to prohibit buy-through but will require licensees to make buy-through to premium channels available from any basic package.

Questions for discussion

1. Apart from distorting competition, how else might bundling be detrimental?

2. BSkyB charges subscribers £11 for one premium film channel, and, if two such channels are taken, £4 for that second channel. Is this likely to be anti-competitive? How might it be to the detriment of viewers?[59]

Following the Consultation Document, the ITC announced new rules on bundling and related practices: minimum carriage requirements were prohibited with effect from 1 July 1998 for all new agreements and for digital television, and from 1 January 2000 for analogue television; viewers should be able to buy premium channels individually although they can still be tied to a basic package; and viewers should be able to buy-through to premium channels from any basic package.[60] Flextech plc and Sci-Fi Channel Europe LLC, channel providers, unsuccessfully sought judicial review of the ITC's rules. It was argued that BA 1990, s 2(2)(a)(ii) did not give the ITC '. . . a free-standing duty to regulate competition in broadcasting, nor . . . to regulate competition in the interests of viewers'.[61] However, Maurice Kay J held that the section '. . . clearly and unambiguously enables the ITC to take steps to ensure fair and effective competition in the circumstances of this case'.

7. CONCLUSION

The regulation of media ownership and of its competitive behaviour is becoming increasingly complex and multi-dimensional. The role of the ITC, compared with its predecessors, is much more pervasive. It is no longer simply concerned with who owns what, but more frequently is having to address the behaviour of licensees. This is a trend which is likely to continue as pay-television becomes more common. Nor is this a matter simply for the

---

[59] The ITC has announced that it is investigating BSkyB's bundling of premium film channels to determine whether its pricing practices are anti-competitive: *The Guardian* (9 July 1999).

[60] ITC, *ITC Confirms End of Minimum Carriage Requirements* (News Release 65/98, 26 June 1998). See also ITC, *Guidance on ITC's Bundling Remedies* (June 1998).

[61] *R v Independent Television Commission, ex parte Flextech plc and Another* (1998) *The Times*, 27 November.

broadcasting regulators. Here again the involvement of other regulatory bodies is apparent – the competition authorities, naturally, but also OFTEL. More and more these bodies are having to work together, developing policies on media practices which may have adverse effects on competition. With the convergence of media and telecommunications, this too is a trend which will not disappear (see Chapter 8). Similarly, the subject matter for the regulatory bodies is becoming more diverse, as media companies become less concerned with owning another broadcasting company or newspaper, and more interested in gaining control of key programming sources, which will strengthen their ability to attract audiences. The importance of controlling access to programming rights has been highlighted in this chapter. The changing nature of the media industry is possibly best exemplified by the recent attempted merger of BSkyB Broadcasting Group plc and a soccer club, Manchester United plc. Following the recommendation of the Monopolies and Mergers Commission (MMC) that the merger would be against the public interest, the Secretary of State for Trade and Industry prohibited it proceeding.[62] While the MMC took into account the impact of the merger on soccer, it was the consequences for broadcasting which primarily concerned it. In this final extract, one can discern why control of a soccer club might be attractive to a media company in today's market and why media ownership and control calls for a sophisticated regulatory response.

Extract 7.7.1

Monopolies and Mergers Commission, *British Sky Broadcasting Group plc and Manchester United plc: A Report on the Proposed Merger*, Cm 4305 (1999), paras 1.4–1.5 and 1.7–1.8

1.4. We have concluded that the relevant football market in which Manchester United operates is no wider than the matches of Premier League clubs. We considered whether the broadcasting market in which BSkyB operates ought to comprise both pay TV and free-to-air TV and concluded that it was more appropriate to treat pay TV as a separate market. Based primarily on considerations of substitutability we concluded that the relevant market for our purposes was for sports premium TV channels.

1.5. Except for small niche channels, BSkyB is currently the only provider of sports premium channels. Entry into this market depends crucially upon the ability of a channel provider to obtain the appropriate live sports rights. We think it unlikely that there are enough such rights to sustain many sports premium channels and BSkyB currently provides three. BSkyB's very high market share together with the difficulties of entry lead us to conclude that BSkyB has market power in the sports premium channel market.

. . .

---

[62] Department of Trade and Industry, *Stephen Byers Blocks BSkyB/Manchester United Merger* (P/99/309, 9 April 1999).

1.7. Our first scenario involved the continuation of existing collective selling arrangements and no other mergers between broadcasters and Premier League clubs. We have concluded that under this scenario, BSkyB would, as a result of the merger, gain influence over and information about the Premier League's selling of rights that would not be available to its competitors. It would also benefit from its ownership stake in Premier League rights, providing a further advantage in the bidding process.

1.8. Taken together, these factors would significantly improve BSkyB's chances of securing the Premier League's rights. We would expect this to influence the behaviour of BSkyB's competitors causing them to bid more cautiously . . . and, in some cases, even not to bid at all. This would enhance BSkyB's already strong position arising from its market power as a sports premium channel provider and from being the incumbent broadcaster of Premier League football.

8

CONVERGENCE

1. INTRODUCTION

One of the recurring themes of this book has been the differences in approach to press and broadcasting regulation. In Chapter 1 the justifications for this were canvassed (Chapter 1, Section 3). While the press has largely been regulated by the general law, radio and television have been subjected to close regulatory control on matters such as who can broadcast and what can be broadcast, in other words structural and content regulation. Spectrum scarcity has been one of the reasons put forward for this special treatment. Traditionally in a book on media law, the regulation of telecommunications would be outside the scope of such a work, but because of current developments, the telecommunications industry and its regulation have an increasing relevance to the regulation of broadcasting.

The model of telecommunications regulation has differed from broadcasting. Regulation of telecommunications has adopted what is known as a common carrier model. The carrier simply acts as a distributor of all messages received and does not exercise any control over content. Unlike broadcasting, legal control over content is essentially a matter for the general law. Telecommunications services, previously provided by a public monopoly, are now offered by private operators in a competitive market, regulated by the Office of Telecommunications (OFTEL). The separate regulation of the broadcasting and telecommunications sectors made sense because there seemed to be little overlap between the two industries: broadcasting provided sound and, in the case of television, also image from one point to many points simultaneously (point to multipoint communication) while telecommunications provided the opportunity for one to one communication via mainly voice telephony services (point to point communication). A third sector which seemed far removed from broadcasting was the computing industry. The computing industry has been treated like any other industry subject to regulation by the general law.

These three sectors have developed separately and have been treated by the law separately. However, this established pattern is changing and it is digital technology which is contributing to this change, producing the convergence of these sectors into what is frequently referred to as 'multi-media'. Until the introduction of digital television in 1998 (see Chapter 3, Section 6), radio and television programmes were transmitted using analogue technology. Digital technology means that sound and pictures are converted into digital bits (a series of noughts and ones) and then reconverted by receivers into broadcasting programmes.[1] The most immediate impact of digital technology on broadcasting, as explained in Chapter 3, is that it increases the number of services which can be broadcast as well as improving picture and sound quality. However, a more significant consequence is that broadcasting now shares a transmission technology with telecommunications and computing. It is becoming increasingly feasible, both technically and economically, for the same network or receiver, that is television set, computer or telephone, to deliver any type of content, whether it be picture, sound, data or text. The delivery technology, and thus, the means of delivery, is becoming less relevant in determining what content will be carried. Thus the traditionally distinct sectors which we described above are converging. The practical effects of this are illustrated in Extract 8.1.1.

Extract 8.1.1

European Commission, *Green Paper on the Convergence of the Telecommunications, Media and Information Technology Sectors, and the Implications for Regulation: Towards an Information Society Approach*, COM (97) 623, 3 December 1997, http://www.ispo.cec.be/ convergencegp/97623.html, executive summary

There is widespread agreement that convergence is occurring at the techno-logical level. That is to say that digital technology now allows both traditional and new communication services – whether voice, data, sound or pictures – to be provided over many different networks.

Current activity in the market suggests that operators from the sectors affected by convergence are acting on the opportunities provided by techno-logical advances to enhance their traditional services and to branch out into new activities. Telecommunications, Media and Information Technology sectors are seeking cross-product and cross-platform development as well as cross-sector share-holding. Examples of new products and services being delivered include:

- Home-banking and home-shopping over the Internet;
- Voice over the Internet;
- E-mail, data and World Wide Web access over mobile phone networks, and the use of wireless links to homes and businesses to connect them to the fixed telecommunications networks;
- Data services over digital broadcasting platforms;

---

[1] Department of National Heritage, *Digital Terrestrial Broadcasting: The Government's Proposals*, Cm 2946 (1995), p 25.

- On-line services combined with television via systems such as Web-TV, as well as delivery via digital satellites and cable modems;
- Webcasting of news, sports, concerts and of other audiovisual services.

While convergence appears to open up possibilities, through multimedia, for access to a much greater array of communication services, with increased flexibility and control for the user of these services, its impact upon the broadcasting regulatory framework cannot be ignored. Convergence has already generated regulatory measures. For example, digital television increases the capacity for subscription services, thereby increasing the ability of the viewer to select more precisely the broadcasting programmes which he or she receives. However, it is necessary to ensure that the viewer is able to have access to the range of programmes available. Rules on what is termed 'conditional access' have been introduced (see Section 2 below). More fundamentally, however, convergence calls into question the traditional approach to broadcasting regulation. If it is possible to download a television-like programme via the Internet (webcasting), or to use one's telephone to order a film (video-on-demand) it must be asked how this affects regulation of programmes delivered via radio and television receivers. Maintaining traditional approaches to regulation becomes problematic when convergence opens up the scope for regulatory bypass. Moreover, attempting to apply broadcasting regulatory models to other delivery mechanisms would probably be impractical. The Internet, for example, reflects an approach to regulation more akin to that applying to the press. Earlier analysis has shown how the imposition of positive programme requirements on broadcasters can be viewed as a means of promoting broadcasting freedom. However, to impose such requirements on the operation of the Internet would almost certainly be viewed as an infringement of freedom of expression, just as if such requirements had been imposed upon the press. In the next extract, Wacks explores some of the difficulties of regulating the Internet.

Extract 8.1.2

R Wacks, 'Privacy in Cyberspace: Personal Information, Free Speech, and the Internet' in P Birks (ed), *Privacy and Loyalty* (Clarendon Press, 1997), pp 93, 95–96, 97 and 102

The Internet has no physical existence. A huge network, it interconnects innumerable smaller groups of linked computer networks. It is a network of networks. Many networks are linked to other networks, which are in turn connected to other networks, so that each computer in any network can communicate with computers on any other network in the system. This global web of linked networks and computers is the Internet . . .

This mosaic of computers and computer networks – some owned by government and public institutions, some by non-profit organisations, and some privately owned, is a decentralised, unrestricted global medium of communications – or what the science-fiction writer, William Gibson, called 'cyberspace' – that links individuals, institutions, corporations and governments around the world. It permits the tens of millions of people with access to the Internet to exchange ideas, software, images, literature, sound or simple e-mail. These communications are almost instantaneous, and can be directed either to specific individuals, to a group of individuals interested in a particular subject, or to the world as a whole.

. . . It would seem that no entity – academic, corporate, governmental, or non-profit-making – controls, or indeed runs, the Internet. It functions solely as a result of the fact that hundreds of thousands of separate operators of computers and computer networks independently decided to use a common data transfer protocol to exchange communications and information with other computers . . . There is no centralised storage location, control point, or communications channel for the Internet, and it would be impossible for any single entity to regulate the information conveyed on it.

. . .

There is nothing new about the law's struggle to keep abreast with technology. In the present context, however, the contest may not be worth the candle. Attempts to control the Internet, its operation or content, have been notoriously unsuccessful. Its anarchy and resistance to regulation is, in the minds of many, its strength and attraction.

. . .

Inevitably, the advances in electronic media will continue to test the appropriateness of existing standards. Can the same regulation that is applied, for example, to broadcasting be applied to cable television or to computer networks? The print media appear to enjoy a preferred position, and seem less susceptible to regulation than the electronic word, notwithstanding that the latter is now already the dominant means of communication in advanced societies. As the differences between the media dissolve, there is clearly a need to establish a regime that recognises the rights of both the users and the operators of the new technology. It should no longer matter whether the information you receive (and which you regard as obscene, racist, intrusive) appears in the pages of your newspaper or on the screen of your computer or television.

Yet though the form in which a message is transmitted may cease to be a significant factor, users of the Internet experience communication in a fundamentally different way from other electronic media. Thus in the case of television and radio, the number of speakers is limited by the available spectrum, the ability to speak is limited by the high cost of speaking, and listeners are (at least for the present) merely passive recipients of the communications. With the Internet, on the other hand, the number of speakers is infinite, anyone can speak for a few pence a day (or none) and listeners can respond and engage the speaker in an interactive and continuing dialogue. Moreover, unlike television and radio, on the Internet viewers and listeners normally receive only the communications they request, and are not a passive or 'captive' audience. And, unlike television and radio, on the Internet a speaker can reach the entire world (at no additional cost), yet at the same time can direct his or her speech to individuals who share an interest in a particular subject.

In 1998 the House of Commons Culture, Media and Sport Committee conducted an inquiry into multimedia. In its Report it also recognised the inappropriateness of the UK trying to exert existing regulatory patterns over the Internet.

Extract 8.1.3

Culture, Media and Sport Committee, *The Multi-Media Revolution*, Fourth Report (HCP 520-I, 1998) vol I, paras 106–107 and 114 (footnotes omitted)

106. There are technical barriers to the transmission of high quality audio-visual material over the Internet, but these are diminishing and show signs of all but disappearing. The relationship between the regulation of Internet content and that of broadcasting of a more traditional kind will thus be of growing importance. The Government's approach to Internet regulation is to encourage voluntary action backed up by the full force of the existing law, based on the application of the general law on-line as off-line. Thus, the Obscene Publications Act applies to the producer of a web-site in the same way as it does to other forms of publication. Self-regulation is being taken forward by the Internet Watch Foundation, funded by the United Kingdom Internet service provider industry, whose Chief Executive, Mr David Kerr, submitted evidence. Self-regulation can take two main forms: the creation of hotlines so that users can alert Internet service providers to offensive material; and systems for content rating or filtering, so that users can either block or be forewarned about what might be regarded by some as objectionable content.

107. Mr Kerr pointed out that the Internet Watch Foundation's approach depended on the reporting of material and was developed for static material. It could not easily be applied to transitory audio-visual material. Legal regulation would only be viable if broadcasters were required to keep a record of their output. This in turn would require licensing. The number of potential licensees was immense, indeed incalculable. . . . Mr Kerr argued that liability could only apply where the service provider was aware of the content and could reasonably have acted upon that knowledge. This would be extraordinarily difficult to apply to live sound and video broadcasts over the Internet.

. . .

114. The Internet will become increasingly a platform for audio-visual content barely distinguishable from broadcast content. This does not mean it can be subject to regulation comparable to broadcasting. Self-regulation through service providers is in its early stages and should be encouraged. We are far from persuaded that any particular legislative provision for regulation for Internet content (as opposed to legislation to clarify the application of the current general law to the Internet) is viable. This is first of all a matter of scale. Second, it is a matter of means of access: an audio-visual transmission over the Internet could be one of millions of one-to-one transactions, over which there can be no legislative control. Third, it is a function of the Internet's economic and social potential. The potential of the Internet as an engine of

economic growth and social progress is enormous; it would be an act of self-indulgence to purport to jeopardise this unique opportunity by means of a virtually unenforceable law. Finally the Internet is international; any framework for its regulation must equally be international.

Although not explicit, the Committee is discussing the two types of content regulation which were considered in Chapter 4 above: negative regulation and positive programme requirements or regulation. Negative regulation will aim to prevent the transmission of, for example, obscene material or material which depicts excessive violence, whereas positive regulation will require material to meet certain standards or to have particular characteristics, for example, of quality or diversity. With respect to negative regulation, the Committee, while recognising the practical difficulties, sees this as being most appropriately a matter for the general law and self-regulation. Notwithstanding the Committee's recognition of the growing similarities between the Internet and the broadcasting platforms in terms of what they can deliver, it is clear that it recognises as impractical any attempt to impose positive regulation on the former. While also recognising the practical limitations, Wacks is more alive to the parallel to be drawn between the Internet and the press in terms of the way they operate. As he appears to recognise, the question for policy makers and regulators is not simply what regulation should be applied to the Internet, but what regulation remains appropriate for broadcasting. He emphasises the different relationship users have with the Internet compared with other electronic media, particularly broadcasting, and this may provide some clue to the approach which needs to be taken in devising regulatory structures for the multimedia environment. These matters are still under consideration in the UK and the European Community (see Section 3 below). In the meantime some regulatory measures are in place and it is these which we will now consider.

2. CURRENT REGULATORY MEASURES – CONDITIONAL ACCESS

One regulatory consequence of the introduction of digital television, with implications for the regulation of converged industries generally, is the regulation of 'conditional access'. Briefly, this is the process whereby scrambled, or encrypted, broadcasting services are delivered and decoded to the subscribing viewer. Access to a service or a particular programme is conditional upon payment. In one sense, conditional access is not new, nor is it a direct result of the development of digital technology. Access systems have been operating with existing analogue satellite and cable services. However, the introduction of digital technology means that they become more significant because of the potential for a greater number of subscription broadcasting services and interactive services to be delivered to the viewer. It is common

291

to refer to operators of conditional access systems as 'gatekeepers'. They are gatekeepers in the sense that they control the means by which viewers can access services. They can also act as gatekeepers because those wishing to supply broadcasting or other services might be dependent upon them to reach viewers. This would not be a concern if there were many conditional access systems available and competing, but this is unlikely, as will be explained shortly, and therefore the control of conditional access operators becomes an important element of the regulatory framework. There are a number of elements to the conditional access system:[2]

(1) the encryption process – the broadcast programme is sent in an encrypted or scrambled form which can be decoded or unscrambled by the viewer inserting a smart card into the set-top box. Viewers who can 'unlock' this scrambled message are those who have paid for the service. Until digital television receivers become widely available, another aspect of this process will be the conversion of the digital signal so that it can be received on conventional analogue televisions;

(2) subscription management services – these include the preparation and delivery of smart cards, and the enabling or disabling of access to services, for example, because a viewer has not maintained a subscription or has chosen not to receive a particular pay-per-view service;

(3) electronic programme guides (EPGs) – these guides will perform the function which listing magazines have previously performed. With so many services becoming available it will be impractical to rely on paper versions of programme guides. An EPG can display services which are available and in time will be the means by which the viewer can access the desired service.

In the absence of sufficient competition, each of these elements of the conditional access system could result in harmful gatekeeper activity. The anxiety that only one or two conditional access systems could control the market has some foundation in the UK. The encryption system which became established in the UK as a result of the introduction of analogue satellite broadcasting is known as the VideoCrypt system. This was developed by News Datacom, a company which is owned by News International plc which in turn has a share in BSkyB.[3] Because of understandable viewer resistance to possession of more than one set-top box, VideoCrypt has become the established system through which all other satellite companies must pass in order to gain access to viewers. With the introduction of digital television, VideoGuard (the digital version of VideoCrypt) will be well placed to become the industry standard for digital satellite television conditional access.

[2] B Middleton, 'Conditional Access: Looking Forward' (1997) 7(6) *Consumer Policy Review* 201, at 202 and J Hurt, 'Conditional Access for Digital Television Broadcasts' [1998] *Computer and Telecommunications Law Review* 154.

[3] Office of Fair Trading, *The Director General's Review of BSkyB's Position in the Wholesale Pay TV Market* (December 1996), pp 51–52.

Given News Datacom's association with BSkyB, one of the major UK satellite programme companies, the concerns about conditional access systems acting as gatekeepers are not merely fanciful. In the following extract, OFTEL describes the likely scenario for digital services in the UK, having concluded that competition among conditional access systems is unlikely in the foreseeable future.[4]

Extract 8.2.1

Office of Telecommunications, *The Pricing of Conditional Access Services for Digital Television, Consultative Document* (October 1997), paras 2.3–2.5, 2.7–2.8, 2.11–2.12 and 2.15–2.16

2.3. The equipment in most viewers' homes will only give access to pay television services using the particular conditional access system incorporated into the set top box. Conditional Access System B is therefore not a substitute for Conditional Access System A for a broadcaster wishing to reach the population of boxes equipped with Conditional Access System A. Since set top boxes will, at least initially, be relatively expensive,[5] there are likely to be significant switching costs for households wishing to change to a different conditional access system requiring the use of a different set top box.

2.4. Because of the importance of switching costs, consumers are likely to adopt the system which provides access to the widest range of content. Content providers are likely in turn to use the system giving access to the greatest number of subscribers. This position is therefore likely to be one which is self-reinforcing and which rival systems are likely to find difficult to break.

2.5. There is therefore a substantial risk that the first conditional access system to be widely adopted will constitute a bottleneck. Other service providers wishing to use conditional access to sell subscription services into the market would have to use this system.

. . .

2.7. There has been considerable discussion about whether future market developments might reduce the importance of this barrier to entry. For example, new generations of TV receivers may be equipped either with the circuitry to support more than one conditional access system, or the *common interface* which would allow the conditional access circuitry to be incorporated on a plug-in module (a PCMCIA card as used with a laptop computer).

2.8. This 'multicrypt' approach, if adopted, might facilitate network competition by enabling consumers to switch between competing networks without having to replace all their equipment. However, enabling consumers to switch easily between channels using different conditional access systems would require provision for more than one conditional access system to be

---

[4] Office of Telecommunications, *The Pricing of Conditional Access Services for Digital Television, Consultative Document* (October 1997), para 2.9.
[5] It is envisaged that within five years the cost of a decoder will be about £50: *The Guardian* (19 April 1999), p 20.

293

incorporated in the box at the same time. This does not at the present moment appear to be a likely outcome in the near to medium term future. Even if, at some point in the future, such receivers were to become widespread, a new entrant, or potential new entrant, would still be left with the problem of how to gain access to the population of single system receivers.

. . .

2.11. The large majority of English-language services broadcast by satellite to the UK will be broadcast from the Astra 2A satellite . . . Organisations which have leased, or taken options on transponders on Astra 2A include, BSkyB, Flextech, the BBC for its free-to-air channels, as well as other broadcasters such as CNN.

2.12. It is anticipated that with the exception of services broadcast 'in the clear',[6] these services will use the conditional access system operated by Sky Subscribers Services Ltd (SSSL) using the VideoGuard technology developed by News Digital Systems. SSSL is a wholly-owned subsidiary of BSkyB Limited. It will provide conditional access services to BSkyB in respect of pay television services which are part of the BSkyB bouquet as well as for services provided by third-party broadcasters. . . .

. . .

2.15. Cable and Wireless Communications, Telewest and General Cable have announced their intention to launch digital services.[7] OFTEL understands that each company will operate its own conditional access system separately from the others.

2.16. British Digital Broadcasting [ONdigital] has been awarded the licence for three digital terrestrial multiplexes. It will require a conditional access system for its pay services. . . . Although most of the capacity on the non-BDB multiplexes will be used for simulcasting of existing analogue services and new free-to-air services, there may also be new subscription services. These will require the use of a conditional access system, most probably BDB's.

In an earlier discussion, the government explored other likely consequences of a dominant conditional access operator.

Extract 8.2.2

Department of Trade and Industry, *The Regulation of Conditional Access Services for Digital Television*, Consultation Paper (January 1996), http://www.dti.gov.uk/cii/c16/index.htm, para 17

17. Regulatory safeguards are therefore necessary to guard against the possibility of the abuse of this dominant position. Such abuse could result in consumers paying higher prices and receiving a narrower range of services than would otherwise have been the case, with the further consequence that investment in new services would be deterred. Particular problems could also occur if the provider of conditional access services was also itself involved or

---

[6] 'In the clear' are services broadcast in unscrambled form.
[7] Digital cable services are expected to begin in November 1999.

connected with others involved in the provision of programming material. This would provide an incentive for the operator to use its market power in conditional access to improve its position elsewhere in the market, especially by favouring its own or a connected business and discriminating against competitors. There is also the potential that providers of SMS [subscriber management systems] could acquire a similar gatekeeper position. It may well be very difficult and expensive to set up a new subscriber management service in competition with existing well-established services and this may mean that programme service providers may have little realistic alternative to going through an existing operator with a well-established subscriber base.

There may be other concerns about control of the subscriber management system. If the operator of that service is also a broadcaster or associated with a broadcaster, other programme providers may be concerned that the operator will have access to commercially sensitive information, such as forthcoming pay-per-view events, which could give the operator a competitive advantage.[8] EPGs can also allow the operator to influence viewers in their choice of services, as OFTEL discusses.

Extract 8.2.3

Office of Telecommunications, *The Regulation of Conditional*
Access for Digital Television Services: OFTEL Guidelines
(March 1997), paras 25, 27 and 29

25. The Electronic Programme Guide (EPG) will be of great significance in the competition amongst service providers for customers. It will not be the only method by which viewers can scan different service offerings and choose one but it may well turn out to be the most important. In the absence of rules to the contrary, an EPG might be designed to give greater prominence to one group of services than the rest or to facilitate the selection of one group while making selection of another group considerably more difficult. Either of these effects would be likely to distort competition and would hence be unacceptable.

. . .

27. Because of the central part the EPG is likely to play in the process by which customers choose, select and purchase programmes, and because this process will be significantly determined by the way information is presented, 'fair, reasonable and non-discriminatory' access to this aspect of conditional access services will mean much more than just the price of any 'listing'. It will also cover, inter alia, the ordering of the display of different potential programmes, the branding of pages within the EPG, the display of channel brands, the ease of 'purchasing' pay per view options, access to information on viewers' use of pay per view and other services.

. . .

---

[8] Department of Trade and Industry, *The Regulation of Conditional Access Services for Digital Television: Final Consultation Paper on Detailed Implementation Proposals* (November 1996), http://www.dti.gov.uk/cii/c18/index.htm, para 65.

29. OFTEL draws a number of main messages from consultation:

- in the early stages of the market there is likely to be only one EPG per delivery mechanism. But the possibility of the emergence of third party EPGs should not be precluded;
- both channels and brands will be important as a method by which viewers may wish to sort and select. This will be a central issue in considering whether the design and operation of an EPG is or is not competitively neutral between broadcasters;
- it would expect that viewers should have the same easy and direct access to free-to-air channels that they will have to pay-TV programming. . . .
- where the EPG provider is associated with a broadcaster, branding of EPG pages with the logo of the EPG provider could have the effect of distorting competition amongst providers of television services.

The European Commission's attempts to impose a common standard for conditional access failed, largely because of opposition from broadcasters dominant in the analogue pay-television market, such as BSkyB, who had already developed their own conditional access systems.[9] A common standard would have ensured that no one decoder would have become the industry standard for digital television. An alternative approach canvassed by the Commission was the adoption of a multicrypt system whereby decoders would include a common interface (referred to in Extract 8.2.1 above). A viewer would purchase a card (similar to those used with portable computers) from the chosen broadcaster and insert this into the decoder, and if the viewer wished to change services would simply purchase another card from another broadcaster.[10] An advantage of the multicrypt approach (compared with the simulcrypt approach – that is reliance on individual proprietary systems, such as VideoGuard) is that it would avoid the need for broadcasters to negotiate access with other, possibly competing, operators. However, here too the Commission failed to achieve agreement on the adoption of a mandatory common interface.

In 1995 a directive, *On the Use of Standards for the Transmission of TV Signals*,[11] was adopted setting standards for the transmission of digital television signals.[12] It made no provision for the adoption of a multicrypt system,

---

[9] C Llorens-Maluquer, 'European Responses to Bottlenecks in Digital Pay-TV: Impacts on Pluralism and Competition Policy' (1998) 16 (2–3) *Cardozo Arts and Entertainment Law Journal* 557, at 561.

[10] Ibid, at 561–562.

[11] Directive 95/47/EC of the European Parliament and of the Council of 24 October 1995 on the use of standards for the transmission of television signals, [1995] OJ L281/51.

[12] In 1998 a further directive on conditional access was adopted: Directive 98/84 EC of the European Parliament and the Council of 20/11/98 on the legal protection of services based on, or consisting of, conditional access [1998] OJ L/320/54. This Directive addresses unauthorised access to encrypted services, whether broadcasting or other information services, via, for example, unauthorised decoders or smart cards. Members States have until 28 May 2000 for its implementation. This Directive will not be further considered here.

leaving it open for both simulcrypt and multicrypt systems to develop and operate in the market: '[b]y so doing, the Directive in effect favors the proprietary simulcrypt system and largely supports the existing market structure. However, it is important to remember that at this time there was no specification of the common interface standard'.[13] As a result of pressure from the European Parliament, the Directive does incorporate provisions to prevent a conditional access operator abusing its position.

Extract 8.2.4

Directive 95/47/EC of the European Parliament and of the Council of 24 October 1995 on the use of standards for the transmission of television signals, [1995] OJ L281/51, art 4(c) and (d)

(c) Member States shall take all the necessary measures to ensure that the operators of conditional access services, irrespective of the means of transmission, who produce and market access services to digital television services:

– offer to all broadcasters, on a fair, reasonable and non-discriminatory basis, technical services enabling the broadcasters' digitally-transmitted services to be received by viewers authorized by means of decoders administered by the service operators, and comply with Community competition law, in particular if a dominant position appears,

– keep separate financial accounts regarding their activity as conditional access providers.

Broadcasters shall publish a list of tariffs for the viewer which takes into account whether associated equipment is supplied or not.

A digital television service may take advantage of these provisions only if the services offered comply with the European legislation in force;

(d) when granting licences to manufacturers of consumer equipment, holders of industrial property rights to conditional access products and systems shall ensure that this is done on fair, reasonable and non-discriminatory terms. Taking into account technical and commercial factors, holders of rights shall not subject the granting of licences to conditions prohibiting, deterring or discouraging the inclusion in the same product of:

– a common interface allowing connection with several other access systems, or

– means specific to another access system, provided that the licensee complies with the relevant and reasonable conditions ensuring, as far as he is concerned, the security of transactions of conditional access system operators.

---

[13] Llorens-Maluquer, note 9, above, at 563.

Where television sets contain an integrated digital decoder such sets must allow for the option of fitting at least one standardized socket permitting connection of conditional access and other elements of a digital television system of the digital decoder;

The UK has implemented Directive 95/47/EC by the Advanced Television Services Regulations 1996 (SI 1996/3151).[14] The Regulations, consistent with the Directive, cover digital television services only, satellite, terrestrial and cable. However, the government proposes to introduce further regulation so that conditional access systems for all digital services, whether they are delivered via broadcast networks or switched networks (that is, telecommunications networks) will be brought within the regulatory regime. It is likely that this will occur in the second half of 1999.[15] When this unified regulation is put into place, it will be the clearest acknowledgement yet of the regulatory reality of convergence.

Regulations 11 and 12 of the Advanced Television Regulations 1996 implement art 4(c) of the Directive and regs 13 and 14 implement art 4(d). Like the Commission, the government was not prepared to mandate a common interface, despite requests to do so, and it seems that this would not be permissible under Community law.[16] Difficulties arose, under the Regulations, when, in early 1999, it became known that BSkyB was arranging to market digital television sets, which were constructed to receive BSkyB services, rather than allow the connection of decoders for receipt of other services (see Directive 95/47/EC, art 4(d), Extract 8.2.4 above).[17] The government clarified the guidance given under the Regulations, insisting that television sets should be fitted with, or capable of being fitted with, standardised sockets permitting connection of other digital equipment.[18] The government consented to television sets, already in production, which might not comply with the Regulations, being completed and sold.

Responsibility for regulating conditional access systems has been conferred on OFTEL, working in co-operation with the ITC. The decision to regulate conditional access within the telecommunications framework was justified by the government in the following terms.

[14] The Regulations were amended by the Advanced Television Services (Amendment) Regulations 1996 (SI 1996/3197). The amendments were primarily to complete arrangements for enforcement of the regulations in Scotland.

[15] Note 8, above, paras 11–14. See also OFTEL and Department of Trade and Industry, *A Joint OFTEL and DTI Notice and Consultation: Extending the Regulatory Regime for Conditional Access Services* (July 1997).

[16] Note 8, above, para 52. The DTI noted that the Commission has already registered its opposition to attempts by Italy to prescribe a common interface. Spain's attempt to do the same also encountered difficulties and it eventually abandoned such proposals: Llorens-Maluquer, note 9, above, at 575.

[17] *The Guardian* (23 April 1999), p 23. BSkyB denied that the sets would be contrary to the Regulations.

[18] *Compliance Guidance, Revised Version* (June 1999) http://www.dti.gov.uk/cii/lacotsso.htm.

Extract 8.2.5

Department of Trade and Industry, *The Regulation of Conditional Access Services for Digital Television* (11 January 1996), para 12

The Government announced in August [1995] that it had decided to regulate conditional access for digital services under the Telecommunications Act framework. There are two key reasons:

– conditional access systems work through streams of data sent over a telecommunications system, and themselves form an inherent part of the infrastructure used to deliver subscription television. They require licensing and regulation under the Telecommunications Act in any case;

– conditional access systems are economically-important parts of the telecommunications infrastructure used to deliver broadcasting services. Those who control conditional access systems are important potential gatekeepers in this part of the communications market – just as those who control the transmission systems are in a similar position, and are regulated under the Telecommunications Act.

Questions for discussion

1. Do you find the reasons advanced here by the government convincing?
2. What arguments would you advance to support regulatory responsibility being conferred on the ITC?

As well as the Advanced Television Services Regulations 1996, all operators of conditional access services for digital television are governed by a class licence issued by the Department of Trade and Industry, the Conditional Access Services Class Licence, which sets out in further detail the obligations arising under the Regulations. Conditions in the Class Licence supplement the requirement to give fair, reasonable and non-discriminatory access. The Class Licence and the Regulations came into force on 7 January 1997. Detailed guidelines on its approach to the regulation of conditional access services have also been produced by OFTEL.[19]

As already noted an important part of the conditional access system will be the provision of EPGs. These come within the remit of both OFTEL and the ITC, because EPGs require channel space to function.[20] As with conditional access systems in general, it is likely that there will be only one EPG for each type of digital television service. If the EPG for digital satellite services is to be operated by BSkyB, it could face temptations in the way information about programmes is presented to the viewer. The importance of EPGs is illustrated by Graham.

[19] OFTEL, *The Regulation of Conditional Access for Digital Television Services*, Oftel Guidelines, March 1997.
[20] The ITC will regulate both analogue and digital transmissions whereas the Regulations and Class Licence are concerned only with digital systems. However, the ITC is only concerned with EPG providers who are licensed by the ITC: *ITC Code of Conduct on Electronic Programme Guides* (June 1997), paras 13 and 14.

Extract 8.2.6

A Graham, 'Broadcasting Policy and the Digital Revolution' in J Seaton (ed), *Politics and the Media: Harlots and Prerogatives at the Turn of the Millennium* (Blackwell Publishers, 1998), p 30, at pp 36–37

They will set the agenda and, by highlighting some things rather than others, they will have the ability to guide both consumers and citizens to the areas the designer of the EPG wishes them to see first. Indeed as EPGs become more sophisticated they will become a major marketing and advertising tool. . . . So important are these EPGs likely to be, that, in the UK, the digital satellite system BSkyB is planning . . . to devote . . . the equivalent of more than five full channels [to its EPG]. It is hard to imagine that such a massive commitment of resources is being done with no thought except the promotion of the public interest. What is needed from a public interest point of view is a source of information that is impartial and trusted. Not what we are likely to get if it is left to the proprietary interests of the market.

Both OFTEL and the ITC aim to ensure that EPG services are provided on a basis that is fair, reasonable and non-discriminatory. OFTEL emphasises that an EPG should operate in a competitively neutral manner.[21] What will be expected of EPG providers is illustrated by the Code of Conduct produced by the ITC, some of which is extracted below.

Extract 8.2.7

Independent Television Commission, *ITC Code of Conduct on Electronic Programme Guides* (June 1997), paras 17–20 and 22

17. An EPG Provider should not discriminate between free to air and pay television services either in determining the services to be included on the EPG, including through the specification of the receiver application software, or in the operation of the EPG service.

18. The EPG Provider shall also ensure that use of his EPG service does not prevent or hinder viewers from being able to access free to air services easily and quickly and must ensure that viewers will not require additional equipment or commercial agreements over and above those required for the acquisition of the receiving equipment. Access to free to air services must be capable of being achieved without routing via a page or pages containing details of pay services.

19. The EPG Provider must give due prominence to any Public Service Channels [the BBC, Channels 3, 4 and 5, and S4C or S4C Digital] included on the EPG. Access to such channels should not be more difficult for viewers than access to any other services included on the EPG.

20. If the EPG Provider is also a Broadcaster [for these purposes, also includes a multiplex provider], or is connected to a Broadcaster, then any

---

[21] Note 19, above, para A119.

listing or display should not give prominence (e.g., in terms of size, ranking, colour or image, or the inclusion of a logo or other brand identification) to his own or connected television services over the television services of other Broadcasters, or preclude other Broadcasters from obtaining similar prominence on fair, reasonable and non-discriminatory terms.

. . .

22. Where an EPG Provider is also a Broadcaster or is connected to a Broadcaster, he must ensure that access to and from all television services included in the EPG service is easily available to all viewers equipped to use the EPG service and to receive the relevant programme services, i.e., there should be no distinction between access to his own or connected services and those of other Broadcasters.

Question for discussion

Why is there so much emphasis on the treatment of free-to-air services?

The decision to confer on OFTEL the regulation of conditional access highlights some of the regulatory difficulties which arise with convergence. The view has been taken that conditional access is more akin to telecommunications than to broadcasting, and hence OFTEL, and not the ITC, is the more logical regulator (Extract 8.2.5 above). Yet the operation of a conditional access system may have a significant influence over what programmes and programme information are available to the viewer. Should this raise concerns about the relationship between conditional access systems and the protection of pluralism? OFTEL has noted that it will consult fully with the ITC,[22] and it is intended that OFTEL's Conditional Access Guidance and the ITC's Code of Conduct will be amalgamated.[23] However, it is worth comparing the regulatory objectives of the two bodies, for OFTEL, in respect of conditional access systems generally, and for the ITC, in relation to EPG provision.

Extract 8.2.8

OFTEL, *The Regulation of Conditional Access for Digital Television Services: OFTEL Guidelines* **(March 1997), para A4**

A4. OFTEL's goal is to secure the best deal for the consumer in terms of quality, choice and value for money. In this context OFTEL has five key objectives:
- to ensure that control of conditional access technology is not used to distort, restrict or prevent competition in television and other content services . . . ;

---

[22] Ibid, A24.
[23] ITC, *ITC Publishes Code of Conduct on Electronic Programme Guides* (News Release 48/97, 13 June 1997), p 1.

- to ensure that control of conditional access technology does not lead to consumer choice being unreasonably constrained, whether in relation to consumer equipment, the range of services available via that equipment or the packaging of those services;
- to facilitate, so far as possible, consumers being able to access services on more than one delivery mechanism, or switch between delivery mechanisms, without having to incur unnecessary additional expense;
- to facilitate consumer choice by ensuring ease of access to comprehensive information about the range of services available and ease of selection of services;
- to ensure that control of conditional access technology is not exploited via excessive pricing for the use of that technology.

<hr>

Extract 8.2.9

<hr>

Independent Television Commission, *ITC Code of Conduct on Electronic Programme Guides* (June 1997), para 1

1. Section 2(2) of the Broadcasting Act 1990 requires the Independent Television Commission (ITC) to discharge its functions as respects the licensing of services in the manner which it considers is best calculated to ensure that a wide range of services is available throughout the UK and to ensure fair and effective competition in the provision of licensed services and services connected with them. . . . The ITC wishes to ensure in licensing EPG services that the terms on which an EPG service is provided are consistent with the ITC's functions. The ITC would be concerned if the terms on which an EPG service is offered limited viewers' access to a wide range of services, particularly to those services which viewers watch most. The ITC's duties to ensure the availability of a wide range of services and fair and effective competition are interlinked in that the existence of a wide range of services is more likely to ensure fair and effective competition and vice versa. . . .

It can be seen from Extracts 8.2.8 and 8.2.9 that both OFTEL and the ITC are concerned with ensuring a properly competitive environment, although one can also see more explicitly, in relation to the ITC, the concerns about diversity. However, for both regulators, effective regulation of conditional access is dependent upon monitoring behaviour. There are no pre-emptive controls, limiting, for example, who can operate these systems. When the government was reviewing media ownership and control in 1995, which led to the BA 1996 (Chapter 7, Section 4), the opportunity was there to consider all aspects of digital broadcasting and to provide comprehensive regulation of all its constituent parts: broadcasters; programme suppliers; multiplex operators; and conditional access operators. Yet the government did not do this, choosing to retain structural regulation for some parts only of the broadcasting framework, and to rely upon competition regulation for other parts, such as conditional access. While the regulation of conditional access is welcome, both the European Commission and the government have failed to take the opportunity to make a holistic regulatory assessment of the new digital environment. In the following extract, Graham explains why he considers competition law insufficient for the regulation of conditional access.

Extract 8.2.10

A Graham, 'Exchange Rates and Gatekeepers' in T Congdon, A Graham, D Green and B Robinson (eds), *The Cross Media Revolution: Ownership and Control* (John Libbey, 1995), p 38, at pp 47–48

First, competition law is primarily *negative* being concerned with preventing monopolies or controlling anti-competitive practices. It is not concerned with setting standards nor with the need to intervene *positively* to reap the full benefits of network externalities. . . .

Second, . . . there is the importance of conditional access to the future shape of the media. Here especially, competition law is not sufficient. Suppose, for example, that several manufacturers compete to produce set-top boxes and that, because of the competition, there is no monopoly pricing. Suppose further that the channels supplied via these boxes are also at competitive prices. The requirements of competition are thereby satisfied. Yet, if the boxes are incompatible, a major problem remains. Many consumers, reluctant to buy more than one box and facing significant 'switching costs' in moving from one supplier to another, will effectively be dependent upon a single supplier. In other words *individual* consumers might well face an undesirable monopoly of media influence *even when no such concentration was apparent at the level of the industry as a whole.* Moreover, the fact that other channels were available at similar prices and so, in this sense, consumers were offered choice, would not be an adequate defence. In the case of the media it is a requirement of a democratic society that citizens should have *actual* access to a diversity of views and opinions. Potential access is not good enough. But these are not considerations that are predominant with competition law.

. . .

The fact is that if one takes seriously the requirement that there should be a diversity of media suppliers, then common standards are essential. In this industry, *common standards are the prerequisite for common carriers and common carriers are the prerequisite for media competition and for unhindered access to information.* In other words the right public policy for these critical points in the Information Superhighway may prove to be far more important than direct market dominance both in determining access *now* and in having a critical influence on the *future shape* of the media industry.

Questions for discussion

1. Do you agree with Graham when he says that it is necessary for citizens to have 'actual access to a diversity of views and opinions'?
2. Does the regulatory system established for conditional access provide you with confidence that Graham's objections will be met?

3. FUTURE REGULATION OF THE CONVERGED ENVIRONMENT

As observed in the previous section, the introduction of digital television, and, more generally, convergence, is exacerbating the tendency, already present within the UK, for a number of regulatory bodies to have overlapping responsibilities for media regulation. The regulation of conditional access also highlights another consequence of convergence: the need to decide whether we are regulating telecommunications or broadcasting, or indeed, something else. Obviously, given the different regulatory models applying to these sectors (outlined in Section 1 above), the answer could have significant ramifications for the regulatory tools selected. Both the government and European Commission have been addressing the question of regulation in a converged environment. There are two issues here. First, how should communication services be characterised and regulated and, secondly, by whom?

(a) The nature of regulation

It may be tempting to suggest that because of convergence and the likely abundance of programme outlets, a case need no longer be made for regulation of media in the manner that we have traditionally experienced. But, as Gibbons argues, that would be to confuse the reasons for specialised regulation of media with its means of delivery. What we have to keep in mind are the reasons why media is special and, therefore, requires special regulation.

Extract 8.3.1

T Gibbons, *Regulating the Media*, 2nd ed (Sweet & Maxwell, 1998), pp 301–302

The development and adoption of new, especially digital, technology may raise the possibility that media regulation will no longer be necessary in the middle to long term, but that depends on characterising media products as purely commercial and without political and social significance. While it is true that the media are primarily concerned with entertainment, they also provide a major resource for communication and cannot be wholly shaped by market mechanisms. Indeed, it is the potentially *mediating* character of the media which makes them important and distinguishes them from simple information services. Newspapers, radio and television do more than convey ideas in a neutral way; they are part of our culture and provide a means of obtaining and presenting knowledge and engaging in political activity. As a result of their ability to select information and order priorities, they have a profound influence on the way we think about the world. Furthermore, it is doubtful whether information services can be completely neutral about the way they package material and make it available to consumers; they also select and shape what they convey. There is, therefore, a public interest in activities which are mediating, one which denies the mediators complete control over their goals and practices.

That is not to say that new forms of media will have no implications for media regulation, but the issue is one of re-regulation, rather than de-regulation,[i] the need to tailor regulation to fit the values which are sought to be promoted. Here a functional approach is required, one which does not depend on technology or forms of delivery, but which recognises the nature of the service being provided and the character of the audience receiving it. The early justification for regulating broadcasting, that it was *broad*-casting, rests on the belief that material which is transmitted to a universal audience, both in terms of geographic reach and personal profile, requires special treatment. The reason is that the audience has no effective control over the scheduling and content of the material received. For universal programming, then, there will always be a need for sensitivity to audience membership, regardless of the public service or commercial quality of the content. To the extent that programming is made available in progressively segmented forms, either by 'narrow-casting' or subscription, the case for content regulation becomes correspondingly weaker,[ii] although there will continue to be a public interest in the overall provision of media output.

[i] See W. Hoffman-Reim, *Regulating Media* (1996); P. Humphreys, *Media and Media Policy in Western Europe* (1996); T. Prosser, *Law and the Regulators* (1997), chap. 10. See also Culture, Media and Sport Select Committee, *Fourth Report: The Multi-Media Revolution* – Volume I (1997–1999) HC 520–1, para. 116.

[ii] See J. Balkin, 'Media Filters, the V-Chip and the Foundations of Broadcast Regulation' (1996) 45 *Duke Law Journal* 1131–1175.

The approach suggested by Gibbons, whereby focus needs to be on the type of service being delivered can be seen reflected in the government's consideration of these issues. In a Green Paper prepared jointly by the Department of Trade and Industry and the Department for Culture, Media and Sport, the government set out its preliminary views on regulation in the converging environment. In the following extract, the continuing case for regulation of broadcasting content is assessed.

<hr>

Extract 8.3.2

<hr>

Department of Trade and Industry and Department for Culture, Media and Sport, *Regulating Communications: Approaching Convergence in the Information Age,* Cm 4022 (1998), paras 2.18–2.19 and 2.21–2.23

Providing diversity of content

2.18   Four of the five terrestrial broadcasters reach virtually the whole population, and it is important that their programming is inclusive, catering for a wide range of interests and involving all significant demographic, geographic and ethnic groups. Programming designed to meet these requirements is not always commercially attractive, and intervention has been necessary to ensure that the needs of all sections of the community are met. This has been especially important hitherto, given the limited number of services. The experience of cable and satellite broadcasting suggests that universal access is very difficult to achieve when viewers have to pay for special receiving equipment and services are not free-to-air.

2.19 Digital technology offers the prospect of far more services, which of itself can be expected to help increase diversity and choice. However, the delivery of information by public service broadcasters as a public good will remain an important element in this diversity and choice. The importance of information as a resource is widely recognised, and the Government is committed to ensuring that all our citizens have timely access to the information they need. . . .

Upholding taste and decency

2.21 Specific rules governing taste and decency in broadcasting are needed because of its wide availability and ease of access. Acceptable standards will vary according to the characteristics of the service and its delivery. Text and data services are distinguishable from moving pictures, and those where access is controlled via subscription, pay-per-view or password are distinguishable from free-to-air services. The aims must be to protect minors and prevent affront to public feeling. . . .

The impact of new services

2.22 The Government believes that broadcasting will remain distinctive, and retain its unique place in the public mind. Policy-makers must continue to give particular attention to the content of broadcasting, which still matters greatly and about which people care deeply. The policy aims set out above retain their relevance in the multimedia future.

2.23 Nevertheless, the changes which are unfolding in broadcasting and telecommunications will call into question existing approaches to the achievement of those aims. Some of the ends which have been achieved in the past through regulation may in the multi-channel, multimedia environment be achieved by various means such as competition and self-regulation, underpinned by legal provisions. Where regulation continues to be necessary, the current approach may need to be reassessed in the light of the emergence of new services and the rapid growth of provision. New services, provided to consumers on demand, by subscription or other forms of payment at the point of use, will require different treatment.

It is apparent from this extract that there will not be a radical change in the nature of broadcasting regulation and indeed the government specifically rejected such an approach, preferring instead '. . . an evolutionary path'.[24] Nevertheless the Green Paper acknowledges that regulatory patterns will have to change.[25] Like Gibbons, the government seems to be suggesting that

---

[24] Department of Trade and Industry and Department for Culture, Media and Sport, *Regulating Communications: Approaching Convergence in the Information Age*, Cm 4022 (1998), 4.
[25] Ibid.

the focus for regulation will not be, purely, on how the service is delivered, but also on the nature of the service, and the degree of control the recipient has over it. This reflects also the view taken by Wacks when he describes the different relationship a viewer/user has with the electronic media compared with the Internet (Extract 8.1.2 above). Having assessed the case for regulation, the government concludes that competition law alone cannot be relied upon and that there will still be a need for some sector-specific regulation.[26] In the following extract the Green Paper develops this, setting out how it envisages regulation of content-based services.

Extract 8.3.3

Department of Trade and Industry and Department for Culture, Media and Sport, *Regulating Communications: Approaching Convergence in the Information Age*, Cm 4022 (1998), paras 4.33–4.34, 4.38–4.40, 4.44, and 4.50–4.52

Regulating content

4.33 The trends . . . indicate a move from distinct segments of service provision based on delivery platform towards a continuum of services, each available on a variety of platforms. At one end, a segment with much the same characteristics as today's universal public service broadcasting is likely to persist for the foreseeable future. At the other end, a diverse and dynamic market of pay-TV, niche, on-demand and interactive services.

4.34 In this environment, policy objectives need to be pursued using methods which take account of the different characteristics of each segment. While the case for ensuring acceptability of content, for example, remains strong, it will typically need to be applied through a variety of measures and, at least in those newer service areas, with a lighter touch, while ensuring there is consistency in the way it is applied across the various types of services.

. . .

Positive content controls

4.38 It is possible that a market supplied by a large number of sources will of itself, over time, widen the extent of access to new services, and provide the quality and variety of content which the public expects. Commercial imperatives may lead to the creation of both generalist and niche offerings catering for a wide range of interests, and create a demand for high quality original productions. In that event, it would be hard to justify continuing positive programming requirements for commercial broadcasters.

4.39 However, that is not the only possible outcome. Total broadcasting hours will inevitably expand more rapidly than will viewing and listening. Revenue streams may grow at a modest rate, leading broadcasters to concentrate on

---

[26] Ibid, para 4.5.

those forms of programming most likely to attract large audiences and generate substantial revenue. This may or may not generate a programming mix which meets these policy objectives.

4.40   Policy must be reassessed realistically in the light of the reality which emerges in the market. In so far as positive programming requirements remain necessary, they should be set at a level and delivered in a way which minimises market distortion and allows providers as far as possible to compete on equal terms.

. . .

Public service provision

4.44   Increasing fragmentation of the services will mean that the public faces a bewildering and possibly confusing choice. Many of the new services will offer a view of the world which is partial (perhaps in both senses of the word), and their programming will be determined by commercial factors. Public service broadcasting cannot be seen merely as filling in gaps. Its positive role will be more important than ever.

. . .

General services

4.50   Some services will always be universally available and freely accessible. Today this segment is represented by television and radio services broadcast free-to-air for general reception. Here public expectation about standards of taste and decency are at their highest. There seems to be a continuing case for licensing, bringing conditions over and above the provisions of general law, giving effect to those general provisions by specific measures appropriate to audience expectations.

4.51   An increasing number of broadcast channels provided on a commercial basis will be accessed only on the basis of choice. Channels provided on a subscription basis may nevertheless be readily accessed by any member of the customer's household, including children. Consequently the case for retaining some additional licensing provisions for both free-to-air and subscription-based services which are provided for general, or universal, reception throughout the UK, is likely to remain strong.

Selective services

4.52   The growth in service provision will make it impossible to extend existing licensing controls to all forms of service delivery: the regulatory burden on both operators and on regulators with necessarily finite resources would be intolerable. In particular, where specific regulation of newer services is required it should proceed with a lighter touch. Contrasting with freely available and subscription services provided for general or universal reception throughout the UK, there will be many new services which can only be accessed specifically at the request of the consumer, often after payment of a fee. Such 'selective' services might properly not be subject to specific controls at all, but would of course be subject to the general law. This is likely, however, to depend to some extent upon the effectiveness of the controls in place to prevent access to these services by young people.

The government has published a review of the responses to its Green Paper (see Extract 8.3.4 below), which confirms its intention to make gradual regulatory changes. The Review also announces details of measures which the government proposes to initiate in response to the Green Paper; one of these is to review, with the ITC, current regulation of television services with the aim of removing unnecessary regulation.[27]

Extract 8.3.4

Department of Trade and Industry and Department for Culture, Media and Sport, *Regulating Communications: The Way Ahead, Results of the Consultation on the Convergence Green Paper* (17 June 1999), paras 1.9–1.10, 1.13–1.14 and 1.19

1.9   In general, the responses supported an evolutionary approach to developing regulation, though some specific improvements were seen to be necessary in the short term. New services are beginning to emerge. Many respondents expected a steady take-up of digital television, and continued growth in the market penetration of pay-TV. Interactivity was expected to be a major agent of change in the way television is used by consumers, but some respondents felt it would be some time before it was embraced by the majority of viewers. 1.10   It was noted that growth of Internet use in the home has exceeded most projections. Although electronic commerce is likely to be one of the main drivers for the Internet, alongside access to information services including e-mail and increased social and leisure use, some companies are investigating it as a means of distribution for television services. Many believe it is likely to have an impact on the nature and method of delivery of television services in the longer term. However, the majority will continue for some time to rely on traditional, free-to-air broadcast services to meet their information and entertainment requirements.

. . .

1.13   Most argued that the regime would require modification as convergence accelerated, and that the Government must be prepared to make changes to address specific issues as they arise. Respondents accepted that competition law should gradually replace some sector-specific regulation. The potential abuse of a strong market position in, for example, gateways or electronic programme guides, was a particular concern, as, in the non-economic area, were privacy and data protection. Better transparency and

---

[27] Department of Trade and Industry and Department for Culture, Media and Sport, *Regulating Communications: The Way Ahead, Results of the Consultation on the Convergence Green Paper* (17 June 1999), para 3.11. The government also proposes to review the duration of radio licences and renewal procedures: ibid, para 3.31.

co-ordination between regulators were seen as essential and would increase in importance as new developments accelerated.

1.14   Self-regulation of content received much support as a general ideal. However, statutory regulation of broadcast services remained valid in most views. It should however, be graduated according to the degree of control the viewer exercised over access to a particular service. It was important to keep regulatory requirements under review to ensure they remained appropriate as consumer expectations evolved with changes in markets and services.

. . .

1.19   In the light of these responses, **the Government will continue with the evolutionary approach to adapting communications regulation set out in the Green Paper.**

Questions for discussion

1.   Gibbons argues for a functional approach to regulation (Extract 8.3.1), one which does not focus on forms of delivery. If, as the Internet develops, it delivers more content, of a type similar to broadcasting content, does this make the case for regulation of the Internet stronger?

2.   Is the Green Paper's assessment of developments realistic?

3.   Based on the Green Paper's discussion, can you suggest how regulation of broadcasting services should change from its current model?

4.   Can an argument be made for a radical regulatory approach instead of an evolutionary one? How would communications regulation change if such an approach was adopted?

(b) Who should regulate?

Reference has already been made to overlapping regulation in the broadcasting sector, but the question which more recently has been under consideration is whether, because of convergence, there should be a single regulator or regulatory body overseeing this converged sector. The Culture, Media and Sport Committee favoured a single regulator.

Extract 8.3.5

Culture, Media and Sport Committee, *The Multi-Media Revolution*, Fourth Report (1998, HCP 520–1), vol I, paras 157–159 (bold text and footnotes omitted)

157. The current system for statutory regulation of audio-visual communications, composed as it is of numerous bodies with confusing and overlapping jurisdictions and powers often ill-fitted for digital technologies, is more reminiscent of a feudal State than a regulatory structure for the multi-media age. The

case for change is unanswerable. Any new structure should have clarity and coherence, but recognise the distinctive nature of broadcasting provision. It is possible to establish a structure which combines these characteristics.

158. We recommend the absorption of all current regulatory bodies into one Communications Regulation Commission with overall responsibility for statutory regulation of broadcasting, telecommunications and the communications infrastructure. We recommend that its duties include:

- regulation of access to communications platforms by both systems operators and service providers, including all issues relating to gateways, competition law, and cross-media ownership;
- the compilation of information and the duty to report to Government on policy issues;
- all regulatory actions in support of universal broadband provision;
- strong encouragement of the development of self-regulation by Internet service providers; and
- oversight, for all broadcasters, including the BBC, of broadcast content regulation and the commercial activities of broadcasters, with direct oversight of their implementation.

There shall be a Chairman of the Commission who is a member of the Commission and not a statutory regulator. There shall be two Deputy Chairmen responsible respectively for delivery and content. . . .

159. In order to ensure that all classes of broadcasters and narrowcasters are adequately administered – and we take cognisance of the evidence that radio was neglected when it was a division within the former Independent Broadcasting Authority – we believe a sub-commission structure should be created to ensure proper fulfilment of the Commission's several functions. Each sub-commission shall have its own small board. Each sub-commission shall have the power to publish its own reports and recommendations subject to approval of the Commission which shall not unreasonably be withheld. We further recommend that one or more members of the Communications Regulation Commission should have a duty to represent the interests of consumers, supported by appropriate research capacity within the staff of the Commission.

A single regulator has attracted support elsewhere. Collins and Murroni in a study of new media policy also recommended a single regulatory body. Their proposal for bringing regulation under one regulator, 'Ofcom', included not just broadcasting and telecommunications but the print media also.

Extract 8.3.6

R Collins and C Murroni, *New Media New Policies* (Polity Press, 1996), pp 173–175

On balance we find arguments for fewer regulators compelling, and argue for a single regulator in the communications sector. Media and communications are becoming increasingly interconnected and it is less troublesome to conceive of them as an interconnected whole than as a series of discrete phenomena. Although content regulation and the regulation of markets are different tasks, they are not necessarily best done by separate bodies. Indeed the ITC and Radio Authority now regulate both structure and content. Each regulatory task is more efficiently discharged because both are done by the same body. The leverage which accrues from structural and carriage regulation assists enforcement of content regulation. Carriage and structural regulatory decisions, such as those concerning diversity of outlets, are influenced by considerations of content. To regulate concentration of ownership effectively, both the individual and the aggregate UK media and communication markets must be considered together. Consumers will be better served by one stop regulatory shopping. . . .

What is required is a single regulator – we suggest 'Ofcom' – applying common content guidelines and codes with different standards of severity and exactitude for different media and types of communication. For communications that can be consumed involuntarily, i.e. public media (posters on street, advertising sites and free-to-air radio and television), content codes will apply with greater severity than with media that are unlikely to be consumed involuntarily . . .

Adjudication on complaints of misrepresentation and invasion of privacy should fall within the remit of Ofcom. Press regulation should be performed with a notably lighter touch than regulation of non-print media. Ofcom, moreover, will have some responsibilities for the structural, pro-competition regulation of the press – issues such as concentration of ownership. However, Ofcom shall have no powers of prior restraint over publication of the written word. . . .

There are significant advantages in subsuming the functions presently discharged by Oftel, the ITC, the BSC, the Radio Authority, [. . .] and the statutory responsibilities of the BBFC [British Board of Film Classification] in a single regulatory body. There would be further advantages if this body, Ofcom, also oversaw allocation of the radio frequency spectrum and undertook the regulatory functions presently discharged by the Governors of the BBC, who now have the unenviable task of being judge and jury in their own case.

Concentration of regulatory functions in a single agency would offer economies of scale and help to ensure that Ofcom was sufficiently well resourced to do its job effectively.

At first glance, the notion of a single regulator appears attractive bringing together all regulatory functions for all aspects of communications, while avoiding the difficulties of how to define the remit for sector-specific regulators. Yet, even the model proposed by the Culture, Media and Sport Committee implicitly acknowledges that there will be a need for a separation of functions within the single regulator, and it is likely that the all-embracing proposal of Collins and Murroni would also necessitate internal divisions. How such divisions are made could also have a significant impact. Gibbons has expressed reservations about adopting a single regulator.

Extract 8.3.7

T Gibbons, *Regulating the Media*, 2nd ed (Sweet & Maxwell, 1998), p 304 (footnotes omitted)

Problems in deciding the appropriate scope of regulation may lead to the conclusion that the establishment of a single, 'super' regulator would be the most effective solution. The advantages would be that regulatory policy could be co-ordinated in one body and regulatory compliance would be made easier. However, there are strong arguments against such a move. It would be a delusion to believe that the existence of one regulator would remove any conflict between regulatory objectives. Instead, such conflict would be hidden from public gaze and become a matter of office politics rather than democratic debate. There would be a real risk that economic arguments would prevail, given the liberalising trends in the industry. There would also be a rather extreme concentration of power in one regulator for an industry which is so important to democratic aims. Both considerations suggest that it would be much healthier to have more than one regulator, with each defending its own corner through public and Parliamentary discussion. To create a single regulator would actually serve to pre-empt such debate, since it would not be policy-neutral.

Questions for discussion

1. Do you find the arguments in favour of a single regulator convincing?
2. Is the Culture, Media and Sport Committee's proposal an admission that a single regulator is not feasible?
3. Is there a need to bring the print media into a single regulatory structure as Collins and Murroni suggest?

The Green Paper reviewed several regulatory models, and while clearly aware of the need to rationalise the present proliferation of regulatory bodies, seemed reluctant, to favour a single regulator.

Extract 8.3.8

Department of Trade and Industry and Department for Culture, Media and Sport, *Regulating Communications: Approaching Convergence in the Information Age*, Cm 4022 (1998), paras 5.10–5.19

Regulatory models for the longer term

5.10 A number of possible structural models can be conceived for the longer term, when the evolution of the markets in response to convergence is more complete; any of these, with appropriate definition of duties and powers, could provide for greater coherence in dealing with competition and other economic issues, and greater consistency in content regulation.

Model 1: separate infrastructure and content regulators

5.11   One structure which has been suggested by a number of comment-ators is that there should be separate regulators for the infrastructure and content industries. However, increasing integration between these and the growth of joint venture projects mean that important regulatory issues – particularly in promoting competition – can straddle the two.

5.12   This model corresponds reasonably well to current market segmenta-tion and to largely distinct sets of regulatory concerns: open access and wide coverage on the one hand; quality and diversity on the other. But it may not be sufficiently flexible to cater for further convergence and consequent market integration.

Model 2: economic and content regulators

5.13   An alternative would be to split the structure according to regulatory function: i.e. separate bodies with responsibility for economic (essentially com-petition) and content issues. Again, however, the structure does not avoid overlap. Content regulation has important economic effects: for example, re-quirements for plurality of voice, and diversity of content have important eco-nomic consequences; while the impact of competition rules on the structure of the industry may affect the range of content which is provided.

Model 3: a horizontal split

5.14   It would be possible to divide regulation according either to model 1 or model 2 above, or indeed on various other bases, including the current, service-based one, but to add a co-ordinating body to span both areas of regulation. Its function would be to ensure there was a coherent and co-ordinated approach between the regulators.

5.15   This overarching body could in principle co-ordinate the activities of a number of regulators. While there is a clear need to remove regulatory over-laps and simplify the structure, different segments of the converging market are likely to persist and to retain distinctive characteristics for some time. . . .

Model 4: a single regulator

5.16   A further development of this approach is to create a single regulator, or at least a single regulatory umbrella. This body would be able to take a broad view of the converging sectors, would be able to respond flexibly to the emergence of new services and would ensure a consistent approach to regu-lation of related activities. A regulator with this breadth of scope and expertise might prove the most effective as organisations diversify their activities across the convergent sectors. . . .

5.17   However, some question whether a single organisation is appropriate when many of the convergent sectors nevertheless retain distinctive charac-teristics and each may raise sector-specific issues. There are concerns also about the unwieldiness, transparency and accountability of a single regulatory body. While the idea of a 'one-stop shop' has attractions, the internal structure of large organisations can be complex and more confusing to those outside than a series of separate organisations with clearly defined responsibilities.

Preliminary conclusions

5.18   As convergence unfolds, regulators will have to work together more closely. This suggests that an integrated structure for the whole range of services and for every aspect of their regulation will at some stage be desirable. This does not necessarily imply a single organisation, but it does suggest a need to consider how regulatory responsibility should be allocated, co-ordinated and structured in the longer term.

5.19   For the immediate future we will make full use of the considerable flexibility which is incorporated in the present regime. In order to avoid regulatory uncertainty in exploiting that flexibility, it will be necessary for the regulators to co-operate closely to identify and resolve overlaps and to agree where regulatory responsibility should lie for new services which do not fall clearly within established regulatory categories.

While there has been some support from the regulatory bodies for a single regulator,[28] this seems to have weakened. In its response to the Green Paper, the ITC questioned whether a single regulator would ensure a more coherent approach to regulation, and noted that single regulation of carriage and content would result in content issues being marginalised by telecommunications.[29] OFTEL favoured one regulator for content issues and another for infrastructure, access and services.[30] The government's review of the responses to the Green Paper showed no strong consensus for a particular regulatory structure, but did recognise a need for greater co-ordination between the regulatory bodies.[31] Two committees have been established: the G3 Committee consists of representatives from the ITC, OFTEL and the Office of Fair Trading (OFT); and the G6 Committee includes officials from the Department for Culture, Media and Sport and the Department of Trade and Industry. Both committees are chaired by the OFT.[32]

(c) European responses to convergence

Within the European Community, investigation of the impact of convergence has also been underway. In December 1997, the Commission issued a

---

[28] D Goldberg, T Prosser and S Verhulst, *Regulating the Changing Media: A Comparative Study* (Oxford University Press, 1998), p 112.

[29] ITC, *The Independent Television Commission's response to questions raised in 'Regulating communications: approaching convergence in the information age (Cm. 4022)'* (11 January 1999), para 50.

[30] OFTEL, *OFTEL's response to the UK Green Paper – Regulating communications: approaching convergence in the information age* (January 1999), para 1.81.

[31] Note 27, above, paras 1.17–1.18.

[32] Ibid, para 2.2.

Green Paper, *Convergence of the Telecommunications, Media and Information Technology sectors, and the implications for Regulation towards an Information Society Approach.*[33] This was followed by a Working Paper in July 1998 which reported on the results of the public consultation, *Working Document of the Commission, Summary of the Results of the Public Consultation on the Green Paper on the Convergence of the Telecommunications, Media and Information Technology Sectors; Areas for Further Reflection.*[34] Finally, a Communication was issued in March 1999, *Communication to the European Parliament, the Council, the Economic and Social Committee and the Committee of the Regions, The Convergence of the Telecommunications, Media and Information Technology sectors and Implications for Regulation, Results of the Public Consultation on the Green Paper.*[35] The Green Paper was intended to stimulate debate on the role of regulation in the converging communications sector. The Commission now intends to put forward proposals for reform of both infrastructure and content regulation. What is noticeable in the Communication is the similarity of the preliminary conclusions reached with those of UK Green Paper. For example, the Communication recognises the continuing importance of public interest objectives, the need for sector-specific regulation, and the need to ensure that content regulation is appropriate for the type of service being regulated.[36]

4. CONCLUSION

Although there have been fairly intensive examinations of the implications of convergence, it is apparent, at both national and European level, that regulatory changes will be gradual, occurring as the practical consequences of convergence themselves emerge. It is clear that the familiar world of radio and television regulation described in Chapter 3 is disappearing. However, it is unlikely that these changes will be sudden. A comparative study of new media developments has recently been completed. In their concluding comments, the authors suggest that there is a need to be realistic about the changes taking place and to avoid falling into a kind of technological determinism. Like Gibbons (Extract 8.3.1 above), the authors recognise a need to keep in mind the underlying reasons for regulation of media. In reading this extract, consider the extent to which the Green Paper reflects their conclusions.

---

[33] COM (97) 623 (3 December 1997), http://www.ispo.cec.be/convergencegp/97623.html.
[34] SEC (98) 1284 (29 July 1998), http://www.ispo.cec.be/convergencegp/gpworkdoc.html.
[35] COM (99) 108 EN final, http://www.ispo.cec.be/convergencegp/Com(99)108%20ENfinal.html.
[36] Ibid.

Extract 8.4.1

D Goldberg, T Prosser and S Verhulst, *Regulating the Changing Media: A Comparative Study* (Oxford University Press, 1998), pp 296–297, 298–299 and 314

A further point which needs reiteration, however, is of great importance for regulatory policy-making. This is that the degree of convergence in services is not only highly varied but relatively slow in many cases, and a radically new media world dominated by the new services is far off, and indeed in some cases may never arrive.... [H]owever, the inevitability of the so-called 'converged environment' is taken for granted, particularly at the European level.[i] One of the problems in much of the debate is the assumption that technological change is the only determinant of this growth. However, this not only assumes the unimportance of particular legal and regulatory cultures..., it also assumes that new technologies will always prove marketable and that different markets are shaped by technology, not by social or cultural factors. This is why the area is dogged by false predictions... The implication from the uncertainty of how far convergence should advance is that we should treat with caution suggestions that the brave new world of media abundance is imminent, and be slow to abandon the protections developed in the old world of a limited number of media outlets and services.

A further point of some importance is that there is no single new media form or market, and there is never likely to be such uniformity. Markets remain distinct; for example, there is still a clear distinction between television-type services and on-line services. Technological convergence may be imminent in the form of television Internet access (or Web TV) becoming cheaply available, but the cultures remain radically different. Indeed, in the context of television, it seems likely that, though delivery forms may change, the culture may not, and that new types of media may supplement rather than replace existing ones.[ii] ...

These radical differences between new forms of media market have contradictory implications for regulation. On the one hand, they lessen the likelihood of the sort of dull uniformity based on the broadcasting of similar, cheap programmes which has been feared in the context of the development of new television services.... The newer media will be much more complex than this and will have the *potential* to differentiate many markets more effectively than has been the case in the old media; in this sense the popular convergence model is misleading since it suggests narrowing, whereas what is happening is some degree of broadening through market differentiation. The implication could be drawn that the market can be successful in maintaining forms of diversity beyond the reach of regulatory controls. On the other hand, fragmentation of markets means that regulatory concerns will need to be addressed not across media markets, for example through controls on percentage ownership, but instead by concentrating on regulation of particular technological or economic instruments which might give control of each or several of the fragmented markets; an argument for behavioural rather than structural regulation...[iii]

...

... [T]here are influential arguments to the effect that the days of ... [media] regulation are numbered with the ending of spectrum scarcity as a justification for regulation – although the European Commission's Green Paper on Convergence makes the point that '[f]requency remains a key, but finite resource even in the digital age'[iv] – the ending of the uniquely pervasive and intrusive role of television in the household as it is supplemented by other media delivery systems, and with the promise of a diversity of content undreamt of in public service broadcasting with the arrival of multi-channel digital broadcasting.

We would suggest that these arguments for the withering away of regulation should also be treated with considerable caution. Firstly, as already described, it will be a long time before convergence has reached a stage in which the new media supplant the old, or, in key markets, offer effective competition to them. Secondly, it is very likely that the elimination of the scarcity of transmission frequencies will intensify new and other scarcities.[v] Scarcity of available media content and programme software is already a large problem. Moreover the problem becomes even bigger when considering the qualitative aspect of programming. Other major scarcity problems are concerned with user attention and shared knowledge, the latter dealing with the role of media in providing a 'cultural cohesion to the nation'.[vi] As Hoffman-Riem stated: '[s]carcity constellations of all kinds are at the same time power constellations. The crucial topic of regulation is the problem of use and abuse of power'. Concerning the newer media he concludes that 'the basic normative idea of necessary protection against the one-sided use of power, however, continues to apply, even if there is a shift in scarcity constellations and new abuse potentials become identifiable.'[vii]

...

Of course, the future media world will be very different from that of today, but to suggest that this removes our responsibility to address issues of law and regulation would be to allow technological change (complex enough in itself) to mask even more difficult problems of economic, social, and legal organisation. We have suggested in these conclusions that legal regulation will, and should, continue to have an important place in the new media world; indeed, we suspect that political crises and political concerns so evident around issues such as Internet pornography will ensure that this remains high on the political agenda.

[i] Commission of the European Communities, *Green Paper on the Convergence of Telecommunications, Media and Information Technologies,* COM (97) 623 (1997).

[ii] See, e.g., 'US Entertainment and Information: Traditional Media Stay in Fast Lane', *Financial Times,* 29 July 1997.

[iii] For an early statement of this theme see Graham, A, 'Exchange Rates and Gatekeepers' in Congden, T *et al* (eds), *The Cross Media Revolution* (London: John Libbey, 1995), 38–49.

[iv] Note i, above, 19.

[v] For a discussion see Hoffmann-Riem, W, 'New Challenges for European Multimedia Policy', *European Journal of Communication,* Vol 11(3), 1996, 327–46.

[vi] Negrine, R, *Politics and the Mass Media in Britain* (London: Routledge, 1994).

[vii] Note v, above, 333.

9

INTERNATIONAL REGULATION OF
BROADCASTING

1. INTRODUCTION

From earlier chapters, it is evident that broadcasting regulation has moved
beyond the national sphere, necessitating regulation at a European level.
Launching a satellite to enable broadcasting will also fall within an international regulatory framework. It might be thought curious that the law of
outer space should have any relevance to who can and what should be
broadcast, but in a very real sense the international regulatory framework has
consequences for these issues. As has been seen with terrestrial broadcasting,
access to limited resources can raise important concerns about the ability to
impart and receive information and ideas. Devising a regulatory framework
for access to outer space, a limited resource, has been difficult and with
increased demand, given the growing interest in satellite exploitation, remains a topical issue.

Satellite broadcasting, which enables broadcasting across frontiers, can
also raise concerns because the content of the broadcasts may conflict with
domestic policies on broadcasting. Within Europe, the European Community and the Council of Europe, through the Television without Frontiers
Directive and the European Convention on Transfrontier Television respectively, have found mechanisms to reconcile this potential conflict (see Chapter 5, Sections 4 and 5). At the international level, there has also been a
debate over whether states should have a right to control the broadcasts they
receive, or whether there should be no restrictions. This debate, which has
been known as the 'free flow of information/prior consent' debate, is one
which has continued for some time although the nature of the debate and its
participants have changed somewhat during that period. There has still not
been a satisfactory legal resolution to this debate. This chapter provides an
introduction to the international regulatory framework, first outlining the
regulatory framework, and then considering the two issues just mentioned:
access to outer space and the right to broadcast.

2. THE INTERNATIONAL REGULATORY FRAMEWORK[1]

There is no legal definition of outer space even though there is a treaty on its use (see below). However, outer space is generally understood to mean the '. . . space between the innumerable planets and stars, beyond their respective atmospheres where these exist'.[2] This includes interplanetary and interstellar space, and in the Outer Space Treaty (and subsequent United Nations treaties) also includes the moon and other celestial bodies in that region.[3] What has not been settled is the point at which air space ends and outer space begins, although there is general acceptance that it has begun at a point of altitude 100 kilometres above sea level.[4] However, there is no doubt that communication satellites are launched into outer space, since they occupy a space within the geostationary orbit (see below) which is situated approximately 36,000 kilometres from the Earth.[5]

The United Nations has been responsible for much of the development of general international space law, largely through the work of its specialist committee, Committee on the Peaceful Uses of Outer Space (COPUOS), while the International Telecommunication Union (the ITU), an agency of the United Nations, is responsible for the more specialised and technical international space regulation.[6] The most important legal instrument on the use of outer space is the Treaty on Principles Governing the Activities of States in the Exploration and Use of Outer Space including the Moon and other Celestial Bodies (the Outer Space Treaty). The Outer Space Treaty was produced by the United Nations and came into force in 1967. Although expressed in general terms, the Treaty is important is setting out guiding principles about the use of outer space, and in declaring that outer space is for the free use of all. The articles of the Outer Space Treaty most relevant to the discussion in this chapter and illustrating these general principles are set out in the following extract. As well as the prohibition on national appropriation of outer space, it can also be observed that there is an emphasis placed on parties to co-operate and to act transparently.

---

[1] Much of the information for this Section has been obtained from M L Smith, *International Regulation of Satellite Communication* (Martinus Nijhoff, 1990) and S White, S Bate and T Johnson, *Satellite Communications in Europe: Law and Regulation*, 2nd ed (Sweet & Maxwell, 1996).

[2] B Cheng, *Studies in International Space Law* (Clarendon Press, 1997), p 18.

[3] Ibid.

[4] M L Smith, *International Regulation of Satellite Communication* (Martinus Nijhoff, 1990), p 183.

[5] Satellites are launched at lower altitudes, for example around 800 kilometres, but these satellites are generally used for military, maritime or weather surveying purposes. Satellites launched at lower altitudes do not give the same coverage as a satellite launched in the geostationary orbit. However, there is increasing interest in what are called 'low earth orbiting satellites' and middle earth orbiting satellites, which orbit the Earth up to around 10,000 kilometres: S White, S Bate and T Johnson, *Satellite Communications in Europe: Law and Regulation*, 2nd ed (Sweet & Maxwell, 1996), para 1.12. Increasingly satellites in these orbits are being exploited for telecommunications, particularly mobile telephony and internet access. Launching satellites in these orbits has particular advantages for developing countries because they are less costly.

[6] Cheng, note 2, above, p 150.

Treaty on Principles Governing the Activities of States in the Exploration and Use of Outer Space including the Moon and other Celestial Bodies (27 January 1967) 610 United Nations Treaty Series 205, UK Treaty Series No 10, Cmnd 3519 (1968) arts I–III, VI and IX

Article I

The exploration and use of outer space, including the moon and other celestial bodies, shall be carried out for the benefit and in the interests of all countries, irrespective of their degree of economic or scientific development, and shall be the province of all mankind.

Outer space, including the moon and other celestial bodies, shall be free for exploration and use by all States without discrimination of any kind, on a basis of equality and in accordance with international law, and there shall be free access to all areas of celestial bodies.

. . .

Article II

Outer space, including the moon and other celestial bodies, is not subject to national appropriation by claim of sovereignty, by means of use or occupation, or by any other means.

Article III

States Parties to the Treaty shall carry on activities in the exploration and use of outer space, including the moon and other celestial bodies, in accordance with international law, including the Charter of the United Nations, in the interest of maintaining international peace and security and promoting international co-operation and understanding.

Article VI

States Parties to the Treaty shall bear international responsibility for national activities in outer space, including the moon and other celestial bodies, whether such activities are carried on by governmental agencies or by non-governmental entities, and for assuring that national activities are carried out in conformity with the provisions set forth in the present Treaty. The activities of non-governmental entities in outer space, including the moon and other celestial bodies, shall require authorization and continuing supervision by the appropriate State Party to the Treaty.

. . .

Article IX

In the exploration and use of outer space, including the moon and other celestial bodies, States Parties to the Treaty shall be guided by the principle of co-operation and mutual assistance and shall conduct all their activities in outer space, including the moon and other celestial bodies, with due regard to the corresponding interests of all other States Parties to the Treaty. . . . If a State Party to the Treaty has reason to believe that an activity or experiment planned by it or its nationals in outer space, including the moon and other celestial bodies, would cause potentially harmful interference with activities of other States Parties in the peaceful exploration and use of outer space, including the moon and other celestial bodies, it shall undertake appropriate international consultations before proceeding with any such activity or experiment. A State Party to the Treaty which has reason to believe that an activity or experiment planned by another State Party in outer space, including the moon and other celestial bodies, would cause potentially harmful interference with activities in the peaceful exploration and use of outer space, including the moon and other celestial bodies, may request consultation concerning the activity or experiment.

Article VI of the Outer Space Treaty requires the states which are party to the Treaty to take responsibility for the outer space activities of persons connected with that state. In the UK, this is achieved through the Outer Space Act 1986. This legislation provides for the licensing and regulation of space objects, such as satellites, which are being launched into outer space or otherwise operated, and of any other outer space activity.

It has been mentioned that for communication satellites the most appropriate orbit in outer space is the geostationary orbit. Its advantage is that any satellite placed in this orbit will revolve around Earth at the same speed, so that viewed from Earth it will appear as stationary. A satellite operating in the geostationary orbit will be able to cover about a third of the Earth's surface. For a satellite to operate and communicate with Earth, it will require a position within this geostationary orbit, and it must also make use of the radio frequency spectrum.[7] The radio frequency will enable the transmitted material to be communicated from Earth (the earth station) up to (the up-link) the satellite, and then to be communicated, via a different frequency, from the satellite back to (the down-link) Earth, being received by antennae, including the now ubiquitous 'dish' attached to satellite television viewers' homes.[8] The geostationary orbit and the radio frequency spectrum is generally referred to as the 'orbit/spectrum resource'.[9] This is a limited resource. Although in time technological developments may make it less scarce, this possibility has to be balanced by the growing demand for satellites.[10] First, there is a limit on the number of satellites which can be placed in the

---

[7] The bands (groups of frequencies) which are used are the C Band, the Ku Band and the Ka Band, although the latter is less useful at present.

[8] For a more detailed description of the geostationary orbit and the radio frequency spectrum and their relationship to satellites see Smith, note 4, above, pp 5–10.

[9] Ibid, 5.

[10] It has been estimated by a NASA/National Science Foundation report that the value of all satellite services will grow from $11.4 billion in 1992 to $38.3 billion in 2002: *Financial Times*, 28 October 1997.

geostationary orbit if a collision is to be avoided. About 2,000 satellites can be placed there.[11] Secondly, because of the physical nature of radio waves, only certain radio frequencies are suitable for communication satellites.[12] A further limitation arises because of the possibility of one user creating interference with another user of the spectrum; thus there is a need to co-ordinate each country's use of the radio frequency spectrum.[13]

Technological developments have affected the type of satellites which can be used for different purposes and this in turn has affected the regulatory framework (see further below). The main types of communication satellites using the geostationary orbit are fixed satellite services (FSS), broadcasting satellite services (BSS) and mobile satellite services (MSS)[14], although these distinctions have become less significant. Initially telecommunication services, for example, international telephony, were provided by low and medium powered satellites which required very large antennae, and it was thought that these were not suitable for satellite broadcasting.[15] These were the FSS and they were known as such because they transmitted to a fixed earth station, that is an antenna. FSS are the most numerous type of satellites in the orbit.[16] Technical developments made it possible for these satellites to carry television signals, although initially they were transmitted to large antennae and then retransmitted terrestrially, usually by cable. The size of the antennae meant that broadcasting direct to viewers' homes was not feasible unless high powered satellites were used. These were used to enable satellite broadcasts to reach individual homes, using only a small receiving antenna. These services were BSS. This type of broadcasting was known as Direct Broadcasting by Satellite (DBS) or Direct to Home Broadcasting (DTH). Initially it was thought that all DBS services would be BSS services and planning of the orbit/spectrum resource was carried out on this assumption (see below). However, technological developments have meant that the use of high powered satellites has become less significant because low and medium powered satellites have the technical capacity to transmit television signals of good quality, not just to large antennae, but also to the small antennae which could be located at viewers' homes. Thus it is the FSS which have become the most prevalent type of satellite service, both for telecommunications and broadcasting. It is these satellites which have given rise to the difficult problem of how to ensure equitable access to the orbit/spectrum resource (see Section 3 below).

[11] J C Thompson, 'Space for Rent: The International Telecommunications [sic] Union, Space Law, and Orbit/Spectrum Leasing' (1996) 62 *Journal of Air Law and Commerce* 279, at 284.

[12] Smith, note 4, above, p 7.

[13] White, Bate and Johnson, note 1, above, para 1.4.

[14] MSS are outside the scope of this chapter. MSS are communication satellites which involve communication with a moving location, for example ships and aircraft.

[15] A satellite's power, that is high, medium or low, is determined by the size of the transponders carried by a satellite. A satellite, depending on its size, will carry a certain number of transponders. These transponders receive the signals from the Earth and transmit them back to Earth.

[16] Smith, note 4, above, p 7.

The ITU has been referred to as an agency of the United Nations. Among other functions, the ITU has responsibility for the allocation of frequencies on the radio frequency spectrum and orbital positions. Although it is essentially meant to be responsible for technical matters, many of its activities have had considerable political significance, as issues, such as access to the geostationary orbit, have highlighted tensions between member countries, particularly between the developed and developing countries. The ITU is the oldest international organisation, having descended from the International Telegraph Union which was formed in 1865.[17] Its members are nation states although there is a membership category for those belonging to the telecommunications industry and for members of international satellite organisations.[18] These 'industry' members are not involved in the main decision-making elements of the ITU. With the increased involvement of the private sector in telecommunications, the ITU has been under pressure to give the private sector a greater role. However, for the present, it remains committed to being an intergovernmental organisation.[19] The ITU is governed by its Constitution and Convention. The Constitution sets out its general purposes and functions, the role of members, the structure and so forth, while the Convention provides more detailed provisions about its operation. In the following extract, one can see its central purposes and functions. Their relevance to satellite broadcasting is clear.

Extract 9.2.2

International Telecommunication Union, Constitution and Convention of the International Telecommunication Union, with Optional Protocol, Resolutions and Recommendation (22 December 1992) UK Treaty Series No 24, Cm 3145 (1996) Preamble, art 1, Annex

Preamble

While fully recognizing the sovereign right of each State to regulate its telecommunication and having regard to the growing importance of telecommunication for the preservation of peace and the economic and social development of all States, the States Parties to this Constitution, as the basic instrument

---

[17] G A Codding, Jr, 'The International Telecommunications [sic] Union: 130 Years of Telecommunications Regulation' (1995) 23(3) *Denver Journal of International Law and Policy* 501. It was renamed in 1934 and agreed to become an agency of the United Nations in 1947.

[18] J Wilson, 'The International Telecommunication Union and the Geostationary Satellite Orbit: An Overview' (1998) 23 *Annals of Air and Space Law* 241, at 246. An example of an international satellite organisation would be INTELSAT, the International Telecommunications Satellite Organisation, which launches and operates satellites for telecommunication purposes on behalf of the countries which are its members.

[19] ITU, *Press Report on the Minneapolis Plenipotentiary Conference: Main Highlights*, http://www.itu.int/newsroom/press/PP98/PressRel-Features/PP98press_report.html.

of the International Telecommunication Union, and to the Convention of the International Telecommunication Union (hereinafter referred to as the 'the Convention') which complements it, with the object of facilitating peaceful relations, international co-operation among peoples and economic and social development by means of efficient telecommunication services, have agreed as follows:

Article 1, Purposes of the Union

1. The purposes of the Union are
    (a) to maintain and extend international co-operation between all Members of the Union for the improvement and rational use of telecommunications of all kinds;
    (b) to promote and to offer technical assistance to developing countries in the field of telecommunications, and also to promote the mobilization of the material and financial resources needed for implementation;
    (c) to promote the development of technical facilities and their most efficient operation with a view to improving the efficiency of telecommunication services, increasing their usefulness and making them, so far as possible, generally available to the public;
    (d) to promote the extension of the benefits of the new telecommunication technologies to all the world's inhabitants;
    (e) to promote the use of telecommunication services with the objective of facilitating peaceful relations;
    (f) to harmonize the actions of Members in the attainment of those ends;
    (g) to promote, at the international level, the adoption of a broader approach to the issues of telecommunications in the global information economy and society, by co-operating with other world and regional intergovernmental organizations and those non-governmental organizations concerned with telecommunications.
2. To this end, the Union shall in particular:
    (a) effect allocation of bands of the radio-frequency spectrum, the allotment of radio frequencies and registration of radio-frequency assignments and any associated orbital positions in the geostationary-satellite orbit in order to avoid harmful interference between radio stations of different countries;
    (b) co-ordinate efforts to eliminate harmful interference between radio stations of different countries and to improve the use made of the radio-frequency spectrum and of the geostationary-satellite orbit for radiocommunication services;
    . . .
    (d) foster international co-operation in the delivery of technical assistance to the developing countries and the creation, development and improvement of telecommunication equipment and networks in developing countries by every means at its disposal, including through its participation in the relevant programmes of the United Nations and the use of its own resources, as appropriate;

. . .

325

Annex

For the purpose of the above instruments of the Union [Constitution, Convention and Administrative Regulations, which includes the Radio Regulations (see text below)], the following terms shall have the meanings defined below:

. . .

Harmful Interference: Interference which endangers the functioning of a radionavigation service or of other safety services or seriously degrades, obstructs or repeatedly interrupts a radiocommunication service operating in accordance with the Radio Regulations.

. . .

Radiocommunication: Telecommunication by means of radio waves.

. . .

Telecommunication: Any transmission, emission or reception of signs, signals, writing, images and sounds or intelligence of any nature by wire, radio, optical or other electromagnetic systems.

. . .

Question for discussion

In what ways do the purposes and functions of the Constitution reflect the principles of the Outer Space Treaty?

The ITU is a complex structure comprising different conferences, sectors and administrative bodies – only the most relevant to this discussion are mentioned here. The most important component is the Plenipotentiary Conference. This is the supreme organ of the ITU,[20] responsible for policy-making, and attended by delegations from the member countries. It meets every four years and has the power to amend, and replace, the Constitution and Convention, which it does regularly. The World Radiocommunication Conferences (formerly known as World Administrative Radio Conferences or WARCS) are held every two years. Their most important function is maintaining the Radio Regulations. These are detailed technical rules governing, inter alia, the allocation of frequencies and orbital positions and their registration. They are binding on all member countries. As will be clear from the following Section, these essentially technical matters have often been the subject of considerable dispute, raising fundamental questions about who should have access to the orbit/spectrum resource and on what basis. The basis of voting within the ITU is one vote for each member, and most voting is done on majority basis.[21] An interesting aspect of ITU membership, and largely the reason for the policy tensions, has been the growing domination of the developing countries. The majority of ITU members are now developing countries and certainly from the mid 1960s they have been willing to use their majority power to influence its direction.[22]

---

[20] Smith, note 4, above, p 24.

[21] Amending the Constitution requires a two thirds majority (Constitution, art 55(4)) while a simple majority only is required to amend the Convention (Convention, art 42(4)).

[22] Codding, note 17, above, at 504–505.

3. ACCESS TO THE ORBIT/SPECTRUM RESOURCE

Article II of the Outer Space Treaty (Extract 9.2.1 above) precludes national appropriation of outer space. However, in 1976 a group of eight equatorial nations[23] put forward a declaration claiming sovereignty over those parts of the geostationary orbit located directly above their countries. This claim has been consistently rejected by almost all other countries, and, given the terms of the Outer Space Treaty, it seems relatively easy to dismiss its validity, as Thompson suggests in Extract 9.3.2 below. The Bogota Declaration, however, reflects a more serious concern felt by developing nations generally. For those not yet in a position to exploit satellite technology, their concern is how to ensure, given the limitations of the orbit/spectrum resource, that they will be able to find space when they are ready to use it. This has become known as the issue of 'equitable access'. In the following extract, one can see how the Bogota Declaration reflected these concerns. The references to Article 33 of the ITU Convention will be discussed shortly.

Extract 9.3.1

International Telecommunication Union, *Declaration of the First Meeting of Equatorial Countries*, WARC-BS (1977) Doc 81-E (17 January 1977) reproduced in (1978) 6(2) *Journal of Space Law* 193–196

1. The geostationary orbit as a natural resource

. . .

The equatorial countries declare that the synchronous geostationary orbit is a physical fact arising from the nature of our planet, because its existence depends exclusively on its relation to gravitational phenomena caused by the Earth, and that for that reason it must not be considered part of outer space. Therefore, the segments of the synchronous geostationary orbit are an integral part of the territory over which the equatorial States exercise their national sovereignty. The geostationary orbit is a scarce, natural resource whose importance and value is increasing rapidly with the development of space technology and with the growing need for communication; therefore, the equatorial countries meeting in Bogota have decided to proclaim and defend on behalf of their peoples the existence of their sovereignty over this natural resource. . . .

. . .

The solutions proposed by the International Telecommunication Union . . . with a view to achieving a better use of the geostationary orbit and preventing its imminent saturation are at present impracticable, and are also unfair, because they would considerably increase the cost of utilizing this resource, especially for developing countries. Such countries do not have the same technological and financial resources as industrialized countries, which enjoy an evident

---

[23] Brazil, Colombia, Congo, Ecuador, Indonesia, Kenya, Uganda and Zaire.

monopoly in the exploitation and use of the synchronous geostationary orbit. In spite of the principle established by article 33, paragraph 2, of the 1973 International Telecommunication Convention . . . [see Extract 9.3.4 below], we can see that both the geostationary orbit and the frequencies have been used in a way that does not allow equitable access to the developing countries, which do not have the technical and financial means that the great Powers have. . . .

. . .

3. Legal status of the geostationary orbit

Bearing in mind the existence of sovereign rights over the segments of the geostationary orbit, the equatorial countries consider that the legal system applicable in this area must take into account the following:

a) The sovereign rights put forward by the equatorial countries are directed towards rendering real benefits to their respective peoples and to the world community, in complete contrast to the present state of affairs, in which the orbit is used primarily for the benefit of the most developed countries.

. . .

c) The equatorial States do not object to free orbital transit or the transit of communications requiring satellites covered and authorized by the International Telecommunication Convention, when these satellites pass through their space territory in gravitational flight outside their geostationary orbit.

d) Devices to be placed in a fixed position on an equatorial State's segment of the geostationary orbit shall require previous and express authorization on the part of the State concerned, and the operation of the device shall be governed by the national law of that State.

. . .

e) The equatorial States do not acquiesce in the presence of satellites on their segments of the geostationary orbit and declare that the existence of such satellites does not confer any right to place satellites there or to use the segment unless expressly authorized . . .

Extract 9.3.2

J C Thompson, 'Space for Rent: the International Telecommunications [sic] Union, Space Law, and Orbit/Spectrum Leasing' (1996) 62 *Journal of Air Law and Commerce* 279, at 306–308

Acknowledgement of the nearly universal applicability of the non-appropriation principle can be seen in the response to an attempt by a group of nations to claim portions of the orbit as sovereign territory [the Bogota Declaration] . . .

This viewpoint, however, has been rejected by both the nations that have launched satellites into geostationary orbit and developing nations which have not yet launched such satellites.[i] A claim of sovereignty would be directly antithetical to the underlying principles of the International Telecommunications Convention in that granting exclusive rights to the equatorial countries would violate the mandate of equitable access.[ii] The claim in the Bogota Declaration is clearly inconsistent with the underlying justification propounded to support it because any sovereignty granted over all or part of the geostationary orbit would be the opposite result of that required by the principles of equitable access which the equatorial states used to base their arguments upon. If ownership is granted, access to the portions claimed would obviously not be equitable – it would be foreclosed altogether.

Despite their protestations, it has been questioned whether the signatories to the Declaration were 'serious about gaining property rights to the geostationary orbit',[iii] or were simply exercising political pressure 'on a few developed countries that [were] monopolizing the geostationary orbit and consequently restraining the use of the orbit by late-comer developing countries.'[iv] Despite its futility, the Declaration nonetheless did serve to 'assert [the] position [of the equatorial nations] vis a vis the developed nations.'[v]

The overwhelming rejection of the view espoused in the Bogota Declaration firmly validated the principle of non-appropriation of the geostationary orbit and, by extension, the electromagnetic spectrum. At the same time, however, it further illustrated the tension between the developing nations' desire for guaranteed access (despite a lack of technological capability to utilize the resource) and the position of the administrations with existing and proposed satellite systems.

[i] Michael J. Finch, Note, *Limited Space: Allocating the Geostationary Orbit*, 7 Nw. J. Int'l. L. & Bus. 788, 790 (1986).
[ii] Milton L. Smith, *International Regulation of Satellite Communications* 203 (1990).
[iii] Note i, above, 796.
[iv] Ram Jakhu, *The Legal Status of the Geostationary Orbit*, 7 Annals Air and Space L. 333, 341 (1982).
[v] Note i, above, 796.

The Bogota Declaration, although never successful in its claim, highlights the problem of determining access to the orbit/spectrum resource. This may seem a remote concern in the context of a book on media law, however, it is linked to a general theme of this book, that broadcasting regulation has been influenced by the scarcity of natural resources. Although the scarcity rationale has usually had more relevance to individuals' rights to impart and receive information, access to the orbit/spectrum resource raises essentially similar questions, albeit on a different stage. Here the allocation of the resource will affect, at least in the first instance, the rights of one nation in relation to another, but, this may also affect that nation's ability to provide its citizens with the opportunity for information and ideas to be expressed and received. The question of broadcasting freedom in the international context is more usually considered in relation to the free flow/prior consent debate (see Section 4 below), but in the ongoing debate about orbit/spectrum access, there is an underlying principle of broadcasting freedom at stake.

The system for allocation of frequencies and orbital positions for communication satellites was developed well before the exploitation of satellites was even contemplated, as the following extract describes.

Extract 9.3.3

J C Thompson, 'Space for Rent: the International Telecommunications [sic] Union, Space Law, and Orbit/Spectrum Leasing' (1996) 62 *Journal of Air Law and Commerce* 279, at 290–292 (some footnotes omitted)

The regulations and procedures governing the use of telecommunications satellites in space were initially based on the system established to regulate radio stations which dates back to 1927.[i] At that time, the primary concern was harmful interference in terms of frequency allocation. The registration system protected stations which were already operating from infringement by later users. This *a posteriori* method utilizing notification and registration of frequency assignments is essentially a 'first-come, first-served' process.[ii] An *a posteriori* approach entails the granting of rights as a specific need arises. An *a priori* approach grants future rights to each nation 'on the basis of agreed principles.'[iii]

. . . At first, the system seemed adequate to the task given the moderate use of the orbit/spectrum resource and a perception of the resource as being unlimited.[iv] The rapid development of satellite communications, however, eventually led to an increased demand for the orbit/spectrum resource, and a growing perception of its scarcity created pressures on the system and concerns on the part of developing countries.[v] These countries feared that the 'first-come, first-served' process would result in a situation where the advanced countries could ultimately monopolize the available frequencies.[vi] . . . These growing concerns set the stage for the development of the present allocation system.

. . .

Whereas the developed countries wished to apply the first-come, first-served approach to the new realm of satellite telecommunications, the developing countries feared that such an approach would penalize their lack of technology and they would be denied access to the resource.[vii] Developed countries generally prefer the first-come, first-served *a posteriori* approach because it provides for efficient access while not allowing segments of the resource to be left unused.[viii] Developing nations, on the other hand, prefer an *a priori* approach in which frequencies and orbits are pre-coordinated . . .[ix]

The 1963 Extraordinary Administrative Radio Conference (EARC) squarely addressed the concerns of the developing nations. The conference included a debate on U.N. General Assembly Resolution 1721 (XVI), which stated that 'communication by means of satellites should be available to the nations of the world . . . on a global and non-discriminatory basis'.[x] Despite these proclaimed goals, the developed countries prevailed and the *a posteriori* system was adopted for space telecommunications.[xi] Consequently, some developing countries 'expressed fears that the radio spectrum would be preempted by the developed countries if the practice of first-come, first-served continued.'[xii] The quest for equitable access was on.

The 1971 WARC [World Administrative Radio Conference] resulted in few changes to the regulatory scheme.[xiii] Still, the principle of equitable access appeared yet again in Resolution Spa 2–1. The resolution considered that 'all countries have equal rights in the use of both the radio frequencies . . . and the geostationary satellite orbit.' The Resolution, while 'taking into account' that the orbit/spectrum resources are 'limited' and 'should be most effectively and economically used', concluded that the system of regulation 'should not provide any permanent priority for any individual country . . . and should not create an obstacle to the establishment of space systems by other countries.' Nonetheless, the first-come, first-served approach was retained yet again.

[i] Milton L. Smith, *International Regulation of Satellite Communications* 57 (1990).
[ii] *Ibid.*
[iii] *Id.*, 65.
[iv] Steven A. Levy, *Institutional Perspectives on the Allocation of Space Orbital Resources: The ITU, Common User Satellite Systems and Beyond*, 16 Case W. Res. J. Int'l L. 171, 173 (1984).
[v] *Id.*, 171.
[vi] Note i, above, 59. . . .
[vii] *Id.*, 59–60, 71 n.21.
[viii] E. D. DuCharme et al., *The Genesis of the 1985/87 ITU World Administrative Radio Conference on the Use of the Geostationary-Satellite Orbit and the Planning of Space Services Utilizing It*, 7 Annals Air & Space L. 261, 261 n.1 (1982).
[ix] *Ibid.*
[x] G. A. Res. 1721, U.N. GAOR, 16th Sess., Supp. No. 17, at 6, U.N. Doc. A/5100 (1962).
[xi] Note i, above, 60. . . .
[xii] Ram Jakhu, *The Evolution of the ITU's Regulatory Regime Governing Space Radiocommunication Services and the Geostationary Satellite Orbit*, 8 Annals Air and Space L. 381, 400 (1983).
[xiii] Note viii, above, 266.

Although a resolution is not binding it may be significant in highlighting policy, and in leading, at subsequent conferences, to binding provisions. Resolution Spa 2–1 was important, not only in its own terms, but because it did result in the incorporation of the equitable access concept into the Convention[24] at the 1973 Plenipotentiary Conference. The relevant provision is set out in the next extract, while Extract 9.3.5 analyses art 33, and the developments within the ITU following its adoption.

Extract 9.3.4

International Telecommunication Union, International Telecommunication Convention with Final Protocol, Additional Protocols I to VI and Optional Additional Protocol (25 October 1973) UK Treaty Series No 104, Cmnd 6219 (1975) art 33

Rational Use of the Radio Frequency Spectrum and of the Geostationary Satellite Orbit

1. Members shall endeavour to limit the number of frequencies and the spectrum space used to the minimum essential to provide in a satisfactory

---

[24] Prior to 1992, what is now termed the 'ITU Constitution and Convention' was referred to only as the 'Convention'.

manner the necessary services. To that end they shall endeavour to apply the latest technical advances as soon as possible.

2.   In using frequency bands for space radio services Members shall bear in mind that radio frequencies and the geostationary satellite orbit are limited natural resources, that they must be used efficiently and economically so that countries or groups of countries may have equitable access to both in conformity with the provisions of the Radio Regulations according to their needs and the technical facilities at their disposal.

Extract 9.3.5

M L Smith, 'Space WARC 1985: The Quest for Equitable Access' (1985) 3 *Boston University International Law Journal* 229, at 237–241 (some footnotes omitted)

Although the term 'equitable access' has never been defined in the Convention, it is generally agreed that equitable does not mean equal. Rather, equity implies fairness and justice, taking all relevant circumstances into consideration.[i] . . .

At the 1979 WARC, the developing countries secured passage of Resolution No 3.[ii] This Resolution recognizes the growing requirements for use of the orbit/spectrum resource and resolves 'that a world space administrative radio conference shall be convened . . . to guarantee in practice for all countries equitable access to the geostationary-satellite orbit and the frequency bands allocated to space services . . .' . . .

In addition to calling for the Space WARC, Resolution No 3 also addresses the issue of equitable access. It provides that 'there is a need for equitable access to, and efficient and economical use of [the orbit/spectrum resource] by all countries as provided for in Article 33 . . .' Two aspects of this provision are of paramount importance. First, while Resolution 3 recognizes the need for equitable access, the goal is tempered by the requirement that such access be 'efficient and economical'. Thus, these objectives are linked and are of equal importance. Second, Resolution 3 makes reference to Article 33 . . .

Article 33 . . . provides that countries are to have equitable access to the orbit/spectrum resource 'according to their needs and the technical facilities at their disposal.' This language implies that a country without a need for access to the orbit/spectrum resource or without the technical facilities to enable its use does not require equitable access. Article 33 can be interpreted to exclude countries without a present need and ability to use the orbit/spectrum resource from present considerations of equitable access. As in Resolution No 3, Article 33 also provides that the orbit/spectrum resource 'must be used efficiently and economically.' Thus, Article 33 both emphasizes the present or near-term capability to use the orbit/spectrum resource and reaffirms the link between equitable access and efficient and economical use.

. . .

The provision in Article 33 regarding needs and technical facilities was unpopular with developing countries who were concerned about their future access to the orbit/spectrum resource. At the 1982 Plenipotentiary Conference, those countries succeeded in amending Article 33 [see Extract 9.3.6 below]. . . .

The proposal to amend Article 33 sparked considerable debate at the Plenipotentiary Conference. Most developing countries supported deletion of the phrase 'according to their needs and the technical facilities at their disposal', because they believed it to be discriminatory. The developed countries, on the other hand, were generally concerned that deletion of the phrase and substitution of language identifying the 'special needs of the developing countries', would 'imply the introduction of a degree of inequality in favor of developing countries . . .' [a delegate from the USSR]

Thus, the threshold issue raised by the amendment to Article 33 is whether it created a priority favoring the developing countries. Several arguments exist against reaching this conclusion. First, it appears that only equal treatment was sought by the nations supporting the change. For example, during the negotiation of the amendment to Article 33, a delegate from one of the countries that proposed the amendment stated that '[f]ar from instituting an inequality in favor of the developing countries, the text aimed at establishing a fair balance in the use of a limited resource . . .'. [a delegate from Colombia] Second, specification of the special needs of the developing countries does not necessarily mean that the needs of other countries cannot be taken into consideration. . . . Finally, a legal priority favoring developing countries would contravene the Outer Space Treaty [see Article I, extract 9.2.1] . . .

Article 33 of the 1982 ITU Convention provides that use of the orbit/spectrum resource must be made 'efficiently and economically . . .' Use of this resource in the manner most needed by the developing countries, however, may not constitute the most efficient and economical use. Moreover, when they are ready to use the orbit/spectrum resource, developing nations may be unable to afford the advanced technologies that would provide the most efficient and economical use. Finally, the needs of the developing countries for assured future access, if taken into account currently, may not lead to the most efficient and economical use. Therefore, the special needs of the developing countries are for current and future uses which are not the most efficient and economical.

ⁱ Christol, *National Claims for the Using/Sharing of the Orbit/Spectrum Resource*, Proceedings of the Twenty-Fifth Colloquium on the Law of Outer Space 295, 298 (1982); Gorove, *Principles of Equity in International Space Law*, Proceedings of the Twenty-Sixth Colloquium on the Law of Outer Space 17, 18 (1983).

ⁱⁱ *1982 Radio Regulations* (Geneva, 1982), Resolution No 3.

Extract 9.3.5 referred to the amendments to Article 33, which were adopted as part of the 1982 Convention. Article 33 has essentially remained in the same form since then. The only substantive change has been the insertion of the word 'rationally' as indicated in square brackets in the following extract.

Extract 9.3.6

International Telecommunication Union, International Telecommunication Convention with Final Protocol, Additional Protocols I to VII and Optional Additional Protocol (6 November 1982) UK Treaty Series No 33, Cmnd 9557 (1985) art 33(2)

(2) In using frequency bands for space radio services Members shall bear in mind that radio frequencies and the geostationary satellite orbit are limited natural resources and that they must be used [rationally,] efficiently and economically, in conformity with the provisions of the Radio Regulations, so that countries or groups of countries may have equitable access to both, taking into account the special needs of the developing countries and the geographical situation of particular countries.

Questions for discussion
1. Do you agree with Smith's analysis of art 33?
2. Is it possible to reconcile the apparently conflicting principles of art 33?
3. Do the terms of the Outer Space Treaty give any scope for making allowances for developing countries?

Despite the vagaries of art 33 (now art 44), the long debate over equitable access has brought some changes to the system of allocation of frequencies and orbital positions. There has been a move away from the first-come, first-served system of allocation to a planned system, although its effectiveness may be questioned. Smith referred to the Space WARC. In fact two sessions of this Space WARC took place, in 1985 and 1988, and the outcome was to provide for planned access for FSS positions.[25] Thus, each Member State was allocated one orbital position and relevant frequency. However, the planned system applied only to parts of the C and Ku bands[26] so that much of the orbit/spectrum resource remains under the *a posteriori* or first-come, first-served basis (that is, unplanned).[27] Positions and frequencies have also been allocated for BSS, although, as mentioned earlier, BSS are now less important. Although, the allocation of positions provides some form of protection for those countries not yet able to exploit satellite technology, it is clear that those countries which are more technically advanced will be better placed to access the resource.

That tensions continue to exist can be seen in the growing problem of 'paper satellites'. The problem relates to the bands of the orbit/spectrum resource left unplanned, and arises because countries apply for positions

---

[25] In fact only a nominal position is allocated within a specified arc and this position can be moved: Smith, note 4, above, p 145.
[26] Ibid, p 90.
[27] Thompson, note 11, above, at 295.

within these bands which they may not be ready to use.[28] There may be valid reasons for such applications, for example, a satellite operator may need spare slots in case an existing satellite fails.[29] It has been estimated that more applications for positions over Asia have now been filed than there are places.[30] A recent and illustrative example of the dilemmas facing the ITU, was the application by Tonga for 16 positions in the Pacific Rim region. These were the only remaining positions in the region which could link Asia, the Pacific and the USA and, hence, were extremely valuable.[31] At the time Tonga had no satellite programme in operation or planned, and it made it clear that it intended to sell or lease some of the orbital positions.[32] There was considerable protest at the Tongan application, particularly from INTELSAT. Ultimately, the matter was resolved when Tonga agreed to give up ten of the applications and recent ITU conferences have been addressing the paper satellite problem.[33] The Tongan incident demonstrates the continuing pressure on the orbit/spectrum resource, and the concern still felt by some countries that they may be the losers in the race to access this increasingly important resource.

Question for discussion

Would Tonga's plans to sell or lease the orbital positions have been valid under the Outer Space Treaty?[34]

4. THE PRIOR CONSENT/FREE FLOW DEBATE

A connection between access to the orbit/spectrum resource and freedom of expression has been suggested in Section 3 above. However it is the free flow/prior consent debate which especially highlights the relationship between freedom of expression and satellite broadcasting. That the concept of freedom of expression is relevant to the international sphere is clear from the Universal Declaration of Human Rights.

---

[28] H Wong, 'The Paper "Satellite Chase" The ITU Prepares For Its Final Exam in Resolution 18' (1998) 63 *Journal of Air Law and Commerce* 849, at 850–851.

[29] For example, when an INTELSAT satellite failed, it was able to launch immediately a replacement satellite: ibid, at 859.

[30] Ibid, at 859, note 42. Paper satellites also cause delays in the processing of genuine applications: ITU, *Press Report on the Minneapolis Plenipotentiary Conference: Main Highlights*, http://www.itu.int/newsroom/press/PP98/PressRel-Features/PP98press_report.html.

[31] E L Andrews, 'Tiny Tonga Seeks Satellite Empire in Space', *N Y Times*, 28 August 1990, A1 cited in A N Delzeit and R E Beal, 'The Vulnerability of the Pacific Rim Orbital Spectrum Under International Space Law' (1996) 9(1) *New York International Law Review* 69, note 1.

[32] Thompson, note 11, above, at 281.

[33] Wong, note 28, above, at 866–875.

[34] For a discussion of the validity issue see Thompson, note 11, above, at 302–308.

Extract 9.4.1

United Nations General Assembly, *Universal Declaration of Human Rights*, General Assembly Resolution 217, UN Doc A/810 (1948), arts 19 and 29(2)

Article 19

Everyone has the right to freedom of opinion and expression; this right includes freedom to hold opinions without interference and to seek, receive and impart information and ideas through any media and regardless of frontiers.

Article 29(2)

In the exercise of his rights and freedoms, everyone shall be subject only to such limitations as are determined by law solely for the purpose of securing due recognition and respect for the rights and freedoms of others and of meeting the just requirements of morality, public order and the general welfare in a democratic society.

Satellite broadcasting allows broadcasters of one state to transmit programmes directly to citizens in another state (see also Chapter 5 above). In one sense, this is not a new phenomenon. With terrestrial broadcasting, there was always an element of 'overspill' across borders, but clearly satellite broadcasts can operate over a much wider area. But what have been the concerns about satellite broadcasting at the international level?

Extract 9.4.2

M E Price, 'The First Amendment and Television Broadcasting by Satellite' (1976) 23 *UCLA Law Review* 879, at 881–882 (footnotes omitted)

In its final flower, the direct broadcast satellite undoubtedly will be a potent instrument for reaching across national borders to transmit information, education, cultural events and commercials. It is hailed as a new device for binding the world together and serving the cause of peace. But its coming is also feared. The satellite is seen as another step in a kind of information imperialism leading to substantial control, whether intentional or not, over the less developed countries through direct media access to community centers or individual homes from sources in the major developed nations.

With its potential ability to reach into homes with ease, the direct broadcast satellite expands the opportunity for the free flow of information. But it can also disrupt the delicate techniques now used to balance the inward flow of information against the need to preserve and enhance national identity. In some cases, the governments may be concerned that the information and views that directly reach the people will lead to greater political opposition. Some governments fear the impact of Soviet information and propaganda. Others may fear ideas and information coming from the United States. Some envision a future in which two systems of direct broadcast satellites, each dominated by a superpower, rain signals on the nations within their sway. Another concern is the lack of a genuine exchange among the nations. The principle of free flow of information would be more palatable if it were not unidirectional or almost so. The less developed countries are media poor and information poor, in the Western sense. Each piece of external information takes on great significance. Often the nations are only recently independent. They yearn to develop their own political and national identity. Control over communications is a way to reach that goal; foreign-source information is an obstacle.

Price was writing in the early days of direct satellite broadcasting and the concerns outlined by him have changed greatly. Much of the early debate reflected the political situation at the time. With the collapse of the communist bloc, the debate has shifted, although it is certainly true that some states will still wish to keep control over broadcasting content for political and security reasons. However, concerns about direct satellite broadcasting are now more likely to focus on the other issues raised by Price. Many countries are concerned that satellite broadcasting will lead to a form of cultural imperialism because broadcasting will be dominated by foreign, particularly North American, programming.[35] This concern is reflected in the imposition, within the European Community, of European programme quotas (see Chapter 5, Section 5(d)). These concerns, whether political or cultural, have led to calls by some countries for international recognition of a right by receiving countries to control foreign satellite broadcasting. In other words, a right of prior consent. The need arises because controlling foreign direct satellite broadcasts is increasingly unfeasible, as technology has enabled satellite receiving dishes to become so small and relatively inexpensive. Those who advocate prior consent have met with opposition from those states which support the right of all citizens to receive information and ideas from any source.[36] These conflicting opinions have influenced attempts to introduce into international law regulations affecting direct satellite broadcasting. Reference has been made to art 19 of the Universal Declaration of Human Rights, which, while a statement of a well-recognised principle, is not legally binding. The Declaration may be said to form part of a customary law of human rights, although this remains a matter of debate.[37] Thus, it seems unlikely that the Declaration

---

[35] For a critique of this fear see J Sinclair, E Jacka, and S Cunningham, 'Peripheral Vision' in J Sinclair, E Jacka, and S Cunningham (eds), *New Patterns in Global Television* (Oxford University Press, 1996), pp 1–32.

[36] B A Hurwitz, 'The Labyrinth of International Telecommunications Law: Direct Broadcast Satellites' (1988) 35 *Netherlands International Law Review* 145, at 147.

[37] P Malanczuk, *Akehurst's Modern Introduction to International Law*, 7th ed (Routledge, 1997), p 217.

itself can be relied upon to support the advocates of free flow. However, the International Covenant of Civil and Political Rights (along with the International Covenant on Economic, Social and Cultural Rights) has transformed the Declaration into law. The Covenant came into force in 1976.[38] While it incorporates a similar provision to art 19, like the Universal Declaration, this is not an unrestricted right to freedom of expression. Nor, however, does it give any general rights to prohibit communications indiscriminately.

Extract 9.4.3

International Covenant on Civil and Political Rights, General Assembly Resolution 2200, UN Doc A/6316 (1966), arts 19 and 20

Article 19

1.   Everyone shall have the right to hold opinions without interference.
2.   Everyone shall have the right to freedom of expression; this right shall include freedom to seek, receive and impart information and ideas of all kinds, regardless of frontiers, either orally, in writing or in print, in the form of art, or through any other media of his choice.
3.   The exercise of the rights provided for in paragraph 2 of this Article carries with it special duties and responsibilities. It may therefore be subject to certain restrictions, but these shall only be such as are provided by law and are necessary:
    (a) For respect of the rights or reputations of others;
    (b) For the protection of national security or of public order (*ordre public*), or of public health or morals.

Article 20

1.   Any propaganda for war shall be prohibited by law.
2.   Any advocacy of national, racial or religious hatred that constitutes incitement to discrimination, hostility or violence shall be prohibited by law.

It is clear that the Covenant offers neither unqualified support for the advocates of free flow, nor does it give those who would support prior consent an absolute right to prevent communication, although it clearly recognises that there may be circumstances when it will be permissible to restrict the information being communicated. The first attempt to reach international agreement about satellite broadcasting came in 1972 with a Declaration from the United Nations Educational, Scientific and Cultural Organisation (UNESCO).

---

[38] As at 31 July 1996, 134 states had become parties to the Covenant, although reservations have been entered by a large number of countries: ibid, 215. The USA is not a signatory.

Extract 9.4.4

UNESCO, Declaration of Guiding Principles on the Use of Satellite Broadcasting for the Free Flow of Information, the Spread of Education and Greater Cultural Exchange, 15 November 1972, UNESCO, General Conference 17th Session (1972), UN Doc A/AC 105/109 (1973), reprinted in (1972) 11 *International Legal Materials* 1476, arts II(1), VI, VII, IX and X

Article II(1)

1. Satellite broadcasting shall respect the sovereignty and equality of all States.

. . .

Article VI

1. The objectives of satellite broadcasting for the spread of education are to accelerate the expansion of education . . .
2. Each country has the right to decide on the content of the educational programmes broadcast by satellite to its people . . .

Article VII

1. The objective of satellite broadcasting for the promotion of cultural exchange is to foster greater contact and mutual understanding between peoples by permitting audiences to enjoy, on an unprecedented scale, programmes on each other's social and cultural life including artistic performances and sporting and other events.
2. Cultural programmes, while promoting the enrichment of all cultures, should respect the distinctive character, the value and the dignity of each, and the right of all countries and peoples to preserve their cultures as part of the common heritage of mankind.

. . .

Article IX

1. In order to further the objectives set out in the preceding articles, it is necessary that States, taking into account the principle of freedom of information, reach or promote prior agreements concerning direct satellite broadcasting to the population of countries other than the country of origin of the transmission.
2. With respect to commercial advertising, its transmission shall be subject to specific agreement between the originating and receiving countries.

Article X

In the preparation of programmes for direct broadcasting to other countries, account shall be taken of differences in the national laws of the countries of reception.

The UNESCO Declaration clearly shows a move towards prior consent, but its significance must not be overstated. The Declaration is not legally binding, and there were doubts about UNESCO's competence to address this question.[39]

Another attempt to reach agreement arose through protracted negotiations within the United Nations, particularly during the 1970s. These negotiations led to a General Assembly Resolution in 1982. The nature of the debate over free flow and prior consent can be seen in the account of the negotiations leading to the Resolution in the following extract.

Extract 9.4.5

H C Anawalt, 'Direct Television Broadcasting and the Quest for Communication Equality' in Michigan Yearbook of International Legal Studies, *Regulation of Transnational Communications* (Clark Boardman Company, 1984), p 361, at pp 363–365 (footnotes omitted)

The debate began in earnest in the late 1960s, but shifted into high gear when the Soviet Union put forth a proposal in 1972. This proposal set the stage for the formal and informal legal discussions on direct television broadcasting. The USSR proposed an international convention that would bind nations to observe, among items, the following:

1. *Prior consent.* Transmission from broadcasting states to receiving states would be illegal, unless the express consent of the receiving state were obtained.

2. *Content regulation.* In addition to the content regulation implicit in a prior restraint regime, the Soviet proposal banned broadcasting of programs publicizing war, militarism, Nazism and racial hatred. . . . The proposal also prohibited other broader categories of content including violence, pornography, use of narcotics and 'broadcasts undermining the foundations of local civilization, culture, way of life, tradition or language'.

3. *State responsibility.* Finally, the proposal provided that the nation or state 'shall bear international responsibility for all national activities connected with the use of artificial earth satellites for the purposes of direct television broadcasting, irrespective of whether such broadcasting is carried out by governmental agencies or by non-governmental organizations . . .'

The USSR enlisted considerable support for this approach. First of all, the prior consent regime could be seen as a necessary protection of national sovereignty and national self-development. The specific prohibitions on content might be viewed as further protection against abusive communications and assurances of use of a powerful medium for generally peaceful purposes. Finally, the insistence on state responsibility could be seen as assuring that the less powerful nations would be able to demand accountability from those, like the United States, that possess great communications power.

---

[39] J Freeman, 'Toward the Free Flow of Information: Direct Television Broadcasting via Satellite' (1979) 13 *Journal of International Law and Economics* 329, at 341.

The United States and certain other western nations opposed the USSR's proposal primarily on the basis that it violated a fundamental international norm or general principle safeguarding the free flow of information. These nations frequently cited Article 19 of the Universal Declaration of Human Rights. . . . The United States urged that no special regulation of direct broadcast satellites was appropriate, and that whatever legal responsibility there might be for such broadcasts should be resolved by application of existing provisions of international law. . . .

Canada and Sweden attempted to create a middle position between those of the Soviet Union and the United States. Their compromise formula eliminated the prohibition of certain types of content, retained state responsibility, and offered a prior consent regime under which the sending and receiving states would be obliged to confer and reach agreement or arrangements giving due consideration to the facilitation of 'the freer and wider dissemination of information of all kinds.'

. . .

Finally, it should be noted that the . . . [Canadian/Sweden] working draft strongly supported the principle of free flow of information at a most important juncture. The most difficult item to resolve in the years of negotiation was the problem of prior consent or agreement on the part of the receiving state. The 1979 draft retained a prior consent requirement in that the broadcasting state was required to consult and obtain agreement on the part of the recipient state, but both parties were obliged to bear in mind an overriding purpose of the agreement, namely that it was to be entered into 'in order to facilitate the freer and wider dissemination of information of all kinds and to encourage cooperation in the field of information and the exchange of information with other countries'. . . .

The Swedish/Canadian proposal of 1979 was a useful and concrete proposal. Its key feature was that it articulated principles to guide the conduct of nations rather than establish rules which might appear inflexible in the growing area of communications. The principles referred to existing international law, especially the Outer Space Treaty, and created specific boundaries for bargaining in good faith concerning reception of television broadcasting. The proposal offered a basis for meeting the concerns of cultural independence and of advancing the principle of free flow. It urged protection of the dignity of individual national cultures and created a growing basis for a right to receive information, including by way of satellite broadcast.

In the resulting Resolution (Extract 9.4.6 below), one can discern a similar approach to the UNESCO Declaration, but again it is necessary to be cautious about the significance of this later instrument. It is not a legally binding instrument and while it was passed by a large majority,[40] most Western nations opposed it, including Germany, the USA and the UK, with Canada

---

[40] 107 countries voted in favour of the resolution, 13 against and 13 countries abstained: H C Anawalt, 'Direct Television Broadcasting and the Quest for Communication Equality' in Michigan Yearbook of International Legal Studies, *Regulation of Transnational Communications* (Clark Boardman Company, 1984), p 361, at p 374, note 19.

and Sweden among those countries which abstained.[41] That it was necessary to take a vote might also be said to undermine the influence of the Resolution, since all treaties in the space law area and resolutions prepared by COPUOS have, with the exception of this Resolution, been agreed by consensus rather than by majority vote.[42]

Extract 9.4.6

Principles Governing the Use by States of Artificial Earth Satellites for International Direct Television Broadcasting, 10 December 1982, UN Resolution 37/92 of 10 December 1982, paras 1–2, 6 and 13

A. Purposes and objectives

1. Activities in the field of international direct television broadcasting by satellite should be carried out in a manner compatible with the sovereign rights of States, including the principle of non-intervention, as well as with the right of everyone to seek, receive and impart information and ideas as enshrined in the relevant United Nations instruments.
2. Such activities should promote the free dissemination and mutual exchange of information and knowledge in cultural and scientific fields, assist in educational, social and economic development, particularly in the developing countries, enhance the qualities of life of all peoples and provide recreation with due respect to the political and cultural integrity of States.
. . .

D. International co-operation

6. Activities in the field of international direct television broadcasting by satellite should be based upon and encourage international co-operation. Such co-operation should be the subject of appropriate arrangements. Special consideration should be given to the needs of the developing countries in the use of international direct television broadcasting by satellite for the purpose of accelerating their national development.
. . .

J. Consultations and agreements between States

13. A State which intends to establish or authorize the establishment of an international direct television broadcasting satellite service shall without delay notify the proposed receiving State or States of such intention and shall promptly enter into consultation with any of those States which so requests.

---

[41] Ibid.
[42] Malanczuk, note 37, above, p 203.

Notwithstanding the limitations of the Resolution in terms of both its legal and persuasive impact,[43] it is nevertheless clear that there was, at that time, strong support for restraints. How practical the proposed restraints were, particularly with the benefit of hindsight, is questionable, but in one respect they are consistent with existing instruments and statements on freedom of expression, because it is clear, when one examines the Declaration on Human Rights, for example, and the European Convention on Human Rights, that the right to freedom of expression is qualified. It is always a matter of balancing competing interests. As Price points out, even the USA, which has been the most vociferous advocate of the free flow argument accepts that there must be some constraints; he cites regulation of international mail as an example.[44] Curiously, it is within the ITU that one can find a legally binding statement which might offer support for a rule on prior consent. The 1971 WARC adopted a new Regulation designed to minimise the degree to which a satellite broadcasting signal might spill over into another territory.[45]

Extract 9.4.7

International Telecommunication Union, Final Acts of the WARC for Space Telecommunications, 1971, Radio Regulation 428A [now Radio Regulation, art S23.13 (1998); the words in square brackets are now omitted from the text]

In devising the characteristics of a space station in the broadcasting-satellite service, all technical means available shall be used to reduce, to the maximum [extent practicable], the radiation over the territory of other countries unless an agreement has been previously reached with such countries.

For those countries keen to see a system of prior consent in place, Regulation 428A appeared to provide an answer, having the obvious advantage also of being legally binding.[46] However, there are two difficulties with accepting this answer. The first relates to the nature of a satellite signal. Satellite broadcasting signals will cover an area known as a 'footprint'. It is not possible to confine that signal precisely to the territory at which it is being directed, so

---

[43] It is also thought that the Resolution is unlikely to be evidence of a customary law given the lack of uniformity and the identity of the countries which opposed it. It was also significant that in general the countries which supported it lacked satellite broadcasting capability: A N Delzeit and R M Wahl, 'Redefining Freedom of Speech Under International Space Law: The Need for Bilateral Communications Alliances to Resolve the Debate Between the "Free Flow of Information" and "Prior Consent" Schools of Thought' (1995) 2 *ILSA Journal of International and Comparative Law* 267, at 275.

[44] M E Price, 'The First Amendment and Television Broadcasting by Satellite' (1976) 23 *UCLA Law Review* 879, at 890–891.

[45] This regulation came into force on 1 January 1973: S F Luther, *The United States and the Direct Broadcast Satellite* (Oxford University Press, 1988), p 101.

[46] Ibid.

spillover will naturally occur.[47] Secondly, the countries opposed to a prior consent principle respond that Regulation 428A is a technical provision addressing only unintentional spillover.[48] This argument would seem to have some merit, since as Hurwitz points out '. . . the ITU is a *technical* regulatory organization and not a *political–legal* regulatory body with power to restrict the use by States of frequencies allocated to them. The ITU tells States *where* (i.e., on which frequencies) to broadcast, not *what* to broadcast.'[49]

It is clear that despite these efforts it has not been possible to establish a clear legal regime for satellite broadcasting content. As already observed, since the debate over prior consent/free flow was at its height, political developments have changed its nature. However, as Delzeit and Wahl discuss in the following extract, tensions still exist, perhaps even more so, because the potential for satellite broadcasting, along with the convergence of communications (see Chapter 8), is now being exploited on a scale and in a manner not envisaged in the 1960s and 1970s when this debate was most active. At the same time the scope for a state's control of foreign satellite broadcasting is limited. Traditional mechanisms, for example, jamming signals or controlling the acquisition by citizens of aerials, are unpractical.

Extract 9.4.8

A N Delzeit and R M Wahl, 'Redefining Freedom of Speech Under International Space Law: The Need for Bilateral Communications Alliances to Resolve the Debate Between the "Free Flow of Information" and "Prior Consent" Schools of Thought' (1995) 2 *ILSA Journal of International and Comparative Law* 267, at 276–282 (some footnotes omitted)

The fantastic technical capacity of DBS has admittedly created unprecedented opportunities to promote world peace and understanding, to supplement the education of people located in remote areas, to disseminate news of impending disasters, and to present cultural events.[i] . . .

Yet, the above view remains simplistic, given the fact that if past is prologue, DBS technology could also be used for commercial exploitation and cultural imperialism, if all nations followed the free flow philosophy.[ii] Hence, . . . the freedom to impart information without interference is not absolute . . .

When they are read in their entirety, the Outer Space Treaty, United Nations Charter, and Universal Declaration of Human Rights protect the national sovereignty of the receiving state. . . . The same international documents thus simultaneously embody both the idea of 'free flow of information' and the principles of 'sovereignty of state'.

---

[47] Hurwitz, note 36, above, at 161–162.

[48] Luther, note 45, above, p 102. For an analysis of the arguments over Regulation 428A, see ibid, pp 101–105.

[49] Hurwitz, note 36, above, at 161.

The restrictions on freedom of speech are understandable, given that the sovereignty of state forms an undisputed component principle of general international law. It is universally recognized that a state possesses the sovereign right to regulate all activities within its jurisdiction.[iii] The so-called 'prior consent' school of thought is therefore correct in asserting that a nation's sovereign prerogative includes the exclusive right to regulate sources of information that come within its domestic jurisdiction,[iv] and to determine for itself what information may be supplied to its citizens.[v]

. . . The unregulated use of DBS could pose a substantial threat to a state's ability to determine the character of its television system.[vi] It is conceivable that the New World Information Order [that is, communications satellites and new communication technologies] can be used to incite hatred or dissatisfaction by raising socio-economic expectations.[vii] DBS can also be used to erode the cultural independence of a country by an uninterrupted flow of television programs from foreign sources.[viii] . . .

The primary objective of the prior consent philosophy is that information and communication represent a social good, a cultural value, and each country should have a right of self-determination in this field. . . .

The major problem with the prior consent view is that it greatly overemphasizes the notion of 'negative' territorial sovereignty, which is based on the exclusion of the activities of other states. This negative view of territorial sovereignty fails to recognize that self-determination of a state entails not only a right to remain free from foreign interference, but also certain human rights of its citizens.[ix] A state cannot enjoy exclusive rights within its own territory under international law without assuming corresponding obligations for its own populace.[x] Accordingly, the concept of territorial sovereignty does not extend nearly as far as the prior consent philosophy. . . .

. . . The current tension between the free flow of information and prior consent philosophies seems somewhat antique, given the recent passing of the Cold War and the corresponding shift from bipolar superpower relations to multipolar international relations.

A third, yet neglected stance, perceives the debate as more than a question of differences between two schools of thought. . . . The bilateral agreement view calls for a middle-ground approach to the resolution of the so-called New World information order issue.[xi] This position accepts as undisputed the prior consent belief that every state has the right to regulate all DBS transmissions within it's [sic] borders. However, this position also rejects a rigidly implemented content code derived from the notion of 'negative' territorial sovereignty, which overemphasizes the exclusion of other states from a nation's borders.[xii]

Instead, there needs to be dynamic localized content guidelines in the form of regional arrangements between nations which share a cultural homogeneity. The use of localized content guidelines would insure that all recipient states participate in the production of imported programming.[xiii] Moreover, such organizations would emphasize cooperation over dominance and provide transnational methods to pool resources so that more countries could become involved in the New World Information Order. A step in this direction has already occurred with the July 15, 1976 formation of Arab Satellite Communications System (ARABSAT). ARABSAT consists of twenty Arab nations and the Palestine Liberation Organization (PLO), and was chartered to provide telecommunications [including television] services for the Arabic speaking countries. . . .

Similar regional alliances in the Americas, Asia and Africa encouraged on the basis of mutual respect, would not only allow significantly cheaper access to the New World Information Order, they would also benefit all participants with each other's individual experience.[xiv] In a world that is increasingly interdependent since the Cold War, the next step beyond regional alliances could be intercontinental, multilateral alliances between the developed and lesser developed regions.

[i] E.R. Brown III, 'Direct Broadcast Satellites and Freedom of Speech', 4 *Cal.W.Int'l L.J.* 374, 376 (1974); M. Masmoundi, 'The New World Information Order and Direct Broadcasting Satellites' 8 *Syracuse J. Int'l L. & Com.* 321, 331 (1981).

[ii] Comment, 'Direct Satellite Broadcasting and the First Amendment', 15 *Harv. Int'l L.J.* 514, 515 (1974).

[iii] M.N. Taishoff, *State Responsibility and the Direct Broadcast Satellite* 109 (1987); K. Kelson, *Principles of International Law* 242 (1952); J. Powell, 'Direct Broadcast Satellites: The Conceptual Convergence of the Free Flow of Information and National Sovereignty', 6 *Cal. W. Int'l L.J.* 1, 13 (1975).

[iv] H. Kandil, 'Panel 1: The New World Information Order' in 2 *Issues in International Information: A Workshop on the New World Information Order and Other Key Issues* 13 (1981).

[v] K.M. Queeney, *Direct Broadcast Satellites and the United Nations* 48 (1978).

[vi] Note ii, above, 515.

[vii] C. Delfen, 'The International Legislative Process: Direct Broadcasting and Remote Earth Sensing by Satellite Compared', 1972 *Can. Y.B. Int'l L.* 186, 192.

[viii] Powell, note iii, above, 21–24.

[ix] I. Detter de Lupis, *International Law and the Independent State* 13 (1987).

[x] *Id.*, 5. . . .

[xi] M.A. Dauses, 'Direct Television Broadcasting by Satellites and Freedom of Information' 3 *J. Space L.* 59 (1975). . . .

[xii] *Id.*, 64.

[xiii] T.M. Hagelin, 'Prior Consent or the Free Flow of Information Over International Satellite Radio and Television: A Comparison and Critique of U.S. Domestic and International Broadcasting Policy' 8 *Syracuse J. Int'l L. & Com* 265, 269 (1981).

[xiv] R.S. Jakhu & R. Singal, 'Satellite Technology and Education', 6 *Ann. Air & Space L.* 399, 402 (1981).

Questions for discussion

1. To what extent should a state be free to control the broadcasts received within its territory?

2. Is the approach suggested by Delzeit and Wahl, to develop regional arrangements, an adequate response to the prior consent/free flow debate?

3. Are the European Community programme quotas (see Chapter 5, Section 5(d)) an example of their regional approach? Would they serve as a useful model for other regions?

What is most noticeable now, about the free flow/prior consent debate, is that it is no longer played out within an international forum, such as the ITU or the COPUOS, nor, it would seem, are solutions sought there. As Delzeit and Wahl acknowledge, international relations are now more complex and multi-dimensional. Simple divisions cannot be drawn up: the free world vs the communist bloc; the developed countries vs the developing countries. However, perhaps there has also been a more fundamental change which has influenced this debate. Satellite broadcasting is now much more likely to be carried out by private commercial interests, eager to establish themselves in markets with potential, and possibly untapped, revenue sources. A good example of this is STAR TV, a satellite service operating in Asia, owned by Rupert Murdoch's News Corporation, which began in 1991.

Extract 9.4.9

J M Chan, 'National Responses and Accessibility to STAR TV in Asia' in A Sreberny-Mohammadi, D Winseck, J Mckenna and O Boyd-Barrett (eds), *Media in a Global Context: A Reader* (Arnold, 1997) p 94, at p 104

STAR TV has set an Asian precedent that potentially defies the 'prior consent' principle that the World Administrative Radio Conference and the United Nations adopted for controlling signal spillovers. . . . While some countries still find the impact of STAR TV to be too insignificant for serious concern, others have adopted either an open or restricted policy toward it.

So far, no country has asked the Hong Kong government [from where the service operates] to limit the coverage of STAR TV by appealing to the prior consent principle; nor has any nation raised the issue of the possible infringement of information sovereignty. . . . In effect, this leaves regulation of the international flow of information via STAR TV in the hands of national governments and information ministries rather than through international negotiations. If the virtually mute response to STAR TV on the international level continues, it will serve as a tacit recognition of the breakdown of the prior consent principle.

As Chan notes, there has been a move away from resolving these matters on the international stage, but this does not necessarily mean that the prior consent principle is no longer relevant. When, in the early 1990s, STAR TV hoped to gain admission to the Chinese market, it discontinued its carriage of the BBC World Service, because it understood that the BBC's reporting of Chinese current affairs would not be acceptable to the Chinese government.[50] STAR TV's efforts to enter this market were unsuccessful, and, with limited exceptions, direct reception of satellite broadcasts remains prohibited in China.[51] Contrary to Chan's conclusion, STAR TV offers evidence that 'prior consent' may be very relevant in practice. This is worrying, because

---

[50] It has since been restored. Chan comments that other countries have been concerned about STAR TV but have considered that preventing it would be impractical.

[51] Under Chinese law, possession of satellite receiving equipment is prohibited unless licensed: Regulations on Radio and Television Administration (1997), art 26.

private broadcasters might be only too willing to sacrifice values, such as freedom of expression, in order to preserve their commercial interests. While reaching consensus at the international level has proved difficult, debate in a public international forum does at least have the advantage that it is conducted within a transparent framework of certain recognised principles. The debate about free flow and prior consent, which took place in the 1960s through to the early 1980s, may now, as Delzeit and Wahl suggest, seem antiquated, but it may be one which is worth preserving at an institutional level.

10

DEFAMATION

1. INTRODUCTION

One of the most important restrictions on media freedom is that imposed by the law of defamation. As prosecutions for criminal libel are uncommon,[1] the media are concerned with the civil law of defamation. They are particularly troubled by the risk that the jury will award a successful plaintiff substantial damages. Jury decisions are notoriously unpredictable; it may be impossible to foresee whether it will believe the plaintiff or the press (or other defendant). Moreover, there is a presumption that defamatory allegations are false; it is for the media to show that the allegations were true or amounted to fair comment: see Section 5 of this chapter.[2]

Defamation law is complex. Fortunately, two fundamental points are of no importance in the context of media law. First, the requirement that a defamatory allegation is only actionable when it is published to a third party is easy to satisfy; the allegation will have been published in a newspaper, magazine, or book, or will have been broadcast or communicated in some other public way. Secondly, the distinction between libel and slander is of no relevance. It is a libel to publish defamatory allegations in a *permanent* form; a verbal publication amounts to slander. Under the Defamation Act 1952, broadcast statements are to be treated as publication in permanent form.[3] Defamation actions against the media are, therefore, for libel, rather than for slander; as a consequence, the terms 'defamation' and 'libel' are used interchangeably in this chapter.

Section 2 explains what amount to a 'defamatory' allegation, while Section 3 discusses who can bring a libel action. Section 4 is concerned with the range of defendants; not only the author, but also the publisher and distributor,

---

[1] Under the Law of Libel Amendment Act 1888, s 8, no prosecution may be brought against a newspaper or periodical without the consent of a judge in chambers, who must be satisfied that the libel is serious and that the public interest requires the start of criminal proceedings.

[2] These difficulties are discussed by E Barendt, L Lustgarten, K Norrie, and H Stephenson, *Libel and the Media: The Chilling Effect* (Oxford University Press, 1997).

[3] Section 1. In *Youssoupoff* (Extract 10.2.1) two members of the Court of Appeal held that spoken words in a film amount to libel.

say, of a book or newspaper can be sued. The longest part of the chapter is Section 5 which describes the defences available to the media. The remedies for libel, principally an award of damages, are discussed in the following section, while Section 7 briefly outlines important procedural reforms which may reduce the inhibiting effects of libel law on the media.

2. WHAT IS DEFAMATORY?

(a) Definition of defamatory

The law draws a distinction between defamatory allegations, for which the plaintiff may sue in libel, and remarks which, however offensive or abusive, are not actionable. In principle, a claimant should be able to bring an action only for those allegations which infringe the right to reputation, that is, the right each individual enjoys to protect the esteem in which he is held in the community.[4] The media would be placed in an intolerable position if an action could be brought in respect of any irritating newspaper article or item on radio or television. One question, therefore is what does 'defamatory' mean in abstract? In practice, however, a second question is more important: are the particular words in their context defamatory of the plaintiff? The next two extracts bring out the various definitions of 'defamatory'. In the *Youssoupoff* case, the plaintiff was a Russian Princess who claimed that she had been libelled in the film, *Rasputin, the Mad Monk*, produced by the defendants, inasmuch as it suggested that Princess Natasha, a character in the film identifiable as the plaintiff, had been seduced or raped by Rasputin.

Extract 10.2.1

***Youssoupoff v MGM Pictures Ltd* (1934) 50 TLR 581, at 587 (CA)**

SLESSER LJ: I, for myself, cannot see that from the plaintiff's point of view it matters in the least whether this libel suggests that she has been seduced or ravished. The question whether she is or is not the more or the less moral seems to me immaterial in considering this question whether she has been defamed and for this reason, that, as has been frequently pointed out in libel, not only is the matter defamatory if it brings the plaintiff into hatred ridicule, or contempt by reason of some moral discredit on her part, but also if it tends to make the plaintiff be shunned and avoided and that without any moral discredit on her part. It is for that reason that persons who have been alleged to have been insane, or to be suffering from certain diseases, and other cases where no direct moral responsibility could be placed upon them, have been

---

[4] For a discussion of why the law protects the right to reputation, see R C Post, 'The Social Foundations of Defamation Law: Reputation and the Constitution' (1986) 74 *California Law Review* 691.

held to be entitled to bring an action to protect their reputation and their honour.

One may, I think, take judicial notice of the fact that a lady of whom it has been said that she has been ravished, albeit against her will, has suffered in social reputation and in opportunities of receiving respectful consideration from the world. It is to shut one's eyes to realities to make these nice distinctions, but in this case I see no reason to suppose that this jury did come to a conclusion on this film that the imaginary lady depicted in the film, the Princess Natasha, was ravished and not seduced. I have looked at the pictures carefully, I have read the language, and it seems to me perfectly consistent with either view, and to assume at the outset that this film does represent a ravishment and not a seduction seems to me itself to assume that which the jury might have refused to assume at all.

Extract 10.2.2

Sim v Stretch [1936] 2 All ER 1237, at 1240 (HL)

LORD ATKIN: The question, then, is whether the words in their ordinary signification are capable of being defamatory. Judges and textbook writers alike have found difficulty in defining with precision the word 'defamatory.' The conventional phrase exposing the plaintiff to hatred, ridicule and contempt is probably too narrow. The question is complicated by having to consider the person or class of persons whose reaction to the publication is the test of the wrongful character of the words used. I do not intend to ask your Lordships to lay down a formal definition, but after collating the opinions of many authorities I propose in the present case the test: would the words tend to lower the plaintiff in the estimation of right-thinking members of society generally? Assuming such to be the test of whether words are defamatory or not there is no dispute as to the relative functions of judge and jury, of law and fact. It is well settled that the judge must decide whether the words are capable of a defamatory meaning. That is a question of law: is there evidence of a tort? If they are capable, then the jury is to decide whether they are in fact defamatory.

Whether allegations are defamatory or not will generally depend on their precise context. But one general point is well-established. The allegations are assessed by reference to the standards of 'right-thinking' members of society. It is not libellous to suggest that someone has reported a crime to the police or otherwise behaved with propriety, even though as a result many colleagues or friends might think less highly of him. In *Byrne v Deane*[5] the majority of the Court of Appeal ruled that a member of a golf club could not sue in libel in respect of the allegation that he had reported the club to the police for keeping illegal gaming machines on the premises.

[5] [1937] 1 KB 818.

Questions for discussion

1. Which of the definitions formulated by Slesser LJ and Lord Atkin do you prefer?

2. In general, should it now be regarded as defamatory to allege (inaccurately) that X is 'gay', is 'too ill to attend a conference', or 'eats too much and is terribly overweight'. Consider this question again when you have read the remainder of the chapter.

(b) Meaning in context

Often the most important question in a libel action is the meaning of the words; it may in contrast be relatively easy to determine whether that meaning is 'defamatory of the plaintiff' under one of its definitions.

Extract 10.2.3

Lewis v Daily Telegraph [1964] AC 234, at 258–260 (HL)

An article in the *Daily Telegraph* stated: 'Officers of the City of London Fraud Squad are inquiring into the affairs of Rubber Improvement, Ltd . . . The investigations were requested after criticisms of the chairman's statement and the accounts by a shareholder at the recent company meeting.' The plaintiffs, the Rubber Improvement company and its chairman, Lewis, argued that the meaning of this article was that their affairs were conducted fraudulently or, at least, that the police suspected fraud.

LORD REID: The gist of the two paragraphs is that the police, the City Fraud Squad, were inquiring into the appellants' affairs. There is no doubt that in actions for libel the question is what the words would convey to the ordinary man: it is not one of construction in the legal sense. The ordinary man does not live in an ivory tower and he is not inhibited by a knowledge of the rules of construction. So he can and does read between the lines in the light of his general knowledge and experience of worldly affairs. I leave aside questions of innuendo where the reader has some special knowledge which might lead him to attribute a meaning to the words not apparent to those who do not have that knowledge. That only arises indirectly in this case . . .

What the ordinary man would infer without special knowledge has generally been called the natural and ordinary meaning of the words. But that expression is rather misleading in that it conceals the fact that there are two elements in it. Sometimes it is not necessary to go beyond the words themselves, as where the plaintiff has been called a thief or a murderer. But more often the sting is not so much in the words themselves as in what the ordinary man will infer from them, and that is also regarded as part of their natural and ordinary meaning. Here there would be nothing libellous in saying that an inquiry into the appellants' affairs was proceeding: the inquiry might be by a statistician or other expert. The sting is in inferences drawn from the fact that it is the fraud squad which is making the inquiry. What those inferences should be is ultimately a question for the jury, but the trial judge has an important duty to perform.

Generally the controversy is whether the words are capable of having a libellous meaning at all, and undoubtedly it is the judge's duty to rule on that. I shall have to deal later with the test which he must apply. Here the controversy is in a different form. The respondents admit that their words were libellous, although I am still in some doubt as to what is the admitted libellous meaning. But they sought and seek a ruling that these words are not capable of having the particular meaning which the appellants attribute to them. I think that they are entitled to such a ruling and that the test must be the same as that applied in deciding whether the words are capable of having any libellous meaning . . .

In this case it is, I think, sufficient to put the test in this way. Ordinary men and women have different temperaments and outlooks. Some are unusually suspicious and some are unusually naïve. One must try to envisage people between these two extremes and see what is the most damaging meaning they would put on the words in question. So let me suppose a number of ordinary people discussing one of these paragraphs which they had read in the newspaper. No doubt one of them might say – 'Oh, if the fraud squad are after these people you can take it they are guilty.' But I would expect the others to turn on him, if he did say that, with such remarks as – 'Be fair. This is not a police state. No doubt their affairs are in a mess or the police would not be interested. But that could be because Lewis or the cashier has been very stupid or careless. We really must not jump to conclusions. The police are fair and know their job and we shall know soon enough if there is anything in it. Wait till we see if they charge him. I wouldn't trust him until this is cleared up, but it is another thing to condemn him unheard.'

What the ordinary man, not avid for scandal, would read into the words complained of must be a matter of impression. I can only say that I do not think that he would infer guilt of fraud merely because an inquiry is on foot. And, if that is so, then it is the duty of the trial judge to direct the jury that it is for them to determine the meaning of the paragraph but that they must not hold it to impute guilt of fraud because as a matter of law the paragraph is not capable of having that meaning. So there was here, in my opinion, misdirection of the two juries sufficiently serious to require that there must be new trials.

In contrast, the Court of Appeal considered that two articles in the *Sunday Telegraph* could be understood to imply guilt. The articles, one under the headline 'TWO MORE IN SCOTT AFFAIR', reported that the names of various people, one of them the claimant, had been given to the police in connection with allegations of conspiracy to murder. Distinguishing the *Lewis* case, Lord Denning MR said that 'on a first reading any ordinary person' might consider the claimant was involved in the plot.[6]

---

[6] *Hayward v Thompson* [1982] QB 47, at 61 (CA).

Although meaning is a jury matter, the judge can rule whether the words are capable of bearing a particular meaning; he must withdraw from them any interpretation which no reasonable man could place on the words.[7] Some difficulties are nicely illustrated by the *Charleston* case. In a report on a new computer game, the *News of the World* published photos of the faces of two actors, who played well-known soap stars in *Neighbours*; their faces were superimposed on the bodies of other persons engaged in pornographic poses. While the photos and headline suggested the actors had willingly engaged in the poses, the captions and full text made it plain that this was an illusion.

Extract 10.2.4

Charleston v News Group Newspapers Ltd [1995] 2 AC 65, at 73–74 (HL)

LORD NICHOLLS OF BIRKENHEAD: My Lords, newspapers get thicker and thicker. The 'News of the World' published on 15 March 1992 contained 64 pages. Everybody reads selectively, scanning the headlines and turning the pages. One reader, whose interest has been quickened by an eye-catching headline or picture, will pause and read an article. Another reader, with different interests or less time, will read the headline and pass on, leaving the article unread. What if a headline, taken alone or with an attached picture, is defamatory, but the text of the article removes the defamatory imputation? That is the question of law raised by this appeal.

At first sight one would expect the law to recognise that some newspaper readers will have seen only the banner headline and glanced at the picture. They will not have read the text of the accompanying article. In the minds of these readers, the reputation of the person who is the subject of the defamatory headline and picture will have suffered. He has been defamed to these readers. The newspaper could have no cause for complaint if it were held liable accordingly. It has chosen, for its own purposes, to produce a headline which is defamatory. It cannot be heard to say that the article must be read as a whole when it knows that not all readers will read the whole article.

To anyone unversed in the law of defamation that, I venture to think, would appear to be the common sense of the matter. Long ago, however, the law of defamation headed firmly in a different direction. The law adopts a single standard for determining whether a newspaper article is defamatory: the ordinary reader of that newspaper. I leave aside cases where some readers may have special knowledge of facts which would cause them to give the words a different meaning.

In principle this is a crude yardstick, because readers of mass circulation newspapers vary enormously in the way they read articles and the way they interpret what they read. It is, indeed, in this very consideration that the law

---

[7] In order to save time and legal costs, either party can now apply before trial for an order that the words are incapable of bearing a particular meaning placed on them by the other party in his pleading: see CPR, Sched 1, RSC Ord 82, r 3A.

finds justification for its single standard. The consequence is that, in the case of some publications, there may be many readers who understand in a defamatory sense words which, by the single standard of the ordinary reader, were not defamatory. In respect of those readers a plaintiff has no remedy. The converse is equally true. So a newspaper may find itself paying damages for libel assessed by reference to a readership many of whose members did not read the words in a defamatory sense.

I do not see how, consistently with this single standard, it is possible to carve the readership of one article into different groups: those who will have read only the headlines, and those who will have read further. The question, defamatory or no, must always be answered by reference to the response of the ordinary reader to the publication.

This is not to say that words in the text of an article will always be efficacious to cure a defamatory headline. It all depends on the context, one element in which is the layout of the article. Those who print defamatory headlines are playing with fire. The ordinary reader might not be expected to notice curative words tucked away further down in the article. The more so, if the words are on a continuation page to which a reader is directed. The standard of the ordinary reader gives a jury adequate scope to return a verdict meeting the justice of the case.

The present case is well on the other side of the borderline. The ordinary reader could not have failed to read the captions accompanying the pictures. These made clear that the plaintiffs' faces had been superimposed on other actors' bodies. The plaintiffs had not themselves been indulging in the activities shown in the pictures. The ordinary reader would see at once that the headlines and pictures could not be taken at their face value. And the reader's eye needed to travel no further than the 'victims' caption to the smaller photographs, and to the second sentence, at the top of the article, to find confirmation that the plaintiffs were 'unwitting' stars in the sordid computer game.

Accordingly, when the ordinary reader put down the 'News of the World' on 15 March 1992, he or she would have thought none the worse of the two actors who are well known for their roles in the 'Neighbours' television serial. The ordinary reader might have thought worse of the producers of the pornographic computer game, and of the 'News of the World,' but that is a different matter. In agreement with my noble and learned friend, Lord Bridge of Harwich, I, too, would dismiss this appeal.

But often courts refuse to withdraw a question of meaning from the jury. In *Gillick*,[8] an action for libel was brought for remarks made by Susan Pearce, an agony aunt, in a BBC discussion programme about the work of the Brook Centres which provide girls with contraceptive advice. Mrs Pearce said to Victoria Gillick, also participating in the programme: 'But after you won that battle . . . there were at least two reported cases of suicide by girls who were pregnant.' (The reference was to a court declaration obtained by Mrs Gillick that a government circular was unlawful inasmuch as it encouraged the

---

[8] *Gillick v BBC* [1996] 4 EMLR 267 (CA).

provision of contraceptive advice.) A majority of the Court of Appeal held this remark was reasonably capable of the meaning that Mrs Gillick was to blame and morally responsible for the girls' death. In the *Berkoff* case, on the other hand, there was no question about the meaning of the words; the issue was whether two reviews in the *Sunday Times*, written by Julie Burchill, intimating that the actor and director Steven Birkoff was 'hideously ugly' were capable of being defamatory. The majority of the Court of Appeal held that they were.[9]

Extract 10.2.5

Berkoff v Burchill [1997] EMLR 139, at 151, 153 (CA)

NEILL LJ: It may be that in some contexts the words 'hideously ugly' could not be understood in a defamatory sense, but one has to consider the words in the surroundings in which they appear . . .

It is trite law that the meaning of words in a libel action is determined by the reaction of the ordinary reader and not by the intention of the publisher, but the perceived intention of the publisher may colour the meaning. In the present case it would in my view be open to a jury to conclude that in the context the remarks about Mr Berkoff gave the impression that he was not merely physically unattractive in appearance but actually repulsive. It seems to me that to say this of someone in the public eye who makes his living, in part at least, as an actor, is capable of lowering his standing in the estimation of the public and of making him an object of ridicule.

MILLETT LJ: The line between mockery and defamation may sometimes be difficult to draw. When it is it should be left to the jury to draw it . . . A decision that it is an actionable wrong to describe a man as 'hideously ugly' would be an unwarranted restriction on free speech. And if a bald statement to this effect would not be capable of being defamatory, I do not see how a humorously exaggerated observation to the like effect could be. People must be allowed to poke fun at one another without fear of litigation. It is one thing to ridicule a man; it is another to expose him to ridicule. Miss Burchill made a cheap joke at Mr Berkoff's expense; she may thereby have demeaned herself, but I not believe that she defamed Mr Berkoff.

Questions for discussion

1. Would you have agreed with the majority in *Berkoff* or with Millett LJ?
2. Consider the arguments for and against judicial reluctance to withdraw issues from the jury.

---

[9] Phillips LJ held the jury should decide whether the words so exposed the plaintiff to ridicule that they damaged his reputation. Compare *Norman v Future Publishing* [1999] EMLR 325, where the Court of Appeal held the attribution of vulgar and undignified language to the opera singer, Jessye Norman, was not capable, in the context of the whole article, of bearing a defamatory meaning.

3. WHO CAN SUE IN DEFAMATION?

(a) Public authorities and corporations

In principle any person, natural or legal, may bring an action for libel. Companies, including banks, and partnerships are entitled to sue; trades unions, on the other hand, cannot sue in their own name, since they are not treated as having legal personality.[10] (But their officers may bring an action, so in practice this disability does not much matter.) Nor can a dead person sue, or for that matter be sued. It may be in bad taste to criticise the dead, let alone defame them, but they are fair game for the media.

However, the House of Lords established an important exception to the general rule when a local authority brought an action in respect of allegations about the propriety of some investments made for its superannuation fund.

Extract 10.3.1

Derbyshire County Council v Times Newspapers
[1993] AC 534, at 547–549 (HL)

LORD KEITH: There are, however, features of a local authority which may be regarded as distinguishing it from other types of corporation, whether trading or non-trading. The most important of these features is that it is a governmental body. Further, it is a democratically elected body, the electoral process nowadays being conducted almost exclusively on party political lines. It is of the highest public importance that a democratically elected governmental body, or indeed any governmental body, should be open to uninhibited public criticism. The threat of a civil action for defamation must inevitably have an inhibiting effect on freedom of speech. In *City of Chicago v Tribune Co.* (1923) 139 N.E. 86 the Supreme Court of Illinois held that the city could not maintain an action of damages for libel. Thompson C.J. said, at p. 90:

'The fundamental right of freedom of speech is involved in this litigation, and not merely the right of liberty of the press. If this action can be maintained against a newspaper it can be maintained against every private citizen who ventures to criticise the ministers who are temporarily conducting the affairs of his government. Where any person by speech or writing seeks to persuade others to violate existing law or to overthrow by force or other unlawful means the existing government, he may be punished . . . but all other utterances or publications against the government must be considered absolutely privileged. While in the early history of the struggle for freedom of speech the restrictions were enforced by criminal prosecutions, it is clear that a civil action is as great, if not a greater, restriction than a criminal prosecution. If the right to criticise the government is a privilege which, with the exceptions above enumerated, cannot be restricted, then all civil as well

---

[10] *EETPU v Times Newspapers* [1980] QB 585, O'Connor J.

as criminal actions are forbidden. A despotic or corrupt government can more easily stifle opposition by a series of civil actions than by criminal prosecutions . . .'

These propositions were endorsed by the Supreme Court of the United States in *New York Times Co. v Sullivan* (1964) 376 U.S. 254, 277. While these decisions were related most directly to the provisions of the American Constitution concerned with securing freedom of speech, the public interest considerations which underlaid them are no less valid in this country. What has been described as 'the chilling effect' induced by the threat of civil actions for libel is very important. Quite often the facts which would justify a defamatory publication are known to be true, but admissible evidence capable of proving those facts is not available. This may prevent the publication of matters which it is very desirable to make public. In *Hector v Attorney-General of Antigua and Barbuda* [1990] 2 A.C. 312 the Judicial Committee of the Privy Council held that a statutory provision which made the printing or distribution of any false statement likely to undermine public confidence in the conduct of public affairs a criminal offence contravened the provisions of the constitution protecting freedom of speech.

. . .

It is of some significance to observe that a number of departments of central government in the United Kingdom are statutorily created corporations, including the Secretaries of State for Defence, Education and Science, Energy, Environment and Social Services. If a local authority can sue for libel there would appear to be no reason in logic for holding that any of these departments (apart from two which are made corporations only for the purpose of holding land) was not also entitled to sue. But as is shown by the decision in *Attorney-General v Guardian Newspapers Ltd. (No. 2)* [1990] 1 A.C. 109, a case concerned with confidentiality, there are rights available to private citizens which institutions of central government are not in a position to exercise unless they can show that it is the public interest to do so. The same applies, in my opinion, to local authorities. In both cases I regard it as right for this House to lay down that not only is there no public interest favouring the right of organs of government, whether central or local, to sue for libel, but that it is contrary to the public interest that they should have it. It is contrary to the public interest because to admit such actions would place an undesirable fetter on freedom of speech.

Later cases have extended this principle to deny the capacity of public corporations[11] and political parties[12] to bring libel actions. But as Lord Keith made plain in *Derbyshire*,[13] an individual whose reputation is damaged by the allegations remains free to bring an action. In that event, however, the media may be able to rely on the defence of qualified privilege; see Section 5(c) below, and the decision of the House of Lords in the *Reynolds* case, discussed in the Appendix.

[11] *British Coal Corporation v NUM*, 28 June 1996, unreported, French J.
[12] *Goldsmith and Another v Bhoyrul and Others* [1997] 4 All ER 268.
[13] [1993] AC 534, at 550.

(b) Identification of the claimant

The claimant must show that the defamatory allegations were made about him. Clearly there is no problem where he is expressly named. In other cases the question is whether the ordinary reader would understand the allegations to refer to the claimant; evidence may be given to the court to show that some readers (or viewers) did understand the material in this way.[14]

Does it make any difference if the author, say, of a novel has made up a name, without any intention of defaming the plaintiff, of whose existence he was unaware?[15] The answer to this question was given by the House of Lords in *Hulton v Jones*; the *Sunday Chronicle* published a sketch about English holiday makers enjoying themselves in Dieppe, referring to an 'Artemus Jones with a woman who is not his wife, who must be, you know – the other thing!' The paper argued, rather disingenuously,[16] that it had never heard of Artemus Jones, the plaintiff, a sober Welsh barrister.

Extract 10.3.2

Hulton v Jones [1910] AC 20, at 24 (HL)

LORD LOREBURN LC: If the intention of the writer be immaterial in considering whether the matter written is defamatory, I do not see why it need be relevant in considering whether it is defamatory of the plaintiff. The writing, according to the old form, must be malicious, and it must be of and concerning the plaintiff. Just as the defendant could not excuse himself from malice by proving that he wrote it in the most benevolent spirit, so he cannot shew that the libel was not of and concerning the plaintiff by proving that he never heard of the plaintiff. His intention in both respects equally is inferred from what he did. His remedy is to abstain from defamatory words.

It is suggested that there was a misdirection by the learned judge in this case. I see none. He lays down in his summing up the law as follows: 'The real point upon which your verdict must turn is, ought or ought not sensible and reasonable people reading this article to think that it was a mere imaginary person such as I have said – Tom Jones, Mr. Pecksniff as a humbug, Mr. Stiggins, or any of that sort of names that one reads of in literature used as types? If you think any reasonable person would think that, it is not actionable at all. If, on the other hand, you do not think that, but think that people would suppose it to mean some real person – those who did not know the plaintiff of course would not know who the real person was, but those who did know of the existence of the plaintiff would think that it was the plaintiff – then the action is maintainable, subject to such damages as you think under all the circumstances are fair and right to give to the plaintiff.'

---

[14] *Morgan v Odhams Press Ltd* [1971] 1 WLR 1239 (HL).

[15] For a discussion of the impact of libel law on writers of fiction, see E M Barendt, 'Defamation and Fiction' in M Freeman and A Lewis (eds), *Law and Literature* (Oxford University Press, 1999), p 481.

[16] It is clear that the writer of the sketch knew and disliked Jones, who had previously worked for the paper: see P Mitchell (1999) 20 *Journal of Legal History* 64.

In short, there is liability if a newspaper, however innocently, publishes material which reasonable readers may link to someone they know.[17] Writers and broadcasters must, therefore, be precise in their description of a suspect or offender in order to minimise the risk of a libel action by another person of the same name. The difficulties faced by the media were made plain by the Court of Appeal in the *Newstead* case; a newspaper had published an account of a bigamy trial, stating that 'Harold Newstead, 30-year-old Camberwell man, who was jailed for nine months, liked having two wives at once.' That was true of a Camberwell barman of that name, but not of the claimant, a hairdresser, of the same name, who was also living in Camberwell!

Extract 10.3.3

Newstead v London Express Newspapers Ltd
[1940] 1 KB 377, at 388 (CA)

SIR WILFRID GREENE MR: After giving careful consideration to the matter, I am unable to hold that the fact that defamatory words are true of A, makes it as a matter of law impossible for them to be defamatory of B, which was in substance the main argument on behalf of the appellants. At first sight this looks as though it would lead to great hardship. But the hardships are in practice not so serious as might appear, at any rate in the case of statements which are ex facie defamatory. Persons who make statements of this character may not unreasonably be expected, when describing the person of whom they are made, to identify that person so closely as to make it very unlikely that a judge would hold them to be reasonably capable of referring to someone else, or that a jury would hold that they did so refer. This is particularly so in the case of statements which purport to deal with actual facts. If there is a risk of coincidence it ought, I think, in reason to be borne not by the innocent party to whom the words are held to refer, but by the party who puts them into circulation. In matters of fiction, there is no doubt more room for hardship. Even in the case of matters of fact it is no doubt possible to construct imaginary facts which would lead to hardship. There may also be hardship if words, not on their faces defamatory, are true of A, but are reasonably understood by some as referring to B, and as applied to B are defamatory. But such cases must be rare. The law as I understand it is well settled, and can only be altered by legislation.

Questions for discussion

Do you think the principle established in *Hulton v Jones* and the *Newstead* case is right? Would it be fairer to require the claimant to show that the media had been negligent in making defamatory allegations about him?

---

[17] But the media may rely on the offer of amends defence: see Section 5(d) below.

(c) Groups

A group cannot sue in libel to protect its collective reputation. The media are free to say that 'all politicians are corrupt' and 'lawyers are greedy', because no individual can show that the allegations implicate him. But in some circumstances an individual member may be able to sue in defamation for an attack on that group. *Knupffer* is the leading case on this aspect of the law. A newspaper article was published about the activities of a pro-Nazi group in the Soviet Union, which was described as a 'minute body professing a pure Fascist ideology . . .'.

Extract 10.3.4

Knupffer v London Express Newspaper Ltd
[1944] AC 116, at 124–125 (HL)

LORD PORTER: No doubt, it is true to say that a class cannot be defamed as a class, nor can an individual be defamed by a general reference to the class to which he belongs . . . Nevertheless, the words or the words combined with the relevant circumstances may be shown to refer to some person or persons individually . . .

The question whether the words refer in fact to the plaintiff or plaintiffs is a matter for the jury or for a judge sitting as a judge of fact, but as a prior question it has always to be ascertained whether there is any evidence on which a conclusion that they do so refer could reasonably be reached. In deciding this question the size of the class, the generality of the charge and the extravagance of the accusation may all be elements to be taken into consideration, but none of them is conclusive. Each case must be considered according to its own circumstances. I can imagine it being said that each member of a body, however large, was defamed where the libel consisted in the assertion that no one of the members of a community was elected as a member unless he had committed a murder.

Whatever the tribunal, the first question is: Are the words in conjunction with the relevant circumstances reasonably capable of being understood to apply to the plaintiff? In the present case that question must, I think, be answered in the negative. It is true that the appellant was and is a member of a body on which very grave reflections have been cast, that he is the representative of that body in England, and that there are only twenty-four members of it in this country, but the newspaper article makes no reference to England. It confines itself to allegations about 'a minute body' 'established in France and the United States.' Minute, no doubt, its membership of 2,000 is when compared with the vast population of Russia, but in itself it forms a considerable body. Out of that body there was nothing to point to the appellant, nor indeed to any individual in this country. Nor do I think the appellant's case is improved by the allegations of his friends that 'their minds turned to' him when they read the article. Apart from the vagueness of the question, I can see no justification for an inference that he was the person aimed at. If it could be said, as it is conceded it could not, that each member of the body, wherever resident, could claim to be defamed, some case might be made on behalf of the appellant as one of its members, but as the evidence stands I see nothing to point to him in contra-distinction to the rest. Indeed, inasmuch as he is a member of the English group, he is the less likely to be referred to. I agree that the appeal should be dismissed.

The risks run by newspapers in this context are highlighted by two actions brought by police officers. In one of them,[18] ten CID officers stationed in Banbury successfully brought an action in respect of reported allegations of rape and violence by unnamed officers stationed there. There were only 12 CID officers at this station; had there been, say, a hundred, it would have been impossible for the plaintiffs to show the libel identified them. In the second case, the Court of Appeal held an action brought by ten officers could proceed, when the *Police Review* disclosed that a police dog-handler was resigning from the force because of anti-semitism on the part of his colleagues; there were only 27 dog-handlers in the particular dog-handling section, so the plaintiffs could claim to be individually identifiable by readers of the journal.[19]

4. WHO CAN BE SUED?

Anyone involved in the publication of a defamatory allegation may be sued. So, in a newspaper or magazine case, the claimant may sue the author of the libellous article, the editor, proprietor, printer, distributor, and newsagent, for each is involved in its publication. Similarly, a broadcasting company is liable for anything said in the course of a studio discussion or phone-in programme, for it transmits the allegation to the general public.[20]

This position has been exploited by claimants, notably the late Robert Maxwell and Sir James Goldsmith. They often served libel writs on the distributors and retailers of magazines such as *Private Eye*. While authors and publishers are often prepared to attempt to justify the allegations, usually distributors are anxious to avoid legal action, by, for example, removing an 'offending' book or magazine from their shelves. Moreover, the distributor may be in a better position to pay substantial damages than the publisher. A majority of the Court of Appeal refused to hold that an action by Goldsmith against distributors of *Private Eye* should be dismissed as an abuse of court process. Scarman LJ said that if the consequence of the law was to diminish press freedom, it was for Parliament to amend it. He referred, however, to the argument that 'the existing law provides in the action against the

---

[18] See Robertson and Nicol, p 52.
[19] *Aiken v Police Review Publishing Co*, 17 April 1995, unreported (CA).
[20] See, for instance, *Gillick v BBC* [1996] EMLR 267, where the BBC, as well as Mrs Pearce, was sued.

secondary distributor a valuable additional remedy for an individual who is defamed by a scurrilous or financially dubious publication'.[21]

However, in addition to the general defences discussed in the next section, the common law recognised a specific defence of 'innocent dissemination'. It protected distributors (for instance, booksellers, newsagents, and libraries), but not printers, from liability for defamation, unless they knew or ought to have known that the publication contained libellous material.[22] The law has now been modernised by the Defamation Act 1996.

Extract 10.4.1

Defamation Act 1996, s 1

1.—(1) In defamation proceedings a person has a defence if he shows that—

    (a) he was not the author, editor or publisher of the statement complained of,

    (b) he took reasonable care in relation to its publication, and

    (c) he did not know, and had no reason to believe, that what he did caused or contributed to the publication of a defamatory statement.

(2) For this purpose 'author', 'editor' and 'publisher' have the following meanings, which are further explained in subsection (3)—

    'author' means the originator of the statement, but does not include a person who did not intend that his statement be published at all;

    'editor' means a person having editorial or equivalent responsibility for the content of the statement or the decision to publish it; and

    'publisher' means a commercial publisher, that is, a person whose business is issuing material to the public, or a section of the public, who issues material containing the statement in the course of that business.

(3) A person shall not be considered the author, editor or publisher of a statement if he is only involved—

    (a) in printing, producing, distributing or selling printed material containing the statement;

    (b) in processing, making copies of, distributing, exhibiting or selling a film or sound recording (as defined in Part I of the Copyright, Designs and Patents Act 1988) containing the statement;

    (c) in processing, making copies of, distributing or selling any electronic medium in or on which the statement is recorded, or in operating or providing any equipment, system or service by means of which the statement is retrieved, copied, distributed or made available in electronic form;

---

[21] *Goldsmith v Sperrings Ltd* [1977] 1 WLR 478, at 501 (CA). Lord Denning MR vigorously dissented from the majority decision.

[22] Among the leading cases were *Emmens v Pottle* (1885) 16 QBD 354, and *Vizetelly v Mudie's Select Library Ltd* [1900] 2 QB 170.

(d) as the broadcaster of a live programme containing the statement in circumstances in which he has no effective control over the maker of the statement;

(e) as the operator of or provider of access to a communications system by means of which the statement is transmitted, or made available, by a person over whom he has no effective control.

In a case not within paragraphs (a) to (e) the court may have regard to those provisions by way of analogy in deciding whether a person is to be considered the author, editor or publisher of a statement.

(4) Employees or agents of an author, editor or publisher are in the same position as their employer or principal to the extent that they are responsible for the content of the statement or the decision to publish it.

(5) In determining for the purposes of this section whether a person took reasonable care, or had reason to believe that what he did caused or contributed to the publication of a defamatory statement, regard shall be had to—

(a) the extent of his responsibility for the content of the statement or the decision to publish it,

(b) the nature or circumstances of the publication, and

(c) the previous conduct or character of the author, editor or publisher.

(6) This section does not apply to any cause of action which arose before the section came into force.

The range of persons who may take advantage of the defence has been significantly expanded. They are not defined in positive terms, but rather negatively: they must not be 'authors', 'editors', or 'publishers'.

Questions for discussion

1. Does the imposition of defamation liability on distributors amount to an infringement of press freedom?

2. Does Defamation Act 1996, s 1 provide a defence for (a) the publisher of occasional pamphlets, for example a student union; (b) a radio station broadcasting a live interview; (c) an Internet service provider, for example Compuserve?

It has recently been held that an Internet service provider was in a similar position to a bookseller or library, when it distributed defamatory material to subscribers; it could not avail itself of the statutory defence when it failed to remove a defamatory posting, of which it was aware.[23]

5. DEFENCES

(a) Justification

It is a complete defence for the media to justify the defamatory allegation. It must be proved true on the balance of probabilities. In English civil law, in

---

[23] *Godfrey v Demon Internet* [1999] EMLR 542.

contradistinction to the little-used criminal law and the legal position in some Commonwealth jurisdictions, the defence does not also have to show that publication was in the public interest. The defence succeeds, even if the publisher was malicious.[24] Moreover, the defence does not have to prove the truth of every allegation.

Extract 10.5.1

Defamation Act 1952, s 5

5. In an action for libel or slander in respect of words containing two or more distinct charges against the plaintiff, a defence of justification shall not fail by reason that the truth of every charge is not proved if the words not proved to be true do not materially injure the plaintiff's reputation having regard to the remaining charges.

But the media cannot justify libellous allegations, merely by showing that such allegations are current. So a tabloid cannot carry a headline – 'Widespread rumours of adultery by Cabinet Minister' – unless it can prove that the Cabinet Minister about whom the rumour is circulating has in fact committed adultery. This is known as the repetition rule. Recent cases have emphasised its standing as a rule of law.[25] Its effect is to limit the circulation by the media of gossip and rumour, without evidence that the allegations in them are true. (But media reports of allegations made in court or legislative proceedings or at public meetings may be covered by the defence of qualified privilege – see below Section 5(c) – which mitigates, therefore, the operation of the repetition rule.)

(b) Fair comment on a matter of public interest

The defence of fair comment enables the media to express their opinion on matters of public interest. The courts have taken a broad view of 'public interest' in this context.

Extract 10.5.2

London Artists Ltd v Littler (1969) 2 QB 375, at 391 (CA)

LORD DENNING MR: There is no definition in the books as to what is a matter of public interest. All we are given is a list of examples, coupled with a

---

[24] There is one exception to this rule: under the Rehabilitation of Offenders Act 1974, s 8(5), the media cannot plead the truth of a reference to a 'spent' conviction as a defence to a libel action, if it was made maliciously.

[25] *Stern v Piper* [1997] QB 123 (CA); *Shah v Standard Chartered Bank* [1998] 4 All ER 155 (CA). Cf *Aspro Travel v Owners Abroad Group plc* [1996] 1 WLR 132 (CA).

statement that it is for the judge and not for the jury. I would not myself confine it within narrow limits. Whenever a matter is such as to affect people at large, so that they may be legitimately interested in, or concerned at, what is going on, or what may happen to them or to others; then it is a matter of public interest on which everyone is entitled to make fair comment... Here the public are legitimately *interested*. Many people are interested in what happens in the theatre. The stars welcome publicity. They want to be put at the top of the bill. Producers like it too. They wish the house to be full. The comings and goings of performers are noticed everywhere. When three top stars and a satellite all give notice to leave at the same time – thus putting a successful play in peril – it is to my mind a matter of public interest, in which everyone, Press and all, are entitled to comment freely.

A classic statement of the defence is to be found in a summing-up to the jury by Diplock J. A prominent Labour politician sued a newspaper for alleging that he was insincere in expressing political hostility to Germany when he was chairman of a company which marketed German cars.

Extract 10.5.3

Silkin v Beaverbrook Newspapers Ltd [1958] 1 WLR 743, at 746–747 (QBD)

DIPLOCK J: Let us look a little more closely at the way in which the law balances the rights of the public man, on the one hand, and the rights of the public, on the other, in matters of freedom of speech. In the first place, every man, whether he is in public life or not, is entitled not to have lies told about him; and by that is meant that one is not entitled to make statements of fact about a person which are untrue and which redound to his discredit, that is to say, tend to lower him in the estimation of right-thinking men.

The first point, therefore, is that you should not misstate the material facts on which you are commenting. That is common sense and it is the common law. In a great many libel actions one of the matters which the jury have to consider is whether the facts are materially misstated. . . .

[His Lordship said that the second and very important requirement was that the subject of the comment should be a matter of public interest. In the present case the plaintiff's attitude to Germany and the Germans was a matter of public interest, not a mere matter of private interest, and his Lordship so directed the jury. He continued:] What are the limits of the right of comment? Quite rightly they are very wide. First of all, who is entitled to comment? The answer to that is 'everyone.' A newspaper reporter or a newspaper editor has exactly the same rights, neither more nor less, than every other citizen, and the test is no different whether the comment appears in a Sunday newspaper with an enormous circulation, or in a letter from a private person to a friend or, subject to some technical difficulties with which you need not be concerned, is said to an acquaintance in a train or in a public-house. So in deciding whether this was fair comment or not, you dismiss from your minds the fact that it was published in a newspaper, and you will not, I am sure, be influenced in any way by any prejudice you may have for or against newspapers any more than you will be influenced in any way by any prejudice which you may have for or against Lord Silkin's politics. Those are matters which you will, I am sure, all of you, dismiss from your minds.

I have been referring, and counsel in their speeches to you have been referring, to fair comment, because that is the technical name which is given to this defence, or, as I should prefer to say, which is given to the right of every citizen to comment on matters of public interest. But the expression 'fair comment' is a little misleading. It may give you the impression that you, the jury, have to decide whether you agree with the comment, whether you think it is fair. If that were the question you had to decide, you realize that the limits of freedom which the law allows would be greatly curtailed. People are entitled to hold and to express freely on matters of public interest strong views, views which some of you, or indeed all of you, may think are exaggerated, obstinate or prejudiced, provided – and this is the important thing – that they are views which they honestly hold. The basis of our public life is that the crank, the enthusiast, may say what he honestly thinks just as much as the reasonable man or woman who sits on a jury, and it would be a sad day for freedom of speech in this country if a jury were to apply the test of whether it agrees with the comment instead of applying the true test: was this an opinion, however exaggerated, obstinate or prejudiced, which was honestly held by the writer?

Though the comment must not misstate the facts on which it is based, the defence will not fail just because the defendant is unable to substantiate every allegation of underlying fact, provided that the comment was fair in relation to those facts which are proved.[26] Nor need the comment itself set out the facts on which it is based. It is enough to refer to them, as happens in the course of a theatre or film review.

But the fair comment defence can only be made when the defamatory imputation is an expression of opinion, rather than an allegation of fact. It will not always be easy to characterise a statement as one or the other. The issue in the next case was whether, in characterising allegations, the jury should have regard only to the letter (to a newspaper) in which they were made, or could also take into account the article to which it was a reply. The claimant had written an article in the *Daily Telegraph* criticising the BBC Russian Service for its recruitment policies. The defendant's letter, published in the same newspaper five days later, suggested (in paragraphs 6 and 7) that the article in effect demanded a blood test for employment in the Russian Service and the dismissal of non-Russian staff.

[26] Defamation Act 1952, s 6.

Extract 10.5.4

Telnikoff v Matusevitch [1992] 2 AC 343, 352–353 (HL)

LORD KEITH OF KINKEL: The question then arises whether it is permissible to have regard to the whole terms of the plaintiff's article, not only the sentence from it quoted in the letter, in determining whether paragraphs 6 and 7 of the letter contain statements of fact or are pure comment. In my opinion the letter must be considered on its own. The readers of the letter must have included a substantial number of persons who had not read the article or who, if they had read it, did not have its terms fully in mind. If to such persons the letter appeared in paragraphs 6 and 7 to contain statements of fact about what the plaintiff had written in his article, which as I have already indicated might well be the case, then in the eyes of those persons the plaintiff would clearly be defamed. The matter cannot turn on the likelihood or otherwise of readers of the letter having read the article. In some cases many readers of a criticism of some subject matter may be familiar with that subject matter but in other cases very few may be, for example where that subject matter is a speech delivered to a limited audience. The principle must be the same in either case.

Lloyd L.J. in the course of his judgment in the Court of Appeal was troubled by what he regarded as the anomaly that the jury should not be allowed to consider the terms of the article in deciding whether or not the letter contained only comment, but should be allowed to look at the article, if they decided that question affirmatively, for the purpose of deciding whether or not the comment was fair. For my part, I can see nothing undesirable about that situation. The jury would simply be directed in deciding the first question, to consider the effect of the letter on the mind of a person who had not read the article. Lloyd L.J. also considered that if juries were not allowed to consider the terms of articles upon which newspaper correspondents chose to comment, the whole text of the article would have to be set out in the letter, a condition which would be unacceptable to newspaper editors, so that free discussion of matters of public interest would be restricted. That apprehension is not, in my view, well founded. The writer of a letter to a newspaper has a duty to take reasonable care to make clear that he is writing comment, and not making misrepresentations about the subject matter upon which he is commenting. There is no difficulty about using suitable words for that purpose, such as those which Lloyd L.J. thought capable of being implied. Likewise any newspaper editor should be under no difficulty in observing whether his correspondent has used language apt to make clear that what he writes is pure comment and does not contain misrepresentations about what he is commenting on.

Lord Ackner, dissenting, argued that the majority decision posed real difficulties for the publication of readers' letters and reviews of plays and films. Editors might feel it prudent to set out substantial extracts from the original material for any opinion on its merits to be treated as comment, rather than a statement of fact. However, the *Telnikoff* decision also held that for the defence to succeed the publisher does not have to show that the comment represented his own honest opinion.[27] It is enough that it was objectively fair, an opinion which could have been held by someone. But the claimant may rebut the defence by proving that it was made maliciously: see Section 5(d) below.

(c) Absolute and qualified privilege

It is a defence to show that the allegations were published on a privileged occasion. A privilege may be absolute or qualified. The former provides a complete defence; it is immaterial whether the allegations were true or whether the defendant was malicious. In contrast, proof of malice defeats qualified privilege. But unlike fair comment the facts need not be true where a defence of qualified privilege is raised; further, it is immaterial in libel whether the defendant made the statement carelessly.[28]

Some privileges are recognised by common law, while others have been conferred by statute. Perhaps the best known absolute privilege, the immunity of Members of Parliament from liability for anything said or written during the course of parliamentary proceedings, was conferred by the Bill of Rights 1689.[29] For the media the most useful privileges, absolute and qualified, are those formulated in the Defamation Act 1996. Previously, the privileges had given protection only to newspapers and broadcasters;[30] now they cover all branches of the media, including book and journal publishers. The 1996 legislation makes it clear that the privilege for fair and accurate reports of court proceedings is absolute.[31] Moreover, it has extended qualified privilege to cover the reporting of a wider range of meetings and reports. It is no longer, for instance, limited to the reports of proceedings of the legislature and courts of Commonwealth countries.

Extract 10.5.5

Defamation Act 1996, s 15, and Sched 1, paras 1–12

15.—(1) The publication of any report or other statement mentioned in Schedule 1 to this Act is privileged unless the publication is shown to be made with malice, subject as follows.

---

[27] Lord Keith of Kinkel did not agree with the decision of the Supreme Court of Canada in *Cherneskey v Armadale Publishers* (1978) 90 DLR (3rd) 321.

[28] But there may be liability for the tort of negligent misstatement, if a reference covered by qualified privilege is given carelessly: *Spring v Guardian Assurance* [1995] 2 AC 296. It is unclear whether this decision might undermine the effectiveness of qualified privilege for the media.

[29] Article 9. The privilege may be waived to enable evidence to be given of parliamentary proceedings in the course of a libel action brought by an MP: Defamation Act 1996, s 13, removing the difficulty highlighted by *Allason v Haines and Another* [1996] EMLR 143.

[30] Law of Libel Amendment Act 1888, s 3; Defamation Act 1952, ss 7 and 9.

[31] Defamation 1996, s 14. The privilege extends to reports of proceedings before any court in the UK, the European Court of Justice, the European Court of Human Rights, and international criminal tribunals.

(2) In defamation proceedings in respect of the publication of a report or other statement mentioned in Part II of that Schedule, there is no defence under this section if the plaintiff shows that the defendant—

    (a) was requested by him to publish in a suitable manner a reasonable letter or statement by way of explanation or contradiction, and

    (b) refused or neglected to do so.

For this purpose 'in a suitable manner' means in the same manner as the publication complained of or in a manner that is adequate and reasonable in the circumstances.

(3) This section does not apply to the publication to the public, or a section of the public, of matter which is not of public concern and the publication of which is not for the public benefit.

(4) Nothing in this section shall be construed—

    (a) as protecting the publication of matter the publication of which is prohibited by law, or

    (b) as limiting or abridging any privilege subsisting apart from this section.

SCHEDULE 1
QUALIFIED PRIVILEGE

PART I
STATEMENTS HAVING QUALIFIED PRIVILEGE WITHOUT EXPLANATION OR CONTRADICTION

1. A fair and accurate report of proceedings in public of a legislature anywhere in the world.

2. A fair and accurate report of proceedings in public before a court anywhere in the world.

3. A fair and accurate report of proceedings in public of a person appointed to hold a public inquiry by a government or legislature anywhere in the world.

4. A fair and accurate report of proceedings in public anywhere in the world of an international organisation or an international conference.

5. A fair and accurate copy of or extract from any register or other document required by law to be open to public inspection.

6. A notice or advertisement published by or on the authority of a court, or of a judge or officer of a court, anywhere in the world.

7. A fair and accurate copy of or extract from matter published by or on the authority of a government or legislature anywhere in the world.

8. A fair and accurate copy of or extract from matter published anywhere in the world by an international organisation or an international conference.

PART II
STATEMENTS PRIVILEGED SUBJECT TO EXPLANATION OR CONTRADICTION

9.—(1) A fair and accurate copy of or extract from a notice or other matter issued for the information of the public by or on behalf of—

    (a) a legislature in any member State or the European Parliament;

    (b) the government of any member State, or any authority performing governmental functions in any member State or part of a member State, or the European Commission;

    (c) an international organisation or international conference.

(2) In this paragraph 'governmental functions' includes police functions.

10. A fair and accurate copy of or extract from a document made available by a court in any member State or the European Court of Justice (or any court attached to that court), or by a judge or officer of any such court.

11.—(1) A fair and accurate report of proceedings at any public meeting or sitting in the United Kingdom of—

(a) a local authority or local authority committee;

(b) a justice or justices of the peace acting otherwise than as a court exercising judicial authority;

(c) a commission, tribunal, committee or person appointed for the purposes of any inquiry by any statutory provision, by Her Majesty or by a Minister of the Crown or a Northern Ireland Department;

(d) a person appointed by a local authority to hold a local inquiry in pursuance of any statutory provision;

(e) any other tribunal, board, committee or body constituted by or under, and exercising functions under, any statutory provision.

(2) [*Omitted*]

(3) [*Omitted*]

12.—(1) A fair and accurate report of proceedings at any public meeting held in a member State.

(2) In this paragraph a 'public meeting' means a meeting bona fide and lawfully held for a lawful purpose and for the furtherance or discussion of a matter of public concern, whether admission to the meeting is general or restricted.

Common law qualified privilege covers communications made by a person with a duty or interest, legal or social, in making it to a person with an interest or duty in receiving it. It protects, for instance, personal references from employers and communications between local councillors and their staff. It has been argued that the media should enjoy such a privilege to communicate to the public 'fair information of public interest', at least if it is believed on reasonable grounds to be accurate. Its recognition, whether by development of the common law or by statute, would significantly widen the freedom of the media to report and comment on matters of political interest, without the 'chilling effect' created by apprehension of a libel action.[32] The US Supreme Court, for example, has held that under the First Amendment (see Extract 1.1.2 above) public officials and figures can only succeed in libel, if they prove actual malice, that is, that the defendant knew the allegations were false or was reckless as to their truth.[33] But the suggestion that English law should recognise a privilege of this kind was rejected by the Faulks Committee in its review of libel law in 1975,[34] and also more recently by a Supreme Court Committee on Defamation Practice and Procedure under the chairmanship of Neill LJ.[35]

---

[32] For the 'chilling effect' of libel law, see *Derbyshire Country Council v Times Newspapers* (Extract 10.3.1 above).

[33] *New York Times v Sullivan*, 376 US 254 (1964).

[34] Cmnd 5909 (1975), paras 211–15.

[35] *Report on Practice and Procedure in Defamation*, July 1991, Chapter XIX.

The recognition of a broad privilege for the media, akin to the constitutional defence in the US, was rejected by the Court of Appeal in *Blackshaw v Lord*. A journalist for the *Daily Telegraph* wrongly identified the claimant, a former civil servant in the Department of Energy, as responsible for the loss of a large sum of public money. His name had been mentioned in a telephone conversation between the journalist, Lord, and Smith, the Department's press officer.

Extract 10.5.6

Blackshaw v Lord [1984] QB 1, at 35–36 (CA)

DUNN LJ: In *Webb v Times Publishing Co. Ltd.* [1960] 2 Q.B. 535, 568 Pearson J. accepted that there must be an appropriate status for the report as well as the need for appropriate subject matter, which must be of interest to the public concerned. He held in that case that there was the ready made status of a fair and accurate report of foreign judicial proceedings, and I think that his judgment can be supported on the narrower ground that the privilege was analogous to the well-established privilege attaching to reports of English judicial proceedings, once he had found (as he did) that the report in the newspaper was a matter of legitimate and proper interest to English readers. As in so many of the cases there was no question as to the status of the report, and the only question was whether there was sufficient public interest.

This review of the authorities shows that, save where the publication is of a report which falls into one of the recognised privileged categories, the court must look at the circumstances of the case before it in order to ascertain whether the occasion of the publication was privileged. It is not enough that the publication should be of general interest to the public. The public must have a legitimate interest in receiving the information contained in it, and there must be a correlative duty in the publisher to publish, which depends also on the status of the information which he receives, at any rate where the information is being made public for the first time. Different considerations may arise in cases such as *Adam v Ward* and *Dunford Publicity Studios Ltd. v News Media Ownership Ltd.* [1971] N.Z.L.R. 961 where the matter has already been made public, and the publication in question is by way of defence to a public charge, or correction of a mistake made in a previous publication.

As Cantley J. pointed out in *London Artists Ltd. v Littler* [1968] 1 W.L.R. 607, if the law were otherwise, and if the wider principle on which Pearson J. decided *Webb's* case were applicable, then there would be no need for a plea of fair comment, and anyone could publish any untrue defamatory information provided only that he honestly believed it, and honestly believed that the public had an interest in receiving it.

Apart from *Adam v Ward*, no case before 1952 was cited to us in which a statement issued by or on behalf of a government department was held to be privileged. It may be that in the circumstances of a particular case privilege might have been held to cover such a statement, but it is significant that in that year the position was apparently sufficiently unclear to require legislation.

It is true that the Defamation Act 1952 preserved the common law, and included within its provisions some categories of documents which were already privileged at common law. But the absence of authority before 1952 indicates that the inclusion of such statements would have involved the extension of the doctrine of qualified privilege as it was understood at that date.

However, the question has recently been reconsidered by the courts in litigation brought by the former Prime Minister of Ireland, Albert Reynolds, in respect of an article in the *Sunday Times* alleging that he had misled the Dail and Cabinet colleagues on a sensitive matter. The Court of Appeal held that for the purposes of qualified privilege the media did have a duty to inform the public with regard to matters of public interest and the public had an interest to receive such information. But the privilege extended only to stories from a reliable source; further, they should be checked and the person defamed given a chance to rebut the allegations.[36] There is an extract from the House of Lords decision in this case in the Appendix.

Questions for discussion

1. Do you agree with the *Telnikoff* decision? How should statements of fact be distinguished from expressions of opinion?
2. Should English law recognise a qualified privilege akin to the US rule in *New York Times*?

(d) Malice

Both the qualified privilege and fair comment defences may be defeated if the claimant proves the defendant published the allegations with 'express malice'. This term has a broad meaning.

Extract 10.5.7

Horrocks v Lowe [1975] AC 135, at 149–150 (HL)

LORD DIPLOCK: My Lords, as a general rule English law gives effect to the ninth commandment that a man shall not speak evil falsely of his neighbour. It supplies a temporal sanction: if he cannot prove that defamatory matter which he published was true, he is liable in damages to whomever he has defamed, except where the publication is oral only, causes no damage and falls outside the categories of slander actionable per se. The public interest that the law should provide an effective means whereby a man can vindicate his reputation against calumny has nevertheless to be accommodated to the competing public interest in permitting men to communicate frankly and freely with one another about matters in respect of which the law recognises that they have a

---

[36] *Reynolds v Times Newspapers* [1998] 3 All ER 961.

duty to perform or an interest to protect in doing so. What is published in good faith on matters of these kinds is published on a privileged occasion. It is not actionable even though it be defamatory and turns out to be untrue. With some exceptions which are irrelevant to the instant appeal, the privilege is not absolute but qualified. It is lost if the occasion which gives rise to it is misused. For in all cases of qualified privilege there is some special reason of public policy why the law accords immunity from suit – the existence of some public or private duty, whether legal or moral, on the part of the maker of the defamatory statement which justifies his communicating it or of some interest of his own which he is entitled to protect by doing so. If he uses the occasion for some other reason he loses the protection of the privilege.

So, the motive with which the defendant on a privileged occasion made a statement defamatory of the plaintiff becomes crucial. The protection might, however, be illusory if the onus lay on him to prove that he was actuated solely by a sense of the relevant duty or a desire to protect the relevant interest. So he is entitled to be protected by the privilege unless some other dominant and improper motive on his part is proved. 'Express malice' is the term of art descriptive of such a motive. Broadly speaking, it means malice in the popular sense of a desire to injure the person who is defamed and this is generally the motive which the plaintiff sets out to prove. But to destroy the privilege the desire to injure must be the dominant motive for the defamatory publication; knowledge that it will have that effect is not enough if the defendant is nevertheless acting in accordance with a sense of duty or in bona fide protection of his own legitimate interests.

The motive with which a person published defamatory matter can only be inferred from what he did or said or knew. If it be proved that he did not believe that what he published was true this is generally conclusive evidence of express malice, for no sense of duty or desire to protect his own legitimate interests can justify a man in telling deliberate and injurious falsehoods about another, save in the exceptional case where a person may be under a duty to pass on, without endorsing, defamatory reports made by some other person.

Apart from those exceptional cases, what is required on the part of the defamer to entitle him to the protection of the privilege is positive belief in the truth of what he published or, as it is generally though tautologously termed, 'honest belief.' If he publishes untrue defamatory matter recklessly, without considering or caring whether it be true or not, he is in this, as in other branches of the law, treated as if he knew it to be false. But indifference to the truth of what he publishes is not to be equated with carelessness, impulsiveness or irrationality in arriving at a positive belief that it is true. The freedom of speech protected by the law of qualified privilege may be availed of by all sorts and conditions of men. In affording to them immunity from suit if they have acted in good faith in compliance with a legal or moral duty or in protection of a legitimate interest the law must take them as it finds them. In ordinary life it is rare indeed for people to form their beliefs by a process of logical deduction from facts ascertained by a rigorous search for all available evidence and a judicious assessment of its probative value. In greater or in less degree according to their temperaments, their training, their intelligence, they are swayed by prejudice, rely on intuition instead of reasoning, leap to conclusions on inadequate evidence and fail to recognise the cogency of material which might cast doubt on the validity of the conclusions they reach. But despite the imperfection of the mental process by which the belief is arrived at it may still be 'honest,' that is, a positive belief that the conclusions they have reached are true. The law demands no more.

Even a positive belief in the truth of what is published on a privileged occasion – which is presumed unless the contrary is proved – may not be sufficient to negative express malice if it can be proved that the defendant misused the occasion for some purpose other than that for which the privilege is accorded by the law. The commonest case is where the dominant motive which actuates the defendant is not a desire to perform the relevant duty or to protect the relevant interest, but to give vent to his personal spite or ill will towards the person he defames. If this be proved, then even positive belief in the truth of what is published will not enable the defamer to avail himself of the protection of the privilege to which he would otherwise have been entitled. There may be instances of improper motives which destroy the privilege apart from personal spite. A defendant's dominant motive may have been to obtain some private advantage unconnected with the duty or the interest which constitutes the reason for the privilege. If so, he loses the benefit of the privilege despite his positive belief that what he said or wrote was true.

Judges and juries should, however, be very slow to draw the inference that a defendant was so far actuated by improper motives as to deprive him of the protection of the privilege unless they are satisfied that he did not believe that what he said or wrote was true or that he was indifferent to its truth or falsity.

(e) Offer of amends

The Defamation Act 1952 provided an offer of amends defence to an action for 'unintentional defamation', where, for example, the media were unaware that a reasonable man would understand the allegations to refer to the claimant (see Extracts 10.3.2 and 10.3.3). But it was rarely used. The Defamation Act 1996, implementing the Neill Committee proposal,[37] should give the defence a more prominent role. An offer to make amends is an offer to publish a suitable correction and sufficient apology in a reasonable manner, and to pay compensation to be agreed by the parties or assessed by the court.[38] It will be valuable to newspapers which realise they have got the facts wrong and are prepared to make amends. If the claimant accepts an offer of amends, he may not bring defamation proceedings, but is only entitled to enforce the offer. In default of agreement, compensation is to be determined by a judge, not a jury, on the same principles as damages in libel proceedings.[39] But if the plaintiff considers the media knew or 'had reason to believe' its allegations were false, it can decline the offer and sue for damages in the usual way.[40]

---

[37] *Report on Practice and Procedure in Defamation*, July 1991, Chapter VII. Also see LCD Consultation Paper, *Reforming Defamation Law and Procedure*, July 1995.
[38] Defamation Act 1996, s 2.
[39] Ibid, s 3.
[40] Ibid, s 4. Note that the claimant must prove the defendant knew the allegations were false and defamatory.

6. REMEDIES FOR LIBEL

(a) The presumption against interim injunctions

While permanent injunctions to restrain publication are frequently granted, the courts are reluctant to grant interim (formerly, interlocutory) injunctions to restrain publication of an alleged libel before trial. This is an aspect of the hostility to prior restraints on the media, discussed in Chapter 1. The application of this principle to libel law is known as the rule in *Bonnard v Perryman*.

Extract 10.6.1

Bonnard v Perryman [1891] 2 Ch 269, at 284 (CA)

LORD COLERIDGE CJ: But it is obvious that the subject-matter of an action for defamation is so special as to require exceptional caution in exercising the jurisdiction to interfere by injunction before the trial of an action to prevent an anticipated wrong. The right of free speech is one which it is for the public interest that individuals should possess, and, indeed, that they should exercise without impediment, so long as no wrongful act is done; and, unless an alleged libel is untrue, there is no wrong committed; but, on the contrary, often a very wholesome act is performed in the publication and repetition of an alleged libel. Until it is clear that an alleged libel is untrue, it is not clear that any right at all has been infringed; and the importance of leaving free speech unfettered is a strong reason in cases of libel for dealing most cautiously and warily with the granting of interim injunctions. . . . In the particular case before us, indeed, the libellous character of the publication is beyond dispute, but the effect of it upon the Defendant can be finally disposed of only by a jury, and we cannot feel sure that the defence of justification is one which, on the facts which may be before them, the jury may find to be wholly unfounded; nor can we tell what may be the damages recoverable. Moreover, the decision at the hearing may turn upon the question of the general character of the Plaintiffs; and this is a point which can rarely be investigated satisfactorily upon affidavit before the trial, – on which further it is not desirable that the Court should express an opinion before the trial.

Defendants may even claim the protection of the *Bonnard v Perryman* rule when they published the libel out of self-interest or vindictiveness.[41] It is unclear whether the rule survives the Human Rights Act 1998 provision that no interim relief is to be granted unless the court is satisfied the applicant is likely to establish at trial that publication should not be allowed.[42] Arguably, the statutory test will be easier to satisfy than the rule which precludes interim relief unless the court is 'sure' that any defence will fail.

---

[41] *Holley v Smyth* [1998] 1 All ER 853 (CA).
[42] Human Rights Act 1998, s 12(3): see Extract 1.5.3 above.

(b) Damages

Damages are the principal remedy for libel. In contrast to continental European legal systems, there is no legally enforceable right of reply: see Chapter 2, Section 3(b). Nor is there any right to have a libellous allegation corrected, though the publication of a correction, or statement by way of explanation or contradiction, may be required as part of an accepted offer of amends or as a condition for reliance on the qualified privilege defence: see Sections 5(c) and (e) above.

Libel damages may be classified in a number of ways. One distinction is between *general* and *special* damages. The latter compensate the plaintiff for any particular financial loss, for example cancellation of a contract, shown to have resulted from the publication. They are much less important than general damages, which are presumed to follow publication of the libel.[43] The claimant does not have to prove the particular respects in which it has damaged his reputation or injured his feelings.[44] General damages can be classified as *compensatory*, *aggravated*, and *exemplary* (sometimes known as punitive) damages.

The subjective character of general damages – 'damages at large', as they are sometimes described – was emphasised by Lord Hailsham LC in *Broome v Cassell & Co*, a leading authority on the award of exemplary damages. *Sutcliffe v Pressdram* is notable for its exposition of the role of the jury in awarding damages; Nourse LJ also explains the distinction between 'aggravated', really an element of compensatory, damages and exemplary damages.

Extract 10.6.2

Broome v Cassell & Co [1972] AC 1027, at 1071 (HL)

LORD HAILSHAM OF ST MARYLEBONE LC: In actions of defamation and in any other actions where damages for loss of reputation are involved, the principle of restitutio in integrum has necessarily an even more highly subjective element. Such actions involve a money award which may put the plaintiff in a purely financial sense in a much stronger position than he was before the wrong. Not merely can he recover the estimated sum of his past and future losses, but, in case the libel, driven underground, emerges from its lurking place at some future date, he must be able to point to a sum awarded by a jury sufficient to convince a bystander of the baselessness of the charge. As Windeyer J. well said in *Uren v John Fairfax & Sons Pty. Ltd.*, 117 C.L.R. 115, 150:

'It seems to me that, properly speaking, a man defamed does not get compensation *for* his damaged reputation. He gets damages *because* he

---

[43] In contrast, damages must generally be proved in the case of slander.
[44] See E M Barendt, 'What is the point of libel law?', (1999) 52 *Current Legal Problems* 110.

was injured in his reputation, that is simply because he was publicly defamed. For this reason, compensation by damages operates in two ways – as a vindication of the plaintiff to the public and as consolation to him for a wrong done. Compensation is here a solatium rather than a monetary recompense for harm measurable in money.'

This is why it is not necessarily fair to compare awards of damages in this field with damages for personal injuries. Quite obviously, the award must include factors for injury to the feelings, the anxiety and uncertainty undergone in the litigation, the absence of apology, or the reaffirmation of the truth of the matters complained of, or the malice of the defendant. The bad conduct of the plaintiff himself may also enter into the matter, where he has provoked the libel, or where perhaps he has libelled the defendant in reply. What is awarded is thus a figure which cannot be arrived at by any purely objective computation. This is what is meant when the damages in defamation are described as being 'at large.'

Extract 10.6.3

Sutcliffe v Pressdram Ltd [1991] 1 QB 153, at 182–184 (CA)

NOURSE LJ: When one turns to the matter of damages the primacy of the jury is seen to be even more firmly established. I do not know that it was ever doubted that the amount of the damages should be left to the jury. The rule received the unqualified support of Scrutton L.J. in *Youssoupoff v Metro-Goldwyn-Mayer Pictures Ltd.* (1934) 50 T.L.R. 581, 584:

'The constitution has thought, and I think there is great advantage in it, that the damages to be paid by a person who says false things about his neighbour are best decided by a jury representing the public, who may state the view of the public as to the action of the man who makes false statements about his neighbour, the plaintiff.'

This rule had nothing to do with the freedom of the press, being only an application of the general practice of the common law courts for the amount of the damages to be assessed by the jury and not by the judge. It may be that until recently the press were as content with the rule as was anyone else. But Mr. Lightman, for the defendants, has said that the recent large awards of damages in libel cases against newspapers, in some of which at any rate no claim for exemplary damages has been made, have put the press in fear, perhaps even in despair, of the law. It is said that they have endangered the freedom of the press to investigate and report fearlessly on matters of public interest. That is without doubt a consideration of great importance, although it must be said that the value of any freedom cannot properly be estimated without asking whether there has been an acceptance of the responsibilities which go with it, an acceptance with which not every section of the press can justly be credited. Be that as it may, these recent large awards have raised an important question in the public mind. Ought damages in defamation cases to be assessed not by the jury but by the judge?

In most early systems of law injuries committed by the spoken or written word were treated as remediable not by compensation to the injured but by punishment of those who committed them; the substitution of public opprobrium for private revenge. It was therefore only natural in systems such as our own, where the civil action has been developed out of the criminal and has virtually replaced it, that juries should have tended to include a punitive, now called an 'exemplary', element in their awards of damages and, moreover, that judges should not have discouraged them from doing so. In the 18th century a similar tendency had been seen in the actions brought before Lord Camden, then Sir Charles Pratt C.J., in the Court of Common Pleas for trespass and false imprisonment arising out of the illegality of general warrants; see e.g. *Wilkes v Wood* (1763) Lofft. 1 and *Huckle v Money* (1763) 2 Wils. 205. For the greater part of this century (and I assume throughout the 19th century) it was thought to be the law that an award of general damages in defamation cases could include an exemplary element if the conduct of the defendant had been so wanton as to merit punishment. But in *Broome v Cassell & Co. Ltd.* [1972] A.C. 1027 the House of Lords, affirming and applying to defamation cases their earlier decision in *Rookes v Barnard* [1964] A.C. 1129 (an intimidation case), authoritatively held that exemplary damages can only be awarded in three instances, of which the only one with any practical relevance to defamation cases is where the defendant, either with knowledge of the tort or recklessly, decides to publish because the prospects of material advantage to him outweigh the prospects of material loss. In all other cases the damages may be compensatory only.

The rule having been settled at the highest level, it has ever since been loyally applied by judges at trial and in this court. But I cannot help thinking that the occasions on which exemplary damages are now claimed in defamation cases are rarer than the framers of the rule would have expected. More significantly, it is possible that they did not well appreciate the difficulties which its application would cause to juries, and perhaps to judges also. The difficulty most in point is that compensatory damages may include compensation for the natural injury to the plaintiff's feelings at having been written or spoken of in defamatory terms, injury which can be aggravated by the defendant's subsequent conduct. In *Broome v Cassell & Co. Ltd.* [1972] A.C. 1027, Lord Reid, speaking of the wide bracket within which an amount of compensation might reasonably fall and echoing the words of Pearson L.J. in *McCarey v Associated Newspapers Ltd. (No. 2)* [1965] 2 Q.B. 86, 104, said, at p. 1085:

> 'It has long been recognised that in determining what sum within that bracket should be awarded, a jury, or other tribunal, is entitled to have regard to the conduct of the defendant. He may have behaved in a high-handed, malicious, insulting or oppressive manner, in committing the tort or he or his counsel may at the trial have aggravated the injury by what they there said. That would justify going to the top of the bracket and awarding as damages the largest sum that could fairly be regarded as compensation.'

There are statements to the same effect in the speeches of Lord Devlin in *Rookes v Barnard* [1964] A.C. 1129, 1221, and of Lord Hailsham of St. Marylebone L.C. in *Broome v Cassell & Co. Ltd.* [1972] A.C. 1027, 1073, and of Lord Diplock, at p. 1124. In a case where compensation for injury to the plaintiff's feelings, original or aggravated, is claimed, the attention of the jury may thus be directed towards the reprehensible conduct of the defendant. And however carefully the judge might seek to protect them against it, it would not be surprising if an element, even a large one, in their award exceeding a due consideration for the plaintiff's feelings and trespassed into punishment of the defendant's conduct.

The conduct of a defendant which may often be regarded as aggravating the injury to the plaintiff's feelings, so as to support a claim for 'aggravated' damages, includes a failure to make any or any sufficient apology and with-drawal; a repetition of the libel; conduct calculated to deter the plaintiff from proceeding; persistence, by way of a prolonged or hostile cross-examination of the plaintiff or in turgid speeches to the jury, in a plea of justification which is bound to fail; the general conduct either of the preliminaries or of the trial itself in a manner calculated to attract further wide publicity; and persecution of the plaintiff by other means. I think it likely that many of these misconducts were featured in many of the recent cases in which these large awards have been made. Nobody could say that the jury were not entitled to view them with abhorrence. Nobody could really blame the jury if, as representatives of the public and not as lawyers, they included an exemplary element in their award.

The size of jury awards has frequently been criticised, particularly by the media. The award of £1,500,000 to Lord Aldington against the author and distributor of a pamphlet – alleging he had been responsible in 1945 for handing over Cossack prisoners of war to the Soviet authorities – led to an application to the European Court of Human Rights. It held unanimously that UK law did not afford adequate safeguards against disproportionately large awards; the award of such a large sum violated freedom of expression.[45]

Jury awards have been criticised as excessive in relation to awards in personal injury cases. In the *Rantzen* case,[46] the Court of Appeal held it would be inappropriate to refer juries to awards in previous libel actions or to awards for personal injuries. But it did permit them to be referred to awards made by the Court of Appeal. Subsequently in the *Elton John* case, it changed its approach.[47] The case arose from the publication of a feature in the *Sunday Mirror* alleging that the entertainer practised bizarre eating habits. The Master of the Rolls admitted that libel awards had given rise to justified criticism, though that was not the fault of juries, acting without adequate guidance from the courts. He agreed with *Rantzen*, insofar as it had held that juries should not for the time being be reminded of previous awards, which in the absence of direction from the judge would provide unreliable pointers, and insofar as

---

[45] *Tolstoy v UK* [1996] EMLR 152.

[46] *Rantzen v Mirror Group Newspapers* [1994] QB 670 (CA).

[47] The award of exemplary (or punitive) damages is controversial in principle; the defendant is punished on the civil burden of proof, and the plaintiff receives a windfall in terms of damages which go beyond what is appropriate to compensate him. The Law Commission has however proposed their retention: see *Aggravated, Exemplary and Restitutionary Damages*, Law Com No 247, 1997, Part V.

it had held that reference could be made to awards made or approved by the Court of Appeal. But then his judgment took a more radical turn.

Extract 10.6.4

Elton John v MGN Ltd [1996] 2 All ER 35, at 53–55, 57–58 (CA)

SIR THOMAS BINGHAM MR: In [*Rantzen*] the Court of Appeal essentially adopted the approach of Lord Hailsham LC in *Cassell & Co Ltd v Broome* in concluding that there was no satisfactory way in which conventional awards in actions for damages for personal injuries could be used to provide guidance for an award in an action for defamation. Much depends, as we now think, on what is meant by guidance: it is one thing to say (and we agree) that there can be no precise equiparation between a serious libel and (say) serious brain damage; but it is another to point out to a jury considering the award of damages for a serious libel that the maximum conventional award for pain and suffering and loss of amenity to a plaintiff suffering from very severe brain damage is about £125,000 and that this is something of which the jury may take account.

It is of interest that in the present case Drake J, who has much recent experience in this field, expressed some criticism of the existing rules. He observed:

> '. . . counsel made submissions on the extent to which it is proper to address the jury in speeches or in the summing up on the quantum of damages. I need only say that although I think the law is in need of change, I shall have regard to the guidelines given by the Court of Appeal in *Rantzen v Mirror Group Newspapers (1986) Ltd* [1993] 4 All ER 975, [1994] QB 670. I shall therefore not make any comparison with awards in personal injury cases. I shall invite the jury to consider the purchasing power of any award they make.'

It has often, and rightly, been said that there can be no precise correlation between a personal injury and a sum of money. The same is true, perhaps even more true, of injury to reputation. There is force in the argument that to permit reference in libel cases to conventional levels of award in personal injury cases is simply to admit yet another incommensurable into the field of consideration. There is also weight in the argument, often heard, that conventional levels of award in personal injury cases are too low and therefore provide an uncertain guide. But these awards would not be relied on as any exact guide, and of course there can be no precise correlation between loss of a limb, or of sight, or quadriplegia, and damage to reputation. But if these personal injuries respectively command conventional awards of, at most, about £52,000, £90,000 and £125,000 for pain and suffering and loss of amenity (of course excluding claims based on loss of earnings, the cost of care and other specific financial claims), juries may properly be asked to consider whether the injury to his reputation of which the plaintiff complains should fairly justify any greater compensation. The conventional compensatory scales in personal injury cases must be taken to represent fair compensation in such cases unless and until those scales are amended by the courts or by Parliament. It is in our view offensive to public opinion, and rightly so, that a defamation plaintiff should recover damages for injury to reputation greater, perhaps by a significant factor, than if that same plaintiff had been rendered a helpless cripple or an insensate vegetable. The time has in our view come when judges, and counsel, should be free to draw the attention of juries to these comparisons.

Reference to an appropriate award and an appropriate bracket

It has been the invariable practice in the past that neither counsel nor the judge may make any suggestion to the jury as what would be an appropriate award . . .

In *Sutcliffe v Pressdram* [1990] 1 All ER 269 at 292, [1991] 1 QB 153 at 190 Russell LJ gave his reasons for rejecting the argument that counsel or the judge might be allowed to refer to figures. He approved the following passage in the summing up by Michael Davies J in that case:

'Well, supposing I were to suggest a figure to you or a bracket. Supposing I were to say: "If she succeeds, what about giving her between so much and so much." Well, there are two possibilities. One is that you would say I was quite wrong and you would either give much more than I suggested or much less. Well now, can you imagine what would happen then? The party that did not like it, the plaintiff if you have given much less, or the defendant if you have given much more than I suggested, would be off to the Court of Appeal saying: "Well, look at that jury, they were quite unreasonable. Here was this experienced judge suggesting a figure to them and they ignored it." You can see readily how that would happen. Supposing you did give the figure, or very close to the figure, that I suggested to you, well then, you would have been wasting your time here on damages, you would simply be acting as a rubber stamp for me . . . So we look to you, as representatives of the public, applying the principles I have indicated, if you come to damages, to come to that figure.'

We have come to the conclusion, however, that the reasons which have been given for prohibiting any reference to figures are unconvincing. Indeed, far from developing into an auction (and we do not see how it could), the process of mentioning figures would, in our view, induce a mood of realism on both sides.

In personal injury actions it is now commonplace for the advocates on both sides to address the judge in some detail on the quantum of the appropriate award. Any apprehension that the judge might receive a coded message as to the amount of any payment into court has not to our knowledge been realised. The judge is not in any way bound by the bracket suggested, but he finds it helpful as a check on his own provisional assessment. We can for our part see no reason why the parties' respective counsel in a libel action should not indicate to the jury the level of award which they respectively contend to be appropriate, nor why the judge in directing the jury should not give a similar indication. The plaintiff will not wish the jury to think that his main object is to make money rather than clear his name. The defendant will not wish to add insult to injury by underrating the seriousness of the libel. So we think the figures suggested by responsible counsel are likely to reflect the upper and lower bounds of a realistic bracket. The jury must, of course, make up their own mind and must be directed to do so. They will not be bound by the submission of counsel or the indication of the judge. If the jury make an award outside the upper or lower bounds of any bracket indicated and such award is the subject of appeal, real weight must be given to the possibility that their judgment is to be preferred to that of the judge.

The modest but important changes of practice described above would not in our view undermine the enduring constitutional position of the libel jury. Historically, the significance of the libel jury has lain not in their role of assessing damages, but in their role of deciding whether the publication complained of is a libel or no. The changes which we favour will, in our opinion, buttress the constitutional role of the libel jury by rendering their proceedings more rational and so more acceptable to public opinion.

Exemplary damages

. . .

We . . . consider that where exemplary damages are claimed the jury should in future receive some additional guidance to make it clear that before such damages can be awarded the jury must be satisfied that the publisher had no genuine belief in the truth of what he published. The publisher must have suspected that the words were untrue and have deliberately refrained from taking obvious steps which, if taken, would have turned suspicion into certainty.

Secondly, the publisher must have acted in the hope or expectation of material gain. It is well established that a publisher need not be shown to have made any precise or arithmetical calculation. But his unlawful conduct must have been motivated by mercenary considerations: the belief that he would be better off financially if he violated the plaintiff's rights than if he did not. Mere publication of a newspaper for profit is not enough.

We do not accept, as was argued, that in seeking to establish that the conditions for awarding exemplary damages have been met the plaintiff must satisfy the criminal, rather than the civil, standard of proof. But a jury should in our judgment be told that as the charge is grave, so should the proof be clear. An inference of reprehensible conduct and cynical calculation of mercenary advantage should not be lightly drawn. . . .

It is plain on the authorities that it is only where the conditions for making an exemplary award are satisfied, and only when the sum awarded to the plaintiff as compensatory damages is not itself sufficient to punish the defendant, show that tort does not pay and deter others from acting similarly, that an award of exemplary damages should be added to the award of compensatory damages. Since the jury will not know, when making their decision, what costs order will be made, it would seem that no account can be taken of the costs burden which the unsuccessful defendant will have to bear, although this could in itself have a punitive and deterrent effect. It is clear that the means of the defendant are relevant to the assessment of damages. Also relevant are his degree of fault and the amount of any profit he may be shown actually to have made from his unlawful conduct.

The authorities give judges no help in directing juries on the quantum of exemplary damages. Since, however, such damages are analogous to a criminal penalty, and although paid to the plaintiff play no part in compensating him, principle requires that an award of exemplary damages should never exceed the minimum sum necessary to meet the public purpose underlying such damages, that of punishing the defendant, showing that tort does not pay and deterring others.

The Court of Appeal reduced the jury award of compensatory damages from £75,000 to £25,000, and exemplary damages from £275,000 to £75,000.

But the Court of Appeal is not always willing to interfere with jury awards. It dismissed an appeal from an award of £45,000 against the *Sunday Times* in respect of an article in its business section, wrongly alleging the plaintiff was being sued for defaulting on a loan and was filing for bankruptcy.

Extract 10.6.5

Kiam v Neil (No 2) [1996] 4 EMLR 493, at 507–508, 510 (CA)

BELDAM LJ: It is, I think, necessary to bear in mind that Parliament has repeatedly declined to attenuate the right of a plaintiff who claims trial by jury in a libel action ... Whilst it is tempting to think that the greater the guidance given by judges, the more rational the jury's conclusion is likely to be, it seems to me that if the failure of the jury to keep its award within bounds indicated by a judge gives rise merely to the possibility that their judgment is to be preferred to that of the judge, the court may appear to preserve only the semblance of a right which Parliament has repeatedly affirmed.

. . .

Unless the *Times* establishes that the award ... is out of proportion, this court would not be entitled to substitute its own assessment, nor would it be sensible to accede to [counsel for *The Times'*s] invitation to lay down guidelines for this or similar cases.

. . .

... [W]as an award of £45,000 excessive in the sense that it exceeded the sum which a jury could reasonably have regarded as proportional to the injury done to Mr Kiam? The jury were entitled to have regard to the fact that the *Times* publication was irresponsible. No effort was made to check its accuracy ... The jury could properly take into account the prominence of Mr Kiam's reputation when deciding what figure was required to vindicate it. They were also entitled to take account of the fact that it struck at the core of his life's achievement and personality and that ... it had a prolonged and significant effect on him personally. Judged by the criteria of reasonableness and proportionality, I do not find an award of £45,000 for a widespread, grave and irresponsible assertion of insolvency against a prominent entrepreneur to be excessive and would dismiss the appeal.

It is therefore unclear how far the *Elton John* decision marks a radical step in controlling jury awards.[48]

Questions for discussion
1. Are the principles in the *Elton John* decision satisfactory?
2. Should the jury assess damages in libel cases?

7. REFORM: THE NEW SUMMARY PROCEDURE

The principal object of the Defamation Act 1996 is to remove trivial cases from jury trial.[49] That will be achieved partly by the revision of the offer of amends defence to encourage the defendant to offer the publication of a correction and apology, with the incentive that any compensation will be assessed by a judge without a jury (see Section 5(e) above). But the most radical reform is the introduction of a summary procedure.[50]

Extract 10.7.1

Defamation Act 1996, s 8

8.—(1) In defamation proceedings the court may dispose summarily of the plaintiff's claim in accordance with the following provisions.

(2) The court may dismiss the plaintiff's claim if it appears to the court that it has no realistic prospect of success and there is no reason why it should be tried.

(3) The court may give judgment for the plaintiff and grant him summary relief (see section 9) if it appears to the court that there is no defence to the claim which has a realistic prospect of success, and that there is no other reason why the claim should be tried.

Unless the plaintiff asks for summary relief, the court shall not act under this subsection unless it is satisfied that summary relief will adequately compensate him for the wrong he has suffered.

(4) In considering whether a claim should be tried the court shall have regard to—

    (a) whether all the persons who are or might be defendants in respect of the publication complained of are before the court;

    (b) whether summary disposal of the claim against another defendant would be inappropriate;

---

[48] But see *Jones v Pollard* [1997] EMLR 233, where the Court of Appeal applied the principles of *Elton John* to reduce a jury award of £100,000 to £40,000.

[49] The Defamation Act 1996 has also reduced the normal limitation period for bringing a libel action to one year, with a broad judicial discretion to extend the period in appropriate cases: s 5.

[50] For the background to this proposal, see LCD Consultation Paper, *Reforming Defamation Law and Procedure* (July, 1995), Chapter 6.

(c) the extent to which there is a conflict of evidence;

(d) the seriousness of the alleged wrong (as regards the content of the statement and the extent of publication); and

(e) whether it is justifiable in the circumstances to proceed to a full trial.

(5) Proceedings under this section shall be heard and determined without a jury.

Under s 9 of the Defamation Act 1996, summary relief may include an award of damages, limited (at the moment) to £10,000, a declaration that the statement was false and defamatory of the claimant, and an order that the defendant publish a suitable correction and apology. The impact of these reforms will largely depend on the attitudes of the media and of the judges. It is uncertain how far newspapers and other media defendants will attempt to insist on their 'right' to jury trial or will accept summary disposal of many cases. Equally, it is unpredictable how willing judges will be to exercise their power to resolve libel claims instead of sending them for full jury trial. The courts remain attached to the role of the jury in libel law and so may be reluctant to exercise the power of summary trial. If that is the case, the 1996 reforms may turn out to be relatively insignificant, and libel law will continue to exercise a serious 'chilling effect' on media freedom.

11

PRIVACY AND BREACH OF CONFIDENCE

1. INTRODUCTION

English law has hitherto not recognised an independent tort of privacy. The media have, therefore, been free to reveal details of, say, a politician's or an entertainer's private life, in particular his current or previous sexual relationships. On the other hand, the courts may prevent the disclosure of confidential information. There is considerable overlap between this remedy for breach of confidence and the protection of privacy; it may mean that in many situations the former remedy in effect protects personal privacy.[1]

The elements of the jurisdiction to restrain breach of confidence will be discussed in Section 2, while Section 3 is concerned with the defences to that action. Many of them would also apply to a statutory privacy right (discussed in Section 4), and would protect the freedom of the media to report matters of real interest to the public. Other remedies for infringement of privacy by the press and broadcasters are discussed in Section 5; the final part of this chapter raises the implications of the Human Rights Act 1998 for privacy and the media.

In contrast to the venerable history of defamation law, the need for some protection for privacy has only been felt over the last 100 years. To some extent the rise of the popular press at the end of the 19th century was responsible for this concern, best expressed in a classic article by Louis Brandeis (later a Justice of the US Supreme Court) and his law partner, Samuel Warren.

Extract 11.1.1

**Samuel D Warren and Louis D Brandeis, 'A Right to Privacy'
(1890) 4 *Harvard Law Review* 193, at 196**

Of the desirability – indeed of the necessity – of some such protection, there can, it is believed, be no doubt. The press is overstepping in every direction

---

[1] See in particular R Wacks, *Privacy and Press Freedom* (Blackstone Press, 1995), especially Chapters 3 and 4; W Wilson, 'Privacy, Confidence, and Press Freedom: A Study in Judicial Activism' (1990) 53 *Modern Law Review* 43.

the obvious bounds of propriety and of decency. Gossip is no longer the resource of the idle and of the vicious, but has become a trade, which is pursued with industry as well as effrontery. To satisfy a prurient taste the details of sexual relations are spread broadcast in the columns of the daily papers. To occupy the indolent, column upon column is filled with idle gossip, which can only be procured by intrusion upon the domestic circle. The intensity and complexity of life, attendant upon advancing civilization, have rendered necessary some retreat from the world, and man, under the refining influence of culture, has become more sensitive to publicity, so that solitude and privacy have become more essential to the individual; but modern enterprise and invention have, through invasions upon his privacy, subjected him to mental pain and distress, far greater than could be inflicted by mere bodily injury. Nor is the harm wrought by such invasions confined to the suffering of those who may be made the subjects of journalistic or other enterprise. In this, as in other branches of commerce, the supply creates the demand. Each crop of unseemly gossip, thus harvested, becomes the seed of more, and, in direct proportion to its circulation, results in a lowering of social standards and of morality. Even gossip apparently harmless, when widely and persistently circulated, is potent for evil. It both belittles and perverts. It belittles by inverting the relative importance of things, thus dwarfing the thoughts and aspirations of a people. When personal gossip attains the dignity of print, and crowds the space available for matters of real interest to the community, what wonder that the ignorant and thoughtless mistake its relative importance. Easy of comprehension, appealing to that weak side of human nature which is never wholly cast down by the misfortunes and frailties of our neighbors, no one can be surprised that it usurps the place of interest in brains capable of other things. Triviality destroys at once robustness of thought and delicacy of feeling. No enthusiasm can flourish, no generous impulse can survive under its blighting influence.

The article had a large impact in the USA, where a number of states introduced privacy rights. Interestingly, Warren and Brandeis based their argument that the common law implicitly recognised a right of privacy on English decisions. The most important of these arose from an action to restrain the unauthorised publication of etchings drawn by Queen Victoria and Prince Albert and of a catalogue of their work. The defendant had obtained the drawings from an employee of the printers to whom they had been given (in confidence, as it would now be phrased) for the purpose of private publication.

Extract 11.1.2

Prince Albert v Strange (1849) 64 ER 293, at 312–313; 2 De G & Sm 652, 697–698 (Ch)

KNIGHT BRUCE V-C: Addressing the attention specifically to the particular instance before the Court, we cannot but see that the etchings executed by the Plaintiff and his Consort for their private use, the produce of their labour, and belonging to themselves, they were entitled to retain in a state of privacy, to withhold from publication. That right, I think it equally clear, was not lost by the limited communications which they appear to have made, nor confined to prohibiting the taking of impressions, without or beyond their consent, from the plates their undoubted property. It extended also, I conceive, to the prevention of persons unduly obtaining a knowledge of the subjects of the plates from publishing (at least by printing or writing), though not by copy or resemblance, a description of them, whether more or less limited or summary, whether in the form of a catalogue or otherwise . . .

I think, therefore, not only that the Defendant here is unlawfully invading the Plaintiff's right, but also that the invasion is of such a kind and affects such property as to entitle the Plaintiff to the preventive remedy of an injunction; and if not the more, yet certainly not the less, because it is an intrusion – an unbecoming and unseemly intrusion – an intrusion not alone in breach of conventional rules, but offensive to that inbred sense of propriety natural to every man – if intrusion, indeed, fitly describes a sordid spying into the privacy of domestic life – into the home (a word hitherto sacred among us), the home of a family whose life and conduct form an acknowledged title, though not their only unquestionable title, to the most marked respect in this country.

2. BREACH OF CONFIDENCE

The decision in the *Prince Albert* case is generally regarded as a seminal authority on breach of confidence. Until relatively recently the equitable jurisdiction to restrain breaches of confidence was used primarily to prevent the improper disclosure of trade secrets. The next two cases show how it may also be employed to stop publication by the media of confidential material of political interest.[2] The first case involved an application by the Attorney General to stop the publication of diaries kept by Richard Crossman, a Cabinet Minister in the Labour government from 1964 to 1970.[3] The second extract is taken from Lord Goff's speech in the *Spycatcher* case, where the government, in the end unsuccessfully (see Section 3 below), attempted to stop publication by English newspapers of extracts from the memoirs of a retired secret service agent.

Extract 11.2.1

Attorney General v Jonathan Cape Ltd [1976] 1 QB 752, at 769–770 (QBD)

LORD WIDGERY CJ: However, the Attorney-General has a powerful reinforcement for his argument in the developing equitable doctrine that a man

---

[2] For its coverage of personal information, see *Argyll v Argyll* [1967] Ch 302 (referred to in Extract 11.2.1) and *Stephens v Avery* [1988] 1 Ch 449.

[3] The application failed on the facts because in the view of Lord Widgery CJ the information had lost its confidential character, as the publication was to take place several years after the events described in the diaries.

shall not profit from the wrongful publication of information received by him in confidence. This doctrine, said to have its origin in *Prince Albert v Strange* (1849) 1 H. & T. 1, has been frequently recognised as a ground for restraining the unfair use of commercial secrets transmitted in confidence. Sometimes in these cases there is a contract which may be said to have been breached by the breach of confidence, but it is clear that the doctrine applies independently of contract: see *Saltman Engineering Co. Ltd. v Campbell Engineering Co. Ltd.* (1948) 65 R.P.C. 203. Again in *Coco v A. N. Clark (Engineers) Ltd.* [1969] R.P.C. 41 Megarry J., reviewing the authorities, set out the requirements necessary for an action based on breach of confidence to succeed. He said, at p. 47:

'In my judgment three elements are normally required if, apart from contract, a case of breach of confidence is to succeed. First, the information itself, in the words of Lord Greene M.R. . . . must "have the necessary quality of confidence about it." Secondly, that information must have been imparted in circumstances importing an obligation of confidence. Thirdly, there must be an unauthorised use of that information to the detriment of the party communicating it.'

It is not until the decision in *Duchess of Argyll v Duke of Argyll* [1967] Ch. 302, that the same principle was applied to domestic secrets such as those passing between husband and wife during the marriage. It was there held by Ungoed-Thomas J. that the plaintiff wife could obtain an order to restrain the defendant husband from communicating such secrets, and the principle is well expressed in the headnote in these terms, at p. 304:

'A contract or obligation of confidence need not be expressed but could be implied, and a breach of contract or trust or faith could arise independently of any right of property or contract . . . and that the court, in the exercise of its equitable jurisdiction, would restrain a breach of confidence independently of any right at law.'

This extension of the doctrine of confidence beyond commercial secrets has never been directly challenged, and was noted without criticism by Lord Denning M.R. in *Fraser v Evans* [1969] 1 Q.B. 349, 361. I am sure that I ought to regard myself, sitting here, as bound by the decision of Ungoed-Thomas J.

Even so, these defendants argue that an extension of the principle of the *Argyll* case to the present dispute involves another large and unjustified leap forward, because in the present case the Attorney-General is seeking to apply the principle to public secrets made confidential in the interests of good government. I cannot see why the courts should be powerless to restrain the publication of public secrets, while enjoying the *Argyll* powers in regard to domestic secrets. Indeed, as already pointed out, the court must have power to deal with publication which threatens national security, and the difference between such a case and the present case is one of degree rather than kind. I conclude, therefore, that when a Cabinet Minister receives information in confidence the improper publication of such information can be restrained by the court, and his obligation is not merely to observe a gentleman's agreement to refrain from publication.

Extract 11.2.2

Attorney General v Guardian Newspapers (No 2) [1990] 1 AC 109, at 281–282 (HL)

LORD GOFF OF CHIEVELEY: I start with the broad general principle (which I do not intend in any way to be definitive) that a duty of confidence arises when confidential information comes to the knowledge of a person (the confidant) in circumstances where he has notice, or is held to have agreed, that the information is confidential, with the effect that it would be just in all the circumstances that he should be precluded from disclosing the information to others. I have used the word 'notice' advisedly, in order to avoid the (here unnecessary) question of the extent to which actual knowledge is necessary; though I of course understand knowledge to include circumstances where the confidant has deliberately closed his eyes to the obvious. The existence of this broad general principle reflects the fact that there is such a public interest in the maintenance of confidences, that the law will provide remedies for their protection.

I realise that, in the vast majority of cases, in particular those concerned with trade secrets, the duty of confidence will arise from a transaction or relationship between the parties – often a contract, in which event the duty may arise by reason of either an express or an implied term of that contract. It is in such cases as these that the expressions 'confider' and 'confidant' are perhaps most aptly employed. But it is well settled that a duty of confidence may arise in equity independently of such cases; and I have expressed the circumstances in which the duty arises in broad terms, not merely to embrace those cases where a third party receives information from a person who is under a duty of confidence in respect of it, knowing that it has been disclosed by that person to him in breach of his duty of confidence, but also to include certain situations, beloved of law teachers – where an obviously confidential document is wafted by an electric fan out of a window into a crowded street, or where an obviously confidential document, such as a private diary, is dropped in a public place, and is then picked up by a passer-by. I also have in mind the situations where secrets of importance to national security come into the possession of members of the public – a point to which I shall refer in a moment. I have however deliberately avoided the fundamental question whether, contract apart, the duty lies simply 'in the notion of an obligation of conscience arising from the circumstances in or through which the information was communicated or obtained' (see *Moorgate Tobacco Co. Ltd. v Philip Morris Ltd. (No. 2)* (1984) 156 C.L.R. 414, 438, *per* Deane J., and see also *Seager v Copydex Ltd.* [1967] 1 W.L.R. 923, 931, *per* Lord Denning M.R.), or whether confidential information may also be regarded as property (as to which see Dr. Francis Gurry's valuable monograph on *Breach of Confidence* (1984), pp. 46–56 and Professor Birks' *An Introduction to the Law of Restitution* (1985), pp. 343–344). I would also, like Megarry J. in *Coco v A. N. Clark (Engineers) Ltd.* [1969] R.P.C. 41, 48, wish to keep open the question whether detriment to the plaintiff is an essential ingredient of an action for breach of confidence. Obviously, detriment or potential detriment to the plaintiff will nearly always form part of his case; but this may not always be necessary. Some possible cases where there need be no detriment are mentioned in the judgment of Megarry J. to which I have just referred (at p. 48), and in Gurry, *Breach of Confidence*, at pp. 407–408. In the present case the point is immaterial, since it is established that in cases of Government secrets the Crown has to establish not only that the information is confidential, but also that publication would be to its 'detriment' in the sense that the public interest requires that it should not be published. That the word 'detriment' should be extended so far as to include such a case perhaps indicates that everything depends upon how wide a meaning can be given to the word 'detriment' in this context.

To this broad general principle, there are three limiting principles to which I wish to refer. The first limiting principle (which is rather an expression of the scope of the duty) is highly relevant to this appeal. It is that the principle of confidentiality only applies to information to the extent that it is confidential. In particular, once it has entered what is usually called the public domain (which means no more than that the information in question is so generally accessible that, in all the circumstances, it cannot be regarded as confidential) then, as a general rule, the principle of confidentiality can have no application to it. I shall revert to this limiting principle at a later stage.

The second limiting principle is that the duty of confidence applies neither to useless information, nor to trivia. There is no need for me to develop this point.

The third limiting principle is of far greater importance. It is that, although the basis of the law's protection of confidence is that there is a public interest that confidences should be preserved and protected by the law, nevertheless that public interest may be outweighed by some other countervailing public interest which favours disclosure. This limitation may apply, as the learned judge pointed out, to all types of confidential information. It is this limiting principle which may require a court to carry out a balancing operation, weighting the public interest in maintaining confidence against a countervailing public interest favouring disclosure.

Some implications of Lord Goff's remarks concerning the duty of confidence were explored in the *Shelley Films* case. A production company wished to keep secret the filming of 'Mary Shelley's Frankenstein'; it obtained an interlocutory (now termed 'interim') injunction against a photographic agency which had supplied a photograph of a scene involving Robert de Niro to a newspaper. Entry to the studios was by permission only, and it was clearly indicated that photography was forbidden without written consent.

Extract 11.2.3

Shelley Films Ltd v Rex Features Ltd [1994] EMLR 134, at 148 (Ch D)

MARTIN MANN QC, Deputy High Court Judge: For present purposes it is necessary only to decide whether there is a serious question whether equity should in all the circumstances of this case impose such an obligation. What then are the relevant circumstances? So far as Shelley is concerned they are in my judgment the obvious and stated commercial interest in protecting its substantial investment by, minimally, being able to provide an undisrupted production environment and to control the timing and manner of release of information about the film, which it has endeavoured to achieve by selecting facilities at Shepperton Studios and endeavouring, so far as practicable to keep out intruders by reasonable, though not overburdensome entry disciplines and preventing by contractual provisions and restrictions upon photographers the dissemination to the public of information unavoidably imparted.

So far as the photographer is concerned, there are the circumstances in which he came to be present at Shepperton Studios and to take the photograph within the set − it matters not in my judgment whether he took the photograph from a vantage point within the set or without it yet still within Shepperton Studios − while knowing that photographs within the studio were prohibited, though I am not convinced that the express photography ban is necessarily an essential ingredient. These, coupled with Shelley's assertion that the release of information in this way is deleterious to its commercial interests, are sufficient in my judgment to establish a serious question with respect to the photographer.

Questions for discussion

1. What are the requirements for a breach of confidence action to succeed? Is a confidential relationship essential?
2. How far might breach of confidence actions prevent spread of the gossip deplored by Warren and Brandeis (Extract 11.1.1 above)?

3. DEFENCES TO BREACH OF CONFIDENCE ACTIONS

The most important remedy for breach of confidence is an injunction to restrain disclosure. Claimants also invariably apply for an interim injunction (previously known as interlocutory injunction) to restrain publication until full trial. Claims for both permanent and interim injunctions are most often resisted by the defendant, particularly by the media, with the argument that there is a public interest in the disclosure.[4] Further, the media may contend that the information has already been published so that it is in the public domain and no longer confidential.

In one leading case concerning the scope of these defences, the claimants were a group of pop stars. After termination of his employment contract,

---

[4] The public interest in the disclosure of criminal and other wrong conduct by employers has been recognised by the Public Interest Disclosure Act 1998 under which workers who make such disclosure may be protected from victimisation.

their press agent wrote disparaging articles about their behaviour for the *Daily Mirror*.

Extract 11.3.1

Woodward v Hutchins [1977] 1 WLR 760, at 763–764 (CA)

LORD DENNING MR: In a proper case the court will be prepared to restrain a servant from disclosing confidential information which he has received in the course of his employment. But this case is quite out of the ordinary. There is no doubt whatever that this pop group sought publicity. They wanted to have themselves presented to the public in a favourable light so that audiences would come to hear them and support them. Mr. Hutchins was engaged so as to produce, or help to produce, this favourable image, not only of their public lives but of their private lives also. If a group of this kind seek publicity which is to their advantage, it seems to me that they cannot complain if a servant or employee of theirs afterwards discloses the truth about them. If the image which they fostered was not a true image, it is in the public interest that it should be corrected. In these cases of confidential information it is a question of balancing the public interest in maintaining the confidence against the public interest in knowing the truth. That appears from *Initial Services Ltd. v Putterill* [1968] 1 Q.B. 396; *Fraser v Evans* [1969] 1 Q.B. 349 and *D. v National Society for the Prevention of Cruelty to Children* [1976] 3 W.L.R. 124. In this case the balance comes down in favour of the truth being told, even if it should involve some beach of confidential information. As there should be 'truth in advertising,' so there should be truth in publicity. The public should not be misled. So it seems to me that the breach of confidential information is not a ground for granting an injunction.

There is a further point. The injunction is so vaguely worded that it would be most difficult for anyone – Mr. Hutchins, or the newspaper or any court afterwards – to know what was prohibited and what was not. It speaks of 'confidential information.' But what is confidential? As Bridge L.J. pointed out in the course of the argument, Mr. Hutchins, as a press agent, might attend a dance which many others attended. Any incident which took place at the dance would be known to all present. The information would be in the public domain. There could be no objection to the incidents being made known generally. It would not be confidential information. So in this case the incident on this Jumbo Jet was in the public domain. It was known to all the passengers on the flight. Likewise with several other incidents in the series. The injunction is framed in such wide terms that it would be impossible for the newspaper or Mr. Hutchins to know where the line should be drawn.

. . .

Finally, there is the balance of convenience. At this late hour, when the paper is just about to go to press, the balance of convenience requires that there should be no injunction. Any remedy for Mr. Tom Jones and his associates should be in damages and damages only. I would allow the appeal, and discharge the injunction.

Extract 11.3.2

Lion Laboratories Ltd v Evans [1985] 2 QB 526, at 536–538 (CA)

The claimant applied for an interlocutory injunction to restrain publication in the *Daily Express* of a report, based on confidential documents supplied to the newspaper by its former employees, alleging defects in breath-test machines (Intoximeters) which it manufactured. The Court of Appeal upheld the defendants' argument that there was a serious defence of public interest to justify the breach of confidence.

STEPHENSON LJ: The problem before the judge and before this court is how best to resolve, before trial, a conflict of two competing public interests. The first public interest is the preservation of the right of organisations, as of individuals, to keep secret confidential information. The courts will restrain breaches of confidence, and breaches of copyright, unless there is just cause or excuse for breaking confidence or infringing copyright. The just cause or excuse with which this case is concerned is the public interest in admittedly confidential information. There is confidential information which the public may have a right to receive and others, in particular the press, now extended to the media, may have a right and even a duty to publish, even if the information has been unlawfully obtained in flagrant breach of confidence and irrespective of the motive of the informer. The duty of confidence, the public interest in maintaining it, is a restriction on the freedom of the press which is recognised by our law, as well as by article 10(2) of the Convention for the Protection of Human Rights and Fundamental Freedoms (1953) (Cmd. 8969); the duty to publish, the countervailing interest of the public in being kept informed of matters which are of real public concern, is an inroad on the privacy of confidential matters. So much is settled by decisions of this court, and in particular by the illuminating judgments of Lord Denning M.R. in *Initial Services Ltd. v Putterill* [1968] 1 Q.B. 396; *Fraser v Evans* [1969] 1 Q.B. 349; *Hubbard v Vosper* [1972] 2 Q.B. 84; *Woodward v Hutchins* [1977] 1 W.L.R. 760; and *per* Lord Denning M.R. (dissenting) in *Schering Chemicals Ltd. v Falkman Ltd.* [1982] Q.B. 1. I add to those the speeches of Lord Wilberforce, Lord Salmon and Lord Fraser of Tullybelton in *British Steel Corporation v Granada Television Ltd.* [1981] A.C. 1096.

There are four further considerations. First, 'there is a wide difference between what is interesting to the public and what it is in the public interest to make known' said Lord Wilberforce in *British Steel Corporation v Granada Television Ltd.*, at p. 1168. The public are interested in many private matters which are no real concern of theirs and which the public have no pressing need to know. Secondly, the media have a private interest of their own in publishing what appeals to the public and may increase their circulation or the numbers of their viewers or listeners; and (I quote from Sir John Donaldson M.R. in *Francome v Mirror Group Newspapers Ltd.* [1984] 1 W.L.R. 892, 898B, 'they are peculiarly vulnerable to the error of confusing the public interest with their own interest.' Thirdly, there are cases in which the public interest is best served by an informer giving the confidential information, not to the press but to the police or some other responsible body, as was suggested by Lord

Denning M.R. in *Initial Services Ltd. v Putterill* [1968] 1 Q.B. 396, 405–406 and by Sir John Donaldson M.R. in *Francome v Mirror Group Newspapers Ltd.* [1984] 1 W.L.R. 892, 898. Fourthly, it was said by Wood V.-C. in 1856, in *Gartside v Outram* (1856) 26 L.J.Ch. 113, 114, 'there is no confidence as to the disclosure of iniquity'; . . .

But I nowhere find any authority for the proposition, except perhaps in the judgment of Ungoed-Thomas J. in *Beloff v Pressdram Ltd.* [1973] 1 All E.R. 241, 260, that some modern form of iniquity on the part of the plaintiffs is the only thing which can be disclosed in the public interest; and I agree with the judge in rejecting the 'no iniquity, no public interest' rule; and in respectfully adopting what Lord Denning M.R. said in *Fraser v Evans* [1969] 1 Q.B. 349, 362, that some things are required to be disclosed in the public interest, in which case no confidence can be prayed in aid to keep them secret, and '[iniquity] is merely an instance of just cause or excuse for breaking confidence.'

Griffiths L.J. put this case in argument. Suppose the plaintiffs had informed the police that their Intoximeter was not working accurately nor safe to use, and the police had replied that they were nevertheless going to continue using it as breath test evidence. Could there then be no defence of public interest if the defendants sought to publish that confidential information, simply because the plaintiffs themselves had done nothing wrong but the police had? There would be the same public interest in publication, whichever was guilty of misconduct; and I cannot think the right to break confidence would be lost, though the public interest remained the same.

Bearing this last consideration in mind, in my opinion we cannot say that the defendants must be restrained because what they want to publish does not show misconduct by the plaintiffs.

We have then, with the other three considerations in mind and remembering that confidentiality is admitted, to ask what the judge called the 'sole question,' namely:

> 'whether the defendants have shown that they have an arguable defence to the plaintiffs' claims in respect of breach of confidentiality and breach of copyright . . .'

. . . To be allowed to publish confidential information, the defendants must do more than raise a plea of public interest; they must show 'a legitimate ground for supposing it is in the public interest for it to be disclosed.' Then as Lord Denning M.R. said in *Woodward v Hutchins* [1977] 1 W.L.R. 760, 764, we 'should not restrain it by interlocutory injunction, but should leave the complainant to his remedy in damages' after (I will assume, though I am not sure that Lord Denning M.R. would have agreed) considering and weighing in the balance all relevant matters such as whether damages would be an adequate remedy to compensate the plaintiffs if they succeeded at the trial.

The public domain defence was upheld in the *Spycatcher* case, after publication of the memoirs of the former secret service agent in the USA and other countries.

Extract 11.3.3

Attorney General v Guardian Newspapers (No 2)
[1990] 1 AC 109, at 260 (HL)

LORD KEITH OF KINKEL: The newspapers which are the respondents in this appeal were not responsible for the world-wide dissemination of the contents of *Spycatcher* which has taken place. It is a general rule of law that a third party who comes into possession of confidential information which he knows to be such, may come under a duty not to pass it on to anyone else. Thus in *Duchess of Argyll v Duke of Argyll* [1967] Ch. 302 the newspaper to which the Duke had communicated the information about the Duchess was restrained by injunction from publishing it. However, in that case there was no doubt but that the publication would cause detriment to the Duchess in the sense I have considered above. In the present case the third parties are 'The Guardian' and the 'Observer' on the one hand and 'The Sunday Times' on the other hand. The first two of these newspapers wish to report and comment upon the substance of the allegations made in *Spycatcher*. They say that they have no intention of serialising it . . . 'The Sunday Times' for their part, wish to complete their serialisation of *Spycatcher*. The question is whether the Crown is entitled to an injunction restraining the three newspapers from doing what they wish to do . . . For the reasons which I have indicated in dealing with the position of Mr. Wright, I am of the opinion that the reports and comments proposed by 'The Guardian' and the 'Observer' would not be harmful to the public interest, nor would the continued serialisation by 'The Sunday Times.' I would therefore refuse an injunction against any of the newspapers. I would stress that I do not base this upon any balancing of public interest nor upon any considerations of freedom of the press, nor upon any possible defences of prior publication or just cause or excuse, but simply upon the view that all possible damage to the interest of the Crown has already been done by the publication of *Spycatcher* abroad and the ready availability of copies in this country.

It is possible, I think, to envisage cases where, even in the light of widespread publication abroad of certain information, a person whom that information concerned might be entitled to restrain publication by a third party in this country. For example, if in the *Argyll* case the Duke had secured the revelation of the marital secrets in an American newspaper, the Duchess could reasonably claim that publication of the same material in England would bring it to the attention of people who would otherwise be unlikely to learn of it and who were more closely interested in her activities than American readers. The publication in England would be more harmful to her than publication in America. Similar considerations would apply to, say, a publication in America by the medical adviser to an English pop group about diseases for which he had treated them. But it cannot reasonably be held in the present case that publication in England now of the contents of *Spycatcher* would do any more harm to the public interest than has already been done.

Questions for discussion

1. Did Lord Denning MR and Stephenson LJ take the same approach to the scope of the public interest defence?

2.   Does, or should, the law admit a public interest in the disclosure of all *truthful* information, at least if it corrects a false impression?

3.   Should the public domain defence be accepted whenever confidential information has already been published in another country or in another branch of the media? Suppose a national newspaper proposes to publish material already available on the Internet or previously published in a local paper?

4. PRIVACY IN ENGLISH LAW

(a) The absence of a privacy tort

In contrast to many states in the USA and to continental European countries,[5] English law has not developed a general tort of privacy. This has implications outside media law. For instance, an individual whose telephone has been tapped, either by the police or by a private detective agency, cannot bring an action for infringement of privacy.[6] (But media publication of information obtained as a result of an unlawful interception might be restrained as a breach of confidence.[7]) In the media law context, the absence of a tort of privacy was deplored in *Kaye v Robertson*, although the Court of Appeal was able to grant a limited interlocutory injunction on the basis of malicious falsehood.[8]

Extract 11.4.1

Kaye v Robertson [1991] FSR 62, at 70 (CA)

Gordon Kaye, a television actor, had been seriously injured while driving his car. After being in intensive care, he was moved to a private ward; notices were posted at its entrance asking visitors to see a member of staff. Ignoring them, journalists from the *Sunday Sport* interviewed and took photographs of Kaye. Medical evidence was given to the effect that he was in no fit condition for an interview; apparently he had no recollection that he had given one. Potter J granted an injunction to stop publication of the photographs and any story to the effect that Kaye had posed for them and granted an interview. The Court of Appeal granted a more limited injunction to restrain publication of the false story that Kaye had consented to the interview.

BINGHAM LJ: Any reasonable and fair-minded person hearing the facts which Glidewell L.J. has recited would in my judgment conclude that these defendants

---

[5]   See B Markesinis (ed), *Protecting Privacy* (Oxford University Press, 1999) for essays on privacy law in European countries and in the USA.

[6]   *Malone v Commissioner of the Police for the Metropolis (No 2)* [1979] 1 Ch 344 (Megarry V-C).

[7]   See *Francome v Mirror Group Newspapers Ltd* [1984] 1 WLR 892 (CA).

[8]   This is generally brought for false and malicious statements about a business or the quality of goods. Damage must be proved.

had wronged the plaintiff. I am therefore pleased to be persuaded that the plaintiff is able to establish, with sufficient strength to justify an interlocutory order, a cause of action against the defendants in malicious falsehood. Had he failed to establish any cause of action, we should of course have been powerless to act, however great our sympathy for the plaintiff and however strong our distaste for the defendants' conduct.

This case nonetheless highlights, yet again, the failure of both the common law of England and statute to protect in an effective way the personal privacy of individual citizens. This has been the subject of much comment over the years, perhaps most recently by Professor Markesinis (*The German Law of Torts*, 2nd edn., 1990, page 316) where he writes:

> 'English law, on the whole, compares unfavourably with German law. True, many aspects of the human personality and privacy are protected by a multitude of existing torts but this means fitting the facts of each case in the pigeon-hole of an existing tort and this process may not only involve strained constructions; often it may also leave a deserving plaintiff without a remedy.'

The defendants' conduct towards the plaintiff here was 'a monstrous invasion of his privacy' (to adopt the language of Griffiths J. in *Bernstein v Skyviews Ltd.* [1978] Q.B. 479 at 489G). If ever a person has a right to be let alone by strangers with no public interest to pursue, it must surely be when he lies in hospital recovering from brain surgery and in no more than partial command of his faculties. It is this invasion of his privacy which underlies the plaintiff's complaint. Yet it alone, however gross, does not entitle him to relief in English law.

The plaintiff's suggested cause of action in libel is in my view arguable, for reasons which Glidewell L.J. has given.[9] We could not give interlocutory relief on that ground. Battery and assault are causes of action never developed to cover acts such as these: they could apply only if the law were substantially extended and the available facts strained to unacceptable lengths. A claim in passing off is hopeless. Fortunately, a cause of action in malicious falsehood exists, but even that obliges us to limit the relief we can grant in a way which would not bind us if the plaintiff's cause of action arose from the invasion of privacy of which, fundamentally, he complains. We cannot give the plaintiff the breadth of protection which I would, for my part, wish. The problems of defining and limiting a tort of privacy are formidable, but the present case strengthens my hope that the review now in progress may prove fruitful.[10]

Laws J has suggested that an action for breach of confidence could be brought to prevent the disclosure to members of the public of photographs of suspects held on police files. But the remarks were obiter; no interlocutory injunction was given as he also found the police would have a clear public interest defence.

---

[9] It was arguable that the article defamed Kaye by implying that he had sold 'exclusive' rights to his story, but the courts are reluctant to grant an interim injunction for libel unless it is inevitable that the claimant will succeed at trial.

[10] Bingham LJ is referring to the review conducted at that time by Sir David Calcutt: see Extract 11.4.4 below.

Extract 11.4.2

Hellewell v Chief Constable of Derbyshire
[1995] 1 WLR 804, at 807 (QBD)

LAWS J: The time came when there was a request to the police to provide photographs of individuals known to be causing particular problems because in some shops new staff might not recognise such troublemakers, and as a result fail to bar them from the premises. Sergeant Portman, who had a particular responsibility for crime prevention work, discussed the request with his superior, the divisional commander, who agreed that it should be complied with. As a result, photographs were copied from the police file onto A4 sheets and handed to shop watch members at a meeting on 16 November 1992.

One such sheet bore a photograph of the plaintiff. It is plain that it was one of those taken at the police station in May 1989. The nature of the photograph, which is subscribed with the plaintiff's name, a number and the date, is such that it would be tolerably clear to anyone looking at it that it was taken in police or prison custody: it is, in common parlance, a 'mugshot.' It would thus at least convey the information that the plaintiff was known to the police.

The Chief Constable's evidence is that guidelines were given to the effect that the photographs were not to be publicly displayed so that only the shopkeepers or their staff might see them. But in June 1993 the plaintiff learnt that his photograph was in use in the Beeston and Long Eaton area. He brings these proceedings for declaratory relief and an injunction to restrain the defendant, the Chief Constable, from disclosing to the public or a section of the public any photograph taken at the police station when he was charged in May 1989.

. . .

There is only one potential cause of action in play here, namely breach of confidence. Although that is not made explicit in the statement of claim, it clearly emerges from the plaintiff's further and better particulars where it is pleaded that: 'the use to which the photograph was put was a breach of . . . confidence.'

I entertain no doubt that disclosure of a photograph may, in some circumstances, be actionable as a breach of confidence. If a photographer is hired to take a photograph to be used only for certain purposes but uses it for an unauthorised purpose of his own, a claim may lie against him: *Pollard v Photographic Co.* (1888) 40 Ch.D. 345. That case concerned portrait photographs of a lady taken for her private use by a hired photographer who then used one of the pictures for a Christmas card which was put on sale in his shop. North J. upheld the plaintiff's claim, both in contract and breach of confidence. If someone with a telephoto lens were to take from a distance and with no authority a picture of another engaged in some private act, his subsequent disclosure of the photograph would, in my judgment, as surely amount to a breach of confidence as if he had found or stolen a letter or diary in which the act was recounted and proceeded to publish it. In such a case, the law would protect what might reasonably be called a right of privacy, although the name accorded to the cause of action would be breach of confidence. It is, of course, elementary that, in all such cases, a defence based on the public interest would be available.

400

Questions for discussion

1. Could Kaye have obtained an injunction on the basis of breach of confidence? (The point does not seem to have been argued.)

2. Are there any good reasons why the courts should not formulate an explicit privacy right in cases such as *Kaye* and *Hellewell*?

(b) The introduction of a statutory privacy right?

Despite the introduction of Bills by back-bench MPs to establish a privacy right, governments have been unwilling to take this step. Perhaps they fear that it would incur the wrath of the press: see Chapter 2, Section 2. But there are also arguments of legal policy for caution. In 1972, the Younger Committee concluded it would be wrong to introduce a general privacy right; instead, so far as the media were concerned, it preferred to rely on breach of confidence and voluntary regulation (at that time, of the Press Council).

Extract 11.4.3

**Younger Committee Report on Privacy, Cmnd 5012
(1972) paras 665–667**

665 We have found privacy to be a concept which means widely different things to different people and changes significantly over relatively short periods. In considering how the courts could handle so ill-defined and unstable a concept, we conclude that privacy is ill-suited to be the subject of a long process of definition through the building up of precedents over the years, since the judgments of the past would be an unreliable guide to any current evaluation of privacy. If, on the other hand, no body of judge-made precedent were built up, the law would remain, as it would certainly have to begin, highly uncertain and subject to the unguided judgments of juries from time to time. It is difficult to find any firm evidential base on which to assess the danger to the free circulation of information which might result from a legal situation of this kind. The press and broadcasting authorities have naturally expressed to us their concern about any extension into the field of truthful publication of the sort of restraints at present imposed on them by the law of defamation, especially if the practical limits of the extension are bound to remain somewhat indeterminable for a period of years. We do not think these fears can be discounted and we do not forget that others besides the mass media, for instance biographers, novelists or playwrights, might also be affected. We already have some experience of the uncertainties which result, for instance in obscenity cases, when courts of law are asked to make judgments on controversial matters, where statutory definitions are unsatisfactory, and social and moral opinion fluctuates rapidly.

666 It would, in our view, be unwise to extend this kind of uncertainty into a new branch of the law, unless there were compelling evidence of a substantial

wrong, which must be righted even at some risk to other important values. Within the area covered by our terms of reference, evidence of this kind has been conspicuously lacking and we therefore see no reason to recommend that this risk should be taken.

667 Finally, we repeat what we said at the outset of this chapter. Privacy, however defined, embodies values which are essential to a free society. It requires the support of society as a whole. But the law is only one of the factors determining the climate of a democratic society and it is often only a minor factor. Education, professional standards and the free interplay of ideas and discussion through the mass media and the organs of political democracy can do at least as much as the law to establish and maintain standards of behaviour. We have explained in this report that we see risks in placing excessive reliance on the law in order to protect privacy. We believe that in our recommendations we have given to the law its due place in the protection of privacy and we see no need to extend it further.

Nearly 20 years later, the Calcutt Committee also rejected the introduction of a privacy right against the press. It preferred to give it another chance to introduce a system of effective self-regulation: see Chapter 2, and Section 5 below. In its view, that would be more likely to provide speedy and cheap relief than a tort remedy. Only if it failed, should further consideration be given to the introduction of a legal privacy right. Calcutt, however, did not think that it was impossible to define privacy.

Extract 11.4.4

Calcutt Committee Report on Privacy and Related Matters, Cm 1102 (1990) paras 12.17–12.19, 12.22–12.25

12.17 We are satisfied that it would be possible to define a statutory tort of infringement of privacy. This could specifically relate to the publication of personal information (including photographs) . . . Personal information could be defined in terms of an individual's personal life, that is to say, those aspects of life which reasonable members of society would respect as being such that an individual is ordinarily entitled to keep them to himself, whether or not they relate to his mind or body, to his home, to his family, to other personal relationships, or to his correspondence or documents.

12.18 We would not see any advantage in laying down a more detailed definition of personal information on the face of any statute. The courts could develop their interpretation on a case by case basis . . .

. . .

12.19 All proposals for a tort of infringement of privacy have included a number of defences. These have been of two kinds: the specific and the general. Specific defences have included consent, legal privilege, lawful authority and absence of intent. Defences of this kind would clearly be necessary if a tort were ever to be introduced . . .

. . .

12.22 ... we have serious reservations about a general defence merely labelled 'public interest'. We would not consider it appropriate for any tort of infringement of privacy. A defence to cover the justified disclosure of personal information would, however, clearly be necessary, but it would need to be tightly drawn and specific. The possible definition of personal information which we have set out (see *paragraphs 12.17–12.18*) would already provide for flexible interpretation by the courts. We would see difficulty in introducing a further variable which would be likely to mean different things to different people.

12.23 We consider, therefore, that the additional defence would have to be limited to any infringement where the defendant had reasonable grounds for believing that:

a. publication of the personal information would contribute to the prevention, detection or exposure of any crime or other seriously anti-social conduct; or

b. it would be necessary for the protection of public health or safety; or

c. there would, but for the publication, be a real risk that the public, or some section of the public, would be materially misled by a statement previously made public by or on behalf of any individual whose privacy would otherwise be infringed (whether the plaintiff or otherwise).

...

12.24 A number of arguments of principle, many of them relating to freedom of speech, have been advanced against the creation of a statutory tort of infringement of privacy. We do not accept that such a tort would be the thin end of a wedge leading towards censorship. A law designed solely for the protection of individual citizens and their personal lives should offer no scope for Government interference. Furthermore, there is no necessary interrelationship between protection of individual privacy (in the terms in which we discuss it in this report) and censorship by Government. We cannot, therefore, accept the argument that no tort of infringement of privacy should be introduced unless balanced by some provision for the entrenchment of freedom of speech or a Freedom of Information Act.

12.25 Nor do we agree that a narrowly-drawn tort would inhibit serious investigative journalism or that responsible newspapers would suffer for the misdeeds of others. Serious investigative journalism would be outside the scope of such a law, especially when exposing serious wrong-doing. There is a clear distinction between infringements of privacy deriving from prurient curiosity and those associated with legitimate journalism ... Most people have little difficulty in recognising where the boundary lies.

Questions for discussion

1. Do you think it is possible to define privacy for the purposes of a right of action against the media in tort?

2. Do you agree with the approach of the Calcutt Committee to a public interest defence?

3. What are the advantages of a legal privacy right over the protection afforded by voluntary regulation? What are the disadvantages?

5. OTHER REMEDIES FOR INVASION OF PRIVACY

As noted earlier in this chapter, the jurisdiction to restrain breaches of confidence may protect privacy where it is infringed by the publication of personal information, correspondence or diaries. But the media may violate it in other ways. Journalists may use long-lens photography to take pictures or they may besiege a home, the practice known as 'doorstepping', where it is less clear that a breach of confidence action would succeed.[11] In any case, however privacy is infringed, the victim may prefer recourse to an informal, extra-legal remedy; a complaint to the Press Complaints Commission (PCC) for infringement by newspapers and magazines, the Broadcasting Standards Commission (BSC) for infringement by broadcasters.

(a) Privacy and the Press Complaints Commission

Extract 11.5.1

Press Complaints Commission Code of Practice, clause 3

(1) Everyone is entitled to respect for his or her private and family life, home, health and correspondence. A publication will be expected to justify intrusions into any individual's private life without consent.

(2) The use of long-lens photography to take pictures of people in private places without their consent is unacceptable.

Note – Private places are public or private property where there is a reasonable expectation of privacy.

Clause 4 of the PCC Code of Practice precludes harassment. Journalists must not try to obtain information by harassment and intimidation, must not persist in telephoning, photographing, or questioning individuals after a request to stop, and must not follow them. A number of provisions protect the privacy of children.

Extract 11.5.2

Press Complaints Commission Code of Practice, clause 6(i), (v)

(i) Young people should be free to complete their time at school without unnecessary intrusion.

. . .

(v) Where material about the private life of a child is published, there must be justification for publication other than the fame, notoriety or position of his or her parents or guardian.

---

[11] But see *Hellewell* (Extract 11.4.2 above) and the European Commission of Human Rights decision in *Spencer* (Extract 11.6.2 below).

Complaints brought under any of these heads, and also others,[12] may be contested by the press on the ground that the publication (or harassment, etc) was in the public interest.

Extract 11.5.3

Press Complaints Commission Code of Practice, Public Interest Defence[13]

1. The public interest includes:
    (i) Detecting or exposing crime or a serious misdemeanour;
    (ii) Protecting public health and safety;
    (iii) Preventing the public from being misled by some statement or action of an individual or organisation.
2. In any case where the public interest is invoked, the Press Complaints Commission will require a full explanation by the editor demonstrating how the public interest was served.
3. In cases involving children editors must demonstrate an exceptional public interest to override the normally paramount interests of the child.

Privacy complaints constitute about 13–14% of the Commission's case load.[14] They attract disproportionate publicity, particularly when they are brought by a member of the Royal Family, a politician, or an entertainment celebrity.

Extract 11.5.4

Complaint against *News of the World*, PCC Report No 29 (1995), pp 6–7

The Earl Spencer complains that in publishing a story covering the first three pages of its 2 April 1995 edition the News of the World unjustifiably intruded into the privacy of his wife in breach of Clauses 4 (Privacy), 6 (Hospitals and similar institutions) and 8 (Harassment) of the Code of Practice.[15]

Earl Spencer has informed the Commission that the complaint is made on behalf of his wife and with her consent.

The story was headlined *'DI'S SISTER IN BOOZE AND BULIMIA CLINIC ... ROYAL EXCLUSIVE ... Earl Spencer's ailing wife has secret therapy'* and reported that *'Victoria Spencer, 29, is suffering from bulimia ... is*

---

[12] These include complaints of intrusion in hospitals and misrepresentation (clauses 9 and 11 respectively), and of cheque-book journalism (clause 16): see Chapter 2, Section 3(e) above.

[13] The Defence was provided by a numbered provision, most recently clause 18; the provision now appears in the Code unnumbered.

[14] The PCC has appointed a member, Professor Robert Pinker, to act as a Privacy Commissioner to investigate complaints and bring them quickly to the Commission.

[15] These are now clauses 3, 9, and 4 respectively; some of the terms have now been redrafted, though the changes are not material.

also believed to have a drink problem' and was being treated in a private addiction clinic. The article went into considerable detail about the circumstances of Countess Spencer's alleged problems and featured, on the front page and again on page three, a photograph of Countess Spencer walking in the grounds of the clinic. The photograph had clearly been taken using a telephoto lens without her permission and was captioned '*BATTLING: Victoria in the clinic grounds . . . SO THIN: Victoria walks in the clinic's grounds this week*'.

. . .

The associate editor of the newspaper responded to the complaint on behalf of the News of the World. He argued that Earl Spencer was a public figure whose privileges by birth made him open to a degree of public examination. He claimed that Earl Spencer was no stranger to publicity in the press and had on many occasions encouraged media interest in his home and family in return for fees or publicity. He cited a number of examples in this respect, arguing that Earl Spencer had by putting his family in the public arena on so many occasions waived their rights to privacy. With regard to the issue of the Countess's health the associate editor drew the Commission's attention to two particular matters. First, he referred to an item in the social diary column of Harpers and Queen magazine dated August 1993 which reported on '*an evening of music and champagne in aid of the Eating Disorders Association*' in which the writer claimed that Countess Spencer had attended the evening as a guest of honour with her husband and had told her in a private conversation that she '*had suffered from the condition for many years*'. The second was a reference to the Daily Mail dated 5 August 1993 containing an interview with Earl Spencer about his family estate. This stated that Earl Spencer '*revealed that Lady Spencer worked part-time at St. Andrew's Hospital, Northampton, where she voluntarily helps young girls suffering from anorexia, which plagued her own teenage years*'.

. . .

The newspaper maintained that Countess Spencer's illness had been put firmly into the public domain by her actions and those of her husband and she was not entitled to rely on the privacy provisions of the Code of Practice. It claimed that the clinic was not a hospital but a health centre offering no medical treatment and having no doctor on the staff.

Clause 6(ii) of the Code states that '*The restrictions on intruding into privacy are particularly relevant to enquiries about individuals in hospitals or similar institutions*'.[16] In the view of the Commission, the 'similar institutions' referred to in Clause 6 clearly include the type of clinic involved in this case.

Two further matters arise in relation to the PCC's Code of Practice: the specific question of the publication of the photograph of the Countess in the grounds of the clinic and the more general issue of alleged intrusion into her privacy raised by the publication of the story by the newspaper.

The photography of individuals on private property without their consent specifically constitutes harassment under Clause 8(ii) of the Code unless such action can be justified in the public interest under Clause 18.

---

[16] Now clause 9(ii), formulated in identical terms.

406

In the absence of such public interest justification, the Commission does not accept that the publication of a photograph taken with a telephoto lens of an indisputably unwell person walking in the private secluded grounds of an addiction clinic can be anything other than a breach of the Code. The Commission notes the 'apology' published to the Countess as part of the newspaper's comment on her husband but does not accept that this can reasonably be seen to remedy the complaint or exculpate the newspaper from a failure to observe the Code in the first place. The contention that the newspaper published the photograph to demonstrate the veracity of the article is rejected by the Commission, which concludes that the newspaper is guilty of a serious breach of one of the most unequivocal parts of the Code of Practice.

The Commission has no doubt that matters of health fall within the terms of an 'individual's private life' described in Clause 4 (Privacy) of the Code. On Earl Spencer's complaint of intrusion into privacy the Commission therefore considered whether Countess Spencer was entitled to be protected from any intrusion into her privacy in the face of the newspaper's arguments to the contrary.

In arguing that the Countess's privacy had not been invaded, the newspaper made allegations concerning the Earl's character and his attitude and behaviour towards the press.

ADJUDICATION

While the Commission considers that the Earl's past relationship with the press . . . affects the extent to which he may now be entitled to privacy in respect of particular aspects of his own life, it does not believe that this necessarily leaves the press free to report on any matter concerning the Countess. The fact that Earl Spencer may have sought publicity in the past cannot reasonably be taken to mean that, henceforward, every aspect of the private affairs of his wife is a matter which the press has a right to put into the public domain. In the view of the Commission, this must apply particularly to matters affecting her health and psychological well-being. The magazine diary piece cited by the newspaper is, in the view of the Commission, an insufficient basis on which to build a case that the Countess had opened her illness to public scrutiny or that there is a public interest justification for the articles and photographs printed. The Daily Mail article put forward was an interview with the Earl containing a passing comment about the Countess's health in the past.

To justify the intrusion of which the complaint is made the newspaper is required under the Code of Practice to demonstrate that publication was in the public interest. The newspaper has failed to offer any sufficient argument to sustain its position on this point.

The complaints are all upheld.

The Commission takes a particularly serious view of this matter. The article by the newspaper was not justified as being in the public interest under Clause 18 of the Code. This breach was compounded through a flagrant breach of Clause 8(ii) by the publication of the photograph of the Countess in the private grounds of the clinic.

National Lottery winners must not be identified by its organiser, Camelot, without their written consent. In 1994 a resident of Blackburn won a jackpot prize of £17.8 million, a matter which excited media interest; two newspapers offered rewards for information about the winner, while three others identified him. The question was whether his privacy had been infringed.

Extract 11.5.5

Complaint with regard to identification of National Lottery winner, PCC Report No 29 (1995), pp 30–31 (paras 23–28)

23. . . . So far as the Commission is concerned, the matter is mainly governed by the provisions of Clause 4 of the Code of Practice which states that intrusions and enquiries into an individual's private life without his or her consent are generally not acceptable and publication can only be justified when in the public interest. The Commission takes the view that inquiries into the financial affairs of private individuals clearly comes within the terms of Clause 4 of the Code.

24. The Commission accepts that individuals taking part in The National Lottery have an expectation of anonymity, if they should so wish, as a result of the terms of the licence which has been granted to the lottery organisers. In this circumstance it would be unfair if that expectation were to be rendered nugatory by an editorial decision taken by newspapers or other media to publish the name of prize winners at their choosing. However, the Commission accepts that the press cannot be expected to act as a back-stop in maintaining the anonymity of winners, irrespective of all circumstances including the actions of the operator or the winners themselves. In this particular case, it is perhaps understandable that problems should have arisen from the first test of the privacy arrangements, involving a win of an unparalleled amount and some resulting media and public frenzy. In view of the confusion which resulted, the Commission has decided not to censure any particular newspapers on this occasion for identifying the winner. It is possible that as a result of the actions of Camelot some journalists were encouraged to search for and narrow down a list of possible people who were the recipients of the large prize. In such circumstances the Commission finds it difficult to believe that such a large win would have gone unnoticed locally and the name not known within a relatively short time within a wide area. Indeed, there is evidence that some newspapers were aware of the winner's identity before Camelot gave out any information. Information may also pass into the public domain as a result of winners or their families informing others of their good fortune.

25. The Commission can foresee that there may be some circumstances where there might be a justification in the press naming a previously anonymous winner for public interest reasons. However, the Commission does not accept that the Press are entitled to make enquiries of, or to interview winners who have chosen to remain anonymous, their family, friends or those who work with them in circumstances which would amount to harassment under Clause 8 of the Code of Practice.

26.   In those cases in the future where the press wishes to publish information about the identity of a winner who has chosen to remain anonymous
they will generally need to justify that fact by reference to the public interest
defence provided by Clause 18 of the Code of Practice. The Commission
does not accept that the size of the win itself will necessarily provide such
justification.

27.   The Commission recognises that there are occasions where a newspaper may be justified in offering a reward for information. However it is difficult
to see circumstances where a reward for information about the identity of a
lottery winner could be justified as being in the public interest except, perhaps,
where there was prima facie evidence that uncovering information about the
winner was necessary, for example, to expose a fraud or some other serious
misdemeanour. None of these circumstances existed in the case of the 10
December winner.

28.   Accordingly, the Commission condemns the decision of some newspapers to offer rewards for information to help them to identify the jackpot
winner in this case. The Commission is pleased to note that the newspapers
concerned have ceased to make such offers and did not, in the event, publish
the name concerned.

Among the most sensitive complaints were those brought against four newspapers in respect of articles concerning the fathering by a homosexual of a
child born to a surrogate mother in the US; the PCC declined to censure
them, primarily on the ground that overall the publications were in the
public interest or that the matter was already in the public domain.[17]

Extracts 11.5.6

Complaint by William Zachs against *Sunday Mail*, PCC Report
No 38 (1997), pp 9–12

COMPLAINT

Mr William Zachs of Edinburgh complained that coverage in the Sunday Mail
about himself, his baby daughter and his partner during the week commencing 1 September 1996 gave details of their situation, named his daughter
and revealed their address in breach of Clause 4 (Privacy) of the Code of
Practice . . .

The complainant had fathered a child, born to a surrogate mother in the
U.S. and the baby was brought to Edinburgh to live with the complainant and
his male partner. The complainant objected that, while the issues of surrogacy
and homosexual parenting might be a matter for public debate, the particulars
of the birth of his daughter were a private matter – publication of which was
not in the public interest. He considered that publishing a photograph of the

---

[17]   The PCC also rejected most of Zach's complaints against *The Herald*, *The Express* and the
Scottish Daily Mail.

front of their house and giving the street name made them vulnerable. So too did an article headlined 'STOP THIS EVIL BABY TRADE' which was illustrated by the photograph of another baby, prominently naming his own, saying she was 'born in America and cost a fortune' and lives in Scotland 'with no mum . . . only two gay dads', possibly putting his daughter at risk.

The editor said the newspaper stood by its view that this was a story in the public interest illustrating its stance against what it saw as importing children for gay couples; the couple and the baby they had 'bought' were news throughout Britain and the newspaper had legitimately followed up on what was already in the public domain . . .

ADJUDICATION

The unique circumstances of this case posed complex problems relating to privacy and public interest for the Commission to consider. In doing so, it judged this complaint solely on its merits and was concerned that its adjudication should not be seen as a precedent.

The Commission agreed with the newspaper that the twin issues of surrogacy and homosexual parenting are clear matters of legitimate public interest. It is right – and important – that the press reports and comments on them.

That said, the Commission also agreed with the complainant that the privacy of all those involved in this particular story was, in principle, subject to the provisions of Clause 4 of the Code. In particular, the Commission considered that privacy should attach to the infant involved as much as to a child or an adult: one of the aspects of privacy is how intrusion into it affects the unfolding lives of those involved, and is therefore arguably all the more important where an infant is concerned. Under the Code, intrusions into an individual's private life are only acceptable where there is a legitimate matter of public interest at stake; in practice, where those directly involved in a contemporary story in effect act to put private information into the public domain, entitlement to privacy is also undermined.

Even though there was great public interest in this case and there was legitimate debate on an important issue, the Commission did not believe that, in principle, the newspaper needed to report all the details of the family's private life. *However*, the mother of the surrogate baby had herself put some information into the public domain.

The matter for the Commission to consider, therefore, was how much of that information the newspaper was right to publish. In doing so, it found that while the news of the birth and the details of the men's names had in effect been made public by one of those involved, it was unsatisfactory for the newspaper to have published the forenames of the infant and details of the men's address including a photograph of their house, regardless of whether the house number was legible or not. As details which added nothing to legitimate public debate – providing only colour to a story which could have been written without them – publication was not within the spirit of the Code.

With that important caveat, the Commission found – however – that *overall* the newspaper could not be censured for its reporting when a considerable amount of information was in the public domain; the complaint of intrusion into privacy under Clause 4 was therefore not upheld.

The Commission also considered the general complaints raised under Clause 8 of the Code and was greatly concerned to learn of the harassment experienced by the complainant and his partner as a result of the 'media scrum' outside their Edinburgh home.

The Commission noted that such pressure inevitably resulted from the presence of a large number of journalists – from the broadcast as well as the print media – which to a large extent exacerbated the pressures on the family at a time when the stress of nurturing a new born baby would have been most acute. As in some other similar cases, the Commission believed this to be an example of collective if unintentional harassment – and it had great sympathy with the complainant and his family.

Although the Commission found no clear evidence of intended harassment of this type from the newspaper, and therefore made no finding on this part of the complaint, it will not hesitate to do so if in a future case it becomes apparent that an individual newspaper or reporter either played a leading part in collective unjustified harassment, or did not withdraw when individually asked to do so.

Questions for discussion:

1. Does the PCC adopt a consistent approach to the 'public domain' defence? Is it relevant that the winner of a lottery or a homosexual father has told, say, friends and neighbours about the matter? Or that another person – the mother of the surrogate baby – has given an interview?

2. Was the PCC right to decline to censure the newspapers in the *National Lottery* and the *Zachs* cases?

3. Did the PCC resolve the harassment complaint in *Zachs* satisfactorily?

Two recent developments show how difficult it is to balance privacy and freedom of the press. First, in the spring of 1999 the PCC issued a general statement on reporting the Royal Princes.[18] It concluded that while it was not right for young boys to be exposed to weekly stories about them, 'there *cannot* be a total blackout on all stories about the Princes at school. The public interest means that newspapers should print *occasional* stories and general information – and not just on subjects such as health and safety, where the public interest is obvious and clear cut.'[19] Secondly, the Commission adjudicated a complaint by the Prime Minister and Mrs Blair about articles and an editorial in the *Mail on Sunday* implicitly alleging that their daughter had been unfairly admitted to a Catholic school in preference to local children. The PCC concluded that the articles were misleading and so

---

[18] The PCC does occasionally issue general statements, a practice which runs counter to Calcutt's recommendation that it concentrate on the adjudication of complaints: see Chapter 2, Section 2.

[19] PCC Report No 46 (1999), Statement, para 3.3 (emphasis in the original).

infringed clause 1 of the Code; but it also decided that there was a breach of clause 6 protecting the privacy of children.

Extract 11.5.7

Complaint against *Mail on Sunday*, PCC Report No 47 (1999), pp 7–8

The second question which the Commission had to decide was whether there was any justification for making Kathryn Blair the focus of the article and the leader about the admission policy of the school solely because of her relationship to her parents. The newspaper said that the references had arisen during the course of interviews with the parents of unsuccessful children and it should be free to report them.

The Commission believes that an article about the selection procedure at the school could have been written without reference to Kathryn Blair or making her the centre of the story. By herself, she could have been no more responsible for denying a place to the large number of unsuccessful candidates than any other of the girls actually admitted who equally could have been individually highlighted by the articles. To focus on Kathryn Blair in circumstances where there was a breach of Clause 1 of the Code was clearly not within the terms of Clause 6 of the Code and appeared to arise solely because of the position of her father.

Notwithstanding its conclusion on the above question, the Commission went on to consider whether there was any exceptional public interest which justified the reference to Kathryn Blair in the articles and leader. The Commission believes that it would be permissible under the editors' Code to name the children of public figures in newspaper articles – in a manner proportionate to the issues and facts involved – in circumstances where:

- there is reasonable substance to a charge or allegation that provides the exceptional public interest required by the Code; and
- it is necessary to report the story and to identify the child because that child, and that child alone, had to be the centre of the story.

Applying these criteria, the Commission could find no justification for naming Kathryn Blair alone in connection with complaints about the admission criteria of the school. There was no evidence of special treatment in her favour. An opposition spokesman who alleged 'hypocrisy' on Mr Blair's part did so on an inaccurate factual basis that the allegations were true. The newspaper's leader did no more than suggest that Mr Blair would be embarrassed if the unproved allegations of an 'under-the-counter policy of selection' proved to be correct. Finally, the newspaper noted in its submission that Mr Blair had publicly made reference to his children. The complainants' response to this emphasised the great lengths that the Prime Minister and Mrs Blair go to in order to avoid publicity for their children. The Commission agrees with the contention made to it that if every story about the Prime Minister's children, which relates to their education, is to be justified on the basis that he has made statements about education, then Clause 6 provides no protection for his children or others in a similar position. The Commission intends the industry's Code – drawn up by editors themselves – to be effective and to provide real protection for all children.

(b) Privacy and the Broadcasting Standards Commission

A complaint of invasion of privacy in the context of broadcasting may be made to the Broadcasting Standards Commission (BSC), formerly the Broadcasting Complaints Commission: see Chapter 4, Section 4.

Extract 11.5.8

Broadcasting Act 1996, s 110 (1)

. . . it shall be the duty of the BSC to consider and adjudicate on complaints which are made to them . . . and relate—
  (a) [*Omitted*]
  (b) to unwarranted infringement of privacy in, or in connection with the obtaining of material included in, such programmes.[20]

Only a person 'whose privacy was infringed' (or a person authorised to make a complaint on his behalf) may complain;[21] standing issues do not raise the same difficulties as they do in the context of 'unfair treatment' complaints.[22]

The BSC has drawn up a Code, giving guidance on principles and practices to be adopted to avoid 'unwarranted' infringements of privacy. It reflects rulings of the former Complaints Commission, and court rulings on applications for judicial review. It can usefully be compared with the much terser provisions of the PCC Code.

Extract 11.5.9

Broadcasting Standards Commission Code on Fairness and Privacy (June, 1998), paras 17–19, 22–23, 25–26

17.   People in the public eye, either through the position they hold or the publicity they attract, are in a special position. However, not all matters which interest the public are in the public interest. Even when personal matters become the proper subject of enquiry, people in the public eye or their immediate family or friends do not forfeit the right to privacy, though there may be occasions where private behaviour raises broader public issues either through the nature of the behaviour itself or by the consequences of its becoming widely known. But any information broadcast should be significant as well as true. The location of a person's home or family should not normally be revealed unless strictly relevant to the behaviour under investigation.

[20] The term 'such programmes' covers all BBC, Welsh Authority, and licensed commercial services: BA 1996, s 107(3).
[21] BA 1996, s 111, and see definition of 'person affected' in s 130(1).
[22] See Chapter 4, Section 4 for discussion of standing to complain about unfair treatment.

The Use of Hidden Microphones and Cameras

18.   The use of secret recording should only be considered where it is necessary to the credibility and authenticity of the story, as the use of hidden
recording techniques can be unfair to those recorded as well as infringe their
privacy. In seeking to determine whether an infringement of privacy is warranted, the Commission will consider the following guiding principles:
  (i) Normally, broadcasters on location should operate only in public where
     they can be seen. Where recording does take place secretly in public
     places, the words or images recorded should serve an overriding public
     interest to justify:
       • the decision to gather the material;
       • the actual recording;
       • the broadcast.
 (ii) An unattended recording device should not be left on private property
     without the full and informed consent of the occupiers or their agent
     unless seeking permission might frustrate the investigation by the pro-
     gramme-makers of matters of an overriding public interest.
(iii) The open and apparent use of cameras or recording devices on both
     public and private property, when the subject is on private property, must
     be appropriate to the importance or nature of the story. The broadcaster
     should not intrude unnecessarily on private behaviour.
19.   When broadcasting material obtained secretly, whether in public or on
private property, broadcasters should take care not to infringe the privacy of
bystanders who may be caught inadvertently in the recording. Wherever it is
clear that unfairness might otherwise be caused, the identity of innocent parties should be obscured.
  . . .

Telephone Calls

22.   Broadcasters should normally identify themselves to telephone inter-
viewees from the outset, or seek agreement from the other party, if they wish
to broadcast a recording of a telephone call between the broadcaster and the
other party.
23.   If factual programme-makers take someone by surprise by recording a
call for broadcast purposes without any prior warning, it is the equivalent of
doorstepping (see paragraphs 25, 26, 27) and similar rules apply. Such approaches should only take place where there is reason to believe that there is
an overriding public interest and the subject has refused to respond to reasonable requests for interview, or has a history of such failure or refusal, or there
is good reason to believe that the investigation will be frustrated if the subject
is approached openly.
  . . .

Doorstepping

25.   People who are currently in the news cannot reasonably object to being
questioned and recorded by the media when in public places. The questions

should be fair even if they are unwelcome. If the approach is made by telephone, the broadcaster should make clear who is calling and for what purpose. Nevertheless, even those who are in the news have the right to make no comment or to refuse to appear in a broadcast. Any relevant broadcast should make clear that a person has chosen not to appear and mention such person's explanation, if not to do so could be materially unfair. . . .

26.   Outside the daily news context, different considerations apply. But surprise can be a legitimate device to elicit the truth especially when dealing with matters where there is an overriding public interest in investigation and disclosure. Doorstepping in these circumstances may be legitimate where there has been repeated refusal to grant an interview (or a history of such refusals) or the risk exists that a protagonist might disappear.

Like its predecessor, the BSC receives relatively few privacy complaints compared to the number concerning unfair treatment.[23] It has jurisdiction to consider a privacy complaint, only when the programme, the making of which is alleged to have involved an infringement of privacy, is in fact broadcast. But it is immaterial whether the infringement occurred in the course of obtaining material, for example, film, which itself was broadcast. These nice distinctions emerge from two judicial review rulings, the first of which is summarised in the following extract from the later case.

Extract 11.5.10

R v BCC, ex parte Barclay [1997] EMLR 62, at 65–66

The Barclay twins, joint proprietors of a major newspaper, owned and lived on a small island in the Channel Islands. Despite their refusal, a reporter for the BBC landed on the island and sought an interview. The Barclays' complaint of privacy infringement to the BCC was lodged before the programme was broadcast.

SEDLEY J: At first blush this appears to be a simple and homogeneous scheme, directed not to the preparation but to the broadcasting of a programme. Even the fourth category (infringement of privacy in connection with obtaining of material) is predicated upon the inclusion of the material in a broadcast programme. But it is not quite so. In *R. v Broadcasting Complaints Commission ex p. BBC and Another* [1993] EMLR 419 MacPherson of Cluny J. had to consider the Commission's claim that it had power to deal with a complaint, made after the transmission of a programme, that there had been an unwarranted infringement of an individual's privacy in the course of an investigative expedition which, however, had not furnished material included

---

[23] In 1995, of the 73 complaints adjudicated on, only seven involved purely privacy complaints, while 45 raised solely unfair treatment, and 21 both privacy and unfair treatment. Comparable figures for 1996 were: 61, 6, 36, 19: see Annual Report of BCC for 1995, HC 640, and Annual Report of BCC for 1996, HC 479.

in the programme. MacPherson J. accepted without hesitation the Commission's contention that the words 'in connection with' were sufficiently wide in their meaning to permit the Commission to adjudicate on the manner of obtaining the material which, though not broadcast, was linked to what was broadcast. He said:

> 'It seems to me verging on the absurd that if a single "flash" of the visit to the Lloyds' home [the topic of complaint] had been included in the programme the position would have been acceptable to the BBC, but that by contrast the actual position [the non-transmission of such material] should be outside the Act. Provided there was some nexus or connection between the material actually broadcast and the visit I am convinced that what took place must be within the words "in connection with obtaining of material included in . . .". To some extent of course that is a factual decision based upon the individual facts of any individual case.'

. . .

MacPherson J., as I have indicated, drew attention to the absurdity of distinguishing between material which has been obtained by an unwarranted infringement of privacy but has not been transmitted and similarly obtained material, closely linked to it, which has been transmitted. His conclusion, albeit in relation to a programme which had been broadcast by the time the complaint was made, resolved the anomaly. In the present case the literal reading of the Act produces a comparable anomaly. If material is obtained by means of an unwarranted infringement of privacy but is excluded from the programme, it can be the subject of a complaint so long as the programme when broadcast contains related material. But if – perhaps because the infringing material is simply of technically unusable quality, or perhaps because a conscientious editorial decision has been taken that the infringement is so gross that it would be unethical to use any of it – the programme is spiked and never broadcast, or if nothing related to the infringing material gets into the programme when it is broadcast, on a literal reading of section 143 [of BA 1990] the Commission will never have power to adjudicate and the invasion of privacy will go unredressed in English law.

Sedley J felt unable to depart from the literal meaning of the legislation; the Commission lacked power to 'entertain an anticipatory complaint even where, once the programme is broadcast, the complaint is bound to succeed'.[24] But if the Commission does have jurisdiction, the courts may be reluctant to interfere with a decision that there has been an 'unwarranted infringement of privacy'.[24a] This reluctance is evidenced by the judgment from which the following extract is taken; the Broadcasting Complaints Commission had held that two *Granada* programmes unwarrantably infringed privacy inasmuch as they included photographs of children who had died in tragic circumstances

---

[24] *R v BCC, ex parte Barclay* [1997] EMLR 62, at 70.

[24a] But in *R v BSC, ex parte BBC* [1999] EMLR 858 Forbes J held the Commission had wrongly decided that a company is entitled to privacy and that its privacy is violated by secret filming of sales transactions in public.

without warning their parents that this material would be included. The approach of the former Broadcasting Complaints Commission is now reflected in the terms of the BSC Code.[25]

Extract 11.5.11

R v BCC, ex parte Granada TV [1995] EMLR 163, at 168–169 (CA)

BALCOMBE LJ: In my judgment it is clear that the fact that a matter has once been in the public domain cannot prevent its resurrection, possibly many years later, from being an infringement of privacy. Whether in such a case there is an unwarranted infringement of privacy is a matter of fact and degree and as such for the decision of the BCC with which the Court cannot interfere.

. . .

In my judgment it would be an unacceptably narrow interpretation of the meaning of privacy, and contrary to common sense, to confine it to matters concerning the individual complainant and not as extending to his family. Such an interpretation would also be inconsistent with the existing jurisprudence:

(1) Article 8(1) of the European Convention of Human Rights provides that:

Everyone has the right to respect for his private and family life . . .

(2) The French law of privacy covers family, personal and sexual matters – the Calcutt Report, para. 5.12.

(3) The Calcutt Committee adopted a formulation of privacy for working purposes in the following terms:

. . . the right of the individual to be protected against intrusion into his personal life or affairs, *or those of his family* [my emphasis] . . . – para. 3.7.

(4) At least some American jurisdictions seem to recognize that a father's privacy may be invaded by a reference to his daughter. Thus in *Cox Broadcasting Corporation v Cohn* (1975) 95 SC 1029, the father of a deceased rape victim sued a broadcasting company for damages for the invasion of *his* privacy, by reason of the publication of his daughter's name. The Supreme Court of Georgia did not rule out the claim as inadmissible, and the Supreme Court of the United States made no adverse comment on this part of the case, although that was not the issue before it.

Again this is a matter of degree for the decision of the BCC. While a reference to a distant relative is unlikely to infringe a person's privacy, a reference to a person's child, particularly where that child has died in tragic circumstances, may well do so.

---

[25] Under para 31 of The Code, failure to inform surviving victims or families of those involved in a traumatic event about the transmission of a programme revisiting it may amount to an infringement of privacy.

Questions for discussion

1. Does the decision in *Ex parte Barclay* show a serious gap in the protection of privacy? If so, how should it be filled?

2. Compare the approach of the PCC and Balcombe LJ to the 'public domain' argument. Is it entitled to less weight as a justification for broadcasts revisiting past events than it is in the case of articles in the press?

6. THE IMPACT OF THE HUMAN RIGHTS ACT 1998

The implications of incorporation of the European Convention on Human Rights (ECHR) for privacy were keenly debated during the passage of the Human Rights Act 1998: see Chapter 1, Section 2(b). The Convention rights which the courts must protect against interference by a public authority include not only freedom of expression (see Extract 1.2.1), but the right to respect for private life guaranteed by art 8 of the ECHR.

Extract 11.6.1

European Convention on Human Rights and Fundamental Freedoms, art 8

(1) Everyone has the right to respect for his private and family life, his home and his correspondence.

(2) There shall be no interference by a public authority with the exercise of this right except such as is in accordance with the law and is necessary in a democratic society in the interests of national security, public safety or the economic well-being of the country, for the prevention of disorder or crime, for the protection of health or morals, or for the protection of the rights and freedoms of others.

The implication of the opening words of art 8(2) might be that only public bodies need comply with the right to respect for private life, etc. The right does not have 'horizontal effect' by limiting the freedom of private institutions such as newspapers and other commercial media. But the European Court of Human Rights has held (in a case not involving the media) that a state may be required to take positive steps to protect the right to private life.[26] In 1998 the European Commission of Human Rights considered a complaint that English law had infringed the rights of the Earl and Countess Spencer in failing to prohibit the taking and publication of photographs relating to their private lives (see also Extract 11.5.4).

---

[26] *X & Y v Netherlands* (1986) 8 EHRR 235.

Extract 11.6.2

Earl Spencer and Countess Spencer v UK **(1998) 25 EHRR CD 106, at 112 (European Commission of Human Rights)**

The Commission recalls that the obligation to secure the effective exercise of Convention rights imposed by Article 1 of the Convention may involve positive obligations on a State and that these obligations may involve the adoption of measures even in the sphere of relations between individuals . . .

. . . the Commission would not exclude that the absence of an actionable remedy in relation to the publications of which the applicants complain could show a lack of respect for their private lives. It has regard in this respect to the duties and responsibilities that are carried with the right to freedom of expression guaranteed by Article 10 of the Convention and to Contracting States' obligation to provide a measure of protection to the right of privacy of an individual affected by others' exercise of their freedom of expression . . .

However, the application was inadmissible because the claimants had not exhausted their domestic remedies by bringing an action for breach of confidence, which might have been successful.[27]

The press, supported by Lord Wakeham, Chairman of the PCC, campaigned for changes to the Human Rights Bill to prevent the application of art 8 of the ECHR to the media and to exempt the Commission from any obligation it might have as a 'public authority' to act compatibly with the Convention. The government resisted these moves, but instead added s 12 to the Human Rights Act 1998 (see Extracts 1.2.5 and 1.5.3). It directs the courts to pay special attention to the right to freedom of expression. In particular, they must take account of the extent to which the material is available (the 'public domain' defence) and to which its publication would be in the public interest. Further, s 12 will clearly have an impact on breach of confidence actions; the requirement that no relief before trial is to be granted unless the court is satisfied that the applicant is 'likely to establish that publication should not be allowed' will make it more difficult to obtain an interim injunction in these cases.[28]

What is less clear is whether the Human Rights Act 1998 establishes a privacy right against the media. It does not matter that the European Court of Human Rights has (yet) to uphold such a right under art 8, for the UK courts are only bound to take account of its judgments,[29] and are, therefore, free to take a more expansive view of the scope of Convention rights. A widespread view is that the courts may require public authorities such as the Independent Television Commission, the BSC, the BBC, and perhaps the PCC, to act compatibly with the Convention; but they are under no obligation

[27] It is not certain that a breach of confidence action would have succeeded; see the discussion in Sections 2 and 4 above.

[28] Human Rights Act 1998, s 12(3).

[29] Ibid, s 2, and see Chapter 1, Section 2(b).

to develop the common law to recognise a right to privacy against a private party such as a newspaper or a commercial broadcaster.[30] Two points may be made in conclusion. First, whether or not the courts are now required to develop a right to privacy, judges have increasingly regretted its absence in the law. Perhaps incorporation of the Convention will encourage them finally to formulate an autonomous privacy right. But secondly, if they do take this step, they are required by the Human Right Act 1998 to pay particular regard to freedom of expression in any circumstances when the rights of privacy and the media conflict.

---

[30] See M Hunt, 'The "Horizontal Effect" of the Human Rights Act' [1998] *Public Law* 423; I Leigh, 'Horizontal Rights, The Human Rights Act and Privacy: Lessons from the Commonwealth?', (1999) 48 *International and Comparative Law Quarterly* 57.

12

CONTEMPT OF COURT

1. INTRODUCTION

Contempt of court is a complex area of law.[1] Some of its varieties have little relevance for media law; for instance, it is a contempt to interrupt a trial or physically to prevent the parties or witnesses from attending proceedings. But many contempts do typically involve the media. Indeed, for journalists and editors contempt of court is as significant a restraint on their freedom as that imposed by the law of libel. This chapter examines those parts of contempt law which are concerned to restrict media publications which may prejudice the fair conduct of legal proceedings. The freedom of the press and the broadcasting media conflicts with the right of the parties to a fair trial. Both freedoms are fundamental rights guaranteed by the European Convention on Human Rights (ECHR): art 10 freedom of expression covers the media (see Chapter 1, Section 2), while art 6 guarantees the right to a 'fair and public hearing': see Extract 13.2.3 below. Other instances of the conflict between these freedoms are considered in the next chapter, where a number of restrictions on the freedom of the media to attend and report legal proceedings are discussed.

The principal type of contempt considered in this chapter is the 'strict liability rule', under which a publication amounts to a contempt if it creates a significant risk of prejudice to forthcoming legal proceedings. The leading common law authority in this area of law before its statutory reform in 1981 is the famous *Sunday Times* thalidomide case. The Attorney General took proceedings against the newspaper which had proposed to publish an article suggesting that Distillers had not taken proper care before putting its drug on the market. An earlier article had criticised the company for not offering the parents of the children concerned more generous compensation. Lord Reid explains why the later, but not the earlier, article amounted to contempt of court.[2]

---

[1] The most authoritative work is D Eady and A T H Smith (eds), *Arlidge, Eady & Smith on Contempt*, 2nd ed (Sweet & Maxwell, 1998).

[2] Lords Diplock and Simon would also have upheld the application on the ground that the article would have amounted to public pressure on Distillers to abandon its right to have its liability determined by a court of law.

Extract 12.1.1

Attorney General v Times Newspapers **[1974] AC 273, at 299–300 (HL)**

LORD REID: The crucial question on this point of the case is whether it can ever be permissible to urge a party to a litigation to forgo his legal rights in whole or in part. The Attorney-General argues that it cannot and I think that the Divisional Court has accepted that view. In my view it is permissible so long as it is done in a fair and temperate way and without any oblique motive. 'The Sunday Times' article of September 24, 1972, affords a good illustration of the difference between the two views. It is plainly intended to bring pressure to bear on Distillers. It was likely to attract support from others and it did so. It was outspoken. It said: 'There are times when to insist on the letter of the law is as exposed to criticism as infringement of another's legal rights' and clearly implied that that was such a time. If the view maintained by the Attorney-General were right I could hardly imagine a clearer case of contempt of court . . . And it could not be said that it created no serious risk of causing Distillers to do what they did not want to do. On the facts submitted to your Lordships in argument it seems to me to have played a large part in causing Distillers to offer far more money than they had in mind at that time. But I am quite unable to subscribe to the view that it ought never to have been published because it was in contempt of court. I see no offence against public policy and no pollution of the stream of justice by its publication.

Now I must turn to the material to which the injunction applied. If it is not to be published at this time it would not be proper to refer to it in any detail. But I can say that it consists in the main of detailed evidence and argument intended to show that Distillers did not exercise due care to see that thalidomide was safe before they put it on the market.

If we regard this material solely from the point of view of its likely effect on Distillers I do not think that its publication in 1972 would have added much to the pressure on them created, or at least begun, by the earlier article of September 24. From Distillers' point of view the damage had already been done. I doubt whether the subsequent course of events would have been very different in its effect on Distillers if the matter had been published.

But, to my mind, there is another consideration even more important than the effect of publication on the mind of the litigant. The controversy about the tragedy of the thalidomide children has ranged widely but as yet there seems to have been little, if any, detailed discussion of the issues which the court may have to determine if the outstanding claims are not settled. The question whether Distillers were negligent had been frequently referred to but, so far as I am aware, there has been no attempt to assess the evidence. If this material were released now, it appears to me to be almost inevitable that detailed answers would be published and there would be expressed various public prejudgments of this issue. That I would regard as very much against the public interest.

There has long been and there still is in this country a strong and generally held feeling that trial by newspaper is wrong and should be prevented. I find, for example, in the report in 1969 of Lord Salmon's committee dealing with the Law of Contempt in relation to Tribunals of Inquiry (Cmnd. 4078) a reference to the 'horror' in such a thing (p. 12, para. 29). What I think is regarded as most objectionable is that a newspaper or television programme should seek to persuade the public, by discussing the issues and evidence in a case before the court, whether civil or criminal, that one side is right and the other wrong. If we were to ask the ordinary man or even a lawyer in his leisure moments why he has that feeling, I suspect that the first reply would be – 'well, look at what happens in some other countries where that is permitted.' As in so many other matters, strong feelings are based on one's general experience rather than on specific reasons, and it often requires an effort to marshal one's reasons. But public policy is generally the result of strong feelings, commonly held, rather than of cold argument.

. . .

There is ample authority for the proposition that issues must not be pre-judged in a manner likely to affect the mind of those who may later be witnesses or jurors. But very little has been said about the wider proposition that trial by newspaper is intrinsically objectionable. That may be because if one can find more limited and familiar grounds adequate for the decision of a case find more limited and familiar grounds adequate for the decision of a case it is rash to venture on uncharted seas.

I think that anything in the nature of prejudgment of a case or of specific issues in it is objectionable, not only because of its possible effect on that particular case but also because of its side effects which may be far reaching. Responsible 'mass media' will do their best to be fair, but there will also be ill-informed, slapdash or prejudiced attempts to influence the public. If people are led to think that it is easy to find the truth, disrespect for the processes of the law could follow, and, if mass media are allowed to judge, unpopular people and unpopular causes will fare very badly. Most cases of prejudging of issues fall within the existing authorities on contempt. I do not think that the freedom of the press would suffer, and I think that the law would be clearer and easier to apply in practice if it is made a general rule that it is not permissible to prejudge issues in pending cases.

It used to be common to bring contempt proceedings for abusive criticism of a judge, in particular if a publication suggested that he was biased. For example, the *New Statesman* was held guilty of this type of contempt, known as 'scandalising the court', when it doubted whether the birth control pioneer, Marie Stopes, could receive a fair hearing of her libel action from Mr Justice Avory, a Roman Catholic.[3] Frequent use of this type of contempt proceeding would constitute a significant fetter on the freedom of the media to discuss uninhibitedly the quality of the judiciary and the merits of their decisions.

It is now nearly 70 years since a successful contempt application for scandalising has been brought in England, though applications have been upheld in Commonwealth cases.[4] Clearly, good faith criticism, however abusive, will

---

[3] *R v New Statesman, ex parte DPP* (1928) 44 TLR 301 (DC).
[4] See Robertson and Nicol, pp 296–299; E M Barendt, *Freedom of Speech* (Oxford University Press, 1987), pp 218–223. For the most comprehensive treatment of this topic, see C Walker, 'Scandalising in the Eighties' (1985) 101 *Law Quarterly Review* 359.

not be regarded as amounting to a contempt,[5] and it is unlikely that use of this type of contempt will be revived in this country.

Questions for discussion

1. Why is 'trial by newspaper' wrong? What is the argument for a general rule prejudging issues in forthcoming cases? (Consider here the decision of the European Court of Human Rights: Extract 1.2.2 above.)

2. If it is wrong to prejudge issues in pending cases, is it less wrong to criticise a judge in abusive terms for his rulings?

2. THE STRICT LIABILITY RULE

(a) Introduction

The European Court of Human Rights held that the absolute rule formulated in the *Sunday Times* case was incompatible with the right to freedom of expression provided by art 10 of the ECHR (see Extract 1.2.2). The Contempt of Court Act 1981 (CCA) was enacted partly in order to bring UK law into line with this ruling, though it was also framed to implement recommendations of a committee which had reviewed contempt of court.[6] The legislative provisions reformulating the 'strict liability rule' are of particular significance.

Extract 12.2.1

Contempt of Court Act 1981, ss 1–3, 5, 7

1. In this Act 'the strict liability rule' means the rule of law whereby conduct may be treated as a contempt of court as tending to interfere with the course of justice in particular legal proceedings regardless of intent to do so.

2.—(1) The strict liability rule applies only in relation to publications, and for this purpose 'publication' includes any speech, writing, broadcast or other communication in whatever form, which is addressed to the public at large or any section of the public.

(2) The strict liability rule applies only to a publication which creates a substantial risk that the course of justice in the proceedings in question will be seriously impeded or prejudiced.

(3) The strict liability rule applies to a publication only if the proceedings in question are active within the meaning of this section at the time of the publication.

---

[5] See *Ambard v Attorney General for Trinidad & Tobago* [1936] AC 322 (PC), and *R v Metropolitan Police Commissioner, ex parte Blackburn* [1968] 2 QB 150 (CA).
[6] Phillimore Committee on Contempt of Court, Cmnd 5794 (1974), paras 73–154.

(4) Schedule 1 applies for determining the times at which proceedings are to be treated as active within the meaning of this section.

3.—(1) A person is not guilty of contempt of court under the strict liability rule as the publisher of any matter to which that rule applies if at the time of publication (having taken all reasonable care) he does not know and has no reason to suspect that relevant proceedings are active.

(2) A person is not guilty of contempt of court under the strict liability rule as the distributor of a publication containing any such matter if at the time of distribution (having taken all reasonable care) he does not know that it contains such matter and has no reason to suspect that is is likely to do so.

(3) The burden of proof of any fact tending to establish a defence afforded by this section to any person lies upon that person.

(4) [*Omitted*]

. . .

5. A publication made as or as part of a discussion in good faith of public affairs or other matters of general public interest is not to be treated as a contempt of court under the strict liability rule if the risk of impediment or prejudice to particular legal proceedings is merely incidental to the discussion.

. . .

7. Proceedings for a contempt of court under the strict liability rule (other than Scottish proceedings) shall not be instituted except by or with the consent of the Attorney General or on the motion of a court having jurisdiction to deal with it.

(b) Contempt in the course of the discussion of public affairs

The case from which the next extract is taken shows the value of s 5 of the CCA 1981. An article in the *Daily Mail*, written to support a pro-life candidate at a by-election, suggested that in the prevailing medical climate the chances of a physically handicapped baby surviving would be low, as 'someone would surely recommend letting her die of starvation, or otherwise disposing of her'. The trial of a doctor charged with murdering a mongoloid baby had started two days before this publication. (He was later acquitted.) Does Lord Diplock's interpretation of 'substantial risk', as applying to all risks which are not remote, mark any real change from the approach of the House of Lords in the *Sunday Times* case, of which he appears to approve?

Extract 12.2.2

Attorney General v English [1983] 1 AC 116, at 141–144 (HL)

LORD DIPLOCK: There is, of course, no question that the article in the 'Daily Mail' of which complaint is made by the Attorney-General was a 'publication' within the meaning of section 2 (1). That being so, it appears to have been accepted in the Divisional Court by both parties that the onus of proving that the article satisfied the conditions stated in section 2 (2) lay upon the

Attorney-General and that, if he satisfied that onus, the onus lay upon the appellants to prove that it satisfied the conditions stated in section 5. For my part, I am unable to accept that this represents the effect of the relationship of section 5 to section 2 (2). Section 5 does not take the form of a proviso or an exception to section 2 (2). It stands on an equal footing with it. It does not set out exculpatory matter. Like section 2 (2) it states what publications shall *not* amount to contempt of court despite their tendency to interfere with the course of justice in particular legal proceedings.

For the publication to constitute a contempt of court under the strict liability rule, it must be shown that the publication satisfies the criterion for which section 2 (2) provides, viz., that it 'creates a substantial risk that the course of justice in the proceedings in question will be seriously impeded or prejudiced.' It is only if it falls within section 5 that anything more need be shown. So logically the first question always is: has the publication satisfied the criterion laid down by section 2 (2).

My Lords, the first thing to be observed about this criterion is that the risk that has to be assessed is that which was created by the publication of the allegedly offending matter at the time when it was published. The public policy that underlies the strict liability rule in contempt of court is deterrence. Trial by newspaper or, as it should be more compendiously expressed today, trial by the media, is not to be permitted in this country. That the risk that was created by the publication when it was actually published does not ultimately affect the outcome of the proceedings is, as Lord Goddard C.J. said in *Reg. v Evening Standard Co. Ltd.* [1954] 1 Q.B. 578, 582 'neither here nor there.' If there was a reasonable possibility that it might have done so if in the period subsequent to the publication the proceedings had not taken the course that in fact they did and Dr. Arthur was acquitted, the offence was complete. The true course of justice must not at any stage be put at risk.

Next for consideration is the concatenation in the subsection of the adjective 'substantial' and the adverb 'seriously,' the former to describe the degree of risk, the latter to describe the degree of impediment or prejudice to the course of justice. 'Substantial' is hardly the most apt word to apply to 'risk' which is a noumenon. In combination I take the two words to be intended to exclude a risk that is only remote. With regard to the adverb 'seriously' a perusal of the cases cited in *Attorney-General v Times Newspapers Ltd.* [1974] A.C. 273 discloses that the adjective 'serious' has from time to time been used as an alternative to 'real' to describe the degree of risk of interfering with the course of justice, but not the degree of interference itself. It is, however, an ordinary English word that is not intrinsically inapt when used to describe the extent of an impediment or prejudice to the cause of justice in particular legal proceedings, and I do not think that for the purposes of the instant appeal any attempt to paraphrase it is necessary or would be helpful. The subsection applies to all kinds of legal proceedings, not only criminal prosecutions before a jury. If, as in the instant case and probably in most other criminal trials upon indictment, it is the outcome of the trial or the need to discharge the jury without proceeding to a verdict that is put at risk, there can be no question that that which in the course of justice is put at risk is as serious as anything could be.

My Lords, that Mr. Malcolm Muggeridge's article was capable of prejudicing the jury against Dr. Arthur at the early stage of his trial when it was published,

426

seems to me to be clear. It suggested that it was a common practice among paediatricians to do that which Dr. Arthur was charged with having done, because they thought that it was justifiable in the interest of humanity even though it was against the law. At this stage of the trial the jury did not know what Dr. Arthur's defence was going to be; and whether at that time the risk of the jury's being influenced by their recollection of the article when they came eventually to consider their verdict appeared to be more than a remote one, was a matter which the judge before whom the trial was being conducted was in the best position to evaluate, even though his evaluation, although it should carry weight, would not be binding on the Divisional Court or on your Lordships. The judge thought at that stage of the trial that the risk was substantial, not remote. So, too, looking at the matter in retrospect, did the Divisional Court despite the fact that the risk had not turned into an actuality since Dr. Arthur had by then been acquitted. For my part I am not prepared to dissent from this evaluation. I consider that the publication of the article on the third day of what was to prove a lengthy trial satisfied the criterion for which section 2 (2) of the Act provides.

The article, however, fell also within the category dealt with in section 5. It was made, in undisputed good faith, as a discussion in itself of public affairs, viz., Mrs. Carr's candidature as an independent pro-life candidate in the North West Croydon by-election for which the polling day was in one week's time. It was also part of a wider discussion on a matter of general public interest that had been proceeding intermittently over the last three months, upon the moral justification of mercy killing and in particular of allowing newly born hopelessly handicapped babies to die. So it was for the Attorney-General to show that the risk of prejudice to the fair trial of Dr. Arthur, which I agree was created by the publication of the article at the stage the trial had reached when it was published, was not 'merely incidental' to the discussion of the matter with which the article dealt.

My Lords, any article published at the time when Dr. Arthur was being tried which asserted that it was a common practice among paediatricians to let severely physically or mentally handicapped new born babies die of starvation or otherwise dispose of them would (as, in common with the trial judge and the Divisional Court, I have already accepted) involve a substantial risk of prejudicing his fair trial. But an article supporting Mrs. Carr's candidature in the by-election as a pro-life candidate that contained no such assertion would depict her as tilting at imaginary wind-mills. One of the main planks of the policy for which she sought the suffrage of the electors was that these things did happen and ought to be stopped.

I have drawn attention to the passages principally relied upon by the Divisional Court as causing a risk of prejudice that was not 'merely incidental to the discussion.' The court described them as 'unnecessary' to the discussion and as 'accusations.' The test, however, is not whether an article could have been written as effectively without these passages or whether some other phraseology might have been substituted for them that could have reduced the risk of prejudicing Dr. Arthur's fair trial; it is whether the risk created by the words actually chosen by the author was 'merely incidental to the discussion,' which I take to mean: no more than an incidental consequence of expounding its main theme . . .

427

My Lords, the article that is the subject of the instant case appears to me to be in nearly all respects the antithesis of the article which this House (pace a majority of the judges of the European Court of Human Rights) held to be a contempt of court in *Attorney-General v Times Newspapers Ltd.* [1974] A.C. 273. There the whole subject of the article was the pending civil actions against Distillers Co. (Biochemicals) Ltd. arising out of their having placed upon the market the new drug thalidomide, and the whole purpose of it was to put pressure upon that company in the lawful conduct of their defence in those actions. In the instant case, in contrast, there is in the article no mention at all of Dr. Arthur's trial. It may well be that many readers of the 'Daily Mail' who saw the article and had read also the previous day's report of Dr. Arthur's trial, and certainly if they were members of the jury at that trial, would think, 'that is the sort of thing that Dr. Arthur is being tried for; it appears to be something that quite a lot of doctors do.' But the risk of their thinking that and allowing it to prejudice their minds in favour of finding him guilty on evidence that did not justify such a finding seems to me to be properly described in ordinary English language as 'merely incidental' to any meaningful discussion of Mrs. Carr's election policy as a pro-life candidate in the by-election due to be held before Dr. Arthur's trial was likely to be concluded, or to any meaningful discussion of the wider matters of general public interest involved in the current controversy as to the justification of mercy killing. To hold otherwise would have prevented Mrs. Carr from putting forward and obtaining publicity for what was a main plank in her election programme and would have stifled all discussion in the press upon the wider controversy about mercy killing from the time that Dr. Arthur was charged in the magistrates' court in February 1981 until the date of his acquittal at the beginning of November of that year; for those are the dates between which, under section 2 (3) and Schedule 1, the legal proceedings against Dr. Arthur would be 'active' and so attract the strict liability rule.[7]

Such gagging of bona fide public discussion in the press of controversial matters of general public interest, merely because there are in existence contemporaneous legal proceedings in which some particular instance of those controversial matters may be in issue, is what section 5 of the Contempt of Court Act 1981 was in my view intended to prevent. I would allow this appeal.

(c) Substantial risk of serious prejudice

The scope of the strict liability rule has been considered by the Divisional Court[8] on a number of occasions. In particular, it has been asked to determine whether the publication in question created a *substantial* risk of serious prejudice to the course of justice in pending criminal proceedings. (In the *English* case, the proceedings were contemporaneous with the article.) The cases, from which the next three extracts are taken show the court's approach to the question. The *Mirror Group Newspapers* case reveals a particular problem:

[7] Criminal proceedings are 'active' from the moment of arrest, the issue of a warrant for arrest or summons, or oral charge, until acquittal or sentence: CCA 1981, Sched 1, paras 4 and 5.
[8] The Divisional Court usually has exclusive jurisdiction over committal for contempt of court: see C J Miller, *Contempt of Court*, 2nd ed (Oxford University Press, 1989), pp 64–66.

it would seem to follow from Schiemann LJ's judgment that an application cannot succeed when any risk of prejudice to the outcome of a criminal trial has been occasioned by the cumulative impact of publicity in several newspapers.

Extract 12.2.3

Attorney General v ITN and Others [1995] 2 All ER 370, at 383 (DC)

Following the arrest of two Irishmen on suspicion of murdering a police officer, an early evening ITN news bulletin reported that one of the suspects was a convicted IRA terrorist who had escaped from jail. It showed a poor quality photograph of him. The following morning, early editions of three national newspapers and a North of England regional paper carried the story, also referring to the suspect as an IRA fugitive. The report was not broadcast in later ITN news bulletins, nor was it repeated in subsequent editions of the newspapers. The trial took place nine months later in London.

LEGGATT LJ: The broadcast in the late evening news, of which we have watched a replay on video tape, consisted of a report of what Magee had done, accompanied in part by a photograph of him from which he was prob- ably unrecognisable. However horrible the incident that was described, this medium is in its nature ephemeral. It is, moreover, permissible to pay regard to the frequency of reported IRA outrages, which, although they are not, on that account, less untoward, do tend on the other hand to be individually less memorable.

In the result, I am not persuaded so as to be sure that in these circum- stances there was a substantial risk that anyone who saw and heard the broadcast would have remembered it nine months later. Different considera- tions might apply if it had been repeated, but it was not.

In the case of each of the newspapers, the article would have been some- what more likely to be remembered, since even a casual reader has the opportunity of reading a particular passage twice, an opportunity which is denied to a casual viewer. However, in the light of the very limited distributions in London of the offending editions, the risk was on that account diminished, and in the case of the Northern Echo, for practical purposes, annulled. Though the possibility must exist of what has been called 'leakage', I regard it in the circumstances as minimal.

The reason why I am unimpressed by the 'leakage' argument is that, although there may be an outside chance of a person adventitiously reading an article in a newspaper bought by somebody else, the possibility is, in my judgment, so remote in the circumstances of this case, as to be negligible. The risk that one of the newspapers distributed outside the jurors' catchment area might none the less come into the hands of, or be read by, one of them, is so slight as to be insubstantial.

To be coupled with the smallness of the distribution of the relevant publica- tions is the all-important factor, once again, of the lapse of time. During the nine months that passed after anyone had read the offending articles, the likelihood is that he no longer would have remembered it sufficiently to prejudice the trial. When the long odds against the potential juror reading any of the publications is multiplied by the long odds against any reader remembering it, the risk of prejudice is, in my judgment, remote. Since the newspapers too acted with alacrity to ensure that there was no repetition after the edition containing the objectionable material, I am similarly not satisfied so as to be sure that there was a substantial risk that any of the publications might have prejudiced the trial. It is to be noted that in relation both to the broadcast and to the publications, I have expressed myself in terms of the standard of proof. That is because the risk of prejudice can never be excluded, but in the particular circumstances of this case the Attorney General has not made me sure that the risk was substantial.

Extract 12.2.4

***Attorney General v MGN Ltd and Others* [1997] 1 All ER 456,
at 460–461, 466 (DC) (footnotes omitted)**

The trial judge had stayed proceedings against Geoffrey Knights on the charge of wounding with intent contrary to s 18 of the Offences Against the Person Act 1861, on the ground that the pre-trial coverage in five national newspapers of the incident, of Knights's character, and of his relationship with Gillian Taylforth, a well-known actress, made it impossible for him to have a fair trial. The reports had been published in April (shortly after the charge was brought) and May 1995, while the trial started on 29 September 1995. The Attorney General took proceedings against the five papers.

The extract sets out the court's statement of general principles, details of the article in the *Daily Mail*, and the court's conclusions with regard to all the newspapers involved.

SCHIEMANN LJ:

THE PRINCIPLES GOVERNING THE APPLICATION OF THE STRICT LIABILITY RULE

These are as follows and are not the subject of serious dispute.

(1) Each case must be decided on its own facts.

(2) The court will look at each publication separately and test matters as at the time of publication (see *A-G v English* [1982] 2 All ER 903 at 918, [1983] 1 AC 116 at 141 per Lord Diplock and *A-G v Guardian Newspapers Ltd* [1992] 3 All ER 38 at 48–49, [1992] 1 WLR 874 at 885); nevertheless, the mere fact that, by reason of earlier publications, there is already some risk of prejudice does not prevent a finding that the latest publication has created a further risk . . .

(3) The publication in question must create some risk that the course of justice in the proceedings in question will be impeded or prejudiced by that publication.

(4) That risk must be substantial.

(5) The substantial risk must be that the course of justice in the proceedings in question will not only be impeded or prejudiced but *seriously* so.

(6) The court will not convict of contempt unless it is *sure* that the publication has created this substantial risk of that serious effect on the course of justice.

(7) In making an assessment of whether the publication does create this substantial risk of that serious effect on the course of justice the following amongst other matters arise for consideration: (a) the likelihood of the publication coming to the attention of a potential juror; (b) the likely impact of the publication on an ordinary reader at the time of publication; and (c) the residual impact of the publication on a notional juror at the time of trial. It is this last matter which is crucial.

One must remember that in this, as in any exercise of risk assessment, a small risk multiplied by a small risk results in an even smaller risk.

(8) In making an assessment of the likelihood of the publication coming to the attention of a potential juror the court will consider amongst other matters: (a) whether the publication circulates in the area from which the jurors are likely to be drawn, and (b) how many copies circulated.

(9) In making an assessment of the likely impact of the publication on an ordinary reader at the time of publication the court will consider amongst other matters: (a) the prominence of the article in the publication, and (b) the novelty of the content of the article in the context of likely readers of that publication.

(10) In making an assessment of the residual impact of the publication on a notional juror at the time of trial the court will consider amongst other matters: (a) the length of time between publication and the likely date of trial (b) the focusing effect of listening over a prolonged period to evidence in a case, and (c) the likely effect of the judge's directions to a jury.

This last matter in particular has been the subject of extensive judicial comment in two different contexts: in the context of a trial or an appeal from a trial verdict and in the context of contempt proceedings. There have been many cases where, notwithstanding such prejudicial publications, the convictions have not been quashed. However, undoubtedly there have also been occasions where convictions have been quashed notwithstanding judicial directions to the jury to ignore prejudicial comments in the media.

. . .

THE DAILY MAIL

13 May 1995

The article by Lynda Lee-Potter purports to be based on an interview given by Miss Taylforth in which she described the stormy and violent relationship between herself and Mr Knights. There were, in that article, references to the fact that he had previously been convicted of an offence of violence and in particular a reference to the evidence which he had given in the libel action when he had been asked about his previous convictions. Despite the fact that the article occupied two pages with large photographs of Miss Taylforth and

Knights, the reference to the incident on the night of the 17/18 April was really only one short paragraph with no detail as to how Mr Davies had received his injuries. The inference, however, from the context of the remainder of the article is that Knights had caused them and caused them unlawfully.

Applying the principles set out earlier in this judgment we do not consider that this publication created a substantial risk that the course of justice in the proceedings would be seriously impeded or prejudiced.

CONCLUSION

There is no doubt that the so called 'news items' or 'articles', excluding for the moment the article on 13 May in the Daily Mail, were all written in typical graphic tabloid style. They include large banner headlines, large photographs of all three of those involved in the incident. There is a measure of exaggeration in the description of the injuries sustained by Mr Davies and the language used is undoubtedly emotive. However, all in all it is difficult to see how any one of the publications in April and May 1995 created any greater risk of serious prejudice than that which had already been created.

We are not called upon to rule upon the correctness of Judge Sanders' decision to stay the proceedings in front of him and nothing in this judgment should be taken as doing so. A consequence of the need in contempt proceedings, in which respondents face imprisonment or a fine, to be sure and to look at each publication separately and the need in trial proceedings to look at risk of prejudice created by the totality of publications can be that it is proper to stay proceedings on the ground of prejudice albeit that no individual is guilty of contempt. One may regret that situation or one may take the view that this is the best answer to a difficult problem. We are not called upon to express our view on that matter.

What however clearly follows from our findings is that each of these applications by the Attorney General is dismissed.

Extract 12.2.5

Attorney General v BBC, Hat Trick Productions [1997] EMLR 76, at 78–79, 82–83 (DC)

AULD LJ: This is a motion by Her Majesty's Attorney-General for committal of the British Broadcasting Corporation and Hat Trick Productions Limited for contempt of court arising out of the BBC's television broadcast on BBC2 of a programme produced by Hat Trick in the series 'Have I Got News for You'. The programme was broadcast on April 29, 1994 between 10 and 10.30 p.m., and was repeated on April 30, 1994 between 9.30 p.m. and 10 p.m.

. . .

The broadcasts were six months before the trial, which was fixed to start on October 31, 1994, of two counts on an indictment charging Kevin and Ian Maxwell with conspiracy to defraud the trustees and beneficiaries – many of the latter, employees of the Mirror Group – of pension funds managed by a company established by their late father and former employer, Robert Maxwell. In the first of those two counts Robert Maxwell was named as a co-conspirator.

'Have I Got News for You' is a popular, humorous and irreverent quiz programme in which two teams of two 'celebrities' compete in a light hearted way in answering questions on current affairs put to them by Angus Deayton the programme's 'presenter' and chairman. At the time it was regularly broadcast on a Friday night and repeated at about the same time on Saturday. Ian Hislop and Paul Merton, who appeared frequently on the programme, were two of the 'celebrities' on the programme broadcast on April 29 and 30, 1994. During a round of questions entitled 'Odd One Out' four photographs were displayed, one of which was of pensioners of the Mirror Group allegedly defrauded by the late Robert Maxwell and his two sons, Kevin and Ian, holding up placards.

After the competitors had attempted to identify the odd photograph of the four, Angus Deayton said:

'All who profited from misfortune except for the Mirror pensioners from whose misfortune others have profited. No mentioning no Maxwells, er no names. The BBC are in fact cracking down on references to Ian and Kevin Maxwell just in case programme-makers appear biased in their treatment of these two heartless scheming bastards.'

The time spent on the topic, including this remark, took about one and a half minutes, the photograph of the Mirror pensioners remaining on display throughout, though not always readily visible as the camera moved from speaker to speaker.

At the end of the programme, and after the credits, Angus Deayton's unpleasant reference to the Maxwell brothers was highlighted by the following broadcast exchange:

Ian Hislop:	You're not going to leave in that bit about the Maxwell brothers being heartless scheming bastards?
Angus Deayton:	Well.
Ian Hislop:	Nothing personal Angus, contempt of Court has a statutory two year imprisonment. TV's Mr Wandsworth Prison. You will find a lot of inmates will fancy you in there, Angus . . .
Angus Deayton:	What a shame we are not recording.

Keith Maxwell's solicitor, Mr Keith Oliver, along with several million others, watched the programme on April 29. He was so concerned about it that, on the morning of April 30, he telephoned the BBC and spoke to its duty solicitor, Mrs Shelley Bradley. He told her that he regarded the matter as one of contempt, that he intended to refer it to the Attorney-General and to Phillips J., the trial judge in the forthcoming criminal trial, and asked that the programme should not be repeated that evening. However, the BBC did broadcast it again that evening, in exactly the same form. According to a cutting from the *London Evening Standard* of May 11, 1994, the combined audience for the two broadcasts was 6,140,000 people, being the largest audience for any programmed broadcast on BBC2 that week.

433

. . .

The facts that the remarks were made in a humorous, irreverent and often rude programme, though not themselves humorous, that they were brief and made in the impermanent medium of television all have to be balanced against the following matters:

their obvious relevance to the charges on which the Maxwell brothers were awaiting trial;

the clear implication that they were obviously guilty of fraudulent conduct of the sort charged;

the large, national, audience to whom the words were addressed; and

the focus and emphasis given to the words in their repetition after the credits and in the repeat programme the following night.

As to the length of time – six months – before the trial, there is the question of whether and how the remarks might be remembered by any potential juror or jurors after that period. If remembered, there is also the question what bearing they might have on their consideration of the case. Those matters go to both questions, whether, at the time of the broadcast, there was a substantial risk of prejudice and, if so, to the seriousness of the prejudice.

I have in mind the obvious point that six months is a long time, and that the longer the time between publication and trial the more likely it is that memories will fade. See *e.g. News Group, per* Sir John Donaldson M.R. at 16B and Parker L.J. at 17H. I also have in mind the oft-cited remarks of Lawton J. in *R. v Kray* (1969) Cr.App.R. 412, C.C.C., at 415 (albeit applying the different test of 'probable bias') and of Sir John Donaldson M.R. in *News Group,* at 16B–E, about the short memory of the public and the inward looking effect of a long trial on a jury. See also *Ex. p. The Telegraph plc* [1993] 1 W.L.R. 980, C.A., *per* Taylor L.C.J. at 987E–F. There is also high judicial authority that a jury can generally be relied upon to follow likely directions from the trial judge to decide the case only on the evidence. See *e.g. R. v The Horsham Justices, ex p. Farquharson* [1982] Q.B. 762, C.A., *per* Lord Denning M.R. at 794; *Ex p. The Telegraph, per* Taylor L.C.J. at 987E; and *Re Dagenais v Canadian Broadcasting Corp.* (1994) 94 C.C.C. (3d) 289, *per* Lamer C.J.C. at 322–323. However, those matters, considered individually or together, cannot exculpate the alleged contemner in every long and complex trial some months after publication. That is especially so where, as here, the offending words are strikingly prejudicial and go to the heart of the case which the jury are to try, and when the offending publicity is great both because of its medium and repetition, and because both the speakers and the victims are already much in the public eye. At the end of the day, the matter is, as I have said, one for the Court to assess on the particular facts of the case, an assessment of which it must be sure. However, the threshold of risk is not high, simply of more than a remote or minimal risk of serious prejudice. Putting my conclusion in the framework of the statutory provision, I am sure that the broadcast created such a risk, namely that one or more jurors would not begin and continue their jury duty with an open mind, and thus that there was a substantial risk that the course of justice in the trial would be seriously prejudiced.

Questions for discussion

1. What factors does the Divisional Court take into account in determining whether the risk of prejudice was substantial?
2. How would you distinguish the *Hat Trick Productions* case from the other two decisions?

In *Hat Trick Productions* the court held that the contempt was serious, resulting from risk-taking, rather than carelessness. The respondents were each fined £10,000. It seems to have taken an even more critical view of the press behaviour in the *Morgan* case, where the *News of the World* had published a sensational article detailing the involvement of its own reporter in the investigation of a massive forgery ring. Among other things the article revealed the criminal records of two persons alleged to be parties to a criminal conspiracy; their trial was halted, because of the possible impact of this publicity.

Extract 12.2.6

Attorney General v Morgan [1998] EMLR 294, at 306 (DC)

PILL LJ: Stress has been placed upon the irrelevance of intention to the breach of the strict liability rule in contempt of court cases. The company's approach to publication has been made clear. Where court proceedings are active so that the strict liability rule applies, they make a judgment under section 2(2) as to whether it applies to a proposed publication. If in their judgment it does, they do not publish; if it does not, they assert their freedom of expression and publish. I accept that their judgment was made in that way in the case of both articles under question.

However, if an erroneous judgment is made, as it was in this case, the effect upon the administration of justice may be very serious and that must be reflected in the penalty. The effect is very serious in this case in that, by reason of publication, criminal proceedings were rendered liable to stay (and were in the event stayed) in a major case. The alleged offence was of conspiracy to deliver counterfeits of English, United States and Spanish currency notes intending that they should be passed as genuine. The scale of the alleged offence was indeed asserted in the publication. The effect of the contempt upon the due administration of justice and the public interest is serious and a substantial penalty is required. Deterrence is also a factor in sentence. The means of the company are not in doubt. I bear in mind the co-operation which the *News of the World* often gives to the police in the investigation of crime. The company will be fined £50,000. I do not consider that an additional penalty upon the first respondent [the editor] is required in this case.

(d) Criminal appeals

It is now quite common for a judge to halt a criminal trial, because he accepts the argument that, owing to massive pre-trial publicity, the accused is unlikely to receive a fair trial. This occurred, for instance, in the *MGN/Knights* case (Extract 12.2.4) and the *Morgan* case (Extract 12.2.6). But the trial judge may consider that a clear direction to the jury to consider the case on the basis of the evidence in court and to exclude from their mind anything they may have read in the press is enough to ensure a fair trial. In that event, a convicted defendant may decide to appeal on the ground that the verdict of the jury was unsafe. The next extract shows the circumstances in which the Court of Appeal is prepared to accept the argument. The defendants, charged with conspiracy to murder Tom King, the Secretary of State for Ireland, had exercised their right not to give evidence; they argued that the announcement during the course of their trial of government proposals to modify the right had inevitably prejudiced its fairness. Television news bulletins had reported Tom King as saying that the proposals were aimed at terrorists, and had carried interviews with him and with Lord Denning who supported a change in the law. The trial judge had rejected arguments to halt the trial and discharge the jury.

Extract 12.2.7

R v McCann (1991) 92 Cr App Rep 239, at 252–253 (CA)

BELDAM LJ: When the judge made his ruling, he once again said that if by reason of the publicity which had been engendered he thought that a fair trial of the accused was endangered, as it had been submitted by defending counsel it was, he would have had to discharge the jury. His view was that he could readily cure any harm that could have been done, which he greatly doubted because he had previously told the jury that they must try the case on the basis of the evidence they heard and not on the basis of anything they read in the newspapers or heard on television . . .

The jury were then brought into court and the learned judge directed them, reminding them that the accused had 'certainly so far not given evidence.' That was an inalienable right which any accused person had under the law. No person was obliged to answer any questions put to him or to give evidence in a case. That was their absolute right and nothing could take that away from them. He reminded them that they must try the case on the evidence which they heard and not on anything which they heard on the radio or television, or read in the newspapers, and he told them totally to disregard anything which they might have read in newspapers or seen on television that might have any effect on their minds. . . . On the hearing of the appeal it seemed to the court that the first question which had to be considered was whether this extensive coverage in the media generally and the very pointed statements made in the television broadcasts created a real risk of prejudice to the appellants because the jury might be influenced against them since they had remained silent. Mr. Rawley, who appeared for the Crown, had seen the video recordings [of the television news bulletins] which we have seen. In answer to the court Mr. Rawley agreed that there was such a risk and that it was real in the sense that it was not fanciful. His contention was that such a risk could be, and was, eliminated by the judge's direction to the jury. The court too had formed the impression that the power and nature of the statements which had been made in the course of the broadcasts did constitute a real and not a fanciful risk that the jury might be influenced to the view that, particularly in a terrorist case, a refusal to give an explanation in answer to questions or in evidence was the refuge of the guilty and incompatible with innocence.

The learned judge had said on more than one occasion that if he thought that a fair trial of the accused was in danger, or if he was satisfied there was a serious risk to a proper verdict or a fair trial, he would have discharged the jury. Neither he, nor Mr. Rawley at that time, had had the opportunity to see the recordings. We are satisfied that if the learned judge had seen them he would not have discounted the risk of prejudice to the appellants to the extent that he did, and he would have been bound to be less confident that it could be eliminated by a direction to the jury.

Consequently it seems to us that this is a case in which this Court ought to review the exercise by the judge of his discretion in the light of the evidence which we have seen from the video recordings, and of the concession made by Mr. Rawley in this Court. The statements to which we have drawn attention, which were powerfully made, were on their face of general application but they had a particular relevance to the trial of the accused. Two of them had declined to answer questions after their arrest and all of them had elected not to give evidence and thus to maintain their right to silence. The allegations made against the appellants were that they were part of a terrorist organisation and that they had conspired to murder Mr. King and others unknown. The coincidence that the remarks should have been made when the trial of the appellants had reached such a critical stage and should have been made by the Minister who was alleged to be the victim of the proposed conspiracy would not, in our view, enhance the perception that justice was seen to be done. The learned judge regarded it as important that the trial, which had continued for some length of time, should come properly to its close. Very little of the evidence which was given at the trial was the subject of challenge and much of it was read to the jury. It is difficult to see what injustice the Crown would have suffered if a retrial had been ordered. As Lord Atkin said in *Ras Behari Lal v King Emperor* [1933] All E.R. 723, 726: 'Finality is a good thing: but justice is a better.'

The great controversy and intense media interest sparked off by the Home Secretary's announcement and the press conference would inevitably have subsided and its impact would have waned in a matter of a month or two. It is true that two or three days would have elapsed before the jury retired to consider their verdict and that before they did so they would have had the advantage of the very fair summing-up which the learned judge delivered to them. We were invited to pay regard, as this Court did in the case of *Dubarry* (1977) 64 Cr.App.R. 7, to the time that the jury deliberated before eventually reaching a verdict by a majority of 10:2 after fifteen hours. We have carefully considered the directions which the learned judge gave with a view to dispelling the risk of injustice as he perceived it.

In the final analysis we are left with the definite impression that the impact which the statements in the television interviews may well have had on the fairness of the trial could not be overcome by any direction to the jury, and that the only way in which justice could be done and be obviously seen to be done was by discharging the jury and ordering a retrial. In our judgment that is what the learned judge should have done. It is not open to us in this appeal to consider whether we should exercise the enlarged power given to this Court to order a retrial by section 43 of the Criminal Justice Act 1988. The appellants' notices of applications for leave to appeal were given before that section came into force. Accordingly, being of the opinion that the verdict of the jury should be set aside on the ground that in the circumstances it is unsafe, we allow the appeals and quash the convictions.

The same approach was taken in the *Taylor* case. There had been saturation coverage in the press of the trial of two sisters for the murder of the wife of a man with whom one sister had an affair before his marriage. McCowan LJ pointed out that it was unreasonable in these circumstances to expect defence counsel at the trial to ask for the jury to be discharged; it would entail the defendants spending yet more time in custody.[9]

(e) The strict liability rule and the stay of criminal trials

A contempt application under the strict liability rule may fail, even though the trial judge had earlier stayed the proceedings because extensive media publicity made it impossible for the accused to have a fair trial: see the *MGN/Knights* case (Extract 12.2.4) Conversely, in the *BBC/Hat Trick Productions* case (Extract 12.2.5) the Divisional Court fined the respondents for contempt, although Phillips J had refused to stay the Maxwell brothers' trial. The Divisional Court has emphasised that in contempt proceedings it is not bound by the decision of the trial judge or of the Court of Appeal on an appeal against an 'unsafe' conviction. It should form its own view on the distinct question whether the requirements for strict liability contempt have been met.[10]

These points have recently been emphasised by the Divisional Court when it upheld a contempt application against a regional newspaper. It had inadvertently published, during the course of a murder trial, an article suggesting that the murder had been committed by members of a notorious criminal gang involved in drug dealing. Although none of the defendants was identified, the trial was halted and the jury discharged. (It commenced ten days later at a different venue, and the defendants were convicted.)

---

[9] *R v Taylor* (1994) 98 Cr App Rep 361, at 369 (CA).
[10] Pill LJ in *Attorney General v Morgan* [1998] EMLR 294, at 301 (DC).

Extract 12.2.8

Attorney General v Birmingham Post and Mail Ltd
[1998] 4 All ER 49, at 57, 59 (DC)

SIMON BROWN LJ: It seems to me necessarily to follow (although it is right to say that no specific authority was produced to us which directly establishes the point) that one and the same publication may well constitute a contempt and yet, even though not substantially mitigated in its effect by a temporary stay and/or change of venue, not so prejudice the trial as to undermine the safety of any subsequent conviction.[11] To my mind that can only be because s 2(2) postulates a lesser degree of prejudice than is required to make good an appeal against conviction. Similarly it seems to me to postulate a lesser degree of prejudice than would justify an order for a stay. In short, s 2(2) is designed to avoid (and where necessary punish) publications even if they merely risk prejudicing proceedings, whereas a stay will generally only be granted where it is recognised that any subsequent conviction would otherwise be imperilled, and a conviction will only be set aside (at all events now, since s 2 of the Criminal Appeals Act 1995) if it is actually unsafe . . .

It seems to me to follow from all this that the questions being asked respectively by the trial judge when considering a stay and this court when considering a s 2(2) application are by no means the same and it is for this reason that a decision to grant or refuse a stay will not necessarily be determinative one way or the other of whether a contempt is established.

That said, however, I find it difficult to envisage a publication which has concerned the judge sufficiently to discharge the jury and yet is not properly to be regarded as a contempt. I conclude that the only situation in which realistically that is likely to arise is where, analysed with the benefit of argument from the publishers' counsel, the publication is seen to have been so little prejudicial as not even to have given rise to a seriously arguable ground of appeal had the trial been allowed to continue and proceeded to conviction. I venture to doubt whether many stays will have been granted in these circumstances. Rather, as the cases show, it is altogether more likely that a stay will have been refused (or perhaps not even sought) and yet the publication nevertheless be in contempt.

Simon Brown LJ added that his observations applied to cases where the prejudicial material was published during the course of the trial and where no other prejudicial publications complicated the issue, as in the *MGN/Knights* case (Extract 12.2.4). The newspaper was fined £20,000; the court took into account that it was a first offence, committed by a regional paper with a circulation of 26,000, and that it was negligent, rather than reckless.

[11] Simon Brown LJ had referred to a number of cases, including *Attorney General v English* (Extract 12.2.2) and the *BBC/Hat Trick Productions* case (Extract 12.2.5), where the requirements of the strict liability rule under CCA 1981, s 2(2) were satisfied, although the criminal proceedings had not been stayed.

Questions for discussion

1. Does it make sense to hold a newspaper liable for contempt, even though the trial judge had earlier held that the prejudicial publicity would not render a conviction unsafe?

2. If the judge has stayed the criminal proceedings, will it generally follow that a contempt application will be successful?

3. Was the fine appropriate, bearing in mind the fines imposed on the *News of the World* in *Morgan* (Extract 12.2.6) and on the *BBC/Hat Trick Productions* (Extract 12.2.5)

3. COMMON LAW CONTEMPT

The Contempt of Court Act 1981 is not an exhaustive code for the law of contempt, or even for that part of contempt law concerned to safeguard the administration of justice.

Extract 12.3.1

Contempt of Court Act 1981, s 6

6. Nothing in the foregoing provisions of this Act—
   (a) prejudices any defence available at common law to a charge of contempt of court under the strict liability rule;
   (b) implies that any publication is punishable as contempt of court under that rule which would not be so punishable apart from those provisions;
   (c) restricts liability for contempt of court in respect of conduct intended to impede or prejudice the administration of justice.

Section 6(c) of the CCA 1981 has proved particularly significant for the media. In *Attorney General v News Group Newspapers*,[12] a tabloid offered to fund a private prosecution against a named doctor for rape, although the authorities had decided not to prosecute him for lack of evidence. As the doctor had not at that time been arrested or charged, proceedings were not 'active', and so the strict liability rule did not apply. The Divisional Court, however, held that under s 6(c) an application for common law contempt could be brought, even where the publication might prejudice only the outcome of proceedings which were not imminent. The elements of common law contempt were further considered in the case from which the next extract is taken. An article in the *Sport* newspaper referred in lurid terms to the previous record of a man called Evans whom the police were looking for in connection with the disappearance of a schoolgirl. The strict liability rule did not apply, as Evans had not been arrested and no warrant had been issued.

---

[12] [1989] QB 110 (DC).

Extract 12.3.2

Attorney General v Sport Newspapers Ltd [1991] 1 WLR 1194, at 1207, 1209 (DC)

BINGHAM LJ: In my view section 6(c) was intended to preserve what was understood to be the existing law, that a publisher was liable in contempt for an intentionally prejudicial publication made at a time when proceedings were imminent. I cannot otherwise see what sensible purpose this provision could have been intended to serve.

. . .

If the question were at large, I would be much more hesitant whether that proposition could hold if proceedings were not imminent. *Attorney-General v News Group Newspapers Plc.* [1989] Q.B. 110 is, however, a very clear decision on the point, and in making it this court expressly recognised that it was extending the boundaries of contempt as previously understood. It is a decision with very serious implications in those cases, perhaps increasingly common, where reporters are concerned to highlight an alleged crime, to point an accusing finger at an identified culprit and to stimulate a demand for prosecution. It also has the effect of enlarging a quasi-criminal liability in a field very recently considered by Parliament . . . In a matter of this nature it is very highly desirable that the law should be clear so that it may be understood and observed. I am quite satisfied that we should not be justified in departing from the rule so recently and unambiguously laid down in this court.[13]. . .

Having heard the second respondent [the editor] give evidence, I think it is possible to reconstruct his state of mind at the time of publication. He said, as is obvious, that a newspaper is written for its readers, and I have no doubt that his main (although unadmitted) aim was to publish a story of a kind which his readers could be expected to relish. According to him, his main aim was to alert the public to the danger of this violent and habitual sexual predator, which he felt the police had been wrong to conceal, and thereby perhaps increase the chance of his apprehension. I doubt if this concern was uppermost in the second respondent's mind, but I see no reason to doubt that it played a part in his thinking. I accept his evidence that he gave consideration to the police request not to reveal Evans' previous convictions, and also his evidence that he wondered whether the police were seeking to cover up their own failure to question a rather obvious local suspect before he slipped through the net. The second respondent's belief, as he made plain in evidence, was that there could be no liability in contempt before a warrant had been issued or an arrest made. That belief, although perhaps understandable in 1988, was (as we have held) incorrect. But I accept the second respondent's evidence that at the date of publication he regarded the commencement of criminal proceedings against Evans as speculative and remote. With the benefit of hindsight, of course, we know that a warrant was issued shortly after publication and an arrest made shortly after that. But these facts were not known

---

[13] Hodgson J disagreed on this point, but concurred with Bingham LJ that the respondent lacked the necessary intent.

when the newspaper was published. At that time all that was known was that Evans had disappeared, with some reason to think he had gone abroad. There was nothing to suggest that he had been sighted or that the police were on his scent or that his early apprehension was expected. It was wholly uncertain whether he would be found and, if so, where or when, and uncertain when, if at all, proceedings might follow.

I have not found this factual issue easy to resolve, and I regard it as finely poised. But on balance I conclude that the applicant has not shown beyond reasonable doubt that at the date of publication the second respondent had the specific intention which must be proved against him. If proof of reckless-ness were enough, the answer might be different, but it is not. On the facts here I cannot be satisfied that the second respondent intended to prejudice the fair conduct of proceedings the very existence of which he regarded as speculative and remote. It follows that I would, on this ground, refuse this application against both respondents.

These decisions prompt the question whether the article in the *Sunday Times* case (Extract 12.1.1 above) might now be held liable for common law con-tempt. This would be odd since an object of the CCA 1981 was to imple-ment the decision of the European Court of Human Rights which had held the House of Lords' decision in that case incompatible with the ECHR. The strict liability rule would not apply, since the proceedings the article intended to influence were not 'active'. (Broadly, civil proceedings are 'active' from the time when the case is set down for trial.)[14] But common law contempt applies whether or not proceedings are 'active'.

Common law contempt may also be committed by the publication by one newspaper of material, the publication of which by other media has already been restrained by an injunction to prevent a breach of confidence. This variety of contempt prevented the *Sunday Times* and other papers from pub-lishing extracts from *Spycatcher* when the *Guardian* had been restrained from doing this by breach of confidence injunctions.[15] Lord Oliver explores the implications of the application of contempt law in this context.

Extract 12.3.3

***Attorney General v Times Newspapers Ltd* [1992] 1 AC 191, at 226 (HL)**

LORD OLIVER OF AYLMERTON: Whilst newspapers have a legitimate inter-est and an important and necessary function in disseminating information, their rights are no higher than the right of a private individual to preserve the inviolability of that which he has imparted to another under an obligation of confidence and ought not to be permitted to override that right save where the

---

[14] CCA 1981, Sched 1, paras 12–13.
[15] See Chapter 11, Sections 2 and 3.

public interest compulsively demands. A fortiori is that the case where a competent court has intervened to protect such right. The respondent to this appeal is the Attorney-General, but it has to be stressed as was emphasised in both the courts below, that in this case he was in no different position from any other private citizen entitled to preserve the sanctity of confidential information. In the end, I have found the logic of the respondent's arguments inescapable and I accordingly agree that the Court of Appeal reached the right conclusion and that the appeal must be dismissed. I confess, however, that I do so with a measure of disquiet, not because I doubt the validity of the conclusion, but because of the possibilities that open up. As I have said, I think that this sort of question is unlikely to arise except in cases of threatened publication of confidential material. But in those cases the important stage of the proceedings is almost always and inevitably the interlocutory one and it is, I think, important that a vigilant eye should be kept on the possibility that the law of contempt may be invoked in support of claims which are in truth insupportable. The guidelines laid down by this House in *American Cyanamid Co. v Ethicon Ltd.* [1975] A.C. 396, have come to be treated as carved on tablets of stone, so that a plaintiff seeking interlocutory relief has never to do more than show that he has a fairly arguable case. Thus the effect in a contest between a would-be publisher and one seeking to restrain the publication of allegedly confidential information is that the latter, by presenting an arguable case, can effectively through the invocation of the law of contempt, restrain until the trial of the action, which may be two or more years ahead, publication not only by the defendant but by anyone else within the jurisdiction and thus stifle what may, in the end, turn out to be perfectly legitimate comment until it no longer has any importance or commands any public interest. In cases where there is a contest as to whether the information is confidential at all or whether the public interest in any event requires its publication despite its confidentiality, this could be very important and experience shows that orders for speedy trial do not always achieve the hoped for result. I speak only for myself, but I cannot help feeling that in cases where it is clearly of importance that publication, if it takes place at all, should take place expeditiously, it may be necessary for courts to balance the rights of the parties and to decide the issue, as they sometimes did before the *Cyanamid* case, at the interlocutory stage on the prima facie merits and on the evidence then available.

Questions for discussion

1. Might the *Sunday Times* be held liable for common law contempt for its press campaign against Distillers?

2. Will the Human Rights Act 1998 (see Extract 1.5.3 above) affect the observations of Lord Oliver concerning the impact of common law contempt on the media?

4. POSTPONEMENT ORDERS

(a) Introduction

Extract 12.4.1

Contempt of Court Act 1981, s 4(1)–(2)

4.—(1) Subject to this section a person is not guilty of contempt of court under the strict liability rule in respect of a fair and accurate report of legal proceedings held in public, published contemporaneously and in good faith.

(2) In any such proceedings the court may, where it appears to be necessary for avoiding a substantial risk of prejudice to the administration of justice in those proceedings, or in any other proceedings pending or imminent, order that the publication of any report of the proceedings, or any part of the proceedings, be postponed for such period as the court thinks necessary for that purpose.

The effect of s 4(1) of the CCA 1981 is clear. The media is not liable for contempt of court under the strict liability rule, merely because a fair, accurate and contemporaneous report of legal proceedings might create a substantial risk of prejudice to their outcome (or that of other proceedings). But s 4(2) gives the court power to order that reporting of proceedings be *postponed* in order to avoid such a risk. The provision puts a common law power of uncertain origin on a secure basis.[16] The statutory power is exercised for a number of reasons, among them the need to prevent the reporting of evidence or legal arguments heard in the absence of the jury, and of evidence identifying a defendant who is likely to be involved in subsequent, related proceedings. A third common ground is that reporting may prejudice later trials involving the same or associated offences.[17]

One legal issue is whether it is a contempt of court merely to breach a postponement order or whether it must be shown that the breach would independently amount to a contempt. Another difficulty is whether a court is entitled to order the postponement of the reporting of *all* the proceedings, even though only some *part* of them concerned sensitive matters, the reporting of which might create a substantial risk of prejudice. Answers to these questions were provided by the Court of Appeal in one of the first cases on the statutory power. It may be noted that Lord Denning MR dissented from the view taken by Ackner LJ (set out in the extract) and Shaw LJ concerning the effect of a postponement order under s 4(2).

---

[16] For leading common law cases, see *R v Clement* (1821) 4 B & Ald 218, and *R v Poulson, The Times*, 4 January 1974. The Phillimore Committee recommended that contemporaneous accurate court reporting should never attract contempt proceedings, without the qualification of the postponement power: Cmnd 5794 (1974), paras 134–141.

[17] See C Walker, I Cram, and D Hogarth, 'The Reporting of Crown Court Proceedings and the Contempt of Court Act 1981' (1992) 55 *Modern Law Review* 647, at 658–660.

Extract 12.4.2

R v Horsham Justices, ex parte Farquharson
[1982] QB 762, at 805–807 (CA)

Horsham Justices had made a 'blanket' order postponing the reporting of proceedings to commit the defendants for trial on arms offences; it was feared that sensational allegations might be made during the proceedings which would prejudice the trial. A journalist, a local newspaper, and the National Union of Journalists applied for judicial review; one argument was that the justices could not take into account the risk of prejudice to the subsequent Crown Court proceedings, another was that the order was too wide and that it should have been limited to the reporting of the sensational material.

ACKNER LJ: It would be an odd situation indeed if the contravention of an order of a court that the publication of a report of its proceedings should be postponed for a specified period, made because the court thought that such a postponement was necessary for avoiding a substantial risk of prejudice to the administration of justice, could carry with it no sanction other than the removal of a defence to a charge of contempt under the strict liability rule. To my mind, and in this respect I with diffidence dissent from the view expressed by Lord Denning M.R., it is clear that as a corollary of the onus now being put upon the court to specify whether a report of its proceedings or any part thereof should be postponed, instead of leaving the journalist to publish at his peril, a new head of contempt of court has been created, separate and distinct from the strict liability rule ('that rule' referred to in section 6 (*b*)). If a journalist reports proceedings that are the subject matter of a postponement order under section 4 (2), then he is guilty of a contempt of court.

Understandably Mr. Beloff [counsel for the applicants] refers to the definition of 'court' in section 19 and stresses that since this includes any tribunal or body exercising the judicial power of the state, then a very widespread power has been given not only to make orders, but orders which are not appealable – although as this appeal illustrates they are nevertheless reviewable by the courts. I do not think this is as powerful a point as may seem at first sight. First of all, the power is a power to *postpone*, not to prohibit totally, publication. Secondly, the power may be exercised in relation to only a *part* of the proceedings. Thirdly, that in order for the jurisdiction to be exercised the court must be satisfied that an order is necessary for avoiding a substantial risk of prejudice to the administration of justice. The obvious case for the postponement of a report of proceedings is where the substantive trial or a retrial has yet to take place, or where a fair and accurate report of one trial might still prejudice another trial still to be heard. The prejudice to the administration of justice which is envisaged is the reduction in the power of the court of doing that which is the end for which it exists – namely, to administer justice duly, impartially, and with reference solely to the facts judicially brought before it: *per* Wills J. in *Rex v Parke* [1903] 2 K.B. 432, 438, 444. What the court is generally concerned with is the position of a juryman who, unlike the judge, has neither the training nor the experience to assist him in putting out of his mind matters which are not evidence in the case. I find it difficult to conceive of a case in which *a tribunal*, properly directing itself in the terms of section 4 (2), could find it necessary to order the postponement of the report of its proceedings . . .

If Mr. Beloff was right in his submissions, it would be necessary to look behind every order made under section 4 (2) and not only to reconsider the very basis of the order, but to revive all the old uncertainties recognised to exist at common law as to whether the conduct complained of could have amounted to contempt. This cannot have been Parliament's intention. It would involve a section 4 (2) order having *no effect* at all in regard to committal proceedings and little effect in regard to other proceedings . . .

I further accept Mr. Simon Brown's [counsel for the prosecutors, the Customs and Excise Commissioners] submission that within the language of section 4 (2) there are pointers to the conclusion that there is a liability for a breach of an order under section 4 (2) which is different from liability under the strict liability rule. The substantial risk of prejudice may relate to 'any other proceedings pending or imminent.' This goes wider than proceedings which are 'active' within the meaning of section 2 (3) of and Schedule 1 to the Act. Moreover, I consider that Parliament by use of additional words was contemplating a more stringent test in section 2 (2) than that provided in section 4 (2).

. . .

To my mind the Divisional Court were entirely correct in deciding that the blanket order imposed by the magistrates was too wide. They therefore ordered that the case be remitted to the magistrates for them to consider whether any order should be made postponing publication of reports and, if so, whether it should relate to only part of the committal proceedings. Before the Divisional Court the submission that there was not sufficient material before the justices to enable them to make *any* postponement order was abandoned. . . . There was material before the justices to support the submission that, not only was the prosecution proposing to tender evidence which was irrelevant and therefore inadmissible to the charges which they were hearing, but that such evidence was likely to be the subject of sensational reporting. Therefore, there was a real risk of prejudice to the administration of justice. Potential jurors who would be trying the case at the Crown Court, if the justices committed, might well start the trial with a bias against the accused, having inferred from the press reports that the accused were involved in far more serious offences than those charged.

The Court of Appeal subsequently issued a Practice Direction.

Extract 12.4.3

Practice Direction (Contempt: Reporting Restrictions) [1982] 1 WLR 1475

LORD LANE CJ: . . . It is necessary to keep a permanent record of such [postponement] orders for later reference. For this purpose all orders made under section 4 (2) must be formulated in precise terms, having regard to the decision of *Reg. v Horsham, ex parte Farquharson* [1982] 2 QB 762, and orders . . . must be committed to writing either by the judge personally or by the clerk of the court under the judge's directions. An order must state (a) its precise scope, (b) the time at which it shall cease to have effect, if appropriate, and (c) the specific purpose of making the order.

Courts will normally give notice to the press in some form that an order has been made . . . and court staff should be prepared to answer any enquiry about a specific case, but it is, and will remain, the responsibility of those reporting cases, and their editors, to ensure that no breach of any order occurs and the onus rests with them to make enquiry in any case of doubt.

(b) The requirements for making a postponement order

In a leading case, the Court of Appeal deleted restrictions which would have prevented the reporting of any material identifying the chief prosecution witness and of the closing speeches and summing-up in a trial for serious drugs offences, on the ground that these were not 'necessary' to avoid a substantial risk of prejudice to later trials of defendants for the same offences.

Extract 12.4.4

Ex parte The Telegraph plc [1993] 1 WLR 980, at 984–985, 987–988 (CA)

LORD TAYLOR CJ: [Section 4 (2) of the Act] contains two requirements for the making of a postponement order, first that publication would create 'a substantial risk of prejudice to the administration of justice' and, second, that postponement of publication 'appears to be necessary for avoiding' that risk.

It has been said that there is a third requirement, derived from the word 'may' at the beginning of the subsection, namely, that a court, in the exercise of its discretion, having regard to the competing public interests of ensuring a fair trial and of open justice, considers it appropriate to make an order: see *Reg. v Horsham Justices, Ex parte Farquharson* [1982] Q.B. 762, 789D, *per* Lord Denning M.R.; *Reg. v Saunders* (unreported), 5 February 1990, *per* Henry J. and *Reg. v Brooks* (unreported), 31 July 1992, *per* Buckley J. It seems to us the discretion indicated by the use of the word 'may' in the provision is catered for by the second requirement that the court may only make an order where it appears to it to be 'necessary for avoiding' the substantial risk of prejudice to the administration of justice that it perceives. In forming a view whether it is necessary to make an order for avoiding such a risk a court will inevitably have regard to the competing public considerations of ensuring a fair trial and of open justice. It is noteworthy that whether the element of discretion is to be regarded as part of the 'necessity' test or as a third requirement, the courts as a matter of practice have tended to merge the requirement of necessity and the exercise of discretion: see, e.g., *Reg. v Saunders*, 5 February 1990, *per* Henry J.; *Reg. v Brooks*, 31 July 1992, *per* Buckley J.; *Ex parte Central Television Plc.* [1991] 1 W.L.R. 4, 8E, *per* Lord

Lane C.J. and *Reg. v Beck, Ex parte Daily Telegraph* (1991) 94 Cr.App.R. 376, 379, 381, *per* Farquharson L.J.

As to the first of the two requirements, it should be noted that the risk of prejudice to the administration of justice must be 'substantial.'

As to the second of the requirements, the necessity for an order, it is a statutory recognition of the principle of open justice. There is an abundance of authority emphasising the importance of this principle in this context, and it is sufficient simply to mention some of the more important authorities in which it is expressed, namely: *Attorney-General v Leveller Magazine Ltd.* [1979] A.C. 440, 449H–450B, *per* Lord Diplock; *Reg. v Horsham Justices, Ex parte Farquharson* [1982] Q.B. 762, 793B–794G, 759B–C, *per* Lord Denning M.R.; *Attorney-General v Guardian Newspapers Ltd. (No. 2)* [1990] 1 A.C. 109, 183E–G, *per* Sir John Donaldson M.R. and *Ex parte Central Television Plc.* [1991] 1 W.L.R. 4, 8E, *per* Lord Lane C.J.

It was agreed by all the parties to these appeals that there would be a substantial risk of prejudice to the administration of justice in the subsequent trials of C., M., P. and H. if there were to be any reporting of proceedings in the first trial in the absence of the jury or of material identifying them. There were two other matters in issue.

The first, the subject of paragraph (3) of the judge's order, was whether the publication of material identifying Vukmirovic would create such a risk of prejudice. The judge found that it would, in the event of there being guilty verdicts in the first trial, because wide publicity given to such verdicts in accounts identifying him as the principal prosecution witness could improperly enhance his credibility when he comes to give evidence in the subsequent trials.

The second matter in issue, the subject of paragraph (4) of the judge's order, was whether the verdicts in the first trial should be reported before the conclusion of the later trials. The judge was of the view that they could be reported contemporaneously without risk of prejudice to the subsequent proceedings, but that the reporting of counsel's closing speeches and of his summing up could cause prejudice in the inevitable references to Vukmirovic's status as an accomplice and to his credibility which such speeches and summing up would contain.

The judge, having found that there would be a substantial risk of prejudice to the administration of justice in those four respects, should have proceeded to the second requirement of section 4 (2), namely, whether it was 'necessary' to make an order for avoiding such a risk. He did not do that. His approach was to investigate how the risk could be eliminated. He said:

'I now turn to the question whether, given the conclusion I have reached, there is any other course which I can take which would have the effect of eliminating the substantial nature of the risk of prejudice which I have identified.'

His answer to the question was that the risk could not be avoided by adopting other solutions, such as arranging for the subsequent trials to take place at another court, or by delaying them to give time for the publicity of the first trial to fade, or to reverse his decision as to separate trials. After considering and rejecting all of those options he returned to the question how, not whether, the risk of prejudice he had identified should be dealt with by way of an order under section 4(2).

. . .

In determining whether publication of matter would cause a substantial risk of prejudice to a future trial, a court should credit the jury with the will and ability to abide by the judge's direction to decide the case only on the evidence before them. The court should also bear in mind that the staying power and detail of publicity, even in cases of notoriety, are limited and that the nature of a trial is to focus the jury's minds on the evidence put before them rather than on matters outside the courtroom: see *Reg. v Kray* (1969) 53 Cr.App.R. 412, 415–416, *per* Lawton J.; *Reg. v Horsham Justices, Ex parte Farquharson* [1982] Q.B. 762, 794, *per* Lord Denning M.R.; *Attorney-General v News Group Newspapers Ltd.* [1987] Q.B. 1, 16B–D, *per* Sir John Donaldson M.R. and *Ex parte Central Television Plc.* [1991] 1 W.L.R. 4, 8B–D, *per* Lord Lane C.J.

In this case we should also approach the matter on the basis that in each trial the judge will direct the jury clearly and firmly about the danger of convicting on Vukmirovic's evidence if uncorroborated, that there will be no public reporting of the names of C., H., M. or P. or of any material likely to identify them, and that, in compliance with section 4(1) of the Act of 1981, each of the trials will be reported fairly and accurately.

Having regard to all those considerations, we are of the view that there is only slight potential for prejudice flowing from such publicity as may be given to Vukmirovic's role and the verdicts in the first trial . . .

Even if, which we reject, there were a substantial risk of prejudice in the contemporaneous reporting of material likely to identify Vukmirovic and/or of the verdicts, the arguments of the media applicants on this issue are, in our view, well founded. The case is of importance and one in which there is a considerable and legitimate public interest because of the nature and quantity of the drug involved. It is the first major trial concerned with Ecstasy. Vukmirovic is alleged to have played a central role in the important events founding the prosecution against all the defendants. Any prohibition of contemporaneous reporting of material likely to identify him and his role in the case would make it almost impossible to report. It would also be very difficult for the media to identify what could properly be reported. Accordingly, it is a case in which the public interest in open trial would, in any event, outweigh any possible risk, substantial or not, of prejudice that might result from publication of Vukmirovic's role.

Questions for discussion

1. How do the statutory requirements for a postponement order differ from those for the strict liability rule?

2. Does the decision of the Court of Appeal in *Ex parte Telegraph* give too much weight to the public interest in full reporting of criminal trials?

(c) Protection of the media

The Practice Direction (Extract 12.4.3) encouraged courts to notify the press, when they made postponement orders.[18] Should a court hear representatives

---

[18] It also applies to anonymity orders made under CCA 1981, s 11, discussed in Chapter 13, Section 5 below.

of the press and other media who wish to resist the making of a postponement order, and what remedies do they have if later they wish to challenge it?
The first question has been considered by the Divisional Court.

Extract 12.4.5

R v Clerkenwell Stipendiary Magistrate, ex parte The Telegraph
[1993] QB 462, at 470–471 (DC)

MANN LJ: In the absence of express provision it was my own practice when
sitting in the Crown Court to hear any representations which the press desired
to make in regard to a section 4(2) order and I believe that the practice of
other judges has been, and is, the same. It is a practice which is recognised
by the Court of Appeal: see *Reg. v Beck*, 94 Cr.App.R. 376, 381–382. The
advantages of it are plain. The prosecution and the defence will frequently
share as a prime concern the need to protect the integrity of the present and
future proceedings and an application is often supported or not opposed by
the other party. The interest which an order would adversely affect is best
represented by the news media serving in their capacity as the eyes and ears
of the public: see *Attorney-General v Guardian Newspapers Ltd. (No. 2)* [1990]
1 A.C. 109, 183F, *per* Sir John Donaldson M.R. They can argue, for example,
that there is really no necessity, or no substantial risk, or that the public
interest in knowing should be paramount in the circumstances.

Lord Williams [counsel for the applicant] submitted that it would be wrong if
justices, who hear most of the criminal business in England and Wales, should
be deprived of the assistance of representations from the news media when
considering a section 4(2) order. He pointed to the absurdity of the contrast
between an inability to hear such representations and the locus standi afforded to publishers in this court on a judicial review of any order made by the
justices. Lord Williams suggested that a solution was to be found by treating
the power to hear as inherent in the jurisdiction of magistrates' courts . . .

. . . The news media do not seek a right to be heard on the issue in the
proceedings. They ask that they should be the subjects of a power to hear on
consideration of reporting restrictions. In my judgment there is such a power in
any court which is contemplating the exercise of powers under section 4(2) of
the Contempt of Court Act 1981. I regard it as implicit in the enactment of
section 4(2) that a court contemplating its use should be enabled to receive
assistance from those who will, if there is no order, enjoy the right of making
reports of the proceedings before the court. They are in particular the best
qualified to represent that public interest in publicity which the court has to
take into account when performing any balancing exercise which has to be
undertaken. The need properly to operate section 4(2) requires that a court
should be able to receive the best assistance available when considering the
curtailment of the freedom to report. I accordingly conclude that the magistrate
was wrong when on 17 July he decided that he had no power to hear the
applicants and I would grant a declaration that on that day, and on 4 August,
he had a power to hear the applicants.

The power which I have identified is a discretionary one. The occasion and manner of its exercise are matters for the court invested with the power, but I expect that the power will ordinarily be exercised when the media ask to be heard either on the making of an order or in regard to its continuance. The power will ordinarily be exercised because the court can expect to find assistance in representations from the news media. In practice it will be convenient if the press are able to present a single view thereby avoiding any need for the court to restrain repetition.

In the course of his judgment Mann LJ referred to the steps the media may now take to challenge postponement orders. In the *Horsham Justices* case (Extract 12.4.2) their recourse was by way of an application for judicial review. But on the general principles of judicial review, the Divisional Court can only review an order if it was made outside jurisdiction or was grossly unreasonable. Moreover, there can be no review of an order made by a High Court or Crown Court judge to postpone the reporting of a trial on indictment.[19] Initially, there was no provision for an appeal against postponement, a gap which led to an application to the European Commission of Human Rights on the basis that there was no effective domestic remedy for violation of the Convention.[20] Following this challenge, the government introduced a limited right of appeal.[21]

Extract 12.4.6

Criminal Justice Act 1988, s 159 (1), (5)

159.—(1) A person aggrieved may appeal to the Court of Appeal, if that court grants leave, against—
  (a) an order under section 4 or 11 of the Contempt of Court Act 1981 made in relation to a trial on indictment.
  (b) any order restricting the access of the public to the whole or any part of a trial on indictment or to any proceedings ancillary to such a trial; and
  (c) any order restricting the publication of any report of the whole or any part of a trial on indictment or any such ancillary proceedings, and the decision of the Court of Appeal shall be final.
  . . .

(5) On the hearing of an appeal under this section the Court of Appeal shall have power—

---

[19] Supreme Court Act 1981, s 29(3).
[20] See *Hodgson, Woolf Productions, NUJ, and Channel 4 v UK* (1987) 10 EHRR 503, where the Commission held admissible an application to challenge a court ban on television reconstruction of the Ponting secrecy trial.
[21] The right of appeal also applies to anonymity orders made under CCA 1981, s 11 and to orders restricting access to attend trials: see Chapter 13 below for these orders.

(a) to stay any proceedings in any other court until after the appeal is disposed of;

(b) to confirm, reverse, or vary the order complained of; and

(c) [*Omitted*].

The extent of the Court of Appeal's powers on an appeal were made plain in *Ex parte The Telegraph*.

Extract 12.4.7

Ex parte The Telegraph plc [1993] 1 WLR 980, at 986 (CA)

LORD TAYLOR CJ: The function of this court on an appeal under section 159 of the Act of 1988 is not simply to review the judge's ruling but to form its own view on the material put before it. Section 159(5)(b) gives the court power to confirm, reverse or vary the order of which complaint is made: see *Reg. v Beck, ex parte Daily Telegraph*, 94 Cr. App. R. 376, 379 *per* Farquharson L.J.

There remain some anomalies. There is a right of appeal from orders made in relation to trials on indictment; but there remains only the more limited remedy of judicial review against an order postponing the reporting of summary proceedings. Equally strange is the absence of any right of appeal for a defendant whose request for a postponement order is rejected, though apparently some appeals have been heard in this situation.[22]

5. PAYMENTS TO WITNESSES

The phenomenon of press payments to witnesses first emerged in the context of the famous Moors murder case in 1966 when two witnesses were offered money for their stories; the amount of payment was dependent on whether a conviction was obtained. The Phillimore Committee on Contempt of Court considered the practice sufficiently serious to warrant inquiry, though it did not think it should be covered by the law of contempt of court.[23] The practice again caused disquiet when it appeared that 19 witnesses in the Rosemary West murder trial had been offered or paid money. Indeed, these dealings formed one ground for her unsuccessful appeal against conviction.

---

[22] For discussion, see I Cram, 'Section 4(2) Postponement Orders: Media Reports of Court Proceedings under the Contempt of Court Act 1981' (1996) 2 *Yearbook of Media and Entertainment Law* 111, at 129–131.

[23] Cmnd 7904 (1974), paras 78–79.

Extract 12.5.1

R v West (1996) 2 Cr App Rep 374, 388–389

LORD TAYLOR CJ: Mr Ferguson [counsel for Mrs West] submitted that the money received or contracts made by these four, who were important witnesses for the Crown, rendered their evidence tainted and suspect to the point of making the jury's verdicts unsafe. There was, he said, temptation for such witnesses to exaggerate. The more lurid their account the more valuable the contract. There might have been rehearsals before trial with journalists. Whereas a story given to a police officer would be monitored, logged and disclosed to the defence, statements given to journalists were not handled in that way. There might be a conscious or subconscious desire in the witness to fulfil the agreement with the media. He submitted this was particularly so in the case of Janet Leach. She said in her evidence-in-chief she had not received any money from the press. However, leading counsel for the Mirror Group contacted leading counsel for the Crown to disclose an agreement which had been made between Janet Leach and that Group. The defence were told immediately. In cross-examination Mrs Leach admitted both the contract and the receipt of money.

In reply Mr Leveson made clear that the prosecution deplored the payment of witnesses. Nevertheless, save in respect of Mrs Leach's contract of which the prosecution were unaware until the disclosure mentioned above, all the other contracts were disclosed to the defence before trial so that Mr Ferguson was able to cross-examine about them. The effect can only have been to weaken the Crown's case. Moreover, the trial judge painstakingly went through the contracts in detail in his summing-up and warned the jury to have regard to the commercial motive which the defence suggested these witnesses had.

. . .

We carefully considered the effect of these contracts with the media. We reached the conclusion that they did not in the circumstances of this particular case render the verdicts unsafe. That is not to say that we wish to condone the payment or promise of payment to witnesses in advance of a trial. Far from it. We believe that in some circumstances it could put justice at risk. For example, as Mr Leveson pointed out, in the present case Mrs Leach felt faint during her evidence and had to leave the witness box. That was before the disclosure that she had received payments from the media. Had she not been fit to return to the witness box, when she was able to be cross-examined about the payments she had received, the jury may well have been misled and the verdicts possibly put at risk.

In our view, the whole issue of media payments to witnesses requires to be reviewed – whether they should be prohibited, or if allowed, at what stage of criminal proceedings and with what, if any, control. It is not for us to answer those questions. We were told by Mr Leveson that the Attorney-General was apprised in October 1994 of the material concerning the press payments and that consideration is being given to the problems raised by such payments.

The conduct of the press in offering payments to potential witnesses in the West murder investigation also led to a complaint to the Press Complaints

Commission (PCC).[24] As a result, its Code of Practice was strengthened. In addition to the requirement of an overriding need for payment for a witness's story, editors must show that there is a legitimate public interest at stake. Further, the payment to any witness who is cited to give evidence must be disclosed to the prosecution and defence.[25]

The government elected in 1997 does not consider that self-regulation by the PCC is adequate in this area. Consequently, the Lord Chancellor's Department issued a Consultation Paper to canvass views on its proposal to prohibit the practice of payments (and offers of payment) to witnesses, either by extension of contempt of court or by the institution of a specific offence.

Extract 12.5.2

Payments to Witnesses, LCD Consultation Paper (October 1996), paras 27–30

27. The existence or possibility of payment by the media does increase the danger of a witness's evidence being distorted or unjustifiably discredited. Either situation represents an unacceptable compromising of the standards of justice and in such circumstances the requirements of justice must be paramount. The present law on contempt of court is uncertain. Nor is it certain that the courts will resolve the problem completely, or develop the law in ways appropriate to fill the gap.

28. The Government therefore considers that legislation is needed to deal with the threat which payments to witnesses pose to the proper administration of justice. Press self-regulation did not prevent the payments in the **West** case or in others. It seems clear from the level of public and Parliamentary concern that steps are necessary to restore confidence that the administration of justice will not be prejudiced by such conduct. Legislation offers the most satisfactory solution.

29. In the first instance, the act to be prohibited is the payment, or offer of payment, by the media (whether press, broadcasters or individual authors and journalists) to a witness in judicial proceedings for an interview which is or might be relevant to those proceedings.

30. Although much of the concern over payments to witnesses has been expressed in the form of criticism of the media, the **West** case shows that it may be the witness who approaches the journalist, and the experience of people working in the media is that requests for payment are more frequent than they used to be. It might also be argued that a witness who goes to the media and asks for money is more likely to exaggerate or withhold evidence than a witness who is approached by them. Any offence or contempt should therefore cover the request for payment, as well as the offer and the making of payment.

---

[24] See Complaint against *Daily Mirror*, PCC Report No 40 (1997), pp 27–28.
[25] Clause 16(i): see Extract 2.3.1 above for the text, and Chapter 2, Section 3(e) for the related phenomenon of payment to criminals.

The government's preference is to extend the strict liability rule, so that it covers payments or offers of payment to witnesses with the object of publication which create a substantial risk of serious prejudice to pending or imminent proceedings.[26] The National Heritage Committee of the House of Commons accepted these proposals, adding that, in its view, prejudice to the fairness of a trial is inherent in media payments to witnesses and that proof of the risk of prejudice should, therefore, not be required.[27] Early in 1998 the Lord Chancellor announced the government's intention to introduce legislation at a convenient time.

Questions for discussion
1. Do you think that legislation should be introduced to restrict payments to witnesses or should the matter be left to the PCC?
2. Should it be a requirement of any strict liability contempt in this context that the payment created a substantial risk of serious prejudice to the proceedings?

6. DISCLOSURE OF JURY DELIBERATIONS

Under the CCA 1981, s 8, it is almost always a contempt of court to disclose the jury's deliberations.

Extract 12.6.1

Contempt of Court Act 1981, s 8(1), (2)

8.—(1) Subject to subsection (2) below, it is a contempt of court to obtain, disclose or solicit any particulars of statements made, opinions expressed, arguments advanced or votes cast by members of a jury in the course of their deliberations in any legal proceedings.
  (2) This section shall not apply to any disclosure of any particulars—
    (a) in the proceedings in question for the purpose of enabling the jury to arrive at their verdict, or in connection with the delivery of that verdict, or
    (b) in evidence in any subsequent proceedings for an offence alleged to have been committed in relation to the jury in the first mentioned proceedings,
or to the publication of any particulars so disclosed.

The leading media law authority on the provision involved contempt proceedings in respect of an article in the *Mail on Sunday* revealing the deliberations of the jury in a much publicised serious fraud trial. It was written by the

---

[26] LCD Consultation Paper, paras 35–45.
[27] 2nd Report of National Heritage Committee for 1996–1997, HC 86, paras 4–31.

editor of the paper's city section, on the basis of information given him by 'researchers' who had interviewed members of the jury. The defendants argued that the provision only applied to disclosure by a juror, and not to the further publication by persons, including the media, to whom a juror had disclosed the deliberations. The House of Lords rejected this argument, as well as the contention that it would be incompatible with art 10 of the ECHR to apply the provision to the press.

Extract 12.6.2

Attorney General v Associated Newspapers [1994] 2 AC 238, at 259–260 (HL)

LORD LOWRY: Each party to the appeal advanced arguments based on the supposed absurdity of the other party's interpretation. The appellants contended that the Attorney-General's construction would render in contempt the reader of a newspaper who communicated a part of its contents to a neighbour who was then unaware of what the paper had said. In my view, my Lords, this argument confuses disclosure with republication and I do not find it at all persuasive. If an item has been published in the paper, it has become a matter of public knowledge, and to describe the communication of that item of news as disclosure is, to my mind, a misuse of language.

Mr. Moses, on the other hand, who appeared with Mr. Havers for the Attorney-General, submitted that it would be absurd, when the long deplored activity was the publication of the jury's deliberations, if only the offending juror and his confidant were amenable, while the publisher went scot free. The act of a juror might be innocent and innocuous, whereas the release of the prohibited information to the public was bound to be much more harmful, actually or potentially, to the administration of justice. He further argued that it would be strange if Parliament hoped and intended to control the unwanted and harmful activities of powerful individuals and groups with an interest in the acquisition and dissemination of the prohibited information and the means to pay for it, if necessary, by merely enacting a prohibition and imposing sanctions on individual jurors.

One could instance the case of a jury-keeper who is told about or overhears the jury's deliberations. Can he not be guilty of disclosure if he reveals what he has heard to a newspaper? And are the newspaper's reporter and publisher immune if the deliberations are published? I scarcely think so. So far as the test of absurdity helps to decide the issue, my verdict is overwhelmingly on the side of the Attorney-General. . . .

In order to get home, the appellants rely, as they must, on the submission that the word 'disclose' in its context is ambiguous, but I do not consider that this case poses for your Lordships an example of ambiguity. The appellants say that the word is ambiguous because it can refer either to disclosure by a juror or to disclosure through newspaper publication or by some other means. The true view is that the word 'disclose' describes and includes both (or all) kinds of disclosure. It is a comprehensive word.

13

REPORTING LEGAL PROCEEDINGS

1. INTRODUCTION

This chapter is largely concerned with aspects of the law concerning media reporting of legal proceedings. Other aspects were treated in the previous chapter on contempt of court; but the strict liability rule discussed there is more concerned with publicity which may prejudice future proceedings than with reports of contemporaneous proceedings. The principal topics of this chapter are the right of journalists to attend legal proceedings and the extent to which courts may impose restrictions on their freedom to report them. Another is the question whether television cameras should be allowed in the courtroom.

English law generally adheres to a principle of open justice which requires the courts to sit in public. In other words, the press (and members of the public) have a right of access to attend their proceedings. A further implication is that the media are usually entitled to report them in full.[1] The chapter also discusses a number of exceptions to the principle, some established by common law, others created by statute.

Many of the qualifications to the open justice principle concern legal proceedings involving children and young persons, who, it is argued, should be protected against media publicity likely to harm their development. Quite apart from the context of legal proceedings, the courts may restrict the publication of stories, or elements in the coverage of a story, which might prejudice the welfare of children. These restrictions are also covered in this chapter.

2. THE OPEN JUSTICE PRINCIPLE

The classic statement of the principle is to be found in speeches in *Scott v Scott*. The particular issue before the House of Lords was whether the court was entitled to hold Mrs Scott and her solicitor guilty of contempt for supplying

---

[1] Indeed, accurate contemporaneous reports of judicial proceedings are covered by the defence of absolute privilege to actions for libel (see Chapter 10, Section 5) and are immune from contempt proceedings under the strict liability rule: see Chapter 12, Section 4.

Mr Scott's father with copies of notes of the proceedings for nullity she had initiated against her husband. By order of the judge these proceedings had been held in private, or (to use the legal term current at that time) in camera; he held that it was, therefore, a contempt to publish a report of them. The House of Lords ruled that he had been wrong to hear the nullity petition in private.

Extract 13.2.1

Scott v Scott [1913] AC 417, at 437–439 (HL)

VISCOUNT HALDANE LC: While the broad principle is that the Courts of this country must, as between parties, administer justice in public, this principle is subject to apparent exceptions, such as those to which I have referred. But the exceptions are themselves the outcome of a yet more fundamental principle that the chief object of Courts of justice must be to secure that justice is done. In the two cases of wards of Court and of lunatics the Court is really sitting primarily to guard the interests of the ward or the lunatic. Its jurisdiction is in this respect parental and administrative, and the disposal of controverted questions is an incident only in the jurisdiction. It may often be necessary, in order to attain its primary object, that the Court should exclude the public. The broad principle which ordinarily governs it therefore yields to the paramount duty, which is the care of the ward or the lunatic. The other case referred to, that of litigation as to a secret process, where the effect of publicity would be to destroy the subject-matter, illustrates a class which stands on a different footing. There it may well be that justice could not be done at all if it had to be done in public. As the paramount object must always be to do justice, the general rule as to publicity, after all only the means to an end, must accordingly yield. But the burden lies on those seeking to displace its application in the particular case to make out that the ordinary rule must as of necessity be superseded by this paramount consideration. The question is by no means one which, consistently with the spirit of our jurisprudence, can be dealt with by the judge as resting in his mere discretion as to what is expedient. The latter must treat it as one of principle, and as turning, not on convenience, but on necessity.

. . . But unless it be strictly necessary for the attainment of justice, there can be no power in the Court to hear in camera either a matrimonial cause or any other where there is contest between parties. He who maintains that by no other means than by such a hearing can justice be done may apply for an unusual procedure. But he must make out his case strictly, and bring it up to the standard which the underlying principle requires. He may be able to shew that the evidence can be effectively brought before the Court in no other fashion. He may even be able to establish that subsequent publication must be prohibited for a time or altogether. But this further conclusion he will find more difficult in a matrimonial case than in the case of the secret process, where the objection to publication is not confined to the mere difficulty of giving testimony in open Court. In either case he must satisfy the Court that by

458

nothing short of the exclusion of the public can justice be done. The mere consideration that the evidence is of an unsavoury character is not enough, any more than it would be in a criminal Court, and still less is it enough that the parties agree in being reluctant to have their case tried with open doors.

My Lords, it may well be that in proceedings in the Divorce Court, whether the proceedings be for divorce, or for declaration of nullity, or for judicial separation, a case may come before the judge in which it is evident that the choice must be between a hearing in public and a defeat of the ends of justice. Such cases do not occur every day. If the evidence to be given is of such a character that it would be impracticable to force an unwilling witness to give it in public, the case may come within the exception to the principle that in these proceedings, and not the less because they involve an adjudication on status as distinguished from mere private right, a public hearing must be insisted on in accordance with the rules which govern the general procedure in English Courts of justice. A mere desire to consider feelings of delicacy or to exclude from publicity details which it would be desirable not to publish is not, I repeat, enough as the law now stands. I think that to justify an order for hearing in camera it must be shewn that the paramount object of securing that justice is done would really be rendered doubtful of attainment if the order were not made.

The open justice principle was fully considered by the House of Lords in the *Leveller Magazine* case. It was asked to decide whether it was a contempt to publish the name of a witness who had been permitted by magistrates, during committal proceedings under the official secrets legislation, to give evidence without disclosing his identity. Lord Diplock's doubts concerning the scope of the courts' powers to prohibit such publication have now been resolved by the Contempt of Court Act 1981 (see Section 5 of this chapter), but his discussion of principle remains authoritative.

Extract 13.2.2

Attorney General v Leveller Magazine [1979] AC 440, at 450–453 (HL)

LORD DIPLOCK: If the way that courts behave cannot be hidden from the public ear and eye this provides a safeguard against judicial arbitrariness or idiosyncrasy and maintains the public confidence in the administration of justice. The application of this principle of open justice has two aspects: as respects proceedings in the court itself it requires that they should be held in open court to which the press and public are admitted and that, in criminal cases at any rate, all evidence communicated to the court is communicated publicly. As respects the publication to a wider public of fair and accurate reports of proceedings that have taken place in court the principle requires that nothing should be done to discourage this.

However, since the purpose of the general rule is to serve the ends of justice it may be necessary to depart from it where the nature or circumstances of the particular proceeding are such that the application of the general rule in its entirety would frustrate or render impracticable the administration of justice or would damage some other public interest for whose protection Parliament has made some statutory derogation from the rule. Apart from statutory exceptions, however, where a court in the exercise of its inherent power to control the conduct of proceedings before it departs in any way from the general rule, the departure is justified to the extent and to no more than the extent that the court reasonably believes it to be necessary in order to serve the ends of justice . . .

In the instant case the only statutory provisions that have any relevance are section 8(4) of the Official Secrets Act 1920 and section 12(1)(c) of the Administration of Justice Act 1960. Both deal with the giving of evidence before a court sitting in camera. They do not apply to the evidence given by 'Colonel B' in the instant case. Their relevance is thus peripheral and I can dispose of them shortly.

Section 8(4) of the Act of 1920 applies to prosecutions under that Act and the Official Secrets Act 1911. It empowers but it does not compel a court to sit to hear evidence in private if the Crown applies for this on the ground that national safety would be prejudiced by its publication. Section 12(1) of the Act of 1960 defines and limits the circumstances in which the publication of information relating to proceedings before any court sitting in private is of itself contempt of court. The circumstance defined in section 12(1)(c) is

'where the court sits in private for reasons of national security during that part of the proceedings about which the information in question is published; . . .'

So to report evidence in camera in a prosecution under the Official Secrets Act would be contempt of court.

In the instant case the magistrates would have had power to sit in camera to hear the whole or part of the evidence of 'Colonel B' if this had been requested by the prosecution; and although they would not have been bound to accede to such a request it would naturally and properly have carried great weight with them. So would the absence of any such request. Without it the magistrates, in my opinion, would have had no reasonable ground for believing that so drastic a derogation from the general principle of open justice as is involved in hearing evidence in a criminal case in camera was necessary in the interests of the due administration of justice.

In substitution for hearing 'Colonel B's' evidence in camera which it could have asked for the prosecution was content to treat a much less drastic derogation from the principle of open justice as adequate to protect the interests of national security. The witness's evidence was to be given in open court in the normal way except that he was to be referred to by the pseudonym of 'Colonel B' and evidence as to his real name and address was to be written down and disclosed only to the court, the defendants and their legal representatives.

I do not doubt that, applying their minds to the matter that it was their duty to consider – the interests of the due administration of justice – the magistrates had power to accede to this proposal for the very reason that it would involve less derogation from the general principle of open justice than would result from the Crown being driven to have recourse to the statutory procedure for hearing evidence in camera under section 8(4) of the Official Secrets Act 1920; but in adopting this particular device which on the face of it related only to how proceedings within the courtroom were to be conducted it behoved the magistrates to make it clear what restrictions, if any, were intended by them to be imposed upon publishing outside the courtroom information relating to those proceedings and whether such restrictions were to be precatory only or enforceable by the sanction of proceedings for contempt of court.

My Lords, in the argument before this House little attempt was made to analyse the juristic basis on which a court can make a 'ruling,' 'order' or 'direction' – call it what you will – relating to proceedings taking place before it which has the effect in law of restricting what may be done outside the courtroom by members of the public who are not engaged in those proceedings as parties or their legal representatives or as witnesses. The Court of Appeal of New Zealand in *Taylor v Attorney-General* [1975] 2 N.Z.L.R. 675 was clearly of opinion that a court had power to make an explicit order directed to and binding on the public ipso jure as to what might lawfully be published outside the courtroom in relation to proceedings held before it. For my part I am prepared to leave this as an open question in the instant case. It may be that a 'ruling' by the court as to the conduct of proceedings can have binding effect as such within the courtroom only, so that breach of it is not ipso facto a contempt of court unless it is committed there. Nevertheless where (1) the reason for a ruling which involves departing in some measure from the general principle of open justice within the courtroom is that the departure is necessary in the interests of the due administration of justice and (2) it would be apparent to anyone who was aware of the ruling that the result which the ruling is designed to achieve would be frustrated by a particular kind of act done outside the courtroom, the doing of such an act with knowledge of the ruling and of its purpose may constitute a contempt of court, not because it is a breach of the ruling but because it interferes with the due administration of justice.

So it does not seem to me to matter greatly in the instant case whether or not the magistrates were rightly advised that they had in law no power to give directions which would be binding as such upon members of the public as to what information relating to the proceedings taking place before them might be published outside the courtroom. What was incumbent upon them was to make it clear to anyone present at, or reading an accurate report of, the proceedings what in the interests of the due administration of justice was the result that was intended by them to be achieved by the limited derogation from the principle of open justice within the courtroom which they had authorised, and what kind of information derived from what happened in the courtroom would if it were published frustrate that result.

There may be many cases in which the result intended to be achieved by a ruling by the court as to what is to be done in court is so obvious as to speak for itself; it calls for no explicit statement. Sending the jury out of court during a trial within a trial is an example of this; so may be the common ruling in prosecutions for blackmail that a victim called as a witness be referred to in court by a pseudonym (see *Reg. v Socialist Worker Printers and Publishers Ltd., Ex parte Attorney-General* [1975] Q.B. 637); but, in the absence of any explicit statement by the Tottenham magistrates at the conclusion of the colonel's evidence that the purpose of their ruling would be frustrated if anything were published outside the courtroom that would be likely to lead to the identification of 'Colonel B' as the person who had given evidence in the case, I do not think that the instant case falls into this class.

. . .

My Lords, in cases where courts, in the interests of the due administration of justice, have departed in some measure from the general principle of open justice no one ought to be exposed to penal sanctions for criminal contempt of court for failing to draw an inference or recognise an implication as to what it is permissible to publish about those proceedings, unless the inference or implication is so obvious or so familiar that it may be said to speak for itself.

Difficulties such as those that have arisen in the instant case could be avoided in future if the court, whenever in the interests of due administration of justice it made a ruling which involved some departure from the ordinary mode of conduct of proceedings in open court, were to explain the result that the ruling was designed to achieve and what kind of information about the proceedings would, if published, tend to frustrate that result and would, accordingly, expose the publisher to risk of proceedings for contempt of court.

Attachment to the open justice principle is strengthened by the European Convention on Human Rights (ECHR), now incorporated in UK law by the Human Rights Act 1998.

Extract 13.2.3

European Convention on Human Rights and Fundamental Freedoms, art 6(1)

In the determination of his civil rights and obligations or of any criminal charge against him, everyone is entitled to a fair and public hearing . . . Judgment shall be pronounced publicly but the press and public may be excluded from all or part of the trial in the interests of morals, public order or national security in a democratic society, where the interests of juveniles or the protection of the private life of the parties so require, or to the extent strictly necessary in the opinion of the court in special circumstances where publicity would prejudice the interests of justice.

3. CAMERAS IN THE COURTROOM?

A topic of recent debate has been the question whether television cameras should be allowed in the courtroom to cover legal proceedings. Arguably, this should be regarded as an aspect of the open justice principle.[2] However, in England and Wales it is assumed that their access is precluded by statute.[3]

---

[2] See Robertson and Nicol, pp 360–362.

[3] See the decision of the Chancellor, Judge Ellison, in the Salisbury Consistory Court, *Re St Andrew's, Heddington* [1978] Fam 121, holding that he could not permit BBC filming of its proceedings.

Extract 13.3.1

Criminal Justice Act 1925, s 41(1)

41.—(1) No person shall—

    (a) take or attempt to take in any court any photograph, or with a view to publication make or attempt to make in any court any portrait or sketch, of any person, being a judge of the court or a witness in or a party to any proceedings before the court, whether civil or criminal or,

    (b) publish any photograph, portrait or sketch taken or made in contravention of the foregoing provisions of this section or any reproductions thereof; . . .

In some jurisdictions, notably in the USA, cameras are permitted in the courtroom; for instance, the trials of O J Simpson and Louise Woodward were extensively televised. The legislation of 1925 does not apply to Scotland, so in 1992 the courts there allowed on an experimental basis television filming of legal proceedings, albeit subject to conditions: for instance, the broadcast of current criminal trials was not permitted, and proceedings could only be filmed with the consent of the judge and all the parties involved.[4] The following extract presents arguments for allowing television cameras in the courtroom, while canvassing some points made against taking that step.

Extract 13.3.2

M Dockray, 'Courts on Television' (1988) 51 *Modern Law Review* 593, at 598–602 (some footnotes omitted)

In contrast with the position in 1925, television is today thought to be the single most important source of news for the general public. It is undoubtedly the most important medium in which issues of general concern can be treated and public opinion formed and informed. One special value is its ability to provide a personal experience of current events rather than a merely second-hand reported version. The law itself recognises this value, in some cases preferring film or television to the written or spoken word.

These advantages are no small matter. They give television the potential to play both an important educational and an important political role. Educationally, regular coverage by television of court proceedings could have great value in developing wider public knowledge of the law and its workings. The importance of informing public opinion was recognised recently by the Master of the Rolls who said in the 1987 Court of Appeal (Civil Division) Annual Review that he believed:

---

[4] See the note by Campbell (1995) 16 *Tolley's Journal of Media Law and Practice* 130–131.

'it to be crucially important that the judiciary should explain to the public what they are seeking to achieve, how they are seeking to achieve it, what problems they are encountering, what success is attending their efforts . . .'

. . .

Television could also play an enhanced political role if courtroom proceedings could be recorded by making public scrutiny of the law and its institutions more informed and more effective. Improving the means of scrutiny is not necessarily unconstitutional or hostile to the judiciary. As the Master of the Rolls also said in his 1987 Review 'Independence is in no way inconsistent with public accountability . . .'

The potential benefits of television for the law are neither trivial nor illusory. They are matters of great public importance:[i]

'The democratic form of society demands of its members an active and intelligent participation in the affairs of their community . . . More and more it demands also an alert and informed participation not only in purely political processes but also in the efforts of the community to adjust its social and economic life to increasingly complex circumstances. Democratic society, therefore, needs a clear and truthful account of events, of their background and their causes . . .'[ii]

Television has talents which enable it to provide just this type of account. It would be folly to fail to use those talents unless there are dangers in doing so which outweigh the potential advantages. What are the dangers?

Effect of Cameras: Judges and Jurors

Fears in 1925 that the judiciary would be annoyed by cameras seem, in relation to television, to be over-solicitous. Members of the judiciary have appeared voluntarily on television without noticeable discomfort or resentment. It seems unlikely that a professional judge would be either embarrassed, intimidated or distracted by a video camera, provided physical disruption to the proceedings (see below) was controlled.

Jurors on the other hand, require special consideration. The danger of jurors being distressed by the presence of cameras is greater. Fear of criticism or desire for applause might tempt a juror to reach a popular decision, if television had made the identity of a jury widely known.[iii] It is undeniable that the presence of cameras might occasionally have some such insidious effect.[iv] But the legitimate desire to avoid this danger cannot possibly justify a ban on the use of cameras either in criminal proceedings in which a jury takes no part, or most civil cases[v] or in appellate proceedings. And even in jury cases, the danger could be avoided either barring coverage at the request of the jury, or locating cameras so that pictures of the jury could not be obtained.

Litigants

Here again Parliamentary fears that litigants generally go in terror of the camera seem to have been exaggerated in 1925. The vast majority of litigants

464

have no reason to fear television coverage any more than they at present fear exposure in newspapers. It is ludicrous to imagine that litigants would abandon their rights wholesale if television coverage of courts was allowed. The possibility of being photographed by a newspaper on the way to or from court has not noticeably deterred droves of disputants.[vi]

There are no doubt some litigants each year who, for special reasons, would drop a case rather than see it broadcast on television. In some cases of this type, the court already has power to sit in private: where a court does sit in private, cameras could continue to be excluded. But where the court sits in public and press reports are permitted, the danger that a film report (as distinct from merely written coverage) will deter or harm litigants seems a very remote risk. The present total ban on cameras goes beyond what is needed to manage this risk. It would be sufficient if the court had power to prohibit television coverage on the application of any party who could show cause why this should be done.[vii] Evans J. adopted just this approach in *J. Barber & Sons v Lloyd's Underwriters*[viii] where the defendants sought to discharge an order made pursuant to a request from the California Superior Court that depositions be taken from the defendants before an examiner in England, and that the depositions be videotaped:

'As to discretion, I have heard strongly worded claims by the defendants that the presence of a camera would oppress them and cause additional stress. The defendants are Lloyd's underwriters. I have no evidence that they are not in good health or that they are subject to any personal disability. Of course it is a stressful matter to give evidence and the court is keen to protect those who are under any disability – especially the weak or the old. In the case of these four defendants I cannot accept that there will be additional stress, certainly not enough to outweigh the value and convenience of videotaping the proceedings . . . I can see therefore great value in having a video recording, which far outweighs the other matters. Courts in this country place great emphasis on the demeanour of witnesses, although opinions may differ as to its value. I will not vary the order to delete the reference to videotaping.'

Witnesses

Where a court sits in public and there are no restrictions on newspaper reports, the danger that a film report will deter or prejudicially affect a witness also seems small.

Nevertheless, it is clearly possible that there are some witnesses who would not be affected by having to give evidence in public in the presence of newspaper reporters, but whose evidence would be affected if they were filmed while under oath. It is equally clear that this possibility is insufficient to justify a total ban on all cameras in all cases: it can scarcely justify the present rule in proceedings in which oral evidence is not heard. The danger to the particularly sensitive witness could be avoided without a general ban on cameras if a discretionary power (of the type mentioned above) was conferred on the court to prohibit filming of the testimony of any witness on good cause being shown.

The Pillory of Publicity[ix]

Another reason for banning photography which was mooted both in the debates which preceded the 1925 Act and earlier, was the desire to avoid unfairly pillorying those defendants in criminal cases in whom the press showed a special interest. But experience since 1925 suggests that this argument ought to receive little weight. Some cases, both civil and criminal, have continued to attract great public interest and consequent press attention despite the absence of cameras in court.

Permitting cameras in court would probably add very little to the burden of the participants in such a case. It might in fact ease the burden. If cameras were permitted in court under controlled conditions (see below) there would be no need for packs of photographers to haunt the doors of the court as they now do. Courtroom congestion might also be relieved. There is evidence from jurisdictions[x] in which filming in court is permitted which indicates that newspaper journalists often prefer to follow an important case on television from a press room rather than from the press bench in court.

Dignity

It has been said that it is not 'in keeping with the dignity of the court that it should be used as a studio'.[xi] This argument appears very dated today. Television coverage does not insult or impair the dignity of religious, Parliamentary or Royal occasions. Microphones and tape recorders, used to provide transcriptions, have not harmed the dignity of the Court. The use of video recorders and television monitors to present video evidence has not noticeably undermined respect for the law. There is no reason why a video camera should be any more harmful than a video recorder, provided that noise and physical disruption to the work of the court is kept within acceptable limits. In fact a bit of decent film taken under controlled conditions would be far more dignified than the 'out-of-court' sketches now used or the photographic scrimmage which now often occurs at the doors of the court.

Noise and Physical Disruption

This does not seem to have been regarded as an important factor in the debates preceding the 1925 ban. Probably this was because the courts already had quite adequate powers to deal with disruptive conduct.

But what about television? It is generally assumed that television cameras always require oppressive additional lighting; that cameras and recording equipment are invariably bulky and would leave courtrooms and corridors cluttered and confused; and that with television production a large noisy crew is inevitable.

None of these assumptions is necessarily true. At least in the views of one distinguished American judge, '. . . in the early days of television . . . I think perhaps the noise and lights and so on would have distorted and disrupted the proceedings. But as I understand the present technology, that is hardly a threat anymore. . . .'[xii] In other words, today it is technically possible to obtain sound and pictures of a quality which are acceptable to a general audience without interfering with the smooth running of the court. The quality of the production may not match the standards which audiences have come to expect of broadcast television. But the important point is that material of appropriate quality can be obtained without interfering with the work of a court.

It would however be necessary to regulate in advance a number of matters. It would not be safe simply to throw open the doors of the court and leave everything to the discretion of any producer who came forward. Probably rules of court would be necessary.

[i] It has been objected that televising courts would not be educational because '. . . the news media chooses to cover only the sensational trials (and so) . . . warps public understanding of courtroom proceedings . . . The media would continue to select trials based upon their notoriety. In addition, programs would be edited, most likely to include the dramatic portions and remove the "dull or mundane"': Tongue & Lintott (1980) 16 Williamette L.R. 777, 785. These criticisms cannot be fairly levelled against British television news and current affairs programmes which show a discriminating preference for legal cases of political, social and ethical concern. And the danger of editorial distortion is no greater in the case of film or videotape than it is in the case of traditional written or oral reporting.

[ii] Royal Commission on the Press, 1949, Cmd. 7700, para. 362.

[iii] Zimmerman (1980) 4 Duke L.J. 641 argues that available research evidence shows that cameras have little if any noteworthy impact on participants in trials. See also Netteburg (1980) 63 *Judicature* 467. Cf. *Estes v Texas* (1965) 381 U.S. 532, 545.

[iv] The possible danger of members of a jury reviewing testimony each evening by watching television could be dealt with by warning to the jury or by prohibiting television coverage until the end of a trial. A similar warning to witnesses against watching the testimony of others would also be appropriate in some cases.

[v] In the House of Commons the 1925 Act was debated almost exclusively in the context of the criminal law: the few references to other types of proceedings were concerned for the most part with divorce cases.

[vi] Technical doubts about the meaning of 'precincts' have led to a long-standing reluctance to prosecute where photographs are taken outside the court: the press and television have taken full advantage of this reluctance.

[vii] As originally drafted, clause 41 would have permitted photographs to be taken with leave of the judge [or the presiding or senior judge]: this power was struck from the 1925 Bill at the committee stage of the House of Commons.

[viii] [1987] 1 Q.B. 103.

[ix] *The Times*, leader, February 28, 1924; H.C.Deb., Vol. 188, col. 839 (Sir Wm. Joynson-Hicks).

[x] Davis (1980) 64 *Judicature* 85.

[xi] F. A. Broad, M.P., H.C.Deb., Vol. 188, col. 836.

[xii] Justice Potter Stewart (on retiring from the U.S. Supreme Court): (1981) 67 A.B.A.J. 954.

Questions for discussion

1. Do you find Dockray's arguments persuasive? Does the open justice principle really require admission of the cameras into the courtroom?

2. Are the arguments against admission met by the imposition of strict conditions, for instance, prohibiting the filming of the faces of witnesses as they give evidence, and/or requiring the consent of the parties?

4. EXCEPTIONS TO THE OPEN JUSTICE PRINCIPLE

As Lord Haldane (and other Law Lords) intimated in *Scott*, the open justice principle is not absolute. Exceptions concerning trade secrets litigation and the exercise of the wardship jurisdiction have long been established by case law. Further, a number of statutes enable the courts to sit in private for the whole or part of the proceedings. For example, the prosecution may apply to the court for it to hear the whole, or part, of any proceedings under the official secrets legislation in private (see Extract 13.2.2 above).[5] Magistrates have a discretion not to hear committal proceedings in public, where it appears 'that the ends of justice would not be served by their sitting in open court'.[6] Adoption proceedings in the High Court may, and in the county court and magistrates' courts must, be heard in private.[7]

Proceedings concerning children are generally heard in private, though the press may be allowed to stay. The practice of the courts in these cases has been summarised by the Court of Appeal, in the course of rejecting an argument that a county court judge should exercise its discretion (under the Family Proceedings Rules 1991, r 4.16(7))[8] to hear an application for a residence order in open court.

Extract 13.4.1

Re P-B (A Minor) (Child Cases: Hearings in Open Court)
[1997] 1 All ER 58, at 61–62 (CA)

BUTLER-SLOSS LJ: The long-established practice in the English High Court and county court hearing applications for custody/access (now called residence/contact) or wardship has been and remains to hear the whole of the evidence in private. In the High Court, which hears the more difficult cases and those which create public interest, judgment will often be given in public either in part or in whole where the court believes there to be a public interest in the case or to give guidance to practitioners. . . .

Family proceedings now heard in the magistrates' courts are bound by s 97 of the 1989 Act amending s 69 of the Magistrates' Courts Act 1980, and by r 16(7) of the Family Proceedings Courts (Children Act 1989) Rules 1991, SI 1991/1395. In general the public is not admitted to family proceedings in the magistrates court, but the press often are admitted.

The differences in procedures of the various courts in child cases, in relation to admission of the public, of the press and the right to report proceedings have been usefully set out in a consultation paper, Review of Access to and Reporting of Family Proceedings, provided by the Lord Chancellor's Department in August 1993. In that consultation paper the main arguments for and

---

[5] Official Secrets Act 1920, s 8(4).
[6] Magistrates' Courts Act 1980, s 4(2).
[7] Adoption Act 1976, s 64; Magistrates' Courts Act 1980, s 69(3).
[8] SI 1991/1247.

against opening all or part of child proceedings to the public are set out. The arguments in support of opening the proceedings to the public have been redeployed by the appellant to this court.

Despite the arguments advanced by Dr P, it is abundantly clear that the courts are bound by para (7) to hear child cases generally in private. That was obviously the intention of the Rules Committee and it follows the long-established practice in the hearing of child cases. Paragraph (7) allows for all or part of the case to be heard in public. In the light of the long-established practice it is unlikely that judges will, other than rarely, hear the evidence relating to the welfare of a child in public. The judgment is in a somewhat different position and it may be that the practice of giving judgment in private is partly due to the parties not asking for it to be heard in public and partly because in the county court, where the vast majority of children cases are heard, it is less likely that there will be issues of public interest. Where issues of public interest do arise it would seem entirely appropriate to give judgment in open court providing, where desirable in the interests of the child, appropriate directions are given to avoid identification. If the case raises issues of principle or of law, the judgments are increasingly provided to the law reporters and are published in the large number of law reports which report family cases. But the majority of cases are of no interest to any one beyond the parties and their families.

In some circumstances, the law gives the press a general right of access to attend legal proceedings, from which members of the public may be excluded.[9]

Extract 13.4.2

Magistrates Courts' Act 1980, s 69(2)

In the case of family proceedings in a magistrates' court other than proceedings under the Adoption Act 1976, no person shall be present during the hearing and determination by the court of the proceedings except—
(a) officers of the court;
(b) parties to the case before the court . . . ;
(c) representatives of newspapers or news agencies;
(d) any other person whom the court may in its discretion permit to be present . . .

The arguments for exceptions to the open justice principle in the context of family proceedings have been considered in a Lord Chancellor's Department (LCD) Consultation Paper. These arguments may also justify restrictions on publicity concerning children, a topic considered in Section 7 of this chapter.

---

[9] Also see Children and Young Persons Act 1933, s 47(2). However, magistrates may now exclude the press from family proceedings, when they consider exclusion 'expedient in the interests of the child': Family Proceedings Court (Children Act 1989) Rules 1991 (SI 1991/1395), r 16(7), made under Children Act 1989, s 97(8)).

Extract 13.4.3

Review of Access to and Reporting of Family Proceedings
(LCD, 1993), paras 3.12–3.20 (some footnotes omitted)

3.12 Justifications for departing from the general rule of open justice stem from the premise that there are fundamental differences between family proceedings and other types of proceedings. Much of family law is not concerned with rights and obligations but with providing practical solutions by means of discretionary remedies. More often than not the matters that come before the courts will touch on personal matters and the details of family relationships. Such matters may well fall within the scope of 'private and family life', respect for which is guaranteed by Article 8 of the European Convention on Human Rights.

3.13 Reasons for restricting access and reporting would appear to include the following:

(a) to protect children from harmful publicity;

(b) to provide an informal atmosphere for hearing the evidence;

(c) to respect the privacy and dignity of those seeking a remedy from the court;

(d) to enable justice to be done where people might otherwise refrain from seeking a remedy for fear of publicity; and

(e) to protect public morals.

These are all discussed in turn below. . . .

(a) *Protecting children from publicity*

3.14 Many of the restrictions presently found in the law would appear to be based on this ground. It seems to be the generally accepted wisdom that publicity is harmful to children's welfare and that they should therefore receive special protection. A clear-cut example of where publicity would have been prejudicial to a child's welfare was found in *Re. X (A Minor) (Wardship: Injunction).*[i] In 1968, at the age of 11, Mary Bell was found guilty of the manslaughter of two infants. She was sentenced to detention for life but was released on licence in 1980. Upon her release she assumed a new identity, and in 1984 gave birth to a daughter. The daughter was made a ward of court, and an injunction was granted prohibiting publication of any details which would enable the identification of Mary Bell, the child or the child's father. The court granted the order because of the likelihood that publicity would be detrimental to the stability of the new family's home and therefore damaging to the child's welfare.

3.15 The harm that may be caused to children following publication of details of court proceedings may, however, be less obvious. For example, parents might refuse to allow their own children to mix with a child whom they knew to be a victim of child abuse, or an abused child might be subject to ridicule or taunts from his school peers. In either situation it is easy to imagine the effect which this might have on the child involved. Restrictions on access and reporting may therefore be justified in order to reduce the risk of harm to the welfare of children.

(b) *Informal atmosphere*

3.16 As stated above, much of family law consists of providing practical solutions to the various family situations which have given rise to proceedings. In a high proportion of cases, the court's function is to assess what is the best course of action for the *future*, particularly where the upbringing of children is directly or indirectly involved. Private hearings may contribute to a more relaxed and informal atmosphere which is less stressful for the parties and witnesses and which may encourage openness and frankness in their evidence. This in turn may enable the court better to assess the character and personalities of the persons involved, facilitating the decision-making process in matters where sensitive and emotionally charged family issues are under consideration.

(c) *Dignity and privacy*

3.17 The matters that come before the courts which handle family business tend to be sensitive ones concerning personal affairs and family relationships. The law protects marital confidences,[ii] and may well protect the confidences of other family relationships. In seeking the assistance of the courts to regulate these family relationships, it may seem harsh that those involved should forfeit the protection they might otherwise receive. This is particularly so where the law requires them to seek a judicial resolution of matters which they might prefer to resolve in other ways. Indeed, the very fact that the parties are seeking a judicial remedy may point to a greater need for such protection. Restrictions may therefore be justified in order to respect the dignity and privacy of those who are required in court to recount the details of their personal life and family relationships.

(d) *The deterrent effect*

3.18 Though this is linked to the justification set out at (c) above, it is also a ground for restrictions in its own right. The knowledge that proceedings may be heard in public and/or reported may deter certain people from seeking a judicial remedy to which they are entitled. The danger of this was recognised by the Law Commission following a case where a litigant declined to continue legitimacy proceedings after it was held that the court had no power to sit in private.[iii] The Law Commission was of the opinion that it was:

'wrong in principle and liable to result in a denial of justice that people should be deterred from establishing their legitimacy or that of their children through a reasonable fear of the adverse effects that publicity may have on the children'.[iv]

It recommended a change in the law and legislation was passed to permit private hearings and restrict reporting.[v]

3.19 This ground for restriction is not concerned with any claim of the litigant to privacy. It is, however, concerned with encouraging the use of available judicial remedies, thereby avoiding the risk of injustice to someone who fears publicity. It could be said to be the same justification as provides for the anonymity of complainants of rape and other sexual offences. Restrictions thus serve to prevent injustice and to ensure that those at risk are not discouraged from seeking the courts' protection.

(e) *Public morality*

3.20 Restrictions based on this ground stem from a different society from today's. They do, however, still form part of the current law.[vi]. . .

[i] [1984] 1 W.L.R. 1422, Balcombe J. [see Extract 13.7.1.]
[ii] See *Argyll v Argyll* [1967] Ch. 302.
[iii] *B. (orse P.) v Attorney-General* [1967] p. 119.
[iv] See the Report of the Powers of Appeal Courts to Sit in Private and the Restrictions upon Publicity in Domestic Proceedings, Law Com. No. 8, p. 18.
[v] The Domestic and Appellate Proceedings (Restriction of Publicity) Act 1968.
[vi] See the Judicial Proceedings (Regulation of Reports) Act 1926, s. 1(1)(a).

Questions for discussion

1. Are the arguments in the LCD paper persuasive?
2. Is there a good case for giving the media special rights to attend family proceedings, when the general public is excluded?

As the LCD paper makes plain, the open justice principle is concerned with the freedom of the media (and indeed everyone) to report legal proceedings as much as it is with their right of access to attend them. However, there are a number of statutory exceptions to this aspect of the principle. For example, only the bare details of committal proceedings may be reported.[10] It is feared that otherwise the interests of the accused might be prejudiced by the publicity given to evidence not subsequently given at his trial. The extent to which the media may cover divorce, nullity, and other matrimonial proceedings is limited to a report of the names and addresses of the parties, a concise statement of the charges and defences, legal submissions and rulings.[11]

One well-known limitation on media reporting protects the victims of rape and other sexual offences. They are entitled to anonymity. The initial statute (the Sexual Offences (Amendment) Act 1976) only conferred anonymity from the time a suspect was accused, but the law now protects the victim[12] from the time the allegation was made. Originally confined to the victims of rape, anonymity was extended to the victims of a number of sexual offences in 1992. The position is contained in the Sexual Offences (Amendment) Act 1992, amended by the Youth Justice and Criminal Evidence Act 1999 (to be brought into force in 2000).

[10] Magistrates' Courts Act 1980, s 8.
[11] Judicial Proceedings (Regulation of Reports) Act 1926, s 1(1)(b). This legislation also prohibits the reporting, in relation to any type of proceedings, of any indecent matter or indecent medical or surgical details, the publication of which might injure public morals: s 1(1) (a).
[12] The anonymity rule protects male victims as well as women: Criminal Justice and Public Order Act 1994, s 142.

Extract 13.4.4

Sexual Offences (Amendment) Act 1992, s 1(1)

Where an allegation has been made that an offence to which the Act applies has been committed against a person, no matter relating to that person shall during that person's lifetime be included in any publication.

The court may displace the anonymity rule in certain limited circumstances, for example, if it is necessary to induce potential witnesses to come forward or because the judge is satisfied that it is in the public interest to remove the restriction *and* that otherwise there would be an unreasonable restriction upon reporting.[13] However, the media are free to report the names and other details of the accused, unless publication is likely to lead to identification of the victim.[14]

Questions for discussion

1. What arguments justify giving a victim of sexual offences anonymity? Why does it apply from the time an allegation is made?
2. Why should an accused not enjoy the same protection from media publicity, at least unless and until he is convicted?

5. ANONYMITY ORDERS

In the *Leveller Magazine* case (see Extract 13.2.2 above) the magistrates had allowed a witness to give evidence anonymously, because revelation of his identity might prejudice national security. Such anonymity orders (to be distinguished from the automatic statutory rule imposed in sexual offences cases) are a less extreme measure than a direction that proceedings should be held in private. They are clearly justifiable in blackmail cases, where otherwise witnesses might be reluctant to give evidence.[15] The doubts expressed by Lord Diplock (and other members of the House) in *Leveller* whether this step can be supported by an order prohibiting the publication of the witness's name or other information withheld during court proceedings have now been resolved.

---

[13] Sexual Offences (Amendment) Act 1992, s 3.
[14] The Criminal Justice Act 1988, s 158(5) repealed the provision in the 1976 legislation conferring anonymity on persons charged with rape.
[15] See *R v Socialist Worker Printers and Publishers Ltd, ex parte Attorney General* [1975] QB 637 (DC).

Extract 13.5.1

Contempt of Court Act 1981, s 11

In any case where a court (having power to do so) allows a name or other matter to be withheld from the public in proceedings before the court, the court may give such directions prohibiting the publication of that name or matter in connection with the proceedings as appear to the court to be necessary for the purpose for which it was so withheld.

It should be noted that this provision does not clarify or extend the circumstances in which it is appropriate for a court to make an anonymity order in respect of a party or witness. The scope of this power is determined by the existing common and statutory law. If, but only if, the court exercises such power properly, it may further prohibit the media from publishing material covered by the anonymity order.[16] They may appeal to the Court of Appeal against an order made under s 11, or against any order denying them access to legal proceedings or prohibiting them from reporting such proceedings: see Extract 12.4.6 above.

In the *Evesham Justices* case magistrates had made an order allowing a defendant not to disclose his current address in order to save him from harassment from his former wife who, he said, had thrown things through the window of another home.

Extract 13.5.2

R v Evesham Justices, ex parte McDonagh
[1988] QB 553, 561–562 (DC)

WATKINS LJ: There are undoubtedly cases in which it is necessary for the identity of a witness or even a defendant to be protected from publicity. But they are rare and the circumstances of them bear no comparison with those which obtained in the present case. It is also beyond doubt that justices may do what seems to them to be right properly to control procedures in their courts. They may receive information in the form of a document the nature of which they may not be obliged to reveal . . .

It is not, therefore, right to say that everything which justices receive as evidence has publicly to be revealed. This is because the proper administration of justice commands a measure of confidentiality in respect of certain evidence which, in the public interest, should not be published.

---

[16] No direction can be made in respect of a name or other material actually disclosed in court: *R v Arundel Justices, ex parte Westminster Press Ltd* [1985] 1 WLR 708. The Youth Justice and Criminal Evidence Act 1999, s 46 gives the court power to restrict reports which would identify adult witnesses, for example, if a restriction is likely to improve the quality of evidence, otherwise diminished through fear or distress.

However, I am bound to say that I am impressed with the argument that the action taken by the justices in the present case had nothing to do with the administration of justice. It seems to me that the concern shown by the justices for not giving publicity to Mr. Hocking's home address was solely motivated by their sympathy for his well-being if his former wife should learn of his home address and harass him yet again. That kind of predicament is not, unfortunately, unique. There are undoubtedly many people who find themselves defending criminal charges who for all manner of reasons would like to keep unrevealed their identity, their home address in particular. Indeed, I go so far as to say that in the vast majority of cases, in magistrates' courts anyway, defendants would like their identity to be unrevealed and would be capable of advancing seemingly plausible reasons why that should be so. But, section 11 was not enacted for the benefit of the comfort and feelings of defendants. The general rule enunciated in the passage I have quoted from *Attorney-General v Leveller Magazine Ltd.* [1979] A.C. 440, 450, may not, as is there stated, be departed from save where the nature or the circumstances of proceedings are such that the application of the general rule in its entirety would frustrate or render impracticable the administration of justice. I fail to see how the revelation of Mr. Hocking's home address could in the circumstances in any sense warrant a departure from observance of the general rule of ensuring open justice.

For those reasons I have come to the conclusion that the justices in the present case misused the provisions of section 11 and further were in error in not causing Mr. Hocking to give his home address publicly for the purpose of fully identifying himself to the court in the usual way. By the usual way I mean that whilst no statutory provision lays down that a defendant's address has publicly to be given in court, it is well established practice that, save for a justifiable reason, it must be. I would make the declaration sought.

The general principles governing anonymity orders were considered by the Court of Appeal when a firm of solicitors, seeking judicial review of the decision of the Legal Aid Board which had ended their franchise, applied for anonymity and for an order under s 11 of the 1981 Act. Kay J refused the application for anonymity, but granted a temporary order prohibiting publication of the name of the firm until the appeal had been heard. On appeal, the applicant argued that the firm should have anonymity in relation to the appeal itself, since it would be embarrassing for its name to be associated with the case.

Extract 13.5.3

R v Legal Aid Board, ex parte Kaim Todner [1998] 3 All ER 541, at 550–551 (CA)

LORD WOOLF MR: In deciding whether to accede to an application for protection from disclosure of the proceedings it is appropriate to take into account the extent of the interference with the general rule which is involved. If the interference is for a limited period that is less objectionable than a restriction on disclosure which is permanent. If the restriction relates only to the identity of a witness or a party this is less objectionable than a restriction which involves proceedings being conducted in whole or in part behind closed doors.

The nature of the proceedings is also relevant. If the application relates to an interlocutory application this is a less significant intrusion into the general rule than interfering with the public nature of the trial. Interlocutory hearings are normally of no interest to anyone other than the parties. The position can be the same in the case of financial and other family disputes. If proceedings are ex parte and involve serious allegations being made against another party who has no notice of those allegations, the interests of justice may require non-disclosure until such a time as a party against whom the allegations are made can be heard.

A distinction can also be made depending on whether what is being sought is anonymity for a plaintiff, a defendant or a third party. It is not unreasonable to regard the person who initiates the proceedings as having accepted the normal incidence of the public nature of court proceedings. If you are a defendant you may have an interest equal to that of the plaintiff in the outcome of the proceedings but you have not chosen to initiate court proceedings which are normally conducted in public. A witness who has no interest in the proceedings has the strongest claim to be protected by the court if he or she will be prejudiced by publicity, since the courts and parties may depend on their co-operation. In general, however parties and witnesses have to accept the embarrassment and damage to their reputation and the possible consequential loss which can be inherent in being involved in litigation. The protection to which they are entitled is normally provided by a judgment delivered in public which will refute unfounded allegations. Any other approach would result in wholly unacceptable inroads on the general rule.

There can however be situations where a party or witness can reasonably require protection. In prosecutions for rape and blackmail, it is well established that the victim can be entitled to protection. Outside the well-established cases where anonymity is provided, the reasonableness of the claim for protection is important. Although the foundation of the exceptions is the need to avoid frustrating the ability of the courts to do justice, a party cannot be allowed to achieve anonymity by insisting upon it as a condition for being involved in the proceedings irrespective of whether the demand is reasonable. There must be some objective foundation for the claim which is being made.

Conclusions as to this appeal

This last point is particularly relevant to the claims for anonymity in this court which the appellants are putting forward. It is not a reasonable basis for seeking anonymity that you do not want to be associated with a decision of a court. Nor is it right for an appellant to seek to pre-empt the decision of this court by saying in effect we will not co-operate with the court unless the court binds itself to grant us anonymity. The appellant had secured anonymity until the end of the appeal and they could not reasonably ask for more.

It also cannot be reasonable for the legal profession to seek preferential treatment over other litigants. If the appellants had not raised the issue of anonymity, at the leave stage, it is not likely that their proceedings would have resulted in any publicity at least until the substantive hearing. If publicity did result from the substantive hearing then that publicity, so far as it was unfair, would be mitigated within a short time scale by the judgment of the court. If the judgment was adverse, then it is accepted on their behalf, that publicity could no longer be restrained since their alleged conduct should then be known. If the judgment was favourable, then the judgment would to a substantial extent provide the answer to any adverse publicity.

Kay J came to the right answer in deciding not to grant the application. The appeal against his decision will therefore be dismissed.

Questions for discussion

1.   Do you agree with Lord Woolf MR that anonymity orders should be less readily granted to claimants, since in initiating proceedings they accept the likelihood of a public hearing? Does it follow that courts should be unwilling to grant anonymity, say, to seriously ill or vulnerable applicants for judicial review who request it?[17]

2.   If a court grants an anonymity order, does it follow that it should also grant an order under s 11 of the Contempt of Court Act 1981?

6. THE REPORTING OF PRIVATE PROCEEDINGS

Sections 2 and 4 of this chapter were concerned with the access of the media to legal proceedings and various exceptions to the open justice principle. Is it a contempt of court to report proceedings which have been held in private? Remarks of members of the House of Lords in *Scott* suggested that it was not at common law, though it was held there that it had been wrong to hear a petition for nullity of marriage in private merely to protect the sensitivities of the parties. The legal position has now been clarified by statute.

Extract 13.6.1

Administration of Justice Act 1960, s 12

12.—(1) The publication of information relating to proceedings before any court sitting in private shall not of itself be contempt of court except in the following cases, that is to say

    (a) where the proceedings—

        (i) relate to the exercise of the inherent jurisdiction of the High Court with respect to minors;

---

[17] See *R v Westminster City Council, ex parte Castelli* (1995) 30 BMLR 123 (DC) (anonymity refused to applicant for public housing, who was HIV positive); *T v Secretary of State for Home Department* [1996] AC 742 (HL) (asylum seeker, but active member of terrorist organisation, in fear of his life apparently allowed anonymity).

   (ii) are brought under the Children Act 1989; or

   (iii) otherwise relate wholly or mainly to the maintenance or up-bringing of a minor;

  (b) where the proceedings are brought under [certain provisions] of the Mental Health Act 1969;

  (c) where the court sits in private for reasons of national security during that part of the proceedings about which the information in question is published;

  (d) where the information relates to a secret process . . . which is in issue in the proceedings;

  (e) where the court (having power to do so) expressly prohibits the publication of all information relating to the proceedings or of information of the description which is published.

(2) Without prejudice to the foregoing subsection, the publication . . . of an order made by a court sitting in private shall not of itself be contempt of court except where the court (having power to do so) expressly prohibits the publication.

(3) [*Omitted*]

(4) Nothing in this section shall be construed as implying that any publication is punishable as contempt of court which would not be so punishable apart from this section.

The meaning of this complex provision has to some extent been clarified judicially, notably by the Court of Appeal in *Re F* when it allowed appeals by newspaper owners and editors who had been convicted of contempt when they published, without being aware of the connection, material which was related to continuing wardship proceedings.[18]

Extract 13.6.2

Re F (orse A) (A Minor) (Publication of Information)
[1977] Fam 58, at 105–107 (CA)

GEOFFREY LANE LJ: In short, publication of information relating to proceedings held in private is only an offence in the five cases set out in section 12 (1) (*a*) to (*e*). Even then, subsection (4) makes it clear that unless such publication would have been a contempt at common law it is not punishable under the section. Such a provision may be unusual; it may be difficult to operate; but the court must do its best.

    There are two important questions. First, what is meant by 'proceedings'? Obviously a report of the actual hearing before the judge or part of it is included. But the words must include more than that; otherwise it would have been unnecessary to use the expression 'information relating to proceedings . . .'

---

[18] The decision in *Re F* was approved by Lord Bridge in *Pickering v Liverpool Daily Post and Echo Newspapers plc* [1991] 2 AC 370, at 421–423 (HL).

The object is to protect from publication information which the person giving it believes to be protected by the cloak of secrecy provided by the court. 'Proceedings' must include such matters as statements of evidence, reports, accounts of interviews and such like, which are prepared for use in court once the wardship proceedings have been properly set on foot. Thus in the instant case the reports of the Official Solicitor and the social worker were clearly part of the proceedings and were protected by section 12.

The second and crucial question is whether the person publishing the information is guilty even if he had no knowledge that it related to wardship proceedings held in private or honestly believed that it did not. The judge decided that such lack of knowledge was no defence: that the offence of contempt was one of strict liability; all that had to be proved was the publication of information which related to wardship proceedings held in private and the contempt was complete whatever the publisher's state of knowledge or whatever his belief may have been. There is no indication in the wording of section 12 of the Act that Parliament intended this to be an offence of strict liability. If there had been such an intention it would have been simple to say so. The presumption must be against such an interpretation. It is no deterrent to others if a person acting in all innocence is said to be guilty. Nor does a finding of guilt in such circumstances make it any less likely that the guilty man will offend again. Where both the liberty of the individual and freedom of comment are at stake it would be quite wrong to imply words into a statute making the offence an absolute one.

Section 12 (4) provides:

'Nothing in this section shall be construed as implying that any publication is punishable as contempt of court which would not be so punishable apart from this section.'

The precise meaning of that subsection is obscure: see *Borrie and Lowe, The Law of Contempt*, p. 119. It protects publications made at the request of the court. It certainly means that if knowledge of the existence and nature of the proceedings was necessary at common law it is also necessary under the statute. Decisions on the subject are not easy to find. There is ample authority that marrying or attempting to marry a ward of court was an offence of strict liability: see Warrington J. in *In re H.'s Settlement* [1909] 2 Ch. 260, 264. The same considerations applied to removing a ward from the jurisdiction: *In re Witten (An Infant)* (1887) 4 T.L.R. 36 and *In re J. (An Infant)* (1913) 108 L.T. 554.

Such indications as there are seem to show that so far as publications relating to wardship proceedings were concerned knowledge was considered necessary . . .

. . . the effect of section 12 (1) (*a*) is that any person who is proved to have published without leave what he knows to be information relating to wardship proceedings before any court sitting in private is guilty of contempt. Honest mistake is a defence providing that had the mistaken circumstances been true, no offence would have been committed. The section is not intended to enlarge the scope of the offence as it existed at common law.

The embargo on publication of matters disclosed in a private hearing is not necessarily perpetual. Silence should only be enforced for so long as is necessary to protect the interests of those for whose benefit the rule is made: see

Lord Shaw of Dunfermline in *Scott v Scott* [1913] A.C. 417, 483. Where, for example, what was once a trade secret has become common knowledge, there is no warrant for continuing the ban on the publication of proceedings. Similarly, where all necessity for preserving the confidentiality of information about an infant has with the passage of time disappeared, publication will not be a contempt.

A recent decision of the Court of Appeal concerns the freedom to disclose information about various procedural directions made in private (or 'chambers' to use the traditional term) in a controversial negligence action brought by cancer suffers against cigarette manufactureres. The judge had imposed 'gagging' orders to stop the parties and their advisers making comments to the media in relation to these matters without leave of the court.

Extract 13.6.3

Hodgson v Imperial Tobacco Ltd **[1998] 2 All ER 673, at 686–688 (CA)**

LORD WOOLF MR: Surprisingly, just what can be repeated in public about what occurs in chambers is virtually free from authority. The reasons for this could be at least twofold. First, the fact the great majority of the matters dealt with in chambers are of no interest to anyone except those immediately involved. Secondly, in the normal way the parties and, in particular, their legal advisers recognise that it is desirable to treat in a confidential manner what occurs in chambers, because it is in accord with the 'chambers culture' which has grown up over the years and which contributes to the efficient dispatch of the work of the courts. For the majority of lawyers to treat what happens in chambers in any other way would not be in accord with proper professional behaviour.

However it remains a principle of the greatest importance that, unless there are compelling reasons for doing otherwise, which will not exist in the generality of cases, there should be public access to hearings in chambers and information available as to what occurred at such hearings. The fact that the public do not have the same right to attend hearings in chambers as those in open court and there can be in addition practical difficulties in arranging physical access does not mean that such access as is practical should not be granted. Depending on the nature of the request reasonable arrangements will normally be able to be made by a judge (of course we use this term to include masters) to ensure that the fact that the hearing takes place in chambers does not materially interfere with the right of the public, including the media, to know and observe what happens in chambers. Sometimes the solution may be to allow one representative of the press to attend. Another solution may be to give judgement in open court so that the judge is not only able to announce the order which he is making, but is also able to give an account of the proceedings in chambers. The decision as to what to do in any particular situation to provide information for the public will be for the discretion of the judge conducting the hearing. As long as he bears in mind the importance of the principle that justice should be administered in a manner which is as open as is practical in the particular circumstances, higher courts will not interfere with the judge's decision unless there is good reason for doing so.

. . .

The nature of the hearing being that which is indicated, while lawyers will be expected to continue to exercise self restraint as to what is said, any order, judgment or account of the proceedings in chambers can, except in the special cases, be communicated to those who did not attend without any concern that such a communication will create any risk of the imposition of a penalty. If the court wishes to restrain such communication, then it will have to make an appropriate order, when it has the power to do so. As to those situations it is important to take account of the judgment of Lord Reading CJ in *R v Governor of Lewes Prison, ex p Doyle* [1917] 2 KB 254 at 271 where he drew attention to the fact that it was impossible to enumerate all the circumstances which would justify an exception to the general rule. As the practice of the courts alters, for example because of the developments in relation to alternative dispute resolution, so will the exceptions change.

In relation to hearings in chambers the position may be summarised as follows. (1) The public has no right to attend hearings in chambers because of the nature of the work transacted in chambers and because of the physical restrictions on the room available, but if requested, permission should be granted to attend when and to the extent that this is practical. (2) What happens during the proceedings in chambers is not confidential or secret and information about what occurs in chambers and the judgment or order pronounced can, and in the case of any judgment or order should, be made available to the public when requested. (3) If members of the public who seek to attend cannot be accommodated, the judge should consider adjourning the proceedings in whole or in part into open court to the extent that this is practical or allowing one or more representatives of the press to attend the hearing in chambers. (4) To disclose what occurs in chambers does not constitute a breach of confidence or amount to contempt as long as any comment which is made does not substantially prejudice the administration of justice. (5) The position summarised above does not apply to the exceptional situations identified in s 12(1) of the 1960 Act or where the court, with the power to do so, orders otherwise.

. . .

. . . the normal protection of the administration of justice is to be found in the law of contempt. To rely on the law of contempt for this purpose has the disadvantage that what does or does not amount to contempt cannot be identified with precision before all the circumstances are investigated. The advantage of an order of the class made by the judge on 10 October is that the parties and their legal advisers should know, so far as this can be achieved, precisely where they stand. The advantage of relying on the law of contempt in preference to a precise order of the sort which was made is that upon an application to commit for contempt, the court is required to weigh the conflicting public interests involved. Those interests include not only the need to protect the administration of justice but also the importance of not interfering with freedom of speech and the freedom of the press. Although the order was not made against the media, if they become aware of the terms of the order and become a party to any breach of the order they are liable to be cited for contempt.

Although we therefore recognise that advantages can flow from an order of this sort, we are quite satisfied that it was wrong to make this order. While we would much prefer lawyers not to become engaged in commenting about proceedings to the press (as opposed to communicating facts), we consider that in this case the risk, if any, of the administration of justice being interfered with by communications with the press are far less than the risks which would follow from interference with the entitlement of the media to obtain information about these proceedings. We appreciate that the defendants might find what is said to the media objectionable, but we do not accept that they will be deterred from defending these proceedings because of adverse publicity which could be generated by those comments.

The problem with the order is that it achieves certainty by imposing rigidity. If it is enforced, it will mean that instead of being judged as would normally be the case under the law of contempt the plaintiffs' legal advisers will be judged by whether they have not complied with the order. Whether there has been a failure to comply with the order will become the test for contempt instead of whether there has been unjustified interference with the administration of justice. To produce this result is wrong in principle and the order should not have been made.

7. REPORTS WHICH CONCERN CHILDREN

A number of exceptions to each branch of the open justice principle – access of the media to legal proceedings and the fair reporting of them – have been established to safeguard the privacy and welfare of children. In addition to these, it should be noted that the Children Act 1989 makes provision for magistrates' courts to sit in private in proceedings, in the course of which powers with respect to any child under the legislation may be exercised;[19] further, it prohibits the publication of any material intended or likely to identify any child involved in such proceedings.[20]

Moreover, in addition to the rules prohibiting the identification of wards or other children involved in legal proceedings (see Extracts 13.6.1 and 13.6.2 above), the courts have an inherent power to prohibit media reports which may damage the welfare of young children. On the other hand, in some circumstances, the courts will refuse to make an order, or make only a limited order, out of a concern for freedom of the media to report stories of real public interest which may incidentally prejudice the welfare of children. Their approach depends on the circumstances of each case; as a result the law is hard to state with precision.

---

[19] Children Act 1989, s 97(1).
[20] Ibid, s 97(2).

The cases from which the next two extracts are taken show how the courts sometimes frame injunctions narrowly in order to avoid undue interference with freedom of the press. In the first (mentioned in Extract 13.4.3 above) an injunction was granted to prohibit publications which could identify Mary Bell or her child; Mary Bell was the assumed name of a woman who, 16 years previously, at the age of 11 had been found guilty of the manslaughter of two young boys and who subsequently had been released on licence.[21] Balcombe J first held that the court had jurisdiction to make an order to prohibit publication of information which would enable the identity of Mary Bell and her child to become known to the public. The question was whether it should be exercised.

Extract 13.7.1

Re X (A Minor) (Wardship: An Injunction)
[1984] 1 WLR 1422, at 1427 (Fam D)

BALCOMBE J: I turn now to the only remaining question, whether in the circumstances of this case it is appropriate that I should exercise that jurisdiction. In this context, I do bear in mind what was said by the Court of Appeal in *In re X* [1975] Fam. 47, and in particular by the two judges, Roskill L.J. and Sir John Pennycuick, who in that case made it clear that the court is concerned to hold a proper balance between the protection of the ward and the rights of outside parties. Sir John Pennycuick said, at p. 61:

> 'Specifically, it seems to me, the court must hold a proper balance between the protection of the ward and the right of free publication enjoyed by outside parties and should hesitate long before interfering with that right of free publication. It would be impossible and not, I think, desirable to draw any rigid line beyond which the protection of a ward should not be extended. The distinction between direct and indirect interference with a ward is valuable, though the borderline may be blurred. I am not prepared to say that the court should never interfere with the publication of matter concerning a ward. On the contrary, I think in exceptional circumstances the court should do so.'

I have had evidence put in front of me, particularly by the probation officer concerned, of the harm which publicity identifying Mary Bell by her present name could do to the ward. It requires only a very small exercise of the imagination to appreciate that the original case rightly stirred up very strong feelings; but the criminal law has taken its course, Mary Bell is out on licence, she has this child, and I am concerned with the welfare of the child. It must be apparent, particularly with a child who is still only a little over two months old, that any disturbance to the fragile stability which her mother has achieved

---

[21] For resolution of the complaint to the Press Complaints Commission in respect of payments for serialisation of a book about Mary Bell, see Extract 2.3.9.

must rebound upon that child's welfare. Although, as I said previously, I did not think it right to prohibit any reference to the fact that Mary Bell has grown up and has had a child, equally I am satisfied that it is a proper exercise of this jurisdiction, for the protection of the welfare of the two-month old ward, that I should make an order – and I do make an order – which prohibits any publication which could identify Mary Bell by the name which she is now known, or the child as the child of Mary Bell, or the identity of the child's father.

Extract 13.7.2

Re W (A Minor) [1992] 1 WLR 100, 102–104 (CA)

NEILL LJ: Media interest surrounding children who are wards of court raises difficult issues. These issues have been addressed in a number of recent cases including in particular In re X (A Minor) (Wardship: Jurisdiction) [1975] Fam. 47; In re C. (A Minor) (Wardship: Medical Treatment) (No. 2) [1990] Fam. 39; and In re M. and N. (Minors) (Wardship: Publication of Information) [1990] Fam. 211. From these cases I would venture to extract the following guidelines. (1) The court will attach great importance to safeguarding the freedom of the press. In Attorney-General v Guardian Newspapers Ltd. (No. 2) [1990] 1 A.C. 109, 183, Sir John Donaldson M.R. explained the crucial position occupied by the press:

'It is because the media are the eyes and ears of the general public. They act on behalf of the general public. Their right to know and their right to publish is neither more nor less than that of the general public. Indeed, it is that of the general public for whom they are trustees.'

(2) The court will also take account of article 10 of the Convention for the Protection of Human Rights and Fundamental Freedoms (1953) (Cmd. 8969) which is designed to safeguard the 'freedom to hold opinions and to receive and impart information and ideas without interference by public authority . . .' (3) These freedoms, however, are subject to exceptions which include restrictions upon publication which are imposed for the protection of children. (4) In considering whether to impose a restriction upon publication to protect a ward of court the court has to carry out a balancing exercise. It is to be noted, as Butler-Sloss L.J. pointed out in In re M. and N. (Minors) (Wardship: Publication of Information) [1990] Fam. 211, 223, that 'in this situation the welfare of the child is not the paramount consideration.' (5) In carrying out the balancing exercise the court will weigh the need to protect the ward from harm against the right of the press (or other outside parties) to publish or to comment. An important factor will be the nature and extent of the public interest in the matter which it is sought to publish. A distinction can be drawn between cases of mere curiosity and cases where the press are giving information or commenting about a subject of genuine public interest. (6) It is to be anticipated that in almost every case the public interest in favour of publication can be satisfied without any identification of the ward to persons other than those who already know the facts. It seems to me, however, that the risk of some wider identification may have to be accepted on occasions if the story is to be told in

a manner which will engage the interest of the general public. (7) Any restraint on publication which is imposed is intended to protect the ward and those who care for the ward from the risk of harassment. The restraint must therefore be in clear terms and be no wider than is necessary to achieve the purpose for which it is imposed. It also follows that, save perhaps in an exceptional case, the ward cannot be protected from any distress which he may be caused by reading the publication himself.

I can return to the facts of the present case. It is and always has been common ground that the placement of a male ward with two male foster parents is a matter of legitimate public interest. The council therefore would not, and indeed could not, oppose the publication of an article which discussed the principle of such a placement in general terms. The concern of the council, however, is that any reference to the council by name or to the boy's particular difficulties in the past would lead to his identification and to all the problems that such an identification would cause.

Douglas Brown J. came to the conclusion that the council's submissions 'in this exceptional case' were right. He therefore took what he described as the 'unusual and severe step' of ordering that there should be no publication on the lines of this article of 'anything that will reactivate this sad history of this boy.'

It is clear that the judge recognised that he had to perform a difficult balancing exercise. Furthermore, one must pay careful regard to the fact that the judge granted the injunction now under appeal in the exercise of a discretion vested in him. In these circumstances this court can only interfere if the judge misdirected himself in law or if we are satisfied that he was plainly wrong. I can see no adequate basis for an argument that the judge misdirected himself in law. I am satisfied, however, that on the facts of this case he was plainly wrong. The risk of a possible identification of the ward by someone not already in the know had no doubt to be weighed in the balance. But in my view the judge attached wholly insufficient importance to the fact that this was a matter of great public interest and concern. In the circumstances I consider that this court is entitled to interfere and to substitute its own discretion.

The newspaper recognises that they must use their best endeavours to avoid *any* risk that the article will lead to the identification of the ward to persons other than those who already know the facts. But I am satisfied that the newspaper should be allowed to include in the article *all* the ingredients of the story which are of public concern. In this particular case those ingredients include: (a) the fact that a boy of 15 is being placed with two men as foster parents who have a long-standing homosexual relationship; (b) the fact that the boy has been subjected to grave sexual abuse in the past by other people; (c) the fact that the council is the local authority responsible for this placement; and (d) the fact that the placement was arranged and put into effect without the prior consent of the court and, it seems, despite the disapproval of the mother.

The court has seen a copy of the article to be published by the newspaper. It is not for me to comment on the style of the article. Nor should I comment on the wisdom of the course which the council are taking in the case of this boy, though I am sure that responsible and conscientious officers believe that this course, though unusual, is the right one in the very difficult circumstances.

But I have no doubt whatever that the newspaper should be free to publish this story and to publish it in a manner which will engage the interest of their readers.

In both these cases the decisive question was how the courts should balance the welfare of the child and freedom of the press. However, in others judges have doubted whether the courts' jurisdiction to grant injunctions to protect the welfare of young children, including wards of court, extends beyond circumstances where the publication (or broadcast) relates to the upbringing of the child whose welfare the court is supervising. This view was vigorously expressed in the *Central Television* case; there was an appeal from an order that a television documentary on the work of the Obscene Publications Squad should not be transmitted without deleting pictures of a man identified in the programme as a convicted paedophile. It was argued that the order should be granted to avoid identification of, and distress to, his former wife and their child, aged five.

Extract 13.7.3

R v Central Independent Television plc [1994] Fam 192, 203–205 (CA)

HOFFMAN LJ: . . . I respectfully think that Lord Denning M.R. was right in *In re X (A Minor) (Wardship: Jurisdiction)* [1975] Fam. 47 when he said that the wardship jurisdiction did not permit the courts to balance the competing interests of the child and the freedom of the press. The exceptions to freedom of speech were, he said, at p. 58F 'already staked out by the rules of law.' Section 12(1)(*a*) of the Administration of Justice Act 1960 prohibits the publication of information relating to a private court hearing in proceedings which concern children. It does not however apply to information which relates to the child but not to the proceedings: see *In re F. (orse. A.) (A Minor) (Publication of Information)* [1977] Fam. 58. It would be wrong, said Lord Denning M.R. in *In re X (A Minor) (Wardship: Jurisdiction)* [1975] Fam. 47, 58 to extend the law:

> 'so as to give the judges a power to stop publication of true matter whenever the judges – or any particular judge – thought that it was in the interests of a child to do so.'

As I read the judgment of Roskill L.J., he left the point open. He agreed that the judge did not have power to prevent publication in that case but was not willing to say that a judge might not have such a power in another case. He said, at p. 60C: 'it is not necessary to consider here what, if any, limits there are to [the wardship] jurisdiction.' Sir John Pennycuick, at p. 61F, went further. He thought that 'in exceptional circumstances' the court should be willing to interfere with the publication of matter concerning a ward. But there is no majority for the proposition that such a jurisdiction exists, even in exceptional circumstances.

In any area of human rights like freedom of speech, I respectfully doubt the wisdom of creating judge-made exceptions, particularly when they require a judicial balancing of interests. The danger about such exceptions is that judges are tempted to use them. The facts of the individual case often seem to demand exceptional treatment because the newspaper's interest in publication seems trivial and the hurt likely to be inflicted very great. The interests of the individual litigant and the public interest in the freedom of the press are not easily commensurable. It is not surprising that in this case the misery of a five-year-old girl weighed more heavily with Kirkwood J. than the television company's freedom to publish material which would heighten the dramatic effect of its documentary. This is what one would expect of a sensitive and humane judge exercising the wardship jurisdiction. But no freedom is without cost and in my view the judiciary should not whittle away freedom of speech with ad hoc exceptions. The principle that the press is free from both government and judicial control is more important than the particular case.

It is true that in a series of decisions commencing with *In re C. (A Minor) (Wardship: Medical Treatment) (No. 2)* [1990] Fam. 39 the courts have, without any statutory or, so far as I can see, other previous authority, assumed a power to create by injunction what is in effect a right of privacy for children. The power is said to be based on the powers of the Crown as parens patriae and the 'machinery for its exercise' is the wardship jurisdiction: see Butler-Sloss L.J. in *In re M. and N. (Minors) (Wardship: Publication of Information)* [1990] Fam. 211, 223. The novelty of this jurisdiction is shown by the fact that as recently as 1977, Scarman L.J. in *In re F.* [1977] Fam. 58, 99 was able to say that apart from section 12(1)(a) of the Administration of Justice 1960, 'the ward enjoys no greater protection against unwelcome publicity than other children.' In *In re M. and N.* Butler-Sloss L.J. said, at p. 224, that the power to restrain publication was needed because:

'There has, since *In re X* [1975] Fam. 47, been an upsurge in investigative journalism with an interest in situations affecting children which has led the media to publish or attempt to publish more widely and more frequently than ever contemplated in the early 1970s.'

I would not for a moment dispute either this perception or the fact that a right of privacy may be a legitimate exception to freedom of speech. After all, other countries also party to the Convention have a right of privacy for grown-ups as well. But we do not and there may be room for constitutional argument as to whether in a matter so fundamentally trenching upon the freedom of the press as the creation of a right of privacy, it would not be more appropriate for the remedy to be provided by the legislature rather than the judiciary. In recent years Parliament has not been slow to act in the interests of children. However that may be, the existence of a jurisdiction to restrain publication of information concerning a child and its upbringing is no longer open to dispute in this court.

But this new jurisdiction is concerned only with the privacy of children and their upbringing. It does not extend, as Lord Donaldson of Lymington M.R. made clear in *In re M. and N.*, at p. 231B to 'injunctive protection of children from publicity which, though inimical to their welfare, is not directed at them or those who care for them.' It therefore cannot apply to publication of the fact that the child's father has been convicted of a serious offence, however distressing it may be for the child to be identified as the daughter of such a man. If such a jurisdiction existed, it could be exercised to restrain the identification of any convicted criminal who has young children. It may be that the decision of Balcombe J. in *X County Council v A.* [1985] 1 All E.R. 53 [see Extract 13.7.1] can be brought within Lord Donaldson of Lymington M.R.'s language because the child's mother, at whose past the intended publication was directed, was actually caring for the child at the time of the application. But the events in question had happened long before the child was born. The publication was not directly concerned with the child or its upbringing, and for my part I think that the judge, for wholly commendable reasons, was asserting a jurisdiction which did not exist.

If follows that in my judgment there was in this case no jurisdiction to restrain the television company from publishing pictures of the child's father, or of the house in which he had lived and had been arrested. In fact the television company gave undertakings not to publish the pictures of the house or the mother, or to refer in any way to the fact that the father was married or had a child. In my view it was considerate and responsible of the television company to give these undertakings and I am glad that it did. But it was not obliged to do so and the judge was not entitled to impose the further condition that the father's appearance should be concealed. I therefore agreed that the appeal should be allowed.

The Court of Appeal attempted to formulate clear principles in *Re Z*, which should now be considered the leading authority in this area of law. The well-known parents of Z had secured an injunction prohibiting any publication identifying her or any school attended by her, or any information likely to lead to her identification. Z had special educational needs for which she received help from a specialised institution which had a successful record in treating the problems from which she suffered. Her mother applied for the injunction to be varied to permit the broadcast of a programme about the institution which filmed and identified the child. The Court of Appeal upheld the judge's refusal to vary the injunction. It should be noted that the child was not a ward; but it was held that there was no distinction in this context between the wardship jurisdiction and the courts' inherent jurisdiction to protect children. Further, the court held that the mother's decision to permit the making of the film was an exercise of parental responsibility, which it could control by the issue of a 'prohibited steps order' under the Children Act 1989.[22]

Extract 13.7.4

Re Z (A Minor) (Identification: Restrictions on Publication)
[1997] Fam 1, at 23–24, 24–31 (CA)

WARD LJ: I draw these conclusions from this review of the authorities:
(1) The wardship or inherent jurisdiction of the court to cast its cloak of protection over minors whose interests are at risk of harm is unlimited in

---

[22] Section 8(1).

theory though in practice the judges who exercise the jurisdiction have created classes of cases in which the court will not exercise its powers. . . .

(2) There is now an established category of case, of which *In re X (A Minor) (Wardship: Jurisdiction)* [1975] Fam. 47 and *R. v Central Independent Television Plc.* [1994] Fam. 192 are the examples, where the freedom to publish information has been set beyond the limit of the exercise of the jurisdiction. I would define that category as the case where (a) the child is not already under the court's protective wing in that the court is not exercising some supervisory role over some aspect of the child's care and upbringing but where, on the contrary, the originating summons is issued for the express purpose of seeking the injunctive relief; (b) crucially, the material to be published is not material directly about the child or material directed at the manner of the child's upbringing. In this category the material is only indirectly or incidentally or inferentially referable to the child. Thus the eight pages in the book about X's father was not a story about her or about the way she had been brought up except indirectly in so far as it revealed that her father was a philanderer: see *In re X (A Minor) (Wardship: Jurisdiction)* [1975] Fam. 47. By contrast the story in 1984 about X, Mary Bell's daughter, was directly about the fact that the authorities were permitting her to be brought up by a mother whom some may have thought to be so evil as not to be entrusted with the care of any young child: see *In re X (A Minor) (Wardship: Injunction)* [1984] 1 W.L.R. 1422. The television programme about the arrest and offending of Mr R. was not a programme about the child nor did it carry any hint or suggestion of her upbringing having been affected by the criminal activity of her father: see *R. v Central Independent Television Plc.* [1994] Fam. 192. By contrast the publicity about W. was about the fact that the local authority, and the court, were permitting him, a child already disturbed by involvement in homosexuality, to be brought up in a homosexual household.[23]

(3) It follows that the wardship or inherent jurisdiction will be exercised where the material to be published is directed at the child or is directed to an aspect of the child's upbringing by his parents or others who care for him in circumstances where that publicity is inimicable to his welfare. Thus stories of how the nurses looked after baby C. (*In re C. (A Minor) (Wardship: Medical Treatment) (No. 2)* [1990] Fam. 39) related directly to her upbringing. The story of the removal of M. and N. (*In re M. and N. (Minors) (Wardship: Termination of Access)* [1990] Fam. 211) from their foster parents was a story directly concerned with their upbringing. Here the court is exercising its supervisory role to restrain publication of matters relating to the care and upbringing of children.

(4) A separate aspect of the court's inherent jurisdiction is the power to protect the integrity of its own proceedings. For example, by preserving the anonymity of those who come forward to assist the court, so encouraging full and free disclosure of all material facts impinging on the child's wellbeing, the court serves the administration of justice, the ultimate end of which is to do what is best for the child.

. . .

---

[23] This is a reference to *Re W (A Minor)* [1992] 1 WLR 100: Extract 13.7.2 above.

The test for the exercise of any discretion

1. *When welfare is subordinate to press freedom*

Although, to be pedantic, there is in the *In re X* [1975] Fam. 47 and *R. v Central Independent Television* [1994] Fam. 192 situations an exercise of judgment in deciding that the case falls beyond the proper limit for the invocation of the wardship or inherent jurisdiction, in reality no discretion is exercised at all in the sense that the welfare of the child is not held in balance against the freedom of publication. It must now be recognised that the law has so developed that there is this category where freedom of publication always prevails over the welfare of the child. The child may be harmed by the realisation that he is related to the object of the publicity, and his self esteem may be damaged thereby, but all that has to be accepted as part of the slings and arrows of misfortune of life because the publicity is, as Lord Donaldson of Lymington M.R. expressed it in *In re M. and N. (Minors) (Wardship: Publication of Information)* [1990] Fam. 211, 231, 'but . . . an incidental part of life.' But the freedom of the press is so fundamental that in this category it must triumph over welfare because, to adapt an observation of Lord Shaw of Dunfermline in *Scott v Scott* [1913] A.C. 417, 477: 'To remit the maintenance of constitutional [in this case one would say 'fundamental human'] right to the region of judicial discretion is to shift the foundations of freedom from the rock to the sand.'

2. *When welfare dominates the decision*

I wish to emphasise that freedom of publication is only the subordinate interest 'when a court determines any question with respect to the upbringing of a child:' section 1(1) of the Children Act 1989. It is not always *easy* to decide when a question of upbringing is being determined. . . . In the *In re W.* [1992] 1 W.L.R. 100 category of case on publicity it is also now firmly established, as Neill L.J. stated, at p. 103, in his fourth guideline, citing Butler-Sloss L.J. in *In re M. and N. (Minors)* [1990] Fam. 211, 223, that 'in this situation the welfare of the child is not the paramount consideration.' I have already analysed that line of cases as being in a category where the publication was of the child and was about the way in which he was being brought up but although his care and upbringing was the object of the publication, the court was not having to determine any question with respect to the upbringing. The court was not exercising what Lord MacDermott in *S. v McC.* [1972] A.C. 24, 48 called the 'custodial jurisdiction.'

Sir John Pennycuick made this point in *In re X (A Minor) (Wardship: Jurisdiction)* [1975] Fam 47. He drew attention, at p. 62, to section 1 of the Guardianship of Minors Act 1971 which provided before its repeal by the Children Act 1989:

'Where in any proceedings before any court . . . (*a*) the custody or upbringing of a minor; . . . is in question, the court, in deciding that question, shall regard the welfare of the minor as the first paramount consideration . . .'

490

He said, at p. 62:

'It seems to me that the words 'the custody or upbringing of a minor' do not cover the issue in this present case, namely, the publication of this material. I do not think either the custody or the upbringing of the minor is in question within the meaning of section 1. If it were, then I think the court would be bound by statute to regard the welfare of the minor as the first and paramount consideration in deciding the question. On the other side, the wording of section 1 throws, I think, considerable light on the sphere within which the court in practice should exercise its jurisdiction.'

I agree. In my judgment a question of upbringing is determined whenever the central issue before the court is one which relates to how the child is being reared. If the matter before the court requires the determination of any question which is to be characterised as one with respect to the upbringing of the child, then the child's welfare is the court's paramount consideration and welfare prevails over the freedom for publication.

3. *The balancing exercise*

If welfare is not paramount because a question of upbringing is not being determined, then welfare must be balanced against the freedom of publication. The guidelines are given in *In re W. (A Minor) (Wardship: Restrictions on Publication)* [1992] 1 W.L.R. 100, 103. Neill L.J. and I attempted to explain them and apply them in *In re H.-S. (Minors) (Protection of Identity)* [1994] 1 W.L.R. 1141. There the injunction was granted in divorce proceedings. It was an extraordinary case. The father was a transsexual who later underwent a 'gender re-assignment operation.' He wished to profit by writing a book and giving interviews to tell his story. What he planned to do did not involve an exercise of parental responsibility for he was not requiring any active participation by the children. A balance between the welfare of the children and the freedom of press had to be struck. . . .

4. *Where a duty of confidentiality arises*

The right to preserve confidential material may be absolute in the sense that no one may invade it. The right may, of course, be surrendered. A *'Gillick* incompetent' child (see *Gillick v West Norfolk and Wisbech Area Health Authority* [1986] A.C. 112) can not exercise the right of surrender but the parent may exercise it on his behalf. The parent is not entitled to do so if it is contrary to the welfare of the child.

5. *The exercise of parental responsibility and prohibited steps orders*

The disclosure by a parent of confidential information relating to the child is an exercise of parental responsibility. As already set out, it can be restrained by a prohibited steps order. If the court is considering whether or not steps should be taken by a parent in meeting his parental responsibility for a child, then, beyond question, the court is determining a question with respect to the upbringing of the child. Welfare becomes the paramount consideration. . . .

The application of these principles to the facts of this case

This case is not simply about some third person (the television company) publishing without parental involvement information about the way in which this child is being cared for and brought up as in *In re M. and N. (Minors) (Wardship: Publication of Information)* [1990] Fam. 211 and *In re W. (A Minor) (Wardship: Restrictions on Publication)* [1992] 1 W.L.R. 100 etc. This is not a case where the parent stands by acquiescing in competent teenagers taking their story to the press as they did in *In re W. (Wardship: Discharge: Publicity)* [1995] 2 F.L.R. 466. If there was more than mere acquiescence and if there was active encouragement by the father in that case, it was not argued or presented on that basis. This is not a case like the transsexual father in *In re H.-S. (Minors) (Protection of Identity)* [1994] 1 W.L.R. 1141 who tells the family story but who does not require the children to participate in its telling. This case is one where the mother wishes her child to perform for the making of the film. This mother wishes to bring up her child as one who will play an active part in a television film. This is a case where the mother wishes to exercise her parental responsibility and waive the confidentiality which the child otherwise enjoys in keeping her medical treatment and/or education private. This is a case, quite unlike any of the other cases I have discussed, where the court is being asked to decide whether the child shall take part in the activity. The court is, therefore, required to determine a question with respect to the upbringing of the child. Accordingly section 1 of the Children Act 1989 must apply and welfare is the paramount consideration. The judge was of the clear view that the welfare of the child would be harmed and not advanced by her being involved in the making and publication of this film. It is a conclusion with which I wholeheartedly agree.

Questions for discussion

1. What were the decisive facts in *Re Z*? The fact that the programme would involve the active participation of the child? That there was already in place a wide-ranging injunction?
2. Does the distinction between cases where the court is asked to determine a matter concerning the upbringing of a child, and cases where it is not so concerned, make sense?
3. What cases are left for any third, intermediate category, where the court balances two interests?
4. How should *Re Z* be decided after incorporation of art 10 of the ECHR by the Human Rights Act 1998?

8. REPORTING OF CRIMINAL TRIALS INVOLVING PERSONS UNDER 18

The Children and Young Persons Act 1933 has imposed restrictions on the reporting of legal proceedings involving children and young persons under 18. In the case of proceedings before youth (formerly, juvenile) courts, that is, magistrates' courts dealing with criminal cases against young persons, there has been an automatic ban on reporting which would disclose the name and other details identifying the young persons concerned in them; but the court had power to lift the ban in narrowly defined circumstances.[24] In contrast, the protection of children involved in adult proceedings, whether as the accused or as a witness was more limited; the court had a discretionary power to direct that reports and pictures should not be published.[25] The distinction between the two provisions is nicely illustrated in *Lee*, where the Court of Appeal refused to review the lifting of an order which had restricted the identification of a boy, aged 14, convicted of robbery and (at an earlier trial) of rape.

Extract 13.8.1

R v Lee [1993] 1 WLR 103, at 109–110 (CA)

LLOYD LJ: . . . we have a transcript of the very full and clear ruling which he gave on 26 June. In the course of the argument before him on that day he had been referred to *Reg. v Leicester Crown Court, Ex parte S. (A Minor)*, post, p. 111, and in particular to the following passage from the judgment of the court given by Watkins L.J., at p. 114:

> 'In our judgment, the correct approach to the exercise of the power given by section 39 is that reports of proceedings should not be restricted unless there are reasons to do so which outweigh the legitimate interest of the public in receiving fair and accurate reports of criminal proceedings and knowing the identity of those in the community who have been guilty of criminal conduct and who may, therefore, present a danger or threat to the community in which they live. The mere fact that the person before the court is a child or young person will normally be a good reason for restricting reports of the proceedings in the ways permitted by section 39 and it will, in our opinion, only be in rare and exceptional cases that directions under section 39 will not be given or having been given will be discharged.'

The judge quoted extensively from that passage in his ruling. It may be, he said, that it is now exceptional for the press to be allowed, under the section, to publicise the name or identity of the defendant. At the same time, if an order were never to be made, it would emasculate the court's discretion under the section. Yet Parliament clearly intended that the court should have such a discretion. This was not a case, he said, of a minor offence where the applicant was going straight back into the community. In such a case it would not help the applicant to get back on his feet if everybody knew that he had had a conviction. This was a case at the very opposite end of the spectrum. The applicant's offences were exceptionally grave. He would on any view be detained for a lengthy period. In those circumstances he could see no real harm to the applicant, and a powerful deterrent effect on his contemporaries, if the

---

[24] Children and Young Persons Act 1933, s 49.
[25] Ibid, s 39.

493

applicant's name and photograph were published. The public interest in know-ing the identity of the applicant outweighed any harm to the applicant himself.

That is a brief summary of the judge's ruling. We have not attempted to set out his reasons in full. It is sufficient to say that having read his reasons we can see no basis on which we could in this court interfere with his discretion, even if we were so minded. He directed himself correctly and he is not shown to have omitted any relevant factors. In those circumstances the case is very different from *Reg. v Leicester Crown Court, Ex parte S. (A Minor)*, where Judge Young did not express his reasons or identify in any way the excep-tional circumstances in his view justified lifting the restriction in that case.

Before leaving *Reg. v Leicester Crown Court, Ex parte S. (A Minor)*, we would add this comment. At the conclusion of the passage which we have already quoted from the judgment, the court said that the mere fact that the person before the court is a child will normally be a good reason for restricting reports of the proceedings. It will, the court said, only be in rare and exceptional cases that a direction will not be given or having been given will be discharged. For our part, we would not wish to see the court's discretion fettered so strictly. There is nothing in section 39 about rare or exceptional cases. There must of course be a good reason for making an order under section 39, just as there must be a good reason for lifting the restriction on publicity of proceedings in the juvenile court under section 49, namely to avoid injustice to the child. The rule under section 49, as has been pointed out, is the reverse of the rule under section 39. The onus is, so to speak, the other way round. If the discretion under section 39 is too narrowly confined, we will be in danger of blurring the distinction between proceedings in the juvenile courts and proceedings in the Crown Court, a distinction which Parliament clearly intended to preserve.

These reporting restrictions have recently been tightened. The 1933 legisla-tion did not cover publicity before 'proceedings' began, a matter which was highlighted at the end of 1997 when it was unclear whether the press was free to identify the son of a Cabinet Minister suspected, but not charged, of a drugs offence. The Youth Justice and Criminal Evidence Act 1999 pro-hibits the publication of any 'matter relating to any person involved in [an] offence' while he is under 18 which is likely to identify him, whenever a criminal investigation has started in respect of an alleged offence.[26] Further, the provisions in the 1933 legislation restricting the reporting of criminal proceedings have been amended[27] or replaced. The following extract sets out the principal rules protecting children involved in adult proceedings.[28]

---

[26] Section 44. The ban covers publications identifying young persons as alleged victims of, or witnesses to the commission of, the offence, as well as suspects. The courts may dispense with the restriction if satisfied that is necessary in the interests of justice, taking into account the welfare of the young person involved.

[27] Children and Young Persons Act 1933, s 39, as amended by Sched 2 to the 1999 Act, still governs the reporting of youth proceedings.

[28] The young person may be involved as the person against, or in respect of, whom the proceed-ings are taken or as a witness in the proceedings (not necessarily to the commission of the offence): s 45(7). But these provisions will not be brought into force for youth defendants until 2000, while the government will keep under review the date of their application to youth victims and witnesses.

Extract 13.8.2

Youth Justice and Criminal Evidence Act 1999, s 45 (3)–(5)

44.—(3) The court may direct that no matter relating to any person concerned in the proceedings shall while he is under the age of 18 be included in any publication if it is likely to lead members of the public to identify him as a person concerned in the proceedings.

(4) The court or an appellate court may by direction ('an excepting direction') dispense . . . with the restrictions imposed by a direction under subsection (3) if it is satisfied that it is necessary in the interests of justice to do so.

(5) The court or an appellate court may also by direction . . . dispense . . . with the restrictions . . . if it is satisfied—

(a) that their effect is to impose a substantial and unreasonable restriction on the reporting of the proceedings, and

(b) that it is in the public interest to remove or relax that restriction; but no excepting direction shall be given under this subsection by reason only of the fact that the proceedings have been determined in any way or have been abandoned.

Questions for discussion

1. What justification is there for the extension of the reporting restrictions to cover the investigation of alleged offences?

2. How should the courts exercise their discretion under s 45? Are the factors taken into account in *Lee* still relevant?

14

PROTECTION OF JOURNALISTS' SOURCES AND RELATED ISSUES

1. INTRODUCTION

Journalists consider that they have a moral obligation not to disclose their sources.[1] The media argue that otherwise people would be unwilling to supply information, generally for fear that on identification they would be dismissed by their employers. In the absence, therefore, of a privilege not to disclose the identity of their sources, journalists would find it difficult, perhaps impossible, to obtain enough information fully to report stories of real public interest. In short, this privilege is said to be an integral aspect of freedom of expression, the principle which governs so much of media law.

Yet English common law has been reluctant to recognise a link between freedom of the press and a privilege (or immunity) not to disclose its sources of information. Lord Wilberforce's speech in the *British Steel* case was representative of its approach, while Lord Salmon's dissenting view was generally regarded as heterodox, albeit appreciated by the press itself. The case arose after the broadcast by Granada of a current affairs programme about a steel strike and, it was alleged, the incompetent management of British Steel; it quoted from a number of confidential documents sent to Granada, presumably by an employee of British Steel. The latter sought an order for Granada to disclose its source.[2]

Extract 14.1.1

British Steel Corp v Granada Television Ltd [1981] AC 1096, at 1168–1169, 1174–1175, 1195 (HL)

LORD WILBERFORCE: First, there were appeals, made in vigorous tones to such broad principles as the freedom of the press, the right to a free flow of

---

[1] The principle constitutes clause 15 of the Press Complaints Commission Code.
[2] The application was based on the procedure approved in *Norwich Pharmacal v Customs and Excise Commissioners* [1974] AC 133 (HL), to the effect that a person involved, however innocently, in the tortious conduct of others, is under a duty to assist the injured party by giving him full information with regard to the wrongdoer's identity.

496

information, the public's right to know. In Granada's printed case we find quotations from pronouncements of Sheridan in Parliament and from declarations of eminent judges in cases where the freedom of the press might be involved. I too would be glad to be counted among those whose voice had been raised in favour of this great national possession – a free press: who indeed would not? But this case does not touch upon the freedom of the press even at its periphery. Freedom of the press imports, generally, freedom to publish without pre-censorship, subject always to the laws relating to libel, official secrets, sedition and other recognised inhibitions. It is not necessary to define the concept more closely, for it is clear and *not disputed by Granada*, that B.S.C. could, if they had acted in time, have obtained from the courts an injunction against publishing or reproducing any of the contents of the documents . . . In other words, Granada do not make the case that they had the right to publish. The question before us, as to disclosure of the source, is another question altogether.

Then there is the alleged right to a free flow of information, or the right to know. Your Lordships will perceive without any demonstration from me that use of the word 'right' here will not conduce to an understanding of the legal position. As to a free flow of information, it may be said that, in a general sense, it is in the public interest that this should be maintained and not curtailed. Investigatory journalism too in some cases may bring benefits to the public. But, granting this, one is a long way from establishing a right which the law will recognise in a particular case. Before then it is necessary to take account of the legitimate interest which others may have in limiting disclosure of information of a particular kind. I shall return to this point later. As to an alleged 'right to know,' it must be clear that except in a totally open society (if any such exists) limitations on this not only exist but are considerable, whether one is concerned with the operations of government, or of business, one's neighbours' affairs or indeed any other activity. To keep to the concrete, as regards the British Steel Corporation, the conduct of its affairs and the disclosures and reports which have to be made, are, as one would expect of a public body, regulated by statute, now by the Iron and Steel Act 1975. The legitimate interest of the public in knowing about its affairs is given effect to through information which is a statutory duty to publish and through reports to the Secretary of State who is responsible to Parliament. That some of the internal activities of B.S.C. at particular times are of interest to the public there can be no doubt. But there is a wide difference between what is interesting to the public and what it is in the public interest to make known.

Thirdly, as to information obtained in confidence, and the legal duty, which may arise, to disclose it to a court of justice, the position is clear. Courts have an inherent wish to respect this confidence, whether it arises between doctor and patient, priest and penitent, banker and customer, between persons giving testimonials to employees, or in other relationships. A relationship of confidence between a journalist and his source is in no different category: nothing in this case involves or will involve any principle that such confidence is not something to be respected. But in all these cases the court may have to decide, in particular circumstances, that the interest in preserving this confidence is outweighed by other interests to which the law attaches importance. The only question in this appeal is whether the present is such a case.

497

One final point. There is an important exception to the limitations which may exist upon the right of the media to reveal information otherwise restricted. That is based on what is commonly known as the 'iniquity rule.' It extends in fact beyond 'iniquity' to misconduct generally: see *Initial Services Ltd. v Putterill* [1968] 1 Q.B. 396. It is recognised that, in cases where misconduct exists, publication may legitimately be made even if disclosure involves a breach of confidence such as would normally justify a prohibition against disclosure. It must be emphasised that we are not in this field in the present case; giving the widest extension to the expression 'iniquity' nothing within it is alleged in the present case. The most that it is said the papers reveal is mismanagement and government intervention. Granada has never contended that it had a right to publish in order to reveal 'iniquity.'

So the question is, and remains, whether the court at the instance of B.S.C., would compel disclosure of the source. . . .

I now come more particularly to the law relevant to this case. I start with the proposition that the media of information, and journalists who write or contribute for them, have no immunity based on public interest which protects them from the obligation to disclose in a court of law their sources of information, when such disclosure is necessary in the interest of justice. No such claim has ever been allowed in our courts, and such attempts as have been made to assert such an immunity have failed. A claim for immunity was made before the Parnell Commission in 1888 (C. 5891) and flatly rejected by Sir James Hannen sitting with two other judges. In the two cases arising out of the Vassall inquiry, in which the usual argument was strongly put that if disclosure were ordered in such cases the sources of information would dry up, the claim was firmly repelled (Report of the Tribunal appointed to inquire into the Vassall Case and Related Matters, Cmnd. 2009 (1963)). In *Attorney-General v Clough* [1963] 1 Q.B. 773, 788, Lord Parker C.J. expressed the clear opinion that no such immunity had been recognised or existed. In *Attorney-General v Mulholland; Attorney-General v Foster* [1963] 2 Q.B. 477 a similar claim in respect of communications between journalists and sources of information was rejected by the Court of Appeal . . .

I come then to the final and critical point. The remedy (being equitable) is discretionary. Although, as I have said, the media, and journalists, have no immunity, it remains true that there may be an element of public interest in protecting the revelation of the source . . . The court ought not to compel confidence bona fide given to be breached unless necessary in the interests of justice: see *Science Research Council v Nassé* [1980] A.C. 1028. There is a public interest in the free flow of information, the strength of which will vary from case to case. In some cases it may be very weak; in others it may be very strong. The court must take this into account. How ought the discretion which the court undoubtedly has to be exercised in this case? Sir Robert Megarry V.-C. considered this and exercised it in favour of B.S.C. I would, for myself, give somewhat greater weight to the public interest element involved in preserving, qua the relevant information, the confidence under which it was obtained than he did. But I think that even so the balance was strongly in B.S.C.'s favour. They suffered a grievous wrong, in which Granada itself became involved, not innocently, but with active participation. To confine B.S.C. to its remedy against Granada and to deny it the opportunity of a remedy against the source, would be a significant denial of justice. Granada had, on its side, and I recognise this, the public interest that people should be informed about the steel strike, of the attitude of B.S.C., and perhaps that of the government towards settling the strike. But there is no 'iniquity' here – no misconduct to be revealed. The courts, to revert to Lord Denning M.R.'s formulation in *Attorney-General v Mulholland*; *Attorney-General v Foster* [1963] 2 Q.B. 477, had to form their opinion whether the strong public interest in favour of doing justice and against denying it, was outweighed by the perfectly real considerations that Granada put forward. I have reached the conclusion that it was not. . . .

LORD SALMON: My Lords, it is, I imagine, apparent from what I have said that I have the misfortune to disagree with your Lordships. The immunity of the press to reveal its sources of information save in exceptional circumstances is in the public interest, and has been so accepted by the courts for so long that I consider it is wrong now to sweep this immunity away. The press has been deprived of this immunity only twice, namely, in the *Clough* case [1963] 1 Q.B. 773 and in the *Mulholland* case [1963] 2 Q.B. 477. And the exceptional circumstances in each of those cases were that the security of the nation required that the press's source of information must be revealed. Certainly no such circumstances appear in the present case. I do not say that national security will necessarily always be the only special circumstances but it is the only one which has been effective until now. Moreover, there are no circumstances in this case which have ever before deprived or ever should deprive the press, by discovery, of its immunity against revealing its sources of information in relation to matters of great public importance. The freedom of the press depends upon this immunity. Were it to disappear so would the sources from which its information is obtained; and the public be deprived of much of the information to which the public of a free nation is entitled.

Other jurisdictions have discussed whether the privilege should be recognised as an aspect of the constitutional freedom of the media. The Supreme Court of Canada seems to have doubted the argument that for a court (or in this case the Alberta Labour Relations Board) to compel journalists to testify, and in particular to disclose their sources of information, would endanger their ability to report stories of public interest.

Extract 14.1.2

Moysa v Alberta (Labour Relations Board) (1989) 60 DLR (4th) 1, at 4, 7–8 (Supreme Court of Canada)

SOPINKA J: The board then proceeded to consider the alleged right to a qualified privilege for reporters under s. 2(*b*) of the Charter. The board examined the decision of the United States Supreme Court in *Branzburg v Hayes*, 408 U.S. 665, 33 L.Ed.2d 626, 92 S.Ct. 2646 (1972), which considered whether the guarantee of the freedom of the press under the First Amendment to the

American Constitution permits a reporter to refuse to answer questions before a grand jury. White J. for the majority (speaking for four members of the court) held that the First Amendment accords a reporter no privilege against appearing before a grand jury and answering questions as to either the identity of his or her news sources or information which he or she has received in confidence. In a concurring opinion Powell J. agreed in the result but held that each claim of privilege should be judged on its particular facts by striking a balance between the freedom of the press and the obligation of all citizens to give relevant testimony.

The labour board was of the opinion that Powell J. had identified two criteria that need be demonstrated before the government could compel a journalist to testify. The perceived evidence must be crucial to whomever seeks it and the evidence also must be relevant. The board felt that this was the appropriate test under s. 2(b) of the Charter. However, on the facts presented before the board, it was held that the evidence sought from the appellant was crucial to the union's allegation of unfair labour practices and was also relevant. Further, the board held that if there is a third requirement that the information not be available from an alternative source it, too, had been satisfied. Therefore, the board concluded that the appellant could be compelled to testify . . .

Section 2(b) of the Charter provides:

'2. Everyone has the following fundamental freedoms:

. . . . .

(b) freedom of thought, belief, opinion and expression, including freedom of the press and other media of communication;'

In oral argument counsel for the appellant stated that he was not asserting a special constitutional privilege for members of the press beyond that which is available to everyone generally under the right to freedom of expression. However, it was argued that s. 2(b) was violated when the appellant was required to testify before the Labour Relations Board and was not permitted by the board to avail herself of a claim of qualified privilege. The appellant's argument is premised on s. 2(b) according the same protection to the gathering of news as it extends to the dissemination of news. The appellant contends that the ability to gather news is hindered by the failure to extend testimonial privilege to journalists in situations such as the appellant's.

Even if I assume for the moment that the right to gather the news is constitutionally enshrined in s. 2(b), the appellant has not demonstrated that compelling journalists to testify before bodies such as the Labour Relations Board would detrimentally affect journalists' ability to gather information. No evidence was placed before the court suggesting that such a direct link exists. While judicial notice may be taken of self-evident facts, I am not convinced that it is indisputable that there is a direct relationship between testimonial compulsion and a 'drying-up' of news sources as alleged by the appellant. The burden of proof that there has been a violation of s. 2(b) rests on the appellant. Absent any evidence that there is a tie between the impairment of the alleged right to gather information and the requirement that journalists testify before the Labour Relations Board, I cannot find that there has been a breach of s. 2(b) in this case.

In addition, the Labour Relations Board held that the relationship between the appellant and the persons she spoke with at the Hudson Bay Company was not one based on confidence. The protection of confidence was neither sought nor given. The board also held that the evidence was crucial, relevant and was not available from alternative sources. As well, the board concluded that the appellant would fail in her claim for qualified privilege based on the test proposed by Powell J. in *Branzburg v Hayes, supra*. Therefore, in my opinion, even if this court were to adopt Powell J.'s approach to a qualified privilege, on the facts of this case no possible violation of s. 2(*b*) has been made out.

One argument, referred to in the *British Steel* case, is that the law should respect a confidential relationship between the press and its sources in much the same way as it recognises the relationship of confidence between a lawyer and client, a doctor and patient, or perhaps between priest and penitent. English law, for instance, recognises in some circumstances legal professional privilege, so that a lawyer cannot be required to give evidence about confidential matters discussed with his client. The journalists' privilege is different, however, in that it is concerned not to keep the content of the matters discussed with the source confidential, but rather to keep the latter's identity secret.

Another question is whether the privilege belongs to the journalist or to the source. If it is a privilege for the media (albeit one which is recognised for the public benefit), it might follow that they, rather than the source, should be entitled to waive it. In that case a newspaper editor would be entitled to reveal the source in order to give a story more credibility. However, the US Supreme Court has ruled that a newspaper has no right under the First Amendment to break a promise to its source not to reveal his identity.[3]

Questions for discussion
Do you think that the arguments for recõgnising the privilege not to disclose sources of information are persuasive? Or is the scepticism of the Canadian Supreme Court justified?

2. THE STATUTORY PRIVILEGE

(a) General principles

At most the common law recognised a judicial discretion not to compel the media to disclose its sources, in particular when disclosure was irrelevant to the issues before the court or was unnecessary to their resolution.[4] In principle, this position has been changed by s 10 of the Contempt of Court Act 1981.

---

[3] *Cohen v Cowles Media Co* 111 S Ct 2513 (1991).
[4] *Attorney General v Lundin* (1982) 75 Cr App Rep 90 (DC).

Extract 14.2.1

Contempt of Court Act 1981, s 10

No court may require a person to disclose, nor is any person guilty of contempt of court for refusing to disclose, the source of information contained in a publication for which he is responsible, unless it be established to the satisfaction of the court that disclosure is necessary in the interests of justice or national security or for the prevention of disorder or crime.

The overall aim of this provision was discussed by the House of Lords in the controversial *Guardian* case, when the Secretary of Defence applied for the return of confidential documents sent anonymously to the editor of the paper, a course which would enable the government to determine who had leaked them. The documents discussed the best way for the government to cope with the controversy which would result when news broke that Cruise missiles had arrived in Britain.

Extract 14.2.2

Secretary of State for Defence v Guardian Newspapers [1985] AC 339, 348–350 (HL)

LORD DIPLOCK: Section 10 thus recognises the existence of a prima facie right of ordinary members of the public to be informed of any matter that anyone thinks it appropriate to communicate to them as such, though this does not extend to that information's source. The right so recognised is, so far as members of the public are directly concerned, of imperfect obligation. It encourages purveyors of information to the public, but a member of the public as such has no right conferred on him by this section to compel purveyance to him of any information. The choice of what information shall be communicated to members of the public lies with the publisher alone; it is not confined to what, in an action for defamation would be regarded as matters of public interest, or even, going down the scale, information published in order to pander to idle curiosity and thus promote sales of the publication; nor is the section confined to publications by 'the media' although no doubt the media will in practice be the chief beneficiaries of it. Provided that it is addressed to the public at large or to any section of it every publication of information falls within the section and is entitled to the protection granted by it unless the publication falls within one of the express exceptions introduced by the word 'unless.'

The nature of the protection is the removal of compulsion to disclose in judicial proceedings the identity or nature of the source of any information contained in the publication, even though the disclosure would be relevant to the determination by the court of an issue in those particular proceedings; and the only reasonable inference is that the purpose of the protection is the same

502

as that which underlay the discretion vested in the judge at common law to *refuse* to compel disclosure of sources of information; videlicet – unless informers could be confident that their identity would not be revealed sources of information would dry up.

The words with which the section starts, before it comes to specifying any exceptions, impose a prohibition on the court itself that is perfectly general in its terms: 'No court may require a person to disclose . . . the source of information contained in a publication for which he is responsible . . .' This prohibition is in no way qualified by the nature of the judicial proceedings, or of the claim or cause of action in respect of which such judicial proceedings, if they are civil, are brought. So I am unable to accept Scott J.'s construction of the section as being inapplicable to a claim for detention of goods in which an order for the delivery of the goods, without the option to the defendant to pay damages by reference to their value instead, is sought under section 3(2)(*a*) of the Torts (Interference with Goods) Act 1977. . . .

Again, what the court is prohibited from requiring is not described by reference to the form the requirement takes, but by reference to its consequences, viz. disclosure of the source of information. If compliance with the requirement, whatever form it takes, will, or is sought in order to enable, another party to the proceedings to identify the source by adding to the pieces already in possession of that party the last piece to a jigsaw puzzle in which the identity of the source of information would remain concealed unless that last piece became available to put into position, the requirement will fall foul of the ban imposed by the general words with which the section starts. I therefore, with respect, do not share the doubts expressed by Slade L.J. as to whether section 10 of the Act of 1981 applies to anything other than an order of a court which *in terms* (his italics) directs disclosure of the identity of the source by oral evidence or affidavit; nor do I accept his alternative, though tentative, suggestion that in order to rely upon section 10 of the Act of 1981 to resist delivery up of a document the person responsible for its publication must establish by affirmative evidence that compliance will (not just may) compel him to reveal a source of information. If he can show that there is a reasonable chance that it will do so, then (subject always to the exceptions provided for later in the section) this will suffice to bring the prohibition into effect.

I find myself in full agreement with the judgment of Griffiths L.J., where he says that he sees no harm in giving a wide construction to the opening words because in the latter part of the section the court is given ample powers to order the source to be revealed where in the circumstances of a particular case the wider public interest makes it necessary to do so.

So I turn next to the exceptions that the latter part of section 10 provides to the general ban upon the court requiring disclosure of sources of information that is imposed by the opening words. There are only four interests, and each of these is specific, that are singled out for protection, viz.: (a) justice, (b) national security, (c) the prevention of disorder, and (d) the prevention of crime.

The exceptions include no reference to 'the public interest' generally and I would add that in my view the expression 'justice', the interests of which are entitled to protection, is not used in a general sense as the antonym of 'injustice' but in the technical sense of the administration of justice in the course of legal proceedings in a court of law, or, by reason of the extended definition of 'court' in section 19 of the Act of 1981 before a tribunal or body exercising the judicial power of the State.

The onus of proving that an order of the court has or may have the consequence of disclosing the source of information falls within any of the exceptions lies upon the party by whom the order is sought. The words 'unless it be established to the satisfaction of the court' make it explicit and so serve to emphasise what otherwise might have been left to be inferred from the application of the general rule of statutory construction: the onus of establishing that he falls within an exception lies upon the party who is seeking to rely upon it. Again, the section uses the words 'necessary' by itself, instead of using the common statutory phrase 'necessary or expedient,' to describe what must be established to the satisfaction of the court – which latter phrase gives to the judge a margin of discretion; expediency, however great, is not enough; section 10 requires actual necessity to be established; and whether it has or not is a question of fact that the judge has to find in favour of necessity as a condition precedent to his having any jurisdiction to order disclosure of sources of information.

Lord Diplock took a broad view of aspects of the provision.[5] In particular, the immunity is not confined to the institutional media. The writer of a leaflet or local newsletter can equally claim it. But Lord Diplock was one of the three Law Lords who held that the applicant had shown that disclosure of the source, or more accurately information leading to discovery of her identity, was necessary 'in the interests of national security'. They were persuaded that it was necessary to identify the leaker (subsequently revealed to be a clerk in the Foreign Office, Sarah Tisdall) in order to avert the risk of further leaks.

(b) The meaning of 'necessary'

The privilege is not absolute. The applicant may obtain an order for disclosure if he establishes that it is 'necessary' for one of the four specified purposes. There has been some discussion of the meaning of 'necessary', though its interpretation is inextricably linked with the question how the courts should balance the interest in non-disclosure of the source against the interests of justice, national security, or the prevention of disorder or crime which count in favour of disclosure.

---

[5] The *Guardian* case was followed by Sir Nicolas Browne-Wilkinson V-C, when he held that the privilege precluded an order against a newspaper to hand over photographs (of Madonna and her husband), from which the identity of the persons who had sent them to the newspaper might be discovered: *Handmade Films (Productions) Ltd v Express Newspapers plc* [1986] FSR 463.

Extract 14.2.3

Re An Inquiry under the Company Securities (Insider Dealing) Act 1985 [1988] AC 660, at 704 (HL)

LORD GRIFFITHS: What then is meant by the words 'necessary . . . for the prevention of . . . crime' in section 10? I do not think that much light is thrown upon this question by an elaborate discussion of the meaning of the word 'necessary.' 'Necessary' is a word in common usage in everyday speech with which everyone is familiar. Like all words, it will take colour from its context; for example, most people would regard it as 'necessary' to do everything possible to prevent a catastrophe but would not regard it as 'necessary' to do everything possible to prevent some minor inconvenience. Furthermore, whether a particular measure is necessary, although described as a question of fact for the purpose of section 10, involves the exercise of a judgment upon the established facts. In the exercise of that judgment different people may come to different conclusions on the same facts; for an example of this one has to look no further than *Secretary of State for Defence v Guardian Newspapers Ltd.* But this cannot be avoided and the task of the judge will not be lightened by substituting for the familiar word 'necessary' some other set of words with a similar meaning . . .

I doubt if it is possible to go further than to say that 'necessary' has a meaning that lies somewhere between 'indispensable' on the one hand, and 'useful' or 'expedient' on the other, and to leave it to the judge to decide towards which end of the scale of meaning he will place it on the facts of any particular case. The nearest paraphrase I can suggest is 'really needed.'

Arguably, an order for disclosure is not really 'necessary' if the applicant could identify the source from his own inquiries and investigations. Some dicta suggest that judges will consider whether the applicant has made any attempts to do this before they are prepared to hold that disclosure is 'necessary' in the interest of justice, etc.[6]

(c) For the prevention of disorder or crime

There seems to be no case on the meaning of 'disorder' under s 10 of the Contempt of Court Act 1981, but a few judgments have discussed the phrase, 'the prevention of . . . crime'. Again, the leading authority is *Re An Inquiry*, where a financial journalist, Jeremy Warner, had refused to disclose to inspectors appointed by the Department of Trade and Industry the source of leaks of price-sensitive information which he had published in the *Independent*.

---

[6] *Special Hospitals Service Authority v Hyde* (1994) 20 BMLR 75, at 85, Peter Pain J (Extract 14.2.8); *Saunders v Punch* [1998] 1 All ER 234, at 245, Lindsay J.

Extract 14.2.4

Re An Inquiry under the Company Securities (Insider Dealing) Act 1985 [1988] AC 660, at 704–706 (HL)

LORD GRIFFITHS: The words 'prevention of . . . crime' do, however, admit of more than one construction. Hoffmann J. adopted a narrow construction for which Mr. Warner contends. He held that: 'it must appear probable that in the absence of disclosure by the journalist further crimes are likely to be committed.' And later he said:

'The facts to which the inspectors deposed do not therefore in my judgment show a probability that only the disclosure of his sources by Mr. Warner can prevent further insider dealing.'

No one can be so optimistic as to believe that any measure will ever prevent crime, including 'insider dealing,' being committed in the future. Mr. Kentridge [counsel for Warner] submits that this narrow construction means that 'prevention of . . . crime' is limited to a situation in which the identification of the source will allow steps to be taken to prevent the commission of a particular identifiable future crime or crimes: for example, the source knows the plans for the hijack of a wages van and the police urgently need to question him so that they may take steps to ambush the robbers and thus prevent the crime from being committed. In an inquiry such as this it is highly unlikely that the inspectors will be able to discharge such a burden. It is not the job of the inspectors to take immediate action to frustrate a particular crime. Their task is to probe into and lay bare the whole dishonest web of this suspected insider dealing so that measures can be taken to deter and contain, so far as possible, this type of financial dishonesty. Mr. Kentridge freely acknowledges that on the narrow construction a journalist could rarely, if ever, be called upon to identify his sources in aid of this type of inquiry, and submits that section 10 is designed to ensure that inspectors will get little or no help from the press. If Parliament had wished to confer a complete protection on journalists from revealing their sources in this type of inquiry, they could have specifically provided such protection, as they have for legal professional privilege: see section 177(7) of the Act of 1986. But Parliament has not done so and I am reluctant to believe that it was the intention that, by a side wind, the same effect should be achieved by giving a very narrow construction to the meaning of the words 'prevention of . . . crime' in section 10 of the Act of 1981.

The phrase 'prevention of . . . crime' carries, to my mind, very different overtones from 'prevention of a crime' or even 'prevention of crimes.' There are frequent articles and programmes in the media on the prevention of crime. The subject on these occasions is discussed from many points of view including the social background in which crime breeds, detection, deterrence, retribution, punishment, rehabilitation and so forth. The prevention of crime in this broad sense is a matter of public and vital interest to any civilised society. Crime is endemic in society and will probably never be eradicated but its containment is essential. If crime gets the upper hand and becomes the rule rather than the exception, the collapse of society will swiftly follow. By identifying 'prevention of . . . crime' as one of the four heads of public interest to which the journalist's privilege may occasionally have to yield, I am satisfied that Parliament was using the phrase in its wider and, I think, natural meaning, rather than in the restricted sense for which the appellant contends.

One of the principal objects of the inquiry is to identify the sources of the leaks and another is to establish, so far as is possible, the extent to which the leaks have led to insider dealing. It is because this type of fraud is so difficult to detect and bring home to the culprits that Parliament has given special powers to the Minister to set up this type of inquiry which is conducted by a Queen's Counsel and an accountant who have the special skills needed to investigate and expose this type of financial crime. In the light of the inspectors' report it is to be hoped that steps can be taken towards stamping out this form of insider dealing by exposing and perhaps punishing both those who leak the information and those who trade upon it, and by considering further measures that can be taken to prevent future leaks and insider trading. Mr. Warner himself has recognised that the inspectors are engaged upon an investigation of a criminal nature and I have no doubt that the inquiry is being undertaken for the 'prevention of . . . crime' within the meaning of section 10 of the Act of 1981.

On the other hand, the court will be disinclined to order disclosure if the applicant is not charged with the enforcement of the criminal law. A health authority, therefore, did not succeed in its application for disclosure of the source of a newspaper story that doctors in its employment suffered from AIDS.[7]

(d) In the interests of justice

Much the most difficult question has been the scope of 'interests of justice' as a justification for ordering disclosure. In the *Guardian* case (see Extract 14.2.2 above), Lord Diplock suggested that the phrase referred to the administration of justice in legal proceedings. The implication was that disclosure could only be ordered if it was necessary for the disposition of particular legal proceedings. But the House of Lords in *Morgan Grampian* gave the phrase a broader meaning. An anonymous source had telephoned a trainee journalist, William Goodwin, to give him information about the plaintiff company (later disclosed as Tetra Ltd), taken from a 'strictly confidential' document which had disappeared from its premises. The plaintiff obtained an injunction to stop publication of an article in *The Engineer* and an order requiring Goodwin to disclose the identity of the source and notes of the telephone conversation. Goodwin failed to comply with the order of the Court of Appeal to hand over the notes which were to remain secure in a sealed envelope until final determination of his appeal. Despite this contempt, the House of Lords heard the submissions made on his behalf.

[7] *X v Y* [1988] 2 All ER 648, at 664–665, Rose J.

Extract 14.2.5

X Ltd v Morgan-Grampian Ltd [1991] 1 AC 1, at 40–45 (HL)

LORD BRIDGE OF HARWICH: The courts have always recognised an important public interest in the free flow of information. How far and in what circumstances the maintenance of this public interest operated to confer on journalists any privilege from disclosure of their sources which the common law would recognise admitted of no short and simple answer on the authorities. But the matter is no longer governed by the common law and I do not think any assistance is to be gained from the authorities preceding the coming into force of section 10 of the Contempt of Court Act 1981 . . .

It has been accepted in this case at all levels that the section applies to the circumstances of the instant case notwithstanding that the information obtained by Mr. Goodwin from the source has not been 'contained in a publication.' The information having been communicated and received for the purposes of publication, it is clearly right to treat it as subject to the rule which the section lays down, since the purpose underlying the statutory protection of sources of information is as much applicable before as after publication. It is also now clearly established that the section is to be given a wide, rather than a narrow, construction in the sense that the restriction on disclosure applies not only to direct orders to disclose the identity of a source but also to any order for disclosure of material which will indirectly identify the source and applies notwithstanding that the enforcement of the restriction may operate to defeat rights of property vested in the party who seeks to obtain that material: *Secretary of State for Defence v Guardian Newspapers Ltd.* [1984] Ch. 156, 166–167, *per* Griffiths L.J.; [1985] A.C. 339, 349–350, *per* Lord Diplock. As a statement of the rationale underlying this wide construction I cannot do better than quote from the passage in the judgment of Griffiths L.J. to which I have referred, where he said:

'The press have always attached the greatest importance to their ability to protect their sources of information. If they are not able to do so, they believe that many of their sources would dry up and this would seriously interfere with their effectiveness. It is in the interests of us all that we should have a truly effective press, and it seems to me that Parliament by enacting section 10 has clearly recognised the importance that attaches to the ability of the press to protect their sources. . . . I can see no harm in giving a wide construction to the opening words of the section because by the latter part of the section the court is given ample powers to order the source to be revealed where in the circumstances of a particular case the wider public interest makes it necessary to do so.'

It follows then that, whenever disclosure is sought, as here, of a document which will disclose the identity of a source within the ambit of section 10, the statutory restriction operates unless the party seeking disclosure can satisfy the court that 'disclosure is necessary' in the interests of one of the four matters of public concern that are listed in the section. I think it is indisputable that where a judge asks himself the question: 'Can I be satisfied that disclosure of the source of *this* information is necessary to serve *this* interest?' he has to engage in a balancing exercise. He starts with the assumptions, first, that the protection of sources is itself a matter of high public importance, secondly, that nothing less than necessity will suffice to override it, thirdly, that the necessity can only arise out of concern for another matter of high public importance, being one of the four interests listed in the section.

What assistance is to be derived from the authorities as to the proper tests to be applied in carrying out this balancing exercise? In *Secretary of State for Defence v Guardian Newspapers Ltd.* [1985] A.C. 339, 345, Lord Diplock said:

'The section is so drafted as to make it a question of fact not of discretion as to whether in the particular case a requirement for disclosure of sources of information falls within one of the express exceptions introduced by the word "unless."'

In the same case I said, at p. 372:

'There is no ambiguity in the phrase "necessary in the interests of national security." Whether such a necessity is established by the evidence, and, in the case of an interlocutory application, whether the necessity is established at the interlocutory stage, are both questions of fact which must always depend on the evidence adduced in any particular case.'

. . .

I cannot help wondering whether these dicta do not concentrate attention too much on only one side of the picture.[8] They suggest that in determining whether the criterion of necessity is established one need only look at, in the one case, the interests of national security and, in the other case, the prevention of crime. In the context of cases dealing with those two grounds of exception to the protection of sources, it is perfectly understandable that they should do so. For if non-disclosure of a source of information will imperil national security or enable a crime to be committed which might otherwise be prevented, it is difficult to imagine that any judge would hesitate to order disclosure. These two public interests are of such overriding importance that once it is shown that disclosure will serve one of those interests, the necessity of disclosure follows almost automatically; though even here if a judge were asked to order disclosure of a source of information in the interests of the prevention of crime, he 'might properly refuse to do so if, for instance, the crime was of a trivial nature:' [1988] A.C. 660, 703, *per* Lord Griffiths.

But the question whether disclosure is necessary in the interests of justice gives rise to a more difficult problem of weighing one public interest against another. A question arising under this part of section 10 has not previously come before your Lordships' House for decision. In discussing the section generally Lord Diplock said in *Secretary of State for Defence v Guardian Newspapers Ltd.* [1985] A.C. 339, 350:

'The exceptions include no reference to "the public interest" generally and I would add that in my view the expression "justice," the interests of which are

---

[8] Lord Bridge had quoted the remarks of Lords Griffiths and Oliver in *Re An Inquiry under the Company Securities (Insider Dealing) Act 1985* [1988] AC 660, at 704 (see Extract 14.2.3 above), 708–709.

entitled to protection, is not used in a general sense as the antonym of "injustice" but in the technical sense of the administration of justice in the course of legal proceedings in a court of law, or, by reason of the extended definition of "court" in section 19 of the Act of 1981 before a tribunal or body exercising the judicial power of the state.'

I agree entirely with the first half of this dictum. To construe 'justice' as the antonym of 'injustice' in section 10 would be far too wide. But to confine it to 'the technical sense of the administration of justice in the course of legal proceedings in a court of law' seems to me, with all respect due to any dictum of the late Lord Diplock, to be too narrow. It is, in my opinion, 'in the interests of justice,' in the sense in which this phrase is used in section 10, that persons should be enabled to exercise important legal rights and to protect themselves from serious legal wrongs whether or not resort to legal proceedings in a court of law will be necessary to attain these objectives. Thus, to take a very obvious example, if an employer of a large staff is suffering grave damage from the activities of an unidentified disloyal servant, it is undoubtedly in the interests of justice that he should be able to identify him in order to terminate his contract of employment, notwithstanding that no legal proceedings may be necessary to achieve that end.

Construing the phrase 'in the interests of justice' in this sense immediately emphasises the importance of the balancing exercise. It will not be sufficient, per se, for a party seeking disclosure of a source protected by section 10 to show merely that he will be unable without disclosure to exercise the legal right or avert the threatened legal wrong on which he bases his claim in order to establish the necessity of disclosure. The judge's task will always be to weigh in the scales the importance of enabling the ends of justice to be attained in the circumstances of the particular case on the one hand against the importance of protecting the source on the other hand. In this balancing exercise it is only if the judge is satisfied that disclosure in the interests of justice is of such preponderating importance as to override the statutory privilege against disclosure that the threshold of necessity will be reached.

Whether the necessity of disclosure in this sense is established is certainly a question of fact rather than an issue calling for the exercise of the judge's discretion, but, like many other questions of fact, such as the question whether somebody has acted reasonably in given circumstances, it will call for the exercise of a discriminating and sometimes difficult value judgment. In estimating the weight to be attached to the importance of disclosure in the interests of justice on the one hand and that of protection from disclosure in pursuance of the policy which underlies section 10 on the other hand, many factors will be relevant on both sides of the scale.

It would be foolish to attempt to give comprehensive guidance as to how the balancing exercise should be carried out. But it may not be out of place to indicate the kind of factors which will require consideration. In estimating the importance to be given to the case in favour of disclosure there will be a wide spectrum within which the particular case must be located. If the party seeking disclosure shows, for example, that his very livelihood depends upon it, this will put the case near one end of the spectrum. If he shows no more than that what he seeks to protect is a minor interest in property, this will put the case at or near the other end. On the other side the importance of protecting a source from disclosure in pursuance of the policy underlying the statute will also vary within a wide spectrum. One important factor will be the nature of the information obtained from the source. The greater the legitimate public interest in the information which the source has given to the publisher or intended publisher, the greater will be the importance of protecting the source. But another and perhaps more significant factor which will very much affect the importance of protecting the source will be the manner in which the information was itself obtained by the source. If it appears to the court that the information was obtained legitimately this will enhance the importance of protecting the source. Conversely, if it appears that the information was obtained illegally, this will diminish the importance of protecting the source unless, of course, this factor is counterbalanced by a clear public interest in publication of the information, as in the classic case where the source has acted for the purpose of exposing iniquity. I draw attention to these considerations by way of illustration only and I emphasise once again that they are in no way intended to be read as a code.

In the circumstances of the instant case, I have no doubt that Hoffmann J. and the Court of Appeal were right in finding that the necessity for disclosure of Mr. Goodwin's notes in the interests of justice was established. The importance to the plaintiffs of obtaining disclosure lies in the threat of severe damage to their business, and consequentially to the livelihood of their employees, which would arise from disclosure of the information contained in their corporate plan while their refinancing negotiations are still continuing. This threat, accurately described by Lord Donaldson of Lymington M.R. . . . as 'ticking away beneath them like a time bomb' can only be defused if they can identify the source either as himself the thief of the stolen copy of the plan or as a means to lead to the identification of the thief and thus put themselves in a position to institute proceedings for the recovery of the missing document. The importance of protecting the source on the other hand is much diminished by the source's complicity, at the very least, in a gross breach of confidentiality which is not counterbalanced by any legitimate interest which publication of the information was calculated to serve. Disclosure in the interests of justice is, on this view of the balance, clearly of preponderating importance so as to override the policy underlying the statutory protection of sources and the test of necessity for disclosure is satisfied.

Questions for discussion

1. Do you think Lord Bridge's interpretation of the phrase, 'in the interests of justice', is correct?
2. Does his approach to what he terms 'the balancing exercise' give adequate weight to the value of freedom of expression and the role of the press in that context?

Six years later the European Court of Human Rights held, by a majority of 11–7, that the House of Lords order had violated Goodwin's right to freedom of expression.

Extract 14.2.6

Goodwin v United Kingdom [1996] 21 EHRR 123, at 143–145 (ECHR) (footnotes omitted)

The Court recalls that freedom of expression constitutes one of the essential foundations of a democratic society and that the safeguards to be afforded to the press are of particular importance.

Protection of journalistic sources is one of the basic conditions for press freedom, as is reflected in the laws and the professional codes of conduct in a number of Contracting States and is affirmed in several international instruments on journalistic freedoms. Without such protection, sources may be deterred from assisting the press in informing the public on matters of public interest. As a result the vital public watchdog role of the press may be undermined and the ability of the press to provide accurate and reliable information may be adversely affected. Having regard to the importance of the protection of journalistic sources for press freedom in a democratic society and the potentially chilling effect an order of source disclosure has on the exercise of that freedom, such a measure cannot be compatible with Article 10 of the Convention unless it is justified by an overriding requirement in the public interest.

These considerations are to be taken into account in applying to the facts of the present case the test of necessity in a democratic society under Article 10(2).

As a matter of general principle, the 'necessity' for any restriction on freedom of expression must be convincingly established. Admittedly, it is in the first place for the national authorities to assess whether there is a 'pressing social need' for the restriction and, in making their assessment, they enjoy a certain margin of appreciation. In the present context, however, the national margin of appreciation is circumscribed by the interest of democratic society in ensuring and maintaining a free press. Similarly, that interest will weigh heavily in the balance in determining, as must be done under Article 10(2), whether the restriction was proportionate to the legitimate aim pursued. In sum, limitations on the confidentiality of journalistic sources call for the most careful scrutiny by the Court.

The Court's task, in exercising its supervisory function, is not to take the place of the national authorities but rather to review under Article 10 the decisions they have taken pursuant to their power of appreciation. In so doing, the Court must look at the 'interference' complained of in the light of the case as a whole and determine whether the reasons adduced by the national authorities to justify it are 'relevant and sufficient'.

In the instant case, as appears from Lord Bridge's speech in the House of Lords, Tetra [the anonymous plaintiff in the previous extract] was granted an order for source disclosure primarily on the grounds of the threat of severe damage to their business, and consequently to the livelihood of their employees, which would arise from disclosure of the information in their corporate plan while their refinancing negotiations were still continuing . . .

In the Court's view, the justifications for the impugned disclosure order in the present case have to be seen in the broader context of the *ex parte* interim injunction which had earlier been granted to the company, restraining not only the applicant himself but also the publishers of *The Engineer* from publishing any information derived from the plan. That injunction had been notified to all the national newspapers and relevant journals. The purpose of the disclosure order was to a very large extent the same as that already being achieved by the injunction, namely to prevent dissemination of the confidential information contained in the plan. There was no doubt, according to Lord Donaldson in the Court of Appeal, that the injunction was effective in stopping dissemination of the confidential information by the press. Tetra's creditors, customers, suppliers and competitors would not therefore come to learn of the information through the press. A vital component of the threat of damage to the company had thus already largely been neutralised by the injunction. This being so, in the Court's opinion, in so far as the disclosure order merely served to reinforce the injunction, the additional restriction on freedom of expression which it entailed was not supported by sufficient reasons for the purposes of Article 10(2) of the Convention.

What remains to be ascertained by the Court is whether the further purposes served by the disclosure order provided sufficient justification.

In this respect it is true, as Lord Donaldson put it, that the injunction 'would not effectively prevent publication to [Tetra's] customers or competitors' directly by the applicant journalist's source (or that source's source). Unless aware of the identity of the source, Tetra would not be in a position to stop such further dissemination of the contents of the plan, notably by bringing proceedings against him or her for recovery of the missing document, for an injunction against further disclosure by him or her and for compensation for damage.

It also had a legitimate reason as a commercial enterprise in unmasking a disloyal employee or collaborator who might have continuing access to its premises in order to terminate his or her association with the company.

These are undoubtedly relevant reasons. However, as also recognised by the national courts, it will not be sufficient, *per se*, for a party seeking disclosure of a source to show merely that he or she will be unable without disclosure to exercise the legal right or avert the threatened legal wrong on which he or she bases his or her claim in order to establish the necessity of disclosure. In that connection, the Court would recall that the considerations to be taken into account by the Convention institutions for their review under Article 10(2) tip the balance of competing interests in favour of the interest of democratic society in securing a free press. On the facts of the present case, the Court cannot find that Tetra's interests in eliminating, by proceedings against the source, the residual threat of damage through dissemination of the confidential information otherwise than by the press, in obtaining compensation and in unmasking a disloyal employee or collaborator were, even if considered cumulatively, sufficient to outweigh the vital public interest in the protection of the applicant journalist's source. The Court does not therefore consider that the further purposes served by the disclosure order, when measured against the standards imposed by the Convention, amount to an overriding requirement in the public interest.

The impact of this judgment on the English courts' approach was considered by the Court of Appeal in the *Camelot* case. On the basis of a leak of

Camelot's draft accounts, a journalist published an article strongly critical of the payments made to its directors; the article appeared a few days before Camelot intended to publish its final accounts. It applied for an order compelling the publisher of the newspaper, *Marketing Week*, to return the draft accounts, so it could identify the source of the leak. In reviewing the legal principles, Schiemann and Thorpe LJJ considered that the approach of the House of Lords and the European Court of Human Rights in the *Morgan Grampian/Goodwin* cases were substantially the same; they had simply assessed the facts differently.

Extract 14.2.7

Camelot Group v Centaur Ltd [1998] 1 All ER 251, at 261–262 (CA)

SCHIEMANN LJ: I agree with the conclusion of the judge. My evaluation of the facts of the present case is similar in one respect to that of the Court of Human Rights in *Goodwin's* case. There is no threat now posed to the plaintiffs by further disclosure of the draft accounts. Such threat as there was has been dealt with by injunction or undertaking in relation to that material and the passage of time. There is, however, a continuing threat of damage of a type which did not feature significantly in *Goodwin's* case or in the *X Ltd* case, namely that alluded to in the affidavit of Mr Murphy [the financial director of Camelot] and accepted by the judge. Clearly there is unease and suspicion amongst the employees of the company which inhibits good working relationships. Clearly there is a risk that an employee who has proved untrustworthy in one regard may be untrustworthy in a different respect and reveal the name of, say, a public figure who has won a huge lottery prize. This is not a case of disclosing iniquity. It is not a whistle blowing case.

It did not significantly further the public interest to secure the publication of this item a week earlier than planned. The source knew that publication was planned a week later. I do not regard as a significant factor the point urged by Mr Nicol [counsel for the publisher] that early publication prevented the directors from, in the cant phrase, 'putting a spin on' the presentation of the figures which would make them more palatable to ministers and the public and that the inhibition of this is in the public interest. Whether the public heard the relevant news a week earlier or later is of no significant weight.

There is a public interest in protecting sources. But it is relevant to ask 'what is the public interest in protecting from disclosure persons in the position of the source in the present case?'. Is it in the public interest for people in his position to disclose this type of information? Embargoes on the disclosure of information for a temporary period are a common and useful feature of contemporary life. It does not seem to me that if people in the position of the present source experience the chilling effect referred to by the Court of Human Rights the public will be deprived of anything which it is valuable for the public to have.

It is clear that the public interest in protecting some sources is stronger than that in protecting other sources. So far as the present case is concerned I can see no public interest in protecting him. There remains, however, an important consideration. To some extent the effect of disclosing the identity of one source who has leaked unimportant material can have a chilling effect on the willingness of other sources to disclose material which it is important. If the other sources are put in the position of having to guess whether or no the court will order disclosure of their names then they may well not be prepared to take the risk that the court's decision will go against them. That is a consideration, however, which will only be met if there is a blanket rule against any disclosure. That is, however, not part of our domestic law or of the convention. So the well-informed source is always going to have to take a view as to what is going to be the court's reaction to his disclosure in the circumstances of his case.

The judge took the view that the public interest in enabling the plaintiffs to discover a disloyal employee in their midst who leaked the confidential information which he did leak was greater than the public interest in enabling him to escape detection. I agree with the judge and would dismiss the appeal.

THORPE LJ: I have had the advantage of reading in draft the judgments of Schiemann and Mummery LJJ and at once express my complete agreement with their reasoning and conclusion.

I would only emphasise three points of importance to me on the route to conclusion.

First, I accept Mr Pannick QC's [counsel for Camelot] submission that there is no material difference of principle underlying s 10 of the Contempt of Court Act 1981 as applied by the courts of this jurisdiction and art 10 of the European Convention on Human Rights (Convention for the Protection of Human Rights and Fundamental Freedoms (Rome, 4 November 1950; TS 71 (1953); Cmd 8969)) as applied by the European Court of Human Rights. That the two systems produce different outcomes on the same facts does not establish or perhaps even suggest the contrary. The appreciation of individual factors relevant to the essential balancing exercise is likely to vary in different tribunals. The making of a value judgment on competing facts is very close to the exercise of a discretion dependant on those facts. Furthermore in *Goodwin v UK* (1996) 22 EHRR 123 there was a lapse of six years between the performance of the balancing exercise in London and in Strasbourg. In such a period standards fundamental to the performance of the balancing exercise may change materially.

Second, the material published was en route to the public domain and would have been universally read six days later without the action of the individual whose identity the appellants seek to conceal.

Third, I was not impressed by Mr Nicol QC's submission that his failure on this appeal would have reverberations deterring others from disclosure to the public detriment. An individual case decision would only have that consequence if it were to establish a new boundary or shift an existing boundary. An individual who contemplates giving or selling confidential material to a publisher in breach of his contract of employment knows that he will thereby risk his future security and perhaps that of his dependants. The higher his position presumably the more carefully he will weigh the risks. Surely he would be wise to inform himself as to how the courts apply s 10. If he takes from this decision the message that he is at risk I cannot myself see public detriment. There is a public interest in loyalty and trust between employer and employee.

Questions for discussion

1. Did Schiemann LJ identify and weigh the 'public interests' in this case correctly?
2. What do you think of the argument, made by both Schiemann and Thorpe LJJ, that a 'well-informed' (or 'wise') source should consider how the courts will apply s 10?

(e) Residual judicial discretion

The practice of the courts has been to weigh the interests of justice (or the other interest invoked by the applicant for disclosure) against the public interest in the confidentiality of sources. Lord Bridge in the *Morgan Grampian* case (Extract 14.2.6) emphasised that this process does not really involve the exercise of judicial discretion, as opposed to the assessment of questions of fact. But s 10 states that, '[n]o court may require a person to disclose' a source, unless it is satisfied that disclosure is necessary, not that it must order disclosure, once it is so satisfied. This seems to suggest that the court does have a residual discretion not to order disclosure even where the applicant has shown that it would be 'necessary', say, to identify and fire a dishonest employee.

Support for this conclusion is to be found in a judgment of Peter Pain J, where he refused to make an order to identify the officials at Broadmoor Hospital who had leaked a confidential report on the escape of two inmates.

Extract 14.2.8

Special Hospitals Service Authority v Hyde (1994) 20 BMLR 75, at 84–85 (QBD)

PETER PAIN J: The plaintiffs laid great stress on the importance of the leak. They say that it breached the confidentiality of information between doctor and patient. They also assert that it disclosed certain matters as to security: I have examined those allegations with considerable care with counsel. I have been asked not to disclose further material for which confidence is claimed so I limit myself to saying that I do not regard the actual disclosure that was made as important and that the material that actually was published in the press was not of great importance. What was serious from the plaintiffs' point of view was that there should be a leak at all.

What weighs in my mind, in considering whether it is necessary to make an order are: (1) the failure of Mr Franey [the manager of Broadmoor] or members of the management to make any attempt to discover the source other than making application to this court; (2) the absence of any evidence to show that inquiries, if made, would not have been fruitful; and (3) the fact that the actual disclosure of the matter to be confidential to the press was not of great importance.

In view of these considerations I cannot hold that it is necessary in the interests of justice that Mr Hyde's source should be disclosed. My decision is that I have no jurisdiction to make the orders sought. But as the matter has been canvassed I would also express the view as to what I would have done if I had taken the view that I had jurisdiction. I would then have had to consider whether, in the exercise of my discretion, I should make an order. Again I refer to *X Ltd v Morgan-Grampian* [1990] 2 All ER 1 at 9, [1991] 1 AC 1 at 43 where Lord Bridge makes it clear that that further consideration is necessary.

> 'Construing the phrase "in the interests of justice" in this sense immediately emphasises the importance of the balancing exercise. It will not be sufficient, per se, for a party seeking disclosure of a source protected by s 10 to show merely that he will be unable without disclosure to exercise the legal right or avert the threatened legal wrong on which he bases his claim in order to establish the necessity of disclosure. The judge's task will always be to weigh in the scales the importance of enabling the ends of justice to be attained in the circumstances of the particular case on the one hand against the importance of protecting the source on the other hand. In this balancing exercise it is only if the judge is satisfied that disclosure in the interests of justice is of such preponderating importance as to override the statutory privilege against disclosure that the threshold of necessity will be reached.'

The conflict of interest here lies between the interests of Broadmoor in preserving its confidentiality and the interests of the public in the free supply of information about Broadmoor, a public body.

It is clear from those parts of the reports for which confidence is not claimed that they disclosed material of considerable public concern. In saying this, I make no criticism of the management; that is not for me. I am only concerned to find that there was a legitimate and very lively public interest in security at Broadmoor. I set against this the fact that due in part to the responsible way in which the defendant dealt with his information, no important or serious disclosure was in fact made. If I had held that I did have jurisdiction to make an order for disclosure then I would, in my discretion, have refused to make one.

Accordingly, the application is dismissed.

Questions for discussion

1. Does Lord Bridge's speech in the *Morgan Grampian* case support the distinction between 'jurisdiction' and 'discretion' drawn by Peter Pain J?
2. What factors are relevant to the exercise of judicial discretion in this area?

3. ACCESS TO JOURNALISTIC MATERIAL

Similar issues arise in other contexts. The media argue, for instance, that they should enjoy immunity from the standard police powers of search and seizure. They claim that their ability, say, to report, and publish photographs of, demonstrations might be imperilled, if the police were free to search their premises and seize notes, photographs, and other material, in order to obtain evidence of criminal offences. Further, demonstrators and other potential suspects might attack them if it is thought that their notes and photos could be subsequently used by the police.[9]

To a limited extent the Police and Criminal Evidence Act (PACE) 1984 does recognise the particular position of the media. It imposes special conditions before the police can obtain a warrant to gain access to journalistic material for the purposes of a criminal investigation. Normally, a police constable may obtain a warrant to enter and search premises for evidence of a 'serious arrestable offence' from a magistrate.[10] However, access to 'journalistic material' may only be secured on application to a circuit judge, provided the additional 'access conditions' in respect of 'special procedure material' set out in Sched 1 to the Act are satisfied.[11]

Extract 14.3.1

Police and Criminal Evidence Act 1984, s 13 and Sched 1, paras 1, 2 and 4

13.—(1) Subject to subsection (2) below, in this Act 'journalistic material' means material acquired or created for the purposes of journalism.

(2) Material is only journalistic material for the purposes of this Act if it is in possession of a person who acquired or created it for the purposes of journalism.

(3) A person who receives material from someone who intends that the recipient shall use it for the purposes of journalism is to be taken to have acquired it for those purposes.

Schedule 1

1. If on an application made by a constable a circuit judge is satisfied that one or other of the sets of access conditions is fulfilled he may make an order under paragraph 4 below.[12]

2. The first set of access conditions is fulfilled if
    (a) there are reasonable grounds for believing—
        (i) that a serious arrestable offence has been committed;
        (ii) that there is material which consists of special procedure material . . . on premises specified in the application;

---

[9] For fuller consideration of these arguments and the relevant legal provisions, see Robertson and Nicol, pp 205–208, and the magisterial article by D Feldman, 'Press Freedom and Police Access to Journalistic Material' (1995) 1 *Yearbook of Media and Entertainment Law* 43.

[10] Police and Criminal Evidence Act 1984, s 8. The term 'serious arrestable offence' is defined in s 116.

[11] For the definition of 'special procedure material', see PACE 1984, s 14.

[12] The second set of 'access conditions', not reproduced in the extract, concerns 'excluded material', including journalistic material held in confidence: see PACE 1984, s 11(1)(c).

(iii) that the material is likely to be of substantial value . . . to the investigation . . . ; and

(iv) that the material is likely to be relevant evidence;

(b) other methods of obtaining the material—

(i) have been tried without success; or

(ii) have not been tried because it appeared that they were bound to fail; and

(c) it is in the public interest, having regard—

(i) to the benefit likely to accrue to the investigation if the material is obtained; and

(ii) to the circumstances under which the person of the possession of the material holds it,

that the material should be produced or that access to it should be given.

(4) An order under this paragraph is an order that the person who appears to the circuit judge to be in possession of the material to which the application relates shall—

(a) produce it to a constable for him to take it away; or

(b) give a constable access to it,

not later than the end of the period of seven days from the date of the order or the end of such longer period as the order may specify.

These provisions have been considered on a number of occasions, where the police wanted access to media film of demonstrations. In one case, a newspaper publisher and press agency in Bristol applied for judicial review of an order requiring them to hand over unpublished photographs of riots in that city.

Extract 14.3.2

R v Bristol Crown Court, ex parte Bristol Press and Picture Agency Ltd **(1987) 85 Cr App Rep 190, 195–96 (DC)**

GLIDEWELL LJ: As to the public interest in subparagraph (*c*), the balancing exercise which has to be carried out is between the public interest in the investigation and prevention of crime and the public interest in the press being free to report and to photograph as much as they can of what is going on in our great cities, and particularly in the deprived areas of cities. There is also public interest in the press being able to go about that activity in safety. Both of these are matters about which Mr. Macdonald's clients [the newspaper and the press agency] expressed concern. The judge took both into account. But Mr. Macdonald complains that he did not relate the public interest in the investigation of crime to the specific offences, but merely spoke of them generally. He submits that what must be in issue here is the public interest in relation to these particular crimes or suspected crimes.

The judge said:

'Is it in the public interest that the material should be produced, having regard (i) to the benefit likely to accrue to the investigation if the material is obtained? In my judgment it clearly is. There is a very great public interest that those guilty of crime, and particularly of serious crime involving widespread public disorder, should be brought to justice. Equally, there is great public interest that those who are innocent but who may be suspected of crime should be cleared and, if possible, eliminated from the criminal process. Photographs that are likely to advance either of these objects are of benefit to the investigation. Copies of two photographs published by the first respondents were shown to me. It is quite clear that these and similar photographs would be of great value.'

If the judge had gone on to say that those general considerations, which apply to the investigation of all crime, of course apply to the investigation of the crimes committed here, I cannot think that Mr. Macdonald would have made his submission. The absence of those words is of no significance because of course they are to be implied. The learned judge in the next passage in his judgment on the following page weighed those interests against the other matters to which I have referred – the importance of the impartiality and independence of the press, the importance of ensuring that members of the press can photograph and report what is going on without fear of their personal safety – and, having done so, he concluded in favour of granting the application. If he applied the right test, it is not suggested that he was not entitled to weigh the various factors and come to a conclusion, it was a matter for his discretion. In my judgment he did apply the right test. He made no error of law. He directed himself correctly. He took account of relevant considerations. He did not take account of any irrelevant considerations. His decision is not susceptible of judicial review. The application should fail.

Applications against the media to hand over video material, photographs and notes have, it seems, almost always been successful. But in July 1999 a judge ruled that a number of newspapers and broadcasters should not be required to give the police access to material taken in connection with media coverage of anti-capitalist demonstrations in the City of London.

Similar problems occur when the media argue that they should not be required to produce film for evidentiary purposes. When the BBC was ordered to disclose film of the Broadwater Farm riots in subsequent criminal proceedings, it argued before the European Human Rights Commission that a witness summons requiring it to produce this evidence violated its rights under arts 6 and 10 of the ECHR.[13]

Extract 14.3.3

BBC v United Kingdom (1996) 21 EHRR CD93, at CD95–96
(European Commission of Human Rights)

The duty to give evidence in criminal proceedings is a good example of one of the normal civic duties in a democratic society: any person may be called on to give evidence as to matters witnessed by him, and, at least to the extent

---

[13] For ECHR, art 6(1), see Extract 13.2.3.

that he is not required to say anything which may incriminate himself, may be compelled to give evidence in the interests of the fair and proper administration of justice. The order requiring the giving of such evidence does not involve the determination of any civil obligations of the witness, however, and the position is not different where, as in the present case, the evidence consists of material which has been filmed rather than an individual's oral testimony as to what he witnessed.

The proceedings in which the BBC challenged the witness summons made against it did not, therefore, determine the BBC's civil rights or obligations within the meaning of Article 6(1) of the Convention, with the result that that provision is not applicable to those proceedings . . .

2. The BBC also alleges a violation of Article 10 of the Convention.

The Commission recalls that in the case of GOODWIN V THE UNITED KINGDOM [see Extract 14.2.6] it found that a disclosure order on a journalist to reveal his sources constituted an interference with the right freely to receive and impart information without interference by public authority. The present case is different from the case of Goodwin, since in that case the applicant had received information on a confidential and unattributable basis, whereas the information which the BBC obtained comprised recordings of events which took place in public and to which no particular secrecy or duty of confidentiality could possibly attach. The Commission will, however, assume an interference with the BBC's Article 10 rights for the purposes of the present application.

An interference with the freedoms guaranteed by Article 10(1) of the Convention is permissible only if it is 'prescribed by law' and if it is 'necessary in a democratic society' on one or more of the grounds set out in Article 10(2).

The issuing of witness summonses in England and Wales is regulated by section 2 of the Criminal Procedure (Attendance of Witnesses) Act 1965, which provides for the making of witness summonses for a person to attend court and give evidence or produce documents or things. The same provision enables a person to whom a witness summons is addressed to challenge it on the ground that he 'cannot give any material evidence or, as the case may be, produce any document or thing likely to be material evidence'. The Commission therefore considers that the witness summons in the present case – and the procedure adopted by the Crown Court – was 'prescribed by law' within the meaning of Article 10(2) of the Convention.

As to whether the interference was 'necessary in a democratic society', the Commission has found, at paragraph 1 above, that the duty to give evidence is a normal civic duty in a democratic society. In the ordinary course of events, that duty will suffice to justify an interference created by an obligation to testify on the ground that it is necessary for the maintenance of the authority and impartiality of the judiciary. The BBC considers that the present case is not an ordinary case, because there was no reason to think that the material which the defendants in the criminal trial wished to see could assist the defence, and because it was not necessary to impose an obligation on the BBC to disclose without it being given a proper opportunity to know the issues in the criminal trial. The BBC also claims that the obligation to disclose untransmitted material increases the risk for film crews, as they will be associated with the law enforcement agencies by by-standers if such material is subsequently liable to be used in court.

The Commission recalls that, in a criminal trial, it is for the judge to consider the evidence before the court, and to assess its relevance and admissibility. The judge can only perform this function if he has powers to require the production of evidence before the court in the first place, and it was for this purpose that the witness summons was made in the present case. The domestic law in the present case enables the recipient of a witness summons to claim that he cannot give any material help to the court, but ultimately it is for the court, and not for the potential witness, to take the final decision on the relevance of evidence. It is true that the discussions in the present case were largely between the defence in the criminal case and the BBC, rather than between the trial judge and the BBC, but the principle is the same: the full picture should be before the criminal court.

The Commission is not satisfied that the risks to film crews are greater if untransmitted material is liable to be produced in court. The Commission considers that any risk to film crews flows from their presence at incidents such as the Broadwater Farm riots and from the fact that they are filming such incidents, rather than from any possibility that untransmitted material may subsequently be made available to the courts.

Finally, the Commission does not accept the BBC's argument that the interference was not 'necessary' because the BBC did not fully know the issues in the criminal trial. In particular, the Commission would note that it will often be the case that a person giving evidence will not fully appreciate the impact his evidence will have – that is a matter for the court, rather than the individual witness.

Accordingly, the Commission finds that any interference with the BBC's Article 10 rights was 'prescribed by law' and was 'necessary in a democratic society' for 'maintaining the authority and impartiality of the judiciary'.

It follows that this part of the application is manifestly ill-founded within the meaning of Article 27(2) of the Convention.

Questions for discussion

1. Do you agree with the Commission that the argument for press immunity is weaker in this context than it is in the context of confidentiality of sources?

2. Do you agree with the view that the danger to the safety of journalists arises from their presence at riots or demonstrations, rather than from the chance that they may be ordered to produce film to the police or in the course of criminal proceedings?

APPENDIX

The House of Lords published its judgments in *Reynolds v Times Newspapers* (see Chapter 10, Section 5 (c)) in October 1999. The issue in this case was whether the defendant could argue that an article in the *Sunday Times*, which inaccurately alleged that Albert Reynolds (a former Prime Minister of Ireland) had deliberately misled the Dáil, was published on an occasion of qualified privilege in that it contained political information of public interest. The Court of Appeal had held that the defence of qualified privilege was not confined to communications between particular individuals and associations, such as employers' references, but could extend to communications by the media to the public at large. However, it also held that the media could only claim the privilege if the circumstances of the publication, such as the source of the story and the checks on its reliability, warranted that protection, a hurdle it referred to as a 'circumstantial test'. This test was not satisfied, as the *Sunday Times* had acted on information from a political opponent of the plaintiff and had failed to publish Mr Reynolds' side of the story.

A majority of the House of Lords dismissed the newspaper's appeal. The House was unanimous, however, in its rejection of the appellant's principal argument that the law should now recognise a wide 'generic' privilege for all non-malicious communications by the media to the public at large of information about political matters affecting the United Kingdom. But it accepted the Court of Appeal's decision that *in appropriate circumstances* the media had a duty to disseminate defamatory information to the public and that it could then claim privilege in respect of the publication. Its reasons emerge in the following extracts from the judgments of Lord Nicholls and Lord Steyn, though the latter (with Lord Hope) dissented on the ground that it would be right at the retrial of the case for the judge to reconsider the application of the qualified privilege defence in the light of the judgments in the House.[1]

---

[1] A retrial had already been ordered by the Court of Appeal ([1998] 3 All ER 961) on the grounds of misdirection by the trial judge.

Extract

Reynolds v Times Newspapers Ltd
[1999] 4 All ER 609, 621–623, 625–627, 631, 634–635

LORD NICHOLLS OF BIRKENHEAD: My starting point is freedom of expression. The high importance of freedom to impart and receive information and ideas has been stated so often and so eloquently that this point calls for no elaboration in this case. At a pragmatic level, freedom to disseminate and receive information on political matters is essential to the proper functioning of the system of parliamentary democracy cherished in this country. This freedom enables those who elect representatives to Parliament to make an informed choice, regarding individuals as well as policies, and those elected to make informed decisions. . . .

Likewise, there is no need to elaborate on the importance of the role discharged by the media in the expression and communication of information and comment on political matters. It is through the mass media that most people today obtain their information on political matters. Without freedom of expression by the media, freedom of expression would be a hollow concept. The interest of a democratic society in ensuring a free press weighs heavily in the balance in deciding whether any curtailment of this freedom bears a reasonable relationship to the purpose of the curtailment. In this regard it should be kept in mind that one of the contemporary functions of the media is investigative journalism. This activity, as much as the traditional activities of reporting and commenting, is part of the vital role of the press and the media generally.

Reputation is an integral and important part of the dignity of the individual. It also forms the basis of many decisions in a democratic society which are fundamental to its well-being: whom to employ or work for, whom to promote, whom to do business with or to vote for. Once besmirched by an unfounded allegation in a national newspaper, a reputation can be damaged for ever, especially if there is no opportunity to vindicate one's reputation. When this happens, society as well as the individual is the loser. For it should not be supposed that protection of reputation is a matter of importance only to the affected individual and his family. Protection of reputation is conducive to the public good. It is in the public interest that the reputation of public figures should not be debased falsely. In the political field, in order to make an informed choice, the electorate needs to be able to identify the good as well as the bad. Consistently with these considerations, human rights conventions recognise that freedom of expression is not an absolute right. Its exercise may be subject to such restrictions as are prescribed by law and are necessary in a democratic society for the protection of the reputations of others.

The crux of this appeal, therefore, lies in identifying the restrictions which are fairly and reasonably necessary for the protection of reputation. Leaving aside the exceptional cases which attract absolute privilege, the common law denies protection to defamatory statements, whether of comment or fact, proved to be actuated by malice, in the *Horrocks v Lowe* [1975] A.C. 135 sense [see Extract 10.5.7]. This common law limitation on freedom of speech passes the 'necessary' test with flying colours. This is an acceptable limitation. Freedom of speech does not embrace freedom to make defamatory statements out of personal spite or without having a positive belief in their truth.

In the case of statements of opinion on matters of public interest, that is the limit of what is necessary for protection of reputation. Readers and viewers and listeners can make up their own minds on whether they agree or disagree with defamatory statements which are recognisable as comment and which, expressly or implicitly, indicate in general terms the facts on which they are based.

With defamatory imputations of fact the position is different and more difficult. Those who read or hear such allegations are unlikely to have any means of knowing whether they are true or not. In respect of such imputations, a plaintiff's ability to obtain a remedy if he can prove malice is not normally a sufficient safeguard. Malice is notoriously difficult to prove. If a newspaper is understandably unwilling to disclose its sources, a plaintiff can be deprived of the material necessary to prove, or even allege, that the newspaper acted recklessly in publishing as it did without further verification. Thus, in the absence of any additional safeguard for reputation, a newspaper, anxious to be first with a 'scoop', would in practice be free to publish seriously defamatory misstatements of fact based on the slenderest of materials. Unless the paper chose later to withdraw the allegations, the politician thus defamed would have no means of clearing his name, and the public would have no means of knowing where the truth lay. Some further protection for reputation is needed if this can be achieved without a disproportionate incursion into freedom of expression.

This is a difficult problem. No answer is perfect. Every solution has its own advantages and disadvantages. Depending on local conditions, such as legal procedures and the traditions and power of the press, the solution preferred in one country may not be best suited to another country. The appellant newspaper commends reliance upon the ethics of professional journalism. The decision should be left to the editor of the newspaper. Unfortunately, in the United Kingdom this would not generally be thought to provide a sufficient safeguard. In saying this I am not referring to mistaken decisions. From time to time mistakes are bound to occur, even in the best regulated circles. Making every allowance for this, the sad reality is that the overall handling of these matters by the national press, with its own commercial interests to serve, does not always command general confidence.

As highlighted by the Court of Appeal judgment in the present case, the common law solution is for the court to have regard to all the circumstances when deciding whether the publication of particular material was privileged because of its value to the public. Its value to the public depends upon its quality as well as its subject-matter. This solution has the merit of elasticity. As observed by the Court of Appeal, this principle can be applied appropriately to the particular circumstances of individual cases in their infinite variety. It can be applied appropriately to all information published by a newspaper, whatever its source or origin.

Hand in hand with this advantage goes the disadvantage of an element of unpredictability and uncertainty. The outcome of a court decision, it was suggested, cannot always be predicted with certainty when the newspaper is deciding whether to publish a story. To an extent this is a valid criticism.

A degree of uncertainty in borderline cases is inevitable. This uncertainty, coupled with the expense of court proceedings, may 'chill' the publication of true statements of fact as well as those which are untrue. The chill factor is perhaps felt more keenly by the regional press, book publishers and broadcasters than the national press. However, the extent of this uncertainty should not be exaggerated. With the enunciation of some guidelines by the court, any practical problems should be manageable. The common law does not seek to set a higher standard than that of responsible journalism, a standard the media themselves espouse. An incursion into press freedom which goes no further than this would not seem to be excessive or disproportionate. The investigative journalist has adequate protection. . . .

My conclusion is that the established common law approach to misstatements of fact remains essentially sound. The common law should not develop 'political information' as a new 'subject-matter' category of qualified privilege, whereby the publication of all such information would attract qualified privilege, whatever the circumstances. That would not provide adequate protection for reputation. Moreover, it would be unsound in principle to distinguish political discussion from discussion of other matters of serious public concern. The elasticity of the common law principle enables interference with freedom of speech to be confined to what is necessary in the circumstances of the case. This elasticity enables the court to give appropriate weight, in today's conditions, to the importance of freedom of expression by the media on all matters of public concern.

Depending on the circumstances, the matters to be taken into account include the following. The comments are illustrative only.

1. The seriousness of the allegation. The more serious the charge, the more the public is misinformed and the individual harmed, if the allegation is not true.
2. The nature of the information, and the extent to which the subject-matter is a matter of public concern.
3. The source of the information. Some informants have no direct knowledge of the events. Some have their own axes to grind, or are being paid for their stories.
4. The steps taken to verify the information.
5. The status of the information. The allegation may have already been the subject of an investigation which commands respect.
6. The urgency of the matter. News is often a perishable commodity.
7. Whether comment was sought from the plaintiff. He may have information others do not possess or have not disclosed. An approach to the plaintiff will not always be necessary.
8. Whether the article contained the gist of the plaintiff's side of the story.
9. The tone of the article. A newspaper can raise queries or call for an investigation. It need not adopt allegations as statements of fact
10. The circumstances of the publication, including the timing.

This list is not exhaustive. The weight to be given to these and any other relevant factors will vary from case to case. Any disputes of primary fact will be a matter for the jury, if there is one. The decision on whether, having regard to the admitted or proved facts, the publication was subject to qualified privilege is a matter for the judge. This is the established practice and seems sound. A balancing operation is better carried out by a judge in a reasoned judgment than by a jury. Over time, a valuable corpus of case law will be built up.

In general, a newspaper's unwillingness to disclose the identity of its sources should not weigh against it. Further, it should always be remembered that journalists act without the benefit of the clear light of hindsight. Matters which are obvious in retrospect may have been far from clear in the heat of the moment. Above all, the court should have particular regard to the importance of freedom of expression. The press discharges vital functions as a bloodhound as well as a watchdog. The court should be slow to conclude that a publication was not in the public interest and, therefore, the public had no right to know, especially when the information is in the field of political discussion. Any lingering doubts should be resolved in favour of publication.

. . .

Was the information in the 'Sunday Times' article information the public was entitled to know? The subject matter was undoubtedly of public concern in this country. However, these serious allegations by the newspaper, presented as statements of fact but shorn of all mention of Mr. Reynolds' considered explanation, were not information the public had a right to know. I agree with the Court of Appeal this was not a publication which should in the public interest be protected by privilege in the absence of proof of malice. The further facts the defendants wish to assert and prove at the retrial would make no difference, either on this point or overall. I would dismiss this appeal.

LORD STEYN . . . On balance two particular factors have persuaded me to reject the generic test. First, the rule and practice in England is not to compel a newspaper to reveal its sources: see section 10 of the Contempt of Court Act 1981; R.S.C., Ord. 82, r.6; and *Goodwin v United Kingdom* (1996) 22 E.H.R.R. 123, 143 at para. 39 [see Extract 14.2.6]. By contrast a plaintiff in the United States is entitled to a pre-trial enquiry into the sources of the story and editorial decision-making: *Herbert v Lando* (1979) 441 U.S. 153. Without such information a plaintiff suing for defamation in England will be substantially handicapped. Counsel for the newspaper observed that the House could recommend a reform of the procedural rule. This is an unsatisfactory basis to embark on a radical development of the law. Given the procedural restrictions in England I regard the recognition of a generic qualified privilege of political speech as likely to make it unacceptably difficult for a victim of defamatory and false allegations of fact to prove reckless disregard of the truth. Secondly, a test expressed in terms of a category of cases, such as political speech, is at variance with the jurisprudence of the European Court of Human Rights which in cases of competing rights and interests requires a balancing exercise in the light of the concrete facts of each case. While there is as yet no decision directly in point, it seems to me that Professor John Fleming is right in saying that the basic approach of the European Court of Human Rights has been close to the German approach by insisting on individual evaluation of each case rather than categories: 'Libel and Constitutional Free Speech,' in *Essays for Patrick Atiyah*, ed. Cane and Stapleton (1991), p 333 at pp 337 and 345. Our inclination ought to be towards the approach that prevails in the jurisprudence on the Convention. In combination these two factors make me

sceptical of the value of introducing a rule dependent on general categorisation, with the attendant sacrifice of individual justice in particular cases.
. . .

Returning now to the requirement that the occasion must be one in respect of which it can fairly be said to be in the public interest that the information about political matters should be published, I would accept that it may be objected that this requirement is imprecise. But this is a corner of the law which could do with the minimum of legal rules. And what is in the public interest is a well-known and serviceable concept. It will, of course, have to be given practical content. Inevitably the question will arise in concrete cases whether the newspaper was entitled to rely on the information it had obtained before publishing. This issue can be accommodated within the test of an occasion in the public interest warranting publication. In my view such an approach complies with the requirement of legal certainty. And in practice the issue will have to be determined on the whole of the evidence. If a newspaper stands on the rule protecting its sources, it may run the risk of what the judge and jury will make of the gap in the evidence.

The context in which the qualified privilege of free speech should be applied is all important. It was said by counsel for the newspaper that the English courts have not yet recognised that the press has a general duty to inform the public of political matters and that the public has a right to be so informed. If there is any doubt on the point this is the occasion for the House to settle the matter. It is an open space in the law which can be filled by the courts. It is true that in our system the media have no specially privileged position not shared by individual citizens. On the other hand, it is necessary to recognise the 'vital public watchdog role of the press' as a practical matter: see *Goodwin v The United Kingdom* (1996) 22 E.H.R.R. 123, 143, para 39. . . .

Although the House favoured recognition of a qualified privilege for communications to the public on matters of serious public concern, based on weighing the circumstances of the case, it regarded the Court of Appeal's 'circumstantial test' as an undesirable novelty; it considered that the traditional tests concerning the duty and interest of the publisher and recipient were sufficiently flexible to allow for the development of the common law. The Lords emphasised that it is for the judge to rule whether the publication was covered by qualified privilege, though his ruling might be dependent on the jury's finding of the facts.

The practical implications of this seminal ruling will become apparent as later cases clarify the factors listed by Lord Nicholls as relevant to the decision whether to treat a media publication as privileged. Perhaps the media may feel the outcome of litigation on the scope of this expanded privilege will be so uncertain that they will still hesitate to publish political stories unless they are sure they can justify any defamatory allegations; in other words, the *Reynolds* decision may not significantly reduce the 'chilling effect' of libel law on the media.

The judgments raise a number of difficult issues of principle and practice. How would you answer the following questions:

1. What types of communication might be covered by the expanded qualified privilege? Only the publication of political information or also the
   publication of stories which implicate the conduct of, say, sports and
   film stars or other celebrities?
2. The House of Lords generally discusses the expanded privilege in terms
   of communication by the *media*? Would, or should it, also extend to
   communications on the Internet or to books or privately published leaflets?
3. In what circumstances might a newspaper publish defamatory allegations
   of, say, political significance, without seeking comments from the potential plaintiff or putting his side of the story (see items 7 and 8 in the list
   of relevant factors drawn up by Lord Nicholls)?
4. Are you persuaded by the arguments adopted by Lords Nicholls and
   Steyn against the adoption of a broad 'generic' defence?

SELECT BIBLIOGRAPHY

General works

Courtney, C, Newell, D, and Rasaiah, S, *The Law of Journalism* (Butterworths, 1995)

Craufurd Smith, R, *Broadcasting Law and Fundamental Rights* (Oxford University Press, 1997)

Curran, J, and Seaton, J, *Power without Responsibility – the Press and Broadcasting in Britain*, 5th ed (Routledge, 1997)

Gibbons, T, *Regulating the Media*, 2nd ed (Sweet & Maxwell, 1998)

Robertson, G, and Nicol, A, *Media Law*, 4th ed (Sweet & Maxwell, 1999)

CHAPTER 1: THE PRINCIPLES OF MEDIA LAW

Media freedom

Barendt, E, 'Press and Broadcasting Freedom: Does Anyone Have Any Rights to Free Speech?' (1991) 44 *Current Legal Problems* 63

Barron, J A, 'Access to the Press – A New First Amendment Right' (1967) 80 *Harvard Law Review* 1641

Fiss, O M, 'Free Speech and Social Structure' (1986) *Iowa Law Review* 1405

Lichtenberg, J (ed), *Democracy and Mass Media* (Cambridge, 1990)

Special regulation of the broadcasting media

Barendt, E, 'The First Amendment and the Media' in I Loveland (ed), *Importing the First Amendment* (Hart, 1998)

Bollinger, L C, 'Freedom of the Press and Public Access: Toward a Theory of Partial Regulation of the Mass Media' (1976) 75 *Michigan Law Review* 1

Peacock Committee on Financing the BBC, Cmnd 9824 (1986), Chapter 12

Powe, L A, 'Or of the (Broadcast) Press' (1976) 55 *Texas Law Review* 39

Implications of the Human Rights Act 1998

Wade, Sir William, Kentridge, S, and Marshall, G, *Constitutional Reform in the United Kingdom: Practice and Principles* (Hart, 1998), pp 61, 59, 73

Wadham, J, and Mountfield, H, *Human Rights Act 1998* (Blackstone, 1998), pp 53–55, 101–103

Censorship of the media

Hunnings, N M, 'Video Censorship' [1985] *Public Law* 214

Munro, C R, *Television, Censorship and the Law* (Farnborough, 1979)

Williams Committee on Obscenity and Film Censorship, Cmnd 7772 (1979), Chapters 3 and 12

CHAPTER 2: THE PRESS AND THE PRESS COMPLAINTS COMMISSION

Freedom of the press

Marshall, G, 'Press Freedom and Free Speech Theory' [1992] *Public Law* 40

Royal Commission on the Press, Cmnd 6810 (1977), Chapter 2

Stewart, P 'Or of the Press' (1975) 26 *Hastings Law Journal* 631

Owners and editors

Evans, H, *Good Times, Bad Times* (Weidenfeld, 1983)

Gibbons, T, 'Freedom of the Press: Ownership and Editorial Values' [1992] *Public Law* 279

Neill, A, *Full Disclosure* (Macmillan, 1996)

Royal Commission on the Press, Cmnd 6810 (1977), Chapter 16

Seymour-Ure, C, 'Are the Broadsheets Becoming Unhinged?' in J Seaton (ed), *Politics and the Media* (Blackwell, 1998)

The Press Council and the PCC

Calcutt Report on Privacy and Related Matters, Cm 1102 (1990), Chapters 13–17

Munro, C R, 'Self-Regulation in the Media' [1997] *Public Law* 6

Robertson, G, *People against the Press* (Quartet Books, 1983)

CHAPTER 3: BROADCASTING STRUCTURE AND REGULATION

General works

Barendt, E, *Broadcasting Law: A Comparative Study* (Clarendon Press, 1995)
Prosser, T, *Law and the Regulators* (Clarendon Press, 1997), Chapter 10
Report of the Peacock Committee on Financing the BBC, Cmnd 9824 (1986)
Reville, N, *Broadcasting Law and Practice* (Butterworths, 1997)

Public broadcasting

Barendt, E, 'Legal Aspects of BBC Charter Renewal' (1994) 65(1) *The Political Quarterly* 20
Burns, T, *The BBC: Public Institution and Private World* (Macmillan, 1977)
Coarse, R H, *British Broadcasting: A Study in Monopoly* (Longman, 1950)
Department for Culture, Media and Sport, *The Future Funding of the BBC: Report of the Independent Review Panel* (July 1999)
Department for National Heritage, *The Future of the BBC: A Consultation Document*, Cm 2098 (1992)
Department for National Heritage, *The Future of the BBC: Serving the Nation, Competing World-Wide*, Cm 2621 (1994)
Garnham, N, 'The Broadcasting Market and the Future of the BBC' (1994) 65(1) *The Political Quarterly* 11

Private television broadcasting and its reform

Baldwin, R, 'Broadcasting after the Bill: Gold, Franchises and Murmurings of Discontent' (1990) 11 *Journal of Media Law and Practice* 2
Cave, M, and Williamson, P, 'The Reregulation of British Broadcasting' in M Bishop, J Kay, and C Mayer (eds), *The Regulatory Challenge* (Oxford University Press, 1995), Chapter 7
Gibbons, T, 'Broadcasting in the '90s: Spoilt for Choice?' [1989] *Public Law* 213
Hitchens, L, 'Approaches to Broadcasting Regulation: Australia and United Kingdom Compared' (1997) 17(1) *Legal Studies* 40
Home Affairs Committee, Third Report, *The Future of Broadcasting* (HC 262, 1987–88)
Home Office, *Broadcasting in the '90s: Competition, Choice and Quality*, Cm 517 (1988)
Lewis, N, 'IBA Programme Contract Awards' [1975] *Public Law* 317
Report of the Committee on the Future of Broadcasting (Annan Committee), Cmnd 6753 (1977)

Veljanovski, C G, 'Cable Television: Agency Franchising and Economics' in R Baldwin and C McCrudden (eds), *Regulation and Public Law* (Weidenfeld and Nicolson, 1987), p 267

Veljanovski, C G (ed), *Freedom in Broadcasting* (Institute of Economic Affairs, 1989)

Radio

Baldwin, R, Cave, M, and Jones, T, 'The Regulation of Independent Local Radio and its Reform' (1987) 7 *International Review of Law and Economics* 177

Home Office, *Radio: Choices and Opportunities*, Cm 92 (1987)

Jones, T H, 'The De-Regulation of Independent Radio' [1988] *Public Law* 24

Digital broadcasting

Graham, A, 'Broadcasting Policy and the Digital Revolution' in J Seaton (ed), *Politics & the Media: Harlots and Prerogatives at the Turn of the Millennium* (Blackwell Publishers, 1998), p 30

Hitchens, L, 'Digital Broadcasting: The Government's Proposals – The Doubtful Revolution' (1996) 59 *Modern Law Review* 427

CHAPTER 4: PROGRAMME REGULATION

Programme standards

Coleman, F, 'All in the Best Possible Taste: The Broadcasting Standards Council 1989–1992' [1993] *Public Law* 488

Gibbons, T, 'The Role of the Broadcasting Complaints Commission: Current Practice and Future Prospects' (1995) 1 *The Yearbook of Media and Entertainment Law* 129

Political broadcasting and impartiality

Barendt, E, 'Judging the Media: Impartiality and Broadcasting' in J Seaton (ed), *Politics & the Media: Harlots and Prerogatives at the Turn of the Millennium* (Blackwell Publishers, 1998), p 108

Boyle, A E, 'Political Broadcasting, Fairness and Administrative Law' [1986] *Public Law* 562

Cockerell, M, *Live from Number 10* (Faber and Faber, 1989)

Munro, C, 'The 1997 General Election and Media Law' (1997) 2(5) *Communications Law* 166

CHAPTER 5: EUROPEAN BROADCASTING LAW

General works

Collins, R, 'Unity in Diversity? The European Single Market in Broadcasting and the Audiovisual, 1982–92' (1994) 32(1) *Journal of Common Market Studies* 89

Goldberg, D, Prosser, T, and Verhulst, S, *EC Media Law and Policy* (Addison Wesley Longman, 1998)

Humphreys, P, *Mass Media and Media Policy in Western Europe* (Manchester University Press, 1996), Chapter 8

Loon, A van, 'National Media Policies under EEC Law Taking into Account Fundamental Rights' (1993) 14 *Journal of Media Law and Practice* 17

Winn, D B, *European Community and International Media Law* (Graham & Trotman/Martinus Nijhoff, 1994)

Council of Europe

Hondius, F W, 'Regulating Transfrontier Television – The Strasbourg Option' (1988) 8 *Yearbook of European Law* 141

European Community – The Television Without Frontiers Directive

Commission of the European Communities, *Television Without Frontiers: Green Paper on the establishment of the common market for broadcasting, especially by satellite and cable*, COM (84) 300 final, 14 June 1984

Drijber, B J, 'The Revised Television without Frontiers Directive: Is It Fit for the Next Century?' (1999) 36 *Common Market Law Review* 87

Edwards, S, 'A Safe Haven for Hardest Core' [1997] 4 *Entertainment Law Review* 137

Keller, P, 'The New Television Without Frontiers Directive' (1997/8) 3 *The Yearbook of Media and Entertainment Law* 177

Salvatore, V, 'Quotas on TV programmes and EEC Law' (1992) 29 *Common Market Law Review* 967

Wallace, R, and Goldberg, D, 'The EEC Directive on Television Broadcasting' (1989) 9 *Yearbook of European Law* 175

Witte, B de, 'The European Content Requirement in the EC Television Directive – Five Years After' (1995) 1 *The Yearbook of Media and Entertainment Law* 101

CHAPTER 6: ADVERTISING REGULATION

Fitzgerald, D, 'Self-regulation of Comparative Advertising in the United Kingdom' [1997] 7 *Entertainment Law Review* 250

Munro, C, 'Self-regulation in the Media' [1997] *Public Law* 6

Skouris, W (ed), *Advertising and Constitutional Rights in Europe* (Nomos Verlagsgesellschaft, 1994)

Stevens, J, and Feldman, D J, 'Broadcasting Advertisements by Bodies with Political Objects, Judicial Review, and the Influence of Charities Law' [1997] *Public Law* 615

Veljanovski, C (ed), *Freedom in Broadcasting* (Institute of Economic Affairs, 1989), Chapter 6.

CHAPTER 7: COMPETITION LAW

General works

Craufurd Smith, R, *Broadcasting Law and Fundamental Rights* (Clarendon Press, 1997)

Newspaper mergers

Ainsworth, L, and Weston, D, 'Newspapers and UK Media Ownership Controls' (1995) 16(1) *Journal of Media Law and Practice* 2

Whish, R, *Competition Law*, 3rd ed (Butterworths, 1993), pp 672–678

Regulation of broadcasting ownership and control

Barendt, E, 'Structural and Content Regulation of the Media: United Kingdom Law and Some American Comparisons' (1997/8) 3 *The Yearbook of Media and Entertainment Law* 75

Congdon, T, Graham, A, Green, D, and Robinson, B, *The Cross Media Revolution: Ownership and Control* (John Libbey, 1995)

Feintuck, M, 'The UK Broadcasting Act 1996: A Holding Operation?' (1997) 3(2) *European Public Law* 201

Gibbons, T, 'Aspiring to Pluralism: The Constraints of Public Broadcasting Values on the De-regulation of British Media Ownership' (1998) 16 *Cardozo Arts and Entertainment Law Journal* 475

Glencross, D, 'Television Ownership and Editorial Control' (1996) 2 *The Yearbook of Media and Entertainment Law* 3

Hitchens, L, '"Get ready, fire, take aim": The Regulation of Cross-Media Ownership – An Exercise in Policy-making' [1995] *Public Law* 620

European competition law

Beltrame, F, 'Harmonising Media Ownership Rules: Problems and Prospects' (1996) 7(5) *Utilities Law Review* 172

Commission of the European Communities, *Communication from the Commission to the Council and the European Parliament, Follow-up to the Consultation Process to the Green Paper on 'Pluralism and Media Concentration in the Internal Market: An Assessment of the Need for Community Action'*, COM (94) 353 final, 5 October 1994

Commission of the European Communities, *Pluralism and Media Concentration in the Internal Market: An Assessment of the Need for Community Action*, Green Paper, COM (92) 480 final, 23 December 1992

Craufurd Smith, R, 'Pluralism and Freedom of Expression: Constitutional Imperatives for a New Broadcasting Order' (1996) 2 *The Yearbook of Media and Entertainment Law* 21

Craufurd Smith, R, 'Getting the Measure of Public Services: Community Competition Rules and Public Service Broadcasting' (1997/8) 3 *The Yearbook of Media and Entertainment Law* 147

Doyle, G, 'From "Pluralism" to "Ownership": Europe's Emergent Policy on Media Concentrations Navigates the Doldrums' (1997) 3 *Journal of Information Law and Technology* http://elj.warwick.ac.uk/jilt/commsreg/97_3doyl/

Harcourt, A, 'Regulating for Media Concentration: The Emerging Policy of the European Union' (1996) 7 *Utilities Law Review* 202

Harcourt, A, 'Regulation of European Media Markets: Approaches of the European Court of Justice and the Commission's Merger Task Force' (1998) 9(6) *Utilities Law Review* 276

Hitchens, L, 'Media Ownership and Control: a European Approach' (1994) 57 *Modern Law Review* 585

Humphreys, P, *Mass Media and Media Policy in Western Europe* (Manchester University Press, 1996), Chapter 6 and pp 284–293

Rhodes, D, 'The Impact of EC Competition Law on Satellite Broadcasting' (1997) 2(2) *Communications Law* 66

Winn, D B, *European Community and International Media Law* (Graham & Trotman/Martinus Nijhoff, 1994), Chapter 4

Anti-competitive agreements and practices

Fleming, H, ' "Television without Frontiers": The Broadcasting of Sporting Events in Europe' (1997) 8 *Entertainment Law Review* 281

Sadler, J, *Enquiry into Standards of Cross Media Promotion: Report to the Secretary of State for Trade and Industry*, Cm 1436 (1991)

Williams, M, 'Sky Wars: The OFT Review of Pay-TV' [1997] *European Competition Law Review* 214

CHAPTER 8: CONVERGENCE

Regulation of the new media environment

Collins, R, and Murroni, C, *New Media New Policies* (Polity Press, 1996)

Culture, Media and Sport Committee, *The Multi-Media Revolution*, Fourth Report (HCP 520, 1998)

Department of Trade and Industry and Department for Culture, Media and Sport, *Regulating Communications: Approaching Convergence in the Information Age*, Cm 4022 (1998)

Department of Trade and Industry and Department for Culture, Media and Sport, *Regulating Communications: The Way Ahead: Results of the Consultation on the Convergence Green Paper* (1999)

Goldberg, D, Prosser, T, and Verhulst, S, *Regulating the Changing Media: A Comparative Study* (Oxford University Press, 1998), Chapters 1, 4 and 9

Goldberg, D, and Verhulst, S, 'Legal Responses to Regulating the Changing Media in the United Kingdom' (1997) 8 *Utilities Law Review* 12

Landau, J, 'The Future Regulation of Broadcasting and Telecommunications in the United Kingdom' (1998) 3(1) *Communications Law* 2

Office of Telecommunications, *Beyond the Telephone, the Television and the PC, A Consultative Document* (1995) http://www.oftel.gov.uk/superhwy/multi.htm

Conditional access

Hurt, J, 'Conditional Access for Digital Television Broadcasts' [1998] *Computer and Telecommunications Law Review* 154

Landau, J, 'The Regulation of Conditional Access for Digital Television Services' (1997) 2(2) *Communications Law* 74

Llorens-Maluquer, C, 'European Responses to Bottlenecks in Digital Pay-TV: Impacts on Pluralism and Competition Policy' (1998) 16(2–3) *Cardozo Arts and Entertainment Law Journal* 557

European responses to convergence

Bartosch, A, 'The Green Paper on Convergence – A Contribution to the Discussion on the Road to the Information Society' [1998] *Computer and Telecommunications Law Review* 103

European Commission, *Communication to the European Parliament, the Council, the Economic and Social Committee and the Committee of the Regions, The Convergence of the Telecommunications, Media and Information Technology Sectors and Implications for Regulation, Results of the Public Consultation on the Green Paper*, COM (99) 108 EN final, 9 March 1999

European Commission, *Convergence of the Telecommunications, Media and Information Technology Sectors and the implications for Regulation: Towards an Information Society Approach*, COM (97) 623, 3 December 1997

Sauter, W, 'The EC Commission Green Paper on Regulation for Convergence' (1998) 9(4) *Utilities Law Review* 167

CHAPTER 9: INTERNATIONAL REGULATION OF BROADCASTING

The regulatory framework

Bender, R, *Launching and Operating Satellites: Legal Issues* (Martinus Nijhoff Publishers, 1998)

Codding, G A, Jr, 'The International Telecommunications [sic] Union: 130 Years of Telecommunications Regulation' (1995) 23(3) *Denver Journal of International Law and Policy* 501

Dann, P, 'Law and Regulation of Satellite Communications in the United Kingdom' (1992) 20 *Journal of Space Law* 1

Fawcett, J E S, *Outer Space: New Challenges to Law and Policy* (Clarendon Press, 1984) Chapter 4

Lyall, F, *Law & Space Telecommunications* (Dartmouth, 1989)

Smith, M, *International Regulation of Satellite Communication* (Matinus Nijhoff Publishers, 1990)

White, H M, Jr, and Lauria, R, 'The Impact of New Communication Technologies on International Telecommunication Law and Policy: Cyberspace and the Restructuring of the International Telecommunication Union' (1995) 32(1) *California Western Law Review* 1

White, S, Bate, S, and Johnson, T, *Satellite Communications in Europe: Law and Regulation*, 2nd ed (Sweet & Maxwell, 1996)

The orbit/spectrum resource

Gorove, S, *Developments in Space Law: Issues and Policies* (Martinus Nijhoff, 1991), Chapter 4

Smith, M L, 'Space WARC 1985: The Quest for Equitable Access' (1985) 3 *Boston University International Law Journal* 229

Thompson, J C, 'Space for Rent: the International Telecommunications [sic] Union, Space Law, and Orbit/Spectrum Leasing' (1996) 62 *Journal of Air Law and Commerce* 279

Free flow/prior consent

Delzeit, A N, and Wahl, R M, 'Redefining Freedom of Speech under International Space Law: The Need for Bilateral Communications Alliances to

Resolve the Debate between "Free Flow of Information" and "Prior Consent" Schools of Thought' (1995) 2 *ILSA Journal of International and Comparative Law* 267

Fisher, D I, *Prior Consent to International Direct Satellite Broadcasting* (Martinus Nijhoff, 1990)

Gorove, S, *Developments in Space Law: Issues and Policies* (Martinus Nijhoff, 1991), Chapter 5

Hurwitz, B A, 'The Labyrinth of International Telecommunications Law: Direct Broadcast Satellites' (1988) 35 *Netherlands International Law Review* 145

Luther, S F, *The United States and the Direct Broadcast Satellite* (Oxford University Press, 1988)

Price, M E, 'The First Amendment and Television Broadcasting by Satellite' (1976) 23 *UCLA Law Review* 879

Price, M E, *Television, the Public Sphere, and National Identity* (Oxford University Press, 1995)

CHAPTER 10: DEFAMATION

General works

Barendt, E, Lustgarten, L, Norrie, K, and Stephenson, H, *Libel and the Media: the Chilling Effect* (Oxford University Press, 1997)

Faulks Committee on the Law of Defamation, Cmnd 5909 (1976)

Milmo, P, and Rogers, W V H (eds), *Gatley on Libel and Slander*, 9th ed (Sweet & Maxwell, 1998)

Neill, Sir Brian, and Rampton, R (eds), *Duncan and Neill on Defamation*, 2nd ed (Butterworths, 1983)

The function of defamation law

Barendt, E, 'What Is the Point of Libel Law?' [1999] 52 *Current Legal Problems* 110

Gibbons, T, 'Defamation Reconsidered' (1996) 16 *Oxford Journal of Legal Studies* 587

Post, R C, 'The Social Foundations of Defamation Law: Reputation and the Constitution', (1986) 74 *California Law Review* 691

Libel and freedom of speech

Barendt, E, 'Libel and Freedom of Speech in English Law' [1993] *Public Law* 449

Schauer, F, 'Social Foundations of the Law of Defamation: A Comparative Analysis' (1980) 1 *Journal of Media Law and Practice* 3

CHAPTER 11: PRIVACY AND BREACH OF CONFIDENCE

Breach of confidence

Fenwick, H, and Phillipson, G, 'Confidence and Privacy: A Re-examination' (1996) 55 *Cambridge Law Journal* 447

Gurry, F, *Breach of Confidence* (Oxford University Press, 1984)

Law Commission Report on Breach of Confidence, Cmnd 8388 (1981)

Wilson, W, 'Privacy, Confidence and Press Freedom: A Study in Judicial Activism' (1990) 53 *Modern Law Review* 43

Right to privacy

Barendt, E, 'Privacy and the Press', (1995) 1 *Yearbook of Media and Entertainment Law* 23

Lord Chancellor's Department Consultation Paper, *Infringement of Privacy* (1993)

Prosser, W L, 'Privacy' (1960) 48 *California Law Review* 383

Wacks, R, *Privacy and Press Freedom* (Blackstone, 1995)

Warren S D, and Brandeis, L D, 'The Right to Privacy', (1890) 4 *Harvard Law Review* 193

Younger Committee on Privacy, Cmnd 5012 (1972)

The Press Complaints Commission and privacy

Blom-Cooper QC, Sir Louis, and Pruitt, L, 'Privacy Jurisprudence of the Press Complaints Commission' [1994] *Anglo-American Law Review* 133

Privacy law in European jurisdictions

Markesinis, B (ed), *Protecting Privacy* (Oxford University Press, 1999)

Implications of the Human Rights Act 1998

Leigh, I, 'Horizontal Rights, the Human Rights Act and Privacy: Lessons from the Commonwealth?' (1999) 48 *International and Comparative Law Quarterly* 57

Singh, R, 'Privacy and the Media after the Human Rights Act' (1998) *European Human Rights Law Review* 712

CHAPTER 12: CONTEMPT OF COURT

General works

Eady, Sir David, and Smith, A T H, *Arlidge, Eady and Smith on Contempt*, 2nd ed (Sweet & Maxwell, 1999)

Miller, C J, *Contempt of Court*, 2nd ed (Oxford University Press, 1991)

Strict liability rule

Chesterman, M, 'OJ and the Dingo: How Media Publicity Relating to Criminal Cases Tried by Jury is Dealt With in Australia and America' (1997) 45 *American Journal of Comparative Law* 109

National Heritage Committee Report on Press Activity Affecting Court Cases (HC 86, 1997)

Phillimore Committee on Contempt of Court, Cmnd 5794 (1974)

Walker, C, 'Fundamental Rights, Fair Trials and the New Audio-Visual Sector' (1996) 59 *Modern Law Review* 517

Postponement orders

Beloff, M, 'Fair Trial – Free Press? Reporting Restrictions in Law and Practice' [1992] *Public Law* 92

Cram, I, 'Section 4(2): Media Reports of Court Proceedings under the Contempt of Court Act 1981' (1996) 2 *Yearbook of Media and Entertainment Law* 111

Walker, C, Cram, I, and Bogarth, D, 'The Reporting of Crown Court Proceedings and the Contempt of Court Act 1981' (1992) 55 *Modern Law Review* 647

Disclosure of jury deliberations

Campbell, E, 'Jury Secrecy and Contempt of Court' (1985) 11 *Monash University Law Review* 169

Criminal Law Revision Committee Report, *Secrecy of Jury Room*, Cmnd 3750 (1968)

CHAPTER 13: REPORTING LEGAL PROCEEDINGS

Family proceedings

Cretney, S, '"Disgusted, Buckingham Palace . . ." – The Judicial Proceedings (Regulation of Reports) Act 1926' (1997) 9 *Child and Family Law Quarterly* 43

Law Commission Report, *Powers of Appeal Courts to Sit in Private, and the Restrictions upon Publicity in Domestic Proceedings*, Cmnd 3149 (1966)

Cameras in the courtroom

Biondi, A, 'TV Cameras' Access into the Courtroom: A Comparative Note' (1996) 2 *Yearbook of Media and Entertainment Law* 133

Dockray, M, 'Courts on Television' (1988) 51 *Modern Law Review* 593
Tongue, T, and Lintott, R, 'The Case Against Television in the Courtroom' (1980) 16 *Williamette Law Review* 777

CHAPTER 14: PROTECTION OF JOURNALISTS' SOURCES AND RELATED ISSUES

Privilege not to disclose sources

Cripps, Y, 'Judicial Proceedings and Refusals to Disclose the Identity of Sources of Information' [1984] *Cambridge Law Journal* 266
Palmer, S, 'Protecting Journalists' Sources: Section 10, Contempt of Court Act 1981' [1992] *Public Law* 61

Access to journalistic material

Feldman, D, 'Press Freedom and Police Access to Journalistic Material' (1996) 1 *Yearbook of Media and Entertainment Law* 43

Useful web sites

Advertising Standards Authority http://www.asa.org.uk
Broadcasting Standards Commission http://www.bsc.org.uk
Independent Television Commission http://www.itc.org.uk
Office of Telecommunications (Oftel) http://www.oftel.gov.uk
Press Complaints Commission http://www.pcc.org.uk
Radio Authority http://www.radioauthority.org.uk

Department for Culture, Media and Sport http://www.culture.gov.uk
Department of Trade and Industry http://www.dti.gov.uk

Council of Europe http://www.coe.fr
European Community http://www.europa.eu.int
European Commission, Directorate-General IV, responsible for competition policy http://www.europa.eu.int/comm/dg04/
European Commission, Directorate-General X, responsibilities include culture and audiovisual sectors http://www.europa.eu.int/comm/dg10/

INDEX